Archaeology of Urban America

The Search for Pattern and Process

Studies in
HISTORICAL ARCHAEOLOGY

EDITOR

Stanley South

Institute of Archeology and Anthropology
University of South Carolina
Columbia, South Carolina

ADVISORS

Charles E. Cleland
Roy S. Dickens, Jr.
Leland G. Ferguson
John L. Idol, Jr.
Mark P. Leone
Kenneth E. Lewis
W. Lee Minnerly
Cynthia R. Price
Sarah Peabody Turnbaugh

ROY S. DICKENS, JR., (Ed.) *Archaeology of Urban America: The Search for Pattern and Process*

ROBERT PAYNTER *Models of Spatial Inequality: Settlement Patterns in Historical Archeology*

In Preparation

JOAN H. GEISMAR *The Archaeology of Social Disintegration in Skunk Hollow: A Nineteenth-Century Rural Black Community*

KATHLEEN DEAGAN *The Historical Archaeology of Eighteenth-Century Spanish St. Augustine*

Archaeology of Urban America

The Search for Pattern and Process

EDITED BY

Roy S. Dickens, Jr.

Department of Anthropology
Georgia State University
Atlanta, Georgia

ACADEMIC PRESS

A Subsidiary of Harcourt Brace Jovanovich, Publishers

New York London
Paris San Diego San Francisco São Paulo Sydney Tokyo Toronto

ACADEMIC PRESS, INC.
111 Fifth Avenue, New York, New York 10003

United Kingdom Edition published by
ACADEMIC PRESS, INC. (LONDON) LTD.
24/28 Oval Road, London NW1 7DX

Library of Congress Cataloging in Publication Data
Main entry under title:

Archaeology of urban America.

(Studies in historical archaeology)
Includes index.
1. United States--Antiquities--Addresses, essays, lectures. 2. Archaeology and history--United States--Addresses, essays, lectures. I. Dickens, Roy S., Date. II. Series: Studies in historical archaeology (New York, N.Y.)
E159.5.A73 973.1 82-6804
ISBN 0-12-214980-7 AACR2

PRINTED IN THE UNITED STATES OF AMERICA

82 83 84 85 9 8 7 6 5 4 3 2 1

Contents

2
An Approach to Archaeology of the City: The Roger Williams National Memorial Project
Patricia E. Rubertone

3
The City-Site Approach to Urban Archaeology
Pamela J. Cressey and John F. Stephens

4
Archaeological Implications of a Manufacturing Industry in Eighteenth-Century American Cities
Frederick J. E. Gorman

5
Environmental-Impact Archaeology in the Urban Setting: A View from Atlanta
Roy S. Dickens, Jr. and Timothy J. Crimmins

II SITE FORMATION, STRUCTURE, AND PATTERN

6 Urban Land Use and Artifact Deposition: An Archaeological Study of Change in Providence, Rhode Island

Patricia E. Rubertone

7 The Core–Periphery Relationship and the Archaeological Record in Alexandria, Virginia

Pamela J. Cressey, John F. Stephens, Steven J. Shephard, and Barbara H. Magid

8
Bioarchaeology in the Urban Context

Robert L. Blakely and Lane A. Beck

9
The Weaver Pottery: A Late Nineteenth-Century Family Industry in a Southeastern Urban Setting

Charles H. Faulkner

10
Industrial Site-Building: Implications from the 1978–1979 Investigations at the Rogers Locomotive Works, Paterson, New Jersey

Marjorie Ingle

III
ARTIFACT ANALYSIS AND INTERPRETATION

11
Analyzing Glass Bottles for Chronology, Function, and Trade Networks
Sherene Baugher-Perlin

12
An Examination of Manufacture–Deposition Lag for Glass Bottles from Late Historic Sites
Sarah H. Hill

13
Classification and Interpretation of Late Nineteenth- and Early Twentieth-Century Ceramics
Linda H. Worthy

14

Material Culture, Social Structure, and Changing Cultural Values: The Ceramics of Eighteenth- and Nineteenth-Century Middletown, Connecticut

Stephen L. Dyson

15

Patterns in Urban Food Ways: An Example from Early Twentieth-Century Atlanta

Paula Edmiston Davidson

16

The Milwaukee Garbage Project: Archaeology of Household Solid Wastes

Barry E. Thompson and William L. Rathje

Contributors

Numbers in parentheses indicate the pages on which the authors' contributions begin.

SHERENE BAUGHER-PERLIN (259), Landmarks Preservation Commission, New York, New York 10007

LANE A. BECK (175), Department of Anthropology, Georgia State University, Atlanta, Georgia 30303

ROBERT L. BLAKELY (175), Department of Anthropology, Georgia State University, Atlanta, Georgia 30303

PAMELA J. CRESSEY (41, 143), Alexandria Archaeological Research Center, City of Alexandria, Alexandria, Virginia 22313

TIMOTHY J. CRIMMINS (105), Department of History, Georgia State University, Atlanta, Georgia 30303

ROY S. DICKENS, JR. (105), Department of Anthropology, Georgia State University, Atlanta, Georgia 30303

STEPHEN L. DYSON (361), Department of Classics, Wesleyan University, Middletown, Connecticut 06457

PAULA EDMISTON DAVIDSON (381), Department of Anthropology, Georgia State University, Atlanta, Georgia 30303

CHARLES H. FAULKNER (209), Department of Anthropology, University of Tennessee, Knoxville, Tennessee 37916

FREDERICK J. E. GORMAN (63), Department of Anthropology, Boston University, Boston, Massachusetts 02215

SARAH H. HILL (291), Department of Anthropology, Georgia State University, Atlanta, Georgia 30303

MARJORIE INGLE (237), Denver, Colorado 80218

BARBARA H. MAGID (143), Alexandria Archaeological Research Center, City of Alexandria, Alexandria, Virginia 22313

WILLIAM L. RATHJE (399), Department of Anthropology, University of Arizona, Tucson, Arizona 85721

DIANA diZEREGA ROCKMAN (3), Department of Anthropology, New York University, New York, New York 10003

NAN A. ROTHSCHILD (3), Department of Anthropology, Barnard College, New York, New York 10027

PATRICIA E. RUBERTONE (19, 117), Department of Anthropology, Brown University, Providence, Rhode Island 02912

STEVEN J. SHEPHARD (143), Alexandria Archaeological Research Center, City of Alexandria, Alexandria, Virginia 22313

JOHN F. STEPHENS (41, 143), Alexandria Archaeological Research Center, City of Alexandria, Alexandria, Virginia 22313

BARRY E. THOMPSON (399), Department of Anthropology, University of Wisconsin—Milwaukee, Milwaukee, Wisconsin

LINDA H. WORTHY (329), Department of Anthropology, Georgia State University, Atlanta, Georgia 30303

Foreword

During the past few years, it has become increasingly evident that useful, and sometimes exciting, information about *all* past periods of human activity is waiting to be recovered from urban locations that, 10 years ago, many of us would have written off as hopelessly disturbed. Today, most historical archaeologists would probably agree with my 1978 suggestion that, "since all human activity 'disturbs' the locale in which it occurs, the evidence of past construction and destruction may be the very resource that gives an area its historical and cultural importance. It follows that urban, heavily built-up areas must be accorded the same thought and attention that is accorded more bucolic ones. Logically, they deserve *more* attention, since they have been the loci of much more human activity [Salwen 1978:458]."

Not only have archaeologists come to recognize the possibilities inherent in work in cities, but a number of recent articles in the popular press suggest that this field of endeavor has captured the attention of a surprisingly large segment of the non-archaeological public, and that "urban archaeology" has become the trendiest new specialty within historical archaeology. But, despite this popular recognition, it is probably prudent to ask ourselves if this area of work is really entitled to its own status as a separate and distinct subfield. Do its practitioners require special training and experience? Does its successful operation depend upon the development of special theories and methods? Should its findings be reported in separate volumes and in separate sessions at professional meetings?

Without ever forgetting that urban archaeological research, like any other archaeological activity, should be conducted primarily to answer anthropological and historical questions, it is still legitimate and useful to stress the fact that both the theoretical orientations and the technical procedures of urban archaeology must be somewhat different from those appropriate to less crowded places. All aspects of the archaeological program, from survey through excavation, analysis, and interpretation, must be tailored to the complexities of the city, both as subject for study and as setting for fieldwork.

At the most basic physical level, any excavation in a city—whether for a building foundation or for purposes of archaeological research—is almost certain to be more technically complex, more disruptive of the normal routines of more people, and considerably more expensive than the removal of an equal volume of fill from a less heavily utilized setting. The archaeologist who chooses to work in the city must be ready to face these "practical" problems, as well as some equally tough theoretical ones.

Because urban archaeology is always relatively expensive and very often disruptive, as well as highly visible, its practitioners are under particularly strong pressures to plan and conduct their work in an orderly, logical manner, designed to produce the maximum amount of information for the least amount of excavation. Before we accept large sums of money to dig big holes in the middle of someone else's road, stopping traffic for a month or two, we should be fairly certain that we are right about both the actual existence of the archaeological resource and its true historic and scientific importance. Therefore, urban archaeologists have devoted a proportionately large amount of effort to the development of effective methods for prediction and evaluation. This emphasis is reflected in many of the chapters in this volume.

Predictions about the presence of features are most likely to be correct when thorough documentary research, followed by an adequate on-site testing program, precedes any major excavation. In the city, adequate evaluation of resources requires an appreciation of the complexity of the urban cultural universe as it has changed through time, as well as knowledge of the alternatives available for sampling it archaeologically. It is becoming apparent that archaeological manifestations in cities can be effectively predicted and properly evaluated only in the context of information compiled through broad-scale, comprehensive historic resource survey, in which the city itself, in its entirety, is viewed as the "site" under investigation (Cressey 1979; Dickens and Crimmins, this volume).

Because archaeological materials in cities are frequently and intimately associated with standing structures and other above-ground historic features, such surveys are best produced through close interdisciplinary collaboration involving—minimally—historians, architectural historians, and archaeologists. Information about past patterns of land use, as identified through background research, and at least partially verified through field testing, can be used to produce a series of land-use maps, one for each of the major periods in the history—and prehistory—of the locality. Individually, each map is a useful aid in the study of cultural configurations at some particular period in time. Considered sequentially, they provide insights into historical and cultural developments through time. Superimposed, they summarize existing information about archaeological materials of all periods and provide the only adequate and practical method yet devised for predicting the probable locations and characteristics of still undiscovered urban features.

Within the past few years it has been demonstrated that there are important materials under streets and structures in all of our cities. But it has also become clear that it will probably never be feasible to locate and identify the great majority of these before they are actually threatened with imminent destruction. Comprehensive surveys, by identifying probable locations and pinpointing "sensitive" areas, become the key to planning for both historic preservation and urban archaeological research. These surveys also provide the contexts that make it possible to evaluate the importance ("significance") of individual archaeological manifestations.

The special nature of urban archaeology is also apparent when the focus is narrowed to the specific archaeological project area. In settings where the archaeologist may encounter multiple strata of superimposed foundations, deep concrete rubble fill, or live electric lines and gas and water mains, and may be required to erect tall fences and employ armed watchmen, excavation is extremely expensive. Hence, there is absolute need for multistage research strategies, in which rapid feedback from one level of testing provides the information to define more limited areas which require more intensive investigation (Rubertone, Chapter 2, this volume).

In situations where the costs mount with astonishing rapidity as excavation time accumulates, the more expensive, but more efficient, methodology may actually be the most cost-effective one. In addition to the more traditional techniques, urban archaeologists have adopted a number of new tools from other fields of endeavor. In some situations, remote-sensing technologies, such as ground-penetrating radar, have proven extremely reliable in identifying buried foundation walls and other features (Grossman 1980). In other cases, augers and corers, both hand-held and truck-mounted, have been used effectively (Rubertone, Chapter 2). Other kinds of powered construction equipment—graders, front loaders, backhoes—have all been put to good use at one time or another.

Up to this point, the discussion has been devoted mainly to the technical and logistical aspects of urban archaeology—to the problems created by the city as the setting for fieldwork. It has been indicated that many of these problems are being solved with gratifying rapidity. Unfortunately, the theoretical questions arising from the special nature of the city as subject for study have been more difficult to answer.

One major theoretical accomplishment in urban archaeology has been our realization that we cannot study the city as if it were simply a large collection of discrete "sites" (privy features, or backyards, or even city blocks), each of which can be considered in isolation from the rest. We have come to understand that the city must be viewed as an entity, a single system, though it was created by many different patterns of behavior interacting through time.

But this does not mean that urban archaeologists, any more than their colleagues in social anthropology and the other social sciences, have been able to agree upon a definition (or definitions) of the city, or even to prepare a list of the attributes—recognizable archaeologically—that distinguish the city from other systems of settlement (Rothschild, Chapter 1). We have certainly not succeeded in developing a broad and generally accepted framework within which to study urban processes. The relatively straightforward ecological and evolutionary models that structure much of the archaeological research dealing with preliterate societies have not met our needs, and we have not yet found viable alternatives. In seeking these alternatives, urban archaeologists have been increasingly attracted to the work of urban social anthropologists and sociologists, economists, geographers, and historians. It is to be hoped that these interdisciplinary explorations will help us to frame coherent sets of meaningful questions about urban cultural change that will provide unifying goals for our often-fragmented activities.

The realization that the city must be considered as a large and complex unit brings with it the realization that we face a monumental sampling problem. If we are to provide useful answers to questions about the city, we must first obtain adequate, statistically valid samples of the material remains of the wide range of behaviors that produced this most complex of all human creations. Is this a realistic goal, particularly in view of the many logistical constraints under which urban research must be conducted? Somewhat paradoxically, although we have not yet adequately defined the universe, or even fully discovered its boundaries, we *have* begun to develop workable methods for sampling its diversity. Some of the chapters in this volume (e.g., Chapter 3 by Cressey and Stephens) are illustrative of the thoughtful efforts now being made in this direction. To date, the most successful sampling strategies have been tied to comprehensive cultural resource surveys of the kind just discussed. There is reason to be optimistic.

As urban archaeology matures, its practitioners will, quite rightly, devote most of their efforts to research designed to answer increasing important anthropological and historical questions. But their work will also result in the identification and recording of physical aspects of earlier stages in the growth of the city that would not otherwise be recognized. The frequent juxtaposition of these archaeological materials with above-ground structures, in urban localities that are visited daily by large numbers of people, should provide opportunities for another kind of mutually beneficial cooperation among archaeologists, historians, and architectural preservationists. The selective preservation and intelligent interpretation of some of these archaeological features, preferably as components of "multiple resource" historic areas, could help to make the city's past, in all of its gritty immediacy, a bit more real to a broad segment of its population.

To date, such urban archaeological exhibits are rare in North America, but their potential educational value is so great that they should be worth the effort and ingenuity needed to overcome the obstacles—including the high cost of downtown real estate. Urban archaeological research can contribute uniquely toward the fuller appreciation of a city's total historical and cultural heritage, by permitting its citizens to view their visible, above-ground landmarks in the context of the physical and social events that created them.

BERT SALWEN
New York University

REFERENCES

Cressey, Pamela J.
1979 The city as a site: Exploring new approaches to urban archaeology. Paper presented at the annual meeting of the Society for Historical Archaeology, Nashville, Tennessee.
Grossman, Joel
1980 Defining boundaries and targeting excavation with ground-penetrating radar: The Case of Raritan Landing. *Environmental Impact Assessment Review* 1:145–166.
Salwen, Bert
1978 Archaeology in megalopolis: Updated assessment. *Journal of Field Archaeology* 5:453–59.

Preface

In the past 15 years, the amount of archaeological research on the American city has increased steadily. Although there was earlier work in the urban context, the recent efforts have differed in their attention to the total spectrum of the development of urban–industrial culture. Remains of the late nineteenth and early twentieth centuries now are being assigned the same importance as those of the Colonial and early Federal periods. Mill communities, pauper cemeteries, and manufacturing works are receiving as much consideration as the sites of founding statesmen and historically documented events.

This movement toward an archaeology "of the city" has come about as a result of two interrelated factors. Recent attention to historic preservation and cultural resource management, resulting from a series of federal legislative acts, laws, and regulations, has given urban archaeological remains legally mandated attention. A second important factor has been the growing recognition by American archaeologists that recent, and even present, material culture can be profitably studied using the techniques, methods, and theory of anthropological archaeology. Thus, American archaeologists have pushed and have been pushed into the city, and as a result they are recognizing that urban culture itself is a viable research subject. Some of us even believe that only through a combined synchronic–diachronic approach—to which archaeology is in a position to make a major contribution—can we ever expect to elucidate the complex developmental processes and potential future directions of urbanized human behavior.

It is my hope that the chapters in this volume will stimulate a dialogue among archaeologists who have chosen the American city as their subject. The book should also be useful to urban sociologists, economists, cultural anthropologists, and historians. The theme is one of *pattern and process*. It suggests that our investigations of individual sites or portions of sites must be undertaken with the goal of defining behavioral patterns—socioeconomic, demographic, ethnic, etc.—within the data at specific time horizons. These patterns should be analyzed as manifestations of ongoing processes in the evolution of city life. Furthermore, urban archaeology must be viewed herein not just as the study of individual cities, but as the study of *urbanization*, which has ramifications beyond the confines of the primary settlements.

The book is divided into three parts; each part is preceded by an introductory statement. The first, titled *Strategies and Methods*, contains chapters that focus on the general questions urban archaeologists are asking of their data, and on the ways they are designing their research to explore those questions. In the second part, *Site Formation, Structure, and Pattern*, the chapters can be classed as "test cases." Some of them emphasize approaches, and others interpretation, and a few represent direct extensions of the larger research designs proposed in the first part. Part III, *Artifact Analysis and Interpretation*, contains what I hope represents a set of useful approaches to the data base itself. Some of these deal with intersite or intrasite patterning of artifact assemblages, whereas others are concerned with a specific class of artifacts.

The inclusion of chapters in all of these categories seems logical. Since urban archaeology is a relatively new field, it is striving to develop its theory, method, and data base all at the same time. The gradual evolution from description, to method, to theory that has characterized prehistoric archaeology will not be possible for urban archaeologists, nor would it even be appropriate at this time. Our challenge is to formulate creative theory, develop useful and productive methods, and compile a sound and well-ordered data base, all *simultaneously*. To be successful, this effort will require rigorous standards in the field and in the laboratory, and speedy communication of research findings.

I am convinced, therefore, that we must establish and maintain some mechanisms for information exchange to help us move forward without duplication of effort and repetition of mistakes. Perhaps this volume can serve as a beginning forum and as a stimulus for permanent lines of communication.

Acknowledgments

In 1973, at the annual meeting of the Society for American Archaeology, I had the opportunity to attend a half-day symposium based partly on the archaeology then underway in downtown Tucson, Arizona. The session, entitled "The Great American Dream Machine: Archaeologists in the Works," had a lasting effect on my personal involvement in American archaeology.

Prior to that meeting, I had paid lip service to the notion that archaeology was not just "the study of past," but in fact was the branch of science that used material remains to study the workings of specific human societies and of culture in general. In the classroom, I had expounded on the value of an archaeological approach to the study of *any* behavioral system, past or present. In practice, however, I had devoted most of my research attention to prehistoric and early historic remains.

The symposium on the Tucson project presented clear-cut examples of how archaeology could contribute to a better understanding of behavioral processes within an urban setting. Some of the examples even extended to the present, with Rathje's *Le Project du Garbage*. The importance of this and other urban work was brought into overall perspective by the final paper of the symposium, in which Reid, Rathje, and Schiffer (later published in *American Antiquity*) proposed that archaeology could be a science of the present as well as the past.

Shortly after returning from the meeting, I was asked to provide recommendations for archaeological resources to be impacted by the construction of an extensive rapid-rail system in my own city—Atlanta, Georgia. An environmental impact study, already prepared for the project, had limited its archaeological attention to several known or potential locations of aboriginal sites on the outskirts of the construction corridors. No mention had been made of known or potential inner-city archaeological remains!

Soon, I found myself immersed in what has become an ongoing effort to maintain a program of survey, assessment, and mitigation of a large body of urban archaeological resources. The project has brought me into almost daily contact with construction workers, engineers, planners, and interested citizens, and consequently has led me to recognize, in a way more vivid than I would have otherwise, the need for better communication between archaeologists and the public. The Metropolitan Atlanta Rapid Transit Authority (MARTA) project also has provided me some unexpected glimpses of the biases that exist within the historic preservation movement in general, and among some archaeologists, regarding the value of recent archaeological remains.

Perhaps most importantly, however, the urban work has given me the opportunity to be associated with an outstanding group of undergraduate students, who have worked with dedication under the most trying of conditions. My deepest gratitude goes to these students, without whose encouragement and intellectual stimulation I probably would not have continued my efforts in "asphalt archaeology" and would not have attempted this book.

I am also grateful to my staff on the MARTA project—Linda Carnes, Rowe Bowen, Robin Futch, Linda Worthy, Joe Evans, Gary Barber, and Jim Chapman—who approached their work with enthusiasm, creativity, and good humor. Their effects are reflected directly and indirectly at numerous places in this book.

I also wish to thank Stanley South and the editorial board of the Studies in Historical Archaeology series for their help and encouragement, the staff of Academic Press for its prompt and forthright attention to my requests and queries, Carol Dickens and Sarah Hill for their editorial assistance, and Jean Reed for typing the manuscripts. Daryl C. White designed the motif for the book cover.

Archaeology of Urban America

The Search for Pattern and Process

I

STRATEGIES AND METHODS

How are archaeologists to develop sound strategies and methods—research designs—for investigating the American city? The chapters in Part I represent several approaches to this important problem. Although the authors use examples from specific projects, their proposals are general in nature and have applicability beyond the cities in question.

Rothschild and Rockman discuss urban site formation and suggest potential archaeological correlates for various behavioral components of urban culture. They use their work at the Stadt Huys Block in New York City to illustrate ways of measuring changing population density and heterogeneity. With examples from the Roger Williams Memorial in Providence, Rhode Island, Patricia Rubertone proposes a multistaged research strategy that combines historical research with archaeological field work. Distributional data from trenching and auger testing are evaluated directly against a model based on documentary findings. Next, Cressey and Stephens investigate the "city-site" using a Core–Periphery Model for interpreting changes in spatial organization related to group hierarchy, formation, and conflict. They use Alexandria, Virginia, as their research laboratory, and, like Rubertone, suggest a multistaged approach that integrates historical and archaeological research. Gorman's chapter explores the archaeological implications of industrialization in the early American city. He proposes a *correlation approach*, in which hypotheses generated from patterns in the documentary record can be tested through archaeological investigation. He concludes his treatise with a cluster analysis of glass factory profiles to evaluate an hypothesis based on market theory, proposed earlier in the chapter. Finally, Dickens and Crimmins examine the conceptual framework and procedural format of environmental-impact archaeology in the urban setting. They express concern about the perpetuation of review-and-compliance practices that fail to view the city as an integrated system to be evaluated and studied using a multidisciplinary and multistaged approach. The MARTA (Metropolitan Atlantic Rapid Transit Authority) project in Atlanta, Georgia, serves as their example.

1

Method in Urban Archaeology: The Stadt Huys Block[1]

Nan A. Rothschild and Diana diZerega Rockman

INTRODUCTION

Cities are the most complex form of environment yet developed by humans, and this complexity has many ramifications for archaeologists conducting projects in urban areas. In this chapter we will discuss several attributes characterizing urban entities as archaeological sites and describe the impact of these attributes on various aspects of an urban archaeological project carried out in New York City. We also will suggest two measures that might be useful to archaeologists working in urban areas. Whereas the material presented is of particular relevance to North American situations, the discussion of urbanization and its archaeological manifestations has general application.

CHARACTERISTICS OF URBAN AREAS

A large body of literature in anthropology, sociology, geography, and history attempts to define the attributes that characterize urban communities (e.g., Adams 1966; Berry 1967; Blanton 1976; Burgess 1926; Christaller 1966; Hauser 1965; Redfield and Singer 1954; Sjoberg 1960; Weber 1958; Wirth 1938). As in all cross-cultural and cross-temporal definitions of complex phenomena, these classifications are most useful in the context for which they were designed. An

[1]Funding for the Stadt Huys Block project was provided by the landowner, the Dollar Savings Bank, Con Edison, and the Durst Foundation.

ISBN 0-12-214980-7

urban area or *city* has not yet been, and probably never will be, defined absolutely. In fact, attempts at universal definition may be pointless, considering the variation within urban communities. In an effort to deal with this variation, some writers have developed classificatory typologies for cities (e.g., Mumford 1938; Redfield and Singer 1954; Sjoberg 1960; Weber 1958). This chapter will discuss cities at a general level and thus avoid such classifications.

Four characteristics of urban areas are particularly relevant to archaeologists: (*a*) demographic features, (*b*) political and administrative features, (*c*) economic features, and (*d*) social heterogeneity. Of these, *a* and *b* will be visible primarily in the analysis of settlement pattern data, whereas *c* and *d* will be manifested primarily in patterns of artifact distribution.

Some of these diagnostic features are apparent only in the relative context of their regional setting. This means that several aspects of these characteristics cannot be evaluated yet, as regional data are not available for much of the world, including North America. However, once regional frameworks have been developed, archaeologists can begin to use data from both urban and rural sites to test hypotheses about the process of urbanization and the relationship between urban places and their surrounding regions. The four characteristics of urban areas and some of their effects on archaeological projects in urban areas are discussed next. The Stadt Huys Block Archaeological Project is used as an illustrative example.

STADT HUYS BLOCK

The Stadt Huys Block is in the Wall Street district of New York City, one of the most heavily urbanized areas in the world. The project was conducted under the auspices of the New York City Landmarks Preservation Commission prior to the construction of a skyscraper on the site. Documentary research on the project area was begun in August, 1979, and the excavations extended from October, 1979, through August, 1980. Analysis of the materials from the site has begun, and a preliminary report is in preparation.

The site was originally identified as archaeologically sensitive because it was one of the few areas within the seventeenth-century Dutch settlement of New Amsterdam that had not yet been disturbed by the construction of a twentieth-century skyscraper. The project area consisted of portions of three adjacent city blocks as well as two intervening streets (Figure 1.1).

The excavations were very productive. They revealed the only remains of Dutch New Amsterdam that ever have been excavated, as well as innumerable artifacts and features dating from the English colonial period through the nineteenth century. These discoveries included land surfaces dating from the mid-seventeenth through the nineteenth century, a seventeenth-century Dutch well, an eighteenth-century English well, and several privies and cisterns. In addition, foundation walls dating from the seventeenth century, including those from the Lovelace Tavern (built in 1670) and one possibly from the Stadt Huys, or Dutch City Hall (built in 1642), were found.

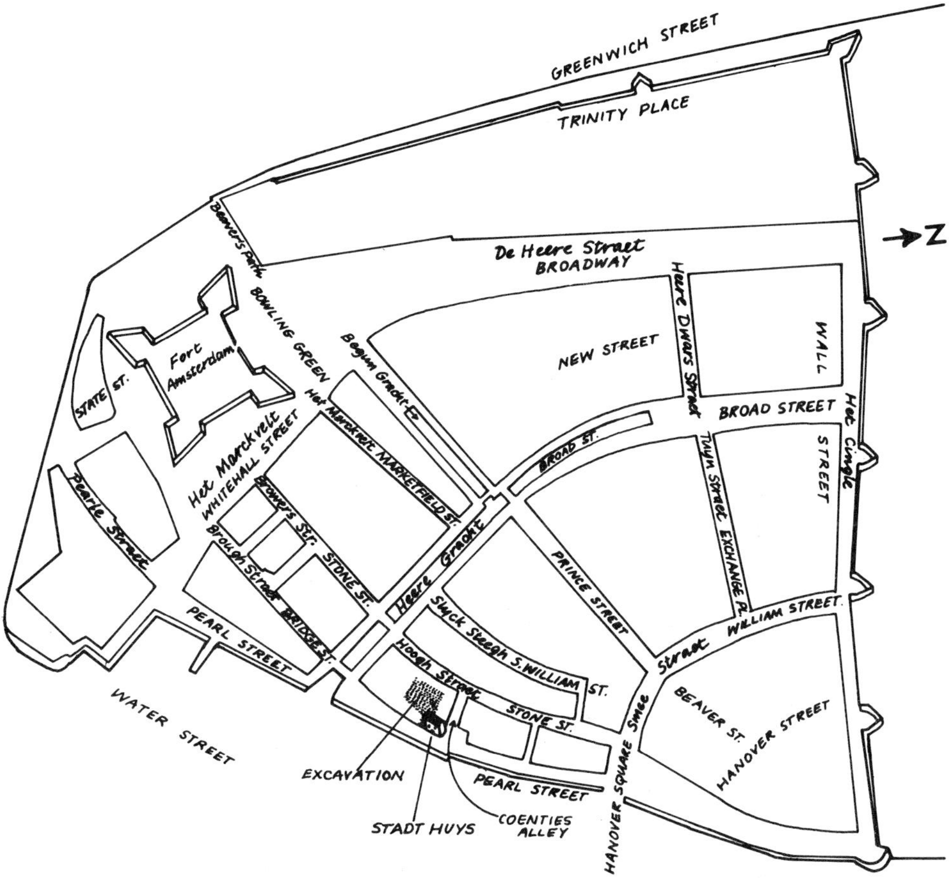

FIGURE 1.1. Map showing the location of the Stadt Huys Block and excavation area.

Throughout all stages of this project, in conducting the documentary research, the field excavations, and the preliminary analysis of the materials, it has been evident that the methods and techniques used in archaeological projects in urban areas are unique, and this uniqueness is directly related to the characteristics of urban areas themselves.

ATTRIBUTES OF URBAN AREAS

Demography: Population Size and Density

Some of the simplest attempts to characterize modern urban areas involve the measure of population size or population density. These definitions usually stipulate that a given population size or density de facto makes a community urban (cf. Davis and Golden 1954). In Scandinavian countries, for example, a settlement of over 250 people constitutes an urban area, while in Greece, Spain, and Switzerland, a community must have 10,000 inhabitants to be so designated (Wheatley 1973:620). Whereas there are serious problems with any "magic number" approach, it is true that cities are more densely settled than other communities within their region. However, it is also true that population density can vary within a single city.

Land Use

The attribute of dense population in urban areas is directly reflected in the use of land. Buildings in cities are relatively closely spaced and land is used and reused intensively. Even public spaces are treated as outdoor structures, in the sense that they are paved or otherwise distinguished from "open" land. The intensive use of urban land is often correlated with the increasing value of land in urban areas (Berry, Simmons, and Tennant 1963). As a city becomes more urban, its land tends to be used by more and more people. This tendency may be manifested in several ways. Land may be subdivided into increasingly smaller parcels. Additional land may be claimed by landfill operations in adjacent submerged and swampy areas. With improvements in architectural technology, land also may be recombined into larger parcels (as in late-nineteenth- and twentieth-century Western cities) and built upward into multistoried skyscrapers.

These processes were expressed on the Stadt Huys Block. The block was originally granted in three large lots in a suburban area in the 1640s, and by the mid-seventeenth century had been further divided into about eight parcels. By the mid-nineteenth century, the block had been further subdivided and covered by 21 separate buildings. In the late nineteenth and early twentieth centuries, architectural innovations allowed this process of subdivision to be reversed, and the block was covered by only 13 larger buildings. Now, in the late twentieth century, the block comprises less than one-half of the ground covered by one 30-story office tower.

Site Formation

The archaeological correlates of the intensive use of land in urban areas are the disturbance and destruction of archaeological deposits and, of course, complex stratigraphy. For the Stadt Huys Block project, the archaeological potential of the project area was explored before fieldwork began by documenting the sequence of disturbance and destruction of archaeological resources. Because the block and street areas within the site had been subjected to different kinds of use, their archaeological deposits had been exposed to different kinds of disturbance and destruction.

The most drastic form of destruction to the archaeological resources of areas within city blocks is usually the construction and alteration of the foundations and basements of the buildings that have been built on the site. It was assumed for the Stadt Huys Block project that areas recently occupied by small buildings with shallow basements and backyards would have the highest archaeological potential.

Information from the New York City Department of Buildings and from borings taken on the site allowed a determination of the backyard locations and the basement depths of many of the most recent buildings in the project area. This information, in turn, provided a way to stratify the site (Redman 1974) into areas of high and low archaeological potential and to concentrate excavations in the former areas.

The most severe forms of destruction to archaeological deposits lying under the streets are street grading and the installation of utility lines, such as gas mains and sewers. Although references to street grading were found in city records, the details of these operations were not documented. Therefore, it was not possible to determine the changes in grades made in the streets surrounding the Stadt Huys Block before fieldwork began. Maps supplied by the city and engineering firms did show the general positions of utility lines under streets. However, the exact locations of these utilities were only schematically represented and proved to be misleading. In fact, under Stone Street, which was documented as containing six different kinds of utilities and numerous concrete vaults extending under the sidewalk from the adjacent buildings to the curb line, we found a large expanse of deposits containing a series of undisturbed earlier land surfaces dating from the mid-seventeenth through the early nineteenth centuries. This was the only area on the site where such early ground surfaces were found.

The high population densities of urban areas and the correlated intensive use of the land also result in complex stratigraphy. The upper portions of most of the features encountered within the Stadt Huys Block had been disturbed by later construction activities. Two early-nineteenth-century buildings, for example, were built over the 1670 Lovelace Tavern, leaving intact only the lower 2 ft (.6 m) of both its foundation walls and the deposits associated with the tavern's use. Both the eighteenth-century English colonial well and a late-eighteenth-century privy had early-nineteenth-century walls built through them. The seventeenth-century Dutch well was covered by a later cistern, which in turn was disturbed by the construction of a twentieth-century basement.

These complexities slow down the excavation process and present problems in accurately recording stratigraphic relationships. For the Stadt Huys Block project, the latter problem has been alleviated by using Harris matrices, which graphically present complex stratigraphy in a concise way (Harris 1979).

Density of Materials

A high population density and the intensive use and reuse of land result in a high density of artifacts. As more and more urban sites are excavated in America, it becomes increasingly difficult to find museums or other appropriate institutions that have the facilities to serve as repositories for these collections, and the artifacts themselves will have to be subjected to a strict sampling procedure in the field. In the Stadt Huys Block project, for example, we counted and weighed the coal, brick, and mortar in the field and kept only a small sample of these materials from each stratum. Even with this procedure, however, we collected almost 5 tons (4.5 metric tons) of material.

Administrative Features

Many towns and cities are defined by administrative criteria. In Turkey, Czechoslovakia, and the United Arab Republic, for example, the existence of a specific form of government is sufficient to establish a community as a town. Conversely, in Japan and the United Kingdom, entities that the central administration decides to define as towns are given a certain kind of government (Jones 1966:4). Cities are noted for their hierarchical, bureaucratic system of management, with a political mode replacing a kinship mode of organization (Adams 1966; Childe 1950; Maine 1917; Wirth 1938). Urban development and state formation are marked by an enlarged population base and the appearance of mechanisms to collect taxes and to distribute information, goods, and services (Adams and Nissen 1972; Blanton 1976; Flannery 1972; Johnson 1978; Wright and Johnson 1975). These administrative characteristics are reflected in the history of land use and have a direct effect on archaeological projects conducted in urban areas.

Public Buildings

In urban centers, public buildings are used to house administrative activities. As the community enlarges, more special-purpose structures may appear. New Amsterdam was originally settled in 1625 by the Dutch West India Company as a company town. The company's administrative offices were located in the central area of the settlement. When the company finally granted New Amsterdam a municipal government in 1653, a large building that originally had been a company tavern was allocated to house these municipal activities. This city hall, or Stadt Huys, located on the block where the excavations took place, continued to serve this function under both the Dutch and English administrations until 1697, when it was declared unsafe for further use. After abandonment of the Stadt Huys, and before construction of a new city hall had been completed, the city's administrative functions were performed in another large public building, the Lovelace Tavern, located next door to the Stadt Huys.

In addition to the Stadt Huys and the Lovelace Tavern, the Stadt Huys Block was also the site of a public school in the late nineteenth and early twentieth centuries. Thus, of the ten lots examined on the Stadt Huys Block, three had been occupied by public buildings at some point in their histories.

Land Management

The administrative functions of cities are also reflected in land management, which shifts from individual to central control in urban areas and is exemplified in the layouts of American towns and cities (cf. Leone 1978, for a nonurban example of the effect of strong central control on town planning). Community layout is also reflective of its socioeconomic structure (Engels 1971; Harvey 1973). Yet another factor influencing land management is the difference between use value and exchange value (Harvey 1973). Working with data from New England, McManis (1975) showed that lot sizes and community layout became standardized when the purpose of land acquisition shifted from individual use to investment and speculation.

The layout of Philadelphia was planned from its inception, with regularly laid-out streets. New York, on the other hand, was founded as a company town with its primary focus on the fur trade, which meant that the regularization of its streets was begun much later. It was only after the American Revolution that the streets of New York City began to be formally laid out on a large scale. Even today, the oldest parts of the city, such as the Wall Street area and Greenwich Village, are noted for their winding and unaligned streets.

The role of the New York City government in land management is also expressed in the landfilling operations that have characterized the physical growth of the city. Since the seventeenth century, the city has owned the area adjacent to the shore of Manhattan Island. Throughout its history, the city has made a practice of raising money by selling water lots in these areas, which were filled in through private enterprise. The central, and therefore, most valuable area of the city was enlarged by the process of filling in and reclaiming land in adjacent rivers. This process was begun as early as the 1680s and continues to the present.

In addition to the information about community growth that has come from the study of the landfill history, the fill itself may constitute a valuable resource. Artifacts from the fill may give insight into earlier occupations, and the excavations may provide information on the topography of the earlier shoreline and the history of the technology of the filling process (cf. Henn 1980; Kardas and Larrabee 1980; Pickman and Rothschild 1981). In Manhattan much of the early landfill consists of materials taken from within the island itself, and often includes artifacts that predate the land's use as fill.

Record Keeping

There is a direct relationship between the degree of administrative activity and the amount of documentation used by the city to record this activity. These records may present the archaeologist with an embarrassment of riches in conducting documentary research before going into the field. For the Stadt Huys Block project, practical restraints required sampling procedures in studying the documents that related to the history of the block. This study had to be restricted to those documents that dealt directly with the history of land use on the lots having greatest archaeological potential. This research was narrowly focused on the occupants of each lot, whether the lot was used for residential or commercial purposes, and, if commercial, the kind of business that was done on the property. Relevant documents included tax assessment records and directories dating after the American Revolution. For the Colonial period, with its relatively sparce documentation, the surviving tax records were supplemented by wills and conveyance records, which often mention the businesses of the occupants of the lot conveyed and those of its immediate neighbors.

Finally, the central administration of an urban area is also reflected in public works projects. One of these projects allowed us to delimit further the focus of the documentary research on the Stadt Huys Block. In the 1840s, the Croton Reservoir system was first put into use in Manhattan (Jones 1978:49). It was assumed, therefore, that most of the backyard features such as wells, cisterns, and privies would not have been used after this period, which eliminated the need to research documents dating after 1850.

Economic Features

Economic attributes have proved useful in studying urban areas. One of these characteristics reflects the division of labor. More than 50 years ago, Pirenne (1925) viewed a city as a "colony of merchants." Several operational definitions of towns and cities include this type of economic criterion. In India, for example, a town has been defined as an area with a population of more than 5000, a density of over 1000 people per square mile, and 75% of the adult male population engaged in work other than agriculture. In Israel a community is not a town if more than one-third of the population is engaged in agriculture (Jones 1966:4). There are, however, some urban entities in which a large proportion of the community is engaged in agriculture, at least on a part-time basis (Church 1959; Milton 1976).

Marketing Centers

Another economic characteristic is the city's function as a marketing center. To study cities in this role, we must use a regional approach, as cities are dependent on their surrounding areas for support in subsistence goods. The geographer's notion of central places (Berry 1967; Christaller 1966) has provided archaeologists with a useful model for studying regional settlement systems characterized by market economies (e.g., Blanton, Appel, Finsten, Kowalewski, Feinman, and Fisch 1979; Johnson 1973; Paynter 1980; Smith 1976). Within such a framework, cities are high-order central places, not only because of their administrative function, but also because of their role as marketing centers, which produce and distribute goods and services.

Artifact Patterns

The city's role as a marketing center suggests certain archaeological correlates that may be expressed in artifact patterns. Specialized markets exist in cities and should leave material remains. And it is expected that technologically new artifact forms will become prevalent in urban areas (active in large marketing networks that allow access to new goods) before they are common in more rural areas (Salwen, Bridges, and Rothschild 1981; and cf. Deetz and Dethlefsen 1967).

Because of this increased access to a variety of goods, it also might be expected that there would be a higher proportion of imported to locally made objects in urban areas than in rural areas. However, the variables controlling trade in a market economy are complex. In a study of the growth of a national-scale American market in the nineteenth century, Spencer-Wood (1979) showed that urban sites yield a higher proportion of locally made glass bottles than rural sites. She explains this by noting that manufacturers would tend to set up business near large-scale marketing areas so that they could economize on transportation costs of importing new materials and marketing finished goods, and benefit from the proximity of the large local market of the city (Spencer-Wood 1979:121).

A similar phenomenon was found in analyzing Dutch materials from the Stadt Huys Block. It was originally predicted that New Amsterdam, being a higher-order central place, would exhibit a higher proportion of imported to locally made ceramics than Fort Orange, a smaller contemporary Dutch settlement in what is now Albany. As it so happens, the opposite is true. The Stadt Huys Block yielded a higher ratio of redware to delft than did Huey's excavations in Fort Orange (Paul Huey, personal communication). Delft is believed to have been imported, whereas some of the redware is assumed to have been locally made. New Amsterdam, with its larger population and local market, and access to a larger trade network, seems to have attracted more potters than the more remote settlement of Fort Orange.

Occupational Specialization

As most of the occupants of cities are not involved in subsistence activities, a high degree of occupational specialization in urban areas is likely to be reflected in the archaeological record. Thus, all things being equal, urban sites should yield a higher ratio of non-subsistence- to subsistence-related artifacts than rural sites.

This economic specialization was evident on the Stadt Huys Block. In the first half of the nineteenth century, the block was occupied by buildings used in a wide range of commercial activities. For example, in the 1840s alone, the ten lots that were identified as having high archaeological potential were occupied by a druggist, a crockery, a hardware store, two grocers, two bootmakers, a clerk, a stevedore, several coopers, a saloon, and a signpainter. The activities in some of these businesses were reflected in the archaeological record. In the lot occupied by the crockery, for example, a 1.3 ft^3 (.027 m^3) level in a small backyard feature yielded more than 2000 pottery sherds.

Social Heterogeneity

Another attribute useful in characterizing cities is that of social heterogeneity (Wirth 1938). This characteristic may be visible along at least two dimensions of variation: cultural or ethnic variation and socioeconomic variation as exemplified by caste or class. Both of these kinds of variation should be reflected in the archaeological record.

Use of Space

The use of space is known to reflect cultural differences (Hall 1966) and these differences are also expressed in house settings, house layouts, room and modular unit size (Deetz 1977; Glassie 1975), and functions performed in each room (Fried and Gleicher 1961; Laumann and House 1970). Dutch architecture in New York, for example, was characterized by houses built so that their stepped gables faced the street, while the later English houses were altered in this respect (Birket 1916; Bridenbaugh 1948). Social class may also be reflected in architectural attributes such as house size, setting, arrangement of rooms, and material of manufacture (Kramer 1979; Watson 1978).

Artifact Patterns

Social heterogeneity may be reflected in the distributions of artifacts of various types. Ethnic heterogeneity may be determined from both the stylistic and functional analysis of artifact distributions. In the analysis of artifacts of similar functions, style may be used as a marker of group identity and in maintaining social boundaries (Barth 1969; Kintigh 1979; Plog 1977; Wobst 1977). South (1977) has pointed out that eighteenth-century British Colonial sites in North America exhibit little stylistic variation in ceramic assemblages, regardless of site function. If style is a marker of group identity, and urban communities are ethnically diverse, this diversity should be reflected in stylistic attributes. Ceramics are an obvious class of artifacts that should reflect stylistic diversity (Watson, LeBlanc, and Redman 1980), but these differences may also be reflected across a number of other artifact types (Hodder 1977), including articles of clothing and pieces of bone showing differences in butchering practices.

The quantitative analysis of functionally different artifacts will also provide insight into ethnic heterogeneity. This might be evident in artifacts related to cuisine. The Dutch in eighteenth-century New York, for example, are noted for not favoring the "Englishman's perpetual dish" of pudding or pie, preferring porridge instead. The Dutch also preferred to drink beer or water and not the Englishman's punch, and the punch bowl did "not make a daily round" in Dutch households (Kalm 1966:603, 614, 628). These ethnically diverse food habits should be directly reflected in the archaeological record.

Socioeconomic differences also are evident in the distributions of artifacts. Certain ceramic wares, for example, were more expensive, and therefore may be expected to be distributed among richer households. Miller (1980) has documented the differences in cost for various kinds of nineteenth-century white earthenwares, and contemporary sources can provide some information on the relative value of wares for earlier periods. The greater socioeconomic heterogeneity found in urban areas should be reflected in the greater diversity of artifact types when typologies are used that reflect economic value (see Worthy, Chapter 13).

URBAN MEASURES

This chapter has focused on some of the ways that an examination of the nature of urban areas can contribute to methods in urban archaeology. It also would seem possible to describe the degree of urbanization in an area in a quantitative fashion. The use of such quantitative assessments will facilitate both the generation of hypotheses to explore specific manifestations of the process of urbanization in a given community and more reliable planning for urban excavations. Archaeologists and others who study cities see them as existing at points along a developmental path. Furthermore, different parts of the same city may differ in their degree of urbanization, and some cities may be more urban than others in terms of the characteristics noted. Quantitative measures will be useful in comparing the degree of urbanization in areas both within and between cities, and within a single community over time. Two measures are proposed to evaluate urbanization in terms of population density and social heterogeneity. The usefulness of these measures has yet to be tested with archaeological data.

One of the archaeological correlates of population density is the intensive use of land in an urban area. This correlate might be measured by:

$$M_1 = \frac{\text{square feet modified land}}{\text{square feet unmodified land}}$$

Modified land might be defined as land occupied by buildings, features, utilities, and paving, and would not include rural modifications such as plowing and terracing. As the ratio increases, the degree of urbanization of the area studied would also increase.

The second urban characteristic which may be measured is that of social heterogeneity. The social heterogeneity of a community should be reflected in the heterogeneity of the artifacts deposited by the members of that community. A measure borrowed from Information Theory, the Shannon-Weaver formula, assesses the diversity of a class of artifacts as they are distributed among a number of types. The formula has been used in ecology to measure species diversity in an ecological community (Hill 1973; Peet 1974; Pielou 1969; Simpson 1949).

Archaeologists have applied diversity measures to a variety of data types (Conkey 1980; Dickens 1980; Gorman 1975; Justeson n.d.; Peebles and Kus 1977; Rothschild 1975, 1982; Saxe 1970; Tainter 1977; Yellen 1977). We suggest the measurement of diversity within the class of ceramics, dividing the class into types based on decorative attributes and ware categories (pearlware, creamware, shell-edged, transfer-printed, etc.).

The formula is

$$H' = -\sum_{i=1} s_{p_i} \log p_i,$$

where p_i refers to the proportion of the class in a particular type and s represents the number of types. This should be corrected for maximum diversity, given a particular s (Pielou 1969):

$$M_2 = J = H'/H_{\max},$$

where $H_{\max} = \log s$.

There are problems with the use of diversity measures relating to sample size effects and the interpretation of the measure. It is our supposition that the sample size problem may be solved in a manner similar to some faunal and palynological solutions (Grayson 1978; Martin 1963), which basically require adequate size samples. We expect diversity to increase with urbanization, as a measure of one or both types of diversity, related to ethnic or socioeconomic variation in the population.

SUMMARY AND CONCLUSIONS

In this chapter we have discussed the relationships between the characteristics of cities and the methods used by urban archaeologists. Four of these characteristics are particularly relevant to the archaeological investigation of cities. These characteristics consist of demographic attributes, and attributes reflecting administrative function, economic function, and social heterogeneity. These characteristics are visible in two sets of archaeological research foci: (*a*) the use of space as reflected in land use, land management, public architecture, and site formation processes; and (*b*) artifact patterns reflecting ethnic and social heterogeneity and economic specialization. We have also proposed measures for two of these characteristics (density of land use and social heterogeneity) that may enable urban archaeologists to compare communities within and between regional systems and over time in order to understand better the process of urbanization.

Although we have used examples from Colonial New York to illustrate some of these points, we hope that they will be relevant to archaeologists working in other urban systems.

ACKNOWLEDGMENTS

We owe a great deal of thanks to many people whose assistance made the Stadt Huys Block project possible. We would especially like to acknowledge the help of Dorothy Miner and other members of the New York City Landmarks Preservation Commission, Bert Salwen of New York University for continuing advice and support, and Carol Kramer and Don Grayson for reading early versions of this chapter. Kathleen Borowitz drew Figure 1.1 (originally published in *Archaeology*) and we appreciate the opportunity to publish it again here.

REFERENCES

Adams, R. McC.
1966 *The evolution of urban society: Early Mesopotamia and prehistoric Mexico.* Chicago: Aldine.

Adams, R. McC., and H. J. Nissen
1972 *The Uruk countryside: The natural setting of urban societies.* Chicago: Univ. of Chicago Press.

Barth, F. (editor)
1969 *Ethnic groups and boundaries: The social organization of cultural differences.* Boston: Little, Brown.

Berry, B. J. L.
1967 *Geography of market centers and retail distribution.* Englewood Cliffs, N.J.: Prentice-Hall.

Berry, B. J. L., J. W. Simmons, and R. J. Tennant
1963 Urban population densities: Structure and change. *Geographical Review* 53:389–405.

Birket, J.
1916 *Some cursory remarks made by James Birket in his voyage to North America.* New Haven, Conn.: Yale Univ. Press.

Blanton, R. E.
1976 Anthropological studies of cities. *Annual Review of Anthropology* 5:249–264.

Blanton, R. E., J. Appel, L. Finsten, S. Kowalewski, G. Feinman, and E. Fisch
1979 Regional evolution in the valley of Oaxaca, Mexico. *Journal of Field Archaeology* **6**:369–390.
Bridenbaugh, C. (editor)
1948 *Gentleman's progress: The itinerarium of Dr. Alexander Hamilton, 1744*. Chapel Hill: Univ. of North Carolina Press.
Burgess, E. W.
1926 *The urban community*. Chicago: Univ. of Chicago Press.
Childe, V. G.
1950 The urban revolution. *Town Planning Review* **21**:3–17.
Christaller, W.
1966 *Central places in southern Germany*, translated by C. W. Baskin. Englewood Cliffs, N.J.: Prentice-Hall.
Church, R. J. H.
1959 West African urbanization: A geographical view. In *Urbanism in West Africa*, edited by K. Little. *Sociological Review* **7.**
Conkey, M. W.
1980 The identification of prehistoric hunger–gatherer aggregation sites: The case of Altamira. *Current Anthropology* **21**:609–630.
Davis, K., and H. H. Golden
1954 Urbanization and the development of pre-industrial areas. *Economic Development and Cultural Change* **3**:6–24.
Deetz, J.
1977 *In small things forgotten: The archaeology of early American life*. New York: Doubleday.
Deetz, J., and E. S. Dethlefsen
1967 Death's head, cherub and willow. *Natural History* **76**:29–37.
Dickens, R. S., Jr.
1980 Ceramic diversity as an indicator of cultural dynamics in the Woodland period. *Tennessee Anthropologist* **5**:34–46.
Engels, F.
1971 *The condition of the working class in England in 1844*, translated and edited by W. O. Henderson and W. H. Chaloner. Oxford: Blackwell.
Flannery, K. V.
1972 The cultural evolution of civilizations. *Annual Review of Ecology and Systematics* **5**:399–426.
Fried, M., and P. Gleicher
1961 Some sources of residential satisfaction in an urban slum. *Journal, American Institute of Planners* 27:305–315.
Glassie, H.
1975 *Folk housing in middle Virginia: A structural analysis of historic artifacts*. Knoxville: Univ. of Tennessee Press.
Gorman, G.
1975 Organization, energy, and extinction: An archaeological evaluation of White's culture trend theory. Paper presented at SAA meeting, Dallas, Texas.
Grayson, D. K.
1978 Minimum numbers and sample sizes in vertebrate faunal analysis. *American Antiquity* **43**:53–65.
Hall, E. T.
1966 *The hidden dimension*. Garden City, N.Y.: Doubleday.
Harris, E. C.
1979 *Principles of archaeological stratigraphy*. New York: Academic Press.
Harvey, D.
1973 *Social justice and the city*. Baltimore, Md.: Johns Hopkins Univ. Press.
Hauser, P. M.
1965 Urbanization, an overview. In *The study of urbanization*, edited by P. M. Hauser and L. Schnore. New York: Wiley.

Henn, R.
1980 The Water Street site: Final report on 209 Water Street. On file at the City Univ. of New York.
Hill, M. O.
1973 Diversity and evenness: A unifying notation and its consequences. *Ecology* **54**:427–432.
Hodder, I.
1977 A study in ethnoarchaeology in western Kenya. In *Archaeology and anthropology*, edited by M. Spriggs. *British Archaeological Review* supplementary series **19**:117–142.
Johnson, G. A.
1973 A test of the utility of central place theory in archaeology. In *Man, settlement and urbanism*, edited by P. J. Ucko, R. Tringham, and G. W. Dimbleby. London: Duckworth. Pp. 769–785.
Johnson, G. A.
1978 Information sources and the development of decision-making organizations. In *Social archaeology: Beyond subsistence and dating*, edited by C. L. Redman, M. J. Berman, E. V. Curtin, W. T. Langhorne, Jr., N. M. Versaggi, and J. C. Wanser. New York: Academic Press.
Jones, E.
1966 *Towns and cities*. Oxford: Oxford Univ. Press.
Jones, P.
1978 *Under the city streets: A history of subterranean New York*. New York: Holt.
Justeson, J. S.
n.d. The design of information theoretic research in archaeology. Manuscript in press.
Kalm, P.
1966 *The America of 1750: Peter Kalm's travels in North America: The English version of 1770*, edited by A. B. Benson. New York: Dover.
Kardas, S., and E. Larrabee
1980 Landmaking in lower Manhattan. *Seaport Magazine* **14**:16–19.
Kintigh, K.
1979 Social structure, the structure of style, and stylistic patterns in Cibola pottery. Manuscript on file, Univ. of Michigan, Ann Arbor.
Kramer, C.
1979 An archaeological view of a contemporary Kurdish village: Domestic architecture, household size and wealth. In *Ethno-archaeology*, edited by C. Kramer. New York: Columbia Univ. Press. Pp. 139–163.
Laumann, E. O., and J. S. House
1970 Living room styles and social attributes. *Center for Research on Social Organization, Department of Sociology Reprint Series* No. 4. Ann Arbor, Michigan.
Leone, M. P.
1978 Archaeology as the science of technology: Mormon town plans and fences. In *Historical archaeology*, edited by R. L. Schuyler. Farmingdale, N.Y.: Baywood Publishing. Pp. 191–200.
Maine, H. S.
1917 *Ancient law*. London: Dent.
Martin, P. S.
1963 *The last 10,000 years, a fossil pollen record of the American Southwest*. Tucson: Univ. of Arizona Press.
McManis, D. R.
1975 *Colonial New England: A historical geography*. New York: Oxford Univ. Press.
Miller, G. L.
1980 Classification and economic scaling of 19th-century ceramics. *Historical Archaeology* **14**:1–40.
Millon, R.
1976 Social relations in ancient Teotihuacan. In *The valley of Mexico: Studies in prehistoric ecology and society*, edited by E. Wolf. Albuquerque: Univ. of New Mexico Press. Pp. 205–248.

Mumford, L.
1938 *The culture of cities*. New York: Harcourt Brace.
Paynter, R.
1980 Long distance processes, stratification and settlement pattern: An archaeological perspective. Unpublished Ph.D. dissertation, Department of Anthropology, Univ. of Massachusetts, Amherst.
Peebles, D. S., and S. M. Kus
1977 Some archaeological correlates of ranked society. *American Antiquity* **42**:421–440.
Peet, R. K.
1974 The measurement of species diversity. *Annual Review of Ecology and Systematics* 7:285–307.
Pickman, A., and N. A. Rothschild
1981 64 Pearl Street: An archaeological excavation in 17th-century landfill. On file, New York State Division of Historic Perservation.
Pielou, E. C.
1969 *An introduction to mathematical ecology*. New York: Wiley Interscience.
Pirenne, H.
1925 *Medieval cities*. Princeton, N.J.: Princeton Univ. Press.
Plog, S.
1977 A multivariate approach to the explanation of ceramic design variation. Unpublished Ph.D. dissertation, Department of Anthropology, Univ. of Michigan, Ann Arbor.
Redfield, R., and M. Singer
1954 The cultural role of cities. *Economic Development and Cultural Change* **3**:53–73.
Redman, C. L.
1974 Archaeological sampling strategies, *Addison-Wesley Module in Anthropology* No. **55**. Reading, Mass.: Addison-Wesley.
Rothschild, N. A.
1975 Age and sex, status and role in prehistoric societies of eastern North America. Ph.D. dissertation, New York Univ., University Microfilms, Ann Arbor, Michigan.
Rothschild, N. A.
1982 *Sex, status and social complexity: An analysis of nine midwestern sites*. In press.
Salwen, B., S. Bridges, and N. Rothschild.
1981 The importance of small samples from disturbed sites. *Historical Archaeology* **15**.
Saxe, A. A.
1970 The social dimensions of mortuary practices. Ph.D. dissertation, Univ. of Michigan, University Microfilms, Ann Arbor.
Simpson, E. H.
1949 Measurement of diversity. *Nature* **163**:688.
Sjoberg, G.
1960 *The preindustrial city, past and present*. Glencoe, Ill.: Free Press.
Smith, C. A.
1976 Regional economic systems: Linking geographical models and socioeconomic models. In *Regional analysis*, Vol. 1, edited by C. A. Smith. New York: Academic Press. Pp. 3–63.
South, S.
1977 *Method and theory in historical archaeology*. New York: Academic Press.
Spencer-Wood, S. M.
1979 The natural American market in historical archaeology: Urban vs. rural populations. In *Ecological anthropological studies of the middle Connecticut River Valley*, edited by R. Paynter. *Research Reports* **18**, Department of Anthropology, Univ. of Massachusetts, Amherst. Pp. 117–128.
Tainter, J. A.
1977 Modeling change in prehistoric social systems. In *For theory building in archaeology*, edited by L. R. Binford. New York: Academic Press. Pp. 327–351.

Watson, P. J.
1978 Archaeological ethnography in western Iran. *Viking Fund Publications in Anthropology* No. 57. Tucson: Univ. of Arizona Press.

Watson, P. J., S. A. LeBlanc, and C. L. Redman
1980 Aspects of Zuni prehistory: Preliminary report on excavations and survey in the El Morro Valley of New Mexico. *Journal of Field Archaeology* 7:201–218.

Weber, M.
1958 *The city*, edited and translated by D. Martindale and G. Neuwirth. New York: Free Press.

Wheatley, P.
1973 The concept of urbanism. In *Man, settlement and urbanism*, edited by P. J. Ucko, R. Tringham, and G. W. Dimbleby. London: Duckworth. Pp. 601–637.

Wirth, L.
1938 Urbanism as a way of life. *American Journal of Sociology* **44**:1–24.

Wobst, H. M.
1977 Stylistic behavior and information exchange. In *Research essays in honor of J. B. Griffin*, edited by C. E. Cleland, *Michigan Anthropological Papers* **61**.

Wright, H. T., and G. A. Johnson
1975 Population, exchange and early state development in southwestern Iran. *American Anthropologist* 77:267–289.

Yellen, J.
1977 *Archaeological approaches to the present*. New York: Academic Press.

2

An Approach to Archaeology of the City: The Roger Williams National Memorial Project[1]

Patricia E. Rubertone

INTRODUCTION

During the last two decades, discussions of archaeological research design have stressed the importance of integrating methods of investigation with analytical procedures and the data base. Of particular interest have been contributions by Binford (1964), Struever (1968), and Redman (1973) that have emphasized the organization of archaeological research designs and have presented strategies for incorporating advances in theory, method, and technique into actual research programs. Although these discussions have provided general guidelines for organizing archaeological research, they have not addressed some of the special problems faced by historical archaeologists. Although the subject of research design in historical archaeology recently has been given some attention (e.g., Klein 1973; House 1977; South 1974, 1977), there have been few published programmatic statements (e.g., Redman, Anzalone, and Rubertone 1979) that broach the issue of research design in urban historical archaeology. Yet, it is in the urban setting that the organizational requirements for effective research are especially demanding.

In this chapter it is argued that there is a need for greater interdependence between our research goals and strategies, so that the various stages of research can

[1]Both the archaeological resource study and the archaeological site examination were conducted by the Public Archaeology Laboratory, Brown University, with the support of the Division of Cultural Resources, North Atlantic Regional Office, National Park Service, United States Department of the Interior, under contracts CX1600-8-0012 and CX1600-9-0038.

ISBN 0-12-214980-7

be integrated in a meaningful way. Whereas this is by no means a new suggestion, it does recognize that, as historical archaeologists working with diverse lines of evidence, we too often approach our data in routine ways without stopping to evaluate the relative effectiveness of various methods in satisfying specific research needs. Furthermore, the urban historical archaeologist is confronted not only with an abundant and highly complex archaeological data base, but also with a very rich and detailed documentary base. This situation necessitates a systematic approach, in which decisions regarding data requirements (e.g., which documents should be reviewed, how much excavated material should be collected, and what level of detail should be recorded for analytical purposes) are tied to the overall research goals and coordinated with the results of each stage in the research process.

The research design formulated for the examination of the Roger Williams National Memorial, Providence, Rhode Island is presented here as an example of an investigative approach to urban historical archaeology. It was designed so that documentary, field, and analytical procedures could be incorporated into a series of interdependent stages through the use of a multistage research design (e.g., Redman 1973). These investigations were directed toward achieving several research goals that would aid the National Park Service in the management and interpretation of the Memorial's archaeological resources. In addition to describing the material inventory and evaluating the significance of archaeological resources, the basic aims of the project were the delineation of depositional processes affecting urban archaeological site formation, and the reconstruction of land-use patterns through time (see also Rubertone, Part II of this volume). The approach has included the systematic study of documentary evidence; the use of random and systematic sampling to select testing locations; deep, stratigraphic testing using power-assisted augers; alternative artifact recording schemes; and computer-based data management, mapping, and analytical procedures.

THE RESEARCH LABORATORY

The Roger Williams National Memorial is presently a small urban park located at the base of the western slope of College Hill, bordering downtown Providence. The archaeological investigations focused on an area that formerly had been the site of six blocks of urban development (Figure 2.1). The changes that have transformed the area through time reflect a trajectory of change that is not at all unusual for many neighborhoods in New England's coastal cities.

For the six-block area, these developments can be traced from the middle of the eighteenth century. At that time, settlement was sparse, with only a few residences in existence. The primary character of the area, however, was influenced by maritime-related activities as evidenced by wharves along its western border. By the middle of the nineteenth century, notable changes had occurred. With the demise of maritime trade, businesses were oriented toward servicing the needs of the local residents, whose numbers continued to increase throughout the century. Although most of the area's initial settlers were Anglo-Americans, the number of non-Anglo immigrants living in the area grew steadily.

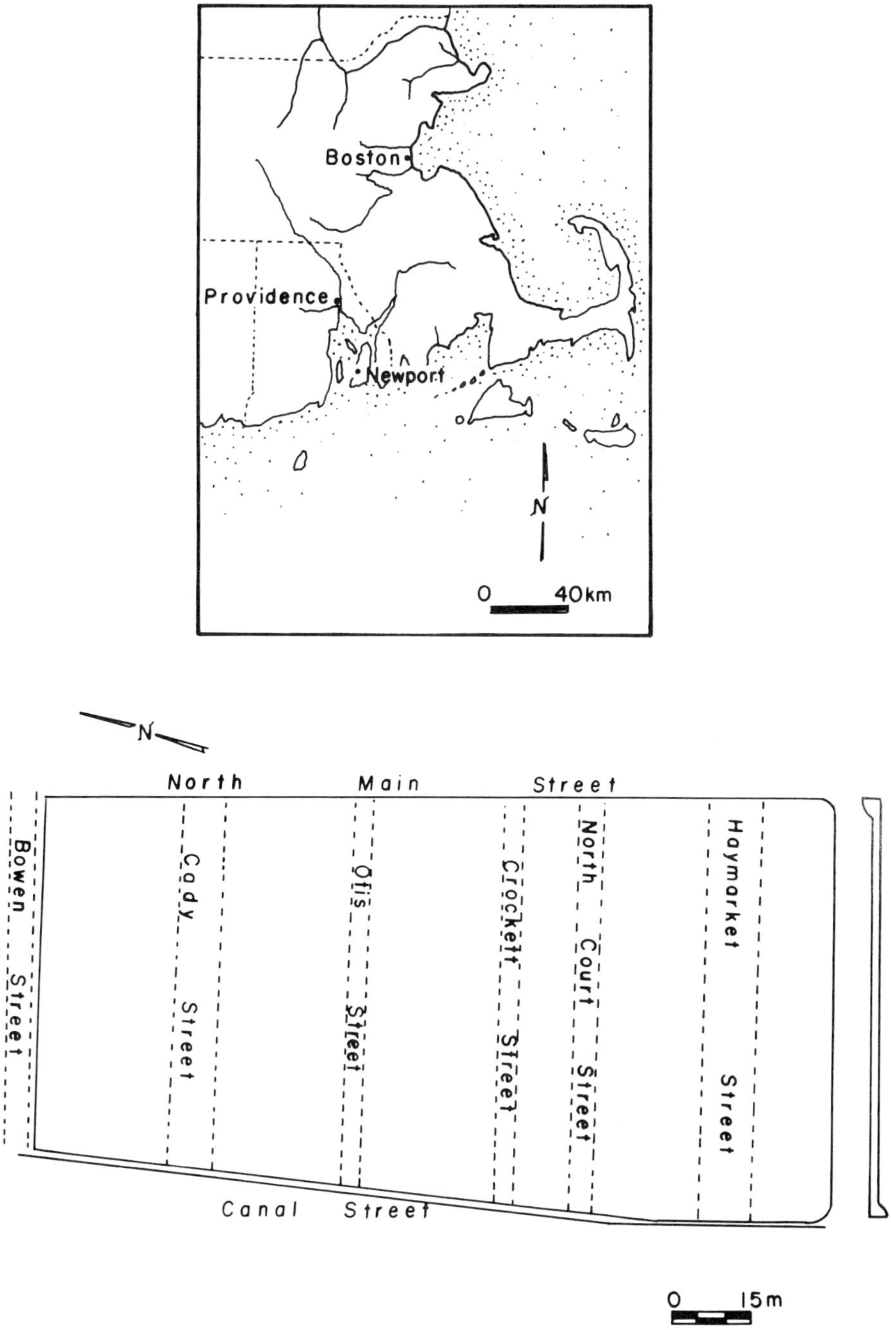

FIGURE 2.1. Map showing location of Providence and other New England coastal cities. Lower plan shows Roger Williams National Memorial Project area.

By the end of the nineteenth century, other major transformations had occurred in the area. The increased competition for land forced many residents from the area. Commercial structures, primarily warehouses, dominated, with only a few tenements scattered throughout the area. These multifamily dwellings served as housing for recent Armenian and Eastern European immigrants. This pattern persisted well into the twentieth century. By this time, a neighborhood that two centuries earlier had played an important political and economic role in Providence's history was completely transformed.

During the late 1960s, the entire 4.56 acre (1.85 ha.) parcel that was to become the Roger Williams National Memorial was purchased by the Providence Redevelopment Authority. At that time, standing structures were razed, thus creating an unobstructed landscape in a prime area that had been the setting for many of the events and developments during Providence's first few centuries. This latest episode in the area's history has made it an ideal laboratory for conducting archaeological investigations into the recent historical past since few historical cities exhibit large expanses of open space such as this in downtown areas. Consequently, in designing the investigations, we were able to treat the six-block area as a whole, rather than having to focus on a series of individual sites or properties.

RESEARCH STRATEGIES

A continuing concern in the research at the Roger Williams National Memorial has been to evaluate and improve methods of investigation in urban historical archaeology. The range of available historical sources, both written and visual, was extensive, and field problems endemic to the archaeological remains of complex societies (e.g., dense architectural debris, abundant artifactural remains, complex depositional patterns, and deeply buried strata) were evident. Faced with this abundance and diversity of archaeological and documentary evidence, we had to draw together these data in an integrated research framework. Therefore, the research design was organized into several complementary stages of documentary and field research (Figure 2.2). It was designed so that the results of each stage could be used to direct subsequent investigations. Within each stage of field research, recording and analytical procedures were formulated that were commensurate with the nature of the data and the specific goals of the operation.

Historical Research

Historical research, undertaken as part of the overall research program for the Roger Williams National Memorial, has been essential in formulating a meaningful approach to the archaeological investigations. In addition to providing a chronological framework for the archaeology, the information has served as an interpretive tool. By outlining known economic and social changes, we have been able to generate hypotheses concerning the relationships between the archaeological remains and these changes. Furthermore, in selected studies, the documentary

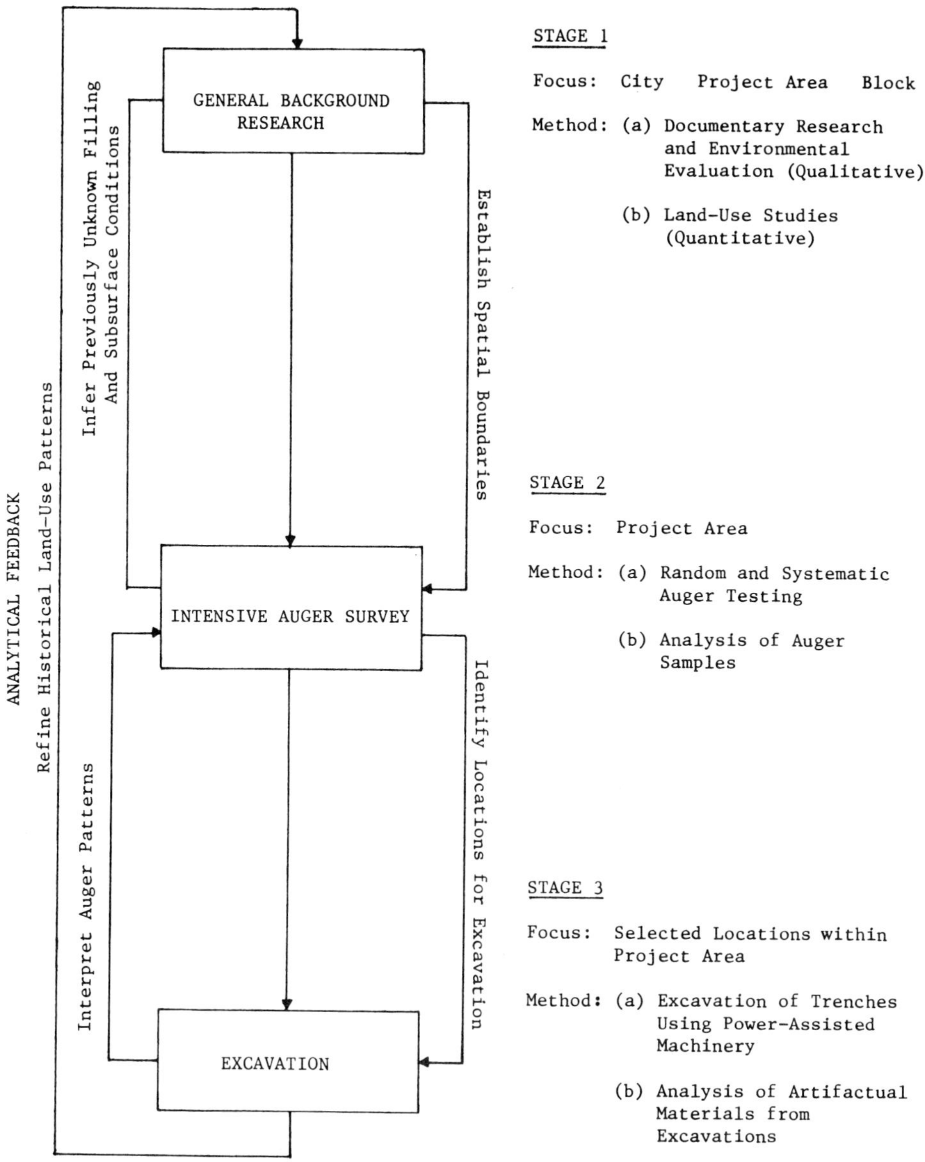

FIGURE 2.2. Organizational framework for multistage research design in urban archaeology.

evidence itself has been treated as an artifact. For example, a quantitative analysis of land-use patterns was based on a series of map reconstructions from cartographic and written evidence.

The preliminary background research for the Roger Williams National Memorial was conducted during 1978–1979, as part of an archaeological resource study (Gibson, Cole, Thorbahn, Wood, and Stachiw 1979). This valuable report served as a basis for the archaeological site examination carried out during the fall of 1979 and the spring of 1980 (Rubertone and Gallagher 1981). Although a major portion of the historical research and environmental studies was done as part of the resource study, subsequent documentary research was undertaken during the archaeological site examination. This ongoing research was necessary in order to collect data for specialized studies (e.g., quantitative analysis of land-use patterns) and to gather information on additional portions of the project area not included in the original resource study. The methods of historical research described here were employed in this latter project, although the work done in the resource study served as a model for these investigations.

Goals of the historical research undertaken as part of the archaeological site examination were (*a*) to outline an interpretative historical framework for urban development in Providence, in general, and the project area, specifically; (*b*) to reconstruct the land-use history of the block between Cady and Bowen Streets (Figure 2.1); and (*c*) to analyze changes in land use and spatial patterning through time. Although a vast amount of historical source materials was available, these varied greatly in quality and amount of detail. Since the goals of this stage of historical research were directed toward three levels of analysis (i.e., the city, the project area, and the individual blocks), it was decided to focus on the sources that were expected to yield the appropriate kinds of information (Figure 2.3).

During initial historical research, secondary sources relating to the history and development of the city of Providence (e.g., state and city histories, anecdotal histories, and scholarly reports) were consulted. Comparative studies of New England's urban centers (e.g., Bridenbaugh 1971) also were useful in developing an interpretative framework for the research. There were, however, problems encountered in developing a working historical framework from these sources. Quite frequently, the information was presented from a single, rather than a holistic, perspective. Often, data were summarized to the point of gross generalization, or were based on patterns inferred from inaccurate measures (see Cook 1976, as an exception). To avoid some of the problems inherent in these historical interpretations and to develop a framework that would be useful to the archaeological research, we had to assess this information from an archaeological perspective. This was done by focusing on information specifically related to several dimensions of change (i.e., population, diversity, and integration) that have been used by other archaeologists in dealing with issues of development and growth (e.g., Flannery 1972; Plog 1974). This approach not only enabled us to integrate information from diverse secondary sources, but it also aided us in organizing the data from primary sources related to the project area and in generating topics that might be pursued in future research.

Subsequent historical research was focused on developments in the project area and those related specifically to each of the six blocks. Both cartographic and written primary sources were employed at this stage of research. Cartographic and visual representations were most useful in establishing spatial relationships between struc-

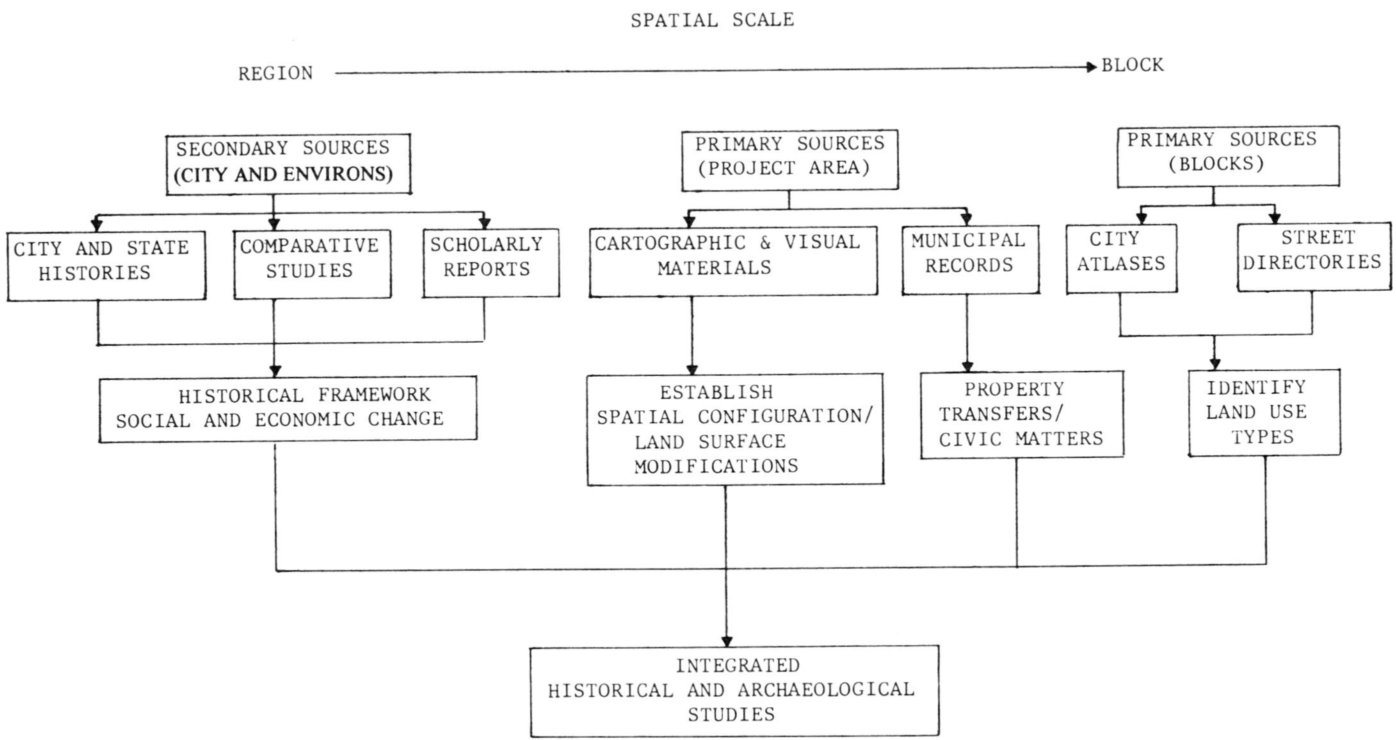

FIGURE 2.3. Organizational framework for levels of historical research.

tures and features of the urban landscape. The earliest maps depicting the area were eighteenth-century plat maps of Providence that indicate property holdings and public lands. It was only after the latter part of the eighteenth century that individual structures, street lines, and other features were labelled. And, it was not until the publication of an 1857 atlas (Cushing and Walling 1857) that there was a detailed cartographic rendering of the land within the Roger Williams National Memorial. City atlases, which were issued regularly beginning in the late nineteenth century, were most useful in reconstructing the land-use history of individual blocks and the project area as a whole.

Among the written primary sources reviewed at this stage of research were the early records of Providence, transactions related to the state and municipal governments, property records, and street directories. The early records contained information on land transfers and other property-related matters up to the middle of the eighteenth century. The municipal records of the nineteenth and twentieth centuries were useful sources of information on matters related to urban management and administrative organization. For example, these contained references to such civic matters as sewage systems, garbage disposal, and the filling of low-lying marshes. The street directories, which were published listings of home and business addresses issued periodically between 1824 and 1853 and annually after that, were a major source of information on specific structures within the parcel. These, along with the maps and atlases, were most useful in identifying the functions of individual buildings for the land-use study.

In summary, the historical research for the Roger Williams National Memorial was conducted in two phases. A previous archaeological resource study (Gibson *et al.* 1979) provided a general evaluation of environmental resources, potential prehistoric land-use, and historical building episodes. Further historical research conducted as part of the present study was directed toward specific interpretative issues at three distinct levels of analysis—the city, the project area, and the individual blocks. By identifying our research goals at each of these analytical levels, we could conduct this research in a fairly efficient manner. Drawing together several different lines of documentary evidence made it possible to trace irregularities and identify possible sources of error in their interpretation. Finally, the results of this research provided information on the location of potential archaeological properties that has been most useful in guiding the archaeological investigations.

Auger Survey

Although the absence of modern habitation in the project area made the archaeological remains considerably more accessible to the archaeologists, the fact that the present landscape was devoid of any visible features made it difficult to discern any foundations or other evidence of spatial patterning from the surface. Previous archaeological testing in the general vicinity had indicated that cultural deposits might extend far below the surface (Gibson *et al.* 1979:70–71). Consequently, these conditions precluded the use of some of the more traditional techniques of initial site examination.

Since power-assisted auger testing has been a successful survey technique in a variety of archaeological situations, such as deeply stratified sites (e.g., Brown 1975) and other urban historic sites (e.g., Deagan, Bostwick, and Benton 1976), an auger survey was employed as part of the field testing strategies at the Roger Williams National Memorial. The aims of the survey were (*a*) to investigate the nature of subsurface conditions, (*b*) to determine the extent of settlement in the area through several historical periods based on archaeological information, and (*c*) to identify areas for excavation. Use of the auger made it possible to achieve these goals in an efficient and relatively nondestructive manner. Furthermore, areas could be tested without requiring a commitment to further and costly excavation.

The type of auger used for the testing was a truck-mounted 6 in. (15.24 cm) solid auger drill, fitted with drill bit segments measuring 60 in. (1.52 m) long. A solid auger was preferable to a coring device since it could penetrate heavy industrial remains and demolition debris. The augering was done in standard increments of 4 ft (1.22 m), with penetration to a maximum depth of 20 ft (6.1 m) below surface, in order to insure a measure of vertical control. Samples of the soil matrix were collected from each vertical increment of each auger boring for later analysis.

A total of 56 auger borings was excavated (Figure 2.4). The use of both random and systematic sampling to locate the auger stations was aimed at providing uniform coverage of the study area, while at the same time generating data that could be used to make probability statements concerning subsurface cultural strata. Thirty systematic auger stations were placed at 15 m (49.2 ft) intervals along four transects aligned north–south across the study area. The testing at regular intervals along linear transects was believed to be the best strategy for locating the former east–west cross-streets, since this interval was approximately the distance between the streets as gauged from cartographic evidence. In addition, 23 auger stations were located using a simple random sampling design. Three judgmental auger stations were placed in areas believed, on the basis of recommendations of the archaeological resource study, to contain remains of historical significance.

In formulating an analytical approach to the auger samples, a major concern was to treat these data in a manner that would be appropriate to answering the stated goals of this stage in the research design, and would, as well, be commensurate with the nature of the data (Figure 2.5). The analysis was aimed at providing information on the form of subsurface deposits and determining the temporal extent of settlement based on archaeological data. Because of the analytical goals, and given the fragmentary condition of artifacts retrieved from the auger bit, the cultural materials were identified simply by material type (e.g., brick, glass, bone). Also, diagnostic ceramics were recorded since these were expected to provide some measure of temporal association. Categories of material type and diagnostic ceramics were recorded in terms of presence or absence.

Following the organization of the multistage research design (Figure 2.2), the processing of auger samples was carried on simultaneously with the field testing so that preliminary results could help direct the next stage of research. The examination of the occurrence of material categories within and among auger borings aided in identifying locations for excavation. This information provided direct archaeolog-

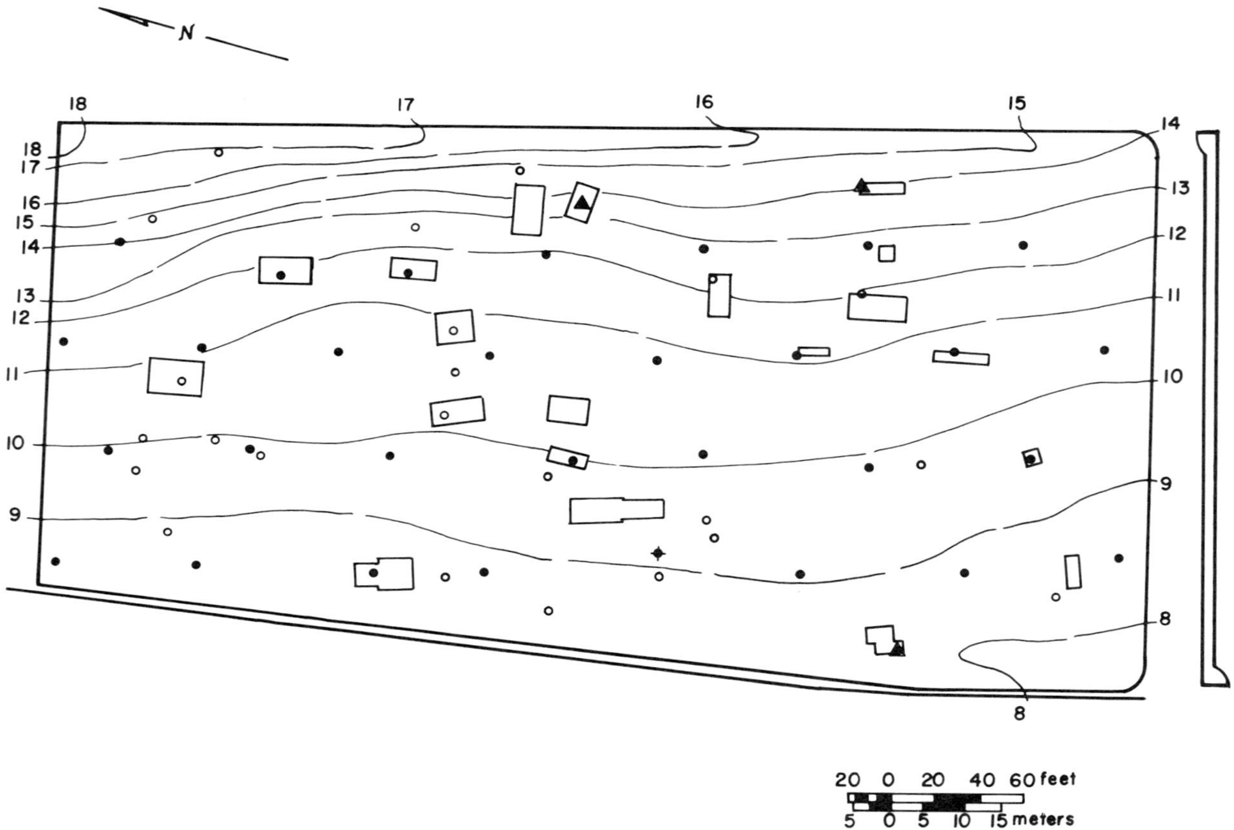

FIGURE 2.4. Plan of project area with locations of auger stations and excavation trenches. (Note: Rectangles denote excavation units; open circles denote random auger stations; dark circles denote systematic auger stations; triangles denote judgmental auger stations.)

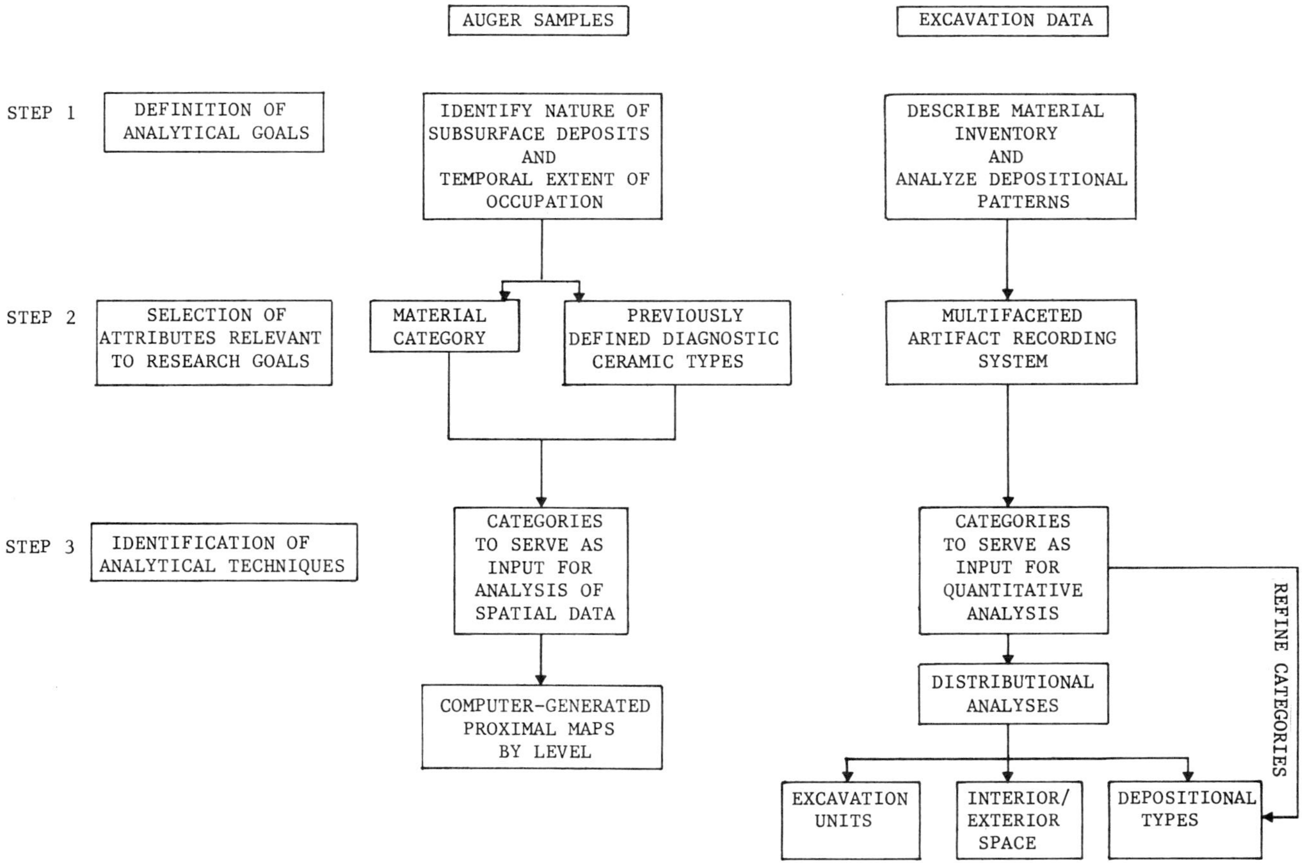

FIGURE 2.5. Organizational framework for alternative approaches to artifact analysis.

ical evidence of the present subsurface conditions, which supplemented what was known from documentary sources. At an analytical level the preliminary results were used to make decisions concerning more intensive analysis of these data, which was ongoing throughout the project. For example, the initial results served to refine categories used in generating spatial maps of the auger stations using SYMAP, a computer graphics package for analyzing spatial data.

The detailed analysis of the cultural materials from the augers revealed several interesting patterns. For example, in an attempt to discover the temporal extent of settlement, we analyzed the patterned distribution of diagnostic ceramics from three temporal phases. The three temporal phases and their associated ceramics were (1) post-1850, including all hard white earthenwares, coarse domestic stonewares, and other modern ceramics; (2) 1800–1850, encompassing all pearlwares and other white earthenwares; and (3) pre-1800, including creamware and all imported stonewares.

The vertical distribution of these temporal components in the augers is depicted graphically in Figure 2.6. The highest incidence of diagnostic ceramics from the post-1850 phase occurs between 0 and 4 ft (0 and 1.22 m) below surface, whereas the highest occurrence of ceramics from phase three (pre-1800) is between 12 and 16 ft (3.66 and 4.88 m) below surface. Comparing all three graphs, several trends can be discerned. There is a sharp drop in the number of augers containing evidence of post-1850 ceramics between 4 and 8 ft (1.22 and 2.44 m) and between 8 and 12 ft (2.44 and 3.66 m). This contrasts with the peak for 1800–1850 ceramics, which occurs between 8 and 12 ft (2.44–3.66 m) below surface. Whereas the incidence of these ceramics declines between 8 and 12 ft (2.44 and 3.66 m) and between 12 and 16 ft (3.66 and 4.88 m), those from the pre-1800 phase peak between 12 and 16 ft (3.66–4.88 m). It is possible that the higher incidence of phase two ceramics compared to phase three ceramics between 16 and 20 ft (4.88 and 6.1 m) reflects legally mandated filling of low-lying areas that took place from 1800 to 1850. However, other activities also could have been responsible for this anomalous pattern. For example, the increased rate of construction activities between 1825 and 1850 would have involved some degree of ground disturbance.

A series of proximal maps was generated using SYMAP in order to analyze the spatial distribution of temporal phases within the various vertical levels. This enabled us to outline the spatial configuration of settlement from archaeological evidence. The distribution of temporal phases indicated fairly consistent evidence of occupation along North Main Street. Evidence from pre-1800 and 1800–1850 phases was the most abundant in this area. The central portion of the project area, however, revealed a different pattern. Here the evidence for a particular temporal phase was much less consistent in terms of its distribution in the auger borings. It suggested that settlement may not have been as concentrated or as continuous as that near North Main Street. Along the western edge of the project area, the incidence of ceramic diagnostic evidence from the augers was low, suggesting that the area was not used primarily for residence. In general, this portion of the site had a greater occurrence of phase two ceramics than those from phase one or three,

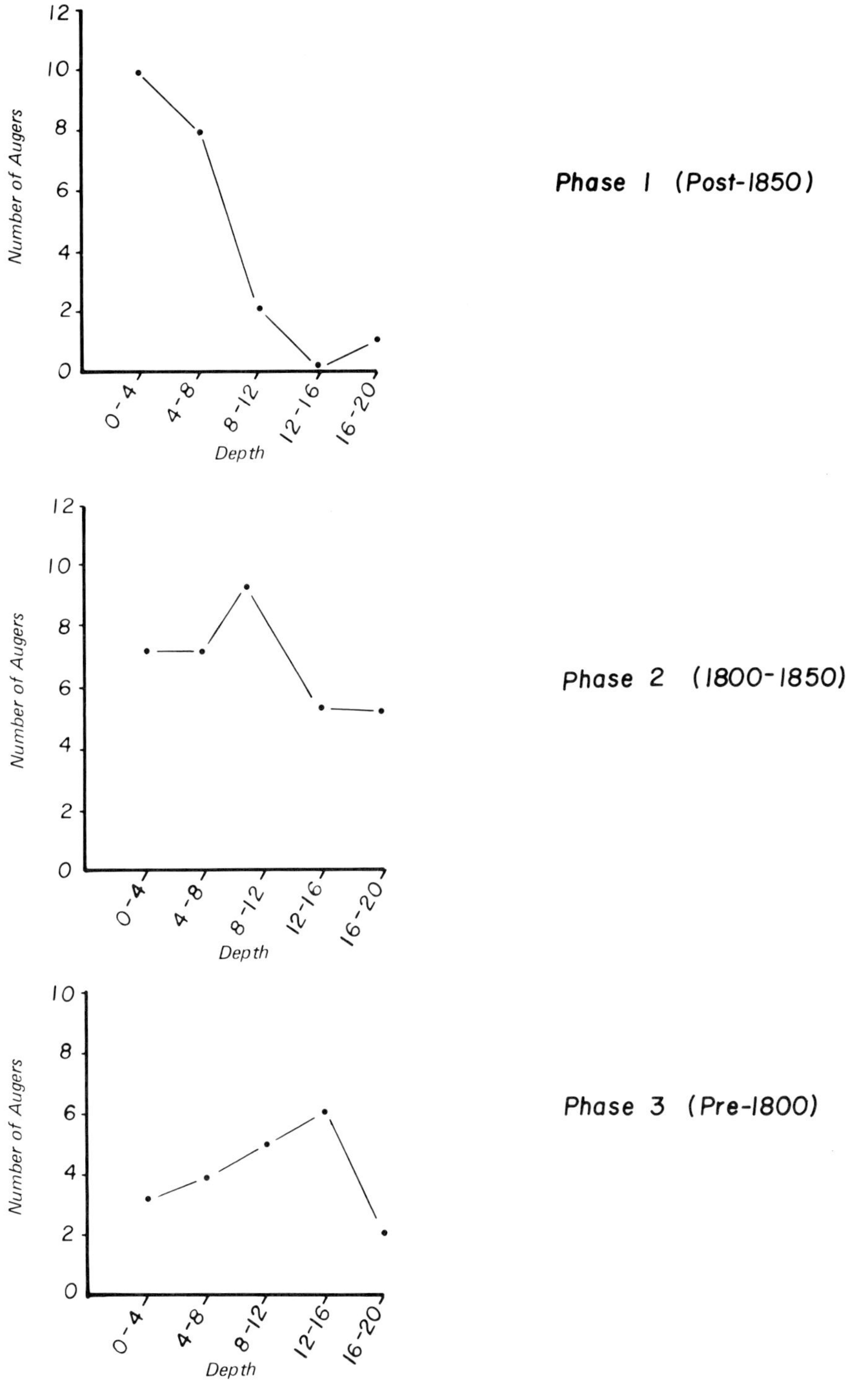

FIGURE 2.6. Distribution of temporal phases among the auger stations by depth.

which may reflect episodes of filling of this former waterfront during the first half of the nineteenth century.

When these patterns for the project area as a whole were compared to a series of land-use maps depicting settlement at four different periods (see Rubertone, Part II of this volume), the results matched favorably. The auger testing, however, did reveal some anomalies when compared to the historical record. For example, discontinuities in the distribution of ceramic phases in the auger tests (in areas that otherwise exhibited continuous patterns) were useful in identifying areas where earlier cultural deposits had been destroyed by intensive, industrial building during the late nineteenth and early twentieth centuries.

Analysis of the results of the random and systematic auger samples was revealing. For example, when the numbers of random and systematic auger borings occurring in streets were compared, we discovered that 13.0% of the random auger borings and 27.3% of the systematic auger borings had been placed in this type of space. The figure from the random auger borings came much closer to predicting the amount of street-associated deposits within the project area since the known relative amounts of street space versus useable space (i.e., space within the blocks) from historical evidence were estimated to be 17.3% and 82.7%, respectively. It would appear that the use of random sampling provides a more reliable measure of the nature of subsurface deposits within the project area. Similar conclusions concerning the use of random sampling in discovering spatial patterning at complex, urban archaeological sites have been reached by other archaeologists (e.g., Redman and Anzalone 1980).

In summary, the power-assisted auger allowed the investigation of compacted, rubble-filled urban deposits that because of their depth could not be reached efficiently either by hand or machine excavation. Analysis revealed distinct patterning in the horizontal and vertical distribution of cultural material. This pattern recognition was possible since a large ($N = 56$) number of auger borings provided extensive coverage of the study area. Furthermore, the use of a random sample, as complementary to the systematic and judgmental auger locations, provided reliable estimates of the nature of subsurface deposits. The value of using augers was verified by the correlation of patterns of artifact deposition with historic documentation. The successive stages of filling, construction, and demolition indicated by the historical record fit closely the material evidence for such activities derived from the auger cores. More importantly, the evidence recovered from the augering supplemented the historic record by suggesting filling sequences not known from documentary material, but which could be empirically determined.

Excavation

Excavations were focused on selected locations identified from the auger survey and from documentary information. The goals of the excavation were (*a*) to examine areas of archaeological interest based on information gained from the preliminary inspection of auger samples, (*b*) to investigate areas expected to contain remains of historical significance, and (*c*) to gather distributional data that could be used in conducting more refined analyses on depositional patterns. Whereas the auger survey produced more information on general spatial patterns and subsurface cultural strata, the excavations exposed information on the vertical and horizontal extents of specific archaeological features and deposits.

Nineteen trenches were excavated using a Gradall. This type of power-assisted machinery was ideal since its telescoping arm could remain stationary during the excavation of an individual trench. This was an important consideration in planning urban archaeological fieldwork where the volume of excavated earth and open trenches greatly inhibits mobility. Although the original scope of work proposed that the excavation units measure 2 × 2 m (6.56 × 6.56 ft), units of that size would have been inappropriate for investigating an urban archaeological site containing the remains of large brick and stone structures. Much larger exposures were needed for architectural examination. Consequently, testing units employed were rectangular trenches measuring approximately 6 × 2 m (19.68 × 6.56 ft). However, due to field conditions during the spring 1980 season, the trenches excavated at that time were widened to approximately 4 m (13.12 ft). All excavation was done by cultural strata, identified on the basis of obvious changes in soil color, texture, and evaluations of the artifactural contents.

At the Roger Williams National Memorial the recording and interpretation of stratigraphy was problematic. Although detailed profiles sequencing the episodes affecting archaeological site formation could be outlined for most trenches, this level of detail was difficult to obtain on an intrasite basis. A system describing profiles was necessary to ensure comparability among trenches and to serve as a basis for more detailed analyses of the depositional processes affecting archaeological site formation. Consequently, a model was devised to reconstruct trench profiles on the basis of excavated cultural strata (Figure 2.7). An assumption inherent in this model was that the trenches were regularly shaped geometric units for which the estimated volume of each excavated stratum (i.e., volume of each backdirt pile) was a percentage of the total excavated trench. The percentage volume of a stratum was assumed to equal a proportion of depth below surface for a trench.

When the formula was applied to all trenches, the stratigraphic data were made comparable. In addition, correspondence was established between the trenches and the units of artifact collection. This allowed for the interpretation of depositional patterns during subsequent analysis and also simplified the description of profiles for the excavation trenches.

The analysis of the artifactual materials collected from the excavations was aimed at providing more precise and detailed information concerning the major interpretive questions posed by the investigations. It was necessary to consider several specific factors in designing the artifact recording system. First, there was an abundance and wide range of ceramic, metal, glass, and other materials. Approximately 30,000 items were recorded from a sample of the screened excavated matrix (i.e., the equivalent of one to five wheelbarrows or 4.5 ft^3 (.13 m^3) per trench stratum). Second, it was important to focus on levels of information that were generally believed to be sensitive to function and, for some artifact classes, time. It was also important that the recording system be fairly streamlined to allow for efficient

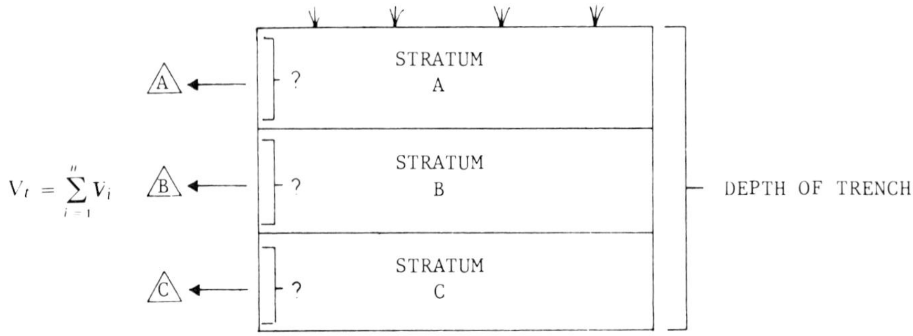

FIGURE 2.7. Model for reconstruction trench stratigraphy. Depth of trench × percentage volume/stratum = depth of stratum. Note: V_i (volume of elliptical cone) = ⅓ Bh, where B = base area of an ellipse (= *p*ab) and h = height of cone.

recording and rapid data entry into a computer-based, data management system for storage and retrieval since it was apparent that the quantity and diversity of the cultural material could not be handled reasonably in any other fashion.

At a more general level, several alternative approaches to artifact classifications were weighed. In selecting attributes for recording, we sought to avoid the particularism characteristic of historic artifact taxonomies. This level of specificity was not considered relevant to the project's research goals, among which was to detect intrasite patterning. On the other hand, some recent approaches to historical artifact recording that are aimed at recognizing patterning (e.g., South 1977) are somewhat problematic in their application to urban archaeological situations where factors contributing to assemblage diversity are more complex and difficult to control.

After weighing these factors, we designed a multifaceted artifact recording system that would handle the diverse range of categories in the inventory. Levels of information were recorded which could be used to detect variability in the functional, stylistic, and material dimensions of the artifacts. This enabled us to satisfy the project goal of adequate description of the artifact inventory and also to investigate specific research questions concerning depositional patterns (Figure 2.5). In all, 11 nonequivalent artifact categories were included (Table 2.1). For each category, only levels of information believed to be relevant to the research were recorded.

All recording was done by level (i.e., stratum) for individual excavation trenches. Counts and, for some categories of material, weights were entered directly onto standardized recording forms. Items in the miscellaneous category were recorded in terms of presence or absence. Information on the forms was structured so that it could be transferred directly by keypunch operators onto 80-column IBM cards. A computer-based data file was created using FOCUS, an interactive data management system. Data stored in the file were used as the basis for producing descriptive tallies of artifacts and in conducting distributional studies of the assemblage in terms of several interpretive frameworks (e.g., spatial; interior–exterior locus).

However, simple comparisons of the vertical or horizontal distribution of artifacts among excavation units or for all excavation units were not carried out. This type of distributional analysis was not considered appropriate for dealing with stratigraphic patterning in urban situations where the processes of archaeological site formation are highly complex. Although the summary data provided some indication of the distribution of cultural materials, it belied the complexity of the processes responsible for the formation of the archaeological record. Consequently, a model was formulated to account for variability in artifact classes among depositional types (see Rubertone, Part II of this volume). From the multifaceted recording system, it was possible to refine artifact categories that were appropriate for testing this model.

In summary, the excavations provided information concerning the project area's archaeological contents and their contextual associations. This type of information was used to pursue the stated goals and to effectively evaluate the area's archaeological resources. Within the multistage research design, analytical procedures were employed that were commensurate with the field testing and the goals of this stage of research. Compared with the auger analysis, the analysis of the excavation data provided more precise and detailed information on the major interpretive questions posed by the investigations. The results of the detailed examinations of the architectural remains and artifact deposits, when integrated with historical information, provided empirical evidence of some of the changes that had occurred over time. By comparing behavioral interpretations with archaeological evidence, this analysis has enhanced our understanding of urban patterns suggested by the historical record.

SUMMARY

The research design for the archaeological examination of the Roger Williams National Memorial has emphasized structuring the research so that diverse lines of evidence would be integrated in the overall project. Organization of the research into three stages—historical research, auger survey, and excavation—made it possible to use the results from one stage in making decisions on subsequent stages. This type of organization promoted the continuous refinement of research results by improving the scope and level of information used in interpreting the project area's urban past.

The limited archaeological testing and related research have produced a wealth of data. In a relatively short time, the analysis of these data has yielded significant information on the six-block area. This has been possible because the investigations have incorporated alternative analytical approaches to enable us to manage and analyze these data in a relatively efficient and rigorous manner. The use of systematic recording and methods of computer and quantitative analysis greatly aided in detecting patterns in both the historical and archaeological data. In the study of land-use patterns, quantitative analysis of cartographic evidence provided detailed information on the changing spatial organization of the area. Computer-generated maps (SYMAP) of data from the auger samples greatly facilitated the detection of spatial patterns at various depths below the surface. With the aid of a computer, the

Table 2.1 Summary of Artifact Recording Categories

Artifact Class	Kind of Information	Categories
ceramics	morphological part	body, diagnostic
	style	plain red earthenware, glazed red earthenware, slip-decorated earthenware, tin-glazed earthenware, creamware, other pearlware, other earthenware, transfer printed ware, hard whiteware, white salt-glazed stoneware, gray stoneware, brown stoneware, coarse domestic stoneware, porcelain, other ceramic, unique ceramic
glass	functional type	window, bottle, other
	style	crown, flat
	decoration	decorated, undecorated
clay pipes	morphological part	bowl, stem
	size (boring)	4/64, 5/64, 6/64, 7/64, 8/64, 9/64
small objects	functional type	buttons (nonmetal), coins, combs, other

nails	style	machine cut, handwrought, wire, can't tell
structural materials (nonmetal)	functional type	brick, plaster/mortar, concrete
	condition	whole, fragmentary
metal	material	yellow metal, white metal, iron, other metal
	functional category	household, building, hand tools, machinery, arms, transportation, personal, recyclable, nonreusable fragments, other
slag	functional category	vitreous, metallic, other, can't tell
bone	functional category	mammal, fish, bird, unidentifiable
	modification	modified, unmodified
shell	functional category	quahog, scallop, oyster, other, can't tell
	condition	whole, fragmentary
miscellaneous	material	wood, charcoal/cinder/ash, coal, lithic asphalt, plastic, leather, seeds, nutshells, others

quantitative treatment of excavation data assisted in describing the cultural remains and in formulating questions for more detailed analyses (e.g., depositional patterns).

Whereas some of the approaches employed in the archaeological site examination at the Roger Williams National Memorial may be of use to other archaeologists planning urban archaeological research, there are still many problems to be faced. For example, there is still the question of how much artifact material to collect in the field. Certainly, more controlled experiments are needed to make informed decisions and gain better estimates of assemblage diversity. Yet, despite the naiveté of our approaches, urban historical archaeology presents many possibilities for refining research methods and for pursuing problems of complex societies.

ACKNOWLEDGMENTS

I appreciate the assistance of the members of the archaeological resource team for producing an excellent report that contributed in many ways to this subsequent study. The archaeological site examination could not have been accomplished without the efforts of the staff of the Public Archaeology Laboratory. I am especially indebted to Joan Gallagher for her contributions at all stages of the research. Larry Manire provided valuable assistance in computer matters. Sarah Bridges, Frank McManamon, and Peter Thorbahn provided helpful comments on preliminary versions of sections of this chapter. And finally, the assistance of Alan Leveillee and Lorry Theroux in the production of this chapter is most appreciated.

REFERENCES

Binford, Lewis
1964 A consideration of archaeological research design. *American Antiquity* 29:425–441.

Bridenbaugh, Carl
1971 *Cities in revolt.* New York: Oxford Univ. Press.

Brown, James
1975 Deep-site excavation strategy as a sampling problem. In *Sampling in archeology*, edited by James Mueller. Tucson: Univ. of Arizona Press. Pp. 155–169.

Cook, Edward M.
1976 *The fathers of the town.* Baltimore, Md.: Johns Hopkins Univ. Press.

Cushing, Samuel, and Henry Walling
1857 *Map of Providence.* Providence, R.I.

Deagan, Kathleen, John Bostwick, and Dale Benton
1976 A sub-surface survey of the St. Augustine city environs. Paper submitted to St. Augustine Restoration Foundation, St. Augustine, Florida.

Flannery, Kent
1972 The cultural evolution of civilizations. *Annual Review of Ecology and Systematics* 3:399–426.

Gibson, Susan, Stephen Cole, Peter Thorbahn, Cynthia Wood, and Myron Stachiw
1979 Archeological resource study, Roger Williams National Memorial, Rhode Island. *U.S. Department of the Interior, National Park Service, North Atlantic Regional Office, Cultural Resource Management Study* 1.

House, John
1977 Survey data and regional models in historical archeology. In *Research strategies in historical archeology*, edited by Stanley South. New York: Academic Press. Pp. 241–260.

Klein, Joel
1973 Models and hypotheses in historical archaeology. *Historical Archaeology* 7:68–77.

Plog, Fred

1974 *A study of prehistoric change*. New York: Academic Press.

Redman, Charles

1973 Multistage fieldwork and analytical techniques. *American Antiquity* **38**:61–79.

Redman, Charles, and Ronald Anzalone

1980 Discovering architectural patterning at a complex site. *American Antiquity* **45**:284–290.

Redman, Charles, Ronald Anzalone, and Patricia Rubertone

1979 Medieval archaeology at Qsar-es-Seghir, Morocco. *Journal of Field Archaeology* **6**:1–16.

Rubertone, Patricia E., and Joan Gallagher

1981 Archaeological site examination: A case study of urban archeology. Roger Williams National Memorial. *U.S. Department of the Interior, National Park Service, North Atlantic Regional Office, Cultural Resource Management Study* **4**.

South, Stanley

1974 Historical archeology reports: A plea for a new direction. *The Conference on Historic Site Archeology Papers*, 1972:151–158. Institute of Archeology and Anthropology, Univ. of South Carolina, Columbia.

1977 *Method and theory in historical archeology*. New York: Academic Press.

Struever, Stuart

1968 Problems, methods, and organization: A disparity in the growth of archeology. In *Anthropological archeology in the Americas*, edited by Betty Meggers. Washington, D.C.: Anthropological Society of Washington. Pp. 131–151.

3

The City-Site Approach to Urban Archaeology[1]

Pamela J. Cressey
John F. Stephens

In recent years the social and historical sciences have developed separate disciplinary approaches to the study of urban development. Because these sciences have offered important insights into specific urban behavioral processes, the spatial and socioeconomic patterns of urban culture now are beginning to emerge; yet they remain unclear in several respects. Two analytical steps can be taken in order to better understand the patterns and processes of urban culture.

First, the methods and concepts of archaeological science should be applied to the urban setting. A concerted effort of urban archaeologists is necessary to define the *material* patterns and processes of urban culture. Second, the interdisciplinary synthesis of the social and historical sciences can provide archaeologists with new methods and concepts, as well as the context within which to interpret the material patterns of urban culture. Archaeologists who seek to discover the general rules of materially expressed behavior share methodological and conceptual ground with other social and historical scientists. The Alexandria Urban Archaeology Program is attempting to complete these two relevant analytical steps.

GOALS AND QUESTIONS

The Alexandria Program was established in 1977 by the city of Alexandria, Virginia, and its public archaeological commission. The Program is now conduct-

[1]The Alexandria Urban Archaeology Program is sponsored by the city of Alexandria, Virginia, and is supported through grants from the U.S. Department of the Interior, the Virginia Historic Landmarks Commission, and the National Endowment for the Humanities.

ISBN 0-12-214980-7

ing a comprehensive study of the relationships between distinct segments of the community's socioeconomic–ethnic hierarchy and the residential patterns of these segments as derived from the documentary record. The study aims at providing an interpretive context for material cultural comparisons (obtained from the archaeological and the architectural records).

The research goals of the Alexandria Program are to (*a*) produce spatial and longitudinal data within Alexandria localities and between rural and urban areas, (*b*) provide cross-cultural and diachronic information relevant to urban developmental studies on other cities, (*c*) examine the relationships between society's material base or substructure (environment, technology, economy, and demography) and its urban organization (stratification system) and developmental processes (group formation and group conflict), (*d*) examine these relationships in terms of their actual physical manifestations in the urban landscape (settlement patterns) and urban material culture (artifact patterns), and (*e*) interpret the component elements of the Alexandria city-site as analytical parts of a conceptually cohesive whole, dependent upon general developmental processes operating within larger historical and social scientific contexts. Furthermore, because of the public setting of the Alexandria Program, an attempt is made to (*a*) integrate research on urban developmental processes into pragmatic decision-making and planning activities in order to facilitate coexistence of the past with a rich and varied contemporary urban landscape, and (*b*) present research findings to the constituents of the Alexandria community and its contiguous metropolitan communities for an increased appreciation of the patterns of urban life.

PROJECT DESIGN

This study attempts a systematic analysis of urban–industrial development from the perspectives of anthropological archaeology, in particular, and the social sciences, in general. Scholars have begun to explore the relationships between material attributes, urban organization, and the level of a society's sociopolitical development in both prehistoric (Millon 1973; Morris 1975; Shimada 1978) and modern (Rathje 1978; Rathje and McCarthy 1977; Schiffer, Downing, and McCarthy 1981) settings. In historic contexts, artifact attributes have been related archaeologically to socioeconomic status (Fairbanks 1974; Otto 1975, 1977, 1980; Watkins 1970) and to ethnicity (Schuyler 1980). Using archival sources, artifact attributes also have been related to price (Miller 1980).

It is now appropriate for archaeologists to create multistage projects within urban settings that will allow comparisons *among* contemporaneous city-types and *between* those of different scales, functions, regions, societies, periods, and levels of industrial development (Fox 1977). With the inclusion of archaeological data in urban developmental studies, the relationships between material culture, group membership, community and state organization, landscape, and level of economic–technological development can be systematically explored (Braudel 1973).

Research already conducted in geography, history, and anthropology can facilitate concept building for an archaeological project that will yield both intercity and intersociety comparisons. What remains to be accomplished, however, is the elucidation of material culture patterns in relation to human organization and changing economy, demography, and technology. Because it is so time consuming to collect relevant data and analyze material culture in an urban–industrial setting, the refinement of artifactual patterns requires a microsetting, or laboratory, before material culture can be used reliably in macrolevel studies.

We are currently using Alexandria, Virginia, as an empirical focus for a study that explores the impact of changing world economic, technological, and demographic factors on the community's socioeconomic–ethnic hierarchical organization and its material culture. To accomplish this general goal, two questions are addressed:

1. How and why did the urban hierarchy in North America become more highly stratified between the eighteenth and twentieth centuries?
2. What are the relationships among residential settlement patterns, material attribute patterns, and the behavior of different socioeconomic–ethnic groups within this changing hierarchy?

As the nineteenth-century American economy shifted from commercial to industrial capitalism, urban social organization was altered by the continuous processes of group formation and conflict, resulting in changing status relationships between groups (Braudel 1973; Wallerstein 1980). Between 1750 and 1910, in Alexandria, as in other cities, the urban hierarchy was composed of changing status groups that can be defined empirically along socioeconomic, ethnic, and legal continua.

Diachronically, the Alexandria study delineates specific status groups, determines their residential locations and neighborhood affiliations, and compares their settlement and material patterns over time to ascertain varying *physical distances* and *material differences* as expressions of changing hierarchical relationships, group formation, and conflict. We expect that as social, economic, and physical distances increase between status groups in an industrial–capitalist society, differences will also increase for categories of material culture.

The settlement and material patterns form two distinct, but analytically related, categories that are defined from different data sources—documents and material culture. Both are derived from the same historical processes, and their integration is necessary for reliable generalizations. Additionally, settlement patterns play a major role in providing (*a*) excavation localities in distinct residential areas and on specific lots occupied by status groups; (*b*) contextual information about these relationships between neighborhoods and groups, thus yielding greater interpretive power for the artifact patterns; and (*c*) an independent test of the general processes that produce the material patterns. By defining Alexandria's city-site type through time and recognizing its specific variations from general urban trends, both the settlement and artifact patterns can be used for subsequent intercity, interregion, and intersociety comparisons.

RESEARCH FRAMEWORKS

Conceptual Framework

In urban archaeology a single area or group within a city should not be the sole object of study, nor should either the settlement pattern or the socioeconomic hierarchy be viewed as independent cultural variables. A more productive approach, leading to generalizations, is to view the individual archaeological area of study—and the pattern or hierarchy of which it is a part—as dependent upon changes within the city as a whole (see Dickens and Crimmins, Chapter 4, for a discussion of the city as a system). This study focuses upon Alexandria as a single archaeological site, whose parts are subject to analysis within the context of the whole. Also, we recognize that any city develops within a regional setting and is influenced by general worldwide processes and that these factors should be incorporated into the research design.

Regional Context

The historic city in North America can be studied for information about urban stratification, group formation, and group conflict during transformations of industrial capitalism. Since the eighteenth century, all cities shared the effects of this set of processes. However, each city's regional location and role has been providing the context for understanding local variations. The regional diversity of North America makes possible a comprehensive analysis of how urban socioeconomic hierarchies function in different geographical settings.

The economic background of regional diversity in the United States lay primarily in the nineteenth-century expansion of American industry and agriculture (North 1961). In the South, with its monopoly on world cotton and tobacco production, the plantation system and Afro-American slavery were firmly established by the beginning of the nineteenth century. The Southern city was characterized by a static and clearly articulated urban hierarchy that mirrored preindustrial settlement and behavioral patterns (Berlin 1976; Goldin 1976; Gutman 1976; Sjoberg 1960). In the North, on the other hand, the expansion of industrial production and the development of an indispensible labor supply and transportation system became the dominant theme (McKelvey 1963; Pred 1966). The dynamic and progressively heterogeneous urban hierarchy of the Northern city translated its changing status relationships into greater physical distances and material differences between groups (Pleck 1979; Thernstrom 1960; Ward 1971).

Because it lies between the industrial North and agricultural South, the Mid-Atlantic region is culturally and geographically well-situated for testing hypotheses about North American urbanization. Although the Mid-Atlantic city was oriented primarily toward commerce and agricultural production upon which trade depended, it also experienced the effects of industrialization. For these reasons, the nineteenth-century Mid-Atlantic city has characteristics of both Northern industrialism and Southern commerce and agrarianism.

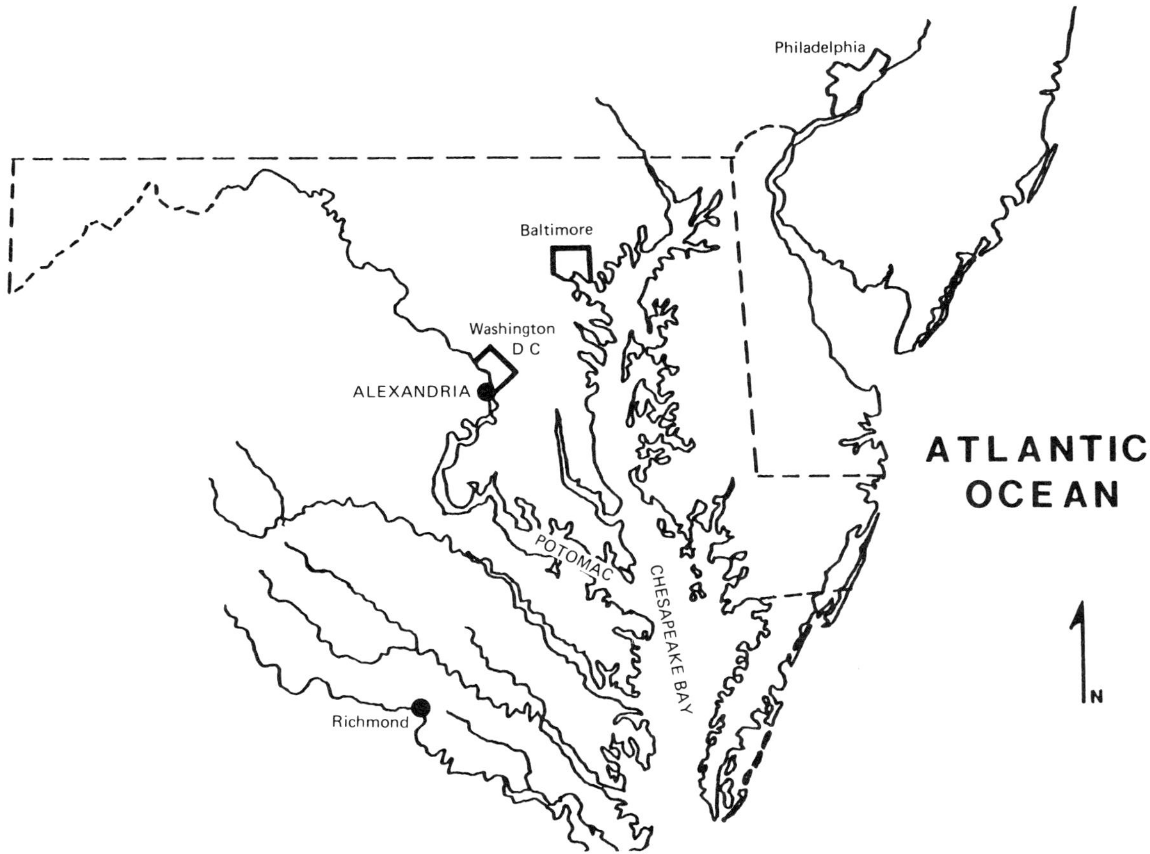

FIGURE 3.1. Mid-Atlantic region.

Local Context

While considering a city's regional location and function, it is also necessary to evaluate its local condition. In this way, variations from general urban patterns can be predicted and scientifically measured. Alexandria, located at the southern tip of the Mid-Atlantic region (Figure 3.1), can be identified as part of the "Upper South" (Berlin 1976). Because of Alexandria's intermediate location between the South and the North, a greater number of newly freed slaves migrated there than to many other cities in the early nineteenth century (Berlin 1976). This was due to Alexandria's proximity to Maryland and the District of Columbia, as well as to the fact that the city lacked harsh sumptuary legislation during the period of its incorporation into the nation's capital (1791–1846). Consequently, the opportunities for free Afro-Americans, generally greater in cities throughout the South (Wade 1964), were further increased. The significant influx of blacks in the early half of the nineteenth century, an increasing number of whom were free, changed the demographic character of Alexandria (Figures 3.2, 3.3, and 3.4). Therefore, we can expect to find group conflict and a resultant residential "sectoralization" (as expressed in increased physical distances) at an earlier time in Alexandria than in most other cities (Coser 1956).

An additional local factor contributed to Alexandria's variation from other Mid-Atlantic city patterns. Alexandria's regional economic role decreased in importance throughout the nineteenth century. Although it was a primary American port in the eighteenth century, Alexandria became a secondary transport center in the mid-nineteenth century, lagging behind Baltimore, Washington, and Richmond. Consequently, as other cities increased their control over resources and the regional economy, Alexandria lost its primary economic role. The city experienced few increases in population, labor supply, and industrial site development, comparable to the primary late-nineteenth-century Mid-Atlantic city. We would not expect to find the large numbers of European immigrants and definable ethnic neighborhoods, which are characteristic of Baltimore or Philadelphia, in Alexandria. Alexandria's settlement and artifact patterns should be compared in detail to other cities that experienced "traditional" late nineteenth-century growth and primacy. By identifying Alexandria's changing regional role and accounting for its specific characteristics, broader studies of urban social organization and group dynamics can be undertaken.

Temporal Framework

The period of our study, 1750–1910, can be described as the most revolutionary era of world history, representing a fundamental break in the continuity of technological, economic, and demographic processes (Cipolla 1964; Landes 1969; Wallerstein 1976, 1980). It also was an era of unprecedented environmental, material, and social change (Braudel 1973). And it was this global upheaval, made possible by the technological transformation of industrial capitalism, that produced

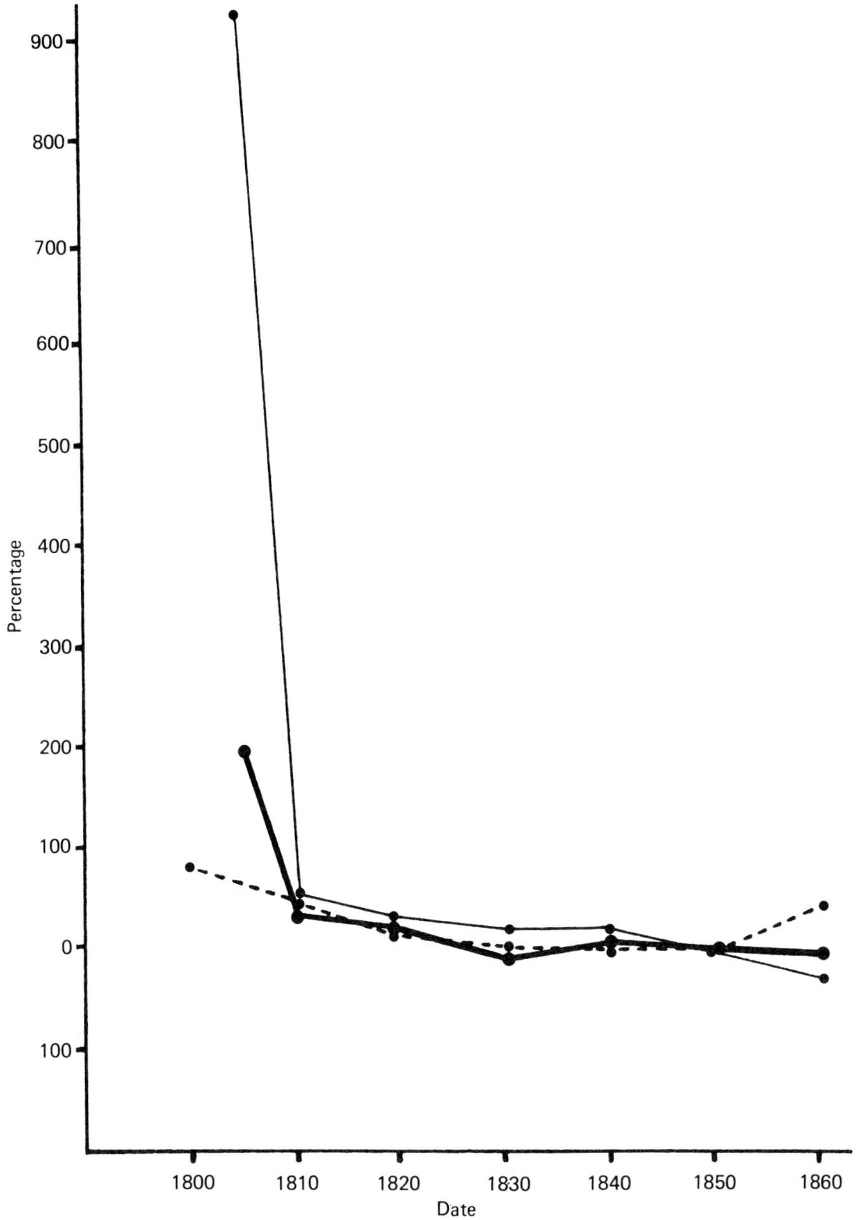

FIGURE 3.2. Population change in nineteenth-century Alexandria. (Dashed lines denote total Alexandria population. Heavy line denotes total Afro-American population. Thin line denotes total free Afro-American population.)

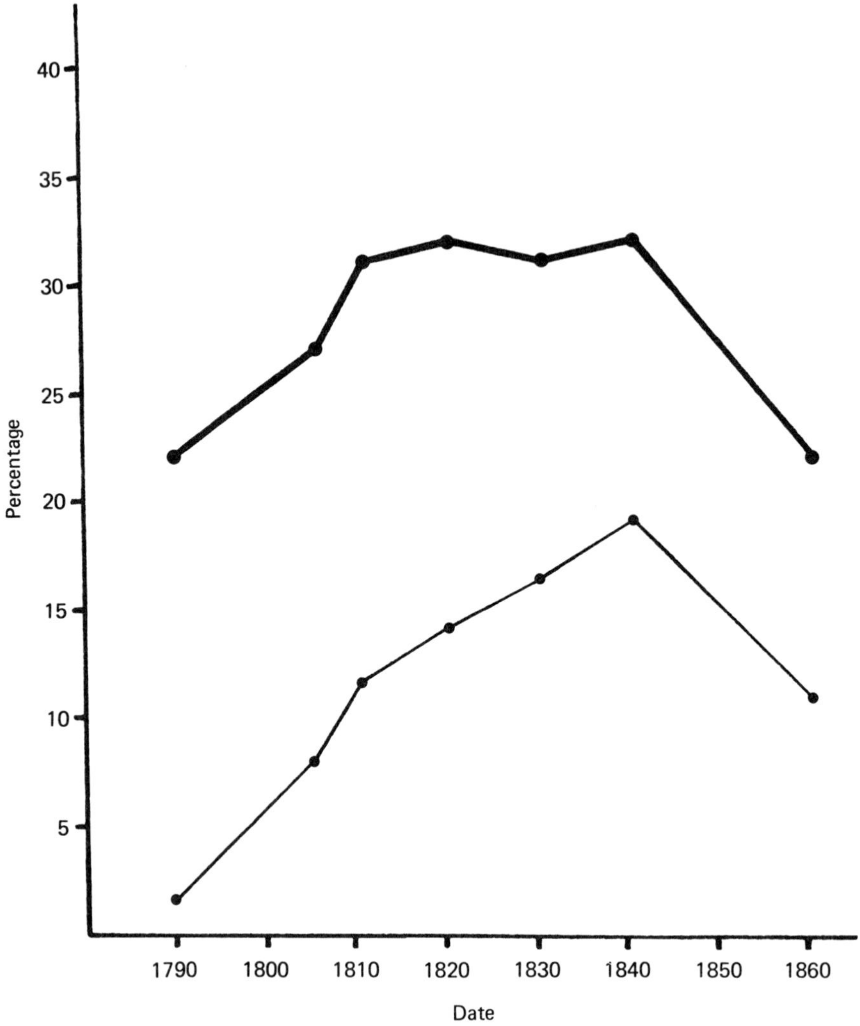

FIGURE 3.3. Afro-American population in nineteenth-century Alexandria. (Heavy line denotes total Afro-American population; thin line denotes free Afro-American population.)

the conflict (Dahrendorf 1959) and segregation (Woods and Kennedy 1962) that profoundly shaped urban development, especially in the historic cities of North America (Goheen 1970; Hershberg 1976; Warner 1962, 1968).

The period 1750–1910 relates particularly well to historical circumstances in Alexandria. Alexandria was incorporated as a town in 1749, and its population can be traced through tax records, census manuscripts, and City directories to 1910. Thus, the period chronicled corresponds to major worldwide changes.

A total city study would take an inordinate amount of time. Consequently, we

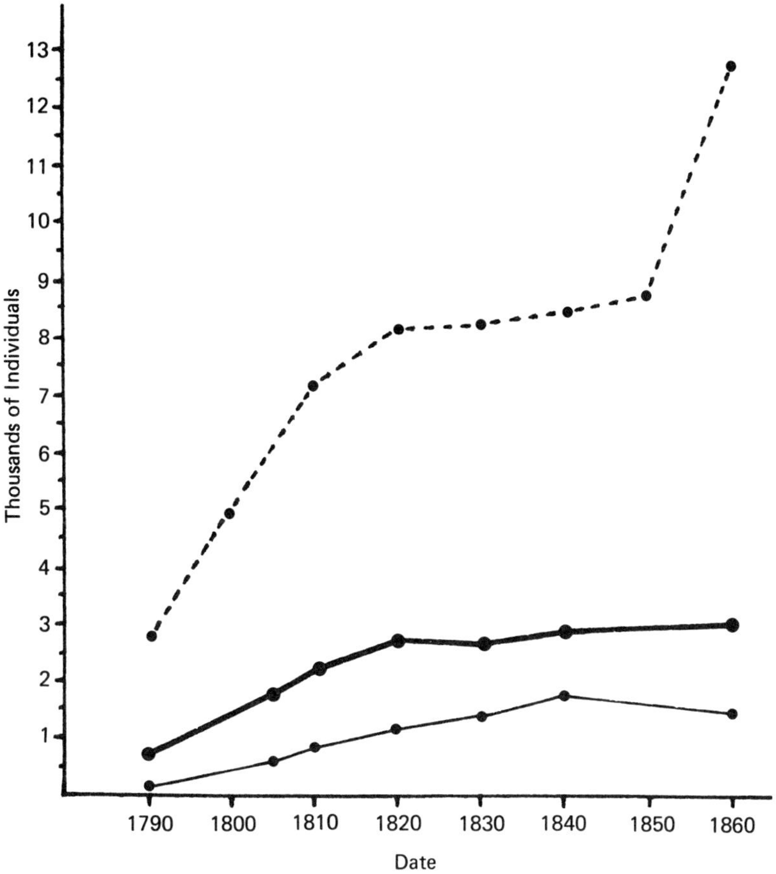

FIGURE 3.4. Nineteenth-century population in Alexandria. (Dashed line denotes total Alexandria population; heavy line denotes total Afro-American population; thin line denotes total free Afro-American population.)

have opted to sample documentary information from 20-year intervals, beginning in 1750, to develop a historical context of the city-site and to describe settlement patterns. The 20-year scale is used since the data collected at these intervals reflect the different functional, economic, demographic, and regional roles of Alexandria. Furthermore, for correlation with archaeological contexts (e.g., backyard midden, privy, and well), a 20-year interval is sufficiently precise.

For analysis, these sample intervals are grouped into temporal segments that reflect economic–technological patterns in North American urban development. They are sufficiently wide to correspond to archaeological layers (usually with 30–40 year bracket dates). The time segments are *Mercantile Capitalism* (mid-eighteenth century), *Indigenous Commercial Capitalism* (late-eighteenth century to mid-nineteenth century), and *Industrial Capitalism* (mid- to late-nineteenth century to early twentieth century). We predict that settlement and artifact patterns, as expressions of social and spatial organization, relate to these economic–techological changes. Artifact contexts with more specific dates can fit appropriately into "upper" or "lower" parts of their respective time segments.

Spatial Framework

City-Site Concept

The term *city-site* refers to the area that incorporates an urban settlement and is tied to it in terms of spatial and socioeconomic organization. Within the urban settlement is a *core* or center of population, wealth, and power. It is smaller than the city measured by conventional standards (legal boundaries or settled areas). The city-site is extended to include *semiperipheral* and *peripheral* areas where appropriate (Figure 3.5). The spatial ties between the urban core and its peripheral areas are essentially those of land use, transportation, and communication (Friedman and Alonso 1964; Pahl 1967). Demographic and economic movements amplify and modulate, but do not undermine the city-centered pattern of organization. The terms *core, semiperiphery,* and *periphery* are more than mere descriptions of geographical location. They connote a set of structural relationships that hold the outlying areas in clear subordination to the center.

The core-periphery model allows one to describe changing settlement patterns in terms of land use and comparative residential activities. It locates archaeological areas of inquiry, not merely in terms of distance from center, but also distance from wealth and power. (Consequently, the actual physical boundaries of the core–peripheral areas can change over time.) This construct aids historical archaeologists who have limited access to much of their urban sites. It allows artifact patterns from specific urban areas, identified through a documentary survey, to be related to specific status groups. Furthermore, it allows the interpretation of material differences to take place within a holistic framework, without excavating an entire neighborhood or city.

Spatial Levels of Study

The whole city-site is the object of investigation, Yet, the parts associated with different status groups need to be delineated, surveyed, and archaeologically excavated to determine urban group material patterns. The need for tangible evidence requires that households and neighborhoods be clearly associated with given status groups. We have developed a strategy that subdivides and samples the whole city-site for intensive documentary research and excavation.

This spatial stratification is necessary in urban archaeological study for a number of reasons, some conceptual and some practical. First, by nature, a city is complexly compartmentalized by land-use and behavioral diversity. Therefore, a sampling strategy that considers the city to be homogeneous would not provide a reliable view (Morris 1975). Second, the Alexandria Program focuses on residential strata

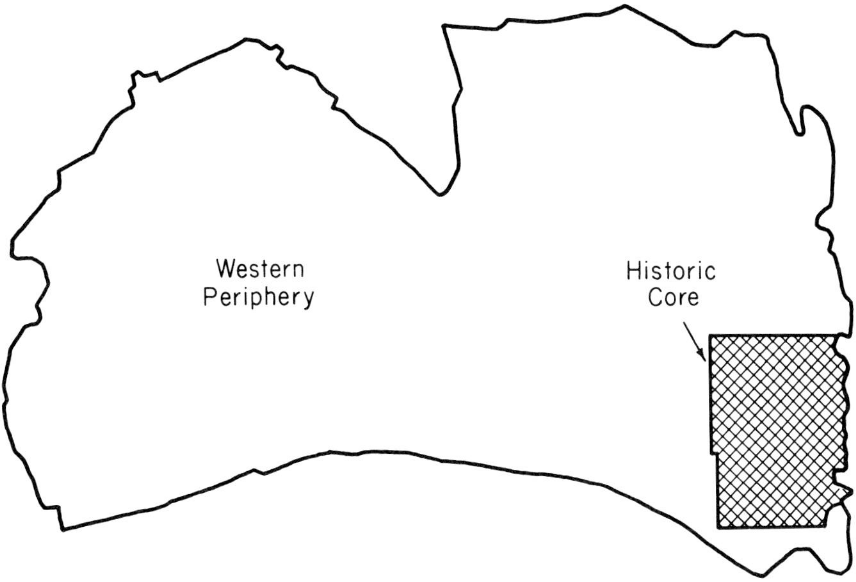

FIGURE 3.5. Core and periphery areas of Alexandria.

for archaeological interpretation. Whereas it is important to delineate where other land-use strata occur to understand urban development and interaction, they need not be sampled for a material study of group behavior. Third, only a portion of the city is sampled since differential developmental processes have destroyed and disturbed archaeological materials or left others in locations that would be too expensive to recover. Urban renewal, new construction, land filling, rising river levels, and flood control projects have all altered the cityscape (in a nonrandom fashion) so that only certain areas are left in each residential stratum that meet the rigid requirements of historic archaeological investigation. Finally, some residential areas in the city have had such a transient and/or mixed nature that they are unreliable for archaeological interpretation. Even though mixed neighborhoods and residential properties are vital to understanding urban life and particular developmental periods, they are, at this time, best left to documentary and architectural study.

In urban research one must control for the major factors that (*a*) define and locate general socioeconomic and ethnic status groups, and (*b*) can be efficiently culled from archives in a citywide study. Urban investigation is further complicated by factors affecting material patterns that must be identified in site selection and interpretation. These factors, which create more specific status groups and affect the kind and amount of archaeological materials, include variables such as household size and composition (Schiffer *et al.* 1981), members' age, education, social mobility, physical mobility, religion, ethnic mixture, and length of time in the

United States and in the urban environment. Thus, for archaeologists, urban study is complicated simply by the need to identify status groups at a given time and the amount of disturbance that might have occurred. By centering research on locations that undergo frequent household replacement or that are part of a heterogeneous residential area, the researcher adds to an already elaborate interpretative process. The changing occupation pattern confounds the archaeological record and increases the amount of time required for background research.

Because of the built-in complexity of city-sites and urban groups, it is desirable at such an embryonic stage in urban archaeological research to reduce problems caused by variability of group occupancy, land uses, disturbances, and alterations. One way to accomplish this is to stratify the city-site based upon the following criteria: *conceptual scheme* (core–periphery); *land use* (residential) and *time frame* (20–50 year segments); homogeneous *areas* (neighborhoods and street-faces), with consistency, continuity, and preservation of specific status groups; and undisturbed and available *zones* in domestic lots that offer information on household material patterns and refuse disposal.

The descending, nested levels of spatial stratification employed in the Alexandria Program are summarized next and are schematically illustrated in Figure 3.6:

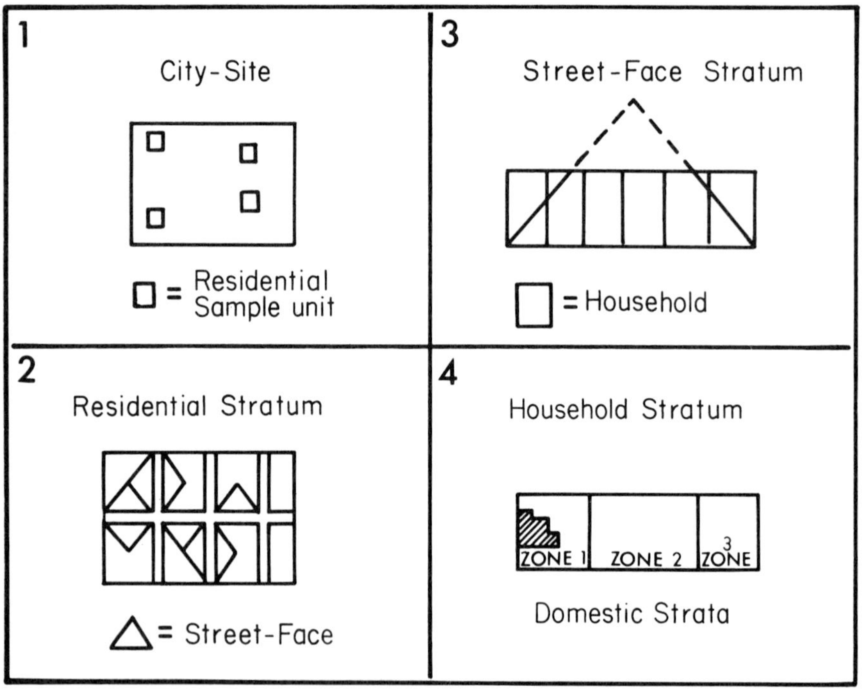

FIGURE 3.6. Spatial stratification schematic of Alexandria.

1. *City-site:* core, semiperiphery, and periphery.
2. *Residential areas:* Neighborhoods associated with homogeneous residential patterns at one or more time phases (e.g., free Afro-American working class, ca. 1810–1850).
3. *Street-faces:* Quarter blocks (shaped like triangles) that face onto a street and have the highest continuous density of the residential behavior defined above. Street-faces are selected, rather than whole, blocks since residences that face one another are more likely to resemble one another in character than those that back onto one another (James Horton personal communication) and since microvariations occur in the nineteenth-century city requiring the precision of quarter-block units.
4. *Household lots:* Domestic properties along the sample street-faces, randomly selected among those that are confirmed to have inhabitants in the specified status group, time phase, and state of preservation.
5. *Domestic zones:* Areas within each household lot that are hypothesized to exhibit distinct artifact patterns (e.g., greater refuse in Zone 3) and that have differential accessibility for archaeological excavation (e.g., Zone 3 is less developed with patios and flowers and can yield a higher sample).

RESEARCH STRATEGY

The methods that determine the time frame and geographical boundaries of an urban archaeological investigation should also delineate a historical context for interpreting land use and socioeconomic–ethnic group dynamics. The significance of an archaeological site is primarily a function of its historical context. Thus, the changing functional role and geographical location of land-use activities and human groups must be delimited *before* putting a trowel into the ground. Working in a continuous city-site also requires additional planning to identify areas of modern development and inaccessibility due to private ownership. A phased research strategy provides a structure to archaeological investigations of a complex urban society and site. The phased approach allows research to proceed systematically through the complex phenomena that describes the site as it developed from a preindustrial to a postindustrial cityscape.

The Alexandria Urban Archaeology Program has embarked upon a four-phased research strategy. Since 1977, the Program has completed the first three phases. Because of the length of time needed to complete archaeological steps, in contrast to archival ones, Phases I and II were proceeded simultaneously. The phases of the research strategy are

I. *City-wide archival survey* producing a historical geography of land-use activities and socioeconomic–ethnic groups occupying the Alexandria city-site between 1770 and 1910.

II. *Residential archaeological testing* of diverse status-related households to select appropriate attributes and methods, as well as to provide preliminary patterns of urban households.

III. *Contemporary survey* of the residential areas to determine current land use, archaeological and architectural continuity, ground disturbance, and accessibility.

IV. *Comprehensive neighborhood survey* of documentary, architectural, and archaeological resources relating to individual historic households sampled from status-related residential areas with continuity and accessibility.

Phase I: City-wide Archival Survey

The archaeological interpretation of urban sites requires alternatives to methods usually employed in traditional historical surveys. First, the historic maps do not record information in relevant land-use, socioeconomic, or ethnic categories needed to define urban residential behavior over time. The first maps of Alexandria that show residential areas as distinct from commercial and industrial areas date from the 1870s. Prior to that time, city maps noted only a few churches, prominent homes, public buildings, and landmarks. Also, the traditional archival tasks conducted prior to excavations may include reviewing deeds, wills, inventories, diaries, and tax and census records. This intensive technique is counterproductive, however, if applied at the initial stage of a city-site project. The rapid growth of the urban population and the concomitant expansion of industrial society's record-keeping functions have produced massive archives for urban historical surveys. To approach households from a city-wide perspective, we must break from traditional, labor-intensive and time-consuming historical surveys. Every household cannot be researched intensively. Furthermore, to focus exclusively on a single area without reference to the full matrix of an urban site and its historic context is to obscure the proverbial forest for the trees.

The delineation of historic context is clearly the major prerequisite to identification, evaluation, and archaeological interpretation of residential localities. Thus, in the Alexandria Project, we turned to methods used in urban geography to differentiate activity areas and the residential localities associated with socioeconomic–ethnic status groups over time. The resulting maps were used to reconstruct the historic residential landscape and to direct us to localities we later excavated for archaeological patterns of urban groups. The settlement patterns derived from this city-wide archival survey simultaneously acted as an independent test of urban developmental process.

The method selected for the Alexandria survey has been used most successfully in Toronto (Goheen 1970). The major feature of the survey is that documents are investigated extensively to provide spatial and longitudinal data that describe the city-site. Moreover, these documents provide consistent data in the same categories over time and are relatively free from collection bias. Although all documents bias information, those developed for governmental statistics or accounting usually have the least idiosyncratic formats. Additionally, they have the greater intercity and intracity analytical value. For example, by cross-referencing tax and census information, social historians and geographers have successfully delineated general status groups and their residential settlement patterns (Duncan and Duncan 1965; Groves and Muller 1975; Ward 1971). In Alexandria the tax assessment rolls and census records meet the conditions of consistency and lack of bias.

In its city-wide archival survey, the Alexandria Program uses the following variables:

A. Condition of tenure of property
  1. Owner
  2. Tenant
B. Assessed value of property—
  Land Value Decile Category (top 10% to bottom 10%)
C. Characteristics of occupant(s)
  1. Ethnicity
    a. Euro-American
    b. Afro-American
  2. Legal status
    a. Free
    b. Slave
  3. Occupation
    a. Professional/entrepreneurial/high white collar
    b. Proprietary/low white collar
    c. Skilled crafts
    d. Service/unskilled specified
    e. Unskilled unspecified or other unskilled
    f. Unclassifiable
    g. No occupation reported
    h. Blank

By using these variables, the city's historic residential areas can be defined, and street-faces with the highest density of occupation over time by specific status groups can be located. The data from a 100% survey, conducted over 2 sample years, were compared to smaller-sized samples (33, 15, and 7%) from the same population. We found that a 100% sample was *not* necessary for yielding accurate settlement patterns on a quarter-block (street-face) scale. In other words a 15% sample allowed us to generalize with accuracy about distribution (residential areas) and density (street-face occupation) of status group populations. Specific households cannot be located precisely along the street-face, a step that requires intensive archival work and occurs *after* street-faces that fit our criteria are selected in the fourth phase of the program. This sampling technique used at systematic time intervals (from 1790 to 1910) provides a diachronic portrait of the city's residential settlement pattern.

The data are collected by community volunteers under supervision of the Project's historian and are recorded, quantified, and placed on a computer for each sample year. First, the tax assessment rolls are sampled, using a 15% random stratified method. The assessment roll pages correspond to geographical units within the city-site and act as the sample strata. Since the assessors walked a patterned route through the city to record property values, they obtained the only records containing locational and site-specific economic information. A street-numbering system was not instituted in Alexandria until the 1880s. The sampled households are identified in the census, which contains information on occupations, ethnicity, legal status, age, and sex. Occupations are ranked and grouped by status criteria (Hershberg 1976; Katz 1972), and a decile scale organizes the property value data by sample year.

The sampled data are first recorded on index cards, then quantified, and finally placed on coding sheets for entry on a computer data file. After we process the data through relevant Statistical Package for Social Sciences Programs (SPSS), frequency charts for each individual variable or specific, analytically significant combinations of variables (e.g., free blacks or slaves) are created by street-faces. The information is printed and mapped, using the SYMAP Program. Acetate overlays, color-coded by analytical value (e.g., ranked 1–5 for occupation), are traced from the computer maps. The acetate overlays, built up in horizontal layers on a base map, provide the composite residential pattern for a 20-year interval. This process, when completed, portrays graphically the residential patterns of each status group in the developing city-site. These patterns define the structure of the city-site, act as a test of hypothesized social and spatial relationships, and highlight the street-faces with the highest degree of consistent and continuous occupation by major socioeconomic–ethnic status groups.

The street-faces identified in this manner are *potential* areas for material studies. However, they must be analytically sorted during Phases III and IV into the *actual* field-sampling localities. The sorting process includes documentary, architectural, and contemporary analysis, and identifies the residential localities for later archaeological sampling and interpretation.

Phase II: Residential Archaeological Testing

Although methods of archival research are clearly described in historical literature, there is little comparable information in archaeological studies. Thus, in the absence of definitions for urban or class artifactual patterns, we found it necessary to conduct a testing phase for clarification of several issues. Through three separate projects, we have developed excavation, processing, dating, and interpretative methodology for use in the Phase IV work.

Because there are few nineteenth-century artifact studies for guidance, type collections for household ceramics, glass, textiles, leather footwear, fauna, and seeds were needed in the laboratory. In addition, specific artifact attributes had to be selected for their value in dating and for their potential to reveal price and function for different households.

For both purposes, a hierarchical classification system, which is a modification of

South's (1977) scheme, has been developed. South's framework has been amplified in two areas—household behavior and nineteenth-century material culture. Although each of the nineteenth-century collections, previously mentioned, has been classified in this manner, the most developed scheme is for ceramics. Ceramics allow for more precise dating than other materials, and they have been studied more frequently in relation to status (Miller 1980; Otto 1975). Ceramic variables in hierarchical relationship are as follows:

- HOUSEHOLD BEHAVIOR
  - USE
    - *Group*: (e.g. Tea Table, Kitchen, Chamber, Decorative)
    - *Function*: (e.g. Consumption, Serving)
    - *Form*: (e.g. Tea Cup, Tea Saucer)
  - RICE
    - DATE
      - *Shape and Size*: (e.g. London-Handleless, 4 in. Diameter)
      - *Ware*: (e.g. Refined/Pearlware)
      - *Type*: (e.g. Handpainted—Cobalt Blue)
      - *Variety*: (e.g. Floral, ca. 1800–1820)

Three different archaeological contexts have been located during Phase II of the Program: privy-wells, middens, and backyard strata. The same attributes are used where possible to analyze artifacts in each context. However, it is often difficult to classify accurately a small sherd found in a backyard stratum by any designation except ware. Wherever appropriate, sherds are crossmended to vessels. In privy-wells and midden features, vessel counts, rather than sherds, are used for analysis. This type of analysis, however, necessitates the independent study of distinct archaeological contexts within and between different urban households. It seems to best represent past behavior since we have found that the different contexts are nonrandomly located (e.g., wells are near back property walls) and distributed between status groups (e.g., black households rarely have wells).

The three project areas that have been tested are not "samples." That is, they were not selected in any fashion from a known universe of localities. The sampling for archaeological purposes must await Phase IV. Rather, residential excavations have been carried out in neighborhoods that have been clearly differented from one another over long periods of time by households with probable status differences. Furthermore, they are spatially and conceptually distinct, occupying core, semiperipheral, and peripheral positions. Finally, since these localities would have been destroyed by modern development, they served as a means of preserving information while methods were developed and goals defined. They did not, however, offer information that could be generalized to class, ethnic, land-use, or neighborhood behavior.

The areas tested were (*a*) King Street—an upper middle class Euro-American area in the urban commerical core; (*b*) The Bottoms (or DIP)—a free Afro-American working-class area in the periphery; and (*c*) The Hill—a free Afro-American and Euro-American middle/working-class area in the semiperipheral "industrial" section of town. Although the latter two projects both concentrated upon black sites, they offered different situations in terms of ground disturbance, property tenure, neighborhood power and wealth, and social mobility. As one might expect from the twentieth-century place names, the Hill's black inhabitants were more affluent than those of the Bottoms. The former lived in an integrated section located only four blocks from downtown King Street, and they also exhibited a degree of upward mobility greater than the inhabitants of the Bottoms. The Hill localities have less disturbance since the Bottoms became the site of a housing development.

This testing phase has resulted in the clarification of significant archaeological attributes and the refinement of analyses for different household contexts. An added benefit has been the elaboration of methods for intensive archival research, which must be conducted at the outset of Phase IV. Consequently, a large degree of potential confusion has been reduced by this approach, and a clear direction has been set for the overall program.

Phase III: Contemporary Survey

The city-wide archival survey has delineated potential areas for archaeological study. However, these areas may contain disturbed household lots, and current owners may refuse access for excavations. Just as Phase II revealed patterned use of backyard space for historic refuse disposal, contemporary attitudes about and uses of the same backyards also are patterned. Because present uses may restrict availability for archaeology, a contemporary survey of potential street-faces is conducted. This survey records (*a*) current land use, (*b*) amount of disturbance, (*c*) legal accessibility, and (*d*) access to different zones on a lot. This information will enable us to discard street-faces that have experienced drastic subsurface changes. And, although most Alexandrians are willing to permit archaeological work on their property, we must disqualify those potential street-faces for which the owners deny legal access.

Phase IV: Comprehensive Neighborhood Survey

The street-faces with relatively little disturbance and whose property owners are willing to facilitate the archaeological process are selected for intensive archival and architectural surveys. For household lots on the eligible street-faces, we search tax and census records, insurance maps, chain-of-title, previous historic resource surveys, and secondary sources. The heads of households are checked at 5-year tax intervals and 10-year census intervals. Also, they are monitored in each census before and after their residency on a particular lot for data on social mobility. Club and church membership provide additional status indexes. To provide a fuller characterization of the residential areas, other land uses are recorded on neighborhood maps, which are used to reconstruct the historic environment of a neighborhood and help explain its residential patterns.

With the criteria just outlined, we are able to list household lots that offer the best opportunity to study residential material culture. From this list, specific lots are randomly selected for field survey of each street-face. The field survey, consisting of architectural analysis along with artifactual study of excavated areas, approaches the built environment from an archaeological perspective. We treat a house as a separate artifact category with its own status-related attributes. Oral histories and historic photographs are searched concurrently to develop an appreciation of the animate and inanimate aspects of urban life.

CONCLUSIONS

The Alexandria Urban Archaeology Program is implementing a multistaged research strategy to explore material relationships between socioeconomic–ethnic stratification, settlement patterns, and urban–industrial development. The hypothesized relationships are tested in an article in Part II of this volume. Although our predictions have a firm theoretical foundation, the lack of previous research on the tangible aspects of historic American urban life make rigidly formulated hypotheses clearly undesirable. We have tried to include in our hypotheses variables and material attributes whose interrelationships previously have gone unrecognized. It is important to realize that walls, alleys, sanitation systems, and even the absence of archaeological features are artifacts of the same developmental processes that produced the specific materials and socioeconomic classes we are studying (see Dickens and Crimmins, Chapter 5). If we recognize that our data units are functional parts of the whole city-site, studies of relationships between them should contribute immensely to our knowledge of urban behavioral patterns and processes.

ACKNOWLEDGMENTS

We would like to thank our colleagues in the Program, D. Katherine Biedleman, Thomas Davidson, Terry Klein, Barbara Magid, Richard Napoli, and Steven J. Shephard, for helping us to develop our research strategies. Appreciation is also expressed to Howard Gillete and James Horton (George Washington University) and Jonathan Haas (University of Denver) for their insights into the nature of a city-site and the material aspects of complex society. William Kelso and Alain Outlaw, Commissioners for Archaeology in the Commonwealth of Virginia, merit special appreciation for their steadfast support of the Program since its inception. Most of all, we are indebted to the members of the Alexandria Archaeological Commission, especially its chairperson Colonel Bernard Brenman, and to the many dedicated volunteers who have made the Program possible.

REFERENCES

Berlin, I.
1976 The revolution in black life. In *The American revolution: Explorations in the history of American radicalism*, edited by A. F. Young. Dekalb: Northern Illinois Press.

Braudel, F.
1973 *Capitalism and material life, 1400–1800*. New York: Harper.

Cipolla, C. M.
1964 *The economic history of world population*. Baltimore: Penguin Books.

Coser, L.
1956 *The function of social conflict*. New York: Free Press.

Dahrendorf, R.
1959 *Class and class conflict in industrial society*. Palo Alto: Stanford Univ. Press.

Duncan, O. D., and B. Duncan
1965 Residential distribution and occupational stratification. *American Journal of Sociology* **60**:210–217.
Fairbanks, C. H.
1974 The Kingsley slave cabins in Duvall County, Florida, 1968. *The Conference on Historic Site Archeology Papers* 1972 7:62–93.
Fox, R. G.
1977 *Urban anthropology: Cities in their cultural settings.* Englewood Cliffs: Prentice-Hall.
Friedman, J. P., and W. Alonso
1964 *Regional development and planning.* Cambridge, Mass.: M.I.T. Press.
Goheen, P. G.
1970 Victorian Toronto, 1850–1900: Pattern and process of Growth. *Department of Geography Research Paper* **127**. Chicago: Univ. of Chicago Press.
Goldin, C. D.
1976 *Urban slavery in the American South, 1820–1860.* Chicago: Univ. of Chicago Press.
Groves, P. A., and E. K. Muller
1975 The evolution of black residential areas in late nineteenth-century cities. *Journal of Historical Geography.* **1**:169–191.
Gutman, H. G.
1976 *The Black family in slavery and freedom, 1750–1925.* New York: Vintage Books.
Hershberg, T.
1976 The Philadephia Social History Project. *Historical Methods Newsletter* **9**:41–184.
Katz, M. B.
1972 Occupational classification in history. *Journal of Interdisciplinary History* **3**:63–88.
Landes, D. S.
1969 *The unbound Prometheus: Technological change and industrial development in western Europe from 1750 to the present.* Cambridge, Mass.: Cambridge Univ. Press.
McKelvey, B.
1963 *The urbanization of America, 1860–1915.* New Brunswick, N.J.: Rutgers Univ. Press.
Miller, G.
1980 Classification and economic scaling of nineteenth-century ceramics. *Historical Archaeology* **14**:1–41.
Millon, R.
1973 *Urbanization at Teotihuacan, Mexico, Vol. I.* Austin: Univ. of Texas Press.
Morris, C.
1975 Sampling in the excavation of urban sites: The case of Huanuco Pampa. In *Sampling in Archaeology*, edited by J. E. Mueller. Tucson, Arizona: University of Arizona Press. Pp. 192–208.
North, D.
1961 *The economic growth of the United States, 1790–1860.* Englewood Cliffs, N.J.: Prentice-Hall.
Otto, J.
1975 *Status differences and the archaeological record—A comparison of planter, overseer, and slave sites from Cannon's Point Plantation (1794–1861).* University Microfilms, Ann Arbor: University of Michigan.
1977 Artifacts and status differences—A comparison of ceramics from planter, overseer, and slave sites on an antebellum plantation. In *Research strategies in historical archeology*, edited by S. South. New York: Academic Press. Pp. 91–118.
1980 Race and class on antebellum plantations. In *Archaeological perspectives on ethnicity in America*, edited by R. L. Schuyler, Farmingdale, N.Y.: Baywood Publishing. Pp. 3–13.
Pahl, P. E.
1967 Sociological models in geography. In *Socioeconomic models in geography*, edited by R. J. Chorley and P. Haggett, London: Metheun. Pp. 217–243.

Pleck, E.
1979 *Black migration and poverty: Boston, 1865–1900*. New York: Academic Press.
Pred, A. R.
1966 *The spatial dynamics of United States industrial growth, 1800–1914*. Cambridge, Mass.: M.I.T. Press.
Rathje, W. L.
1978 Le Project due Garbage 1975: Historic trade-offs. In *Social archeology*, edited by C. Redman. New York: Academic Press.
Rathje, W. L., and M. McCarthy
1977 Regularity and variability in contemporary garbage. In *Research strategies in historical archeology*, edited by S. South. New York: Academic Press. Pp. 261–286.
Schiffer, M. B., T. E. Downing, and M. McCarthy
1981 Waste not, want not: An ethnoarchaeological studv of reuse in Tucson, Arizona. In *The archaeology of Us*, edited by R. A. Gould and M. B. Schiffer. New York: Academic Press.
Schuyler, R. L.
1980 *Archaeological perspectives on ethnicity in America*. Farmingdale, N.Y.: Baywood.
Shimada, I.
1978 Economy of a prehistoric urban context: Commodity and labor flow at Moche V Pampa Grande, Peru. *American Antiquity* **43**:569–592.
Sjoberg, G.
1960 *The preindustrial city*. New York: The Free Press.
South, S.
1977 *Method and theory in historical archeology*. New York: Academic Press.
Thernstrom, S.
1960 *The other Bostonians: Poverty and progress in the American metropolis*. Cambridge, Mass.: Harvard Univ. Press.
Wade, R. C.
1964 *Slavery in the cities: The South, 1820–1860*. Cambridge, Mass.: Oxford Univ. Press.
Wallerstein, I.
1976 *The modern world system, Vol. I*. New York: Academic Press.
1980 *The modern world system, Vol. II*. New York: Academic Press.
Ward, D.
1971 *Cities and immigrants: A geography of change in nineteenth-century America*. New York: Oxford Univ. Press.
Warner, S. B.
1962 *Streetcar suburb: The process of growth in Boston*. Cambridge, Mass.: Harvard Univ. Press.
1968 *The private city: Philadelphia in three periods of growth*. Philadelphia: Univ. of Pennsylvania Press.
Watkins, C. M.
1970 Artifacts from the sites of three nineteenth-century houses and ditches at Darien Bluff, Georgia. *Laboratory of Archaeology Series Report* 9, Athens: Univ. of Georgia.
Woods, R. A., and A. J. Kennedy
1962 *The zone of emergence*. Cambridge, Mass.: Harvard Univ. Press.

4

Archaeological Implications of a Manufacturing Industry in Eighteenth-Century American Cities[1]

Frederick J. E. Gorman

THE STUDY OF INDUSTRY IN EIGHTEENTH-CENTURY CITIES

Economic anthropologists and historians have noted that major industries and cities began to proliferate in the American colonies during the latter half of the eighteenth century (Bridenbaugh 1961; Brinley 1978; Cappon 1976). To my knowledge, however, there is no comprehensive understanding of the significance of industrial manufacture in urban versus nonurban environments of this period. In this chapter, I address the problem of measuring, in ways that are relevant to urban archaeology, the impact of the eighteenth-century city on a constituent manufacturing industry.

My definition of a manufacturing industry excludes operations that depended on the artisanry of silversmiths, gunsmiths, blacksmiths, and cabinetmakers (cf. South 1977a:232). Only eighteenth-century American manufactures of paper, textiles, pottery, glass, iron, and brass (Noël Hume 1975:163) possessed the basic characteristics of industry, in that they were housed in factory structures where raw materials were transformed into bulk-finished or semi-finished goods (Vogel 1967:34).

Manufacturing industries known to have existed in established American cities by 1799 (Bridenbaugh 1961:48–106; Cappon 1976:28–30) are listed in Table 4.1. Inspection of the table shows that Boston, Hartford, New Haven, Norwich, New York, Philadelphia, and Baltimore each sustained at least three different industries

[1]Part of this research was funded through the Historic Preservation Grants-in-Aid Program of the National Park Service

ARCHAEOLOGY OF URBAN AMERICA
The Search for Pattern and Process

ISBN 0-12-214980-7

Table 4.1 Manufacturing Industries Known to Have Operated in Established American Cities by 1799[a]

City	Urban status	Paper mill	Textile factory[b]	Pottery factory	Glass factory	Iron-brass works[c]
Beverly, Mass.	1760			1776-1790(1)		
Salem, Mass.	1760			1760-1790(2)		
Boston, Mass.	1760		1764-1790(1)	1960-1775(1)	1787-1827(1)	
New York, N.Y.	1760	1760-1790(2)	1764-1790(2)	1760-1790(8)	1754-1764(1)	1768-?(1)
Philadelphia, Pa.	1760	1760-1775(1)	1764-1790(6)	1760-1790(12)		1730-1765(3) 1790-?(1)
Charleston, S.C.	1760			1760-1775(2)		
Portsmouth, N.H.	1770		1764-1790(1)			
Newburyport, Mass.	1770			1760-1790(2)		
Providence, R.I.	1770			1760-1775(1)		1790-?(1)
Hartford, Conn.	1770	1776-1790(1)	1764-1790(1)	1776-1790(2)	?-1776(1)	
Norwich, Conn.	1770	1760-1790(3)	1764-1790(1)	1776-1790(2)		1750-1770(2)
Baltimore, Md.	1770	1760-1775(2)	1764-1790(1)		1799-1884(1)	1790-?(3)
New Haven, Conn.	1780	1776-1790(1)	1764-1790(2)		1789-1790(1)	1770-1771(1)

[a] Parenthetical values refer to the number of factories in each period.

[b] Textile factories were quasi-industrial until ca. 1790 (Weeks 1916).

[c] Only smelting furnaces and shaping forges.

during the decade of its urbanization. Other cities, such as Beverly, Salem, and Newburyport, Massachusetts; Portsmouth, New Hampshire; Providence, Rhode Island; and Charleston, South Carolina, incorporated one or two kinds of manufactures at the time of their urbanization. Newport, Rhode Island; New Orleans, Louisiana; St. Augustine, Florida; Detroit, Michigan; Albany, New York; Norfolk, Virginia; and Savannah, Georgia appear to have experienced urbanization without industrial manufacturing during the eighteenth century. Williamsburg, Virginia; Mobile, Alabama; and Santa Fe, New Mexico became urban late in the eighteenth century, and information about their constituent factories is vague at present (cf. Cappon 1976:28–30).

Hypotheses about eighteenth-century industry in the urban environment are derived largely from market theory. For example, Bridenbaugh (1961:69, 84) contends that urban consumer demands stimulated sales of products made in early American cities, while the availability of urban labor promoted specialization in manufacture to a degree beyond that of suburban and rural factories. In a similar vein, he asserts that raw resources and supplies were more readily accessible in cities, which promoted greater productivity among urban factories. The interplay of these supply-and-demand factors led to improvements in the technology and quality of urban manufactures (Bridenbaugh 1961:69).

At present, an archaeological test of this or any other hypothesis about manufacture in eighteenth-century cities is likely to be hindered by problems of data collection and analysis in industrial and urban archaeology. For example, industrial archaeologists can expect to encounter substantial rubble and masses of artifacts during the excavation of an eighteenth-century factory (Noël Hume 1975:79; Starbuck, Gorman, and Wiseman 1976), which complicates the collection of data. Also, the delineation of activity areas within the factory may involve a high degree of uncertainty (Noël Hume 1975:188; 1976:164) that is magnified by the accidental preservation of some components and the nearly complete destruction of others (Cotter and Orr 1975:6). The collection of documentary information about the history of eighteenth-century factories is complicated by the fact that company records, if kept, usually have not been preserved (Filley and Aldag 1975:27; Noël Hume 1975:180; Palmer 1978:224). Frequently, company histories must be compiled from indirect sources such as newpaper accounts, legistlative documents, ledgers of other firms, and diaries. Analyses of both artifactual and documentary data are confounded by a lack of consensus about what industrial archaeology is or should be (Buchanan 1972:20; Foley 1968:67; Ingersol 1971:71). The tendency to study only manufacturing techniques (Buchanan 1972:25; South 1968:52) does not enlarge our understanding of how eighteenth-century factories acquired raw materials, divided their labor forces (Gillmore 1978:77), or disposed of their products. Analysis of a factory as a whole complex of such activities (cf. Landberg 1967:77; Vogel 1967:35) is required to test adequately Bridenbaugh's hypothesis. Regardless of where he begins his task, the industrial archaeologist eventually must consult a technological historian in order to identify the layout of an eighteenth-century factory, its equipment, and its products (Buchanan 1972:30; Foley 1968:68; Heite 1968:43; Noël Hume 1975:161).

The archaeology of eighteenth-century cities is plagued by problems similar to those of purely industrial sites. Collecting artifact data from urban sites that are concealed or distorted by subsequent construction can be frustrating and costly (cf. Bowen 1978:67; Dickens and Bowen 1980:42; Harris 1970:53; Lewis 1977:165; Stone 1968:75). Urban excavations that are arbitrarily delimited by facilities in current use or specific construction projects (Deagan 1974:13; Dickens and Bowen 1980:42; Lewis 1977:165) may generate unrepresentative samples of archaeological data (Landberg 1967:77). Historical information about eighteenth-century urban sites can be collected from a wide variety of documentary sources (Foley 1967a:43; Ingersoll 1971:67; Landberg 1967:73, 75), but there is no agreement about whether it should be used to plan urban excavations or to interpret the archaeological data afterward (cf. Ingersoll 1971:67; Landberg 1967:73). This problem can be attributed to the lack of theory about eighteenth-century urbanism that is necessary to guide analyses of its artifactual and documentary data (Foley 1967a:44; Ingersoll 1971:66). Despite Ingersoll's (1971:68–69) pioneering effort to fill this void, excavation of eighteenth-century remains in the city continues to be undertaken either as a salvage operation in response to the stimulus of urban renewal (Landberg 1967:77; Noël Hume 1975:23; Vogel 1967:34) or as an adjunct to architectural restoration (Foley 1967a:44; MacMurray 1972;56; Noël Hume 1973:4).

The problems of urban and industrial archaeology are likely to be compounded in the study of manufacture in eighteenth-century cities (cf. Cotter and Orr 1975; Ingersoll 1971; South 1968). This implies that an archaeological test of Bridenbaugh's hypothesis would entail a major research effort.

THE CORRELATION APPROACH TO URBAN INDUSTRIAL ARCHAEOLOGY

Any one of four strategies of historical archaeology might be used to evaluate the hypothetical impact of urban environments on the industries in Table 4.1, but one strategy yields more immediate results than the other three. Least fruitful is the traditional "synthetic" stratagem (South 1977a:21), which assumes that the archaeological and the historical records of a site are joint events and that, in the absence of contextual control, gaps in one record can be freely filled by information from the other. This approach is vulnerable to all of the problems of data collection and analysis enumerated above.

The second stratagem also assumes interdependence of historical and archaeological records, but it uses contextual variability of the former to delimit patterning of the latter (South 1972a:148, 1977b:7). This stratagem is relevant insofar as the analysis of artifact inventory profiles of industrial sites from categorically different historical contexts might establish archaeological stereotypes of urban versus nonurban factories (cf. South 1977a:125). Such stereotypes, however, must be derived prior to any test of Bridenbaugh's hypothesis (cf. South 1977b:5). Since the archaeology of eighteenth-century industry is so meager, an approach that will yield more immediate results is needed.

The third stratagem involves the analysis of discrepancies between the historical and archaeological records of a site. This procedure assumes that the records are independent events (cf. Ferguson 1977:7), and it isolates site patterns that are either purely documentary or purely archaeological (cf. South 1972b:155). This lack of correspondence may be attributed to chance factors in the way either record is formed and preserved. For example, a documentary pattern of an eighteenth-century industry that has no archaeological counterpart might reflect an accident in recording manufacturing-curation practices of the past. For fortuitous reasons, a factory's documents may not account for time-lag in the transition of equipment or manufacturing by-products from the historical to the archaeological context (Brose 1968:115; South 1977a:192; Walker 1968:100). Conversely, an undocumented archaeological pattern might be attributed to indeterminant factors that cause relevant industrial records either to be silent or missing altogether (House 1977:242; Schiffer 1977:30). From another viewpoint, the lack of correspondence may be the result of past choice or deliberation (cf. Noël Hume 1975:24; Walker 1968:100) when contradictions between the industrial and archaeological records of a factory are viewed in dialectical terms (Leone 1977:xxi). I can think of no archaeological test implications of Bridenbaugh's hypothesis that are amenable to discrepancy analysis.

In the fourth stratagem, the historical and archaeological records of a site again are assumed to be independent events (cf. Fitting 1977:68), but for a different purpose. Patterning of the form and content of documentary information is analyzed to generate hypotheses that can be tested archaeologically (Klein 1973:68; Stone 1968:76). Prior to archaeological testing, the same documentary pattern can be used to evaluate hypotheses of the sort advanced by Bridenbaugh (cf. Schuyler 1970:88). Later in this chapter, I will implement this procedure in my investigation of the impact of urbanism on eighteenth-century industry. Whichever starting point is chosen, the documentary pattern must be assigned correlates that predict an archaeological pattern (Deagan 1974:13; Lewis 1977:155; Otto 1977:96; Smith and Davidson 1973:35). For this reason, the fourth stratagem is termed the *correlation approach* (cf. South 1977a:321). The assignment of correlates is complicated, however, by the fact that raw documentary classification usually does not make good archaeological classification (South 1977b:12), which means that the application of models from other disciplines is necessary to render both codifications compatible (cf. Klein 1973:68). At the end of this section of the chapter, I introduce one such model to classify documentary information about eighteenth-century industry in ways that are archaeologically sensitive.

Although the correlation approach subordinates archaeology to historical research by restricting archaeological data collection and analysis to sites and phenomena identified in the written record (House 1977:257), it helps us understand what kind of archaeological sample is necessary before excavation (Landberg 1967:77; Schumacher 1967:55; Stone 1968:76). Advance information of this sort can be invaluable in dealing with the aforementioned problems of eighteenth-century urban industrial archaeology. A second advantage of the correlation approach results from the fact that it is ultimately concerned with assessment of the validity and reliability of the historical record. When predictions from historical data diverge from archaeological findings (Fitting 1977:68), the correlation procedure permits the identification of historical data that are either invalid or unreliable as contextual controls. Recall that controlled interpretation of archaeological inventory patterning is a key feature of the second stratagem (cf. Herman, Sands, and Schecter 1973:90; South 1977b:10).

Classification and analysis of the form and content of documentary information are not well developed in the correlation approach to historical archaeology (Baker 1981:247). The method that I employ for these purposes has four aspects. First, I assume that eighteenth-century factories were as complex organizations as their modern counterparts, which implies that my classification scheme should represent this complexity. Specifically, documentary information about an eighteenth-century factory must be classified across a variety of characteristics that covers the spectrum of its actions and interactions, factors that conditioned its effectiveness, and the various outcomes of the behavior in a factory (Filley and Aldag 1975:28). All of this variety can be classified to yield a factory profile that has more predictive value than the use of a few traits in the comparison of an eighteenth-century urban factory with others of the period (Filley and Aldag 1975:27). My profile of a factory includes not only the seven variables hypothesized by Bridenbaugh but more than thirty additional characteristics. In effect, profile classification allows an adequate test of his hypothesis while permitting a much richer understanding of the differences between urban and nonurban manufacturing. Historical archaeologists have advocated profile classification of other kinds of documentary information both in theory (McKay 1974:130) and practice (Brose 1968:114; Brown 1974:87; Herman, Sands, and Schecter 1973:69; Otto 1977:91).

Second, the characteristics that make up an eighteenth-century factory's profile are modeled in terms of the technologies and operations that are commonly observed in modern manufacturing plants (Drucker 1960:28; Mileti, Gillespie, and Morrisey 1978:83; Perrow 1972:48). I assume that the basic technologies and operations of manufacturing have not changed significantly in two centuries. Since modern factories incorporate several different technologies, each of which has a different level of complexity (Mileti, Gillespie, and Morrisey 1978:86), I assume the same approach for factories of the eighteenth century. Then, as now, documentary information about one technology of a manufacturing plant may be incongruous with information about its other technologies, because each is defined in terms of its own types and patterns of activity, equipment, and materials. Moreover, each technology requires different experience or knowledge for one to perform the appropriate tasks (Mileti, Gillespie, and Morrisey 1978:84). For this reason, discordant information about the various technologies of an eighteenth-century factory can impede the derivation of its profile, unless such information is made congruent. Harmony can be achieved by classifying documentary information about each technology in terms of a set of "operations research" variables that are common to all the technologies of a factory. Such variables measure the degrees of diversity, standardization (routine), availability, uniformity, and predictability that underlie all of the factory's technologies (Mileti, Gillespie, and Morrisey 1978:89). Documentary information about formal organizations, such as factories, seems to retain more of its integrity after codification than that for informal organizations of a domestic nature (cf. Buchanan 1972:25; McKay 1974:133–134).

The third aspect of my method is the assignment of archaeological correlates to documentary information that has been codified as the profile of a factory's technological operations. Unfortunately, such criteria have not been developed for industrial archaeology. Therefore, I rely on my knowledge of the preservation of the material remains of eighteenth-century industries to guide the assignment of archaeological correlates to documented technological operations (cf. Schiffer 1977:30). On this basis, I estimate that roughly one-half the variables of a factory's profile have correlates. For example, the profile of each eighteenth-century factory presented in this chapter consists of 152 documented technological operations. Eighty-five of these variables are archaeologically sensitive. These figures may vary somewhat in profiles of pottery, paper, textile, glass, brass, or iron factories, but I believe that their ratio is fairly stable from one of these industries to the next.

The fourth and final aspect concerns the analysis of documentary information about eighteenth-century factories. Historical and industrial archaeologists (Raistrick 1972:10; Schuyler 1970:88; South and Widmer 1977:123; Walker 1968:105) have suggested that the focus of documentary analysis be expanded from the study of event configurations at specific sites to the evaluation of patterns among classes of events that characterize a population of sites. Patterns of industrialization in the nineteenth and early twentieth centuries have been studied in this wider perspective (e.g., Adelman 1980), which I adopt to evaluate the patterning of technological operations among a sample of eighteenth-century factory profiles. A requirement of my analysis is that the sample consist only of those factories that manufactured the same product (Evan 1976:253; Perrow 1972:61). Also, the technological-operations profiles of the factories in my sample must be analyzed as if the factories themselves were functionally autonomous from their urban and nonurban environments (Evan 1976:258). These constraints permit a comparison of how urban and nonurban factories effectively operated the same technologies in different ways (Emery and Trist 1969:286; Evan 1976:194; Trist, Giggin, Murray, and Pollock 1963:152). Operational distinctions between modern factories represent the element of choice in designing the organization of work (Emery and Trist 1969:286). In other words, operational distinctions reflect variations in cultural values (Aiken and Hage 1972:369; Evan 1976:253). If the industrial organization of work two centuries ago had the same implications, it provides a cultural basis of inference about the variability of technological operations among early urban and nonurban factories.

A SAMPLE OF EIGHTEENTH-CENTURY GLASS FACTORIES

In the remainder of this chapter, I test Bridenbaugh's hypothesis by measuring the impact of the eighteenth-century city on one of its constituent heavy industries, that of glass manufacturing. An eighteenth-century glass factory was a major investment in the early American economy, because large amounts of capital were expended on facilities for procuring extensive supplies of fuel and processing raw materials (Noël Hume 1975:166; Palmer 1976b:101). Hundreds of tons of glass sand and thousands of cords of fuel wood were consumed in each of these factories in order to generate almost continuous furnace blasts for 6–9 months a year. All diagnostic activities of glass manufacture, such as sand fritting, batch melting, glass shaping, and product annealing, were performed during this time, and each task involved furnaces. Investment in eighteenth-century glass houses was risky as well. The cost of labor was high because skilled glassmen usually were scarce (Palmer 1967b:101), and expected profits were diminished in many instances by the unforeseen costs of incompetent labor, factory fires, furnace malfunctions, or inappropriate marketing strategies (McKearin and McKearin 1950:12; Wilson 1972:10).

The data in Table 4.1 indicate that five glass factories were located in as many cities by 1799. These factories were (*a*) the New York Glass-House Company in Manhattan (1754–1767), situated today in the Penn Central railyards (Davis 1949:25; Hunter 1950:116, 151–155; Lanmon and Palmer 1976:15; McKearin and McKearin 1950:10–11; Weeks 1884:93); (*b*) the little-known "Glassworks in Hartford," mentioned as defunct in 1776 and of unknown location (Wilson 1972:41); (*c*) the Boston Crown Glass Company (1787–1827), which may be located under a contemporary warehouse (Davis 1949:28–29; Hunter 1950:126; McKearin and McKearin 1950:49–50; Watkins 1940:289–291; Weeks 1884:90; Wilson 1972:58); (*d*) the New Haven Glass Works (1789–1790), of uncertain location (McKearin and McKearin 1950:27); and (*e*) the F. M. Amelung and Company Glassworks (1799–1884), located on Federal Point, Baltimore (Innes 1948:47; Lanmon and Palmer 1976:43; McKearin and McKearin 1950:44; Watkins 1949:364; Weeks 1884:95).

Besides these five, my factory sample consists of nineteen additional glasshouses. Inspection of their chronology and location (Table 4.2) shows that eleven suburban glasshouses (Davis 1949:25, 28–30; Gardner 1935:101–103; Gest and Smith 1939:118–121; Horner 1970; Hunter 1950:144–146; Innes 1948:419; Lanmon and Palmer 1976:15, 18–19, 25–29, 32–39, 56; McKearin 1970:55, 130–138; McKearin and McKearin 1950:12, 24–25, 29–38, 48–49; Noël Hume 1964:310–313; Schwartz 1974:8; Stow 1927:66, 86; Weeks 1884:81, 84, 87, 94–95; White 1930:223; Wilson 1972:41–51, 58–67, 72, 76) and eight rural ones (Davis 1949:25; Davis 1939:294–295; Gest and Smith 1939:120; Hunter 1950:32, 37–47, 116, 146–147, 155, 158, 161–162, 177–180, 224–225, 260; Innes 1948:417–418; Lanmon and Palmer 1976:15–18; McKearin 1926:276–278; McKearin 1950:3; McKearin 1970:142–144; McKearin and McKearin 1950:10–11, 26–30, 48–49, 162; Palmer 1976a:6–15; Palmer 1976b:77–78; Shadel 1970; Sicard 1926:281–282; Watkins 1949:363–365; Weeks 1884:80–83; Wilson 1972:18–19, 52–55) were established during the eighteenth century.

Historical records of the three remaining factories are so sparse as to suggest that they existed only in their planning stages. They are identified in the table as the Darling Venture; the Bowdoin Venture; and the Hubbard, Mosely, Little, and

Table 4.2 Chronology and Location of Eighteenth-century Glass Factories

Factory identity[a]	Dates	State	Community	Settlement
United Glass Company	1739-1778?	N.J.	Alloways town	rural
"Darling Venture"	1747-?	Conn.	?	?
"Bowdoin Venture"	1749-?	Mass.	?	?
Germantown Glassworks	1752-1769	Mass.	Quincy	suburban
New York Glass House Company	1753-1785?	N.Y.	New Windsor	rural
New York Glass House Company	1754-1767	N.Y.	Manhattan	urban
Elizabeth Furnace Glasshouse	1763-1765	Pa.	Lancaster	rural
Manheim Glassworks: American Flint Glass	1765-1780	Pa.	Manheim	rural
Philadelphia Glassworks: John Elliot and Company	1771-1777	Pa.	Kensington	suburban
"Glassworks in Hartford"[b]	? -1776?	Conn.	Hartford	urban
Hubbard, Mosely, Little, and Latimer Glassworks	1780-1780	Conn.	Glastonbury-Lebanon?	?
New England Glassworks	1780-1782	N.H.	Temple	rural
Stanger's "Glass House": N.J. Glass Manufactory: Glassborough: Olive Glass Works	1780-1824[c]	N.J.	Glassborough	rural
Foltz, Kramer, Eberhardt Glasshouse: New Bremen Glass Manufactory: "The New Glass Works"—Amelung, Kohlenberg and Gabler	1780-1813	Md.	Frederick	suburban
Goff Glassworks	1783-1799?	N.Y.	Peterboro	rural
"East Hartford Works"—Pitkin Glassworks	1783-1830	Conn.	East Manchester	suburban
Dowesborough Glasshouse; Albany Glass House	1785-1796	N.Y.	Dowesborough	suburban
Leiper-Butland and Company; Kensington Glassworks[d]	1786-1815	Pa.	Kensington	suburban
Boston Crown Glass Company	1787-1827	Mass.	Boston	urban
New Haven Glass Works	1789-1790	Conn.	New Haven	urban
Etna Glass House	1792-1808	Md.	Frederick	suburban
Thomas Johnson's Glass House	1793-1798	Md.	Frederick	suburban
"Falls of Schuylkill Glassworks"	1794-1808	Pa.	Philadelphia	suburban
New Geneva; Greensboro Glassworks; B.F. Black and Company	1794-1847	Pa.	New Geneva-Greensboro	rural
Hamilton Glassworks	1796-1815	N.Y.	Hamilton	suburban

(Continued)

Table 4.2 (*Continued*)

Pittsburgh Glassworks—Craig and O'Hara Glassworks	1797-1850?	Pa.	Pittsburgh	suburban
F.M. Amelung and Company Glassworks; Barker Brothers	1799-1884	Md.	Baltimore	urban

[a]One or more glasshouses that operated on the same lot and that did not experience joint discontinuity in production and ownership.

[b]This may refer to the earlier and little-known "Darling Venture."

[c]Merged with the nineteenth-century "New Harmony Glassworks" in this year.

[d]Later identity of the Philadelphia Glassworks; John Elliot and Company; partitioned by the discontinuity criterion (see Footnote *a*).

Latimer Glassworks (Hunter 1950:144; Wilson 1972:31, 39). These three are excluded from analysis. I believe that the size of my factory sample closely approximates the true number of eighteenth-century glasshouses because intensive research on this subject during the past decade has not revealed the existence of others (c.f. Wilson 1972).

The independence assumption, which gives every combination of factories an equal chance of appearing in the sample, is violated in two instances. The Philadelphia Glassworks and the Lieper-Butland and Company glassworks consisted of the same physical plant, which I partitioned into two separate firms because production was interrupted for a period of several years, during which ownership and manufacturing policy changed. (This might be construed as an artificial inflation of the sample.) In another case, the Foltz, Kramer, Eberhart factory; the New Bremen Glass Manufactory; and the "New Glass Works" of Amelung, Kohlenburg, and Gabler were classed as one enterprise because each of these three units, despite ownership changes, was successively established on the same property over a 15-year period of uninterrupted operations. (This also might be construed to be an artificial deflation of the sample.)

Archaeological information about these factories is very uneven because many of them have been the subjects of haphazard research conducted, since about 1860, by glass antiquarians. Only a few of the sites have been professionally excavated during the last two decades. For example, the urban New York Glass Company in Manhattan has only been surface collected (Hunter 1950:151). None of the urban glasshouses has been excavated. Two suburban factories—Germantown (Horner 1970) and the Foltz, Kramer, Eberhardt Glasshouse (Innes 1948:417; Noël Hume 1964:310)—have been professionally excavated. Two more were surface collected, while seven others apparently remain undisturbed. One rural factory, the New England Glassworks (Starbuck, Gorman, and Wiseman 1976), has been professionally excavated, while four more have been disturbed by bottle collectors (Hunter 1950:220, 273; Innes 1948:417; Watkins 1953:136; White 1930). The other three may remain untouched.

DERIVATION AND COMPARISON OF GLASS FACTORY PROFILES

Documentary information about each of these glass factories does exist, however, and can be codified as the profile of its *technological operations*. The translation process occurs within the framework of a classic model of operations research (Churchman, Ackoff, and Arnoff 1957). The model framework is defined in terms of the different technologies of a factory and the operations that underlie all of them. There are four basic technologies: (*a*) *the recruitment, holding, and compensation of a labor force*, (*b*) *the procurement of material resources*, (*c*) *the manufacturing process*, and (*d*) *product release* (Churchman, Ackoff, and Arnoff 1957:110). Several archaeologists have differentiated types of manufacturing activity, equipment, and materials along these lines (Buchanan 1972:19; Greer 1970:157–159; Harris, Price, and Price 1977:392; Hudson 1963:55, 63; Kelso and Chappell

1974:59; Outlaw 1974:3–4; Raistrick 1972:10–11, 14; Rowlands 1971:210; Rutsch 1974:40).

Three kinds of operations are common to all of the technologies: (*a*) those that pertain to the *organization* of a factory, (*b*) those that define the factory's *internal environment*, and (*c*) those that reflect factory *decision structure* (Churchman, Ackoff, and Arnoff 1957:13). These categories frame the process by which the different technologies become related to each other (cf. Emery and Trist 1972:270; Evan 1976:274).

The organization of a factory's technological operations is defined in terms of *goals*, *phase controls*, and a *scale of effectiveness*. Factories organized their operations to reach or maintain goals, but the actual objectives that motivated labor recruitment, material resource procurement, glass manufacture, and release among eighteenth-century glasshouses are no less difficult to discern that the goals of their modern counterparts (cf. Churchman, Ackoff, and Arnoff 1957:74–75, 118). Then, as now, goals probably emerged from a glass factory's interaction with its urban, suburban, and rural environments (Thompson and MacEwan 1972:266). It is also likely that the objectives were to maintain (rather than to obtain) the comfort of the owner and the well-being of the glassmen, and to ensure (rather than enhance) the survival of the factory (cf. Churchman, Ackoff, and Arnoff 1957:109; Filley and Aldag 1975:27). Maintenance of these intangibles depended upon (*a*) whether the factory owner(s) had previous experience in organizing the various technologies; (*b*) tolerance limits to the costs of acquiring labor and materials, and manufacturing and releasing glass products; and (*c*) whether cost alleviations were sought.

To the extent that labor and resource procurement, manufacture, and product release represent different phases of glassmaking, organizational objectives also were reflected in the implementation of phase controls to regulate the cost of operating one technology relative to another. This was accomplished by acquiring or relinquishing the finite and discrete commodities of each phase (including labor), either intermittently or continuously, by fixed versus random means (Churchman, Ackoff, and Arnoff 1957:77).

Profits, losses, or quantities produced serve as general scales of effectiveness in measuring how successfully a modern factory maintains its goals. Since much of this information is not preserved in the documentary records of eighteenth-century glasshouses, I substitute effectiveness loss measures such as labor shortage, resource and market transportation distances, and manufacturing delay (cf. Churchman, Ackoff, and Arnoff 1957:13, 120, 279).

Each technology operated within the internal environment of the glass factory. This industrial environment is defined by the *inventory compositions* of the labor forces and of commodities that were either procured, manufactured, or released. It is also defined in terms of the *transition dynamics* of either shifting or fixing the variety and availability of commodities in these inventories (Churchman, Ackoff, and Arnoff 1957:107, 110). The *specific scale of the effectiveness* of each technology in the internal environment is the occurrence of problems that are inherent to labor employment, materials procurement, manufacturing, and sales.

Each technology was operated in accordance with the decision structure of the glass factory. This structure is manifest in a *sequence of choices* made to adjust the costs of one technology independently of the others from one period of production to the next. Consecutive decisions of this sort established a trend either in the alteration or stabilization of the size of the labor force, or in the kinds of commodities procured, manufactured, or released. Alternatively, the lengths of time spent accumulating or disposing of labor or commodities might have been manipulated. I assume that glass factory records of time-size alterations constitute evidence of rational decision making, when, in fact, glasshouses may have had tendencies to make such changes without ever deciding anything (Churchman 1961:44–45, 53). Whether time-size trends were intuitive or rational, they still can be measured in terms of the direction or the rate of change.

Inventory decisions are not structured by a maximizing principle, in which the magnitude of time-size alterations indicates degrees of goal achievement (Nagel and Neef 1976:8). Rather, optimizing principles are more compatible with the goals of a manufacturing organization, because they motivate conscious (or unconscious) decisions that emphasize the persistent search for a more advantageous transaction with the environment, while they simultaneously permit time-size adjustments to be made in order to prevent extinction (Terreberry 1972:160; Thompson and McEwen 1972:266). Environmental search is more crucial to the survival of modern manufacturing firms than either administrative or promotional organizations (Filley and Aldag 1975:28), and I assume this to have been the case two centuries ago. Then, as now, a glass factory's search for advantageous transaction with its environment probably became more difficult with the passage of time, as labor forces, suppliers of materials, and glass product markets became more organized (cf. Davis 1949:28–33; Lanmon and Palmer 1976:47; McKearin 1926:276; Perrot 1961:264; Watkins 1939:68; Weeks 1884:94). In other words, the environment of a factory ultimately becomes "turbulent," and survival of the firm entails more flexible (if not more disjointed) time-size adjustments of its technological inventories (Terreberry 1972:149, 155).

Observation and measurement of these inventory adjustments is complicated by adoption of the optimizing principle. In modern industries, time-size alterations represent continual adjustments of inventory that are made during a period of production in order to approach an optimum by the end of the operation. Since documentary records of short-term decision making in eighteenth-century glass factories usually do not exist, I measure only the long-term trends, which may be less meaningful (cf. Magee and Ernst 1961:480).

The sequence of choices had a *subsequent effect* on a glass factory's viability, depending on whether the decision structure proved to be optimal or suboptimal. I have coded the consequences of decision making about each technology in terms of the stability of the labor force, the locational stability of material resources, the stability of manufacturing schedules, and the stability of product sales.

External factors conditioned the effectiveness of the decision structure of each technology in eighteenth-century glass factories because factors such as wage inflation, material resource taxation, manufacturing disaster, and product markets could be partially controlled at best. If the experience of modern factories is a basis for analogy, then some eighteenth-century glasshouses probably obtained incomplete control of certain external factors only after the first two decades of their existence (Evan 1976:254).

Once codified, the technological operations profiles of the sample glasshouses are compared to each other by means of a hierarchical method of cluster analysis. This clustering technique sorts the glass factories into groups where certain technological operations are more consistently associated among members of the same group than between members of different groups. In other words, the analysis reveals how different groups of factories operated the same technologies in different ways. Such distinctions of choice in designating the organization of work are based on many mutually causal technological operations. Multivariate relationships of this kind are more easily identified by cluster analysis than by inspection (Cowgill 1975:274; Thomas 1978:241).

Cluster analysis is most effective when it is used to generate results that can be compared to intuitively derived groupings of the same data (Read and Christenson 1978:506). Accordingly, I evaluate the demonstrable clustering of glass factories in terms of four alternative outcomes that are logically possible. The first outcome is one in which all urban glasshouses share a unique set of operational distinctions that reflect urban variations of eighteenth-century cultural values. If the operational distinctions involve most of Bridenbaugh's variables, then his hypothesis would be supported. Second, it is possible that all urban and one or more nonurban factories might be assigned membership in the same group because of the hierarchical nature of the clustering technique. As in the first outcome, only those operational distinctions that are unique to city factories reflect urban variants of cultural values. Substantiation of Bridenbaugh's hypothesis depends on whether or not his variables are involved. Third, some, but not all, of the urban glasshouses might be clustered together. This outcome would diminish the validity of Bridenbaugh's hypothesis, depending on what proportion, if any, of the city factories are grouped in terms of his variables. The fourth possible outcome is one in which none of the urban glasshouses is assigned membership in the same cluster. This result would negate Bridenbaugh's hypothesis. It must be borne in mind that my test procedure is subjective since different methods of cluster analysis can group the same data in different ways (Read and Christenson 1978:505).

TECHNOLOGICAL OPERATIONS OF THE GLASS FACTORIES

The complete profile of a glass factory is composed of 152 technological operations. Although 85 of these have archaeological implications, I have selected only 39 of them for cluster analysis. The usefulness of the other 46 archaeologically sensitive variables is vitiated by a lack of documentary data. Each selected technological operation conveys information about 17 or more of the 24 glasshouses. This minimum number includes at least 3 of the 5 urban factories.

There is reason to believe that differences among modern factories are not merely of degree or quantity, but rather of kind or quality (Filley and Aldag 1975:27). I assume that eighteenth-century glass factories also exhibited sharp qualitative differences in the way they performed a technological operation. Accordingly, each technological operation is scaled as a nominal variable consisting of two categorical alternatives. In every instance, these alternatives deliberately maximize the operational distinction between urban and nonurban glasshouses. This differential weighting of the categories favors a cluster solution which supports Bridenbaugh's hypothesis. My bias offsets another that results from the fact that Bridenbaugh's seven variables contribute less to the clustering structure than the other 32 technological operations because they are less numerous. In the remainder of this section, each of the 39 archaeologically sensitive operations is discussed as it pertains to either the organization, the internal environment, or the decision structure of a basic technology.

Acquisition, Holding, and Compensation of the Labor Force

The *organization* of labor technology was motivated by specific goals. These were the acquisition and holding of an adequate number of workers at reasonable wages (cf. Bridenbaugh 1961:134; Watkins 1940:289; Wilson 1972:75). Realization of these goals depended on whether the factory owners or managers were experienced in organizing labor (cf. McKearin and McKearin 1950:33). No less important was managerial knowledge of the maximum wage limits that the factory could tolerate and continue to function.

Estimation of labor costs was difficult because the basic types of workers, such as fuelwood cutters and haulers, glass batch mixers, crucible potters, furnace tenders, glassblowers and their apprentices, glass cutters or engravers, carpenters, blacksmiths, freighters, and superintendents, were variously paid salaries, wages, or for piecework (cf. Hunter 1950:102, 236–239; McKearin and McKearin 1950:52; Palmer 1976b:79; Watkins 1940:288).

A number of glass factories tried to alleviate the financial burden of labor either by securing loans or establishing lotteries (Wilson 1972:54). Not only was labor compensation a problem for some glasshouses, but the acquisition and holding of skilled workers was difficult as well. Certain factories recruited experienced glassmen by securing their exemption from labor taxes, or military and jury duty (McKearin and McKearin 1950:51), while other plants offered them partnerships in the firms (Palmer 1976b:77). Once workers were acquired, a factory might retain its labor force by providing lodging or other facilities, or foods, goods, or services, either free or at cost. Glassblowers might even be given free access to some of their own products (cf. Hudson 1963:103; Lanmon and Palmer 1976:20–24; McKearin and McKearin 1950:50). Most of these goal-seeking labor operations are ineligible for analysis because they do not have obvious archaeological implications. The few that are archaeologically meaningful must be excluded for lack of information.

Glass factories probably attempted to control the cost of labor by altering the size of their work forces from one phase of their existence to the next. Size ranged from a minimum of about 10 workers in some factories to a maximum of 133 in others (Hunter 1950:236; McKearin and McKearin 1950:51; Watkins 1940:291). Also, the ethnic composition of the labor force might be altered from a heterogeneous makeup to a homogeneous one, or vice versa, in an effort to improve the familiarity of workers with equipment and operating methods that originated in specific regions of Europe (cf. Filley and Aldag 1975:28; Wilkinson 1963). Moreover, a glass factory might divide its labor along completely specialized lines, or along partially overlapping ones, in order to improve the effectiveness of labor in relation to its cost (cf. Emery and Trist 1969:286; Even 1976:267). Although all three of these labor operations have archaeological implications (cf. Noël Hume 1976), they are excluded from analysis because of missing information.

The maximum variety of occupational specialists simultaneously employed by a factory is also indicative of its experimentation with divisions of labor. As one of Bridenbaugh's variables, it is important to note that two urban factories, the New Haven Glass Works and the F. M. Amelung Company list one to three specializations, whereas the Boston Crown Glass Company enumerates nine. The maximum variety in any eighteenth-century glass factory is fourteen. This operation is eligible for analysis, and the various specializations of labor should be archaeologically evident in the spatial compartmentalization of activities, equipment, and materials.

Other phase controls, such as the intermittent versus continuous employment of labor, also were adopted to reduce labor costs. Continuous employment required monetary reserves to sustain the labor force during slack periods, which usually lasted from 3 to 6 months of the year (McKearin and McKearin 1950:53). Too much documentary information about this variable is missing for it to be included in the analysis. Labor costs also were controlled by importing glassblowers directly from Europe, rather than hiring locally available American glassmen (Watkins 1949:364). This operation is eligible for analysis, and the source of a factory's glassmen should be evident in the attribution of durable items of clothing and adornment that either were lost or discarded at the plant (cf. Noël Hume 1976; Starbuck, Gorman, and Wiseman 1976). The New York Glass House Company in Manhattan imported glassblowers from abroad, while the New Haven Glass Works and the F. M. Amelung Company obtained them locally. The Boston Crown Glass Company recruited from both sources (cf. Humphreys 1928).

The general effectiveness of labor organization is scaled in terms of documented shortages of workers. Almost half of the glass factories (including three urban ones) experienced this problem. Modern factories often respond to labor crises by adopting innovative manufacturing techniques or equipment (Wilson 1972:256), and it may be assumed that similar responses occurred among some of the eighteenth-century glasshouses. Such alterations of technique or equipment are relevant operations of manufacturing technology, however, and it is not further discussed in the context of labor. As an index of the availability of labor, worker shortages may be considered as one of Bridenbaugh's variables, but it has no obvious archaeological implication. Thus, it must be excluded from this analysis. The organizational effectiveness of labor is also measured in terms of documented complaints by glassmen about their pay. This was a relatively uncommon occurrence at eighteenth-century glasshouses. This variable also is ineligible for analysis for the same reason as worker shortage.

The *internal environment* of labor technology is initially defined in terms of the ethnic composition of material resource procurers, manufacturing personnel, and marketers. The ethnic background of the glassmaking personnel is the only one of these variables eligible for analysis, and its archaeological implications also are based on source identification of the nonperishable personal effects of the glassmen. The New York Glass House Company at Manhattan employed German or Dutch glassblowers. The Boston Crown Glass Company hired a mixture of German-Americans and German blowers, while the F. M. Amelung Company seems to have hired German-American glassmen exclusively.

The labor environment is also defined in terms of whether or not specialists practiced the procurement, manufacturing, and release technologies of glassmaking. This information reveals how eighteenth-century glass manufacture was planned by "those who thought in terms of breaking down the job in terms of a sequence of human actions [Daniels 1970:20]." Elaborate eighteenth-century concepts of manual labor proved to be serious obstacles to inventors of glassmaking machinery. Specialists were employed at the Boston Crown Glass Company to obtain wood fuel, as well as sand and chemical ingredients of the glass batch and clay for the crucibles. None of these resource-procurement specialists are mentioned in the records of the other urban glasshouses. Glassmaking specialists, principally the "gaffers" or master blowers, are known to have worked in the New Haven Glass Works and the F. M. Amelung Company. Gaffers, their apprentices, and glass cutters are recorded as having worked at the Boston Crown Glass Company. Maintenance specialists provided ancillary support for the glassmakers as furnace tenders, glass batch mixers, and crucible potters in several eighteenth-century glasshouses. These personnel are conspicuously absent from the records of all urban glasshouses except the Boston Crown Glass Company, which employed tenders and mixers. It would seem that some glass factories hired resource-procurement and maintenance specialists to expedite the production process, whereas other glass houses chose not to employ these forms of indirect labor because it created an operating economy that diminished profits (cf. Filley and Aldag 1975:28).

These three variables are eligible for analysis, and the archaeological evidence of specialized procurement, manufacturing, and maintenance activities at the remains of eighteenth-century glass factories should be evident as spatially compartmentalized equipment and materials. Glass-product release specialists, such as shipping container carpenters, product freighters, and sales agents, worked in many glass factories, but only sales agents are mentioned in connection with the urban glasshouses. Since these marketing specialists did not conduct their activities at the urban factories, this variable is not archaeologically meaningful for my purposes.

The environment of work was affected by consistent, or fixed, versus variable change in (*a*) the remuneration of labor, (*b*) the size of the labor force, (*c*) the amount of variety in the ethnic composition of the work force, (*d*) the kinds of labor specialization, and (*e*) the annual length of employment. Wide-scale change of personnel and task assignments in a modern factory usually lowers the morale of its workers (Filley and Aldag 1975:28), which I assume to have been the case in eighteenth-century glasshouses. Of these five environmental transition operations, only size and ethnicity are eligible for analysis. Two of the other three also have archaeological implications, but documentary information about them is missing in too many instances. Transitions in the size and ethnic makeup of the work force should be archaeologically evident in the stratigraphic records of eighteenth-century glass factories. Labor force size appears to have been fixed at the New Haven Glass Works and variable at the Boston Crown Glass Company and the F. M. Amelung Company. The labor forces of the Boston Crown Glass Company and the F. M. Amelung Company contained variable amounts of ethnic variety during the lifespans of these factories. Conversely, the amount of ethnic variety among the workers at the New Haven Glass Works and perhaps the New York Glass House Company in Manhattan remained constant.

The effectiveness of the work environment is specifically scaled in terms of documented problems experienced by a factory in retaining its workmen. Employees who resign or are dismissed from a factory can become a source of grief because of the trade secrets they might convey to their next employer (Evan 1976:271). There is some evidence (Gest and Smith 1939:118; Palmer 1976a:31; Watkins 1940:290) that this occurred among eighteenth-century glassmen. Every urban glasshouse, except that Glassworks in Hartford, mentioned having difficulties retaining either gaffers or their apprentices. The impact of their departure should be archaeologically evidenct as temporary discontinuity or decline in the quality of manufactured glass. Either one of these phenomena would be revealed by analysis of stratified deposits of glass waster fragments on factory lots. Employment problems are included in my analysis.

The *decision structure* of the labor technology over the lifespan of an eighteenth-century glasshouse is reflected by the sequence of choices that were made to adjust (*a*) the size of the factory's work force, (*b*) the amount of variety in the ethnic affiliations of its workers, (*c*) the diversification or specialization of its labor, and (*d*) the length of the work period each year. (Note that the third variable is one of Bridenbaugh's.) These trends have important consequences for the stability and survival of modern factories, and I assume that eighteenth-century glasshouses were affected in similar ways. For example, a small firm is more likely to benefit from increases in the size of its labor force than from the progressive diversification of its work (Filley and Aldag 1975:28). Once the factory reaches a certain size, however, increasing the specialization of its labor enhances the adaptability of the factory organization as a whole (Terreberry 1972:159), but it lowers the morale of the workers (Filley and Aldag 1975:28). Although each of these four variables has archaeological implications, none of them contains sufficient information to be included in the analysis.

The four adjustment trends had a subsequent effect upon the viability of a glasshouse. The mobility of its workers is the measure of this impact. Glassmakers participated in the unusual mobility of craftsmen in all American industries during the eighteenth century (Gest and Smith 1939:119; Innes 1948:419; Watkins 1940:288; Watkins 1949:363; White 1937:67). Although the transience of low-level glassmen (apprentices and indentured servants) probably affected only the role sets in a glass factory, the entry and exit of mid-level workers (cutters, engravers, and maintenance personnel) and high-level craftsmen (gaffers and supervisors) were likely to affect the welfare of the firm (cf. Filley and Aldag 1975:28) because of the industrial secrets they carried with them (Daniels 1970:14–15; Evan 1976:271). Mobility seems to have caused the diffusion of technology among eighteenth-century glasshouses (White 1937:67). During their life spans, the Boston Crown Glass Company and the F. M. Amelung Company appear to have acquired more personnel than they lost, while the reverse seems to be true at the New York Glass House Company in Manhattan. None of these urban factories experienced simple turnover in which there was no net gain or loss, as happened at some suburban and rural glasshouses. This variable is included in my analysis. Net gain or turnover should be archaeologically evident as either a shift in the quality of glass manufacture or as an improvement, while net loss might ultimately cause a decline in quality.

One external factor is known to have conditioned the effectiveness of the structure of labor decisions. The ability of eighteenth-century glasshouses to meet their payrolls depended to some extent on factors beyond their control, such as currency supply or warfare. No urban factory suffered in this regard, and neither did most of those in nonurban areas. This variable is excluded from analysis because it has no obvious archaeological correlate.

Procurement of Material Resources

The *organization* of materials-procurement technology at eighteenth-century glass factories was motivated by the need to ensure supplies of wood to fuel furnaces, and to acquire the principal ingredients of glass, which were sand, sodium or potassium flux, and calcium stabilizer. Crucible clay also was an essential resource. Because the logistics of commercial transport were underdeveloped in eighteenth-century America, a glass factory's attainment of these goals depended in part on its decision to locate nearer the geographical sources of these raw materials than to concentrations of available labor and consumers of glass products (cf. Weeks 1884:25–28).

Not all glass factories made this decision, because geographic propinquity either to materials or labor was the primary determinant of the location of most suburban and rural glasshouses, while the urban ones were positioned in the midst of their consumer markets (see the demographic, commercial, and industrial maps of eighteenth-century America by Cappon 1976). This variable is excluded from my analysis because I am uncertain about its archaeological implications. Despite the locational importance of labor and markets, most glass factories tried to ensure supplies of their most critical resources, namely wood fuel and sand (Jarves 1854:33;

McKearin 1970:47; McKearin and McKearin 1950:26; Palmer 1976b:79; Weeks 1884:25, 27–28). Documentary information about factory transport distances from woodlots and sand deposits over eighteenth-century roads and waterways (cf. Cappon 1976) reveals that most glasshouses, including the urban F. M. Amelung Company, maximized their access to fuel rather than sand. In contrast, the New York Glass House in Manhattan and the Boston Crown Glass Company maximized their access to sand instead of fuel. These differential priorities should be archaeologically evident in the presence of facilities for the acquisition and processing of locally available sand on the lots of the urban glasshouses, except Amelung's, which might exhibit the remains of wood procurement and processing facilities.

Minimal transport distance, however, was no guarantee of resource supply. If a glasshouse could not reduce the turbulence of its environment by owning its materials outright (cf. Terreberry 1972:143), then it had to purchase them from domestic or foreign sources. For example, the New York Glass House in Manhattan owned its woodlot, while the New Haven Glass Works, Boston Crown Glass Company, and the F. M. Amelung Company purchased either domestic or foreign sands (cf. Weeks 1884:24). No urban glasshouse is known to have owned its sources of flux or stabilizer; rather, all of them (except the Glassworks in Hartford, for which there is no information) purchased the former from domestic agents and imported the latter from foreign ones (cf. Hunter 1950:125; Weeks 1884:33; Wilson 1972:44). These patterns can be evaluated by comparing the material composition of the trace remains of a resource stockpile or dump on the lot of a city factory with the composition of the relevant resource deposit that is located elsewhere. Too much documentary information about the sources of crucible clays is missing to include this variable in my analysis.

The high cost of each raw material (cf. Palmer 1976b:79; Wilson 1972:38, 43–44) that was tolerated by the factories in pursuit of their resource-procurement goals is excluded from analysis for the same reason and also because each has no obvious archaeological implication. Few glasshouses (including all of the urban ones) attempted to alleviate resource costs. Some factories sought such assistance through loans or lotteries, but this variable is ineligible for analysis because it lacks archaeological evidence. It is unlikely that a glass factory controlled the costs of procuring wood, sand, other glass-batch ingredients, and clay by altering the amounts of their consumption from one phase of production to the next. Documentary information about such manipulations, however, is insufficient to analyze these variables (cf. Palmer 1976b:79; Watkins 1940:290; Wilson 1972:38, 43–44). Alteration of the variety of resources procured from one phase to the next is also a means of controlling expenditures for raw materials. The maximum variety of procured resources listed in the records of a factory is suggestive of its experimentation with this control.

For example, only one kind of raw material is mentioned for the short-lived New Haven Glass Works, whereas records of the New York Glass House Company at Manhattan, the Boston Crown Glass Company, and the F. M. Amelung Company list from four to seven types. Since a categorical difference of this magnitude can be archaeologically evaluated by materials analysis of resource traces, this variable is included in my analysis. An additional phase control was adopted to reduce resource costs. Materials might be procured at a specific time of the year, or periodically, as needed. The latter choice might have lessened capital expenditures for materials at any one time and reduced the costs of warehousing them, but it would have increased the risk of shortage in an absence of surplus. Documentary information about this variable is insufficient for analysis.

The general effectiveness of a factory's organization of its procurement operations can be scaled in terms of distance in miles from its sources of (*a*) fuel, (*b*) sand, (*c*) flux, (*d*) stabilizer, and (*e*) clay (cf. Ashurst 1971:111; Bishop 1861:239; Crossley 1968:80; Crossley and Asberg 1972:108; Harrington 1952:39; Palmer 1978:224; Watkins 1940:288; Weeks 1884:97). Although all of these variables have archaeological implications, only one of them has enough documentary information to be eligible for analysis. Stabilizer was apparently imported by most glass factories (including the urban ones) in the form of limestone nodules or chalk from Great Britain or its Caribbean islands (cf. McKearin 1970:47). The archaeological correlate of this phenomenon can be substantiated by materials analysis.

The *internal environment* of a glass factory's procurement technology can be defined according to whether the capacity and the variety of its procured resources remained consistent (i.e., stable or directional) over the firm's life span. The alternative was to let either capacity or variety (or both) fluctuate as part of the transition from one procurement period to the next. The same decision had to be made about the actual length of time spent procuring materials from one period to the next. All three of these variables lack sufficient documentary information to include in the analysis, and I am uncertain about their archaeological implications.

The effectiveness of these resource-procurement operations depended on whether a glasshouse had difficulty in securing its raw materials. This measure provides insight into the availability of supplies for urban factories, and I consider it to be one of Bridenbaugh's variables. Over half of the sample glasshouses, including most of the urban ones (except the Glassworks in Hartford, which lacks documentary information) experienced difficulties in obtaining one or more of their resources. This variable is eligible for analysis and its patterning should be archaeologically evident as volumetric fluctuations of the stratified traces of resource dumps on factory lots.

The *decision structure* of procurement technology during the lifetime of an eighteenth-century glasshouse is revealed in the sequence of choices either to increase, decrease, or hold constant not only the variety and quantity of its resources, but the lengths of time spent acquiring them as well (cf. Raistrick 1972:243). Expanding the diversity of raw materials ultimately increases the adaptibility of modern factories (Terreberry 1972:159), and I assume this to have been so among eighteenth-century glasshouses. Although this trend and the other two (resource quantity and acquisition time) have obvious archaeological implications, documentary information about them is insufficient to permit their analysis.

The choice sequence had three subsequent effects on the viability of a glasshouse. None of these effects necessarily depended on the occurrence of the others, although some factories experienced combinations of them. First, every factory risked the depletion or disruption of its material supplies. No records of urban factories mention this problem (except the Glassworks in Hartford for which information is missing). The same is true for many of the nonurban plants. This variable is included in my analysis, and it has an archaeological implication. Neither decline nor discontinuity of materials procured from a particular source should be evident in the stratified remains of the resource dumps of these glasshouses. Second, each factory had to consider the possibility of changing its source of a raw material for opportunistic reasons or from necessity. The Boston Crown Glass Company and the F. M. Amelung Company procured new types of sand, while the other urban factories apparently continued to obtain their materials from the same sources. Although this effect has an obvious archaeological implication, it cannot be analyzed because of the lack of documentary information about most other glasshouses in the sample. Third, every firm would have had to consider the possibility of relocating its factory either to insure the continuity of its supplies or to facilitate their procurement. Five glasshouses were moved in order to retain their viability, although none of the urban ones considered this option because their location was determined primarily by market factors. This variable is eligible for analysis and it has obvious implications to an archaeologist.

External factors, such as warfare or customs duties on imported foreign resources (cf. Palmer 1976b:79), conditioned the structure of procurement decisions at only two factories in the sample. None of the urban factories suffered in this regard. This variable is excluded from analysis because it does not have clear archaeological implications.

Manufacturing Process

Glass manufacturing was a technologically conservative industry prior to the nineteenth century. Shortly thereafter, it became one of the first industries to employ machinery in production, but one of the last to experience full automation (Lorrain 1968:36–42). Archaeologists can take advantage of technological conservatism among eighteenth-century glass factories by using it to understand variability in other aspects of glass manufacturing (cf. Hudson 1963:11). This is discussed in several parts of this section.

The *organization* of glassmaking technology may have been motivated by the need to regulate production costs. Attainment of this goal depended in part on the previous experience of a factory manager. The superintendent of the F. M. Amelung Company was technically experienced in glassmaking, whereas managers of the New York Glass House Company in Manhattan and the New Haven Glass Works possessed marketing experience. Both kinds of expertise were combined in the supervision of the Boston Crown Glass Company. Since this variable has no patent archaeological implication, it cannot be analyzed.

Equally important was the amount of capital expenditures on manufacturing facilities and equipment in relation to the costs of the other technologies that were necessary. Documentary information about absolute costs of facilities and equipment is too sparse to permit analysis, and their archaeological implications are not clear. Insight into the relative cost of facilities may be gained, however, by determining (*a*) the number of manufacturing plants in concurrent operation on a company's lot, (*b*) whether the firm was situated in a preexisting community or created its own, (*c*) whether glass was the only item manufactured on the company lot or whether it was part of a complex of other industries, and (*d*) the acreage of the company's lot. The establishment of a glasshouse as a single industry probably enhanced its viability, because a multi-industrial organization would have been less likely to grant the autonomy necessary for flexible decisions. Then, as now, a centralized multi-industrial authority would have been more interested in preventing competition or conflict that might arise between its different factories from overlapping needs for labor or material resources (Evan 1976:127). The patterning of these variables categorically distinguishes the glass factories in cities (except the Glassworks in Hartford for which there is no information) from the nonurban factories. Each urban firm constructed only one glasshouse on its premises; each situated itself within the city, rather than establishing its own community on the urban periphery; and only glass was manufactured on its lot, which was smaller than 50 acres (20.2 ha.). All but the last of these variables are included in my analysis, since there is not enough documentary information about lot size, and all have archaeological implications that are obvious.

Equipment costs depended in large part on the number of blast furnaces that were built to melt glass. This number does not include kilns for drying fuel wood or firing clay crucibles, nor ovens for extracting flux, fusing glass batch ingredients, or annealing glass products (cf. Hudson 1963:111; Powell 1923:12; Watkins 1940:289; Weeks 1884:81; Wilson 1972:38). All of these were ancillary to the blast furnace and most of them were located either in or around the glasshouse. At least three of the urban factories (information about the New York Glass House Company in Manhattan and the Glassworks in Hartford is missing) used only one blast furnace at any time during their lifespans, as did nine of their suburban and rural counterparts. Eight nonurban companies are known, however, to have had two to three main furnaces in simultaneous operation. This variable is eligible for analysis and it has clear archaeological implications. Equipment cost is also indicated by the size of the largest blast furnace on a factory lot. In general, size is a function of the number of glass batch melting crucibles a furnace was built to contain. This number ranges from three to ten in the factory sample. Although it has archaeological implications, documentary information about this variable is missing in too many instances to permit analysis.

Most urban factories did not alleviate production costs by requesting exemption of their physical plants from taxation, nor by attempting to legislate glass-production monopolies and bounties, or by seeking financial assistance through lotteries or loans (cf. Palmer 1976b:79; Wilson 1972:53). Since the archaeological implications of these variables are unclear, I do not include them in my analysis.

Eighteenth-century glasshouses probably regulated manufacturing costs by altering their product inventories from one phase of their existence to the next. Insight into the magnitude of such shifts can be gained from knowledge of the maximum variety of glasswares produced by a factory during its lifetime. For example, the New York Glass House Company in Manhattan and the New Haven Glass Works manufactured either flatware (windowpane) or hollowware (containers), but apparently not both. In contrast, Boston Crown Glass Company and the F. M. Amelung Company manufactured both, as did most of the nonurban factories. The maximum number of types of glass produced is also informative in this regard. During the eighteenth-century, such types consisted of (*a*) window pane and lamp glass, (*b*) utility containers, (*c*) table glass, (*d*) apothecary and chemical containers, (*e*) electrical instruments, and (*f*) industrial tools (cf. Palmer 1976a:16, 18, 1976b:83, 89). The New York Glass House Company in Manhattan, the New Haven Glass Works, and the F. M. Amelung Company are known to have made one to three of these types while the Boston Crown Glass Company produced five of them. Both of these variables are included in my analysis, but the archaeologist will have to identify wares and types from glass fragments concentrated in waste heaps or scattered over the factory lot (Noël Hume 1976:143, 164–165; Starbuck, Gorman, and Wiseman 1976), because whole objects are not likely to be recovered.

Fluctuations in inventory size might be evident to some extent in the limits of the production of flatwares and hollowwares (cf. Wilson 1972:43–45) over a factory's lifespan, but documentary information is missing in too many instances to analyze these variables. The same problem affects the analysis of change in the number of months a glasshouse remained in general production through the years (cf. Raistrick 1972:243).

A glass factory also may have manipulated its production inventory of glass types from one manufacturing period to the next, at random or according to a fixed plan, as part of its effort to control costs, but there is little or no documentary information about this particular phenomenon. Certain types of glass are predominant in the manufacturing histories of most factories, however, and these concentrations of production provide insight into production manipulation. For example, the New York Glass House Company in Manhattan, the New Haven Glass Works, and the F. M. Amelung Company mainly produced utility containers, in contrast to the Boston Crown Glass Company, which concentrated on the manufacture of pane and lamp glass. Although this variable is included in my analysis, the archaeologist should be forewarned that "the popularity of a [glass] item type is not automatically gauged by the number that were dropped [on the factory lot] or otherwise failed to make it to the warehouse [Noël Hume 1976:183]."

The general effectiveness of a company's organization of its manufacturing technology can be measured in terms of the number of years that elapsed between the construction of its glasshouse and initial production. A delay of 1–2 years was experienced by all of the urban factories (information about the Glassworks in Hartford is missing) and most of the nonurban factories. Production at two of the latter factories is known to have been delayed for as much as 4 years. This variable should be archaeologically evident in the stratigraphy of glass and dated artifacts found in and around the glasshouse.

The technological *environment* of manufacturing can be defined in terms of the production of a variety of functionally distinct items within each type of glass. Company records and newspaper advertisements show that real or perceived consumer demand for functional variety was satisfied on the factory floor by altering blowing and shaping techniques. All of the urban glass factories manufactured seven or fewer items of different function, except the Boston Crown Glass Company, which made 18. As many as 51 varieties of glass were produced during the eighteenth century (cf. McKearin and McKearin 1950:31; Noël Hume 1964:312; Palmer 1976a:83; Wilson 1972:47, 64). This variable is eligible for analysis but its archaeological implication must be accepted with caution because Noël Hume (1976:183) notes that "certain kinds of objects such as wineglasses or fragments of small objects are easier to identify than fragments of larger ones." Moreover, handblown objects were often discarded because of asymmetry, and fragments of them amplify the identification problem (cf. Lorrain 1968:35–36).

The transition between periods of manufacture also influenced the technical environment of glassmaking. The amount of functional variety in the product inventory or the quantity of glass items produced may have been fixed (stable or directional) during a factory's transition. The unplanned alternative was to allow one or both of them to fluctuate through time. An identical decision had to be made as well about the length of each manufacturing period. Of these three operations, only product diversity has enough information to be eligible for analysis. The amount of variety in the product inventories of all urban factories, except the New Haven Glass Works, was permitted to fluctuate from one manufacturing period to the next. This oscillation is also documented in the records of most nonurban glasshouses, and it corroborates the observation (Filley and Aldag 1975:28) that product diversification usually occurs as an unplanned event in modern factories because managers often try to limit such growth in order to prevent the adoption of innovative methods. Cyclical changes in product variety should be archaeologically evident in the stratigraphy of glass scrap on the city lots of these factories, if the problematic aspects of object identification can be overcome (cf. Noël Hume 1976:176).

The effectiveness of the technical environment of a factory depended on whether it experienced problems in the mixing, melting, cooling, shaping, or annealing of glass (Davis 1949:366; Hunter 1950:132; Palmer 1976a:260; Powell 1923:116; Weeks 1884:33, 43–45). Manufacturing difficulties are mentioned in the records of all the city factories except the New York Glass House Company in Manhattan. About half of the nonurban glasshouses had similar troubles. Material analysis of glass waster fragments recovered from the remains of the urban factories should substantiate this phenomenon.

The *decision structure* of glass manufacturing is revealed by the sequence of choices made by an eighteenth-century firm to adjust (*a*) the amount of variety in its production inventories, (*b*) its production volume, and (*c*) the length of production time. Documentary information about the first of these three manufacturing trends is sufficient for analysis. It is inadequate for the other two, which must be excluded from my study, despite the fact that one of them (the trend in production volume) is a variable of Bridenbaugh's.

Almost half of the glass factories in my sample ultimately increased the variety of their products. At one rural factory (The United Glass Company), it is known that the glassmen began to expand the diversity of their products as their technical skills increased (Bridenbaugh 1961:63). This factor may explain the occurrence of the same trend at the Boston Crown Glass Company and the F. M. Amelung Company, which makes them the only urban members of this group. If the analogy between modern factories and their eighteenth-century antecedents holds, then expansions of product diversity at these two city glasshouses should have made them more adaptable than the urban ones that did not follow this trend (cf. Terreberry 1972:159). Inspection of the relevant chronological data (Table 10.2) tends to substantiate this interpretation. Factories in the other group, which includes the New York Glass House Company in Manhattan and the New Haven Glass Works, either decreased the amount of variety in their product inventories or held it constant through time. The diversification trend is included in my analysis and its archaeological implications are fairly obvious, if previous warnings about object identification are kept in mind.

Even though consecutive decisions about production volume and manufacturing time remain undocumented, their subsequent effects on the viability of a glasshouse are no less important than the impact of choices about product variety. Decision making in all three areas proved to be either optimal or suboptimal, depending on the length of time required to achieve steady production. For example, manufacturing at the New York Glass House Company in Manhattan became stable 1 year after the construction of its factory, whereas 4 years elapsed before the F. M. Amelung Company was able to establish its production. The Boston Crown Glass Company spent 7 years trying to stabilize production. The maximum delay experienced by an eighteenth-century glass factory was 12 years. This variable is included in my analysis, and minor disruptions of production should be archaeologically evident in the stratigraphy of a factory's glass waster deposits.

The attainment of manufacturing stability, however, did not guarantee the continuous and profitable existence of a glasshouse (cf. Filley and Aldag 1975:27). Production at the New Haven Glass Works and the Boston Glass Company was seriously interrupted late in their development, whereas the New York Glass House Company in Manhattan and the F. M. Amelung Company apparently enjoyed continuity. This subsequent effect is also analyzed and, unlike the archaeological implication of the previous variable, we should expect to find a major disruption in the stratigraphy of waster heaps that does not coincide with the annual cycle of manufacturing. Because either one of these events might easily be mistaken for the other, the potentially ambiguous implication of this variable deserves more careful scrutiny (cf. South 1974:3).

Floods, fires, warfare, or blast furnace malfunction were external factors that conditioned the effectiveness of decision making about production at one-third of the glasshouses in the sample. Among these are the New Haven Glass Works and the Boston Crown Glass Company, which suffered work stoppages as the result of furnace problems. Although this variable is included in my analysis, some of its archaeological implications are less clear than the others. Stratigraphic indications of disaster should be readily apparent, but evidence of military conflict on the factory lot might be less ostensible. Archaeological evidence of furnace malfunction is perplexing because unsatisfactory furnaces were dismantled (McKearin 1970:49–50; Watkins 1940:290; Wilson 1972:76) and much of their clay construction material was probably pulverized to grog for making new firebrick, mortar, or crucibles (cf. Crossley 1968:68; Starbuck, Gorman, and Wiseman 1976).

Product Release

The organization of product-release technology in a modern factory is motivated not only by the desire to make a profit from sales but also to ensure the survival of the firm. The latter goal is attained when the company spends the amount of income necessary to renew its material resources and compensate its labor (Thompson and McEwen 1972:268). If the survival goal of contemporary factories is analogous to that of their eighteenth-century antecedents, then it should explain why so many of the glasshouses failed. For the most part, it does. For example, at least six nonurban factories closed for product marketing reasons. Apparently, they were unable to allocate enough income from sales to procure resources and remunerate labor. The collapse of at least eight other firms, including the New York Glass House Company in Manhattan, is attributed not to market factors, but to difficulties either in procuring material resources or compensating labor. It seems that they were unwilling to reinvest the amount of income in one or the other of these technologies necessary to continue. The analog does not explain the closure of at least four additional factories, including the New Haven Glass Works and the Boston Crown Glass Company, because their demise is attributed to only manufacturing problems.

Profit was the probable motive for the establishment of a glass factory in a particular region of the country at a specific time (cf. Filley and Aldag 1975:28; Terreberry 1972:149). About half the glasshouses, including four in urban areas, were located in colonies or states north of New Jersey. Similarly, about half the factories, including two urban firms, were established before the end of the Revolutionary War, while the remainder came into existence after the war (Table 4.2). Both of these variables were analyzed, and their archaeological implications are obvious.

Early assurance of survival and profit depended on a firm's knowledge of the market for glass in its region from 0 to 5 years before establishing its factory (cf. Lanmon 1969). Great Britain played a significant role in structuring the American market for glass, which it was determined to capture and hold throughout the eighteenth century (Davis 1949:21). Most of the urban glass factories seem to have ignored this foreign competition, for they were established during years when supplies of imported glass were relatively high in their regions and stocks of American-made glass were relatively low. More telling, perhaps, is the fact that almost all of the city glasshouses originated during years when domestic demand for both foreign and American glass was relatively high. Although market demand is one of Bridenbaugh's (1961:61, 64, 68) variables, it must be excluded from analysis because it seems to have no archaeological implications. The same is true of market supply factors.

Early assurance also depended on the company's knowledge of product-transportation conditions in its region (McKearin and McKearin 1950:50). During the eighteenth century, the fragile nature of glass made overland movement of this commodity slow and costly. Water transport was preferred because it was cheaper and lessened the risk of breakage (Palmer 1976b:79). Both methods of conveyance were restricted to seasons of the year when roads and waterways were open to travel, and this constraint limited a factory's ability to expand its market area (Lorrain 1968:35; McKearin and McKearin 1950:45, 50). Slightly more than half the glasshouses in my sample shipped glass to their market destinations on waterways. This includes every urban factory except the Glassworks in Hartford, for which there is no documentary information. The rest of the glass factories freighted their products overland. This variable is included in my analysis, and it has a clear implication. Factories in the first category should yield evidence of facilities for docking and maintaining watercraft, even if the shorelines of their lots were subsequently altered by fill or erosion. The remains of facilities for maintaining draft animals and wagons or sleds should be found on the lots of factories in the second category.

Goal attainment also depended on setting tolerance limits for the total cost of releasing glass products incurred by packing and transporting them to market, franchising sales agents, etc. Almost no documentary information has been published on this subject, which renders it ineligible for analysis. Practically none of the urban glasshouses lowered their release costs by lobbying for a protective tariff on foreign glass, nor by seeking exemption from the sales tax, nor even by encouraging domestic consumption of American glass as an expression of patriotism. Since these variables do not have archaeological implications, they also are excluded from analysis.

The eighteenth-century glass factory may have regulated sales costs and enhanced profits by limiting either the kinds or amounts of glass that it released on the market during one or more phases of its existence. The same motives might have prompted the company to release its products intermittently rather than continuously. Not only is documentary information about these three operations insufficient for analysis, but none of them has archaeological correlates. Other phase controls are known to have been adopted by the glasshouses in order to meet their product-release goals. Two of these concern the number and placement of sales agents commissioned (cf. Lanmon 1969:28). About half the factories in the sample (including two urban firms) retained 1 or 2 sales representatives, whereas the other companies franchised 3–25 glass dealers. Most of the factories commissioned their agents in a single market region, that is, in a rural area, suburban area, or city. The city was preferred by most urban glasshouses. The remaining companies adopted the policy of franchising their dealers in more than one type of market region. Then, as now, this practice increased the risk of failure, because most manufacturing firms have a market niche that permits their existence so long as they do not try to exploit other niches (Filley and Aldag 1975:28). These two phase controls cannot be analyzed because their archaeological correlates are unclear.

The organizational effectiveness of a glass company's product-release technology can be scaled in terms of the transport distance from the factory to primary market place. Plots of these data on Cappon's (1976) maps of eighteenth-century roads and waterways reveal that half of the sample factories conveyed their glass products over distances of less than 12 miles (19.3 km). The New York Glass House Company in Manhattan, together with the Boston Crown Glass Company and the F. M. Amelung Company, are members of this group because they moved most of their products less than a mile (1.6 km) to the markets in their cities. Factories in the other group transported glass to their primary market places over distances that ranged from 17 miles (27.3 km) to 150 miles (241 km). Noteworthy among these is the New Haven Glass Works, which apparently shipped most of its glassware 75 miles (120.6 km) along the coast to New York City. This variable is analyzed, and it has definite archaeological implication. Today, we should find some products of each factory in its primary marketplace. These glass artifacts may exist in public and private collections, or they might be recovered from archaeological excavations of primary marketplaces. Once identified as to type or functional variety, the physiochemical composition of such objects should be the same as that of their counterparts at the factory where they were made (Brill 1976). Of course, attributions of this sort ignore the possibility that the firm might have changed either its raw materials or its glassmaking recipes at some point.

The *environment* of a factory's product-release technology is defined in terms of the inventories of glass that it sold from time to time. Although documentary information about the kinds and amounts of glass actually marketed by an eighteenth-century firm is insufficient for analysis, knowledge of the type of glass released in the greatest quantity by each factory over its life span should provide insight into these subjects. For example, the Boston Crown Glass Company seems to have sold mostly windowpane and lamp glass, whereas the New York Glass House Company in Manhattan and the F. M. Amelung Company are both thought to have concentrated their efforts on the sale of utility containers. Neither of the other two city factories appears to have emphasized the sale of tableware, although some nonurban firms did. This variable must be excluded from analysis, because its implication is not restricted to the factory lot.

The transition dynamics of product sales also are part of the environment. A firm may have released different kinds and amounts of glass from one sales period to the next, according to a fixed plan or at random. In deciding the actual length of each sales period, the glasshouse would have faced the same alternatives. Documentary information about these three variables is insufficient for analysis, and their archaeological implications are unclear.

The effectiveness of the product-release environment depended upon whether a factory experienced problems with the transportation and sale of its glass. Although most of the companies in my sample conveyed glass to their marketplaces without difficulty, half of them (including all urban firms) complained about inadequate sales. Both of these variables are ineligible for analysis because they do not have clear archaeological implications.

The *decision structure* of a factory's release technology should be evident in the sequence of its marketing choices, used to adjust the diversity and volume of glass that it released for sale. Adjustment of the selling time itself was an equally important consideration. Consecutive decisions ultimately increased, decreased, or stabilized the variety and abundance of products marketed, as well as the length of time glass was to be sold. There is not enough documentary information about the trends of these three variables to analyze them, even though one-market volume is an element of Bridenbaugh's (1961:69) hypothesis.

The subsequent effects of a glass factory's marketing trends are better known, however. A decision sequence proved to be optimal when a firm could sell its own glass exclusively. On the other hand, a suboptimal trend probably forced a factory to import foreign glass for sale along with its own products. All of the urban glasshouses escaped this fate (except the Glassworks in Hartford, for which information is lacking), as did most of the nonurban firms. Unfortunately, this variable must be excluded from analysis because it has an archaeological implication that is ambiguous. Assuming that the few factories that imported foreign glass also warehoused these items on their lots, it would be difficult, if not impossible, to distinguish fragmentary remains of this type from cullet (foreign and domestic glass consumed by the citizenry, who sold it as scrap to factories where it was used either to start batch melts of glass or to improve the chemistry [Palmer 1978:222]).

The impact of all three trends on the viability of a firm can be measured in terms of its longevity. Exactly half of the sample factories lasted 16 years or less. The ages of the New York Glass House Company in Manhattan and the New Haven Glass Works fall toward the extremes of this range, at 13 years and 1 year, respectively. The other factories survived from 17 to 85 years. This includes the Boston Crown Glass Company, which remained operative for 40 years, and the F. M. Amelung Company, which enjoyed the longest life of any glasshouse founded in the eighteenth century. The archaeological correlate of this variable is obvious. The year of a factory's closure, extrapolated from its longevity, can be confirmed from dated artifacts (also see Table 4.2).

Three external factors conditioned the effectiveness of a glass factory's decision structure, because they could be controlled only in part or not at all during the eighteenth century. Foremost among these was the prevailing condition of the glass market during the life span of each glasshouse. Roughly two-thirds of the companies in my sample existed during periods when consumer demand for glass generally exceeded supplies from all sources, or when demand and supply tended to balance.

The New York Glass House Company in Manhattan, together with the Glassworks in Hartford and the New Haven Glass Works, enjoyed these favorable market conditions during their existence, whereas the other two urban glasshouses faced markets that were generally unfavorable. This factory cannot be analyzed because it lacks an archaeological correlate.

The effectiveness of decision making about product sales also depended on a glass factory's reputation. This was established largely by public perception of the quality of its glass in comparison to that of foreign imports, and to a lesser extent on claims made by the company itself. Glass made by the F. M. Amelung Company was considered to be comparable to the quality of fine European products, whereas the manufactures of the Boston Crown Glass Company received superior acclaim. Although public consensus about the properties of glass produced by the other city factories is not recorded, we know that the manufactures of at least 14 suburban and rural glasshouses were deemed either comparable or inferior to the common grade of imported glass. Although this pattern lends some support to Bridenbaugh's (1961:69) hypothesis about the excellence of urban industry, it is based on insufficient documentary evidence. For this reason, I exclude it from analysis, even though objective physiochemical criteria are available for archaeological assessments of quality (cf. Weeks 1884).

A third factor also conditioned the effectiveness of product-release decisions of glass factories. Warfare, currency fluctuation, and foreign competition for the American glass market affected the marketing policies of several companies in my sample. Most of the urban glasshouses complained about the unrestricted importation of European glass, as did a number of nonurban firms. A handful of the latter also struggled with marketing problems caused by military conflict and scarce specie. Documentary information about this factor is inadequate for analysis, and I can find no archaeological correlate.

CLUSTER ANALYSIS OF FACTORY PROFILES

In this section I provide a brief, nontechnical description of the clustering technique, which is followed by a discussion of its application to the factory profile data. The clustering solution serves as the basis for my subsequent evaluation of Bridenbaugh's hypothesis.

The P3M Block Clustering Algorithm (Hartigan 1979:643–648), in the BMDP-Series II package of computing programs, is used to sort the eighteenth-century glass factories into groups. The technique simultaneously clusters technological operations in the matrix of profile data in order to identify qualitative differences among the glasshouses. P3M is appropriate for this task because it treats each technological operation as a nominal-scale variable that has very few discrete values. Qualitative differences are identified by a third type of clustering. P3M reorders factories and technological operations so that "blocks" can be recognized in the data matrix. Each block contains technological operations that manifest the same alternative among all the glasshouses in the block. In other words, the discrete values of each nominal-scale variable are constant across the cases within each block. Hartigan (1979:645–646) provides a detailed description of the iterative technique used to identify blocks of variable values. Block clusters completely represent the data, and the blocks themselves form a hierarchy in which any pair is either disjoint or one includes the other. This aspect of the analysis reveals how different groups of factories operated the same technology in different ways.

The block diagram of clusters printed by the computer is too large for effective photographic reduction. Also, the diagram contains much more information than is needed to evaluate Bridenbaugh's hypothesis. Accordingly, I discuss only those aspects of the clustering solution that are relevant to the test. The group structure of the glasshouse sample can be defined in terms of the sequence in which factories join the hierarchy of clusters. The joining sequence of factories is indicated by the number of times P3M passed through the data in order to affiliate one glasshouse with others (Table 4.3). When the list of factories ordered in the rows of Table 4.3 is arrayed against a columnar sequence of pass numbers (from 1 to 89, not shown), the point at which each firm links to others in a tree map is measured by the pass number. For example, the F. M. Amelung Company is the trunk of the tree or "leader" of the hierarchy of clusters, and the Leiper-Butland Company is joined to it at the twenty-fifth pass through the data, which is relatively early in the total sequence. At the opposite extreme, P3M was not able to link either the United Glass Company or the New England Glassworks with the rest of the factories until it had made its eighty-ninth and final pass through the data. Thus, the pass number of a glasshouse is the measure of its branching distance in the tree. Low pass numbers assigned to factories in a group indicate strong similarity, whereas high ones denote weak affiliation. This is most apparent among the factories of Cluster 2, where the low pass number (17) of the New York Glass House Company at New Windsor signifies that many of its technological operations were identical to those of its counterpart in Manhattan. The substantially higher pass number (37) of the New Haven Glass Works in this cluster indicates that it performed only half of the *same* technological operations in identical ways.

Inspection of the settlement data in Table 4.3 shows that the urban factories are members of the first, second, and seventh clusters. The blocks of technological operations that are common to the glasshouses in each of these three groups need to be discussed, because blocks are the criteria of membership, as noted previously.

The factories of Cluster 1 are grouped together because they operated certain aspects of their labor and manufacturing technologies in the same way. For example, all of these firms (except the Falls of Schuylkill Glassworks and the Boston Crown Glass Company) adopted the same phase control of the cost of organizing labor, in that they employed one to three kinds of specialists. Also, the labor environment of each company was affected by seemingly random fluctuations in the amount of ethnic variety in its work force through time. In organizing its manufacturing technology, each firm (except the Falls of Schuylkill Glassworks) dealt with the costs of production facilities by establishing its physical plants in a preexisting community. Furthermore, most of these companies (except the

Table 4.3 Joining Sequence of Factories in the Hierarchy of Clusters

Cluster	Factory identity	Settlement	Pass number
1	F.M. Amelung and Company Glassworks, etc.	urban	(Leader)
	Leiper-Butland and Company, etc.	suburban	25
	"Falls of Schuylkill Glassworks"	suburban	27
	Philadelphia Glassworks, etc.	suburban	33
	Boston Crown Glass Company	urban	33
2	New York Glass House Company (Manhattan)	urban	39
	New York Glass House Company (New Windsor)	rural	17
	New Haven Glass Works	urban	37
3	"East Hartford Works," etc.	suburban	47
	Etna Glass House	suburban	33
	Thomas Johnson's Glass House	suburban	11
	Goff Glassworks	rural	35
	Dowesborough Glasshouse, etc.	suburban	45
	Germantown Glassworks	suburban	25
4	Manheim Glassworks, etc.	rural	49
5	Stanger's "Glass House," etc.	rural	59
	Hamilton Glassworks	suburban	29
	Elizabeth Furnace Glasshouse	rural	37
	Pittsburgh Glassworks, etc.	suburban	37
	Foltz, Kramer, Eberhardt Glasshouse, etc.	suburban	31
	New Geneva, etc.	rural	19
6	United Glass Company	rural	89
7	New England Glassworks	rural	89
	Glassworks in Hartford	urban	46

Philadelphia Glassworks and the Leiper-Butland Company) decided to produce both flatware and hollowware as an effective way to deal with manufacturing costs, especially when one to three types of glass were made (the Philadelphia Glassworks and the Boston Crown Glass Company created more types). The technical environment of manufacturing at these factories was shaped by the fact that they produced fewer than ten varieties of functionally distinct items (again, the Philadelphia Glassworks and the Boston Crown Glass Company made more). This phenomenon is linked to the fact that most of these firms (except the Leiper-Butland Company and the Falls of Schuylkill Glassworks) increased the functional variety of their products toward a maximum of nine different kinds during their lifetime.

The urban and nonurban glasshouses in Cluster 2 tended to make opposite decisions about the *same* technological operations. This predisposition is most evident in the fact that the amounts of ethnic variety in their work forces were fixed either constant or directional. Also, all of the companies in the second group manufactured either flat or hollowware, but not both.

Another block of technological operations distinguishes the second cluster of glass factories from the first. Certain aspects of the labor and production-release technologies were operated uniformly among glasshouses in the second group alone. For example, the labor environments of all factories in Cluster 2 were similar to the extent that their glassmaking personnel came from northern Europe. None of the gaffers in these companies was of American, English, Irish, Scottish, French, Italian, or of mixed origin (cf. Humphreys 1928). The second group of glasshouses also shared some of the same motives and possessed the same knowledge of certain market conditions in organizing their product release technology. These firms (with the exception of the New Haven Glass Works) were established between 1739 and 1780, and they transported their products overland to markets that were only 1–12 miles (1.6–19.3 km) away. The propinquity of all these glasshouses to their markets suggests that each company organized its product-release operations in a comparatively effective manner.

Operational distinctions between factories in the first and second cluster are variations of eighteenth-century cultural values, according to the analogy posited earlier. Note that these alternative choices about the design of work do not depend on the settlement context of the glasshouses. Only one technical operation is sensitive in this regard. Except for the New Haven Glass Works, all of the urban factories in both clusters procured greater varieties of material resources than did the nonurban members of both groups. This suggests that city factories were more willing to experiment with this phase control of resource cost than were the suburban and rural firms in Clusters 1 and 2.

The insight gained from this operational distinction is offset by the uniform patterning of another block of technological operations among both groups. This block forms a higher level in the clustering hierarchy because it unites not only Clusters 1 and 2, but 3 as well. My discussion is restricted to the first two groups, however. The labor environments of all glasshouses in Clusters 1 and 2 were relatively ineffective, because every one of these urban and nonurban firms (except the Leiper-Butland Company) experienced problems in retaining its gaffers and their apprentices. The technical environments of their resource-procurement operations were similarly ineffective, because all of these companies (except the Falls of Schuylkill Glassworks and the New York Glass House Company at New Windsor) met with difficulties in obtaining raw materials. Also, each factory in Clusters 1 and 2 had the same tolerance limits to the costs of facilities and equipment essential to the organization of its manufacturing technology. Only one glasshouse containing a single blast furnace was in operation on the lots of these firms at any given time.

The last urban glasshouse is joined with a rural one in Cluster 7. This group is an artifact of the clustering procedure that simply joined two residual factories because they happen to have been established in the same region around the same time. It is not likely that they have much else in common, but this cannot be discerned, since nothing more than the date and location of the Glassworks in Hartford is known at present (Wilson 1972:41).

In addition to interpreting the blocks of technical operations and factories, I attempt to determine whether or not the overall clustering solution is adequate and plausible. According to Hartigan (1979:647), a good solution should generate a block diagram in which the computer prints less than 10% of all the values in the array of 24 factories and 39 technical operations. A mediocre solution would have 50% of its values printed. My block diagram (not shown) displays 16% of all of its values, which is sufficiently close to Hartigan's optimum.

The clustering solution is believable insofar as time is not the basis of sorting glasshouses into the groups of Table 4.3 (see chronological data in Table 4.2). Alternatively, a possibility exists that the solution is a consequence of sample error, because the results might have been different had I included more technological operations in the analysis. There is substantive documentary evidence, however, to argue against the importance of this quantitative bias. For example, Cluster 1 contains both the Philadelphia Glassworks and the Leiper-Butland Company. The latter firm succeeded the former and used its physical plant to manufacture different types and varieties of glass (Lanmon and Palmer 1976:18; McKearin 1970:130–135; McKearin and McKearin 1950:24–25). In Cluster 2, the New York Glass House Company in Manhattan is closely linked to its counterpart at New Windsor. These two factories were owned by the same corporation (McKearin and McKearin 1950:11). The Etna Glass House is strongly affiliated with Thomas Johnson's Glass House in Cluster 3 for the same reason (Lanmon and Palmer 1976:39; McKearin and McKearin 1950:350). The Manheim Glassworks of Cluster 4 is hierarchically adjacent to Cluster 5, which contains the Elizabeth Furnace Glasshouse. Both of these factories were established by the same individual (Hunter 1950:30–47). In a similar vein, the close connection between the Foltz, Kramer, Eberhart Glass house, New Bremen Glass Manufactory, and New Geneva in Cluster 5 may be attributed to the fact that several gaffers were recruited from the former to build and operate the latter (Gest and Smith 1939; Innes 1948:417–418; McKearin and McKearin 1950:48–49; Weeks 1884:82–83). This kind of evidence certainly lends credence to the clustering solution, although it is not conclusive.

The clustering of urban and nonurban glass factories in Table 4.3 substantiates one of the test implications of Bridenbaugh's hypothesis. Inasmuch as four alternative structures are possible, the results of my analysis meet the third test expectation in which some, but not all, of the urban glasshouses cluster together. This finding lessens the validity of Bridenbaugh's hypothesis to an extent it is related to the proportion of city factories that are grouped together in terms of his variables. Since I have succeeded in measuring only two of the technological operations of his hypothesis, I cannot estimate precisely how much of its validity is lost. Neither of his operations, however, contains distinctions that were unique aspects of urban glass manufacture during the eighteenth century. For example, the amount of labor specialization in the city factories of Cluster 1 tends to differ from that of the two urban members of Cluster 2. All of the urban factories in these two groups experienced difficulties in procuring their raw materials (which contradicts the hypothesis), but so did most of the suburban and rural factories.

Inspection of the pass numbers in Table 4.3 for indications of the strength of each urban factory's association with the other members of its cluster yields additional evidence that diminishes the validity of Bridenbaugh's hypothesis. We might expect the city factories in each cluster to be most closely associated with each other if eighteenth-century urban environments were as influential upon the development of industry as Bridenbaugh believes. The pass number of the Boston Crown Glass Company in Cluster 1 shows that its technological operations were more similar to the suburban Philadelphia Glassworks than to any other company, whereas those of the F. M. Amelung Company in Baltimore were conducted much like the operations of the Leiper-Butland Company, which purchased the Philadelphia Glassworks. The pass numbers of the factories in Cluster 2 indicate that the New York Glass House Company in Manhattan is much more closely associated with its counterpart in rural New Windsor than with the New Haven Glass Works. The pass number data also indicate that the Boston Crown Glass Company is the weakest member of Cluster 1, as is true of the New Haven Glass Works in Cluster 2. These urban factories tended to operate in idiosyncratic ways.

If the operational distinctions among the factories in my sample reflect variations in eighteenth-century cultural values, then I infer that the incipient urbanization of America did not substantially influence the design of heavy industrial work in the city. To be certain, most of the urban glasshouses tend to share some blocks of their technological operations, but these are few in comparison to all the other operations that distinguished these factories from each other, both within and between clusters. Thus, the urban versus suburban or rural elements of choice in designing the organization, the technical environment, and the decision structure of glass manufacture were few indeed, and I suspect that this was also true among other heavy industries of the period. I believe that we shall have to look beyond the city for more adequate explanations of why early American industries operated as they did.

As archaeologists, we can take advantage of the fact that most of the technical operations of urban glass factories are not categorically distinct from those of the nonurban ones. Since comprehensive excavation of the remains of an eighteenth-century glass factory in a modern city will be difficult, substitution of its suburban or rural counterpart in the same cluster would be a feasible way to investigate the block of technological operations that is the basis of membership in the group. Although this research strategy might obviate the need to excavate most of the urban glasshouses in order to test Bridenbaugh's hypothesis further, it will not yield information about the enigmatic Glassworks in Hartford. This may be one of the earliest urban factories in the American colonies, and the details of its operation remain unknown despite efforts of historians. If the urban archaeologist rectifies only part of this problem, he or she will make a significant contribution to the economic history of America.

ACKNOWLEDGMENTS

I am indebted to Stanley South and an anonymous colleague for their constructive criticism of an earlier version of this chapter, which was delivered at the Annual Meeting of the Society for American

Archaeology in Tucson, Arizona, in 1978. Scott Lewis assisted in the collection and codification of the data.

REFERENCES

Adelman, Irma

1980 Patterns of industrialization in the nineteenth and early twentieth centuries: A cross sectional quantitative study. In *Research in economic anthropology* **5**, edited by G. Dalton. Greenwich, Conn.: JAI Press. Pp. 15–41.

Aiken, Michael, and Jerald Hage

1972 Organizational interdependence and intraorganizational structure. In *Complex organizations and their environments*, edited by M. B. Brinkerhoff and P.R. Kunz. Dubuque, Ia.: W. C. Brown. Pp. 367–394.

Ashurst, Denis

1971 Excavations at the Gawber Glasshouse near Barnesley, Yorkshire. *Journal of Post-Medieval Archaeology* **4**:92–140.

Baker, Vernon

1981 Review of research strategies in historical archaeology, edited by S. South. *American Scientist* **66**:247.

Bishop, J. Leander

1861 *History of American manufactures from 1608 to 1860*. Anonymously published.

Bowen, William R.

1978 A consideration of monitoring in urban archaeological survey. In *The Conference on Historical Sites Archeology Papers* **13**, edited by S. South. Columbia, S.C.: Institute of Archeology and Anthropology. Pp. 56–68.

Bridenbaugh, Carl

1961 *The colonial craftsman*. Chicago: Univ. of Chicago Press.

Brill, Robert H.

1976 Chemical analyses and other laboratory studies of glass fragments excavated at the site of New Bremen glassmanufactory. *Journal of Glass Studies* **18**:224–238.

Brinley, Thomas

1978 The rhythm of growth in the Atlantic economy during the eighteenth century. In *Research in economic anthropology* **3**, edited by G. Dalton. Greenwich, Conn.: JAI Press. Pp. 10–32.

Brose, David S.

1968 On the relationship between history and archaeology. In *The Conference on Historic Sites Archaeology Papers* **3**, edited by S. South. Columbia, S.C.: Institute of Archeology and Anthropology. Pp. 112–115.

Brown, Jeffrey L.

1974 Problems with categories of people: Can archaeology help? In *The Conference on Historic Sites Archeology Papers* **9**, edited by S. South, Columbia, S.C.: Institute for Archeology and Anthropology. Pp. 86–95.

Buchanan, R. A.

1972 *Industrial archaeology in Britain*. Middlesex, England: Penguin Books.

Cappon, Lester J. (editor)

1976 *Atlas of early American history: The Revolutionary Era, 1760–1790*. Princeton, N.J.: Princeton Univ. Press.

Churchman, C. West

1961 *The design of inquiring systems: Basic concepts of systems and organizations*. New York: Basic Books.

Churchman, C. West, Russell Ackoff, and E. Leonard Arnoff

1957 *Introduction to operations research*. New York: Wiley.

Cotter, John, and David Orr
1975 The historical archaeology of Philadelphia. *Historical Archaeology* **9**:1–10.
Cowgill, George L.
1975 A selection of samples: Comments on archaeo-statistics. In *Sampling in archaeology*, edited by J. Mueller. Tucson: Univ. of Arizona Press. Pp. 258–274.
Crossley, David W.
1968 Glassmaking in Baggot's Park, Staffordshire in the sixteenth century. *Journal of Post-Medieval Archaeology* **1**:44–83.
Crossley, David W., and F. A. Asberg
1972 Sixteenth-century glassmaking in Yorkshire: Excavations of furnaces at Hutton and Rosedale, North Reading, 1968–1971. *Journal of Post-Medieval Archaeology* **6**:107–159.
Daniels, George H.
1970 The big questions in the history of American technology. *Technology and Culture* **11**:1–22.
Davis, Mary
1939 The glass of Peterboro, New York. *Antiques* 1:294–295.
Davis, Pearce
1949 *The development of the American glass industry.* Cambridge, Mass.: Harvard Univ. Press.
Deagan, Kathleen
1974 Architecture, archaeology and history in Spanish St. Augustine: New data from sealed contexts. In *The Conference on Historic Sites Archeology Papers* 9, edited by S. South. Columbia, S.C.: Institute of Archeology and Anthropology. Pp. 13–29.
Dickens, Roy S., Jr., and William Bowen
1980 Problems and promises in urban historical archaeology: The MARTA project. *Historical Archaeology* **14**:42–57.
Drucker, Peter F.
1960 Work and tools. *Technology and Culture* **1**:28–42.
Emery, F. E., and E. L. Trist
1969 Socio-technical systems. In *Systems thinking*, edited by F. E. Emery. Baltimore, Md.: Penguin Books. Pp. 281–297.
1972 The causal texture of organizational environments. In *Complex organization and their environments*, edited by M. B. Brinkerhoff and P.R. Kunz. Dubuque, Ia.: W. C. Brown. Pp. 268–281.
Evan, William M.
1976 *Organization theory: Structures, systems, and environments.* New York: Wiley.
Ferguson, Leland G.
1977 Historical archaeology and the importance of material things. In *Historical archaeology and the importance of material things*, edited by L. G. Ferguson. *Society for Historical Archaeology, Special Publication Series* **2**:5–8.
Filley, A. C., and R. J. Aldag
1975 An organization typology. In *Man and his artifacts: Quo vadis?* Proceedings: Southeastern Meeting of the Society for General Systems Research.
Fitting, James E.
1977 The structure of historical archaeology and the importance of material things. In *Historical archaeology and the importance of material things*, edited by L. G. Ferguson. *Society for Historical Archaeology, Special Publication Series* **2**:62–68.
Foley, Vincent P.
1967a Pre-1800 historic sites—urban. *Historical Archaeology* **1**:43–46.
1968 On the meaning of industrial archaeology. *Historical Archaeology* **2**:66–68.
Gest, Neil C., and Parke G. Smith
1939 The glassmaking Kramers. *Antiques* **2**:118–121.
Gillmore, Kathleen
1978 The Single Brothers Complex: Old Salem, North Carolina. In *The Conference on Historic*

Sites Archeology Papers 13, edited by S. South, Columbia, S.C.: Institute of Archeology and Anthropology, Pp. 76–84.

Greer, Georgeanna H.
1970 Preliminary information on the use of alkaline glaze for stoneware in the South, 1800–1970. In *The Conference on Historic Sites Archeology Papers* 5, edited by S. South. Columbia, S.C.: Institute of Archeology and Anthropology. Pp. 155–170.

Harrington, J. C.
1952 *Glass making at Jamestown, America's first industry.* Richmond: Dietz Press.

Harris, Donald A.
1970 A French colonial well: Its construction, excavation, and contents. In *The Conference on Historic Sites Archeology Papers* 5, edited by S. South. Columbia, S.C.: Institute of Archeology and Anthropology. Pp. 51–80.

Harris, Suzanne E., James E. Price, and Synthia R. Price
1977 Archaeology of the logging industry of the Little Black River watershed. In *Conservation archaeology,* edited by M. Schiffer and G. Gummerman. New York: Academic Press. Pp. 391–400.

Hartigan, John
1979 P3M: Block clustering. In *BMDP: Series II,* edited by W. J. Dixon. Los Angeles: Univ. of California Press. Pp. 643–648.

Heite, Edward F.
1968 A study of colonial brick technology. In *The Conference on Historic Sites Archeology Papers* 3, edited by S. South. Columbia, S.C.: Institute of Archeology and Anthropology. Pp. 43–49.

Herman, Lynne L., John D. Sands, and Daniel Schecter
1973 Ceramics in St. Mary's County, Maryland during the 1840's: A socioeconomic study. In *The Conference on Historic Site Archeology Papers* 8, edited by S. South. Columbia, S.C.: Institute of Archeology and Anthropology. Pp. 52–93.

Horner, George R.
1970 Report of the excavation of the glassworks at Germantown, Quincy, Massachusetts. Manuscript on file. Department of Anthropology, Bridgewater State College, Bridgewater, Mass.

House, John H.
1977 Survey data and regional models in historical archaeology. In *Research strategies in historical archeology,* edited by S. South. New York: Academic Press. Pp. 241–260.

Hudson, Kenneth
1963 *Industrial archaeology: An introduction.* London: John Baker.

Humphreys, Gregor N.
1928 Foreign influences in American glass. *Antiques* 12:242–246.

Hunter, Frederick W.
1950 *Stiegel glass.* New York: Dover.

Ingersoll, Daniel W.
1971 The problem of urban historical archaeology. *Man in the Northeast* 2:66–67.

Innes, Lowell
1948 Pittsburgh glass. *Antiques* 33:417–419.

Jarves, Deming
1854 *Reminiscences of glass-making.* Boston, Mass.: Eastburn's Press.

Kelso, William M., and Edward A. Chappell
1974 Excavation of a seventeenth-century pottery kiln at Glebe Harbor, Westmoreland County, Virginia. *Historical Archaeology* 8:53–63.

Klein, Joel I.
1973 Models and hypothesis testing in historical archaeology. *Historical Archaeology* 7:68–77.

Landberg, Leif C. W.
1967 Problems of post-1800 urban sites archaeology at Old Sacramento, California. *Historical Archaeology* 1:71–78.

Lanmon, Dwight P.

1969 The Baltimore glass trade, 1780–1820. *Winterthur Portfolio*, **5**:15–48.

Lanmon, Dwight P., and Arlene M. Palmer

1976 John Frederick Amelung and the New Bremen glassmanufactory. *Journal of Glass Studies* **18**:14–125.

Leone, Mark

1977 Foreword. In *Research strategies in historical archeology*, edited by S. South. New York: Academic Press. Pp. i–xxix.

Lewis, Kenneth E.

1977 Sampling the archaeological frontier: Regional models and component analysis. In *Research strategies in historical archeology*, edited by S. South. New York: Academic Press. Pp. 151–201.

Lorrain, Dessamae

1968 An archaeologist's guide to nineteenth-century glass. *Historical Archaeology* **2**:35–44.

MacMurray, Carl D.

1972 Excavations at the Ximinez-Fatio House. St. Augustine, Florida. *Historical Archaeology* **6**:56–64.

Magee, John F., and Martin L. Ernst

1961 Progress in operations research: The challenge of the future. In *Progress in operations research* 1, edited by R. L. Ackoff. New York: Wiley. Pp. 466–481.

McKay, Joyce

1974 A theoretical approach to historical archaeology. In *The Conference on Historical Sites Archeology Papers* **9**, edited by S. South. Columbia, S.C.: Institute of Archeology and Anthropology. Pp. 130–134.

McKearin, George S.

1926 Wistarburg and South Jersey glass. *Antiques* **10**:274–280.

McKearin, Helen

1950 Introduction and notes. In *Stiegel glass*, edited by F. W. Hunter, New York: Dover. Pp. 1–12.

1970 *Bottles, flasks, and Dr. Dyott.* New York: Crown.

McKearin, George S., and Helen McKearin

1950 *Two hundred years of American blown glass.* New York: Crown.

Mileti, Dennis S., David S. Gillespie, and Elizabeth Morrisey

1978 Technology organization: Theoretical deficiencies and methodological lacunae. *Technology and Culture* **19**(1):83–92.

Nagel, Stuart S., and Marian Neef

1976 Operations research methods. Sage University paper on quantitative applications in the social sciences 2. London: Sage Publications.

Noël Hume, Ivor

1964 The search for New Bremen and the glass of John Frederick Amelung. *Antiques* **49**:310–313.

1973 Historical archaeology: Who needs it? *Historical Archaeology* **7**:3–10.

1975 *Historical archaeology.* New York: W. W. Morton.

1976 Archaeological excavations on the site of John Frederick Amelung's New Bremen glassmanufactory, 1963–1964. *Journal of Glass Studies* **18**:138–216.

Otto, John S.

1977 Artifacts and status differences—A comparison of ceramics from planter, overseer and slave sites on an antebellum plantation. In *Research strategies in historical archeology*, edited by S. South. New York: Academic Press. Pp. 91–118.

Outlaw, Alain C.

1974 Preliminary excavations at the Mount Sheppard pottery site. In *The Conference on Historic Sites Archeology Papers* **9**, edited by S. South. Columbia, S.C.: Institute of Archeology and Anthropology. Pp. 1–12.

Palmer, Arlene M.

1976a *The Wistarburgh Glassworks: The beginnings of Jersey glassmaking.* Alloway, N.J.: Alloway Township Bicentennial Committee.

1976b Glass production in eighteenth-century America: The Wistarburgh Enterprise. *Winterthur Portfolio* **11**:75–101.

1978 Through the glass case: The curator and the object. In *Material culture and the study of American life*, edited by I. M. G. Quimby. Charlottesville: Univ. of Virginia Press. Pp. 219–224.

Perrot, Paul N.

1961 Glass: English, Irish or American? *Antiques* **36**:264–268.

Perrow, Charles

1972 A framework for the comparative analysis of organizations. In *Complex organizations and their environments*, edited by M. B. Brinkerhoff and P. R. Kunz. Dubuque, Ia.: W. C. Brown. Pp. 48–67.

Powell, Harry J.

1923 *Glass-making in England*. Cambridge, Mass.: Cambridge Univ. Press.

Raistrick, Arthur

1972 *Industrial archaeology: An historical survey*. London: Eyre Methuen.

Read, Dwight W., and Andrew L. Christenson

1978 Comments on "Cluster analysis and archaeological classification." *American Antiquity* **43**:505–506.

Rowlands, M.

1971 The archaeological interpretation of prehistoric metal working. *World Archaeology* **3**:210–224.

Rutch, E. S.

1974 Symposium on industrial archaeology, Patterson, New Jersey. *Northeast Historical Archaeology* **4**(1–2):39–43.

Schiffer, Michael B.

1977 Toward a unified science of the cultural past. In *Research strategies in historical archeology*, edited by S. South. New York: Academic Press. Pp. 13–40.

Schumacher, Paul J. F.

1967 Financing excavations. *Historical Archaeology* **1**:54–57.

Schuyler, Robert L.

1970 Historical and historic sites archaeology as anthropology: Basic definitions and relationships. *Historical Archaeology* **4**:83–89.

Schwartz, Marvin D.

1974 Introduction. In *American glass*, edited by M. D. Schwartz. Princeton, N.J.: Pyne Press. Pp. 1–10.

Shadel, Jane S.

1970 Robert Hewes, glass manufacturer. *Journal of Glass Studies* **12**:140–148.

Sicard, Hortense F.

1926 Sidelights on the Wistars and their glasshouse. *Antiques* **10**:281–282.

Smith, Samuel D., and William V. Davidson

1973 County seat towns as archaeological sites: Some Arkansas examples. In *The Conference on Historic Sites Archeology Papers* **8**, edited by S. South. Columbia, S.C.: Institute of Archeology and Anthropology. Pp. 33–51.

South, Stanley

1968 What archeology can do to expand historical research. In *The Conference on Historic Sites Archeology Papers* **3**, edited by S. South. Columbia, S.C.: Institute of Archeology and Anthropology. Pp. 50–57.

1972a Evaluation of analysis situations relative to the archeological data bank. In *The Conference on Historic Sites Archeology Papers* 7, edited by S. South. Columbia, S.C.: Institute of Archeology and Anthropology. Pp. 146–151.

1972b Historical archeology reports: A plea for a new direction. In *The Conference on Historic Sites Archeology Papers* 7, edited by S. South. Columbia, S.C.: Institute of Archeology and Anthropology. Pp. 151–156.

1977a *Method and theory in historical archeology*. New York: Academic Press.

1977b *Research strategies in historical archeology*. New York: Academic Press.

South, Stanley, and Randolph Widmer

1977 A subsurface sampling strategy for archeological reconnaissance. In *Research Strategies in Historical Archeology*, edited by S. South. New York: Academic Press. Pp. 119–150.

Starbuck, David R., Frederick Gorman, and James Wiseman

1976 The excavation of a New Hampshire glass factory: The New England Glassworks in Temple, New Hampshire. Paper presented at the 1976 Annual Meeting of the Society for Historical Archaeology, Philadelphia.

Stone, Gary W.

1968 Ceramics in Suffolk County, Massachusetts inventories, 1680–1775. In *The Conference on Historic Sites Archeology Papers* **3**, edited by S. South. Columbia, S.C.: Institute of Archeology and Anthropology. Pp. 73–88.

Stow, Charles M.

1927 A Massachusetts glass factory. *Antiquarian* **13**:66–86.

Terreberry, S.

1972 Evolution of organizational environments. In *Management of change and conflict*, edited by J. M. Thomas and W. G. Bennis, Baltimore, Md.: Penguin Books. Pp. 141–163.

Thompson, James D., and William J. McEwen

1972 Organizational goals and environment: Goal setting as an interactional process. In *Complex organizations and their environments*, edited by M. B. Brinkerhoff and P. R. Kunz. Dubuque, Ia.: W. C. Brown. Pp. 255–268.

Trist, E. L., G. W. Giggin, H. Murray, and A. B. Pollock

1963 *Organizational choice*. London: Tavistock.

Vogel, Robert M.

1967 The New England textile mill survey. *Historical Archaeology* **1**:34–36.

Walker, Ian C.

1968 Comment on Garry Wheeler Stone's ceramics in Suffolk County, Massachusetts inventories, 1680–1775. In *The Conference on Historic Sites Archeology Papers* **3**, edited by S. South. Columbia, S.C.: Institute of Archaeology and Anthropology. Pp. 99–111.

Watkins, C. Malcolm

1949 Glass at the forum: Foreign influences in American glass, I. *Antiques* **46**:363–365.

1953 Some New Geneva and Greensboro glass. *Antiques* **51**:136–137.

Watkins, Laura W.

1939 An antecendent of three-mould glass. *Antiques* **36**:63–68.

1940 The Boston Crown Glass Company. *Antiques* **37**:288–291.

Weeks, Joseph D.

1884 *Report on the manufacture of glass*. Census Office, Department of the Interior, U.S. Government, Washington, D.C.

White, Harry H.

1930 New York State glasshouses. *Antiques* **14**:220–223.

1937 Migrations of early glass workers. *Antiques* **21**:64–67.

Wilkinson, Norman B.

1963 Brandywine borrowings from European technology. *Technology and Culture* **1**:1–14.

Wilson, Kenneth M.

1972 *New England glass and glassmaking*. New York: Thomas Y. Crowell.

5

Environmental-Impact Archaeology in the Urban Setting: A View from Atlanta

Roy S. Dickens, Jr.
Timothy J. Crimmins

INTRODUCTION

This chapter discusses and evaluates the evolving methods and procedures of environmental-impact archaeology in the urban setting. The authors, one an archaeologist and the other a historian, relate their experiences in attempting to develop a unified and workable approach to urban cultural resource management in Atlanta, Georgia. Over an 8-year period, they have worked, at first independently and then together, on various aspects of archaeological, historical, and architectural assessment and mitigation in construction areas of a city-wide rapid transportation system. The experience of working on the Metropolitan Atlanta Rapid Transit Authority (MARTA) project has been, at times, highly rewarding and, at other times, discouraging and frustrating. Setbacks and losses on this urban project, and others, have resulted from the newness of the subfield of urban archaeology, the lack of a multidisciplinary approach to cultural resource assessment, and tendencies at the review-compliance level to force urban resources into a methodological and procedural mold developed mostly for nonurban situations.

THE LEGAL BASE

Since the mid-1960s, a body of federal law has been developed to require assessment and protection of cultural resources that are affected by construction projects receiving public funds. These laws apply equally to projects in urban and

ARCHAEOLOGY OF URBAN AMERICA
The Search for Pattern and Process

ISBN 0-12-214980-7

nonurban areas. In 1966, the National Historic Preservation Act (NHPA) established the National Register of Historic Places and the Advisory Council on Historic Preservation. Later, in 1969, the National Environmental Policy Act (NEPA) expanded the cultural resource responsibilities of an affected agency by requiring a preconstruction Environmental Impact Statement (EIS). Then, in 1971, Executive Order 11593 extended the requirements of the Historic Preservation Act to include evaluation and mitigation of sites deemed eligible for the National Register.

Whereas the law required that sites be evaluated "with respect to historic, architectural, or archaeological significance [Executive Order 11593]," it did not specify the methods and procedures by which the significance of the resources would be assessed and adverse impact properly mitigated. The detailed work of establishing these methods and procedures, left to professionals in government and academia, has slowly evolved by trial and error during the 15-year history of the legislation.

THE URBAN ARCHAEOLOGICAL RESOURCE

American archaeologists have been slow to recognize the importance of urban remains (Salwen 1973). Until recently, attention was concentrated on prehistoric and early historic remains, located mostly in rural areas. The occasional project in an urban area usually was devoted to the recovery of Colonial or early nineteenth-century remains, with little, if any, attention being paid to deposits of the late nineteenth and twentieth centuries. Even the work on early historic urban remains was strongly focused on locations of upper-class habitation, governmental activities, and military actions (e.g., Cotter and Orr 1974). The structural complexities of urban areas further contributed to their receiving little attention, with most projects coming from accidents of discovery during construction and land clearance.

These kinds of circumstantial, small-scale, and culturally biased efforts contributed to several distorted views of the archaeological value of the city. The city was seen as a potential reservoir of information about the early development of Euroamerica, but not as a resource for the study of urbanization itself. Related to this view was an idea generally held by archaeologists and historians that documentary records provided the primary resource for the study of "modern" (urban and industrial) culture and that the material record was of primary value only in temporally remote situations. The fragmented efforts seemed also to have led to an almost unconscious view of urban areas as being composed of disarticulated archaeological units, rather than as components of a larger interconnected city-system.

In the late 1960s and early 1970s, with the instigation of several large-scale urban projects (e.g., Tucson, Arizona; Lowell, Massachusetts; and Patterson, New Jersey), and with a growing recognition of the scientific value of recent material remains (e.g., Rathje 1974; Reid, Rathje, and Schiffer 1974; Salwen 1973; Schuyler 1974), urban archaeology began a rapid ascension within the larger discipline. Projects having city-wide impact (e.g., Tucson, Arizona; San Diego, California; Alexandria, Virginia; and Atlanta, Georgia) have led to the development of more holistic and systematic models for urban archaeological research. Thus, archaeologists have come to recognize the city as a unified and significant body of cultural resources. Such a view of "the city as a site [Cressey 1978]" now must be reconciled within the procedural structure of the federal review-and-compliance process.

RESEARCH MODEL FOR THE MARTA PROJECT

At a very general level, the research model developed for the MARTA project in Atlanta is one in which the city is viewed as a complex, ever-evolving "organism" (Havlick 1974). The underlying principles, derived from ecological theory, hold that the city's cultural components (socioeconomic, political, technological, ideological, etc.) and physical components (physiographic, hydrologic, climatic, geologic, etc.) are interrelated in a dynamic system.[1] Furthermore, it is recognized that changes in one component of the system are likely to produce changes in other components, and that these changes can take the form of complex *feedback relationships*. Thus, for example, one would expect the introduction and spread of the automobile in an early twentieth-century city to affect the entire system. This piece of transportation technology might serve, on the one hand, to enhance suburban residential development and, on the other, to contribute to a "decline" of the inner city. In the former, automobile transportation is functioning to encourage one direction of change (positive feedback), while in the latter, it is functioning to retard or regulate other directions of change (negative feedback). The model also recognizes that a city is not a closed system, but one that is affected by, and in turn affects, larger regional, national, and international systems.

At a more specific level, this model can be characterized as structural and processual. To elucidate the diachronic *processes* (mechanisms and directions) of change in the urban system ("growth" of the organism), the archaeologist must define the *structure* of the system at specific temporal intervals ("anatomy" of the organism). For the MARTA research, processual hypotheses have been developed (Dickens and Bowen 1980:43–46), and these have been tested and revised through studies of structural change, as reflected in the archaeological record. The latter effort is, in many ways, analogous to the method of "pattern recognition" proposed by South (1977).

With this approach, urban archaeological features take on meaning in relation to their potential to contribute to the delineation of specific behavioral *patterns*. Wells, privies, and small garbage deposits, for example, often contain assemblages of material remains representing small, temporally and spatially discrete patterns—that is, a family, a small segment of a community, or a single commercial establishment. A neighborhood dump may define a somewhat larger pattern in time and space, and a municipal dump or landfill, a still larger unit. Small features, or zones within larger ones, often can be used to delineate what might be called *infrapatterns*. These lower-order patterns reflect seasonal and special-occasion behavior (Dickens and Bowen 1980:51–52) that lies within larger ongoing aspects of the

[1] A holistic systemic approach to the analysis of the city has been proposed by cultural anthropologists (e.g., Weaver and White 1972) and social historians (e.g., Lubove 1967).

system. Certain features and groups of features also can be used to define *networks* within the urban system. Roads, alleyways, rail lines, sewer systems, water systems, and military earthworks are in this network category. Such features also may contain "pockets" of more localized and temporally restricted information.

Although urban features, as with those on any archaeological site, can be analyzed and interpreted individually, their importance in elucidating structure and process within the larger system must come from their analysis and interpretation in the context of the whole site and its physical environment. For example, *sequences of filling and abandonment* of features, such as wells, privies, dumps, sewers, alleys, roads, and rail lines, provide important information on technological, socioeconomic, and political changes within the larger system. Well-filling sequences document the spread of municipal water systems; privy-filling sequences mark the spread of municipal sewerage systems; the relocation of dumps reflects decisions on solid-waste management; and changes in the locations of rail lines, roads, and alleys provide a record of shifts in directions of development, transportation, and communication. Changes in the features just discussed and their material contents also reflect *transformations* in the functions of portions of a city; for instance, from residential to commercial, or commercial to industrial.

REVIEW AND COMPLIANCE PROCEDURES

The accepted procedural format for implementing the federal mandates (Section 106 of NHPA) requires a sequence in which the archaeologist (*a*) identifies and bounds the resources, (*b*) evaluates significance, (*c*) completes a determination of eligibility for the National Register, (*d*) defines adverse impact to eligible sites, and (*e*) assists the Advisory Council in developing a mitigation plan. These procedures, devised primarily for dealing with standing structures, ruins, and other above-ground features, have been applied with moderate success to below-ground archaeological sites in rural areas. In these unobstructed situations, preconstruction identification and evaluation of resources usually can be accomplished to the satisfaction of both the archaeologist and the review-compliance official.

In the urban (and even suburban) setting, however, it is seldom possible to identify and evaluate a significant proportion of below-ground resources prior to demolition and construction. In the MARTA project, for example, intensive field surveys and detailed documentary searches have revealed the locations (or approximate locations) of only 53% of the features ultimately investigated. In heavily obstructed inner portions of the city, the figure was 37% (Dickens and Bowen 1980:48–49). Construction monitoring, the single most successful technique for locating and evaluating sites, has not been encouraged by agency officials because it requires on-the-spot decisions and is difficult to specify as to location, time, and cost, prior to construction.[2] The tendency, therefore, is to fit the unique circum-

[2]Just as inappropriate, however, is a procedure that uses construction monitoring outside the bounds of a research design.

stances of the urban setting into a preexisting procedural format, even when such a format does not allow the legal mandates to operate in the best interest of the resources that they are designed to protect.

A SUGGESTED PLAN FOR URBAN ENVIRONMENTAL-IMPACT ARCHAEOLOGY

Successful environmental-impact archaeology in the urban setting requires a multistaged and multidisciplinary plan for identifying, evaluating, and mitigating adverse impact to archaeological resources (Figure 5.1). The major stages can be classed as preconstruction, construction, and postconstruction.

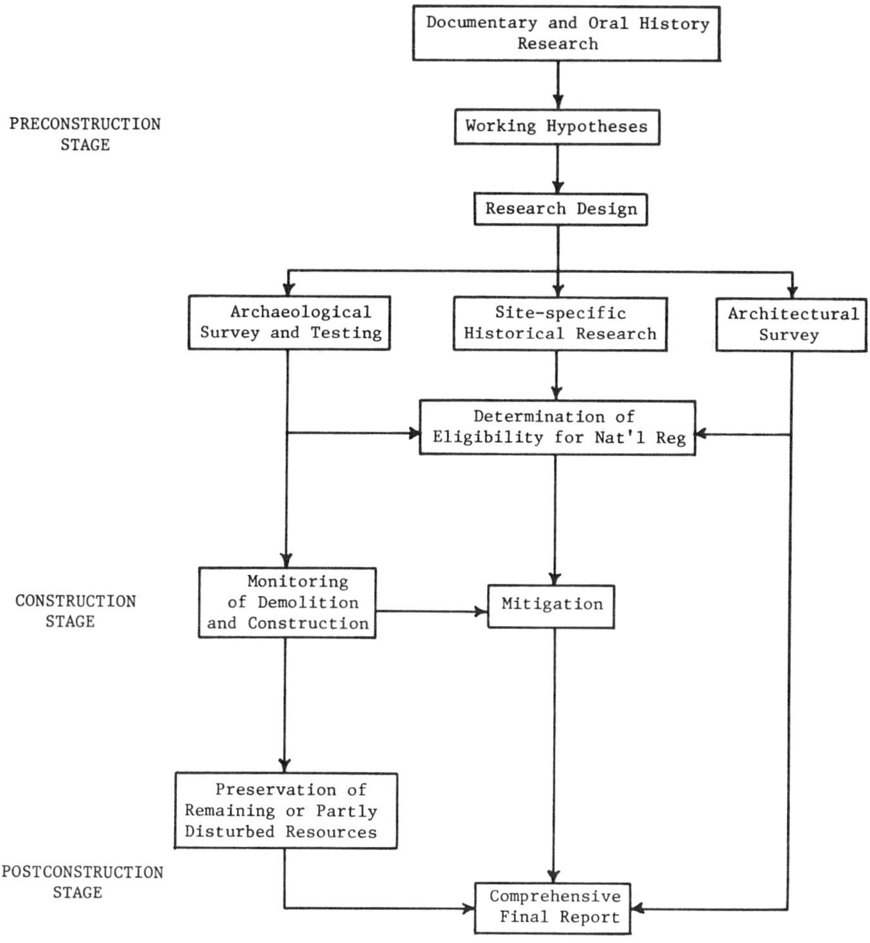

FIGURE 5.1. Suggested plan for conducting urban environmental-impact archaeology.

Preconstruction Stage

A critical first step in urban cultural resource assessment is the preparation of a research design that places archaeology in a multidisciplinary framework. To accomplish this, a team of professionals should be assembled from archaeology, history, and architectural history (and, if possible, cultural anthropology, folklore, and cultural geography) to gather and analyze appropriate literature and oral history about the urban area in question. This work, then, should lead to the development of working hypotheses about the structure and development of the city. Finally, the working hypotheses should be incorporated into a unified research design that will serve as the basis for assessment of all known and potential cultural resources (including archaeological features) in the project impact area.[3]

Following the development of a general research design, and guided by the site-specific documentary findings, archaeological field survey and testing should be undertaken.[4] At this stage, only unobstructed areas can be explored. A number of techniques—metal detector surveys, shovel testing, auger testing, and mechanical testing—have been used in the MARTA Project (Dickens and Bowen: 1980:46–48). Sometimes this initial survey and testing will provide information sufficient to evaluate a feature or group of features and develop a mitigation plan. The archaeologist will want to consult with the historians, and perhaps request additional documentation, in making these decisions.

Demolition and Construction Stage

If an area has standing structures, paving, or other obstructions, demolition will precede construction. Demolition can reveal important archaeological information. In the MARTA project, for example, architectural sequences, road-building sequences, and superimposed rail systems have been documented during demolition. Also, by being present during demolition, the archaeologist often can prevent unnecessary damage to buried features by heavy machinery. If possible, the archaeologist should develop an arrangement with the engineers and construction personnel to provide an interval between demolition and construction for additional archaeological testing.

Construction monitoring is an essential and valuable component of urban environmental-impact archaeology (see Ingle, Chapter 9, for a discussion of monitoring on a complex construction site). Monitoring does not necessarily have to take the form of "salvage" work, but can result in careful, systematic, and technically correct archaeology. The nature of urban archaeological remains often makes on-the-spot evaluation and data recovery more satisfactory than for nonurban sites. Most non-artifact-bearing features (usually architectural remains) can be

[3]A multidisciplinary research design for Atlanta will be described in detail in a forthcoming article by Crimmins and Dickens.

[4]The archaeologist should be careful, however, not to use information from documents, oral history, and standing structures to set up a plan so rigidly that it cannot be modified after the fieldwork begins.

adequately recorded through scaled drawings and photographs. Artifact-bearing features require recovery and documentation, but because of the density of artifacts in most of these features, it usually is preferable to sample them (according to a predetermined design), rather than to attempt total recovery.

Features recovered at the time of construction usually can be adequately evaluated, recorded, and/or excavated without causing significant losses of time to construction. On the MARTA project, the engineer, construction foreman, and archaeologist usually have worked out an arrangement whereby the archaeology is accomplished while construction continues in adjacent areas. In fact, in several instances, the construction crews have volunteered mechanical equipment and other assistance to the archaeological team. This kind of cooperation has alleviated construction personnel's fears that the archaeologists, at some point, would bring their project to a halt.

When a feature is discovered through monitoring, decisions about its significance and the way it is to be investigated (type of recovery and extent of documentation) should be made in the same way as on a nonurban site, that is, in light of its place in the context of the total site and the larger cultural–environmental system. The archaeologist in charge has to be given the legal authority to make these decisions on the spot. Monitoring also allows the archaeologist to trace network features (buried roads, sewerage lines, etc.) through various segments of large construction areas.

Postconstruction Stage

Archaeological features discovered prior to construction, as well as those found by monitoring, should be evaluated with an eye to preservation, if possible. In the MARTA project, where alteration of existing construction plans was not possible, an effort always has been made to work with the construction crews and engineers to preserve portions of threatened sites or features. In several instances, small features (e.g., wells and privies) were capped and reburied in such a manner as to preserve, in situ, part of their structure and artifact content. Portions of two garbage dumps (one a neighborhood deposit and the other a municipal dump) were sealed following construction, and these remaining parts were nominated for the National Register (Bowen, Carnes, and Dickens 1977; Carnes and Dickens 1979). Again, this kind of effort requires close communication and a cooperative relationship between the field archaeologists and construction personnel. In several instances, where such postconstruction preservation was the goal, the archaeologists had to revisit the sites after construction was completed to prevent accidental damage to the protected portions of the features during landscaping, utility relocations, and other "finishing" work. Usually, the workers on these projects have no way of knowing where a preserved feature (even one on the National Register) is located, except by direct contact with the archaeologists.

Finally, and very importantly, the cultural resource team should produce a comprehensive final report that describes its findings and addresses the hypotheses developed at the preconstruction stage (assessment and mitigation phases) and interpretations of data recovered at the construction stage (monitoring phase). This comprehensive report should be an integration, not just a compilation, of the separate reports of the specialists.

CONCLUSIONS AND ADDENDUM

The proper implementation of urban environmental-impact archaeology requires (*a*) a recognition of a city as a site, and its component parts as features within the site; (*b*) the development of procedures that are flexible enough to allow evaluation and mitigation of features discovered during construction; (*c*) the development of a research design by, and continued input from, a multidisciplinary cultural resource team; and (*d*) a concern for preservation, where possible, of features or portions of features.

The major problems in conducting urban archaeology under federal environmental-preservation mandates have resulted from efforts at the review and compliance level to treat features within a city as separate sites that must be discovered and evaluated prior to construction. The nature of the urban environment, however, usually makes this process unworkable. Rather, what is needed is a multistaged approach, where archaeologists and historians work to identify as many resources as possible in advance of construction, and where systematic monitoring is used as a technique for identification, evaluation, and recovery at the time of construction. Such an approach allows the city to be investigated as an integrated whole—as an evolving system in an anthropological–ecological sense—rather than as a disarticulated group of "sites" or "districts" defined exclusively on the basis of known historical events and architectural remains.

The MARTA project in Atlanta has brought the problems of satisfying the law and archaeology into clear focus. Recognition that accepted procedures and approaches are inadequate, however, has been slow and difficult. At the writing of this chapter, there is no longer a systematic plan to recover archaeological data on MARTA construction sites. Over a year ago, archaeological work was halted so that the Urban Mass Transportation Administration (MARTA's parent agency) and the Advisory Council might develop a memorandum of agreement that would bring MARTA into compliance with the environmental and preservation laws.

Thus far, the only document to appear has been a brief "scope of work" for a single small area. This area, Johnsontown, represents an enclave of low-income blacks lying within Atlanta's affluent North Side. Johnsontown, of decided cultural significance, is easily defined and bounded. The fact that the memorandum singles out Johnsontown and ignores the other construction areas is clear evidence that review officials still are trying to treat the urban system as a disarticulated set of "sites." The Johnsontowns, as important as they are, represent the exceptions in urban archaeology, and to emphasize these exceptions, because they fit into an existing procedural mold, is to overlook the larger organism—the city.

It should be possible to approach urban environmental-impact archaeology adequately on a whole-site basis without requiring that an entire city be nominated to the National Register. Although procedures already exist for creating "multiple resource districts," in which all resources have potential National Register eligibility and for which near-instant decisions can be made regarding significance and appropriate mitigation, such provisions have not yet been translated into a form that can be applied to the urban setting.

ACKNOWLEDGMENTS

We are grateful to Annetta Cheek, Carol Dickens, Robert Fishman, and Sarah Hill for commenting on this chapter.

REFERENCES

Bowen, William R., Linda F. Carnes, and Roy S. Dickens, Jr.
1977 Archaeological impact studies on the MARTA east and west lines. Manuscript on file at the Laboratory of Archaeology, Georgia State Univ., Atlanta.

Carnes, Linda F., and Roy S. Dickens, Jr.
1979 Archaeological impact studies on the MARTA north and south lines. Manuscript on file at the Laboratory of Archaeology, Georgia State Univ., Atlanta.

Cotter, John L., and David Orr
1974 Historical archaeology of Philadelphia. *Historical Archaeology* 9:1–10.

Cressey, Pamela J.
1978 The city as a site: The Alexandria model for urban archaeology. *The Conference on Historic Site Archeology Papers* **13**:204–227.

Dickens, Roy S., Jr., and William R. Bowen
1980 Problems and promises in urban historical archaeology: The MARTA project. *Historical Archaeology* **14**:42–57.

Havlick, Spenser W.
1974 *The urban organism: The city's natural resources from an environmental perspective.* New York: Macmillan.

Lubove, Roy
1967 The urbanization process: An approach to historical research. *Journal of the American Institute of Planners* **33**(1):33–39.

Rathje, William L.
1974 The garbage project: A new way of looking at the problems of archaeology. *Archaeology* **27**(4):236–241.

Reid, J. Jefferson, William L. Rathje, and Michael B. Schiffer
1974 Expanding archaeology. *American Antiquity* **39**(1):125–126.

Salwen, Bert
1973 Archaeology in megalopolis. In *Research and theory building in current archaeology*, edited by C. L. Redman. New York: Wiley. Pp. 151–163.

Schuyler, Robert L.
1974 Sandy ground: Archeological sampling in a black community in metropolitan New York. *The Conference on Historic Site Archeology Papers* 7(2):12–52.

South, Stanley
1977 *Method and theory in historical archeology.* New York: Academic Press.

Weaver, Thomas, and Douglas White
1972 Anthropological approaches to urban and complex society. In *The anthropology of urban environments*, edited by Thomas Weaver and Douglas White. *The Society for Applied Anthropology Monograph Series* **11**:109–125. Boulder, Colorado: Society for Applied Anthropology.

II

SITE FORMATION, STRUCTURE, AND PATTERN

The chapters in this section, all of which are concerned with the formation, structure, and pattern of the urban archaeological record, represent a broad range of approaches and data categories. Chronologically, the sites extend from the late eighteenth century to the early twentieth century. The reader should take special note of the uses of sampling strategies, archival data sources, and contextual observation in these projects.

Rubertone, and Cressey, Stephens, Shephard, and Magid provide applications of the research designs they presented in Part I. Rubertone discusses the correlates of land use and artifact deposition in Providence, whereas Cressey, Stephens, Shephard, and Magid focus on the core–periphery model for testing hypotheses about urban culture change in Alexandria. The urban mortuary analysis by Blakely and Beck points out the potential of a little-explored archaeological resource. They suggest that the methods of bioarchaeology and forensic anthropology can be applied profitably to the urban cemetery. The industrial component of the urban system is well represented in this part, with examples ranging from a family-based pottery in Knoxville, Tennessee (Faulkner) to "heavy" industry in the form of locomotive manufacturing in Patterson, New Jersey (Ingle). Faulkner shows how the archaeological record reflects the efforts of a folk industry to adapt to a Southern urban setting; whereas Ingle documents the complexities of conducting salvage archaeology and attempting behavioral interpretations on a large industrial site.

6

Urban Land Use and Artifact Deposition: An Archaeological Study of Change in Providence, Rhode Island[1]

Patricia E. Rubertone

INTRODUCTION

Among urban historical archaeologists there is a growing interest in questions concerning the spatial organization of city and town sites, especially how and why land-use configurations change through time. Traditionally, archaeologists investigating these patterns have relied on either architectural or artifactual evidence. The assumption underlying the use of architecture in the delineation of spatial organization is that architectural space defines the spatial boundaries of activities and thus provides information on the use of space and community layout (Redman and Anzalone 1980). The assumption underlying the use of distributions of artifactual data in the investigation of intrasite spatial organization is that different patterns of behavior (e.g., those related to social, economic, political, and other sociocultural variables) affect the form, composition, and distribution of materials in the archaeological record (Binford 1965; Redman 1978a). Subsequently, the discovery of the patterned variation in these materials and their observed distributions in space can provide information useful for inferring organizational patterns.

In this chapter it is argued that an interdependent use of both architectural and artifactual evidence can enhance the investigation of patterns of land use and the delineation of changing spatial organization in a community. However, the discov-

[1]The archaeological investigations discussed here were supported by the Division of Cultural Resources, North Atlantic Regional Office, National Park Serivce, U.S. Department of the Interior under contract CX 1600-9-0038.

ISBN 0-12-214980-7

ery of patterns of urban land use from architectural space and artifact distribution is not a simple matter. The sites themselves usually are characterized by dense architectural debris with building remains from several construction phases. For continuously occupied sites with multiple building phases, one rarely finds early intact architectural remains. Architectural features dating to the latest phase of construction, however, usually are abundant. Artifact remains at these sites, on the other hand, are characterized by complex patterns of deposition. Artifacts may be quite numerous but are rarely in their primary context. None of this should be surprising if we truly adhere to the belief that cities, as architectural and archaeological sites, are organic entities characterized by differential rates of physical growth and by a range of depositional activities that affect site formation through time. Nevertheless, these complexities do require the development of methods for investigating urban settlement and land-use patterns that take site formation problems explicitly into consideration.

The study of land use and artifact deposition presented here is an example of some ways in which one might approach these problems at complex urban sites. The data patterns are derived from an archaeological project conducted at the Roger Williams National Memorial in Providence, Rhode Island (Rubertone and Gallagher 1981).

THE CASE STUDY AND ITS HISTORY

The Roger Williams National Memorial, located in an area that was the setting for many of the events and developments of Providence's first few centuries, is a 4.56-acre (1.85 ha.) urban park designed to commemorate a spring believed to have been used by Providence's original settlers during the seventeenth century. Although the area has witnessed intensive urban development since the early eighteenth century, in its present state it is an open landscape devoid of standing architecture. The archaeological investigations were focused on the southern portion of the parcel, an area that formerly had covered six urban blocks.

Although the written history of Providence dates to the arrival of Roger Williams and his followers in 1636, the earliest written records for this study area are from the early eighteenth century. During that early period, Providence can be characterized as having been a sprawling agricultural town. By the middle of the century, however, the town had begun to urbanize (Cook 1976:172). This process of urbanization was marked by increasing concentration of property ownership in the hands of the wealthy and an increasingly complex economy in which commerce was elevated to an important role. Within the six-block study area, shops, craft workshops, and residences were established. Wharves occupied the western portion of the blocks, which at that time bordered a salt cove that dominated what is now downtown Providence. The presence of these wharves indicates the importance of maritime trade in the Colonial economy.

Although the American Revolution devastated many urban centers, Providence's economy remained relatively unscathed, and in general, the town experienced considerable growth during the postwar years. It is during this time that Providence gained the status of a primary urban center, surpassing its long-time rival, Newport (Bridenbaugh 1971). Maritime commerce, controlled by a few entrepreneurs, continued to flourish and was marked by specialized long-distance trade and increased involvement in exotic markets.

By the 1820s, however, capital investment increasingly was being diverted to the development of local production—notably, textile manufacturing—and the economy in general was becoming more diversified. Whereas Providence previously had relied primarily on overseas trade, the partial filling of the original shoreline of the salt cove led to a decline of maritime facilities. Wharves surrounding the cove were used for smaller ships that were bound for coastal, rather than international, ports (Cady 1957). Businesses in the area were dominated by retail establishments, providing basic commodities and services to local residents, trades, and craft workshops. In 1828, these changes in the economy were epitomized by the completion of the Blackstone Canal (immediately to the west of the study area) that was supposed to facilitate the transport of goods from the interior hinterlands to the coast.

By the middle of the nineteenth century, another sequence of transformations had begun. With the closing of the financially unsuccessful Blackstone Canal in 1847 and the demise of Providence as an international port, the basic character of this area was changed and would continue to evolve well into the following century. This area and the rest of the city experienced an increase in population resulting partly from the influx of European immigrants beginning in the late 1840s. Businesses, service establishments, and residences dominated the area. This era also was marked by the emergence of a number of civic improvements and the establishment of municipal services that reflected the growing role of bureaucratic decision making in neighborhood affairs. By the turn of the twentieth century, the city contained most of the state's population. Individual neighborhoods declined, with noted deterioration occurring as a result of the growth of industry and unzoned commercial development (Cady 1957).

The most basic question posed by the archaeological investigations focused on how these general changes were reflected in the six-block study area. More specifically, could these changes be seen in localized land use and settlement over time? And, how were they reflected in the archaeological deposits? To answer these questions, researchers examined both architectural and artifactual evidence.

ARCHITECTURAL ANALYSIS OF LAND USE

For the Historic period, architectural studies of land use and intrasite spatial organization can be based on documentary evidence and architectural remains. However, in areas characterized by intensive land use and frequent rebuilding, it is likely that the architectural evidence dating to the earliest phase of an area's history will be scant. Concurrently, although the architectural evidence dating to the latest phase is most abundant, it is also the phase for which the archaeologist has the most information during the earliest stages of a project. Both of these relationships were characteristic of the architectural remains uncovered during the archaeological examination of the Roger Williams study area.

With a lack of standing structures, documentary evidence provided an alternative source of information on the area's architectural and land-use history. Both cartographic and written documents were used in reconstructing spatial relationships among structures and other features for four developmental phases of the area's history. The sources that proved most useful in the spatial reconstruction were (*a*) historical maps rendering the general nature of settlement in the city; (*b*) plat maps indicating individual property holdings and public lands; (*c*) city atlases showing specific locations of houses and shops; and (*d*) city directories alphabetically listing heads of households and their occupations, businesses, and home addresses. The map reconstructions for each of the four developmental phases provided the basis for the architectural analysis of land use and intrasite spatial organization.

The first step in the architectural analysis was the identification of types of space. Several types were defined and used to identify buildings on the basis of their function for each developmental phase. These were

1. *Residential* (R)—any structure used solely as a dwelling
2. *Commercial* (C)—These included the following types of commercial properties:
   a. Shops—any establishment used to provide goods and services (e.g., grocery stores, retail bakeries)
   b. Industrial—any structure that housed businesses engaged in the production of goods (e.g., ironworks, bakery ovens)
   c. Storage facilities—any structure whose storage facilities were operated by a commercial business for a profit (e.g., warehouses)
3. *Mixed residential–commercial* (M)—any building shared by a commercial establishment and a residence
4. *Outbuildings* (O)—any auxiliary structures (e.g., barns, stables, shanties)
5. *Unspecified* (O)—any structure whose function could not be identified based on available historical information
6. *Civic* (Cv)—any structure used for civic and administrative purposes (e.g., schools, police stations, etc.)
7. *Unoccupied* (U)—any portion of land that was not occupied by structures, including both vacant land and potential land surfaces (e.g., land that was covered by water, W)

For each phase, the area occupied by each type of space was calculated by block and for the entire six-block study area. Proportions of each type of land use by area also were computed by block and for the entire area. And finally, a series of land-use maps was constructed depicting the internal configuration of the settlement area over approximately two centuries of development. Using this information, project members were able to make some statements concering land use and urban change in this part of Providence.

A comparison of occupied to unoccupied (i.e., vacant) space clearly indicates that the amount of available space decreases over time (Figure 6.1). This suggests a trend toward the intensification of urban land use from the late eighteenth century onward, with unoccupied space being encroached upon by buildings. In addition,

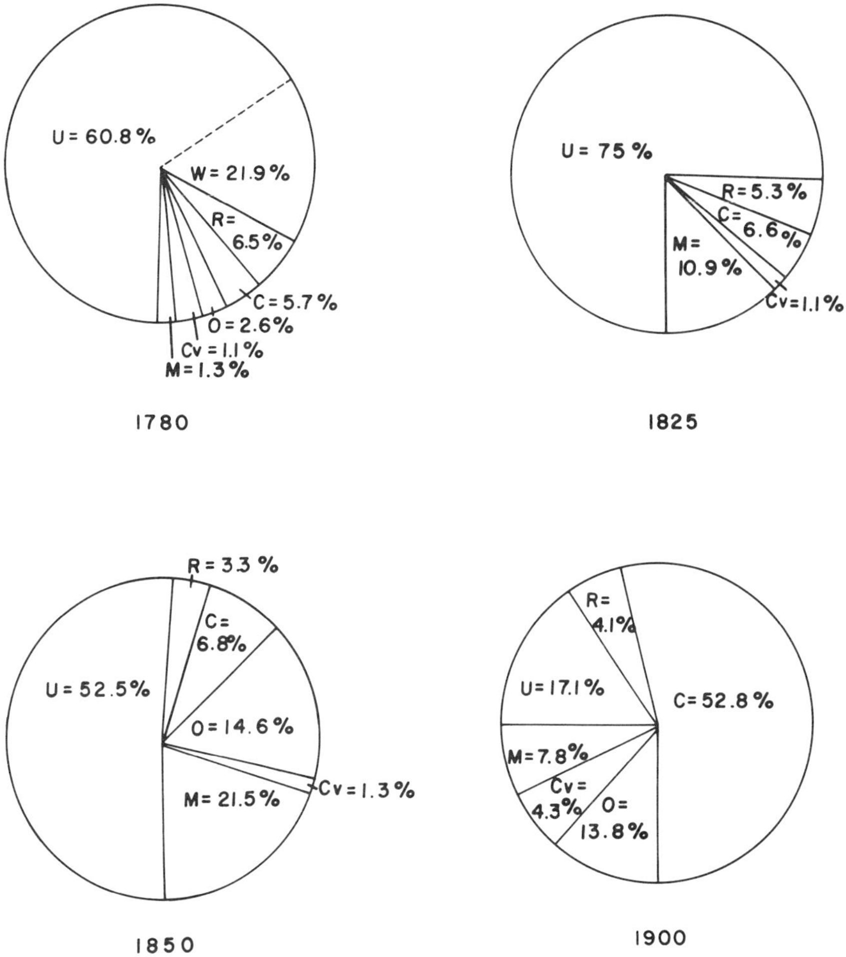

FIGURE 6.1. Percentages of land-use types by phase.

the filling of the western edge of the area during the 1825 phase claimed more available space for development.

An examination of the types of occupied space within each phase indicates that the proportions of residential and commercial land use remained relatively unchanged between 1780 and 1859 (Figure 6.1). By 1900, however, commercial land use jumped to 52.8% of the total space for the entire six-block area. If the proportion of mixed residential–commerical land use is considered along with strictly residential and commerical spaces, an interesting pattern emerges (Figure 6.2). It is suggested that the increasing proportion of mixed residential–commercial land use, plus the decreasing amount of available space, in part may be indicative of increasing competition for urban space and consequent changing urban property values

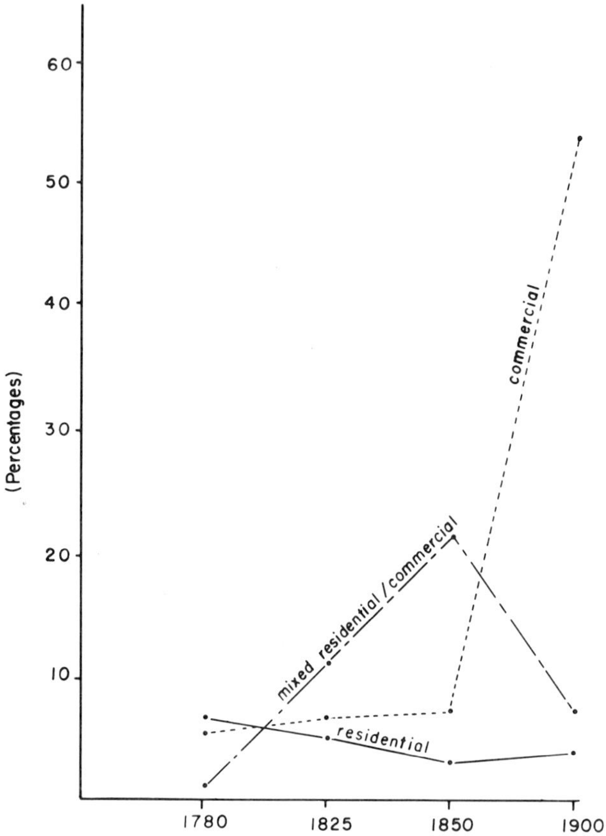

FIGURE 6.2. Percentages of residential, commercial, and mixed residential and commercial use of total space by phase.

during the nineteenth century. These trends usually are indicative of neighborhood transition (Berry 1967). By 1900, commercial land use overwelmingly dominated the six-block area, resulting in a major transformation of this segment of the North Main Street neighborhood.

Using the spatial distribution of the land-use types, one can discuss change in the internal configuration of land use in the six-block area. Early settlement (1780 phase) was concentrated along North Main Street (Figure 6.3), where family residences predominated, together with a few interspersed commercial properties. The rest of the land was unoccupied, except for a few wharves along the waterfront edge of the property. This pattern of segregated land use zones reflects a spatial mode proposed by McManus (1975) for New England's coastal "urban villages" of the late Colonial period. McManus's model consists of a core area, with facilities servicing the overseas trade and its ancillary activities. The core area was surrounded by a zone comprised of local service establishments and residences since it was not

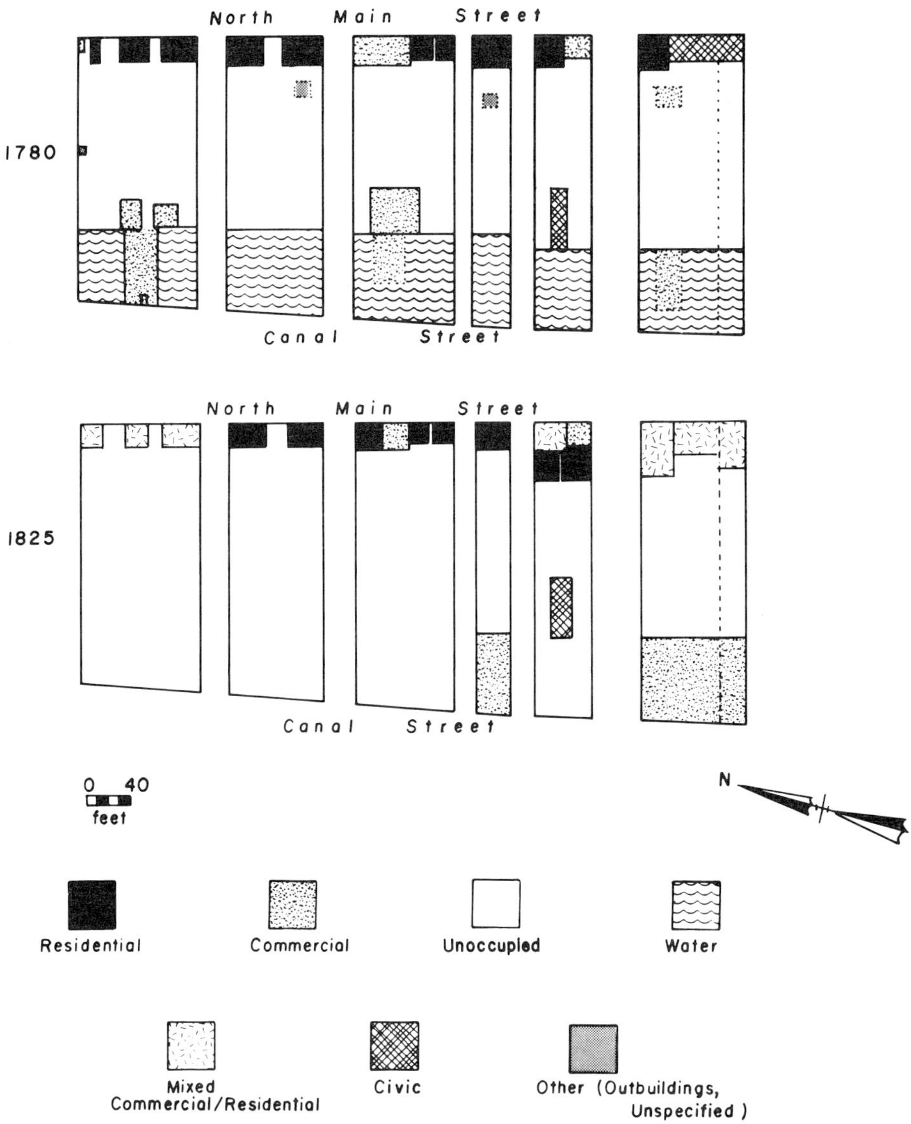

FIGURE 6.3. Land-use maps for 1780 and 1825.

uncommon for these types of land use to be intermixed (McManus 1975:76–79). This pattern of functional zoning continued into the early part of the nineteenth century.

By the 1850 period, the segregation of land use into core area and concentric zones is far less clear (Figure 6.4). Mixed residential–commercial properties covered the entire frontage along North Main Street, which has become an important artery

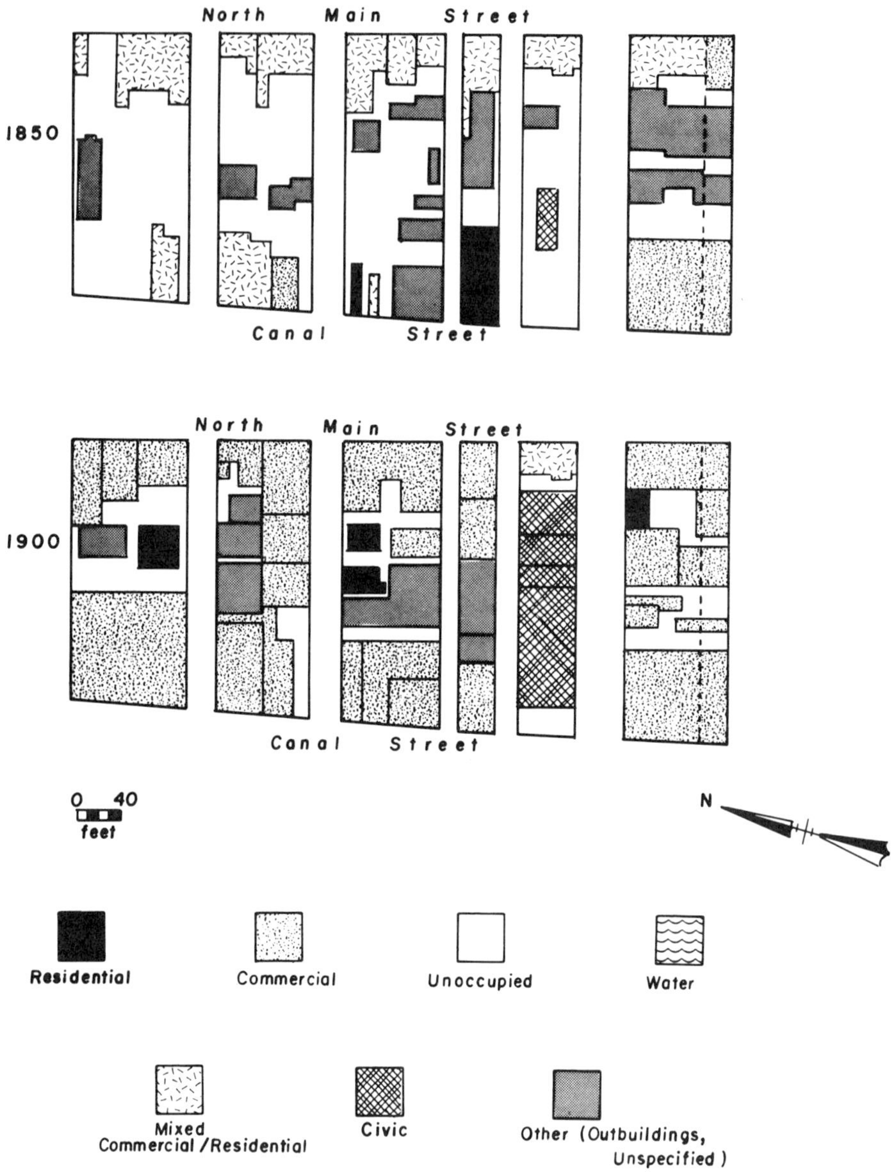

FIGURE 6.4. Land-use maps for 1850 and 1900.

(Gibson, Cole, Thornbahn, Wood, and Stachiw 1979). Buildings now occupy the interior portions of the blocks, and the space along Canal Street is divided into a number of different land-use types. This change in the organization of space within the study area is related to changes that were occurring in Providence as a whole. Prior to this time, there had been two centers of commerce, one being the North

Main Street area of the Roger Williams National Memorial. By the 1859 period, however, the focus of business and enterprise had shifted away from North Main Street to another center on the west side of the Providence River, known as Weybosset (Gibson *et al.* 1979). This shift to a single, dominant, central commercial district affected the character of urban land use and the spatial determinants of the layout of the city.

By the turn of the century, the study area had undergone a major transformation. Commercial properties extended along North Main and Canal Streets, completely dominating the study area. The location of these establishments suggests that high traffic arteries represented increasingly desirable locations for commercial establishments. The few residences were located along secondary streets rather than main roadways. This pattern seems to reflect greater competition for space, which is said to result in sectorization of urban space by land use and class around the central business district (Morrill 1970:165). If these changes are viewed in their wider context, it is clear that the spatial principles that affected the organization of the urban settlement had changed continuously and dramatically from the late Colonial period. The various districts of the city articulated in a different manner, suggesting a more complex set of organizing principles than could be accounted for merely by the expansion of some districts at the expense of others and the dynamic re-sorting of land-use types.

In summary, the quantitative study of architectural change derived from documentary evidence has provided a way of analyzing urban change in terms of land use and spatial patterning. Whereas the changes noted in the six-block study area indicate the specific characteristics of this district over time, they also suggest the nature of the more general changes in urban morphology and internal structure of the city as a whole. It is suggested that different principles have been operative in determining land use and spatial organization at each phase of Providence's urban history.

ANALYSIS OF ARTIFACT DEPOSITION

In recent years the distributional analysis of artifacts has played a major role in studies of intrasite organization and spatial patterning (e.g., Hill 1970; Longacre 1970; Redman 1978b). The assumption underlying these studies is that (*a*) any particular class of artifacts contains different kinds of information concerning past sociocultural systems, and (*b*) the spatial context and distribution of these artifactual materials reflect the patterned distribution of behavior. In fact, most archaeological analysis has posited a direct correlation between frequencies of artifacts and behavior, and relationships among artifacts, their spatial context, and activities. However, these assumptions are somewhat problematic (e.g., Binford 1978; Schiffer 1975). It can be argued that the archaeological record is the product of complex processes of artifact generation, selection, and deposition operating through a series of cultural filters (Rubertone 1978). These cultural processes result in formation processes that not only transform materials quantitatively, but affect spatial patterning as well (Schiffer 1976:67).

Whereas artifact distributions at all types of archaeological sites, from the simplest campsite to the long-term occupation of a city, can be the result of complex formation processes, the urban situation presents a material record that often is more difficult to decipher. Although artifact deposits inside a building may contain evidence for the primary use of that space, such deposits also may provide some indiciation of a building's use after its abandonment, as buildings constructed for one purpose often were reused for another. For example, buildings may be abandoned and used as dumping grounds, or dwellings may be used for commercial purposes or public meetings. Furthermore, villages, towns, and other complex settlements may have more or less formal refuse transport systems. For example, there may be regular dumping areas to which all members of the settlement contribute, or there may be regular mechanisms established for refuse removal to off-site locations (e.g., landfills). In addition, there are potential uses of available space that will leave only subtle evidence that may go unrecognized. For example, open spaces may be used for processing activities or even storage.

These examples point to some of the factors that contribute to the difficulty of interpreting intrasite organization and spatial patterning from artifact distributions at complex urban archaeological sites, particularly when associations are sought between artifacts (i.e., portable archaeological remains) and architectural context (i.e., nonportable archaeological remains). Although these difficulties are not insurmountable, they do indicate that some traditional assumptions and analytical frameworks for examining intrasite artifact distributions are not directly applicable to the urban situation. Furthermore, the classification of deposition into primary and secondary refuse may be too simplistic and even misleading.

Since artifacts, as portable archaeological remains, can provide alternative and perhaps more sensitive indices of the use of space, the analysis of artifact distribution was an important component to the study of spatial organization in the Roger Williams area. However, the analysis of artifacts as a basis for intrasite patterning was not a simple task. The archaeological remains were contained within a matrix composed mainly of cultural fill that was characterized by an almost indistinguishable mass of artifacts. This situation is not unusual in urban historical archaeology. The first task was to examine depositional patterns within these fills, not to dismiss them as having little or no cultural information, as is too often the case in historical archaeology. This was necessary before the more traditional distributional analyses (i.e., space and time) could be undertaken. As Boone (1980:172) has argued, the analysis of depositional variability must be considered in structuring and operationalizing spatial and temporal studies of artifact distribution.

To decipher patterns of artifact distribution, researchers developed a model to account for different rates of deposition in various contexts within the fills. The model includes eleven artifact classes: window glass, brick, metal building artifacts, nails, plaster–mortar, shell, bone, pipes, bottle glass, personal items, and ceramics. These artifact classes are described in terms of their material makeup, reuse value, condition, probable mode of deposition, and expected pattern of distribution among five depositional types that formed the basic analytical units for the study (Table 6.1).

Table 6.1 Model for Expected Distribution of Artifacts among Depositional Types

Artifact	Material	Reuse value	Probable condition in which item entered archaeological record	Probable mode of disposal	Surface	Structural debris	Trash	Fill	Midden
pottery	ceramic	low	broken	disposal	low	low	low	high	low
pipes	ceramic	low	broken	disposal	low	low	low	high	low
bottles	glass	variable	(not recorded)	disposal	low	low	high	high	low
window glass	glass	low	broken	demolition/ decomposition of building	high	high	high	moderate	low
nails	metal	low	(not recorded)	demolition/ decomposition of building	moderate	high	moderate	moderate	low
building metal	metal	variable	(not recorded)	demolition/ decomposition of building	moderate	high	moderate	low	low
personal items	mixed	generally	whole	loss	high	low	low	low	low
bone	faunal	low		disposal	low	low	moderate	high	high
shell	faunal	low		disposal	low	low	low	high	high

(Continued)

Table 6.1 (Continued)

Artifact	Material	Reuse value	Probable condition in which item entered archaeological record	Probable mode of disposal	Surface	Structural debris	Trash	Fill	Midden
brick	—	variable	(not recorded)	demolition/ decomposition of building	high	high	moderate	moderate	low
plaster-mortar	—	low	fragmentary	demolition/ decomposition of building	—	—	—	moderate	low

These depositional types were used to classify provenience units (i.e., strata within excavation trenches) on the basis of the general character of the fill, stratigraphic associations, and architectural context. The assumption underlying the classification of provenience units into categories of depositional types was that the accumulations of artifacts and other debris within the subsurface fills comprising the urban archaeological site were the result of different processes affecting land use and site formation.

The categories of depositional types were

1. *Surface*—These were strata that were observed from the turf layer to above the walls of the buildings or by the presence of a cultural feature. The strata consisted of a loam matrix mixed with rubble.
2. *Structural debris*—These deposits were found within the walls of a building, or immediately adjacent to the walls, and consisted of structural debris resulting from building demolition or decomposition (e.g., structural components) mixed with some rubble and soil.
3. *Fill–trash*—This was material found within the walls of buildings consisting of some structural components and debris that was probably the result of postabandonment or postdemolition disposal activities.
4. *Fill–other*—These materials accumulated in exterior spaces through cultural depositional activities.
5. *Middens*—These were concentrations of rich dark soils mixed with organic refuse and artifacts.

Since these categories are not absolute, they can best be described along a continuum of variation. Nonetheless, it was expected that artifacts usually would be distributed differentially within each category.

In constructing the model, attributes believed to reflect context and rate of artifact deposition were considered. For the most part, archaeological studies that have attempted to account for the *rate* of artifact deposition have focused on factors that contribute to the use-life of a particular item (David and Hennig 1973; Foster 1960; Schiffer 1972). However, recent considerations of the rate of artifact deposition (e.g., Schiffer 1976:64) have indicated that there are other contributing factors, such as the span of manufacture of an artifact (see Hill, Chapter 12).

Variables that affect not only the rate of artifact deposition, but the context of deposition have been suggested by Boone (1980). He has listed size or bulk of an artifact, condition, and the material from which the artifact was made, all of which are closely interdependent. Other possible factors include toxicity, perishability, and accessibility (e.g., nails set in wooden structural components).

For the Roger Williams depositional model, the attributes of material (and its reuse value) and condition were selected. Although these attributes represent only a subset of those that might contribute to variability in the context and rate of artifact deposition, they were considered most relevant in accounting for differential deposition within the fills of this particular urban archaeological situation. These attributes were coded for retrieval from the computer data file that was designed for the management of a large, multifaceted catalogue for historic artifacts (Rubertone and Gallagher 1981).

Material, the substance from which an artifact was made, was considered an important factor in determining rate of disposal since it affects reuse value as well as fragility. For example, artifacts made of precious metals may have a high reuse value. Therefore, items made of these materials should be relatively scarce in the archaeological record. Alternatively, other types of metal (e.g., aluminum) may have a low reuse value and would be expected to be relatively abundant in the archaeological record (e.g., soda cans). Since material also contributes to the fragility of an artifact and subsequently its rate of disposal, artifacts made of glass, for example, may be relatively abundant in the archaeological record.

Condition is a difficult variable to define since the observed condition of an artifact may not reflect its state when it entered the archaeological record. In the present model, it has been assumed that the observed condition of an artifact is an approximate measure of its depositional state. Furthermore, it is expected that the condition of an artifact will affect the context and rate of its deposition. For example, glass artifacts, ceramic vessels, and clay pipes, when broken, have little value and are likely to have high accumulation rates in the archaeological record. Nonetheless, broken glass and pottery can be hazardous and usually are not left on living surfaces or in occupied buildings. Rather, they are removed to dumps or collection areas. In general, the occurrence of whole vessels in the archaeological record is rare under normal conditions of artifact disposal. Exceptions are ceremonial contexts (e.g., graves), accidental-disposal contexts (e.g., privies), or occasionally, living or working space (e.g., special storage facilities, such as vaults and chests). However, other whole items may be found in certain contexts under normal circumstances since these items may be the result of different processes of incorporation. For example, small items (e.g., buttons, fasteners, coins, and combs) may be lost or dropped unintentionally onto living surfaces.

To test the model, researchers examined the differential occurrence of artifact classes among the depositional types. The units of analysis were gathered from limited excavations conducted during the archaeological site examination. From a total of 19 trenches excavated with power-assisted machinery, only a portion of the excavated material per trench level (i.e., provenience unit) was collected for analysis. This portion or sample volume was the equivalent of a unit of 4½ ft^3 (.13 m^3). The number of sample volumes, however, varied from one to five. Because the unequal sample size (i.e., the number of sample volume units) among depositional types would give those depositional types with a larger number of sample volume units higher representation, it was decided to weight the data for the analysis. By weighting the cases, the uneven representation of any one depositional category was eliminated.

The distribution of the weighted percentages for the eleven artifact classes is illustrated in Figures 6.5 and 6.6. In general these percentages compare favorably with the predictions in the model (Table 6.1). For example, shell was expected to have a low rate of deposition in surface strata, structural debris, and trash, and a

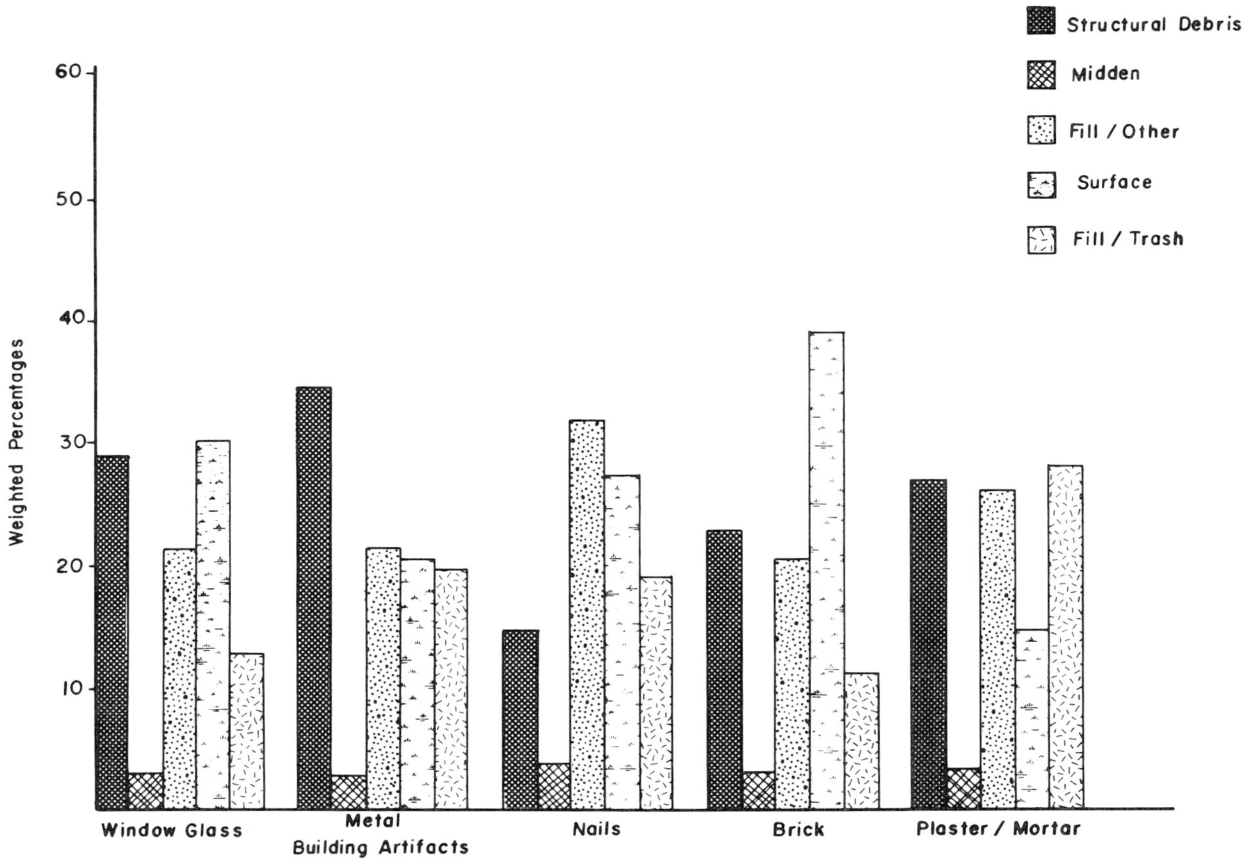

FIGURE 6.5. Weighted percentages by depositional type for classes of structural materials.

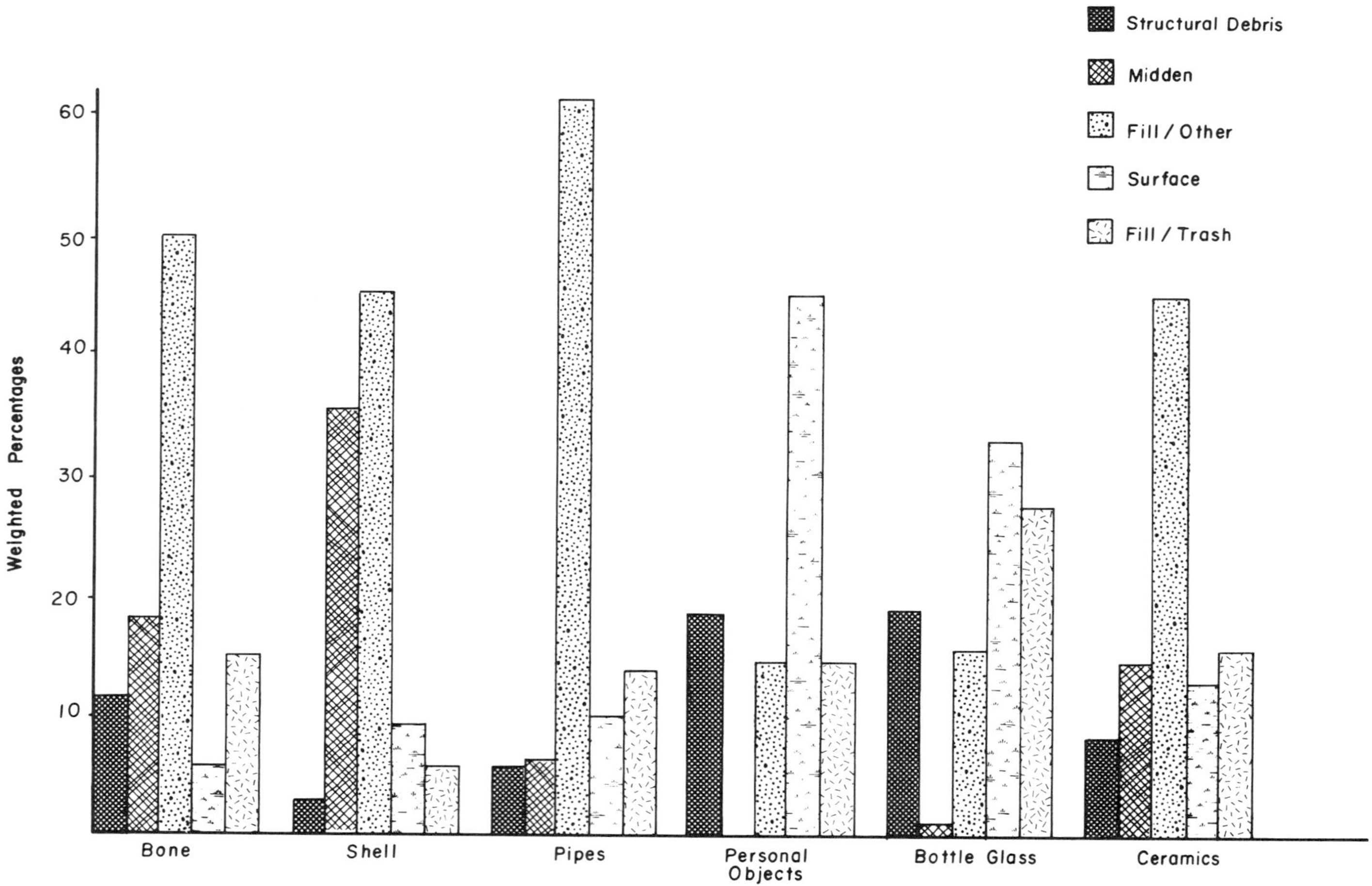

FIGURE 6.6. Weighted percentages by depositional type for bone, shell, pipes, personal objects, bottle glass, and ceramics.

high rate of deposition in fill–other and middens. This pattern of deposition is indicated in the distribution of weighted percentages in Figure 6.6. However, there are several deviations from the predictions in the model. For example, bone was expected to have a high rate of deposition in both fill–other and middens, with generally lower rates of deposition in structural debris, surface strata, and fill–trash. However, the distribution of the weighted percentages (Figure 6.6) indicates that middens did not exhibit the same high values for bone as fill–other. The other predictions for the deposition of bone did conform to the model.

To test the relationship between artifact class and depositional type, researchers selected a chi-square goodness-of-fit test (Siegel 1956:42–47) to compare the observed distributions (i.e., the weighted values of an artifact class by depositional types) to a uniform distribution (Table 6.2). The null hypothesis stated that there were no differences in the distribution of an artifact class among the depositional types. The alternative hypothesis was that there was differential distribution of artifacts among the depositional types when compared to a uniform or normally distributed population. For each artifact class, the chi-square statistic was computed using a program on the *FOCUS* data processing system (Brown University's IBM VS/370 computer).

Although the computed chi-square values for each artifact class indicated that the observed distribution of artifacts, based on the weighted values, differed significantly from a uniform division of artifacts among depositional types at $\alpha = .05$ level, these values were not especially informative since the model describes expected deviations of artifacts among depositional types. Furthermore, the chi-square value does not measure the direction nor the strength of the association. Therefore, in order to compare the observed distributions to the model, one had to add a step to the analysis. This involved comparing the expected value of each cell chi-square with the computed mean cell chi-square (i.e., total chi-square divided by the number of cells) (Table 6.3). This was done to identify those cells that contributed significantly to the total chi-square and, therefore, to the deviation from a uniform distribution of artifacts among depositional types.

To examine the direction of the significant deviations (i.e., those depositional types with cell chi-squares greater than the mean), the *observed frequencies* were compared to the *expected frequencies* (or uniform distribution, Table 6.2). An observed value greater than the uniform frequency would indicate significantly more artifacts of that class in that depositional type. Conversely, an observed value less than the uniform frequency would indicate significantly fewer artifacts of that class in that depositional type. This allowed for the identification of those depositional types that contained significantly more or less of a given artifact class and, therefore, would be directly comparable to the predictions in the model (Reynolds 1977). The results of these comparisons are presented in Table 6.4.

In general, the results compare favorably to the model. However, the relatively high rates of all structural artifact classes (e.g., window glass, metal building artifacts, nails, brick, and plaster–mortar) indicated on the histograms (Figure 6.5) for surface, structural debris, and fill–trash were not found significant for all three

Table 6.2 Observed and Expected Frequencies of Eleven Artifact Classes by Depositional Type on the Basis of Weighted Values

	OBSERVED FREQUENCIES					
	Surface	Structural Debris	Fill/Trash	Fill/Other	Midden	EXPECTED FREQUENCY
Window glass	1404	1306	659	1013	152	906.8
Metal building artifacts	41	69	38	43	7	39.6
Nails	774	476	538	918	115	564.2
Brick	8143	4917	2476	4302	784	4124.4
Plaster/ mortar	1373	2311	2499	2134	369	1737.2
Bone	161	269	331	1188	414	472.6
Shell	895	354	585	4584	3520	1987.6
Pipes	50	26	73	300	31	96.0
Personal objects	50	21	18	18	0	21.4
Bottle glass	1846	1077	1505	963	108	1099.8
Ceramics	1021	624	1269	3429	1130	1494.6

Table 6.3 Results of Chi-Square Goodness-of-Fit Tests to Determine Whether Significant Differences Exist between Five Depositional Types on the Basis of Weighted Values (Individual Cell Chi-Square Values, Total Chi-Square Values, and Mean Chi-Square Values)

	Cell chi-square values						
	Surface	Structural debris	Fill-trash	Fill-other	Midden	Total chi-square	Mean chi-square
Window glass	272.62	175.74	67.72	12.44	628.29	1156.79	231.36
Metal building artifacts	.05	21.83	.06	.29	26.84	49.07	9.81
Nails	78.02	13.79	1.22	221.86	357.64	672.52	134.50
Brick	3915.51	152.32	658.82	7.65	2705.43	7439.72	1487.94
Plaster-mortar	76.35	189.53	334.07	90.63	1077.58	1768.16	353.63
Bone	205.45	87.71	42.43	1082.94	7.27	1425.79	285.16
Shell	600.61	1342.65	989.78	3391.67	1181.45	7506.16	1501.23
Pipes	22.04	51.04	5.51	433.50	44.01	556.10	111.22
Personal objects	38.22	.01	.54	.54	21.40	60.71	12.14
Bottle glass	506.29	.47	149.29	17.02	894.41	1567.47	313.49
Ceramics	150.07	507.12	34.05	2503.62	88.94	3283.8	656.76

Table 6.4 Results of Chi-square Goodness-of-Fit Tests to Determine Whether Significant Differences Exist between Five Depositional Types on the Basis of Weighted Values

Artifact class	Surface (S)	Structural debris (D)	Fill-trash (T)	Fill-other (O)	Midden (M)
Window glass	*(+)				*(-)
Metal building artifacts		*(+)			*(-)
Nails				*(+)	*(-)
Bricks	*(+)				*(-)
Plaster-mortar					*(-)
Bone				*(+)	
Shell				*(+)	
Pipes				*(+)	
Personal objects	*(+)				*(-)
Bottle glass	*(+)				*(-)
Ceramics				*(+)	

Note: Asterisk (*) indicates high cell chi-square compared with mean cell chi-square, and plus (+) and minus (-) indicate whether observed frequency is greater than or less than the expected frequency, respectively.

depositional types. Fill–trash did not exhibit any significantly large cell chi-squares, indicating that this depositional category did not deviate from a uniform distribution of artifacts. This seems to indicate that fill–trash deposition does not result in any particular artifact pattern, which supports the contention that these deposits are the result of mixing. The only deviation for structural debris was in the metal building artifact class. This finding reinforces the earlier suggestion that these depositional types grade into one another. The high values for window glass and brick indicated on the histograms for surface and structural debris were only statistically significant for the surface category. Although the histograms indicated high values for bottle glass in both surface and fill–trash, only the value for surface was statistically significant. This may suggest that surface, structural debris, and fill–trash represent a continuum of variation in which all of these depositional types grade into one another. However, the surface category did exhibit significant deviations in personal objects.

The low values for all structural artifact classes in middens indicated on the histograms (Figure 6.5) represented significant deviations from a uniform distribution. The deposits labeled middens are unique from all other depositional categories in the extremely low values for these artifact classes. Middens also exhibited extremely low values for personal objects and bottle glass. The relatively high values indicated on the histograms for bone, shell, pipes, and ceramics in fill–other were significantly more than what would be expected in a uniform distribution for those artifact classes. Fill–other also exhibited a significantly high frequency of nails.

In summary, the histograms in Figures 6.5 and 6.6 show that the distribution of artifacts among depositional types generally supports the model of artifact deposition and deposit formation that was summarized in Table 6.1. However, when the weighted percentages for the excavated data are compared to the model, several anomalous patterns become apparent. Given the number of sources of error that possibly could have contributed to these discrepancies (e.g., technique of excavation, lack of precise vertical and horizontal control, and postdepositional disturbance), this fact is not surprising. When the distributions of the weighted percentages in the histograms were tested statistically using chi-square goodness-of-fit tests, the results indicated that the method of differentiating provenience units into depositional types was warranted. For example, if units were to be compared in order to make statements concerning activity patterns, either synchronically or diachronically, relative frequencies of artifacts might be misrepresented as differences in actual activity patterns, instead of as differences in depositional types. Furthermore, these results have provided sufficient evidence to indicate differential artifact patterns within the fills in this particular urban case study. If the goal of urban historical archaeology is to delineate patterns and understand the processes as part of long-term and ongoing trajectories of change, it does not make sense to dismiss part of this record as having little or no value for cultural interpretation.

Having demonstrated that artifact accumulations occurring in the different depositional categories are most likely the results of distinct depositional processes, researchers applied the resulting information to an analysis of site formation in the six-block study area. In particular, could these depositional patterns provide information concerning land-use patterns within the study area throughout its history? To answer this question, researchers examined the depositional types temporally and spatially.

Relative temporal associations of the depositional types were determined by calculating mean ceramic dates for each depositional type. Because the relative frequencies of ceramics among the depositional types were variable, it was decided to use general categories of ceramics rather than specific types in calculating the dates. This would eliminate some of the variation that would be caused by introducing rare types into the calculations. The ceramic categories and their estimated dates, based on the mid-points of their known spans of manufacture (South 1977), were

1. Imported ceramics, including tin-glazed earthenwares and imported stonewares (ca. 1750)
2. Creamwares, including all varieties of creamware (ca. 1795)
3. Pearlwares, including all variants of pearlware (ca. 1810)
4. Other earthenwares, including transfer-printed earthenwares and hard-white earthenwares (ca. 1840)
5. Porcelains, including Canton or Nanking wares (ca. 1800)

The calculated mean ceramic dates for the depositional types based on the weighted data were middens (1805.6), fill–other (1814.5), fill–trash (1825.3), structural debris (1825.8), and surface (1820.7). These have been categorized as representing three temporal periods: early (middens), intermediate (fill–other), and late (fill–trash, structural debris, and surface). Given that the deposits of the excavated data can be distinguished into several periods, it was possible to use these temporal groups of deposits as a basis for delineating patterns of space use and site formation for the entire six-block area.

Deposits of the early period (i.e., middens) are restricted to the eastern portion of the study area, bounded by North Main Street. As previously discussed (Figure 6.3), the earliest known settlement within the six-block parcel was concentrated along this street. The deposits themselves were characterized by low values of all classes of structural artifacts. In addition to the expectations set forth in the model of artifact deposition and deposit formation, it is suggested that this pattern of artifact distribution may be explained, in part, by the fact that the activities responsible for these deposits occurred prior to major building demolition in the area. However, other factors also may have been operative. Although not statistically significant, the histograms indicated a relatively high value for shell. This, plus the fact that all midden deposits occurred in exterior loci, suggests that these deposits represent unique depositional events, especially since shell often was used to facilitate drainage (Rubertone and Gallagher 1981).

Deposits that can be dated to the intermediate period (i.e., fill–other), when examined in terms of their location within the study area, occurred primarily in the eastern and east-central portions. Only three provenience units of this depositional type were located near the western end of the area. It is suggested that these deposits can be correlated roughly with the developments that occurred in the area during the first half of the nineteenth century (Figures 6.3 and 6.4). During this time, settlement within the parcel was still concentrated along North Main Street, with the central areas open except for a few outbuildings or unspecified structures. The deposits are characterized by high values of bone, shell, ceramics, and pipes and are found primarily in exterior loci (e.g., streets and yards) or below floors of buildings. Accumulations of these common refuse materials may be used to infer increasing amounts of secondary refuse associated with the intensity of occupation (Schiffer 1972:20–21), as evidenced by the increase in mixed residential–commercial land use during this period. Although the amount of refuse output may have increased, its distribution remained relatively unrestricted.

Deposits dating to the late period include fill–trash, structural debris, and surface. It is suggested that these deposits are related to events occurring after the abandonment of the area in the late 1960s, and not to activities during the latter part of the nineteenth century. Both fill–trash and structural debris are deposits contained within buildings that were the result of postabandonment filling and demolition. No primary deposits were recognized within interior spaces. It is suggested that the deposits classified as surface, which occurred across the entire six-block area, and not within the walls of building foundations, were the result of activities after building demolition. Grading and filling have been mentioned (Gibson *et al.* 1979:9) as landscape modifications prior to the planting of the present parkland. However, the presence of high values of personal objects in surface deposits may provide evidence of the area's use as an open space, facilitating pedestrian traffic between North Main Street and the downtown area.

It is suggested that the lack of secondary refuse deposits dating to the second half of the nineteenth century or later may be explained by several factors: (*a*) the establishment of municipal facilities for refuse removal, (*b*) the reduction in the amount of available space and the intensification of land use that would restrict potential discard areas (Figure 6.4), and (*c*) the type of land use itself since commercial (nonservice) establishments that dominated the area during this time may have had different waste generation patterns compared to residences and retail shops of earlier periods.

SUMMARY AND CONCLUSIONS

Early in this chapter it was argued that while the interdependence of both architectural and artifactual evidence can enhance the investigation of patterns of land use at town or city sites, the discovery of these patterns in the urban historical archaeological situation often is less than straightforward. Two alternative approaches to the study of architectural and artifact patterning have been used to examine changes within a six-block study area of Providence. The first approach employed written and cartographic documentary evidence as a basis for a quantitative study of architectural patterning through time. Given that architectural remains in urban archaeological contexts, particularly those dating to the seventeenth and early eighteenth centuries, are generally categorized as low visibility, documents provide a viable alternative that can be analyzed in the same manner as other material evidence. The second approach involved the construction of a model of artifact deposition and deposit formation to account for depositional variability among artifacts. This model was based on principles affecting the rate and context of artifact deposition as discussed by Schiffer (1976), Boone (1980), and others. Using excavated data from an archaeological site examination of the study area, researchers studied patterns of artifact distribution within different types of fills. Often, such fills have been dismissed as having little or no cultural information.

The examination of land use and its spatial configuration within the six-block study area allowed for inferences concerning the nature of changes that had occurred from the middle of the eighteenth to the end of the nineteenth century. Several processes appear to have been operative, including the intensification of land use, increased competition for commercial locations, and residential succession, in transforming this area over time. Moreover, when the study area is compared to Providence as a whole, it becomes clear that these changes were related to general changes in land use and spatial organization within the city.

The use of artifact deposition to infer land use revealed patterns complementary to those suggested by architectural evidence. For example, alternative uses of space, such as the use of open areas and streets for trash disposal, were evidenced by the artifacts. However, the artifact deposits found in late-nineteenth-century commercial buildings were the result of postabandonment events such as filling or demolition. Neither primary nor secondary deposits of this period were exposed. It is suggested that the sparseness of artifact deposits may be related to a variety of factors, such as waste generation patterns, social control, and civic ordinances. Consequently, the archaeologist's search for artifactual residues of certain types of activities in given temporal periods may result in frustration. In particular, the detection of certain kinds of commercial activities (i.e., those that do not involve specialized tool types or produce residues that are distinct from domestic refuse) may be problematic on the basis of artifactual evidence alone.

ACKNOWLEDGMENTS

Much appreciation is due to those who aided in this research, especially those whose efforts contributed to this chapter: Joan Gallagher, for her assistance in collecting and compiling the documentary data; Peter Thorbahn, for his advice on statistical and nonstatistical matters; and Alan Leveillee, for doing the maps and graphics.

REFERENCES

Berry, Brian

1967 *The geography of market centers and retail distribution.* Englewood Cliffs, New Jersey: Prentice-Hall.

Binford, Lewis

1965 Archaeological systematics and the study of cultural process. *American Antiquity* **31**:203–210.

1978 Dimensional analysis of behavior and site structure: Learning from an Eskimo hunting stand. *American Antiquity* **43**:330–361.

Boone, James

1980 Artifact deposition and demographic change: An archaeological case study of medieval colonialism in the age of expansion. Unpublished Ph.D. dissertation, Department of Anthropology, State Univ. of New York, Binghamton.

Bridenbaugh, Carl

1971 *Cities in revolt.* New York: Oxford Univ. Press.

Cady, John H.

1957 *The civic and architectural development at Providence, 1636–1950.* Providence, R.I.: The Book Shop.

Cook, Edward M.

1976 *The fathers of the town.* Baltimore, Md.: The Johns Hopkins Univ. Press.

David, Nicholas, and Hilke Hennig
1973 The ethnography of pottery: A Fulani case seen in archaeological perspective. *Addison-Wesley Modular Publications* **21**.

Foster, George
1960 Life-expectancy of utilitarian pottery in Tzintzuntzan, Michocán, Mexico. *American Antiquity* **25**:606–609.

Gibson, Susan, Stephen Cole, Peter Thorbahn, Cynthia Wood, and Myron Stachiw
1979 Archeological resource study, Roger Williams National Memorial, Rhode Island. *U.S. Department of Interior, National Park Service, North Atlantic Regional Office, Cultural Resource Management Study* **1**.

Hill, James
1970 Broken-K pueblo: Prehistoric social organization in the American Southwest. *University of Arizona Anthropological Papers* **18**.

Longacre, William
1970 Archaeology as anthropology: A case study. *Univ. of Arizona Anthropological Papers* **17**.

McManus, Douglas R.
1975 *Colonial New England: A historical geography*. New York: Oxford Univ. Press.

Morrill, Richard
1970 *Spatial organization of society*. Belmont, Calif.: Wadsworth.

Redman, Charles L.
1978a Multivariate artifact analysis: A basis for multidimensional interpretations. In *Social archaeology: Beyond subsistence and dating*, edited by Charles L. Redman, M. J. Berman, E. V. Curtin, W. T. Langhorne, Jr., N. M. Versaggi, J. C. Wanser. New York: Academic Press. Pp. 159–192.
1978b Investigating complex settlement structures. Paper presented at the symposium on *Spatial Analysis in Archaeology*, held at Binghamton, New York, October 1978.

Redman, Charles L., and Ronald D. Anzalone
1980 Discovering architectural patterning at a complex site. *American Antiquity* **45**:284–290.

Reynolds, H. T.
1977 *Analysis of nominal data*. Beverly Hills, Calif.: Sage.

Rubertone, Patricia E.
1978 Social organization in an Islamic town: A behavioral explanation of ceramic variability. Unpublished Ph.D. dissertation, Department of Anthropology, State Univ. of New York, Binghamton.

Rubertone, Patricia E., and Joan Gallagher
1981 Archaeological site examination: A case study in urban archaeology. Roger Williams National Memorial. *U.S. Department of Interior, National Park Service, North Atlantic Regional Office, Cultural Resource Management Study* **4**.

Schiffer, Michael B.
1972 Archaeological context and systemic context. *American Antiquity* **37**:156–165.
1975 Behavioral chain analysis: Activities, organization, and the use of space. In *Chapters in the prehistory of eastern Arizona IV*, edited by P. Martin *et al. Anthropology* **65**. Chicago: Fieldiana. Pp. 103–119.
1976 *Behavioral archaeology*. New York: Academic Press.

Siegel, Sidney
1956 *Nonparametric statistics for the behavioral sciences*. New York: McGraw Hill.

South, Stanley
1977 *Method and theory in historical archeology*. New York: Academic Press.

7

The Core–Periphery Relationship and the Archaeological Record in Alexandria, Virginia[1]

Pamela J. Cressey
John F. Stephens
Steven J. Shephard
Barbara H. Magid

It is a complex task to interpret archaeological materials in an historic city-site. Analyzing artifacts from different excavation areas is difficult because of the quantity and technological variety of nineteenth-century items. Although patterns within the archaeological data abound, their meaning may not be clear. The density and mobility of urban populations make it difficult to assign ownership of artifact assemblages to particular individuals or households. This is why we need a conceptual scheme for interpreting the patterns from different excavation localities in relationship to one another and collectively throughout the city-site. The Core–Periphery Model is proposed here as a construct within which these urban patterns may be elucidated.

The core–periphery relationship, represented in both the settlement and artifact patterns of the city-site over time, explains observed patterns and permits them to be compared within the same analytical construct. We shall look at three politicoeconomic sectors of a city-site—the core, the semiperiphery, and the periphery. Then, it will be possible to compare material patterns within and between functional urban areas. Since the Core–Periphery Model describes settlement and artifact patterns simultaneously, it facilitates a holistic interpretation of two data sets that have resulted from separate aspects of the same empirical reality.

[1]The City of Alexandria, the National Endowment for the Humanities, the U.S. Department of the Interior, and the Virginia Historic Landmarks Commission have supported the research presented in this chapter.

ISBN 0-12-214980-7

The analytical integration of the two data sets makes it possible to perceive this reality on a higher interpretative plane than would be possible with either alone.

The purpose of this chapter is to examine the applicability of the Core–Periphery Model for providing information that can be used as an independent test of urban behavioral phenomena. The independent archaeological context offers a material reflection of empirical reality. In addition, we believe there exists a dynamic relationship between settlement and artifact patterns, and therefore the data sets that describe them. The interdependence of settlement and artifact patterns constitutes a dialectical relationship between material and historical reality. The patterns do not develop and cannot be understood except within the context of the historic city-site. Thus, the Core–Periphery Model provides a medium for integrating two data sets that simultaneously are products of the same developmental processes.

The Core–Periphery Model has been used successfully by geographers, economists, and historians to delineate developmental patterns, articulating the relationships between core, semiperiphery, and periphery over time. It is now possible to explore these relationships in the archaeological record, where we would expect different material and discard behavior from different politicoeconomic sectors of a city-site.

CORE–PERIPHERY MODEL

The Core–Periphery Model is applicable on a global scale (Wallerstein 1976, 1980), as well as on regional (Friedman and Alonso 1964) and local (Pahl 1967) levels. In the Model, the economic center, or core, contains localities that usually are wealthier and more developed than those at the semiperiphery and periphery. Additionally, within less-developed peripheral areas, the level of economic growth is considerably lower in the parts farthest from the core area of commercial and governmental activity. Restrictions on economic development are imposed on groups by virtue of their being located in peripheral areas. Hence, the core's economic domination encourages and reinforces increasing distance of peripheral groups from wealth and power.

Traditionally, cultural geographers have referred to a "core–hinterland" relationship (e.g., Chorley and Haggett 1967). This usually is a functional relationship between lowlands and uplands or between urban and rural. The differences between cores and hinterlands are reflected in material culture. In general, the density, variety, and accessibility of material culture is greater in core areas, where there are politicoeconomic centers of more intensive activity.

The core–periphery relationship within any city-site is not static. With changing settlement patterns and economic development, the core expands or contracts, the semiperiphery becomes less or more distant from wealth and power, and the periphery experiences cycles of greater and lesser activity. Within a city-site, the politicoeconomic sectors do not always develop uniformly. Rather, development usually is spread unevenly over the extent of the city-site, centralizing at the core (or core-related points), or along corridors at certain times.

The terms *core* and *periphery* are more than descriptions of geographic location (Friedman and Alonso 1964; Wallerstein 1976). They connote a set of structural relationships that hold the peripheral areas in subordination to the politicoeconomic center. Chief among these relationships is the exploitation of available marine, agricultural, material, and physical resources, and resulting control and assimilation of the peripheral areas. In addition, the core enjoys a monopolistic advantage in commerce that guarantees the flow of sales revenues and taxes from the periphery. Therefore, in the core, specialized land uses—financial, governmental, and large-scale commercial—occur. Operating from a semiperipheral position, business and governmental functionaries serve as intermediaries between core and periphery. In semiperipheral areas, the core–periphery gradient is reflected in core-related economic activities and political subordination. In peripheral areas, marginal retailers and landlords engage in lower-level economic activities, concentrated at nodal points on the transportation network.

The structural relationships between core and periphery can be clarified with an appropriate example—economic centralization. Since capital flows from the periphery to the core in the form of goods and services, taxes, interest, and rents, the core invests the surplus in strategic areas in order to further its competitive advantages. The core invests in construction along transportation corridors, creating clusters of activity and spaces between the clusters. The core also establishes trade and administrative centers within these clusters, thereby strengthening its politicoeconomic control over the resources and occupants of peripheral areas. As a result, the gap between wealth and poverty widens, accentuating material differences between core and peripheral groups.

Two expressions of the core–periphery relationship are especially relevant to the Alexandria city-site. First, the peripheral location of poor whites and Afro-Americans permitted them to maintain distinctive cultural institutions. They were able to resist incorporation into the city's politicoeconomic system, the social order that it represented, and its waterfront-centered lifeways. Although the merchant community possessed superior economic power and bureaucratic organization, it lacked an economic incentive to assimilate the poorest and least developed areas of the city-site. On the other hand, it was advantageous for the core to maintain low-rent and low-income sectors to insure a steady supply of inexpensive labor (Hechter 1975, 1976, 1978).

Second, the economic centralization of the city-site produced both strengths and weaknesses. Its strength lay in superior economic technology and organization, which guaranteed the flow of revenues and surplus from the periphery to the core. Its weakness lay in the fact that major investment projects and bureaucratic operations came to absorb excessive profits relative to neighboring cities. An inability to compete successfully with Baltimore, Washington, and Richmond not only reduced Alexandria's profits, but it also raised the costs of local investment and production. This is a major reason for Alexandria's lower economic position than other Mid-Atlantic cities.

The Core–Periphery Model describes patterns that differentiate functional areas within a city-site. Requiring spatial delineation based on archival data, the Core–Periphery Model describes changes in settlement patterns resulting from differential access to wealth and power. The relationship between core and periphery articulates this patterned reality without necessarily explaining it. Thus, the Core–Periphery Model can be used most powerfully in conjunction with conflict and stratification theory.

The Core–Periphery Model is an important tool for archaeologists because excavation sites (and their occupants) are located not only in terms of *distance from center* of the city-site, but also in terms of *distance from power*. The archaeologist benefits in several ways:

1. Excavation sites can be selected by affiliation with politicoeconomic sectors, allowing artifacts to be interpreted within a total historical system and issues of socioeconomic organization to be addressed without having to excavate the whole city-site.
2. The sectoralization process by which a city specializes in terms of land use and ethnic–socioeconomic residential location can be studied archaeologically, and the results can be used to test theories of urban development.
3. A context is provided within which to examine artifact patterns in relation to status areas and groups described along the core–periphery gradient, thereby eliminating a concern for identifying artifacts with particular individuals.

We expect that material and discard patterns should differ between core and periphery just as the residential patterns of ethnic–socioeconomic groups differ.

THE CORE–PERIPHERY RELATIONSHIP IN ALEXANDRIA

The core–periphery relationship can be studied at different levels. These levels descend from the world-system to a city-system in which core–periphery relationships are nested. The terms *core, semiperiphery*, and *periphery* can be applied in either a broad or a circumscribed manner.

If the broader scale is used, two distinct sections emerge for the historic city-site of Alexandria (see Figure 3.5, p. 51). The historic core area contrasts spatially and functionally with the western periphery. The historic core is a center of relatively dense population and concentrated wealth. The western periphery, which until quite recently was sparsely populated and undeveloped, has been oriented toward agriculture and the transportation networks that link it to the core area. Until recently, the periphery consisted of large farms and plantations that acted as centers of intensive domestic occupation. Additional development of the western periphery focused on mills, light industry, and taverns located at the environmental and transportation nodes that benefited that use. The historic core area, situated on the Potomac River floodplain, has always enjoyed an advantage over the peripheral uplands because of its better access to trade routes and maritime resources. These sections have been linked together by commercial corridors such as roads, rail lines, a canal, trolley lines, and most recently, interstate highways. Yet the sections retained their unique character through the early twentieth century. The historic core functioned as an urban commercial center, and the western periphery was primarily an agricultural area crisscrossed by major transportation arteries.

If a smaller, circumscribed scale is used, the historic core area can be subdivided into its own core, semiperiphery, and periphery, corresponding to politicoeconomic sectors of the urban section of the city-site. This is the scale we are now employing in our study of Alexandria's urban developmental patterns. Hence, the terms *historic core area* and *historic city-site* are being used interchangeably in our present analysis.

The politicoeconomic sectors and residential areas of the historic core area change over time in relation to group dynamics, demographic trends, economic cycles, financial decisions, and technological innovations. To assign archaeological sites to their respective sectors, we must delineate them within the whole city-site. After placing the archaeological sites within their proper geohistorical boundaries, we then identify the successive stages of sector formation reflected in the archival record. Thus, we can place the archaeological localities and the sectors they represent, regardless of their synchronic or diachronic character, along an urban developmental continuum. The core–periphery designations describe the relationship between sectors and localities within them, portraying the city's developmental processes through such relationships (Woods and Kennedy 1962). In so doing, archaeological interpretation is inextricably bound to larger urban issues that arise from economic, technological, and demographic change.

Investigation of Alexandria's politicoeconomic sectors and status-related residential areas from 1770 to 1890 has been the major activity of Phase I of the Alexandria Urban Archaeology Program. The methods for conducting this city-wide survey are outlined elsewhere (Cressey and Stephens, Chapter 3). Using a 20-year interval, the city's tax assessment rolls are sampled by a random, stratified technique. The data are then cross-referenced with the relevant census or city directory. Although the data on sector formation extend back to 1750, it is difficult to include that year in the survey sample because of its meager documentation. The result of the documentary survey is a graphic portrait of sector formation in the historic city-site.

The 20-year intervals can be grouped into analytical units that reflect North American urban developmental patterns in economic and material life. The relevant analytical time periods are (*a*) Mercantile Capitalism (mid-eighteenth century), (*b*) Indigenous Commercial Capitalism (late eighteenth to mid-nineteenth century), and (*c*) Industrial Capitalism (mid–late nineteenth century to early twentieth century). We are predicting that the settlement and artifact patterns will differ from one analytical period to the next. These differences should reflect a restructuring of spatial and socioeconomic organization, resulting from the capitalist transformation of North American life.

Although the settlement patterns derived from the city-wide documentary survey can be articulated for each period of capitalist development, emphasis in this chapter is placed on the two nineteenth-century contexts. This is because the archaeological patterns documented below test the Core–Periphery Model only for the early and middle nineteenth century—the periods of Commercial Capitalism and early Industrial Capitalism.

Settlement Patterns in Alexandria

The Alexandria city-site is not a classic "industrial" site; however, it has been profoundly affected by the general economic processes, especially industrialization, of the capitalist world-system. We expect that the Alexandria settlement pattern and socioeconomic organization will conform to the general pattern and trends of historic city-sites in North America. At the same time, we expect local variations from the general pattern, reflecting Alexandria's particular role within the Mid-Atlantic Region.

In the first three quarters of the eighteenth century, Alexandria was a relatively minor tobacco port within Great Britain's global commercial empire. Specializing in the importation of manufactured goods and slaves, Alexandria became, in the last quarter of the eighteenth century, an important regional market within the British-dominated world economy. By 1790, Alexandria was a locus of international trade and commerce, one of the ten busiest ports in the United States. During the first half of the nineteenth century, however, the economic position of the port community slowly deteriorated (Duffy 1965). The factors undermining the city's commerce included the disruptive effects of the Napoleonic Wars on Euro-Caribbean-American commerce; the rapid industrialization of the Northeast; shifts in trade patterns, such as the expansion of tobacco and wheat trade (Alexandria's major exports between 1750 and 1810) into the Mississippi and Ohio Valleys, away from Virginia; and Virginia's slave economy, which discouraged immigration to that state. The new shipbuilding technology favored deep-water ports (e.g., Baltimore, whose rail links to the interior bolstered its economic preeminence within the Mid-Atlantic region). At the same time, Alexandria invested heavily in a costly canal project that provided less efficient transportation linkages. Occupied by Union troops at the outbreak of the Civil War, Alexandria was relegated to a secondary economic role within the Mid-Atlantic region. In the last half of the nineteenth century, the city functioned as a transport and service center for the northern Virginia region and as a residential suburb of Washington.

Alexandria Settlement in the Mercantile Capitalist Era

The arrival of British settlers in 1733 disrupted Native American subsistence patterns, but continued a sequence of human occupation oriented toward the Potomac River. The Port of Alexandria was a colonial outpost within the European mercantile system. Its commercial activity involved importation of a variety of manufactured goods from Glasgow and London, and fruits, spices, liquor, and wines from other colonial outposts in the Caribbean. Ships were loaded with tobacco, wheat, and fish, commodities eagerly sought by slave masters in the West Indies (Rothgeb 1957).

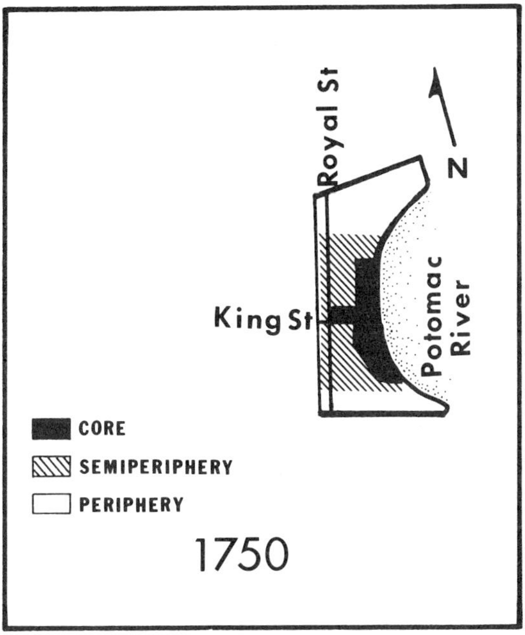

FIGURE 7.1. Alexandria's core, periphery, and semiperiphery in 1750.

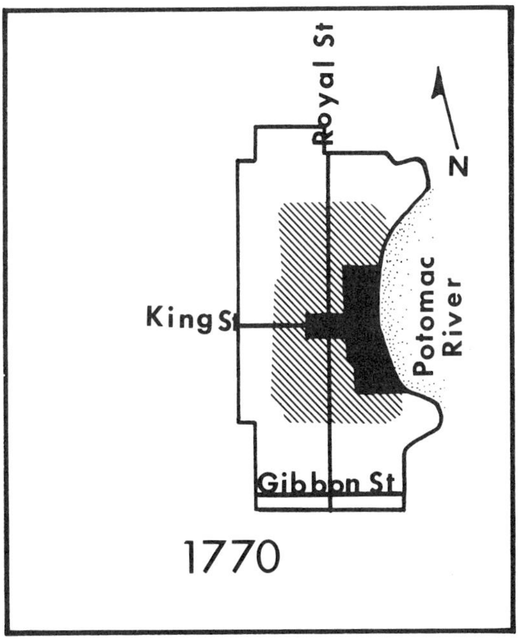

FIGURE 7.2. Alexandria's core, periphery, and semiperiphery in 1770.

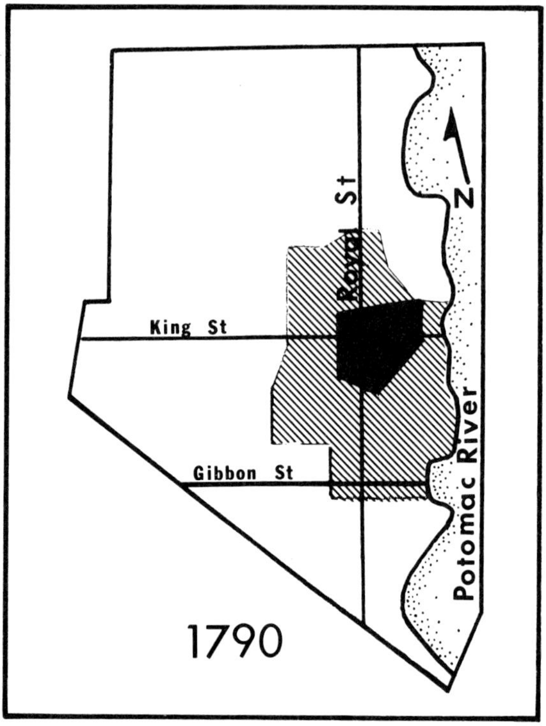

FIGURE 7.3. Alexandria's core, periphery, and semiperiphery in 1790.

In 1749, shortly after European settlement, a 60-acre tract was surveyed, divided into blocks in a regular grid pattern, and cut into half-acre lots, four to a block. In this small area, centered on the waterfront, was a mixture of land uses and status-related residential areas. The Afro-Americans held as slaves lived in the same households as their Euro-American owners. There was small-scale residential clustering by socioeconomic status groups. The core extended along the waterfront on Fairfax Street for two blocks north and south of King Street. Market Square was just one block away on King Street. The most affluent merchants built homes, docks, and warehouses along Fairfax Street. They filled in the waterfront, extending their lots, and thus formed new city blocks (Figures 7.1, 7.2, and 7.3). Middle-status and working-class whites resided in "the Hill" area, which formed a semiperiphery to the waterfront-related core. The different status groups actually occupied the same blocks, but on opposite street-faces, their backyards touching.

Alexandria Settlement and Indigenous Commercial Capitalism

In the late eighteenth and early nineteenth centuries, the economic development of Alexandria was dependent upon maritime activities and international commerce. The city prospered in the 1790s as a marketplace for northern Virginia's farms and plantations, and between 1790 and 1800, its population nearly doubled. In the

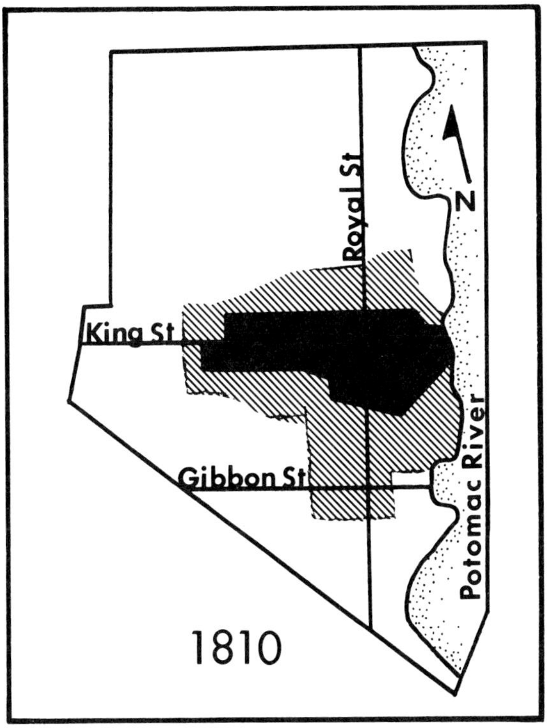

FIGURE 7.4. Alexandria's core, periphery, and semiperiphery in 1810.

1790s, nearly 1000 ships docked at Alexandria's wharves during any 12-month period. Between 1791 and 1795, the city rose from eleventh to seventh place among United States ports (Duffy 1965).

In the first half of the nineteenth century, Alexandria continued to have a jumble of land uses and status-related residential areas. The micro-sectoralization observed in the previous era was perpetuated and intensified with increasing specialization of land-use activities (e.g., maritime, residential, commercial, and light industrial). The core expanded from the waterfront-oriented configuration of the mid-eighteenth century into an elongated commercial corridor reaching toward the western periphery (Figures 7.3 and 7.4). Retail businesses, banks, and residences of the wealthy and upper middle class occupied the core area, bounded by King and Cameron Streets. Most status groups continued to live in close proximity. The microseparation of status groups is revealed in sharp variations in land values and occupational rankings between city blocks (or street-faces).

One status group, the free Afro-American community, experienced a more intensive separation. Rising sharply in total numbers, the Afro-American population, between 1790 and 1810, was composed of a growing percentage of free members (Figure 3.4, p. 49). The first separate Afro-American neighborhood was established in "the Bottoms" on the outskirts of town. The Bottoms evolved from vacant, marshy land into a free black, middle- and working-class neighborhood. On the

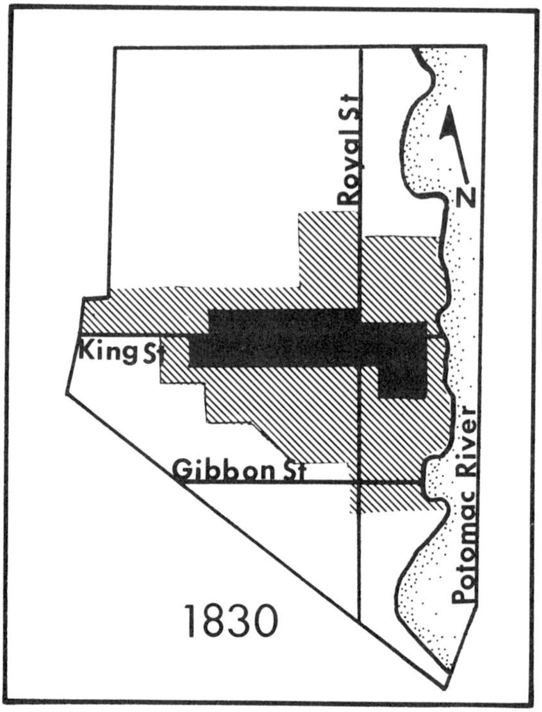

FIGURE 7.5. Alexandria's core, periphery, and semiperiphery in 1830

other hand, "the Hill" became populated on facing blocks by free blacks, whose backyards bordered those of middle-class whites. The Hill functioned as part of a semiperipheral area, with small-scale industry, crafts, and waterfront-oriented railyards. The Bottoms remained peripheral to the city's politicoeconomic core.

During the period of Indigenous Commercial Capitalism, the city annexed new land and added population. The boundaries between core and periphery, and the status-related residential areas associated with them, delineated sectors that became more clearly defined than previously. One result of capitalist enterprise was the expansion of economic opportunities for British immigrants. At the same time, free blacks were situated on the margin of political and economic life, reflecting their peripheral location and social status. In the Northeast, the process of capitalistic expansion attracted greater numbers of immigrants. The Alexandria economy entered a deep recession between 1820 and 1840. The commercial corridor shrank, the number of renters and working-class households living there increased, and the financial position of the middle-class was eroded (Figure 7.5). The process of capitalistic expansion that produced specialized activity and status-related residential areas entered a hiatus. In noncore neighborhoods, the economic climate resulted in the fragmentation of larger properties for quick rental income. Nevertheless, the core dominated the periphery, and the gap between the two sectors remained constant.

Alexandria Settlement during Industrial Capitalism

After the completion of the Alexandria Canal in 1843, the city entered an era of Industrial Capitalism. At the same time, it retroceded to Virginia, whose slave economy discouraged technological innovation. Alexandria never attracted the large number of immigrants who constituted the industrial work-force of Northern cities, and, although it never became industrialized, the city's landscape and socioeconomic organization were profoundly altered by the industrial transformation of the national economy. The Civil War, however, eroded the city's financial and commercial base, and the few local industries (e.g., breweries, brass and iron works, and soap and cotton factories) served predominately local markets. Located at a focal point of rail transportation, Alexandria attracted land developers, financial institutions, and professional, tourist, and commercial services.

The impact of industrial capitalism on the urban landscape and socioeconomic organization of Alexandria was expressed in increasing residential separation and stratification of status groups. The central corridor, with governmental and upper-status white residential areas on the perimeter, was financially and commercially more specialized (Figure 7.6). The semiperiphery, contiguous to the central corridor, experienced residential, retail, and small-scale industrial development. In the 1850s, the Afro-American community formed a concentric band around the core in

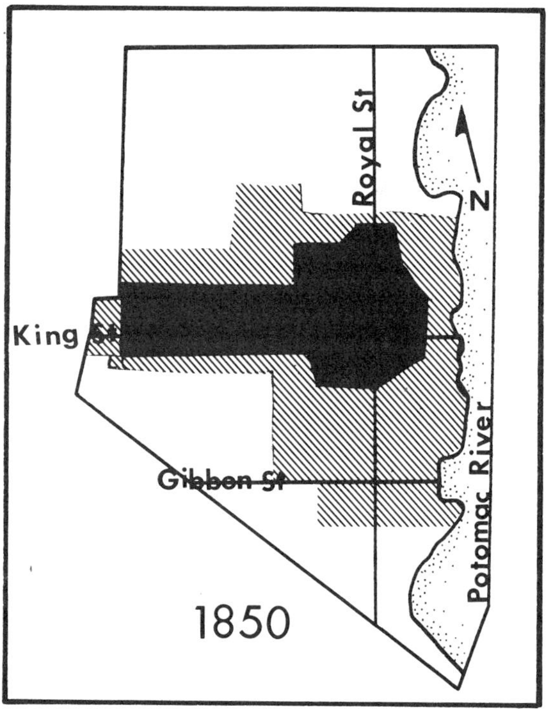

FIGURE 7.6. Alexandria's core, periphery, and semiperiphery in 1850.

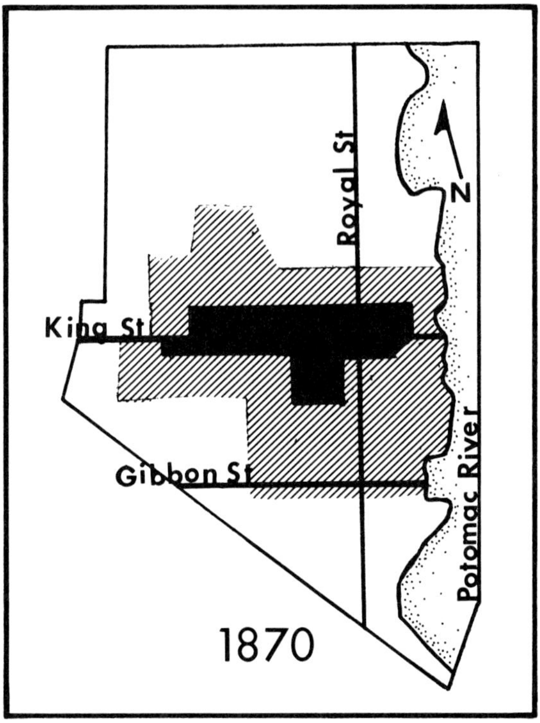

FIGURE 7.7. Alexandria's core, periphery, and semiperiphery in 1870.

semiperipheral and peripheral positions. The core itself was occupied by increasing numbers of upper- and middle-class whites. The upper and middle sections of King Street were occupied by middle-class groups and recent immigrants (mainly Jewish), who were engaged in retail businesses and were upwardly mobile.

In the second half of the nineteenth century, there was clear separation of upper from lower strata, and while Afro-Americans accounted for almost 40% of the city's population after the Civil War, their status progressively declined. Fewer status distinctions existed within the Afro-American community, as most blacks worked as unskilled laborers. Concentration of black residences along transportation arteries circling the core intensified the Afro-American community's distance from the center and distance from power. The possibility of residential choice introduced by the construction of suburban streets and the electric street rail system, reinforced the growing separation of ethnic and socioeconomic groups. New residential suburbs developed on the perimeter of the central corridor (Figures 7.7 and 7.8).

Just as the settlement patterns reflect core and periphery differentiation, so should artifacts recovered from house sites in each of the politicoeconomic sectors. However, the settlement and artifact patterns may not precisely complement one another. For example, households in the core area of a city may not always have the newest and most expensive artifacts, nor the greatest amount of discard (see

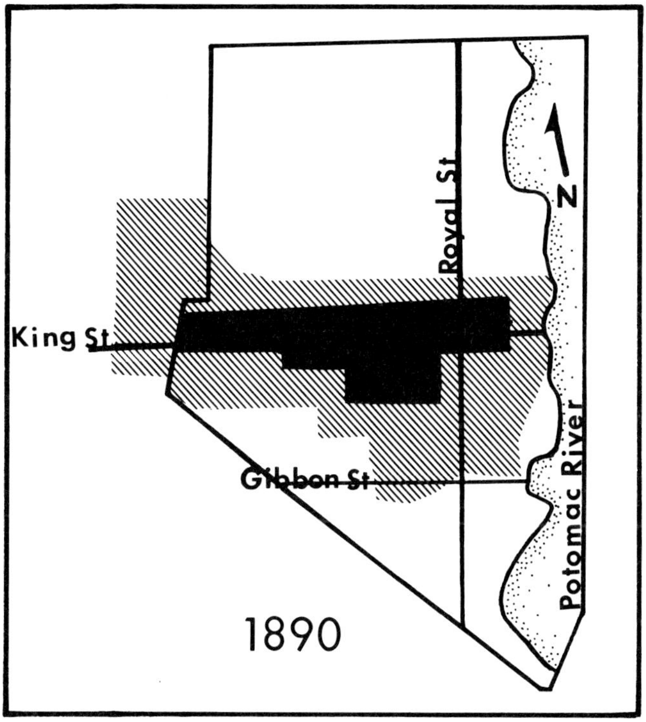

FIGURE 7.8. Alexandria's core, periphery, and semiperiphery in 1890.

Thompson and Rathje, Chapter 16). Nevertheless, it is expected that distinctive patterns reflecting core versus peripheral behavior exist and can be identified by analysis. The purpose of the analysis is to determine to what degree variations occur between core and periphery.

ARTIFACT PATTERNS IN ALEXANDRIA'S CORE AND PERIPHERY

The second phase of the Alexandria Urban Archaeological Program has consisted of excavations on domestic lots in the city's core, semiperiphery, and periphery. The results of these projects provide a relevant material context for the Phase IV comprehensive survey of the city-site. Artifact contexts from these three sectors span all time segments of the study. This chapter, however, is concerned only with a nineteenth-century time frame and tests whether there are differences between the earlier era of Commercial Capitalism and the later period of Industrial Capitalism. The artifacts can be divided into two analytical time segments: ca. 1820–1840 and ca. 1840–1860. Thus, this effort to discern the core–periphery relationship in the material record focuses on a critical transitional period in the world economy.

The Privy-Well Archaeological Context

Two features, one core-related and the other peripheral, are discussed below. Both features (privy-wells) clearly provide comparable archaeological contexts. Built originally to supply a household with drinking water, they were later turned into privies. (The excavations in the semiperiphery centering on free black workers' households did not yield any features of this kind.) A distinguishing aspect of this privy-well context is the high percentage of pottery sherds (approximately 85%) that can be cross-mended into vessels. Thus, function and form, as well as decorative technique and design, can be reliably identified. An additional advantage of privy-wells for archaeological study of urban households is the variety of materials discarded over time into such receptacles. They often contain 50–75 years of ceramics, glass, food remains, clothing, hygienic materials, toys, and tools. Privy-wells offer a good opportunity to select artifact attributes and methods of analysis for studying urban household patterns (see Dickens and Crimmins, Chapter 5).

Each feature was excavated at arbitrary 20 cm (7.9 in.) levels because no stratification was visible. The contents were screened through .25 in. (.6 cm) mesh. Water-screening was used after the water table was reached and dry-screening was impossible. At each level, soil samples were taken for finer screening and flotation to recover small artifacts, bones, and ethnobotanical materials. Although the features differed in construction, size, length of use, and quantity of materials, they did produce artifacts of similar dates. Each feature had components that could be assigned to early-nineteenth-century and mid-nineteenth-century dates. These components satisfy the temporal requirements for analysis.

Dating was carried out using several independent methods. First, in the core feature 44A × 1 Ft. 6), seriation of the type-varieties with known dates (representing about 50% of the sherds) by level produced six components. A cluster analysis (SAS) resulted in dendrograms that conformed to the seriation pattern. A cluster analysis of the periphery feature (44A × 8 Ft. 5) was unnecessary due to the smaller number of vessels ($N=155$ versus $N=815$). It was determined that several of the components in the core feature should be grouped for analysis because of known cross-mending between these components. These analytical components of both features were assigned bracket dates, based on the date of manufacture of their ceramic vessels by ware, type, and variety. After examining the glass artifacts, a final date of deposition was assigned. In both features, the glass dates generally confirmed the ceramic dates, although the dates of the earlier component had to be extended forward.

The Core–Periphery Relationship and the Privy-Well Context

Before discussing the quantitative analysis, the qualitative differences between the two contexts should be elucidated. The privy-wells were considerably different in their size and form. These are important differences that should be fully considered in a study of material patterns within a nineteenth-century urban core area and its periphery. The well in the Alexandria core was dug to a depth of 7.5 m (24.6 ft), far below the current water table. It was made of brick, dry-laid in a spiral form from bottom to top, and represented a large investment of time and money for construction on a private domestic lot. On the other hand, the well in the periphery was only 3.2 m (10.5 ft) deep, and was constructed by placing barrels on top of one another, with clay packed around their exteriors. This construction is similar to that of a slave well at Kingsley Plantation in Florida (Fairbanks 1974:75). The barrel well was easier and less expensive to build than the brick well. This reflects the peripheral status of the lot's occupants, the higher water table in the marshy Bottoms area, and possibly rural construction practices. The two privy-wells are situated at the rear of their respective lots (see Figure 3.6, Zone 3; p. 52).

An important aspect of the material study of core–periphery relations is the analysis of respective *contexts*, as well as contents. Whereas the privy-well context is the norm for the core area, it is exceptional for the periphery (based on information from previous excavations and thorough testing of three blocks in both sectors). Thus, the artifact relationships to be described next are not presented as an "urban core–periphery artifact pattern." The actual artifact patterns associated with these

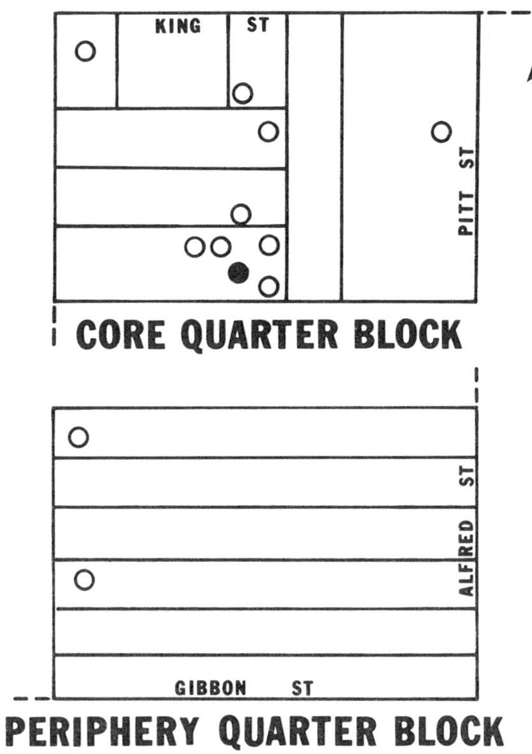

FIGURE 7.9. Brick well and cistern placement on domestic lots in the core and periphery. (Open circles denote brick well. Darkened circles denote filtration cistern.)

sectors must emerge from the Phase IV comprehensive survey. The artifact relationships from these Phase II localities, however, attest to the reliability of the Core–Periphery Model in archaeology by demonstrating material differences in expected ways.

The core has a material pattern of expensive wells on individual properties; the periphery does not. This basic distinction is evidence of the disproportionate amount of economic wealth in the core. It also demonstrates clear differences in material culture, in sanitation and waste-disposal systems, and in access to water and to capital for investment in basic resource development. The fewer number of wells in the periphery may also indicate a communal pattern of the use. Furthermore, the fact that the few brick wells that were built in the periphery were converted into privies and trash dumps in the late nineteenth or early twentieth centuries attests to the continued use of local groundwater (probably contaminated). In the core there had been an earlier, mid-nineteenth-century shift to public water systems and piped-in water supplies (generally pure). Regardless of their core versus peripheral locations, the placement of privy-wells in Zone 3 of domestic lots suggests a similar spatial arrangement of these domestic activities in urban households (Figure 7.9).

Pre- and Early-Industrial Ceramic Patterns

Most studies of artifact variations between historic groups represent diverse situations and archaeological contexts (Deetz 1977; Otto 1975, 1977, 1980; Rathje 1978; Rathje and McCarthy 1977; Schiffer, Downing, and McCarthy 1981; South 1977; Watkins 1970). Other studies have focused on ethnic groups (Fairbanks 1974; Schuyler 1974, 1980 a,b), but it is difficult to compare these findings to nonethnic artifact patterns. One very useful work for comparative purposes is George Miller's (1980) documentary study of price and ceramics in the nineteenth century (see also Worthy, Chapter 13). Miller presents a scale and criteria to measure economic variations. And Schuyler identifies significant material issues relating to economic change in an industrial setting at Sandy Ground, New York (1974, 1980b).

Building on these studies, we have tested the differences between the trash deposits of two households in the pre- and early-industrial contexts of a single city-site. Ceramic form, function, local–import ratio, and price are expected to vary significantly between core and periphery. These differences should occur in both periods and reflect the changing politicoeconomic relationships within the city's hierarchy.

The Two Test Households in the King Street Core and the Gibbon Street Periphery

It is necessary to trace the history of property and occupants to gain an adequate understanding of the artifact patterns that emerge from site-specific excavations of domestic lots. Factors such as social mobility, transience, and household size affected how occupants consumed and discarded materials. These data for nineteenth-century sites can be gathered from documentary records. Following a determination of the location of core and periphery, internal differences within their respective domestic lots must be considered before appropriate comparisons can be offered. One also must determine the activities of individual occupants in a community over time, including their club and office affiliations, friendships, and financial ties. This social–historical analysis can help to qualify the archaeological patterns identified for individual domestic lots at this stage in the research process.

The occupants of the two test households sharply contrast with one another throughout the course of the nineteenth century. Although subsequent research in Phase IV will control for ethnicity and socioeconomic status, spatial clustering of ethnic and socioeconomic variables is the subject of this preliminary investigation. The core is occupied predominately by white, upper-middle status retail merchants. The periphery, in sharp contrast, is occupied almost exclusively by free black, lower-status laborers.

Historical documents tell us that the Gibbon Street residents were much poorer and had significantly less access to resources and power than did their King Street counterparts. The basic contrast (Table 7.1) between neighborhoods is characterized by several factors that are evident both in the early nineteenth century (preindustrial period) and mid-nineteenth century (early-industrial period). The major factors separating the core from the periphery lots are land assessment values, occupations of residents, ethnic affiliation, social mobility, and degree of permanence or transience. On King Street there is high economic and geographical mobility, with relatively transient retailers or professionals renting property for combined residential–commercial purposes. They usually invested their capital in land speculation or other business ventures. Most of the twelve families occupying the King Street property for over 40 years rose from lesser to more prestigious positions within the community. In contrast, a single family bought (and then sold and rented) the Gibbon Street property. The house continued to be occupied by successive generations of the same family for the remainder of the nineteenth century. In addition, while King Street property rose in assessed value from the city's upper one-third to its top one-tenth between the pre- and early-industrial periods, Gibbon Street property remained assessed in the bottom one-tenth of land values over the same period (Figure 7.10). This basic fact emphasizes the increasing economic distance between the King Street core and the Gibbon Street periphery. The distance is further amplified materially by differences in the size and composition of the two buildings. The core house was a three-storied brick structure with an attractive facade, while the peripheral house was a single-storied wood-frame structure.

The artifact patterns that emerge from the privy-wells on these two sites should not be interpreted simply as expressions of elite–poor relations. Other Alexandrian families were far more affluent than those nineteenth-century King Street households. Rather, these people occupied semiperipheral positions within the community's socioeconomic hierarchy, while residing in the core and conducting core-related activities. Compared with the residents of Gibbon Street, the King Street households had significantly less distance separating them from the politicoeconomic elite. This lesser distance from center and distance from power

Table 7.1 Site Histories and Socioeconomic Data

	1820-1850		1851-1860	
Variable	King Street	Gibbon Street	King Street	Gibbon Street
Location	commercial core	periphery	commercial core	periphery
Average property value—house and lot	$3356($3000-$4000)	$195($100-$200)	$4925($3900-$6000)	$200($200)
Property tax percentile	Top 30% to 40%	Bottom 10%	Top 10%	Bottom 10%
Building material	Brick	Wood	Brick	Wood
Number of stories	3	1	3	1
Ethnic affiliation	Euro-American	Afro-American	Euro-American	Afro-American
Tenancy	Rented	Owned 1820-1827 Rented 1827-1850	Rented	Rented
Average number of Euro-American occupants	6	0	6	0
Average number of Afro-American occupants	6	5	0	5
Average number of slave occupants	1	0	0	0

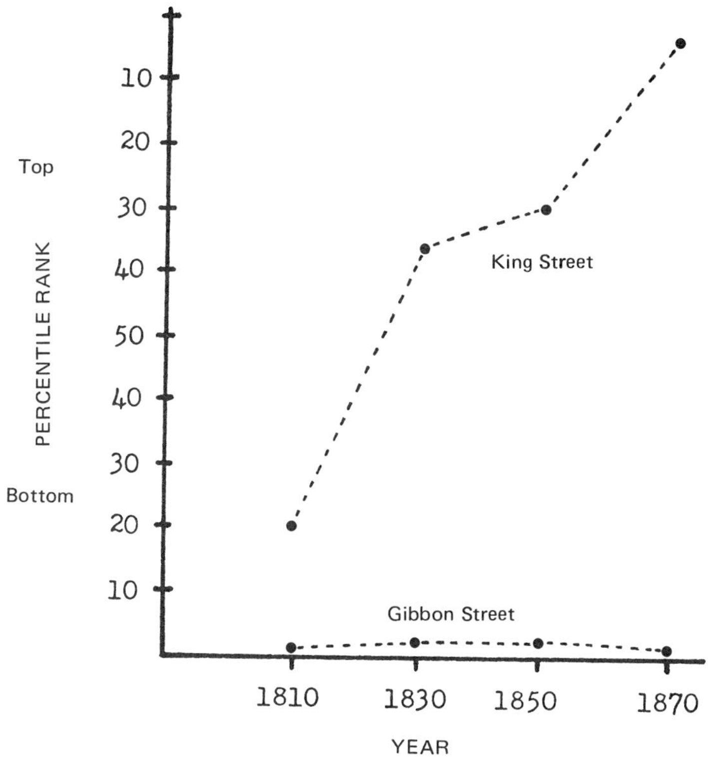

FIGURE 7.10. Property-value ranking for Gibbon and King Streets (house and lot).

was expressed in terms of more proximate residential locations, greater access to capital and material goods, and a central function of exchange between producers and consumers.

It should be noted that it is difficult to determine the actual position of a black family within the Afro-American community. All social evidence derived from the archival analysis suggests that the family was peripheral within the community hierarchy of the whole city-site. However, there are status differences within peripheral groups that reflect inherent stratification. Measuring these differences requires additional documentary research and oral histories. A comparison of this single black family to others in the Afro-American community, indicates that home ownership placed them, initially, in a higher economic position than their counterparts. Yet, their inability to retain ownership of the house and the economic deterioration of the Bottoms neighborhood suggest that the family was downwardly mobile. In addition, after Alexandria's retrocession to Virginia (1846), wealthier blacks emigrated from the Bottoms to escape restrictions, thereby accelerating the economic deterioration of the neighborhood. In contrast, blacks who lived in the semiperipheral Hill neighborhood participated in the city's modest industrialization and were able to improve their economic standing.

This contextual information qualifies the artifact patterns and actually facilitates greater precision in hypothesis formulation. Generally speaking, there should be differences between King and Gibbon Streets in terms of ceramic price and usage. The core's test household should have more expensive wares, more imported wares, more teawares (cf. Otto 1980:9), and more flatwares related to more expensive cuts of meat, served as roasts rather than in stews (cf. Otto 1977:104). The increasing distances between core and peripheral households that developed as a function of industrial capitalism (as evidenced by residential separation and land value differentiation) should be reflected in sharper distinctions within these material categories.

The Core–Periphery Model suggests that artifact differences exist. The contextual information however, qualifies the expected differences. Particularly in the preindustrial period (ca. 1820–1840), these differences should not be as great within the test households as between the city's elite and its most impoverished households. And, previous research indicates that general similarities in domestic behavioral categories (tea, table, kitchen, and chamber wares) may occur.

Patterns in Ceramic Behavioral Groups

Focusing on behavioral categories, we find that artifact distinctions between core and periphery households are evident. Compared to the King Street Core household's ceramics, teawares appear with lower frequency in the preindustrial periphery assemblage (Figure 7.11). Conversely, kitchenwares appear with greater frequency. These differences between core and periphery continue into the industrial period, becoming even more pronounced. Although the frequencies of tea and kitchen wares do vary between core and periphery in the early nineteenth century, a test for statistically significant relationships between all behavioral groups demonstrates that the null hypothesis should be accepted ($\chi^2 = 7.25$, $df = 4$, $p < .20$). As the differences become more pronounced in the mid-nineteenth century, however, we can posit a relationship between core–periphery location and ceramic behavioral groups ($\chi^2 = 27.56$, $df = 4$, $p < .001$). Therefore, when all behavioral groups are considered, there is much more similarity between core and periphery in the preindustrial than in the industrial assemblages.

Taken individually, teawares and kitchenwares (and the inverse relationship between them) may be indexes of core and periphery households, respectively. The presence of fewer teawares in the less affluent household is similar to the situation found by Otto in planter and slave contexts at Cannon's Point Plantation (1977:98). The kitchenwares, however, relate in an opposite way. In Alexandria, higher frequencies of kitchenwares are associated with peripheral location–status, whereas Otto reports higher frequencies of kitchenwares in planter contexts.

Several observations help to clarify the apparent descrepancy in the Alexandria data. First, it should be noted that nineteenth-century rural and urban sociopolitical organizations had different hierarchical arrangements, with potentially different material associations. The differences may have resulted from variances in use, availability, price, household composition, and production in rural and urban

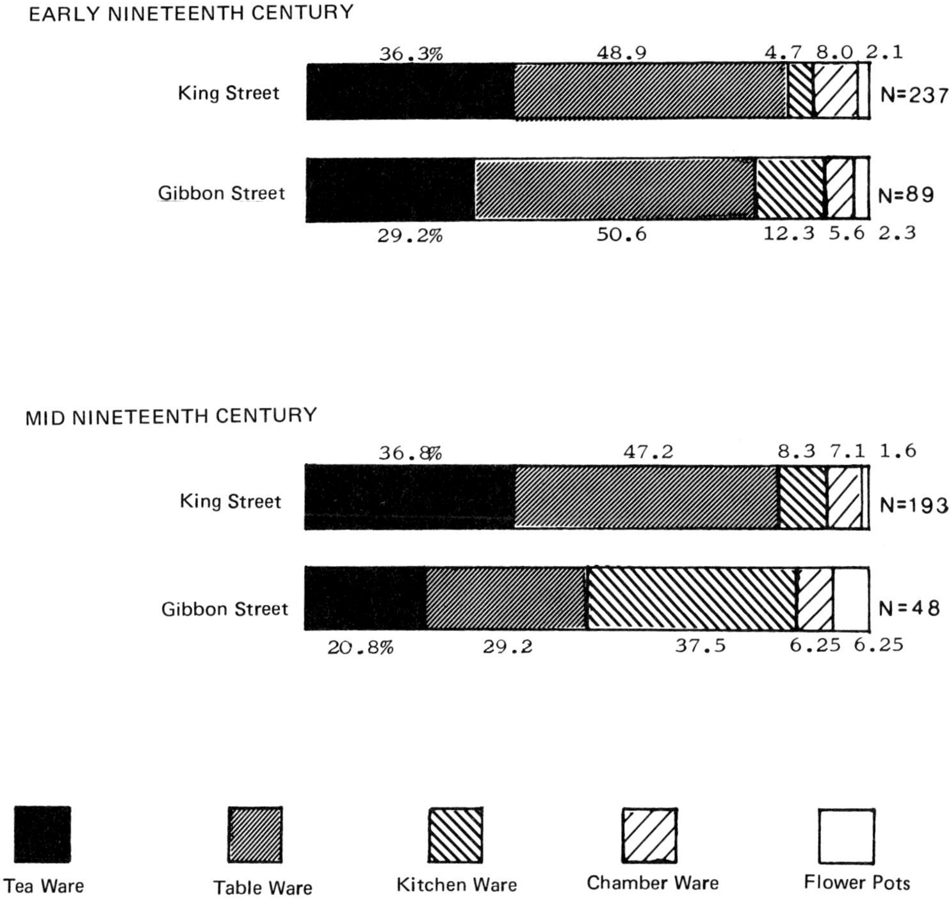

FIGURE 7.11. Relative frequencies of behavioral ceramic groups (percentage of identified vessels).

sociopolitical settings. Second, Otto's archaeological contexts are dissimilar. The planter assemblage is the only one excavated from a kitchen area, which is likely to produce a greater frequency of kitchenwares. Consequently, the results on relative kitchenware frequencies at Cannon's Point are tentative and should be re-examined along with those from comparable rural sites. Finally, two local factors help to shape our interpretation of the Alexandria results. All the kitchenwares from the Gibbon Street site (periphery) are local stonewares. They were less expensive than refined and imported wares. They were also easily accessible to residents of this locality since the manufacturing site was situated only a few short blocks from the Gibbon Street property. In Alexandria, therefore, kitchenware (when locally manufactured) reflects greater accessibility and probably lower prices than other ceramic behavioral groups. This indicates that ceramic behavioral groups should be interpreted not only as measures of household activity (e.g., cooking and tea drinking), but also as measures of access and price (see Worthy, Chapter 13).

We favor an interpretation that consumption of kitchenwares is greater in free black peripheral households because of accessibility and relatively low cost. To be sure, different food preparation and storage practices may also account for variation between core and periphery. There is no evidence, however, of greater cooking activity in the periphery household, but storage vessels do increase from 10% to 33% on Gibbon Street versus 1% to 5% on King Street. It also is possible that more tea and coffee drinking occurred in upwardly mobile, middle-class households than in their black working-class counterparts.

The search for patterns to distinguish core from periphery should not obscure similarities that may occur within the two sectors. These similarities with regard to percentages of the behavioral groups are striking, especially when compared to Otto's findings (1977:98). In both studies, tablewares account for between 40% and 60% of the ceramic assemblages (Figure 7.11). Teawares account for between 20% and 35%, while kitchenwares and chamberwares rarely exceed 10% each. There appears to be a general consistency within the ceramic behavior groups from nineteenth-century domestic contexts. It should be noted, however, that the data from Cannon's Point cannot be compared indiscriminately to the Alexandria data since Otto's calculations included between 6% and 8% unidentified vessels.

Patterns in Ceramic Form and Function

If the use of hollowwares (bowls) is related to consumption of less expensive stews and soups, and flatwares (plates and platters) are associated with larger cuts of meat, then the Alexandria data are consistent with the findings of Otto (1977:99) and Baker (1980:34). Households in the periphery discarded a higher percentage of bowls related to food consumption than did households in the core (Figure 7.12). Much like the trend in kitchenware discard ratios, this dissimilarity in bowl discard behavior increases between the preindustrial and early-industrial contexts. The increasing difference in bowl discard again points to the declining economic position of the free black peripheral household compared to its King Street core counterpart. Chi-square tests indicate a relationship between tableware form and core–periphery location for both the preindustrial period ($\chi^2 = 6.96$, $df = 2$, $p < .05$) and the early-industrial period ($\chi^2 = 20.16$, $df = 2$, $p < .001$). In addition, the preliminary dietary analysis substantiates the hypothesis that different contents were placed in the tablewares of the two households (see Edmiston-Davidson, Chapter 15). Thus, on the Gibbon Street site, animal bones are small and from inexpensive cuts of meat (pig's feet and jowls, ox-tails). In contrast, the King Street site contains evidence of large cuts from beef roasts, pork, and chicken (Wheeler and Weiss 1982).

The quantifications were based on three formal categories—hollowware, flat tablewares, and serving ware. Our serving vessels were not aggregated into the appropriate hollow or flat category, as were Otto's and Baker's. When the percentages of

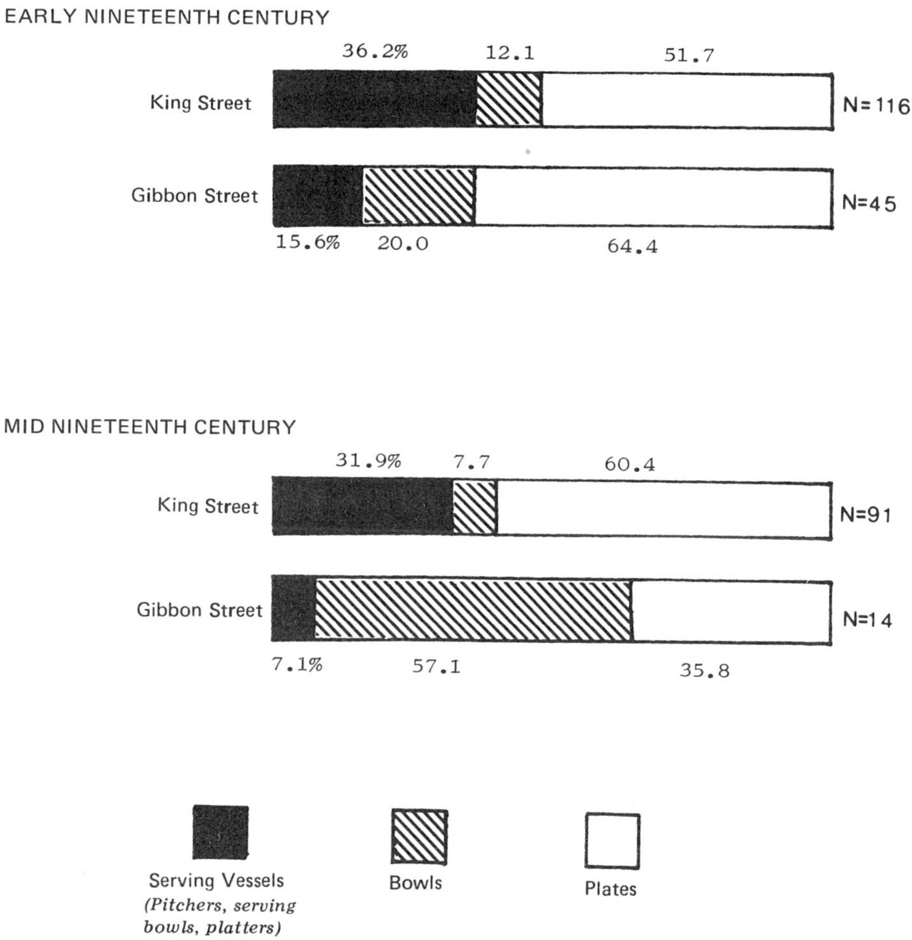

FIGURE 7.12. Relative frequencies of ceramic tablewares by function-form (percentage of all tablewares).

personal tablewares were calculated separately from the communal serving vessels, the relationship between core and periphery is the same as with the behavioral groups. That is, bowl and plate discards were similar in the preindustrial period, but changed dramatically in the early-industrial period (Table 7.2).

Therefore, the rate of serving-vessel discard appears to be a major distinguishing trait between core and periphery patterns relating to form. We have hypothesized that serving vessels were associated with affluent core households. This may be so for two reasons:

Table 7.2 Personal Tablewares

	Early nineteenth century				Mid-nineteenth century			
	Core		Periphery		Core		Periphery	
Hollow	(N = 14)	18.9%	(N = 9)	23.7%	(N = 7)	11.3%	(N = 8)	61.5%
Flat	(N = 60)	8.1%	(N = 29)	76.3%	(N = 55)	88.7%	(N = 5)	38.5%

1. Serving vessels are larger, more specialized in use, produced in lower quantities, and more costly than tableware.
2. They are "luxury" items since food can be served directly from cooking vessels to personal tableware.

Logically, more expensive and less essential items are more likely to be used in wealthier households (Figure 7.12). Serving vessels in the preindustrial period were discarded at twice the rate in the core household (36%) than in the peripheral one (15.6%). The differences escalate between households in the industrial era, so that discards of the core are more than four times those of the periphery.

The analysis of form, function, and behavioral categories of household debris in Alexandria between core and peripheral localities supports the hypothesized differences between the two sectors. Teawares, kitchenwares, tableware bowls, and serving vessels suggest different consumption patterns. Various activities (e.g., tea drinking, entertaining, and food storage) may account in part for the differences; however, in each instance, the price and availability of the ceramic items as well as their contents appear to be powerful explanatory factors. Further study of specific functions of ceramic forms, other materials in the archaeological assemblages, and oral history should aid in explaining these differences.

Patterns in the Origin of Ceramic Wares

With few exceptions, the porcelain and refined wares in both archaeological contexts were manufactured outside of the United States. On the other hand, all coarsewares were produced locally or in nearby towns. Imported porcelain and refined wares should be more expensive than locally produced redware and stoneware. To examine material indicators of price and accessibility, we should look first at the core–periphery relationship between these wares (Figure 7.13).

Chi-square tests support the hypothesis that sector location and ware category are related. For the preindustrial period, the relationship can be expressed as $\chi^2 = 12.41$, $df = 2$, $p < .01$, and for the early industrial period as $\chi^2 = 38.5$, $df = 2$, $p < .001$. The differences in the assemblages were not accounted for over time by the same ware category. In the preindustrial period, the frequencies of local coarsewares are very similar in the core and the periphery. However, porcelain was discarded more often in the core feature (Figure 7.13), a relationship that does not continue into the early industrial period. Rather, the amounts of porcelain become more

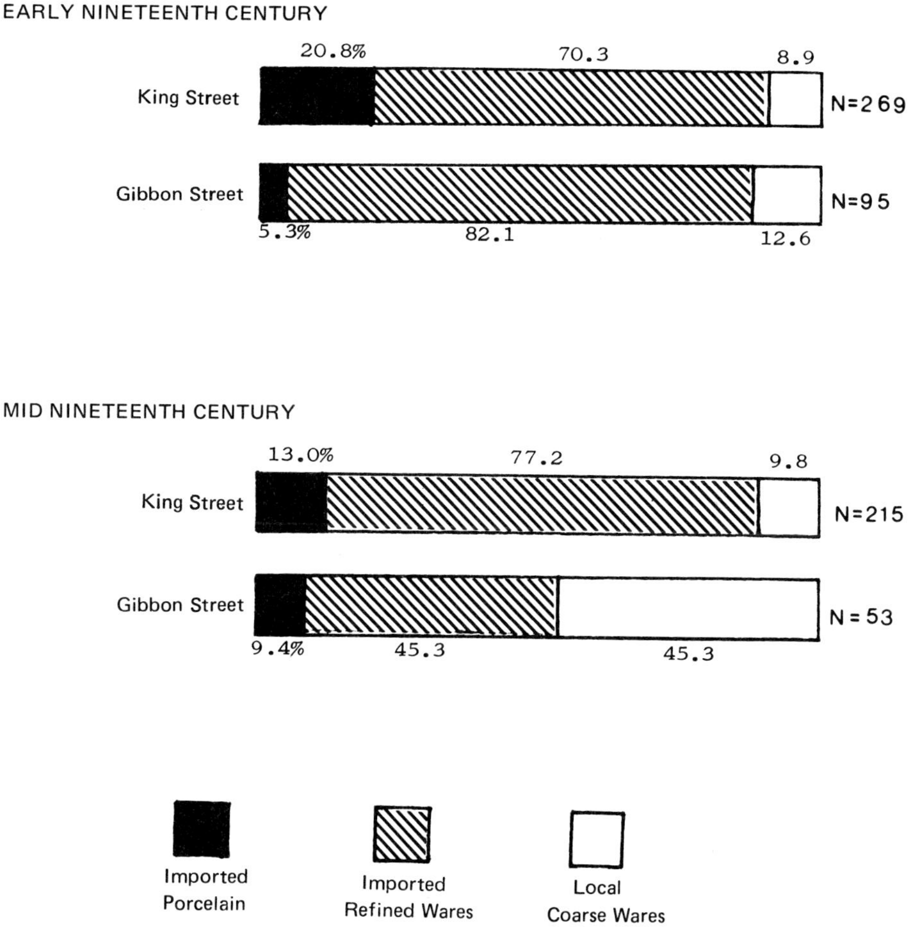

FIGURE 7.13. Relative frequencies of imported and locally produced ceramics (percentage of total ceramic assemblage).

equal, whereas differences between core and periphery increase with regard to refined wares and coarsewares. The decrease in porcelain discard by the King Street residents may be due to the increasing use of refined wares that *match the tablewares* for tea and coffee drinking, rather than to dwindling economic status or changing behavior. (Note that the percentage of teawares in the core assemblage remains constant over time, Figure 7.11.) The use of refined wares may reflect the changing time and function of tea and coffee drinking, as this activity decreases as a specialized entertainment function and is incorporated into meals. Nevertheless, the Alexandria results do support Otto's (1975:183) observation that "the frequency of porcelain does not seem to be an indicator of status differences [in the nineteenth century]."

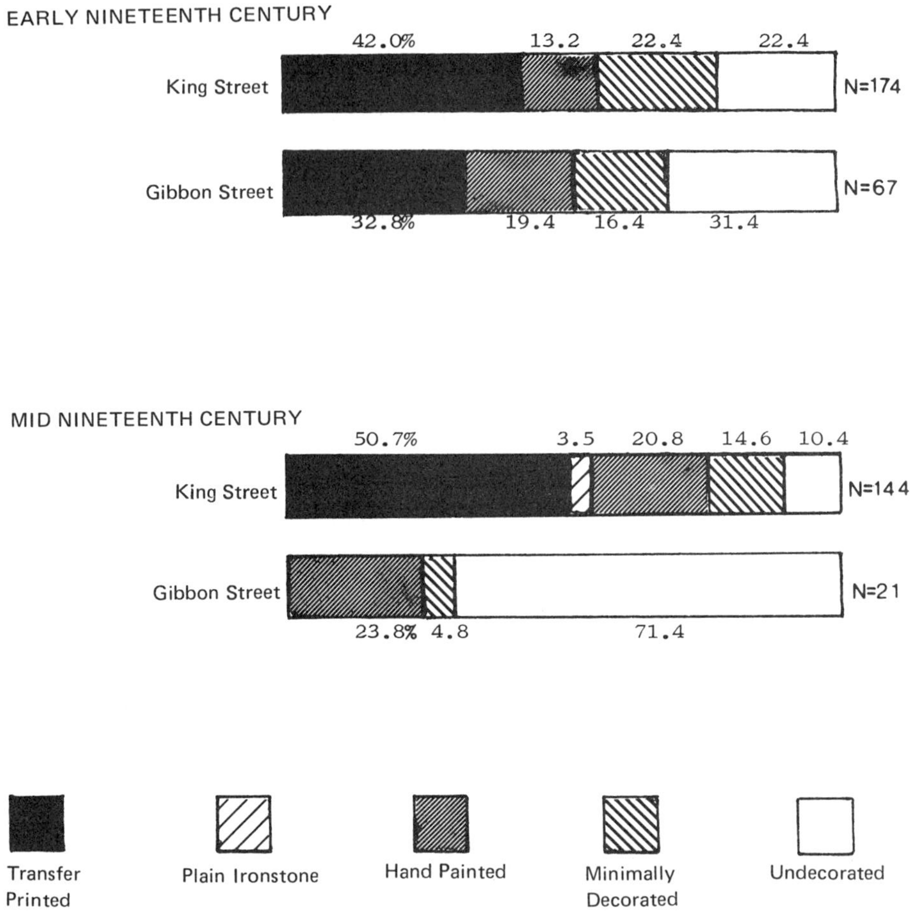

FIGURE 7.14. Relative frequencies of price-related ceramic groups (percentage of refined white earthenwares).

The coarsewares and tablewares present a different picture, one of increasing discard of local, inexpensive wares in the periphery in contrast with the core, where discard occurs in the same percentages over time. Considered together with the Alexandria data on behavioral groups and form-function, the decrease of imported wares in the periphery assemblage is strong evidence that inequality between the two was accelerating during the nineteenth century (Table 7.3).

Thus, although differences by ware exist in the total assemblage in both periods when local ware is compared to imported ware as an aggregate, the differentiation does not occur until the mid-nineteenth century. This phenomenon was previously observed with regard to bowls and behavioral groups.

Although these results must be considered preliminary, possibly skewed by the

Table 7.3 Local Ware versus Imported Ware

	Early nineteenth century		Mid-nineteenth century	
	Core	Periphery	Core	Periphery
Imported ware	(N = 245) 91.1%	(N = 83) 87.4%	(N = 194) 90.2%	(N = 29) 54.7%
Local ware	(N = 24) 8.9%	(N = 12) 12.6%	(N = 21) 9.8%	(N = 24) 45.3%

small number of vessels found in the periphery feature, strong support for our conclusions comes from Bridges and Salwen's Weeksville study (1980:43–45). The dates are later for the Weeksville study, but the two periods (1835–1875 and 1875–1900) correspond to the early growth period of the Alexandria Bottoms and to a later period of stress in the industrial era. Significantly, in the later period, both the Bottoms and Weeksville underwent land speculation, fragmentation of properties, and community dispersal.

In Weeksville, imported wares decrease from the mid- to the late nineteenth century (35% to 4%), while porcelain simultaneously decreases from 34% to 6% in the same periods (Bridges and Salwen 1980:43). The increasing number of domestic ceramics, heavy earthenware, and stoneware are interpreted as indicating "a shift in the economic status of the residents to one of less affluence" (Bridges and Salwen 1980:45.) Thus, the analysis of wares and their imported–local origins can indicate both relative and changing status in a community.

Patterns in Ceramic Price

Previous studies have noted the greater percentages of transfer-printed ceramics and lower frequencies of undecorated refined ceramics in the tableware assemblages of more affluent sites (Fairbanks 1974; Otto 1975, 1977, 1980; Watkins 1970). Miller's (1980) economic scaling of decorative techniques adds to our ability to test hypotheses that relate ceramic decoration (type and variety) to different human groups. The descending order of price-related decorative categories employed is transfer-printed, handpainted, minimally decorated (annular and edged), and plain-undecorated. In the 1850s, plain ironstone prices equaled those of transfer prints. By comparing these rank-ordered categories within the test households, a final test for core–periphery differentiation in the material record can be performed.

The results are similar to those presented for the other ceramic categories (Figure 7.14). Differences do occur in the preindustrial period as the Core–Periphery Model indicates. The core assemblage has more transfer prints and the periphery has a higher percentage of plain wares. But the chi-square test fails to indicate a significant relationship between core–periphery location and price categories ($\chi^2 = 4.68$, $df = 3$, $p < .20$), requiring our acceptance of the null hypothesis.

In the early-industrial period, the assemblages do reflect major differences in price. The periphery feature has no transfer prints, whereas the core's assemblage actually increases. Concurrently, over three-fourths of the periphery feature vessels are in the plain-undecorated category. The chi-square test confirms a relationship between the assemblages ($\chi^2 = 44.76$, $df = 4$, $p < .001$). Again, the small number of vessels, particularly refined tablewares, in the periphery feature qualifies our interpretation. The lack of transfer prints, viewed alone, cannot be taken as conclusive evidence of core–periphery differences. However, in the context of the other tests relating to behavioral activities, price, and accessibility, a growing dissimilarity between the core and periphery in the early-industrial period is indicated.

The relationship of transfer prints to more powerful, affluent households is also confirmed and compares favorably to Otto's results (1980:9). Whereas 62% of planter tableware vessels are transfer prints, middle-class merchant contexts of early- and mid-nineteenth-century Alexandria contain 42% and 51%, respectively (Figure 7.14). In contrast, the Kingsley Plantation slave site records 8% of tableware sherds in the transfer print category and 64% in the predominant undecorated wares category. Fairbanks (1974:77–78) calls the latter "ironstone china," but since he used the criteria of crazing and thickness, they have been grouped here into our category of plain-undecorated. (We place only thick whitewares that are actually marked "ironstone" into that more expensive, mid-nineteenth-century category.)

One more measure can be provided by the decorative type and design variety—the heterogeneity of the tableware assemblage—commented on by both Fairbanks (1974:78) and Otto (1975:173–174). The slave sites have a heterogeneous mixture of tablewares and transfer prints. Fairbanks (1974:79, 90) interprets this mixture in terms of discards from the plantation house. John Otto amplifies this thesis, observing that:

> The planter family appears to have purchased large tableware and teaware sets. . . . Slaves and overseers seem to have purchased individual items or small sets from local shop-keepers; occasionally, they used old and discarded items from the planter family [1975:174].

The situation in Alexandria is comparable, with teawares and tablewares showing marked differences. Not only are the core assemblages more homogeneous than those of the periphery, but the core households also show an increasing number of tableware artifacts belonging to a single set by the mid-nineteenth century. It is difficult to determine whether these differences reflect variations in buying power, use, or discard behavior. To be sure, considerably more artifact vessels from tableware sets were discarded in the core's privy-wells. This appears to reflect the core families' accumulation of capital, permitting them to buy full sets, rather than by the piece, as in peripheral households.

CONCLUSIONS

The artifact patterns from Alexandria's test households substantiate and reinforce the settlement pattern data. Although differences between urban core areas and their peripheries existed early in the nineteenth century, the differences became more pronounced with the initial development of industrial capitalism. The distance between the residences of different status groups became progressively greater and the differentiation between households, as reflected in their consumption of material goods, was progressively heightened. Not only did people come into contact less with those unlike themselves in the mid-nineteenth century, but the lifestyles and quality of life of core and peripheral groups became progressively more distinctive.

The core became more homogeneous, enjoyed technological advances sooner, and discarded material items associated with higher prices, more expensive food, matched sets, and entertainment activities. The periphery also became more homogeneous, with a greater concentration of working class households. As economic pressures increased for free black laborers in the mid-nineteenth century, fewer teawares and tablewares were discarded by them. This is one indicator of the periphery's deteriorating economic position vis-à-vis the core.

The periphery families were in a less favorable economic position than the core families in the second generation. The Church, however, may have assumed a greater role in the Bottoms at the same time, providing for the health care, education, welfare, and spiritual needs of the neighborhood, in contrast to the politico-religious function of churches in the core area. The differential access to resources and capital between core and periphery was reflected in the choices made regarding their use. The free blacks used their resources and capital to develop their church and conserve their neighborhood, in contrast to the King Street merchants, who invested in family businesses, real estate, politics, clubs, entertainment, and the consumption of more expensive foods and goods.

These choices reflect not only the structural constraints of the core–periphery relationship, but also the processes of group formation, conflict, and changing hierarchical relationships in industrial capitalist society. These processes of urban development are elucidated through the study of household consumer behavior and material patterns. Ultimately, the core–periphery relationship, urban organization, settlement patterns, and material behavior should become part of the larger study of the industrial capitalist society, its patterns and its processes.

ACKNOWLEDGMENTS

We wish to thank D. Katherine Biedleman, Thomas Davidson, Susan Henry, Terry H. Klein, Eugenia Luckman, Richard P. Napoli, Sara Revis, Philip Terrie, Richard Wheeler, and Peggy Weiss for helping us develop the methods and data base for this analysis. Special thanks are extended to June Cogswell, Judy Eger, Eugenia Luckman, Vivienne Mitchell, Sara Revis, and June Twing, who contributed their time and effort to the ceramic study over the past 3 years. We also appreciate the efforts of Ruth Baker, Mary Dies, Vivienne Mitchell, Sara Revis, Nancy Sennerwald, and Keith Varner, who researched available documentary records during the course of the excavations.

Members of the Alexandria Archaeological Commission, especially Colonel Bernard Brenman, Chairperson, deserve high recognition for their awareness of the essential importance of archaeological research in assuring proper interpretation of the City's history. Appreciation is also due to the members of the City Council for their continuing support of the Archaeology Program.

REFERENCES

Baker, V. G.
1980 Archaeological visibility of Afro-American culture: An example from Black Lucy's Garden, Andover, Massachusetts. In *Archaeological perspectives on ethnicity in America*, edited by R. L. Schuyler. Farmingdale, N.Y.: Baywood.

Bridges, S. T., and B. Salwen
1980 Weeksville: The archaeology of a black urban community. In *Archaeological perspectives on ethnicity in America*, edited by R. L. Schuyler. Farmingdale, N.Y.: Baywood.

Chorley, R. J., and P. Haggett
1967 *Socio-economic models in geography*. London: Methuen.

Deetz, J.
1977 *In small things forgotten*. Garden City, New York: Doubleday.

Duffy, T. F.
1965 *The decline of the port of Alexandria, Virginia, 1800–1861*. Unpublished M. A. thesis. Georgetown Univ., Washington, D.C.

Fairbanks, C. H.
1974 The Kingsley slave cabins in Duvall County, Florida, 1968. *Conference on Historic Site Archeology Papers* 7:62–93.

Friedman, J. P., and Alonso, W.
1964 *Regional development and planning*. Cambridge, Mass.: M.I.T. Press.

Hechter, M.
1975 *Internal colonialism*. London: Routledge and Kegan Paul.
1976 Ethnicity and industrialization: On the proliferation of the cultural division of labor. *Ethnicity* **3**:214–224.
1978 Group formation and the cultural division of labor. *American Journal of Sociology* **34**:293–318.

Miller, G.
1980 Classification and economic scaling of nineteenth-century ceramics. *Historical Archaeology* **14**:1–141.

Otto, J.
1975 *Status differences and the archaeological record—A comparison of planter, overseer, and slave sites from Cannon's Point Plantation (1794–1861)*. University Microfilms, Ann Arbor, Michigan.
1977 Artifacts and status differences—A comparison of ceramics from planter, overseer, and slave sites on an antebellum plantation. In *Research strategies in historical archeology*, edited by S. South. New York: Academic Press.
1980 Race and class on antebellum plantations. In *Archaeological perspectives in ethnicity in America*, edited by R. L. Schuyler. Farmingdale, N.Y.: Baywood.

Pahl, R. E.
1967 Sociological models in geography. In *Socio-economic models in geography*, edited by R. J. Chorley and P. Haggett. London: Methuen. Pp. 217–243.

Rathje, W. L.
1978 Le Project du Garbage 1975: Historic trade-offs. In *Social archaeology*, edited by C. Redman. New York: Academic Press.

Rathje, W. L., and M. McCarthy
1977 Regularity and variability in contemporary garbage. In *Research strategies in historical archeology*, edited by S. South. New York: Academic Press.

Rothgeb, R. M.
1957 *An analysis of the rise, decline and possible determinants of redevelopment of the seaport of Alexandria, Virginia*. Unpublished M. A. thesis. City College of New York, New York.

Schuyler, R. L.
1974 Sandy Ground: Archaeological sampling in a black community in metropolitan New York. *Conference on Historic Site Archaeology Papers* 7:13–51.

1980a *Archaeological perspectives on ethnicity in America*. Farmingdale, N.Y.: Baywood.
1980b Sandy Ground: Archaeology of a nineteenth-century oystering village. In *Archaeological perspectives on ethnicity in America*, edited by R. L. Schuyler. Farmingdale, N.Y.: Baywood.

Schiffer, M. B., T. E. Downing, and M. McCarthy
1981 Waste not, Want not: An ethnoarchaeological study of reuse in Tucson, Arizona. In *The archaeology of Us*, edited by R. A. Gould and M. B. Schiffer. New York: Academic Press.

South, S.
1977 *Method and theory in historical archeology*. New York: Academic Press.

Wallerstein, L.
1976 *The modern world system, Volume I*. New York: Academic Press.
1980 *The modern world system, Volume II*. New York: Academic Press.

Watkins, C. M.
1970 Artifacts from the sites of three nineteenth-century houses and ditches at Darien Bluff, Georgia. *University of Georgia Laboratory of Archaeology Series, Report* 9.

Wheeler, R., and P. Weiss
1982 Analysis of faunal remains in historic Alexandria. *Alexandria Papers in Urban Archaeology, King Street Series*, edited by P. J. Cressey and S. J. Shephard.

Woods, R. A., and A. J. Kennedy
1962 *The zone of emergence*. Cambridge, Mass.: Harvard Univ. Press.

8

Bioarchaeology in the Urban Context[1]

Robert L. Blakely
Lane A. Beck

INTRODUCTION

This chapter describes a new archaeology in a new setting: *bioarchaeology* in the *urban* context. In the past, many biological anthropologists deceived themselves into thinking that they were part of conjunctive, bioarchaeological investigations when they provided descriptive addenda to site reports. This deception was, of course, but one symptom of a common malaise, revealed also in the traditional monograph through which most anthropologists appeared as technicians or data bearers. Osteologist-anthropologists were, in fact, until recently, preoccupied with counting and measuring "good" (well-preserved adult male) crania, primarily with an eye toward constructing racial typologies and macroevolutionary trends. At the same time, archaeologists were principally concerned with constructing ceramic and lithic typologies and culture histories, which were not necessarily related to issues addressed by biological anthropologists. Thus the goals of the archaeologist and biological anthropologist were, in the past, quite different and, as a result, were unsuited for conjunctive research designs.

Today, however, while some of the procedural tools of the biological anthropologist remain the same as before, they are being put to new uses. The objectives are changing. Following the cross-disciplinary approaches of Buikstra

[1] This research was supported, in part, by grants from Historic Oakland Cemetery, Inc., Marion F. Combs, Chairman; and the Dean's Advisory Committee for the Support of Research, College of Arts and Sciences, Georgia State University.

ISBN 0-12-214980-7

(1972), Peebles (1973), Blakely (1977), and others, both biological anthropologists and archaeologists are beginning to reframe their goals in order to contribute to a more holistic picture of human culture. This bioarchaeological perspective comes, in part, from an increased awareness of the integrated ecological, cultural, and biological systems that contribute to human behavior. It should be pointed out that this recognition in itself is not new to anthropology. In 1942, Chapple and Coon first introduced to the anthropological community the concept of behavioral anthropology and the attendant necessity for a systems approach. It is the widespread acceptance of this cross-disciplinary framework among students of past human biology that is new.

This new orientation is undoubtedly the result of many related and unrelated events. They include Washburn's delineation in 1952 of the "new physical anthropology." He urged that the study of processes should replace descriptive enumeration, that interpretation of population dynamics should supplant typology, and that anthropometry should be but one of many techniques employed to answer specific questions, rather than being an end in itself. In addition, the advent of advanced analytical techniques—for example, multivariate statistics (Howells 1972), the identification of genetic markers on bones (Anderson 1968), trace element analysis (Gilbert 1975), the extension of demographic and epidemiological models to skeletal populations (Weiss 1973), and differential diagnoses of skeletal lesions (Buikstra 1976)—has vastly expanded the resources available for interpretation. And, this new perspective has been enjoined by the invitation for joint endeavors extended to biological anthropologists by advocates of the "new archaeology" and cultural ecology (Binford 1968; Vayda and Rappaport 1968).

BIOARCHAEOLOGY

At present, bioarchaeology is becoming accepted as a viable, indeed necessary, approach to problem solving in the context of prehistoric mortuary sites. It is being used to reconstruct mortuary practices (Buikstra 1972), subsistence patterns (Gilbert 1975), demographic structure (Acsádi and Nemeskéri 1970), and social organization (Blakely 1977) of prehistoric populations. As bioarchaeology has developed, American archaeologists have turned increasing attention to historic investigations in the urban arena. Urban archaeology has come about as a result of heightened public awareness of the need for cultural resource management and stepped-up interest in recent sites and material culture. This movement now raises the attractive possibility of applying the new perspective, objectives, and methods of bioarchaeology to historic mortuary sites, among them, the urban cemetery.

Unique to the bioarchaeology of historic, urban cemeteries is the intriguing prospect of including the methods and findings of forensic anthropology. The combined approaches of bioarchaeology and forensic anthropology are of potentially great value in interpreting the physical remains and behavior patterns of individuals interred in unmarked graves or burial grounds. For example, one could use funeral parlor records of burial plots to identify, by name, people buried in unmarked graves. Dental charts, as employed by medical examiners in modern-day cases of missing persons, also could be used for the same purpose. Trace element and x-ray analyses, coupled with historic records, might permit reconstruction of health environment, diet, and socioeconomic status. Correlation of grave pit sizes with the age and sex of excavated skeletons should permit the assignment of sex and age to skeletons in unexcavated graves, thus allowing the investigator to generate a demographic profile of the larger burial population. Historic records detailing occupational hazards could be employed to elucidate the causes of traumatic skeletal lesions. And historic accounts of epidemic diseases that rarely produce symptoms on bone could be related to the densities of graves, from which differential mortality resulting from such diseases might be inferred.

To date, probably the most ambitious attempt to combine historical research, forensic anthropology, and bioarchaeology was the project directed by Ivor Noël Hume (1979) at the seventeenth-century site of Wolstenholme Towne, Virginia. Historic records indicated that at Martin's Hundred, a part of Wolstenholme Towne, an Indian massacre on March 22, 1622, had resulted in the deaths of many of the town's residents and soldiers. Excavation at Martin's Hundred in 1976 uncovered the skeletons of 23 individuals, apparently victims of the massacre and of disease and famine (Noël Hume 1979). Aided by J. Lawrence Angel, curator of physical anthropology at the Smithsonian Institution, Noël Hume and his colleagues succeeded in tentatively identifying the battered and scalped remains of one Richard Kean, a Wolstenholme lieutenant (Noël Hume 1979:767). Impressive and significant as this piece of sleuthing is, it does not constitute bioarchaeological inquiry in an urban setting.

To illustrate the prospects and problems of bioarchaeology in the urban context, we herein present the results of excavation, analysis, and interpretation of skeletal remains from late-nineteenth-century interments in an unmarked field at Oakland Cemetery in Atlanta, Georgia. Unlike the Martin's Hundred sample of some two dozen interments, Oakland Cemetery contained a potential burial population of several thousand.

The Urban Context

In the United States, large, urban cemeteries such as Oakland were established during the early and middle nineteenth century as alternatives to the small, neglected, unkempt, and potentially hazardous graveyards that pervaded urban areas throughout the seventeenth and eighteenth centuries. By the beginning of the nineteenth century, these old cemeteries were so crowded that they were frequently little more than stinking quagmires, overgrown with vegetation and strewn with bones, fallen markers, rotting coffins, and putrefying flesh. In New York City, for example, it was observed that the yellow fever epidemic of 1822 centered around the Trinity Church burial ground (French 1975). Speaking of this period, French (1975:70–71) states "It is obvious from the dearth of comments about early New England graveyards, from the nature of the comments that do exist and from the grim symbolism of the period's monuments, that graveyards were treated simply as unattractive necessities to be avoided as much as possible by the living."

Thus, by the early nineteenth century, in response to health hazards posed by inner-city graveyards, community leaders began to create large, municipal burial grounds on the outskirts of the cities. The establishment of these facilities—typified by Mount Auburn Cemetery near Boston—marked a change in attitudes about death and burial. Such "garden cemeteries" served not only as places of interment, but as recreational parks with landscaped vistas, walkways, and benches. This shift in attitudes about, and location of, cemeteries is known misleadingly as the "rural cemetery movement." These expansive cemeteries adjoining metropolitan areas stand in stark contrast to nonurban burial grounds such as family plots, church graveyards, and community cemeteries. And today, like Oakland Cemetery in Atlanta, they are surrounded by the residences, factories, and commercial structures that make up the urban milieu.

OAKLAND CEMETERY

Oakland Cemetery was founded in 1850 when the City of Atlanta purchased six acres of land to serve as its municipal burial ground (Figure 8.1). It remained the city's only cemetery until the opening of Westview in 1884. Some sections of the cemetery were assigned to various of Atlanta's churches and private organizations, but nearly everyone who died in the city between 1850 and 1884, from the wealthiest citizen to the poorest slave, was buried in Oakland (Sherry and Combs 1977). As a result of this heavy use, it was not long before Oakland began to run out of burial space. In 1864, the Civil War came to Atlanta, leaving behind a desecrated cemetery and further increasing the number of dead awaiting formal burial. This forced a long-needed expansion of the cemetery (Harwell 1976).

By the end of the war, the city had purchased several adjacent parcels of land, bringing Oakland to its present 88 acres (Sherry and Combs 1977). Much of the newly acquired land was subdivided into burial lots for sale to private owners. Other sections were used for the reburial of the vast numbers of Confederate dead that previously had been interred in hastily dug graves on the battlefields where they had died (Harwell 1976). And a substantial, but unidentified, portion of the acquired land was set aside for pauper interments (Moore 1976).

Writing of the period before 1884, Moore reports that:

> A dramatic increase in Atlanta's black population had been accompanied by related expenses for the city, which could more easily overlook the needs of blacks when alive than the need for the quick disposal of their corpses. The cost of pauper burial weighed on the budget (albeit comparatively lightly), and the space they required reduced Oakland's capacity and revenues. In 1879, for instance, black paupers accounted for nearly thirty-five percent of all Oakland interments and nearly eighty-five percent of the pauper interments [1976:29].

Records dated after 1884 refer to the transferal of pauper interments from one area to another within Oakland, and to other cemeteries, in an attempt to secure more space for the ever-increasing number of corpses brought to Oakland's gates.

Today, Historic Oakland Cemetery, Inc. (HOCI), a nonprofit organization interested in maintaining the cemetery's natural and cultural attributes, is spearhead-

FIGURE 8.1. An 1892 "bird's eye view of Atlanta." Oakland Cemetery is shown in the lower right corner of the painting. (The area covered by this study is marked with a dashed line.)

ing efforts to preserve this historic landmark in downtown Atlanta. In 1976, in a search for new sources of income for Oakland, this association earmarked a 5.7 acre (2.3 ha.) tract of land within the cemetery's walls as a potential area for development. Few monuments or markers were apparent in the field and, except for the record of its purchase in 1866, there were no written records pertaining to this section of the cemetery. Prior to development, however, an assessment of the cultural resources was mandated by two factors:

1. HOCI's application for a federal grant for restoration brought the proposed action under the requirements of the National Historic Preservation Act of 1966 (80 Stat. 915, 16 U.S.C. 470, as amended).
2. In 1976, the cemetery had been placed on the National Register of Historic Places.

In 1978, HOCI took the initial step toward development of the tract when they contracted with the Department of Anthropology at Georgia State University for an archaeological survey, to be conducted under the direction of Roy S. Dickens, Jr. and Robert L. Blakely.

THE STUDY TRACT

The study tract consists of 5.7 acres (2.3 ha.) of undulating terrain in the northeastern section of the cemetery (Figure 8.2). It is roughly hourglass in shape, with a northwest–southeast orientation. The area is a grassy field broken by widely dispersed small trees and is impinged upon by two zones of modern disturbance: a 3-ft (.9-m) deep, oval trash mound (recent city garbage) near the center of the hourglass and a dumping and storage ground near the western periphery.

Preliminary investigation revealed the following evidence that the field had been utilized for interments:

1. Several elderly informants recalled that they had been told that the grounds had once been known as a "potter's field."
2. Former Oakland Cemetery Sexton, Ed Walters, reported stepping through what he assumed was part of a buried wooden coffin near the east edge of the study tract.
3. Rectangular patches of dense grass and scattered bricks suggested the presence of subsurface disturbances in the field.
4. Workers installing a stone monument on the southeast edge of the tract encountered what they described as "human bones."
5. Cemetery records listed the names of at least 10,000 paupers, but with no reference to specific burial location (Dickens and Blakely 1979).

Therefore, it was not unreasonable to suspect that the study tract had been used by the cemetery for the interment of paupers. If it had been put to that use, it could only have been during the period between 1866 and 1884. This conclusion is based upon the following information:

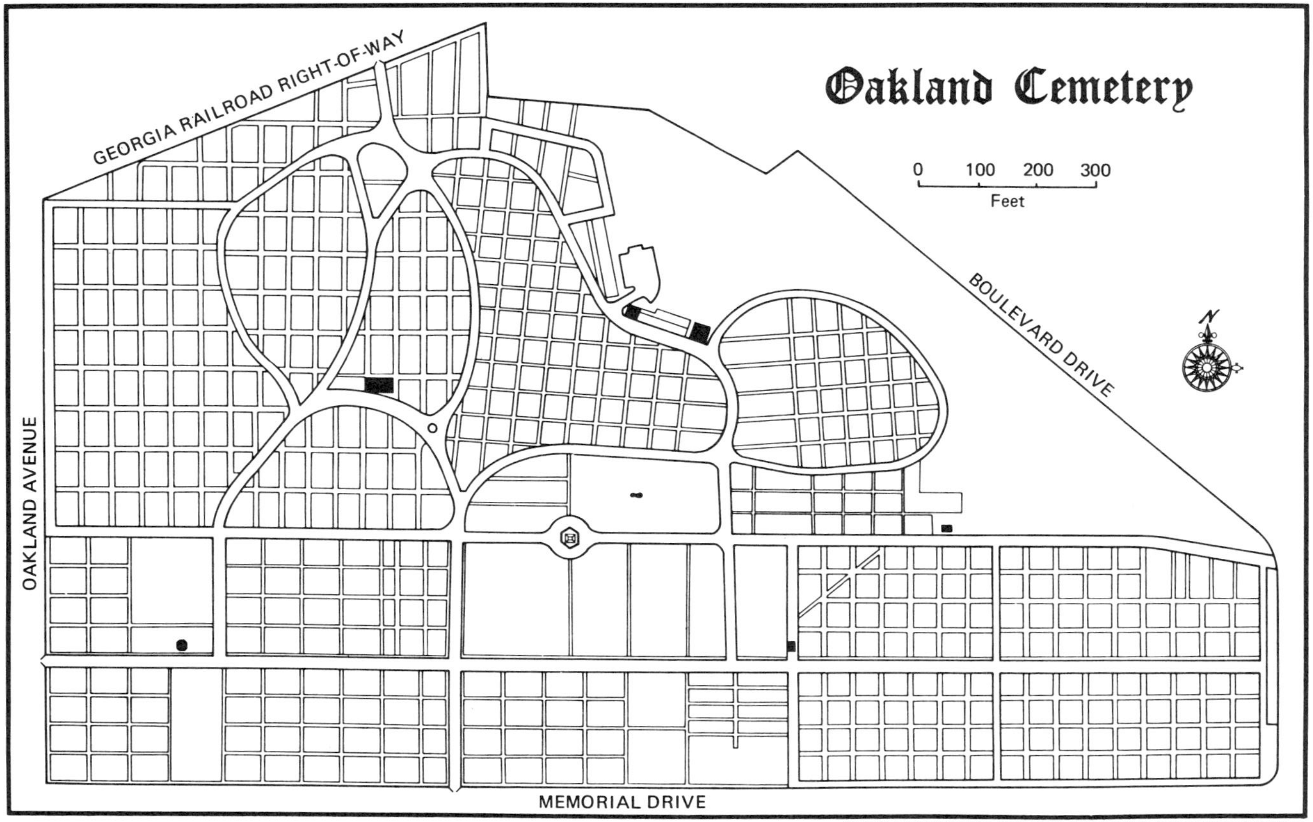

GEORGIA STATE UNIVERSITY, DEPAPTMENT OF GEOGRAPHY, CARTOGRAPHY LABORATORY

FIGURE 8.2. Map of Oakland Cemetery. The study tract is the open area in the upper right, adjacent to Boulevard Drive.

1. The tract was purchased by the city as part of the 1866 expansion of Oakland Cemetery.
2. Written records show that pauper interments at Oakland ceased in 1884 with the opening of Westview Cemetery.
3. A picture taken in the cemetery about 1885 (Sherry 1976:14) shows the study tract overgrown with weeds and scrubby vegetation, suggesting that the area was no longer in use.

In addition to the probability that the grassy field held nineteenth-century interments, the general area had been one of historical significance since Atlanta's beginning. It seemed likely, for example, that the tract contained evidence of Civil War activity. Indeed, Confederate General Hood had positioned himself on one of Oakland's hills to observe the Battle of Atlanta. And a turn-of-the-century mill community had been established adjacent to the field. Clearly, an archaeological investigation would be necessary to evaluate these potential cultural resources.

Sampling Design

Because the study tract encompassed several acres of uneven topography in an irregular shape, it was decided, for sampling purposes, to divide the field into three sections, labeled Area A, Area B, and Area C, proceeding from southeast to northwest and excluding the two major zones of modern disturbance (Figure 8.3). Area A was roughly triangular in shape, and comprised 77,796 ft² (7002 m²) or 1.79 acres (4.4 ha.) of generally sloping terrain, with its highest point at the southwest and its lowest point at the northeast. Area B formed the connection between the two "bulbs" of the hourglass, and contained, 38,736 ft² (3486 m²) or .89 acres (2.2 ha.); it sloped downward from due west to due east. Area C was nearly rectangular in shape and consisted of 78,804 ft² (7092 m²) or 1.81 acres (4.47 ha.), sloping gently from a high point at its west-northwest extension to a low point in the east-southeast, where it was bounded by the oval refuse heap. Each of the three areas was further divided by means of a grid having 50 × 50 ft (15 × 15 m) units. The axes of the grid were oriented north–south and east–west in Areas A and B. In Area C, the long axis was shifted to 300° to align with the configuration of that section of the field.

It was necessary to adopt a sampling strategy that would permit an adequate survey of the possible subsurface intrusions without exposing the entire 5.7 acre (2.3 ha.) tract. To this end, it was decided to employ a "strip-sampling" technique. This method entailed the use of a motor grader to remove the topsoil in shallow trenches systematically cut according to the coordinates of the grid. Motor graders have previously been utilized in archaeological investigations to remove overburden, plowzone, mound fill, and roof fall (e.g., Coe 1964). Dickens (1976) utilized the technique at Horseshoe Bend National Military Park in central Alabama to search for subsurface evidence of an early-nineteenth-century Indian fortification. At that site, parallel trenches were cut perpendicular to the linear fortification in order to transect the feature (which the grading eventually revealed).

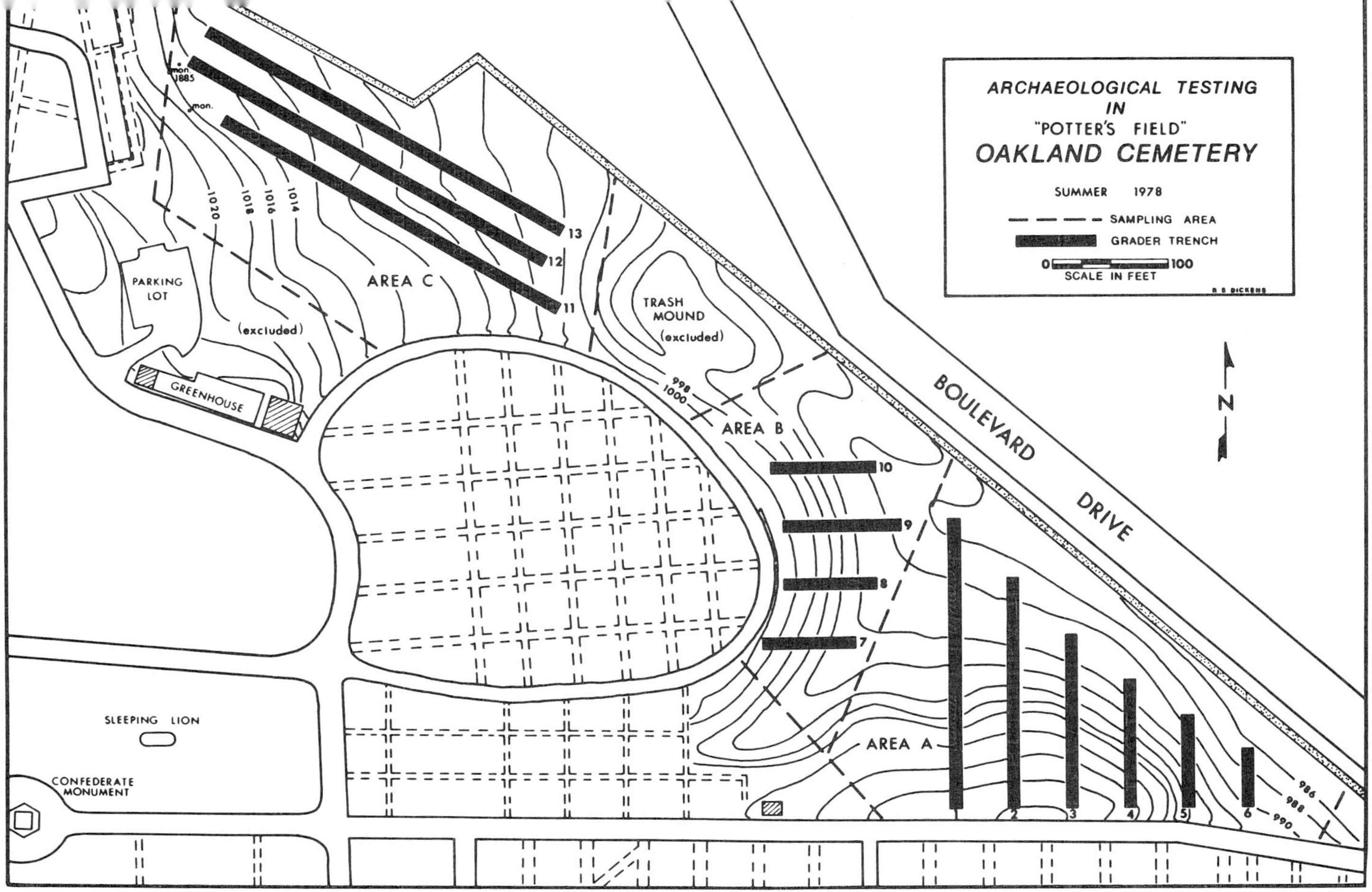

FIGURE 8.3. Map of the east end of Oakland Cemetery, showing the study tract, sampling areas, and grader trenches.

Oakland Cemetery required numerous closely spaced trenches because of the expectation of discontinuous, and possibly scattered, features. Trenches were cut perpendicular to the contour lines of each of the three areas to maximize control of the grading operation. Successive scrapings, each removing about .1 ft (.03 m) of soil, eventually produced "clean" unobstructed surfaces on which intrusions could be easily observed. Six trenches, 40 ft (12 m) apart, were cut in Area A; four trenches, 40 ft (12 m) apart, were cut in Area B; and three trenches, 20 ft (6 m) apart, were cut in Area C. This produced a total of thirteen trenches (Figure 8.3). Each trench was 10 ft (3 m) wide. Some trenches, or portions of them, contained areas disturbed by modern filling and construction, and were subject to deeper stripping. In still other places, it was not possible for the grader to penetrate to subsoil because of the thickness of landfill or erosional deposition. It was felt, however, that this did not appreciably detract from the efficacy of the sampling design. Upon completion of the grading, each exposed intrusion was mapped into the grid of the site. (For a more detailed description of the strip-sampling procedure, see Dickens and Blakely 1979.)

Disposition of Graves

The grader operation revealed grave pits in all three areas of the study tract. In addition, some artifacts, such as a .58-caliber Union regular-issue minie ball, undoubtedly were associated with Civil War activities in and around the cemetery. Several trash middens, which may have resulted from the nearby mill community, also were delineated. And a small prehistoric Indian site in Area B attests to the longevity of human occupation in the area. This site, represented by a scatter of quartz cores and flakes, probably dates to the Middle Archaic Period (ca. 4500 B.C.). These findings notwithstanding, the major resources were the human interments.

In most cases, the grave pits were quite closely spaced. In Areas A and B, some of the graves were placed less than a foot apart. In all sections, they were systematically arranged in parallel rows running north–south (Figure 8.4). Area C seems to have been less intensively utilized for burial purposes, yet the density of graves in this area remains high. In Area A, the grading operation revealed 207 grave pits and exposed 5200 ft^2 (483 m^2) of subsoil. (Exposed footage does not include those parts of the trenches where subsoil could not be penetrated by the grader.) The exposed footage constitutes 6.7% of the total area of Area A. By applying this frequency to the entire square footage of the area (i.e., 207:5200 = x:77,796, where x is the total number of expected burials), it is estimated that Area A contains about 3097 graves. This works out to one burial per 25.1 ft^2 (2.3 m^2), or a grave for every 4 × 6 ft (1.2 × 1.8 m) plot of land in that portion of the study tract. In Area B, 2900 ft^2 (269 m^2) of subsoil were exposed (7.5% of the total area), and 90 features were uncovered. Our formula yields an expectation of 1202 graves for Area B. The density is one burial per 32.2 ft^2 (3 m^2), or one grave for every 4 × 8 ft (1.2 × 2.4 m) section of ground. Area C appears to be the least densely populated of the three zones. In this area, 6% of the subsoil was exposed (4700 ft^2 or 437 m^2), and 94

FIGURE 8.4. Trench 2 in Area A, showing exposed features. View is to the south.

features were uncovered. It is calculated that Area C contains roughly 1576 graves—one burial per 50 ft^2 (4.6 m^2), or a grave for every 5 × 10 ft (1.5 × 3 m) area of soil.

Combining the above data, the grader operation exposed 12,800 ft^2 (1189 m^2) of subsoil, yielding 391 graves. It is estimated that the sampled sections (excluding disturbed zones) contain in excess of 5967 graves in an area of 195,336 ft^2 (18,147 m^2). By extending this estimate to the entire 5.7 acre (2.3 ha.) study tract, the total number of graves is 7575. This extension to the entire tract seems justified for two reasons:

1. The use of these areas for trash dumps and fill postdates the use of the tract for burial purposes.
2. In the spring of 1979, further excavation associated with construction on the western periphery of the tract revealed the same pattern of grave outlines beneath several feet of fill.

This means that, overall, there was an average of one burial per 32.7 ft^2, or a grave in every 4 × 8 ft parcel of land in the field. (Phelps, Green, and Hartsell [1979] report uncovering—by a similar strip-sampling technique—comparable densities of graves in a much smaller late-nineteenth- to early-twentieth-century cemetery near New Bern, North Carolina.)

Mortuary Practices

Regardless of location within the study tract, every exposed grave pit was oriented with its long axis east–west. The outlines were symmetrical, with sharply squared corners. The pits ranged in size from as small as 2.5 × 1.0 ft (.76 × .3 m) to as large as 8.0 × 3.0 ft (2.4 × .9 m). It was later confirmed that the dimensions of a pit were dictated by coffin size, which in turn was determined by the size of the individual being interred.

Many broken and intact artifacts were uncovered in the grader trenches. These items included medicine bottles, ceramic and glass cups and vases, and oyster and conch shells (Dickens and Blakely 1979). Some of the glass and ceramic artifacts were embossed or marked with manufacture dates from the mid-to-late 1800s. Vlach (1977) states that the adornment of burial sites with such artifacts is a common mortuary practice among blacks and their African antecedents. And Combes (1972:56) reports that the grave sites of coastal South Carolina blacks from the nineteenth century were adorned with "cups, saucers, bowls, dishes, tumblers, kerosene lamps, clocks, medicine bottles, pitchers, various cut glass pieces and just about every other household item imaginable . . . [and] many pretty sea shells with the conch being the most popular." The presence of these artifacts in apparent association with the Oakland graves initially suggested that the study tract not only served as a potter's field, but also may have been a segregated burial ground for less affluent black Atlantans in general. The fact that a portion of the cemetery adjoin-

FIGURE 8.5. Burial pit with fill partly removed. Chamber for the coffin is, as yet, unexcavated.

ing the study tract was known as the "black section" added credence to this supposition.

The final phase of the field project involved complete excavation of seventeen graves. These were distributed throughout the study tract, and were selected so as to include a representative sample of the different grave sizes. In addition, each area was sampled according to the relative number of graves it contained.

Excavation revealed that the grave pits had been dug with vertical walls to a depth of approximately 3.5 ft (1 m). At this point, the floor had been leveled off and a smaller excavation made in the exact shape of the coffin (Figure 8.5). The depth of these smaller chambers was determined by the size of the coffin; for adults they averaged 1 ft (.3 m) deep, while for children they were about .7 ft (.2 m) deep. After the coffin had been lowered into the pit, a covering of wooden planks was placed over the coffin and across the dirt ledge at a right angle to the long axis of the grave. The director of an Atlanta funeral home described these planks as "grave arches." They were used with wooden coffins to prevent collapse of the coffin under the weight of the fill dirt. Around 1930, wooden planks were replaced by metal supports, which are still used today whenever a person is buried in a wooden casket (Jane Dillon, personal communication).

In all 17 graves the bodies had been placed in wooden coffins. In most instances the wood of the coffins had completely decayed, leaving only thin lenses of darkened soil and a number of cut nails as clues to their existence. The coffins ranged in shape from rectangular, to oblong hexagonal, to oblong octagonal (Figure 8.6). The presence of three rectangular coffins in the sample confirms that these burials took place after 1850, a date generally accepted for the earliest use of straight-sided caskets (Kline and Kline n.d.). One of the rectangular coffins contained, in the lid and over the face and shoulders of the deceased, an oval glass. Patents for coffins of this style were filed between 1860 and 1900 (Kline and Kline n.d.). Such coffins were more expensive than the plain boxes commonly used during this period. The presence of this relatively expensive casket in the study tract suggests that at least some of the individuals had access to more expensive caskets than one might expect for "paupers." A retired employee of the National Casket Company informed us that the hexagonal or "pigeon-toed" coffins were the earliest of the three styles, and were largely replaced by octagonally shaped coffins. After the introduction of the rectangular casket, the use of octagonal coffins became limited to members of lower socioeconomic classes (Lawrence Moore, personal communication).

The variety of coffin styles was accompanied by a variety of casket fixtures and items of personal adornment. In no instance, however, was there elaborate coffin decoration or expensive personal effects. Items of personal adornment were limited mainly to buttons and buckles from clothing. No shoes were found, but none were expected since custom—and economics—dictated that the dead were buried without shoes (Jane Dillon, personal communication). The modest attire corroborates other information in suggesting that the deceased had been economically disadvantaged in life. (One individual, a young adult male whose remains were poorly preserved, appeared to have had his feet severed. Taylor [1976] notes that, after

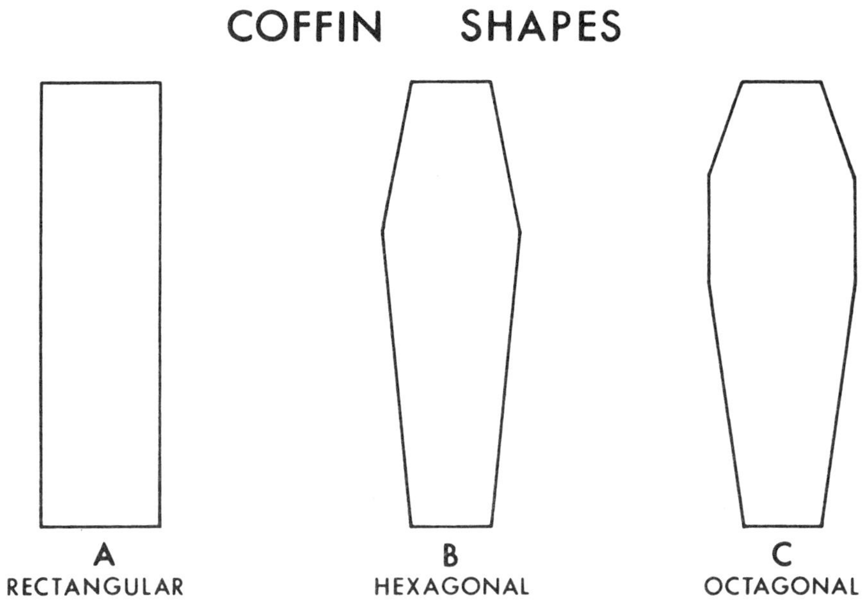

FIGURE 8.6. Coffin shapes encountered in the Oakland Cemetery excavations.

disease, the greatest cause of death among nineteenth-century black men in Atlanta was railroad accidents. And Moore [personal communication] told us that a person killed in a railroad accident most commonly lost either his feet or head.)

Demography

As noted earlier, it became obvious during the course of excavation that the size of the grave pit was determined by the size of the coffin placed in it, which in turn was dictated by the size of the individual interred. Therefore, by correlating the sizes of grave outlines with the ages and sexes of excavated skeletons, one could develop a model for predicting the age and sex of unexhumed remains. Were this the case, meaningful demographic data could be generated without excavating the entire burial population. Although we still adhere to that proposition, the small size of the excavated Oakland sample limited its utility as a predictive model. (It should be pointed out that the archaeological investigations at Oakland were not intended to secure a representative population sample; rather, they were designed to permit assessment of cultural resources within the tract. Neither time nor money was available for more extensive excavation, and the objectives of the project were fully met.) It was observed, however, that infants and children were recovered from grave pits with a size less than 6 × 2 ft (1.8 × .6 m). One 15-year-old was placed in a grave measuring 6.25 × 2.5 ft (1.9 × .76 m) or 15.6 ft^2 (1.45 m^2). All adults were interred in graves that exceeded 6.5 × 2.5 ft (2 × .76 m) or 16.25 ft^2 (1.5 m^2). It is not unreasonable, then, to select 6 × 2 ft (1.8 × .6 m) as a size by which to differentiate the graves of subadults and adults. Using this criterion, of the 204 measurable graves pits in the study tract, about 108 held subadults and 96 contained adults. Thus, roughly 53% of the dead were infants, children, and adolescents, and the remaining 47% were adults. (Interestingly, of the 17 excavated graves, 9 or 53% contained subadults.) If these data are diagnostic, they suggest, not unexpectedly, that over half of the deaths occurred among the young. Taylor (1976:117) reports that for the period 1853–1873, 54–66% of Atlanta's dead were under 10 years of age (blacks and whites combined).

For excavated adults, grave size was a crude indicator of stature and, therefore, of sex. The mean surface area of grave pits containing individuals who stood between 5 ft (1.5 m) and 5 ft 7 in. (1.7 m) was 18.5 ft^2 (1.7 m^2); those ranging in height from 5 ft 9 in. (1.75 m) to 6 ft (1.8 m) were placed in graves with surface areas averaging 19.8 ft^2 (1.8 m^2). The former included only females, and the latter only males. Therefore, a surface area of 19 ft^2 (1.76 m^2) was arbitrarily selected to distinguish grave pits of females from males. But when this criterion was used to assign sex to the excavated adults, three of seven were misclassified.

If a larger excavated sample had been available, we are confident that grave sizes would have yielded the approximate numbers of infants, children, adolescents, adult males, and adult females in the overall study tract. It then would have been possible to construct a demographic profile from which to calculate differential mortality, life expectancy, fecundity, and even population growth rate. If one were armed with these data, together with historic accounts, it then would be possible to interpret the effects of episodic and epidemic diseases upon a segment of Atlanta's citizenry (or any other historic group) for which few medical records exist. Ideally, future archaeological investigations in urban cemeteries should include exposure of a sufficient number of graves and excavation of a large enough skeletal sample to allow biological anthropologists to reconstruct demographic patterns.

FORENSIC ANTHROPOLOGY

An intensive biological analysis of the human skeletal remains was undertaken to augment information gained from excavation. The objectives of this study were to determine the age at death, sex, racial makeup, stature, diet, disease states, and possible causes of death of the individuals exhumed from the cemetery. (For details of the procedures used to derive these data, see Beck 1980 and Blakely and Beck 1982.)

Of the 17 graves excavated, four contained adult females, four contained adult males, one held an adolescent female, and eight contained infants or young children (Table 8.1). Preservation ranged from excellent, with two individuals having traces of human hair clinging to the occipital bones, to burials with no bone present. Most of the graves in the latter category were those of infants. The presence of milk teeth, glass buttons, and cut nails characterized these burials. Only four of the skeletons were complete enough to permit comprehensive analysis. They con-

Table 8.1 Summary of Excavated Features, by Age, Sex, and State of Preservation

Feature	Sex	Age	Preservation
1.13	male	18-25 years	poor (cranial fragments and teeth)
1.16	indeterminate	juvenile	poor (no bone or teeth)
2.3	female	26 years	excellent
2.38	indeterminate	juvenile	poor (no bone or teeth)
3.32	male	50+ years	excellent
7.9	female	79+ years	fair
7.19	male	65+ years	excellent
8.10	female	15 years	fair to poor
9.5	indeterminate	4 years	poor (cranial fragments and teeth)
10.22	indeterminate	juvenile	poor (no bone or teeth)
10.23	male	adult	poor (skeletal fragments)
11.20	indeterminate	2 years	poor (teeth only)
11.48	female	50-60 years	poor (skeletal fragments)
12.34	female	18-30 years	poor (skeletal fragments)
14.1	indeterminate	6 years	poor (skeletal fragments)
14.2	indeterminate	juvenile	poor (no bone or teeth)
14.3	indeterminate	juvenile	poor (no bone or teeth)

sisted of Features 2.3, 3.32, 7.9, and 7.19. To follow is a description and forensic analysis of these burials.

Feature 2.3

Feature 2.3 was a grave containing a hexagonal wooden coffin (Figure 8.7). No wood remained from the coffin, but six metal handles, many nails, and several latches were recovered. A single white glass button, presumed to have been a part of the individual's clothing, was the only item of personal adornment. Preservation of the skeletal remains was excellent and included hair adhering to the back of the cranium.

FIGURE 8.7. Feature 2.3 in situ, the remains of a black female in her mid-twenties. Note the hexagonal shape of the coffin.

The skeleton is that of a female in her middle twenties. Her stature, using the Trotter-Gleser formula (1958), was computed to have been 5 ft 6 in. (1.67 m). Age determination of this skeleton was complicated by contradictory evidence: Her coronal suture had completely closed, suggesting an age over 37 years; but the sagittal suture was active, indicating an age under 29 years. Tooth eruption was complete, although the upper third molars were congenitally absent; dental attrition was slight. The medial epiphysis of the clavicle had not yet fused, but all other epiphyses had united (21–28 years). Thus, the additional aging criteria suggest premature closure of the coronal suture, which supports the age indicated by the sagittal suture (22–29 years). The skull and pelvis clearly demonstrate that this person is female. She has delicate bone structure with a small degree of muscularity. The gonial angle is obtuse and the chin is median. Supraorbital ridges are nonexistent and the forehead is vertically placed. The mastoid processes are small, and frontal and parietal eminences are well developed. On the pelvis, the greater sciatic notch and subpubic arch are wide and shallow.

Her racial attributes strongly suggest that she was black. Of course, American blacks, a sociologically defined ethnic group, evidence varying degrees of Caucasoid admixture upon what is principally a Negroid substratum of phenotypes. Nevertheless, she possesses a clustering of attributes that are quite characteristic of blacks (Figure 8.8). The long cranial vault and broad nasals, as well as the nasal gutters in the lower margin, fit well the craniofacial traits of Negroids listed by Krogman (1962:190). Prognathism is pronounced, producing a downward slant to her facial profile; her interorbital distance is wide and orbital openings square; and the leftward direction of her superior sagittal sinus also suggests African heritage. Although not racially diagnostic, the presence of bilateral septal apertures in the distal portion of the humeri is most common among black females (Trotter 1934). Possible evidence of Caucasoid admixture are the broad face and high, narrow cranial vault. On the other hand, these traits may simply reflect individual variation.

Pathological conditions included moderate-to-severe osteosclerosis of the bones throughout the skeleton. All bones are far heavier than their size would suggest. The surface of the skull is abnormally smooth and resembles marble in both its appearance and texture (Figure 8.8). The removal of a section of bone from the femur for trace element analysis revealed an extremely dense cortex. X-rays confirm this observation (Figure 8.9). This generalized osteosclerosis is probably due to an anemia, possibly sickle-cell anemia (Dan Morse, personal communication). The low level of copper in the bones supports this diagnosis (Gilbert 1977; Underwood 1971).

Dislocation of the left hip is indicated by the presence of an accessory articulating facet for the femur on the back of the pelvis. From the shallow depth of this facet and the lack of new bone growth, it can be assumed that the injury occurred shortly before death. Had the injury occurred earlier, and remained unreduced, the facet would have become much deeper. If the dislocation had been reduced, new bone growth would have begun to fill in the facet.

A circular area of denuded bone, approximately 9 cm in diameter, on the left side

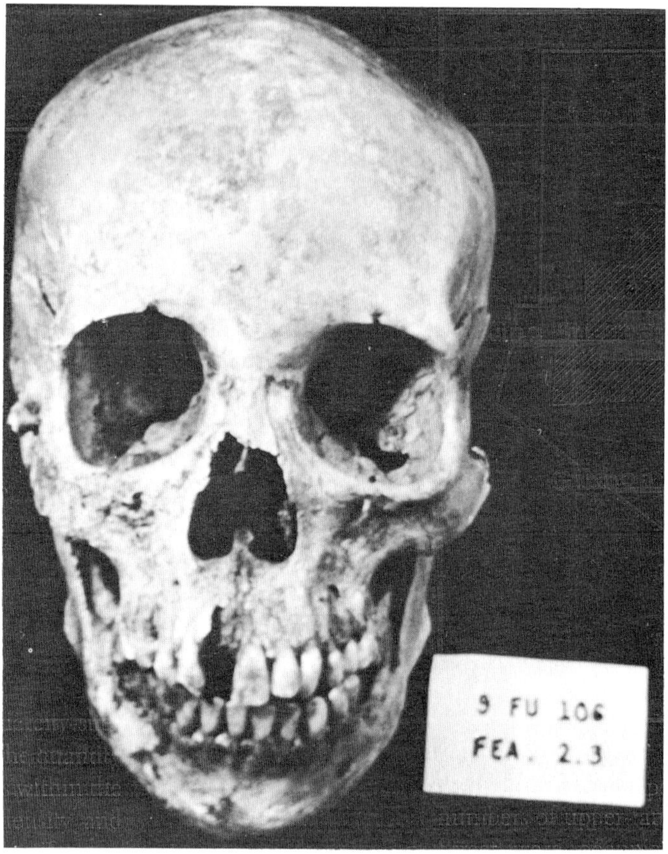

FIGURE 8.8. Anterior view of the skull of Feature 2.3. The "shiny" or marbled appearance of the bone may be indicative of an anemic condition, perhaps sickle-cell anemia.

of the cranial vault is suggestive of soft tissue infection. Within this area is an irregular hole measuring 20 × 5 mm. Close examination shows signs of slight bone regeneration. X-rays of the cranial vault (Figure 8.9) reveal 10–20 small metallic opacities in the area of this lesion. These objects appear to be the remains of a bullet that produced the hole and subsequent infection. Thus, the probable cause of death was infection resulting from a gunshot wound.

Feature 3.32

Feature 3.32 contained the bones of a rather robust and elderly male buried in a rectangular wooden coffin (Figure 8.10). A portion of the lid of the coffin had

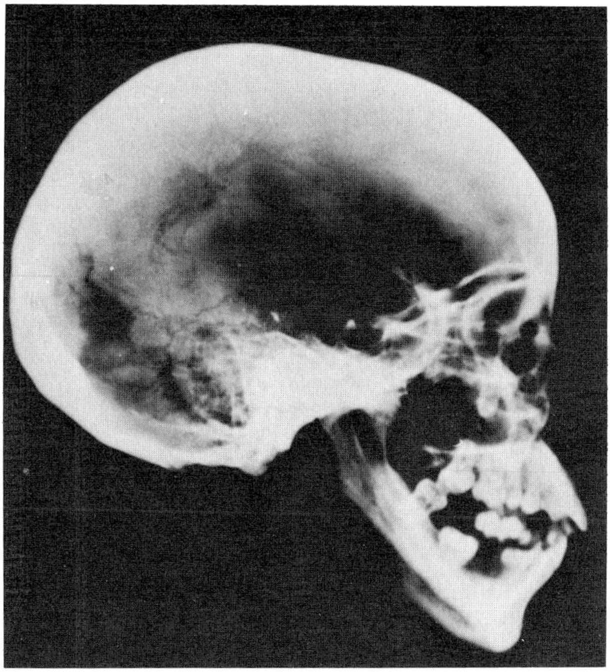

FIGURE 8.9. X-ray photograph of the lateral view of the skull of Feature 2.3. Metal opacities, which appear as minute white dots, probably are fragments of a bullet.

collapsed and was draped over the skeletal remains. The skull rested on a multiple-layered and tasseled pillow. Several small buttons were recovered from the area of the pelvis. A partial brick wall was found around the top of the grave pit, suggesting that it originally had been marked. Combes (1972) cites the use of brick borders around graves, in lieu of stone markers, as a common mortuary practice among nineteenth-century blacks in coastal South Carolina. Several brass objects that appear to have been coffin fittings were recovered from the base of the grave pit. The forehead of the skull is discolored from the coffin wood, and the left parietal shows green discoloration from the pillow upon which the head rested.

Skeletal morphology indicates that 3.32 also was black (Figure 8.11). The skull falls into a qualified version of the formula for "U-type" or Negroid skulls (Todd and Tracy 1930). Qualification is due to the presence of blunt upper orbital margins, usually associated with whites. The brow ridge is undulating, glabella rounded, fronto-nasal junction plain, and interorbital distance wide. Microscopic examination of hair recovered with the skull (and with Feature 2.3) revealed that in cross-section it was ovoid, demonstrating that the hair form was wooly or "afro," a type most commonly found among blacks. The presence of bilateral septal apertures of

FIGURE 8.10. Feature 3.32 in situ, the remains of an elderly black male. Note the wooden remnants of the rectangular coffin draped over the bones.

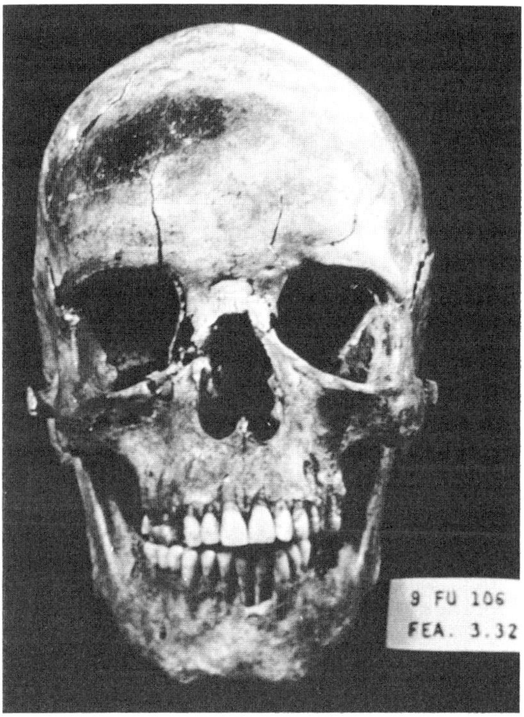

FIGURE 8.11. Anterior view of the skull of Feature 3.32. The dark stain on the forehead is from coffin wood that rested on the skull. The fracture in the right eye orbit resulted from a gunshot wound.

the lower humeri is unusual in males of all races, but is found more commonly among blacks than whites. The presence of an anomalous sixth lumbar vertebra is also more frequent among blacks, but cannot be regarded as conclusive evidence of racial affiliation (Lanier 1939). Stature for Feature 3.32 was computed at 5 ft 9 in. (1.75 m) using the Trotter-Gleser formula.

A highly unusual anomaly is present in the vertebral column where, in addition to 25 presacral vertebrae (instead of the normal 24), there is spondylolysis of the fourth, fifth, and sixth lumbar vertebrae. Spondylolysis is a defect in the neural arch, resulting in its separation from the vertebral body; it is of genetic derivation. Some individuals possessing similar defects have been known to walk with a waddling gait (Morse 1978). Slight arthritic buildup is visible throughout the vertebral column, the tarsals, and the distal femora. Periostitic inflammation is apparent on the posterior-distal femora, anterior surfaces of the proximal ulnae, and inferior surfaces of both clavicles.

A small piece of metal, possibly the tip of an ice pick or knife, is embedded in the left parietal. Sclerotic bone growth surrounding the injury clearly demonstrates healing. A fracture of the right humerus also shows healing, as does a fracture of the left tenth rib. A moderate-to-severe fracture of the right maxilla with callus buildup is easily seen. The inner portion of the right orbital margin and the margin of the right nasal opening are also implicated. X-rays reveal many irregular, metallic opacities in this area (Figure 8.12). It appears that this individual sustained a gunshot wound to the face. Following this diagnosis, a spent .32-caliber bullet was found in laboratory screening of soil from beneath the skull. The fragments in the maxilla match, both in size and shape, sections missing from this bullet. If these are indeed parts of the bullet, it must have remained lodged somewhere in the soft tissues of the nasal or orbital areas, possibly in the brain itself. Such an occurrence matches well the evidence of infection seen in the cranial vault. There is an excessive thickening and porotic appearance to the endocranial aspects of both parietals, with the intensity of disease following the venous drainage of the brain.

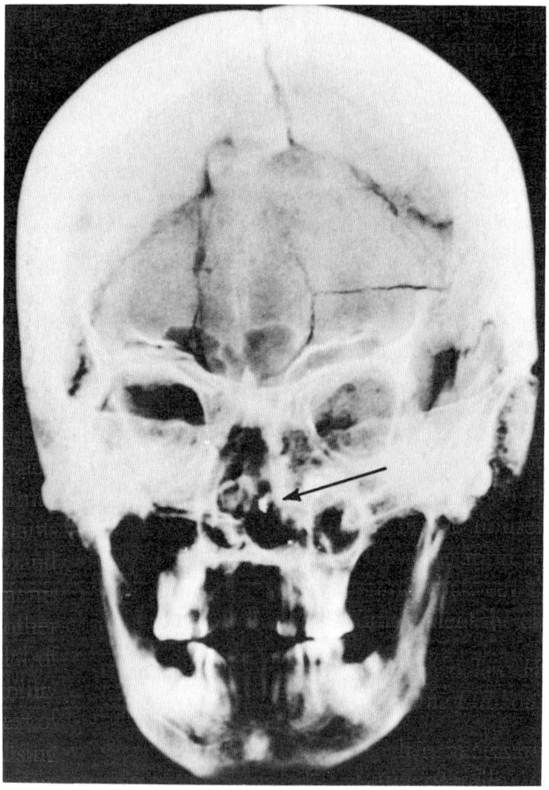

FIGURE 8.12. X-ray photograph of the anterior view of the skull of Feature 3.32. The white speck in the nasal region is an embedded fragment of a .32-caliber bullet, which was later found in dirt taken from beneath the skull.

This suggests a blood infection resulting from the presence of the bullet in the soft tissue. It seems reasonable to suggest that this individual died of an infection resulting from a gunshot wound to the face.

Feature 7.9

Feature 7.9 contained the remains of an elderly female (Figure 8.13). Her coffin was a simple, hexagonal wooden box, without handles. The only items of personal adornment were a brass ring on the middle finger of the right hand, and nearly 600 small, black glass beads from the neck region (possibly decoration on a dress or gown). Four shell buttons also were recovered.

The cranial features and pelvis are small and delicate in appearance. Preauricular sulci on both ilia suggest that she had given birth to children. Her stature, calculated by theTrotter-Gleser formula, was 5 ft 7 in. (1.7 m). The spheno-parietal suture is closed, but the parieto-temporal suture is open. This suggests an age between 65 and 80 years. Extensive arthritic buildup and ossification of cartilage argue for an age near the upper end of that range. Her skull is long and narrow, and the palate and nasal aperture broad (Figure 8.14). These traits, together with the presence of nasal gutters and pronounced prognathism, are suggestive of Negroid ancestry.

All teeth, except the upper canines, lower lateral incisors, and lower right canine, were lost antemortem; bone resorption of the tooth sockets is complete. The five remaining teeth evidence many caries and extreme attrition. And, extensive osteoarthritis is present on the vertebrae. Together with a severe case of gerontal osteoporosis, these attributes are common indicators of progressive aging. However, the severity of their expression in this individual also may reflect advanced states of disease (Dan Morse, personal communication). The low level of copper in her bones suggests a chronic disease state. What appears to be a bony tumor is located in the left maxilla near the molar and premolars. This probably is a benign tumor related to an infection of the tooth roots (Dan Morse, personal communication). An undiagnosed undulating sclerotic buildup of bone is present on the endocranial aspect of both parietals and temporals. Although the condition is widespread in the cranial vault, its etiology remains unknown.

Feature 7.19

Feature 7.19 contained an unusual rectangular coffin (Figure 8.15). Although all of the wood of the coffin had deteriorated, six ornate metal handles and several decorative plates, apparently used as bolt covers, were recovered. An oval piece of glass, which had formed a viewing window in the coffin lid, had collapsed and was broken over the skull and upper torso of the skeleton. Combes (1972) describes a similar coffin from a nineteenth-century black cemetery in South Carolina. These "bust windows" simply may be of decorative origin. Others have argued that they

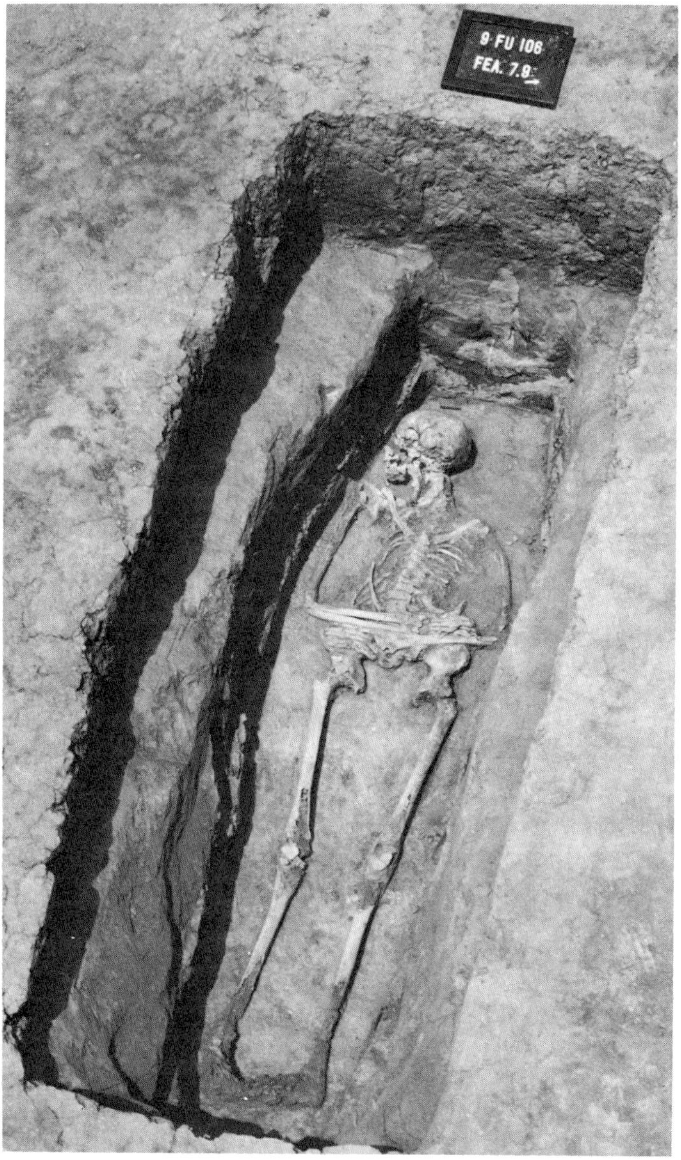

FIGURE 8.13. Feature 7.9 in situ, the remains of an elderly black female.

allowed the body to be viewed without opening the coffin (Dickens and Blakely 1979), an advantage in a time when embalming techniques were less sophisticated than today. The only items of personal adornment associated with this burial were buttons and a metal buckle. Four of the buttons appear to have been two pairs of cuff or glove buttons.

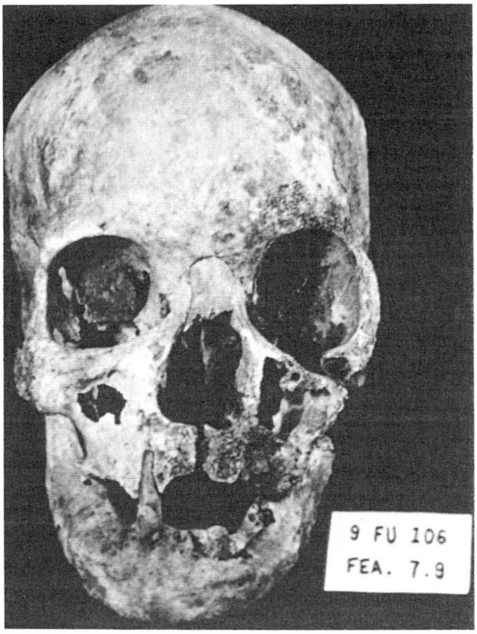

FIGURE 8.14. Anterior view of the skull of Feature 7.9.

The remains are those of a black male, probably in his sixties. His bones are uniformly large and rugged, showing pronounced musculature (Figure 8.16). Using the Trotter-Gleser formula for predicting adult stature, it is estimated that he stood 6 ft (1.8 m) tall. There are few signs of trauma. Slight arthritis is present on the lumbar vertebrae and distal articulating surfaces of both femora. Dental attrition is slight and only two caries are present. The lack of trauma and seemingly good health of this individual, along with burial in an apparently expensive container, suggest that he was not a pauper.

Trace Element Analysis

In general, the trace element analysis showed that these individuals enjoyed a balanced and varied diet. The only consistently low measurement was for copper, yet in all instances except Feature 7.9 the readings fell within the range anticipated for healthy human bone. The level of .9 parts per million of copper for Feature 7.9 may be explained as a result of an extended illness. Macroscopic pathological lesions support the existence of such a disease state. Thus, this reading probably does not reflect a dietary imbalance. All other elements tested (strontium, magnesium, and zinc) had readings within the ranges expected for modern Western diets. No correlation was found between trace element level and burial location, age, or sex.

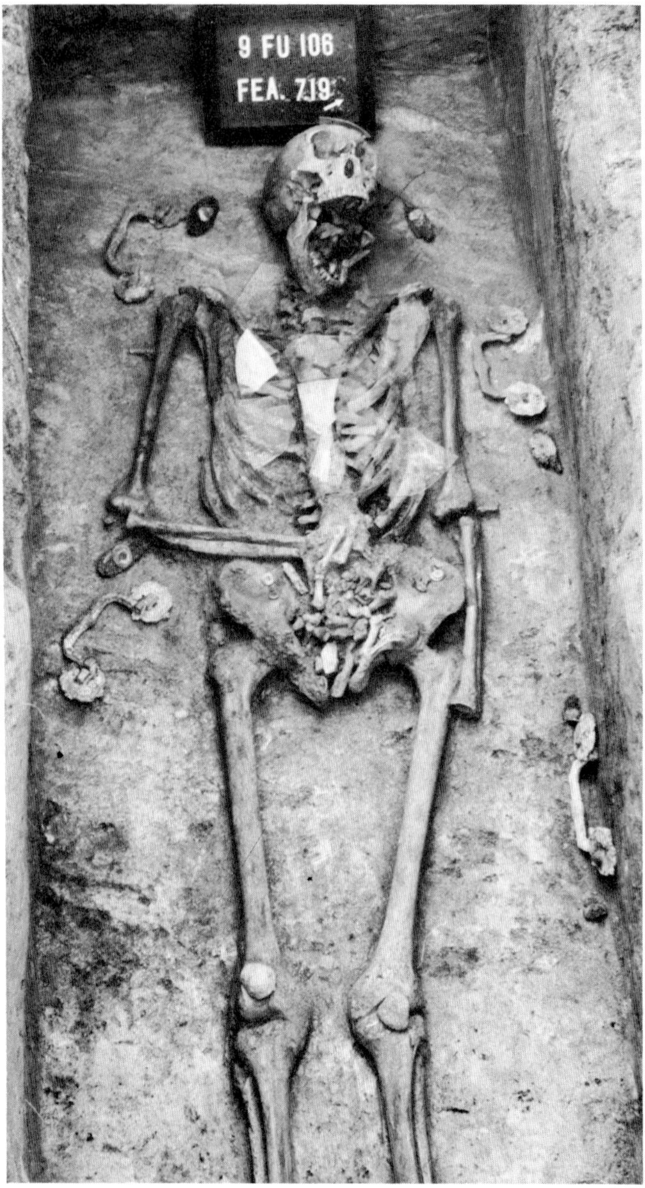

FIGURE 8.15. Feature 7.19 in situ, the remains of an elderly black male. The broken glass once formed an oval viewing window in the lid of the coffin.

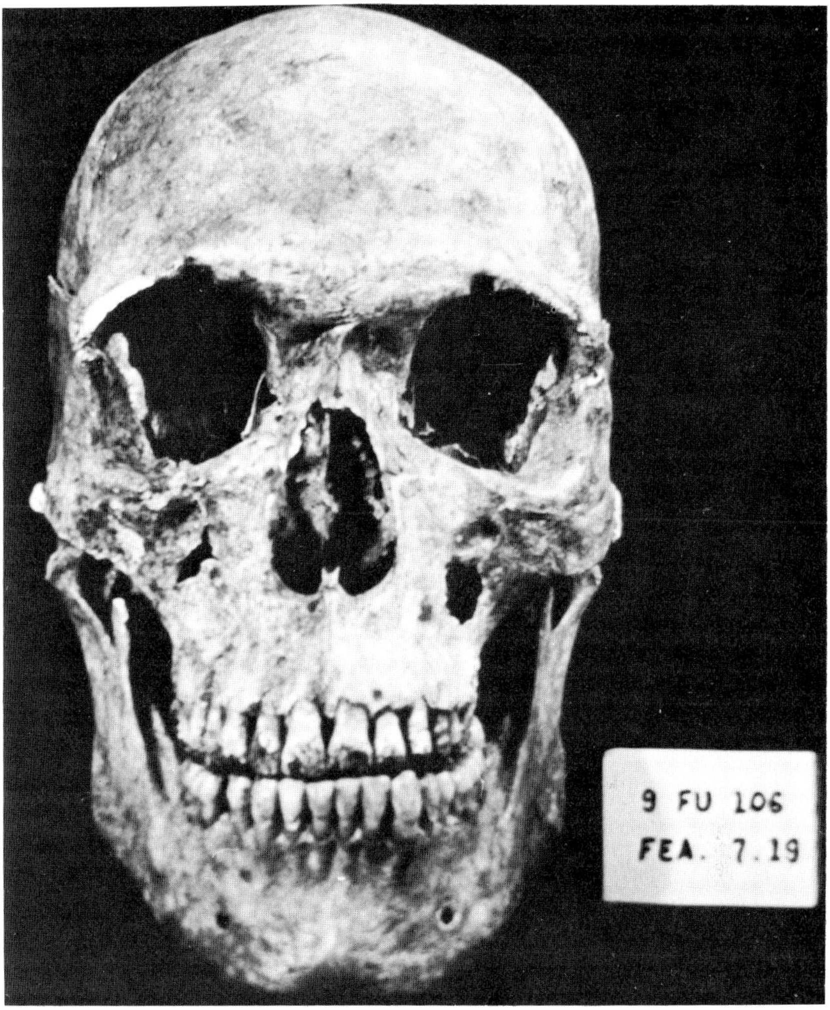

FIGURE 8.16. Anterior view of the skull of Feature 7.19.

CONCLUSIONS

For investigations of archaeological sites containing human skeletal remains, the interpretative power of the bioarchaeological approach is greater than those of either biological anthropology or archaeology alone. This is, of course, true of both historic and prehistoric mortuary sites. But at historic—and particularly urban—sites, the bioarchaeological research design can also include forensic and documentary inquiries. Together, they constitute the most powerful investigative tool yet devised by students of mortuary site archaeology.

Oakland Cemetery was not an ideal laboratory for this approach, however, because of the limited size of the skeletal sample and paucity of historical records. It is to the small sample size that we attribute our failure to generate a predictive demographic model. For the same reason, few generalizations could be reached concerning the health environment and genetic structure of the population from which the skeletal sample was extracted. And the absence of historical records thwarted an attempt to identify, by name, individuals interred in unmarked graves. Full realization of the conjunctive, bioarchaeological approach, therefore, lies in securing a statistically valid skeletal sample and sufficient written records to link skeletal remains to funerary, epidemiological, and dietary behavior.

Regardless of the limitations of the Oakland project, the amount of information gleaned from such a small-scale excavation and analysis is encouraging. The remains represent a segment of southern urban society conspicuous by its absence in written records of the period. By contrast, extensive histories tell of the lives of white Atlantans who helped rebuild the city in the years following the Civil War. In Oakland Cemetery, these more affluent individuals lie in graves marked by elaborate stone monuments. The most imposing monuments in the black section are modest by comparison. "In most instances, less than adequate markers indicate the burial plots of individuals who left behind legacies of valuable service and worthwhile lives in what Reverend E. R. Carter in 1894 referred to as the 'Black Side' [Henderson 1976:58]." This field, assumed to be empty, and apparently long forgotten, is a vivid reminder of an overlooked segment of Atlanta's population.

Most of the interments in the study tract probably are those of paupers buried in simple pine boxes at the city's expense. Other burials appear not to represent paupers in the strictest sense of the word. The glass viewing plate present in one grave indicates a casket of more expensive manufacture than one might expect to have been provided by a city already deeply concerned with the cost of pauper interment. And the range of coffin fixtures, items of personal adornment, and grave offerings suggest that some of the individuals interred in this field were not indigents. This speaks for at least occasional, private, family mortuary preparations. It seems probable, therefore, that in addition to being a potter's field, this area once constituted a segregated burial ground for economically and socially deprived black Atlantans.

ACKNOWLEDGMENTS

We gratefully acknowledge the assistance of Roy S. Dickens, Jr., who directed the field archaeology and assisted in preparing the photographs for publication. Permission to reproduce the photographs in Figures 8.2–8.6 was kindly granted by Stanley South, Editor of the Conference on Historic Site Archaeology. Thanks go to Andy Boorn of the Chemistry Department at the Georgia Institute of Technology for conducting the atomic absorption spectroscopy of trace elements.

REFERENCES

Acsádi, G., and J. Nemeskéri
1970 *History of human life span and mortality*. Budapest: Akadémiai Kiadó.

Anderson, J. E.
1968 Skeletal "anomalies" as genetic indicators. In *Skeletal biology of earlier human populations*, edited by D. R. Brothwell. Oxford: Pergamon Press. Pp. 135–147.

Beck, L. A.
1980 Physical anthropology of skeletal remains from Oakland Cemetery, Atlanta, Georgia. Unpublished honors thesis, Department of Anthropology, Georgia State Univ.

Binford, L. R.
1968 Archaeological perspectives. In *New perspectives in archaeology*, edited by S. R. Binford and L. R. Binford. Chicago: Aldine. Pp. 5–32.

Blakely, R. L.
1977 Sociocultural implications of demographic data from Etowah, Georgia. In *Biocultural adaptation in prehistoric America*, edited by R. L. Blakely. *Proceedings of the Southern Anthropological Society*, No. 11. Athens: Univ. of Georgia Press. Pp. 45–66.

Blakely, R. L., and L. A. Beck
1982 Human skeletal remains. In *Archaeological investigations at the Plum Grove site, Washington County, Tennessee*, edited by R. S. Dickens, Jr. In press.

Buikstra, J. E.
1972 Hopewell in the lower Illinois River Valley: A regional study of biological variability and mortuary activity. Unpublished Ph.D. dissertation, Univ. of Chicago.
1976 The Caribou Eskimo: General and specific disease. *American Journal of Physical Anthropology* **45**:351–367.

Chapple, E. D., and C. S. Coon
1942 *Principles of anthropology*. New York: Holt.

Coe, J. L.
1964 The formative cultures of the Carolina Piedmont. *Transactions of the American Philosophical Society*, New Series, Vol. **54**, Pt. 5.

Combes, J. D.
1972 Ethnography, archaeology, and burial practices among coastal South Carolina Blacks. *Conference on Historic Site Archeology Papers* 7:52–61.

Dickens, R. S., Jr.
1976 Discovery and interpretation of the Indian barricade at Horseshoe Bend National Military Park, Alabama. *Conference on Historic Site Archeology Papers* **11**:1–42.

Dickens, R. S., Jr., and R. L. Blakely
1979 Preliminary report on archaeological investigations in Oakland Cemetery, Atlanta, Georgia. *Conference on Historic Site Archeology Papers* **13**:286–314.

French, S.
1975 The cemetery as a cultural institution: The establishment of Mount Auburn and the "rural cemetery" movement. In *Death in America*, edited by D. E. Stannard. Philadelphia: Univ. of Pennsylvania Press. Pp. 69–91.

Gilbert, R. I., Jr.
1975 Trace element analyses of three skeletal Amerindian populations at Dickson Mounds. Unpublished Ph.D. dissertation, Univ. of Massachusetts, Amherst.
1977 Applications of trace element research to problems in archaeology. In *Biocultural adaptation in prehistoric America*, edited by R. L. Blakely. *Proceedings of the Southern Anthropological Society*, No. 11. Athens: Univ. of Georgia Press. Pp. 85–100.

Harwell, R. B.
1976 Our Confederate dead. *The Atlanta Historical Bulletin* **20**:97–111.
Henderson, A. B.
1976 Paupers, pastors, and politicians: Reflections upon Afro-Americans buried in Oakland Cemetery. *The Atlanta Historical Bulletin* **20**:97–111.
Howells, W. W.
1972 Analysis of patterns of variation in the crania of recent man. In *The functional and evolutionary biology of the primates*, edited by R. Tuttle. Chicago: Aldine. Pp. 123–151.
Kline, K., and J. Kline
n.d. *The meaning and value of the casket*. Brochure of the Casket Manufacturers Association of America, Evanston, Illinois.
Krogman, W. M.
1962 *The human skeleton in forensic medicine*. Springfield, Ill.: Charles C. Thomas.
Lanier, R. R., Jr.
1939 The presacral vertebrae of American white and Negro males. *American Journal of Physical Anthropology* **25**:341–420.
Moore, K.
1976 Atlanta's pride and problem. *The Atlanta Historical Bulletin* **20**:19–41.
Morse, D.
1978 *Ancient disease in the Midwest*. Reports of Investigations, No. 15. Illinois State Museum, Springfield.
Noël Hume, Ivor
1979 First look at a lost Virginia settlement. *National Geographic* **155**:734–767.
Peebles, C. S.
1973 Moundville: The organization of a prehistoric community. Unpublished Ph.D. dissertation, Univ. of California, Santa Barbara.
Phelps, D. S., J. B. Green, and K. C. Hartsell
1979 *An archaeological–historical study of the Bryan Cemetery and site 31Dv25, Simmons-Nott Airport, New Bern, North Carolina*. Publication No. 10. North Carolina Archaeological Council, Raleigh.
Sherry, G. T.
1976 Preface. *The Atlanta Historical Bulletin* **20**:13–14.
Sherry, G. T., and D. W. Combs
1977 *Oakland Cemetery: Atlanta's most tangible link*. Historic Oakland Cemetery, Inc., Atlanta, Georgia.
Taylor, J.
1976 Atlanta mortality trends: 1853–1873. *The Atlanta Historical Bulletin* **20**:112–119.
Todd, T. W., and B. Tracy
1930 Racial features in the American Negro cranium. *American Journal of Physical Anthropology* **15**:53–110.
Trotter, M.
1934 Septal apertures in the humerus of American whites and Negroes. *American Journal of Physical Anthropology* **19**:213–227.
Trotter, M., and G. C. Gleser
1958 A re-evaluation of estimation of stature based on measurements of long bones after death. (Seven figures.) *American Journal of Physical Anthropology* **16**:79–123.
Underwood, E. J.
1971 *Trace elements in human and animal nutrition*. New York: Academic Press.
Vayda, A. P., and R. A. Rappaport
1968 Ecology, cultural and noncultural. In *Introduction to cultural anthropology*, edited by J. A. Clifton. Boston: Houghton Mifflin. Pp. 477–497.

Vlach, J.
1977 Graveyards and Afro-American art. *Southern Exposure* 5(2–3):161–165.
Weiss, K. M.
1973 Demographic models for anthropology. *Memoirs of the Society for American Archaeology*, No. 27.

9

The Weaver Pottery: A Late Nineteenth-Century Family Industry in a Southeastern Urban Setting[1]

Charles H. Faulkner

INTRODUCTION

A major economic development in nineteenth-century America was the industrialization of traditional family crafts such as pottery making. This transformation of the family shop into a mechanized industry was particularly marked during the Reconstruction Period in the South, where a growing population eagerly sought inexpensive, mass-produced consumer products. Although these changes in technology and production were especially rapid in southern cities, the participating small urban-family industries usually are poorly documented in the historic record. Large heavy industries, especially the incorporated establishments, are richly described in the social and commercial histories of these cities, whereas details of small family-run factories usually are forgotten, tucked away in a single entry in a city directory or hidden in the dusty tomes of the county deed office. Although some of these family industries have been virtually obliterated by later intensive industrialization in central city areas, many of their architectural and material remains are still intact, sealed under the protective fill of later construction. This stratified fill, and the architectural and material remains that it contains, can provide considerable data on site layout, manufacturing techniques and products, and the process of industrialization of a traditional family craft in an urban environment.

A widespread traditional craft in the South that felt the full impact of social and

[1]The research for this chapter was made possible by Tennessee Department of Transportation Project No. I-40-7(94)389.

ARCHAEOLOGY OF URBAN AMERICA
The Search for Pattern and Process

ISBN 0-12-214980-7

technological changes in the late nineteenth century was stoneware pottery making. Unfortunately, few of these potteries have been studied archaeologically, especially those located in urban areas. In the late summer of 1980, the Department of Anthropology at the University of Tennessee, Knoxville, had the opportunity to test a nineteenth-century family pottery in downtown Knoxville, Tennessee. The Weaver Pottery site (40KN63) was discovered during an earlier survey of Tennessee potteries (Smith and Rogers 1979), but no archaeological work was planned until the site was extensively disturbed by the rebuilding of an Interstate-40 viaduct directly over the site. At that time, the Tennessee Department of Transportation contracted with the Department of Anthropology to conduct test excavations to determine site significance.

Preliminary archival research indicated that the pottery was established by the Weaver family in 1870 and was closed in 1888. Major products included stoneware vessels and drain pipes. Sanborn Insurance maps of Knoxville for 1884 and 1885 revealed the location of the pottery shop-warehouse and kiln on the north side of McGhee Street and adjacent to the west bank of Second Creek. Since interstate construction revealed a deeply stratified fill over the site, capped by a post-1960 compact-gravelled parking lot, a backhoe was used to remove the recent overburden and determine the depth of the older fill. Using the Sanborn maps as a guide, a 65 ft (19.8 m) east–west trench and a 40 ft (12 m) north–south trench were excavated in the first testing phase (August 23–26, 1980). After major features were located and the stratigraphy was carefully studied, a second testing phase was scheduled (September 10–30, 1980). In the second phase, a wedge-shaped 23.5 × 5 ft (7 × 1.5 m) area was hand excavated in three units within a 10 × 10 ft (3 × 3 m) grid to expose an early kiln and obtain a sample of artifacts from the site strata. In addition, four backhoe trenches were opened, followed by the sinking of eight hand-excavated test pits within these trenches to expose additional features (Figure 9.1).

Eleven features were recorded in the approximately 5 ft (1.5 m) of fill on this site. Five of these features could be related to the Weaver Pottery and the remainder to a furniture company warehouse that stood on the site from about 1905 to 1935. Two other warehouses also had been built here, one about 1890 and the other in 1947, but virtually no archaeological evidence of these structures was found.

FEATURES

Feature 1

This was the foundation of a large circular kiln covered by about 1.8 ft (.5 m) of fill. This kiln was built on a mound of cinders and slag that was raised to a height of 3 ft (.9 m) above the clay subsoil of the creek terrace. The foundation was laid on a prepared surface of pebbles and cinders. Although only the northeast quadrant of this foundation was intact, the remainder being razed and scattered over the site when the pottery closed, it provided data on the method of construction and type of kiln represented. The foundation consisted of rows of bricks and sandstone slabs separated by a band of packed orange-yellow clay. Some of the bricks had been

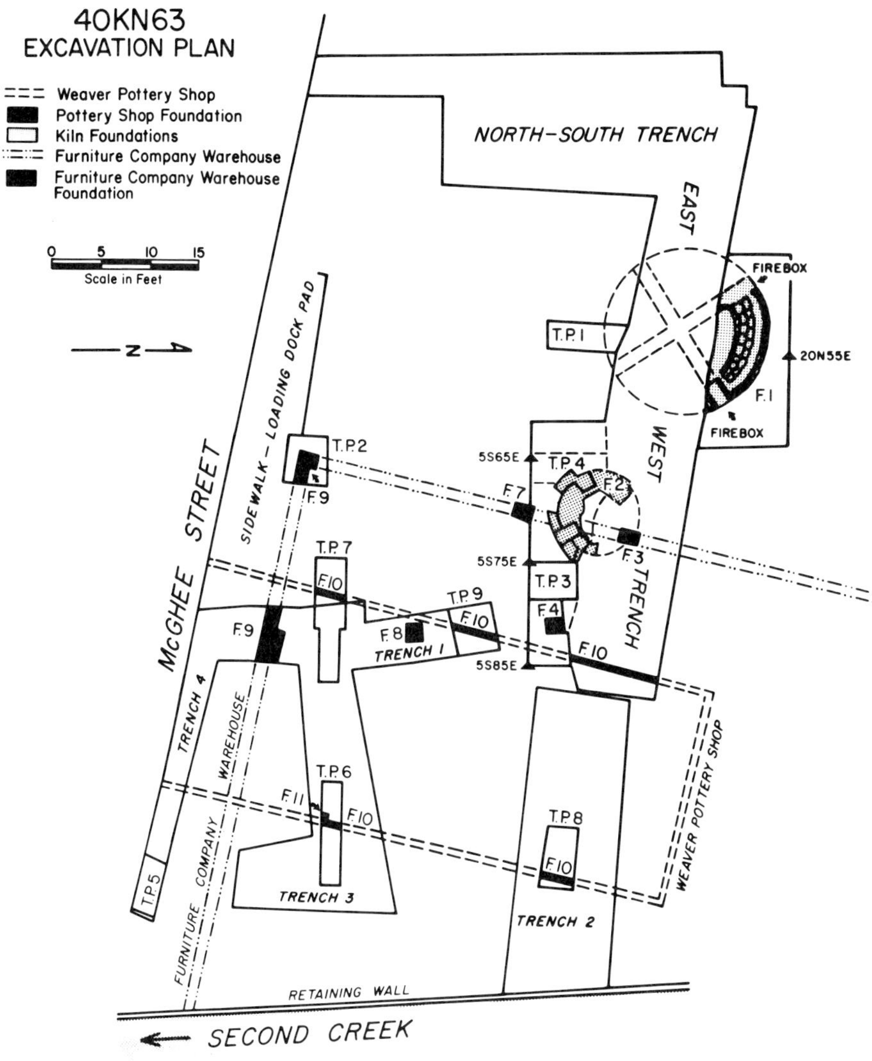

FIGURE 9.1. Site plan, showing excavation units and locations of features (courtesy Tennessee Department of Transportation).

recycled from Feature 2 (next section). The base of a rectangular firebox was preserved in the northeast quadrant, and remnants of a similar structure were found in the northwest quadrant. The presence of thin strata of coal and cinders at the southeast edge of the kiln indicated that another firebox had existed there. Based on this evidence, Feature 1 is believed to have been an updraft kiln about 16 ft (4.8 m)

FIGURE 9.2. Excavated Feature 2 kiln (courtesy Tennessee Department of Transportation).

in diameter, with four equally spaced firing eyes. The fuel used in this kiln appears to have been primarily coal.

Feature 2

This was an earlier updraft kiln built on a low ash mound about 4.5 ft (1.4 m) below the present ground surface and about 1 ft (.3 m) above the original Second Creek terrace. About one-third of the kiln foundation and most of the rubble and clay core had been removed by the later Feature 3 builder's trench and Feature 5 water-line trench. The remainder of the foundation was reasonably intact and measured 8 ft (2.4 m) in diameter, with two complete and one partial firebox openings facing southeast, southwest, and northwest (Figures 9.2 and 9.3). A profile taken through the fill in the well-preserved southwest firebox opening revealed stratified lenses of lime, sand, and charcoal, the lime possibly having been used to neutralize the hydrochloric acid by-product from salt-glazing (James F. Darrow, Associate Professor of Ceramics, personal communication). The sand may have been used to prevent fusing of the pottery to the kiln floor, or perhaps was deposited by flooding. The absence of coal cinders around the firing eyes indicates wood was the principal fuel. Pine (*Pinus* sp.) and oak (*Quercus* sp.) were identified in the charcoal sample (Gary Crites, UTK Paleoethnobotanical Laboratory, personal communication).

The foundation was built of handmade bricks laid with clay mortar. Some of the bricks were reused, glazed kiln bricks or had lime mortar adhering to their surfaces indicating that they were recycled from an earlier dismantled kiln or a building in the vicinity. Previous pottery manufacturing in this locality is also indicated by kiln furniture and stoneware sherds found in the 1 ft high (.3 m high) ash mound on which Feature 2 had been built. The center of the kiln was apparently a core of ash, clay, and brick rubble. This core had been mostly destroyed by later twentieth-century building activities on the site.

Feature 2 was dismantled shortly after the Feature 1 mound had been raised on the site, the west superstructure wall of the earlier kiln having been pushed over on the east slope of the Feature 1 mound. The top of this rubble on both the east and west sides of the dismantled kiln served as a waster dump for stoneware vessels for a short period of time, this fill being followed by interspersed strata of cinders, clinkers (vitrified stony matter), and yellow clay totaling about 1.3 ft (.4 m) thick. The top of this fill sequence then served as a floor between the Feature 1 kiln and the shop-warehouse until the closing of the pottery (see Feature 6).

Feature 3

Feature 3, found in the center of the East–West Trench, was a brick pier measuring 2.1 × 1.4 ft (.6 × .4 m) and set in a deep builder's trench that destroyed part of the foundation and earthen core of Feature 2. The construction and alignment of this pier with Features 7 and 9 indicate that it supported the west wall of the early twentieth-century Knoxville Furniture Company warehouse.

FIGURE 9.3. Detail of southwest firebox of Feature 2 kiln (courtesy Tennessee Department of Transportation).

Feature 4

This feature, a brick pier measuring 1.8 ft^2 (.17 m^2) on top, was exposed in the south profile of the East–West Trench. Alignment with Features 8 and 9 indicates that Feature 4 was one of the central support piers for the furniture company warehouse.

Feature 5

A V-shaped trench, 2.5 ft (.76 m) wide at the top and 2.1 ft (.64 m) deep, containing an iron water pipe was designated Feature 5. The point of origin of this feature and artifacts in the fill indicate that it was laid when a warehouse was built on this site in 1947.

Feature 6

This was a concentration of burned river cobbles resting on a compact pottery clay-and-lime-impacted floor. Since similar cobbles were found scattered throughout a stratum composed primarily of rubble from dismantled Feature 1, it is believed that these cobbles were part of the kiln construction. The compact clay-and-lime stratum was identified as the floor of an open shed that stood between the kiln and the shop-warehouse. The approximately 70 ft^2 (6.5 m^2) of this floor exposed in units 5S75E and 5S65E were completely clean of any artifacts that might indicate specific activities on the shed floor. However, the presence of pottery clay and lime suggests that these materials were processed in this structure.

Feature 7

This was a brick pier, identical in size and construction to Feature 3, that also functioned as a support for the west wall of the furniture warehouse. This feature was located in the south profile of unit 5S65E.

Feature 8

Feature 8, measuring 1.8 ft^2 (.17 m^2) on the top surface and identical in construction to Feature 4, was a brick pier located in Test Trench 1. These two piers and Feature 9 were constructed on 14 ft (4.2 m) centers and functioned as the inner foundation of the furniture company warehouse.

Feature 9

This was the front (McGhee Street) foundation wall of the furniture company warehouse revealed in Test Trench 1 and Test Pit 2. In Test Trench 1, a pilaster, which was 2.2 ft (.66 m) wide and had supported the floor joists that extended from

FIGURE 9.4. Southwest corner of furniture company warehouse, Feature 9 (courtesy Tennessee Department of Transportation).

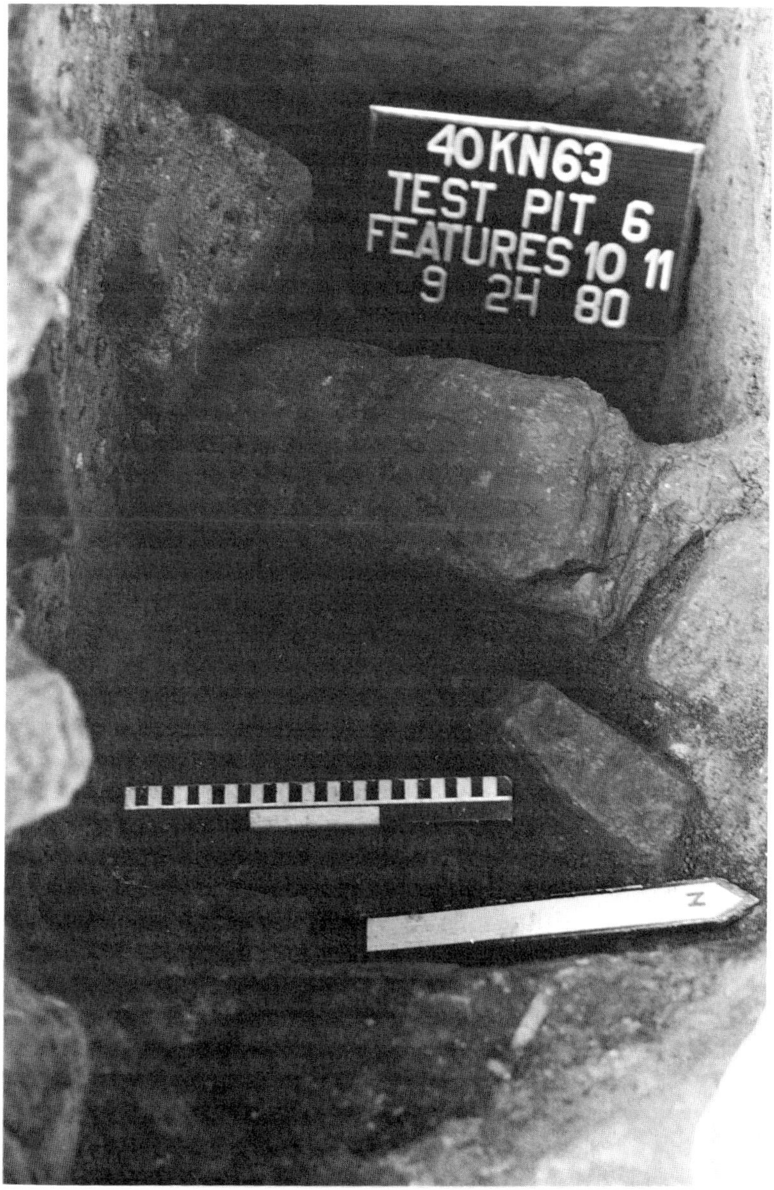

FIGURE 9.5. East wall of pottery shop (Feature 10) and brick pier (Feature 11) in Test Pit 6 (courtesy Tennessee Department of Transportation).

Features 4 and 8, was evident on the inner face of the wall. The main wall, 1.4 ft (.42 m) wide, made a right angle in Test Pit 2 to form the southwest corner of the warehouse and to align with pier-support Features 3 and 7 (Figure 9.4).

Feature 10

Feature 10 was the foundation of the pottery shop-warehouse shown on the 1884 Sanborn map. This foundation indicates that the building was 21 ft (6.3 m) wide, which corresponds to the width of the building on the Sanborn map. According to this map, the building was about 50 ft (15.2 m) long, with its long axis running perpendicular to McGhee Street. It was described as a one-story frame structure with a shingle roof (Sanborn Insurance Map of Knoxville 1884).

The west foundation wall of this structure was revealed in the east profile of the East–West Test Trench, in Test Pit 7, and in Test Pit 9. The east wall was found in Test Pits 6 and 8 (Figure 9.5). The base of the foundation was built of mortared blocks of red shale quarried from bedrock in the immediate vicinity of the site. Bricks had been laid atop this shale foundation, the first course resting on a wooden sill or flooring made of hemlock (*Tsuga canadensis*) or pine (*Pinus* sp.) (Gary Crites, UTK Paleoethnobotanical Laboratory, personal communication). Profiles of the west wall revealed later fill piled against the bricks, an indication that the building had been rebuilt with the brick foundation added later to the shale foundation. When the shop was razed in 1888, the brick foundation was pushed into the open "crawlspace" beneath the building. A layer of plaster on the inner side of several bricks and scattered plaster on the crawlspace floor showed that the brick and frame walls were plastered in the front portion of the building. Windows were indicated by concentrations of glass from small panes on the interior floor. Wood samples in this rubble were evidence that major construction materials of the floor and walls again were hemlock and pine.

Feature 11

This was a small brick pier built just inside the east wall of the shop-warehouse to support the floor of that building (Figure 9.5). The mortar is different from that used between the shale blocks, and appears to be a type of cement. This suggests that this feature was added as a foundational support during the later reconstruction of the building. Although only one of these piers was found in Test Pit 6, it is assumed that pairs of these supports paralleled the foundation walls to support the shop floor.

HISTORY OF THE WEAVER SITE: 110 YEARS OF INDUSTRIAL ACTIVITY

Almost 5 ft (1.5 m) of stratified fill were encountered in the excavation area (Figures 9.6 and 9.7). This stratigraphy and the features of the Weaver Pottery site indicate at least eight formational periods involving construction, demolition, and

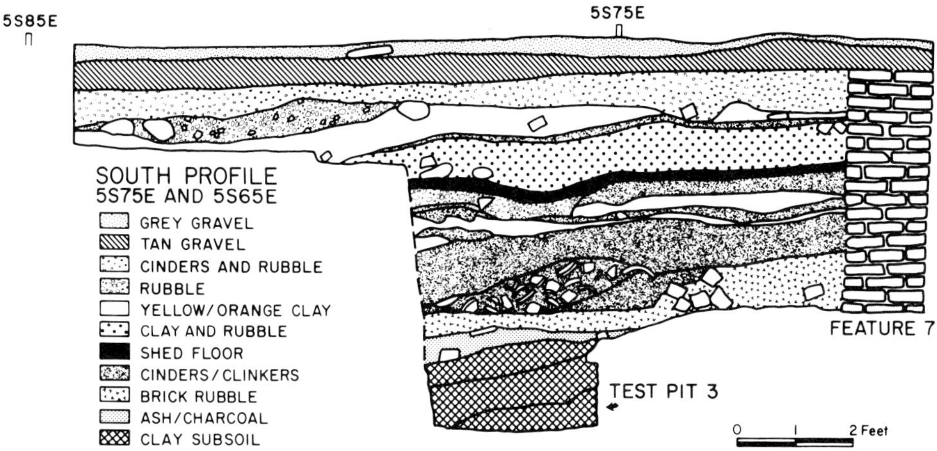

FIGURE 9.6. Stratigraphy in south profile of units 5S75E and 5S65E (courtesy Tennessee Department of Transportation).

filling on this site during the past 110 years. Each period reflects changing industrial and commercial activity, with an initial establishment after the Civil War of family-run industries in a largely residential neighborhood, a peak of industrialization and commercialization of the area about the turn of the century, and the virtual abandonment of the area (now inner city) by 1960.

A total of 4734 vessel sherds, 959 drain pipe sherds, 1862 pieces of kiln furniture, 81 pieces of kiln debris, and 68 unidentified items was recovered in the strata and features during the two testing phases. Whereas intensive analysis of this material has not been completed, preliminary work with selected samples indicates the range of ceramic products manufactured and their frequency through time. Both stoneware and earthenware products were manufactured at the Weaver Pottery, the former being predominant. Most of the ceramic vessels were standard utilitarian food-processing and storage forms that were wheel thrown, with no evidence of machine turning or "jiggering." Two distinctive hand-molded crescent-shaped lug handles often were applied to large crocks and churns (Figure 9.8, D). Some jug handles appear to have been extruded (Figures 9.8,C). Only four sherds with a mold-made decorative relief were recovered (Figure 9.8, A). Two jug sherds exhibited blue (cobalt) decoration on the body and handle terminals (Figure 9.8, B). Generally, however, there is a singular lack of evidence for experimentation with unusual vessel forms. Vessels usually were salt glazed on the exterior and glazed with an "Albany slip" on the interior. A large number of vessels were marked with variations of the stamp "WEAVER & BRO. KNOXVILLE TENN" (Figure 9.9) up to 1882, and a capacity stamp was used on many vessels throughout the 18 years of the pottery's existence. The stamp, distinctive for this pottery, has an ornate numeral encircled by a row of toothed dentates (Figure 9.9).

FIGURE 9.7. South profile of units 5S75E and 5S65E (courtesy Tennessee Department of Transportation).

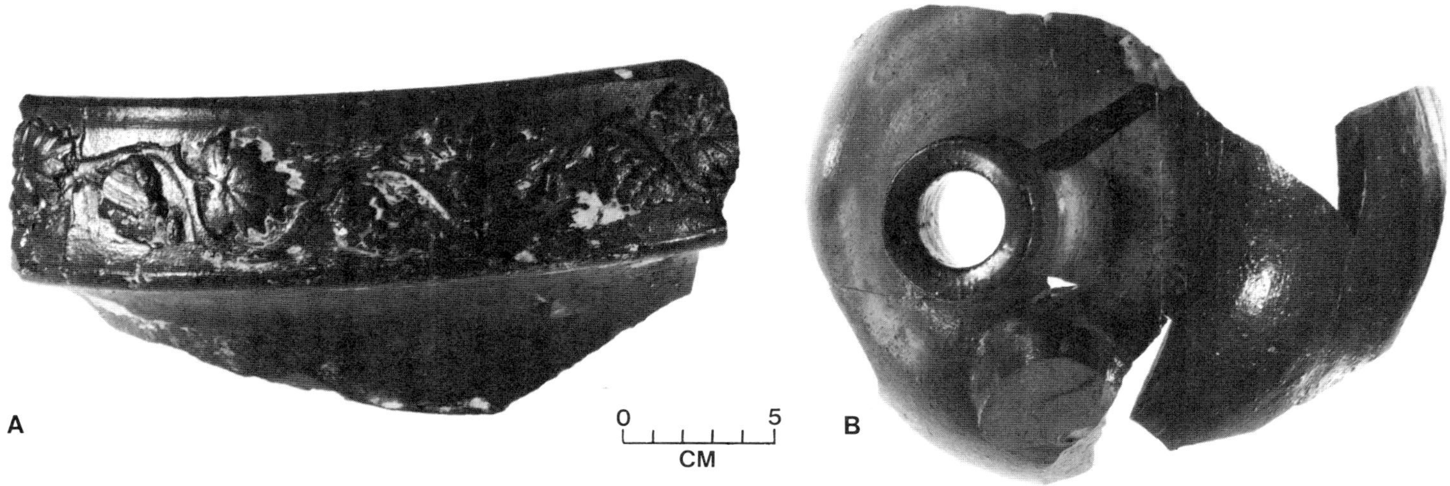

FIGURE 9.8. Weaver vessel forms: (*A*) sherd with mold-made relief, (*B*) slip-painted jug sherd
(continued)

FIGURE 9.8. *(continued)* (*C*) jug with ribbed extruded handle, and (*D*) jar sherd with lug handle (courtesy Tennessee Department of Transportation). (Shown one half actual size.)

Construction and architectural forms include ceramic pipe, chimney flues, and decorative curbing tile. The pipe, most of which is salt glazed, ranges from small-diameter drain pipe to large sewer pipe. Kiln furniture includes stoneware saggers for the firing of jugs, and clay props, wads, and coils (Figure 9.10). The latter three artifacts, handformed pieces of clay that were rolled in sand to prevent them from sticking to the vessels, were used to stack unfired pottery ware in the kiln.

Another ceramic artifact utilized during firing and found on this site is the "draw trial" or "toten piece," a cut and perforated piece of an unfired ("green") vessel placed in the kiln during loading and used to test the firing temperature and glazing conditions in the kiln (Figure 9.10, F). An iron rod was hooked through the hole in the draw trial to retract the pieces during firing.

The first formational period on the Weaver site is represented by ash and waster strata lying 5 ft (1.5 m) below the present ground surface and immediately above the clay subsoil of the creek terrace on which a small pottery kiln (Feature 2) and shop-warehouse (Feature 10) were built. Stoneware vessels marked "WEAVER & BRO.," resting on the subsoil and inclusive in the Feature 1 mound, indicate that the Feature 2 kiln was used by the Weavers, but possibly not constructed by that family.

David H. Weaver, the son and grandson of potters who had moved through Virginia, Pennsylvania, and Kentucky during the late eighteenth and early nineteenth centuries, was the founder of the Weaver Pottery. According to the

FIGURE 9.9. Weaver Pottery mark (courtesy Tennessee Department of Transportation).

family records of his descendants still living in Knoxville and Goodspeed (1887), he came there with his family in late 1869 or early 1870. It was not until September 18, 1872, that the firm Weaver and Brother, owned by David H. and William H. Weaver, purchased from James M. Duncan the lot on which the pottery was located (Knox County Deed Records 1872). The 1869 Knoxville City Directory lists J. M. Duncan and A. P. Ellis as potters who lived nearby on McGhee Street. It is likely, therefore, that Duncan and Ellis built the early kiln and shop, which were rented or leased in 1870 by the Weavers until they could raise enough capital to purchase the property.

Recycled kiln bricks in Feature 2 and salt-glazed stoneware sherds and kiln furniture under the Feature 2 foundation indicate that an even earlier kiln existed somewhere in the area. Perhaps this earlier pottery was operated by Samuel Smith, Jr., whose business was located somewhere along Second Creek in the 1820s (Smith and Rogers 1979:47). A gap in the deed records precludes an association of Smith with this particular lot, but it does provide evidence that a series of potteries was established along Second Creek from about 1820 to the 1880s. The attraction of this locality appears to have been a handy water source and a deposit of pottery clay in the creek terrace.

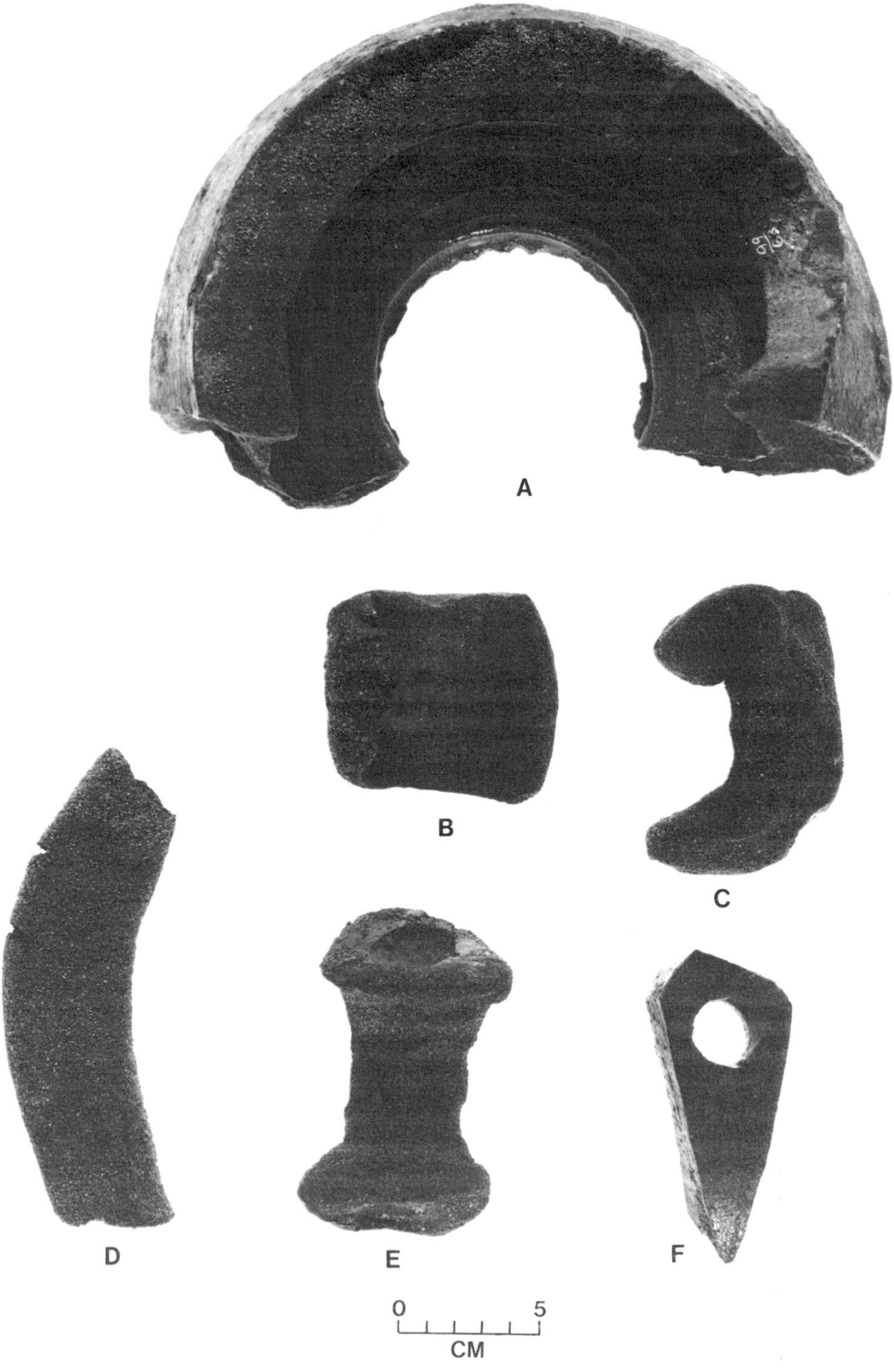

FIGURE 9.10. Kiln furniture: (*A*) jug sagger, (*B*–*C*) wads, (*D*) coil, (*E*) prop, and (*F*) draw trial (courtesy Tennessee Department of Transportation). (Shown one half actual size.)

When the Weavers purchased their shop, it was located on the eastern fringes of what was called the McGhee Addition, a suburb developed by Charles McClung McGhee after the Civil War (McArthur 1976:42), which included both residential areas and small family industries. Because of increasing industrialization of the area, it was later called Mechanicsville. This suburb became the Ninth Ward of the city of Knoxville on January 1, 1883 (Gray and Adams 1976:84). Little is known about the Weaver operation from 1870 to 1874. Because there are no maps of the area from this period, and city directories were not printed from 1870 to 1875, we do not know if other structures besides the kiln and shop-warehouse were present or how many members of the Weaver family were employed there. The size of the kiln suggests that only a modest amount of ceramic products was produced at that time.

Two sherd deposits were found in strata representing the first period of the Weaver operation. Noteworthy characteristics of this collection are the well-developed salted exteriors, the large number of marked pieces (WEAVER & BRO.), the presence of decorated pieces (painting and molding), a variety of domestic vessels, and the virtual absence of drain pipe. One of these deposits was a waster dump of 316 sherds from the top of the clay subsoil in the North–South Trench. Of this collection, 314 are vessel sherds (99%) and only two are drain pipe fragments. Three salt-glazed jugs are present, one a small vessel with a .5 gal. (1.9 liter) capacity and two larger forms with 1.5 and 2 gal. (5.6 and 7.5 liter) capacities, which exhibit cobalt slip-painted decoration. Other salt-glazed vessel forms in this collection include milk bowls or pans, preserve jars, crocks, and three bowl sherds with molded applied strips.

Another collection was from a sherd pocket within the fill of the Feature 1 mound. One-hundred-thirteen vessel sherds and two possible chimney flue sherds were found in this deposit. Salt-glazed vessel forms included a minimum of two churns with lug handles, several crocks, a bowl, and a jug with a collared-type neck and strap handle. Two sherds were from a tall, cylindrical form suggestive of a chimney flue.

The second site-formational period, 1874–1888, can be divided into two phases: the expansion and apparent prospering of the Weaver business from 1874 to about 1882, and the decline of this stoneware industry sometime after this date to the final closing in 1888. The expansion of the pottery is indicated in the archaeological record by four closely occurring events. The initial event was the building of the Feature 1 kiln on the cinder mound. Shortly after this, the Feature 2 kiln was razed and its west wall pushed over on the east slope of the Feature 1 mound. At about this time, the pottery shop also was rebuilt by raising the foundation with several courses of bricks and constructing small piers (Feature 11) to support the floor.

The last event was the sealing of the kiln rubble with several distinct strata. The initial deposit was a waster dump of discarded vessels on the east brick-rubble talus. Immediately overlying this waster pile was a .8 ft (.24 m) thick stratum of cinders and clinkers, probably the discharge from the Feature 1 kiln. There followed a .6 ft (.18 m) thick series of cinders, clinkers, and yellow clay lenses. These strata apparently were laid down over a short period of time since there is no evidence that a stable, compacted floor had been established on any of them. This 1.5 ft (.45 m) of fill was finally capped by a hardened clay-and-lime-impacted floor under a shed (Feature 6) that was built in 1874–1875 between the new kiln (Feature 1) and the west shop wall (Feature 10). Additional evidence that this fill was rapidly laid down to raise the floor to the level of the new kiln is its mean elevation, which varied only .1 ft (.03 m) from the elevation of the Feature 1 foundation.

A total of 2465 vessel sherds (99%) and 10 ceramic drain pipe sherds was recovered in the waster dump on the Feature 2 rubble. Although this large collection is still being analyzed and vessels reconstructed, preliminary analysis reveals a general consistency in color and amount of salt glazing. A few jars were slipped on both the interior and exterior surfaces. Other vessel forms include salt-glazed churns, crocks, bowls, and jugs with plain strap handles.

The rebuilding of the kiln and shop was probably necessitated by the need for flood protection and additional facilities for increased production. The rebuilding and expansion was possibly related to an event cited in a February 26, 1875 article in the *Knoxville Daily Press and Herald* concerning a flood on Second Creek: "The water was, for a while, on the floor of the pottery, but no damage resulted, the proprietors having raised their floor several feet since their rough experience of the freshet of a year ago."

That the rebuilding of the kiln and shop was also motivated by an expansion of the Weaver's business is indicated by three things. First, the new kiln was twice as large as the old one. Second, in October 1874, the Weavers bought the lot immediately north of their property from Charles McGhee (Knox County Deed Records 1874). Since these lots were only 50 ft (15 m) deep (north–south), the structure housing the steam engine and two small outbuildings shown on the 1884 map were situated on this back lot purchased from McGhee. It is possible that the Weavers installed a steam-powered pug mill and extruding machinery at this time and began to use coal as fuel. And third, the increased value of their property is documented by the Knox County tax records, which reveal that in 1874 their property was assessed at $300, while in 1875 the assessment was $1000 (Knox County Tax Records 1874, 1875).

Unfortunately, the second period in the history of the Weaver pottery, probably the most prosperous years of this family industry, left little evidence in the hand-excavated area except for the rebuilding events of 1874–1875. Although the archaeological record is scanty for this period, the city directories and Sanborn map of 1884 provide excellent documentation of which family members worked in the pottery, and descriptions of the operation at this time. Also, the *Tennessee State Gazetteer and Business Directory* for 1876–1877 contains an advertisement for Weaver & Bro. as "Manufacturers of all kinds of stoneware, fruit jars, flower pots, vases, sewer pipe, chimney tops, and dealers in sealing wax, etc."

In July 1882, another important event occurred in the Weaver business; William sold his half of the partnership to his brother for $1400 (Knox County Deed Records 1882). In the 1882 city directory the firm is listed as "David H. Weaver." Stoneware vessels made at the Weaver Pottery after this date are not stamped "WEAVER & BRO." and this fact permits either a pre- or post-1882 date to be assigned to sherd samples collected from each stratum in the test trenches and excavation units. Despite the fact that William was no longer a partner in the business, he continued to be employed by his brother until 1886 (Knoxville City Directories 1880–1886). City directories for this period also indicate that David and William's father, George C. Weaver, and their brother, George W. Weaver, joined the firm by 1880, the latter working there as a potter until he died in 1885 or 1886, and the elder Weaver remaining with the firm as a potter until it closed in 1888. "Eight hands" were listed as employed here on the 1884 Sanborn map. If this includes the proprietor, half the work force in this pottery were family members.

The archaeological excavation of the later kiln (Feature 1), open shed (Feature 6), and shop-warehouse (Features 10 and 11) confirmed their location as shown on the 1884 Sanborn map (Figure 9.11). Unfortunately, the rear portion of the shop area had been destroyed by interstate construction before we were contracted to test the site. The map shows a one-story building containing a 20-HP steam engine and boiler, with a 44 ft (13.2 m) iron smokestack behind the shop. This engine probably powered the pug mill and extruding machinery. Since the shed with the Feature

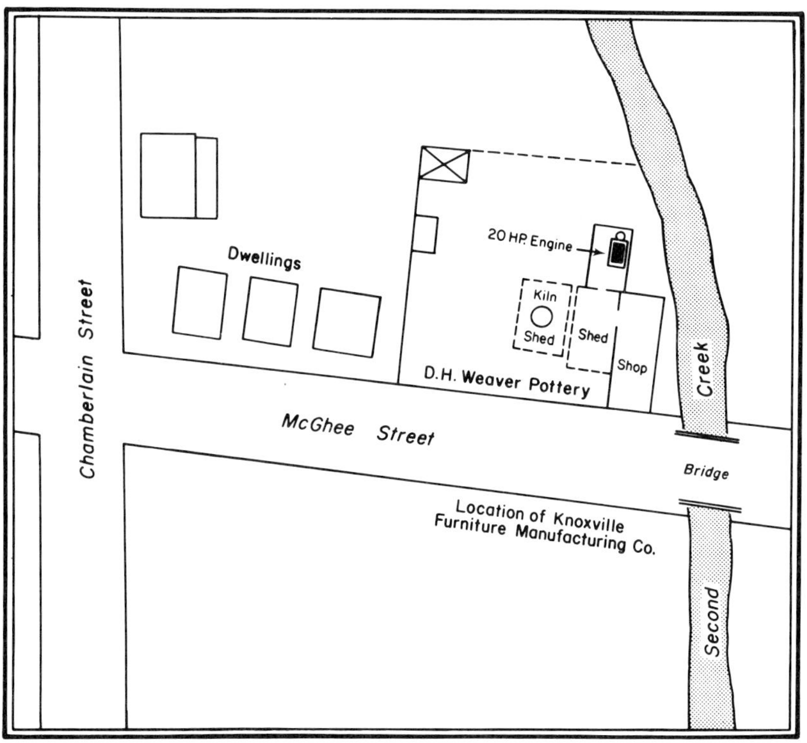

FIGURE 9.11. Map of the Weaver Pottery in 1884 (after 1884 Sanborn map) (courtesy Tennessee Department of Transportation).

6 clay floor is immediately in front of this power source, it could have been used for clay preparation (pug mill) or for extruding pipe.

Feature 10 is identified as a warehouse on the 1884 map, but it is likely that the storage of ceramic products was only one function of this structure. The evidence of windows and especially of plastered walls indicates bright, well-lighted rooms, more in keeping with a turning area and office space. Evidence that this was probably a turning shop is provided by a rare photograph of George C. Weaver, presumably taken in the McGhee Street building and now in possession of the Weaver descendants. This photograph, undoubtedly staged and copyrighted by Knaffl and Bros., Knoxville photographers in the 1880s, shows George throwing a jar on what appears to be a manually operated (kick?) wheel in a room with plastered walls and a large paned window.

The ceramics produced during the waning years of the Weaver operation are represented by 572 sherds found in the clay-and-rubble stratum, deposited when the business was closed and the dismantled kiln rubble spread over the site. Although an advertisement in the *Tennessee State Gazetteer and Business Directory for 1887* (354) for the Knoxville Pottery and Pipe Works, D. H. Weaver, Proprietor, lists "all kinds of stoneware," the large number of pipe sherds found in the stratum dating from this period indicates that drain pipe was now the principal product manufactured there. Of the 572 sherds recovered in the clay-and-rubble stratum, 418 (73%) were from drain pipes.

A total of 154 vessel sherds was recovered in the clay-and-rubble stratum. In contrast to the early deposits on this site, this collection exhibited few vessel forms, lacked painted or molded pieces, was characterized by greater inconsistency in salting and slipping, and contained no pieces marked "WEAVER & BRO." (although several were stamped with the same style of capacity identification used during the earliest period on the site). Identifiable vessel forms included two large—1.5 and 2 gal. (5.6 and 7.5 liter)—salt-glazed jugs (one exhibiting a ribbed, extruded handle), a minimum of two salt-glazed churns with the typical lug handles, and four 1-qt. (.9 liter) preserve jars with Albany-slipped exterior surfaces.

The third period on this site witnessed the closing and razing of the Weaver Pottery. On June 18, 1888, David Weaver sold the property on which his pottery was located to the Knoxville Furniture Company (Knox County Deed Records 1888). Shortly after the property was sold, the kiln (Feature 1) was razed and kiln-brick rubble (about .7 ft or .21 m thick) was spread over the front portion of the site and up to the shop walls. This is the clay-and-rubble stratum of Feature 6. Next, the walls of the shop were pushed into the open foundation, which also was filled with large pieces of sewer pipe and chimney flues. The remaining concavity was then capped with a stratum of virtually sterile, orange clay, which was almost 2 ft (.6 m) thick in some areas. Finally, the clay deposit was leveled with the surface of the kiln rubble stratum, approximately 1.2 ft (.36 m) beneath the present ground surface.

The fourth period on this site, from 1888 to about 1905, is least evidenced in the archaeological record. Almost all of the information concerning activities during this period is from two Sanborn Insurance maps published in 1890 (updated 1898) and 1903. Only one stratum can be definitely attributed to this episode, this being a deposit of cinders immediately above the Feature 1 foundation. Aqua glass fragments and a portion of an embossed glass bottle from the Knoxville Bottling Works indicate an 1880s–1890s date.

The first decade of the twentieth century witnessed the peak of industrial development along McGhee Street. By 1910, the Knoxville Furniture Company had built a three-story warehouse on the Weaver site. This corporation, founded in 1879, was described at the turn of the century as "one of Knoxville's 'biggest and best' and in 1900 made more mantels than any other factory in the United States [Kephart 1901:19]." A 1910 drawing of the Knoxville Furniture Company shows the main plant as being on the south side of McGhee Street, and a three-story warehouse as being on the north side, spanning the creek, and covering the old pottery site (*Greater Knoxville Illustrated* 1910:85).

The building of the warehouse initiated the fifth formational period on the Weaver site. The exact date of this construction has not yet been determined, but it probably was 1905–1906. Archaeological evidence of this warehouse includes the brick piers (Features 3, 4, 7, and 8) and the front brick wall (Feature 9). The concrete retaining walls, which supported the building over Second Creek, are still intact along this stream. These foundations supported a three-story frame building 36 ft (10.8 m) high, over 80 ft (24 m) wide along McGhee Street, and about 100 ft (30 m) long, the structure being somewhat trapezoidal in shape. The walls were covered with sheet metal, each floor was provided with a row of windows on the east and west sides, and the rear wall had a series of loading docks along a spur track that crossed Second Creek on a trestle at the northeast corner of the building (*Greater Knoxville Illustrated* 1910; Sanborn Insurance Map of Knoxville 1917).

The Knoxville Furniture Company closed in 1930. Its buildings are listed as vacant in the 1930 Knoxville City Directory. The warehouse was rented for a couple of years and was finally torn down around 1935. The razing of this structure marks the beginning of the sixth period on this site. After the warehouse was torn down, the terrace slope that it had protected was now filled and leveled to the concrete retaining wall, and the .3–.7 ft (.09–.21 m) cinders-and-rubble layer was spread over the site. Evidence that this latter stratum postdates the destruction of the warehouse includes the presence of the rubble stratum over the brick foundation piers on the terrace slope and of machine-made bottle fragments and silk-screened soda bottle sherds dating from 1920 to 1970 inclusive, within this fill. This area appears to have been used as a storage lot until 1947.

By 1947, the Mechanicsville neighborhood had changed from a primarily industrial area to a commercial area of wholesale fruit and vegetable produce companies. In that year, the Knoxville Farmer's Co-op was built on the site. This was a single-story frame building covered with sheet metal. This seventh period of the site's history is represented archaeologically only by Feature 5, a water line that was laid to this building and a concrete loading dock pad adjacent to McGhee Street (identified as a "sidewalk" during initial field observation). The profile of this feature in Test Trench 1 and Test Pit 2 indicated that it had been laid over the cinders and rubble fill covering the front wall (Feature 9) of the furniture company warehouse and demonstrated its association with the later co-op warehouse.

The Knoxville Farmer's Co-op was torn down in 1960, about the same time as an elevated expressway (now I-40) was completed over the site. The eighth and final period of site formation witnessed the deposition of a tan, compact-gravel stratum capped by grey gravel, apparently for use as a parking lot. This was the surface of the site in the summer of 1980, when interstate improvement began. Although a few commercial establishments still exist in this area, most were closed and demolished at that time.

CONCLUSIONS

A recent survey of pottery making in Tennesse has revealed that, of the 163 pottery sites surveyed, only 31 are classified as "industrial" potteries, that is, large operations, usually employing a number of nonfamily members, using mechanized techniques and equipment, and depending on nonlocal clays (Smith and Rogers 1979:8–11). At least 16 potteries (including the Weaver operation) were found in Tennessee's four largest cities (Memphis, Nashville, Knoxville, and Chattanooga) (Smith and Rogers 1979), but it is not clear how many of these could be characterized as truly industrial. However, it is significant that these represent less than 10% of the potteries found in the survey, a fact suggesting that urban areas may not have been choice locations for the establishment of these industries.

Since the Weaver Pottery is the only urban pottery that has been excavated in the state, it is not possible to determine if it was "typical" for this area of the Southeast in the post-Civil War years; however, features of this pottery do not entirely fit the industrial pattern described above. Folk or family potteries have been described as completely kin-operated with techniques usually being passed down from father to son(s), and utilizing nonmechanized equipment to produce basically conservative utilitarian wares that were distributed locally (Burrison 1975; Guilland 1971; Lasansky 1979). The archaeological evidence gathered at the Weaver Pottery suggests an interesting blend of traditional family and industrial characteristics. This pattern may be typical of small family potteries established in southern urban–industrial settings.

During the first 4 years of its existence, the Weaver operation was a small-scale business, utilizing a small updraft kiln that was typical of a number of traditional pottery manufacturing sites in rural eastern Tennessee (Smith and Rogers 1979:20). Wood was apparently burned in this kiln even though the adjacent railway, the Knoxville and Kentucky, had extended its tracks to the northern Tennessee coalfields by 1868 (Rothrock 1946:228). Although evidence is largely circumstantial (the width of the lot on which the original shop was situated indicates no space for the steam boiler that was present on the later maps of the site), it is probable that the pottery vessels were turned by hand. These vessels were primarily salt-glazed food-preparation and storage types. Few construction materials (e.g., pipe) were found in the older strata. This reflects the basic handcrafted nature of the earliest products and a continuing demand for stoneware vessels in the kitchens, smokehouses, and springhouses of eastern Tennessee. The presence of cobalt slip and applied molded designs indicates some amount of experimentation and innovation in these early years, and although this observation is largely subjective, most of the vessels appear to be more carefully thrown and fired (e.g., thinner and smoother walls and more even and consistent glazing) that the later pieces.

The Weaver operation probably can be called a "factory" after 1875. There is both documentary and archaeological evidence that their business was industrialized after that time. Deed and tax records indicate that adjacent property was acquired by 1874 and that the property value had tripled by the following year. It is believed that this additional property allowed the installation of a steam boiler that probably ran the pug mill and extruding machinery. By 1875, a new kiln, twice as large as the old structure (Feature 2), had been built on a cinder-and-slag mound, and the small, wood-fired updraft kiln had been dismantled. The presence of coal near the firebox of the larger kiln and of the cinder fill immediately above the razed early kiln foundation indicates a shift to coal firing, another characteristic of an industrial pottery.

The position of the four fireboxes and the construction of the one reasonably intact firebox in Feature 1 are so similar to the construction in the Feature 2 updraft kiln that the former also could be identified as an updraft type. However, so little of the foundation was intact that the later construction of a downdraft type cannot be ruled out. Support for the latter interpretation is the fact that the downdraft kiln was superior to the updraft type in providing a more even temperature distribution and economical fuel consumption (Olsen 1973:54). Also, it is noteworthy that the kiln used by the Weavers after they left Knoxville and established a new pottery in northeast Tennessee in the 1890s was definitely a downdraft type.

Although the shop was rebuilt to raise it above the flood zone of Second Creek, there is no evidence that it was increased in size except for the addition of a boiler and engine at the rear of the building. However, if the small brick piers (Feature 11) were added beneath the floor at this time, it is likely that they were necessary to support the weight of additional machinery in this structure.

Despite this evidence of the industrialization of the Weaver Pottery after 1874–1875, certain elements of a traditional family operation still prevailed. The most notable is the continued family involvement in the business during the 1880s. In 1884, for example, half of the workers listed for this establishment were Weavers, the father and his three sons. A perusal of the city directory for that year shows no other persons with the occupation of "potter," which further suggests that the skilled labor in this factory still consisted of family members. Additional evidence of family involvement is found in the conservatism of vessel form and appendage shape through time; even the unmarked pieces usually can be identified as Weaver in origin. Although the increasing number of extruded drain pipe sherds in the later strata of the site attests to the utilization of mechanized equipment, there is one bit of evidence suggesting the continued use of a manually operated wheel. The previously mentioned photograph of George C. Weaver, known to have been taken in the shop during the 1880s, shows no evidence of a power-driven wheel. Although it is certain that this photograph was "staged," the presence of ribs and other tools casually hung on the wall and scattered on the workbench indicates that this truly was a work area.

If half the workers in this factory in 1884 were family members, it is probable that a number of tasks beyond management and pot throwing were done by these kinsmen. Thus, they still can be considered traditional craftspersons, in that they produced their pottery from start to finish. Although unskilled laborers were hired to do such mundane tasks as clay digging and preparing, loading and unloading the kiln, stoking the fires, and delivering the ware to customers, the overall digging, loading, firing, and salting was undoubtedly accomplished under the watchful eyes of the family. A great deal of technical skill was needed to produce a quality, saleable ware because it was so difficult to fire at such a high temperature and achieve a satisfactory uniform salt glaze.

The closing of the Weaver factory in 1888 seems to follow the pattern documented in studies of late-nineteenth-century stoneware manufacturing in the North (Guilland 1971: Lasansky 1979). By the last two decades of the nineteenth century, a number of factors combined to sound the death knell for most of the stoneware potteries. These factors included the mass production of glass containers, especially the Mason canning jar, and various kinds of tin ware, which provided cheaper and more efficient containers for the housewife; the establishment of dairies, which made the milk pan and butter churn obsolete in the cities; the upward spiral of railway rates for the shipment of clay and coal; an increasing scarcity of easily obtainable high-quality clays; and the increasing reluctance, for social and economic reasons, of a son to apprentice in the craft of his father. In the face of this diminishing market and the disappearance of family craftsmen, potteries turned to the mass production of drain pipe, flower pots, or mold-made jugs and crocks that did not require skilled labor. Or, they simply went out of business.

One could routinely explain the demise of the Weaver Pottery in Knoxville as the result of these social and economic changes in late nineteenth-century America. However, data from theWeaver site and a study of the later Weaver family history do not support an explanation simply based on the national experience. Archaeological remains and advertisements for the Weaver business indicate that they shifted to the production of drain pipe by the 1880s, a product that could be mass-produced with unskilled labor and for which there should have been a continuing market in Knoxville during the construction boom of the post-Civil War era. It was during the last three decades of the nineteenth century that Knoxville grew from a town into a city, the population increasing from 8682 in 1870, to 32,673 in 1900 (McArthur 1976:29–30).

Although the Weavers closed the doors of their Knoxville business in 1888, two more generations of this family continued to make ceramic products in rural northeast Tenessee. By 1890, David Weaver and his son Carl M. B. Weaver established another pottery factory in Mohawk, Greene County, Tennessee, called the East Tennessee Pottery and Pipe Works. According to the company letterhead, they specialized in drain tile and sewer pipe, but also continued to manufacture stoneware vessels (letter from David H. Weaver to Carl M. B. Weaver, February 12, 1890). A photograph of this plant made around 1909 shows a large rectangular shop, an open shed, and a crown downdraft kiln, a layout that is strikingly similar to the one found on the Knoxville site. Also noteworthy in Weaver's letter is an explanation by David to Carl about how to build the kiln, thus indicating a continuation of craft knowledge from father to son.

David H. Weaver died on June 1, 1893. Carl continued to operate the Mohawk plant until 1912, when they again moved their operation, this time to the McCloud community in adjacent Hawkins County. The reason for this move was the depletion of the local clay in Mohawk (Lucille Weaver Poates and Lewis L. Poates, personal communications). The Weaver Brick Company in McCloud was operated by Carl's son, David Albert Weaver, until the Tennessee Valley Authority built the John Sevier Steam Plant on the site in 1952.

The fact that the Weavers continued to make ceramics for over 60 years after they closed their Knoxville factory suggests that their move out of the urban area was not merely due to changing consumer demands and increasing manufacturing costs. It is believed that the closing of this small family-run urban factory was primarily due to three factors, one being the competition from heavy industry as Mechanicsville changed from residential light-industry to corporate heavy-industry, and another being the fact that there was a continued greater demand for their ceramic products in rural easternTennessee. A third factor may have been the pollution caused by salt-glazing and the fire hazard from the kiln.

The competition from heavy industry, rather than being economic, was competition for space in this industrial area of Knoxville. The shift to drain pipe and tile production meant local clays could be utilized more readily for their manufacture and more extensive mechanization could be employed. The Weaver Pottery, being a small family-run industry, did not possess the capital to acquire a larger tract of land for clay procurement, nor for an expansion of their extruding plant once they began the mass production of ceramic pipe. Although no analysis has been made of the Weaver ceramics to determine the origin of the clay used in their manufacture, what appears to be a grey pottery clay was found immediately below the historic fill on the site terrace. The fact that at least three potteries were established along Second Creek during the nineteenth century suggests that this clay must have been a factor in their decision to locate there. Although the size of the Weaver lots precluded the extensive mining of clay, it is possible that they mixed this local clay with an imported high-temperature clay. A trait of some southern potters was to mix fine high-firing clay with poorer grade local clays (Guilland 1971:82).

By the 1880s, the Weavers were completely hemmed in by a large bottling works to the north and a furniture factory to the south along McGhee Street. The noxious fumes from their operation and fire hazard to the nearby furniture factory must have been a constant problem. Land prices must have been at a premium in this industrial area, and there was no opportunity for the Weavers to maintain a local clay source or to expand their plant. Their most expedient alternative was to leave the urban location for a rural site where abundant clay was readily available, where there was room for expansion, and where they would constitute less of a hazard to their neighbors.

It is likely that there continued to be a market for stoneware vessels in rural eastern Tennessee after it had virtually disappeared in the larger towns and cities. Pickling, kraut-making, churning of butter, and distilling of corn whiskey are but a few of the activities that would necessitate the continued use of stoneware vessels, especially if a basic conservatism slowed the acceptance of "new-fangled" tin and glass containers. The analysis of household debris from early twentieth-century rural habitation sites in eastern Tennessee would determine how much stoneware continued to be utilized. In addition to continued household uses for the Weaver's products, the clearing of land and the expansion of farms into less-desirable wetlands probably increased the demand for drain tile. Thus, not only was it cheaper to manufacture their products in the rural area, but they were also closer to their new market.

Since the Weaver site is the first family stoneware factory to be archaeologically tested in a southern city, it is not known if its pattern of industrialization of a traditional craft is typical of other late-nineteenth-century stoneware factories in a similar setting. It is probable, nevertheless, that the change from a traditional family-centered craft to full industrialization and the eventual failure of these urban stoneware factories cannot be explained simply by a nationwide decline in the stoneware industry. Whereas the history of each site must be studied in its own unique urban environment, there is a suggestion that small southern potteries never really successfully adapted to an urban environment, even after they became industrialized.

ACKNOWLEDGMENTS

I am grateful to the Tennessee Department of Transportation for permission to publish these data. The following persons provided invaluable assistance during our research on the Weaver Pottery site: Linda F. Carnes, Phase 1 field supervisor and laboratory supervisor; Neil D. Robison, Phase 2 field supervisor; Jeffrey W. Gardner, laboratory assistant; James F. Darrow, Associate Professor of Ceramics at the University of Tennessee, Knoxville; and Lucile Weaver Poates and her son Lewis L. Poates, granddaughter and great-grandson of David H. Weaver. A special note of thanks is due to my wife, Terry J. Faulkner for her steadfast encouragement and for drawing Figures 9.1, 9.6, 9.9, and 9.11. I would also like to thank Linda Carnes, Roy S. Dickens, Jr., Terry Faulkner, Jeffrey Gardner, Georgeanna H. Greer, and Samuel D. Smith for reading and commenting on the preliminary draft of this chapter. Any errors of fact or interpretation are, however, my own responsibility.

REFERENCES

Burrison, John A.

1975 Alkaline-glazed stoneware: A deep-South pottery tradition. *Southern Folklore Quarterly* **39**(4):377–402.

Goodspeed's History of Tennessee

1887 *Goodspeed's history of Tennessee-Knox County.* Nashville, Tenn.: The Goodspeed Publishing Company.

Gray, Aelred J., and Susan F. Adams
1976 Government. In *Heart of the valley: A history of Knoxville, Tennessee,* edited by Lucile Deadrick. Knoxville, Tenn.: East Tennessee Historical Society. Pp. 68–144.
Greater Knoxville Illustrated
1910 *Greater Knoxville illustrated.* Nashville, Tenn.: The American Illustrated Company.
Guilland, Harold F.
1971 *Early American folk pottery.* New York: Chilton Book Company.
Kephart, W. H. (editor)
1901 *The manufacturers of Knoxville, Tennessee.* Knoxville, Tenn.: Bean Waters.
Knox County Deed Records
1872 Warranty Deed, Book K., Vol. 3, pp. 262–263. City and County Building, Knoxville, Tennessee.
1874 Warranty Deed, Book M, Vol. 3, p. 742. City and County Building, Knoxville, Tennessee.
1882 Warranty Deed, Book W, Vol. 3, p. 504. City and County Building, Knoxville, Tennessee.
1888 Warranty Deed, Book 89, p. 136. City and County Building. Knoxville, Tennessee.
Knox County Tax Records
1874 Knox County Tax Records for 1874. City and County Building, Knoxville, Tennessee.
1875 Knox County Tax Records for 1875. City and County Building, Knoxville, Tennessee.
Knoxville, City Directory
1869 *Helms' Knoxville City Directory.* Knoxville, Tenn.: T. Haws.
1876 *Directory of Knoxville and Suburbs 1876–77.* Knoxville, Tenn.: Haddock and Seymour.
1880 *The Knoxville City Directory for 1880–81.* Lynchburg, Va.: Ross A. Smith.
1882 *Knoxville Directory 1882.* Nashville, Tenn.: Standard Directory Company.
1884 *Knoxville Directory 1884.* Chattanooga, Tenn.: Cotton Belt Publishing Company.
1885 *Norwood's Directory of Knoxville, Tennessee, 1885.* Chattanooga, Tenn.: Norwood and Company.
1886 *Crozier's Knoxville Directory 1886.* Knoxville, Tenn.: Crozier and Company.
1888 *Knoxville City Directory, 1888.* Knoxville, Tenn.: R. L. Polk and Company.
1930 *Knoxville City Directory, 1930.* Knoxville, Tenn.: City Directory Company of Knoxville.
Knoxville Daily Press and Herald
1875 Along Second Creek. *Knoxville Daily Press and Herald,* February 26, 1875.
Lasansky, Jeannette
1979 *Made of mud: Stoneware potteries in central Pennsylvania 1831–1929.* University Park, Pennsylvania: Penn State Univ. Press.
MacArthur, William J.
1976 Knoxville history: An interpretation. In *Heart of the valley: A history of Knoxville, Tennessee,* edited by Lucile Deadrick. Knoxville, Tenn.: East Tennessee Historical Society. Pp. 1–67.
Olsen, Fredrick L.
1973 *The kiln book.* Bassett, California: Keramos Books.
Rothrock, Mary U. (editor)
1946 *The French Broad-Holston country: A history of Knox County, Tennessee.* Knoxville, Tenn.: East Tennessee Historical Society.
Sanborn Insurance Map
1884 Knoxville, Tennessee, December, 1884. Map No. 12. Sanborn Map Company, New York.
1885 Knoxville, Tennessee, January, 1885. Map No. 7. Sanborn Map Company, New York.
1890 Knoxville, Knox County Tennessee, May 1890. Map No. 21. Sanborn-Perris Map Company Limited, New York.
1903 Insurance Maps of Knoxville, Tennessee, Map No. 44. Sanborn Map Company, New York.
1917 Insurance Maps of Knoxville, Tennessee, Vol. 1A. Map No. 39. Sanborn Map Company, New York.
Smith, Samuel D., and Stephen T. Rogers
1979 *A survey of pottery making in Tennessee.* Tennessee Department of Conservation, Division of Archaeology, Research Series No. 3. Nashville, Tennessee.

Tennessee State Gazetteer and Business Directory
1876 *Tennessee State Gazetteer and Business Directory, 1876.* Nashville, Tenn.: R. L. Polk and Company.
1887 *Tennessee State Gazetteer and Business Directory, 1887.* Nashville, Tenn.: R. L. Polk and Company.
Weaver, David H.
1890 Letter to Carl M. B. Weaver dated February 12, 1890.

10

Industrial Site-Building: Implications from the 1978–1979 Investigations at the Rogers Locomotive Works, Paterson, New Jersey

Marjorie Ingle

INTRODUCTION

Paterson, New Jersey, located 18 miles west of New York City, has a quiet and struggling inner city status that camouflages an important chapter in American industrial and social history. Historical and archaeological investigations conducted over the last 5 years have established that much of America's first planned industrial city, conceived as our National Manufactory, survives beneath an unassuming veneer of concrete and abandoned residential lots, as well as in fragmented historical documents and in the memories of many of Paterson's citizens. Archaeological studies of Paterson and other industrial cities are increasingly disproving traditional views that both industrialism and urbanism are linear, quasi-evolutionary processes, born ready-formed of the merger of a close supply of immigrant workers, large-scale American capital, and new, well-honed technology. Similarly, the nature and development of the industrial city—usually conceived of as an enormous company town—defies easy generalization. The new immigrant population and their dependence on a manufacturing base of cotton, silk, and locomotives and other iron products appears to have made Paterson distinctly, though subtly, a city *of* workers and *for* workers.

Unknown to the general public and overlooked by academics, Paterson was a large-scale manufacturing center of national importance during a time when the rest of American industrialism was in its infancy. Created in 1791 with the incorporation of the Society for Establishing Usefull (sic) Manufacturers (SUM) (America's

ARCHAEOLOGY OF URBAN AMERICA
The Search for Pattern and Process

ISBN 0-12-214980-7

first corporation), Paterson was to be America's National Manufactory, and, thereby, the first planned industrial city in America. It was to be the physical embodiment of Alexander Hamilton's dream of the nation's becoming economically and politically independent through industrial supremacy, which he promoted in his *Report on Manufactures,* delivered to Congress only a month after the chartering of SUM by the New Jersey State Legislature. Paterson's advantageous location between New York and Philadelphia and its excellent water power source, the Great Falls of the Passaic River (reportedly the second largest waterfall in the eastern United States), recommended it as the site for the National Manufactory. In the succeeding 50 years, a pastoral village of Dutch farmers was transformed into a collection of smoke-spewing, red brick factories.

Paterson's national prominence as an industrial center was predicated on its initial, however uneven, cotton manufacturing period (1791–1830); its later strong iron, machinery, and locomotive base (1830–1880); and, finally, its silk and mosquito netting production (1870–1910). Designated a National Historic Landmark by the Secretary of the Interior, Paterson is unique as "the site of the first planned industrial development in the United States. . . . The completed raceway system [an ingenious, three-tiered system built and controlled by the SUM], the dam across the river, and the buildings erected to accommodate the great variety of industrial processes that developed over a period of 119 years represent the finest and most extensive collection of engineering, planning, and architectural works of the period when the United States was becoming a major industrial nation [National Register of Historic Places, Nomination Form, 1969]."

Locomotive manufacturing was an all-important component of Paterson's considerable iron and machining industry. From a population of 75 ironworkers employed in eleven blacksmith shops, two millwright shops, and an iron foundry in 1825, 3172 of Paterson's 5300 ironworkers, or 9% of the town's total population, were employed in locomotive manufacture in 1873 (Gutman 1976:217,221). It was the "big three"—the Rogers Locomotive Works, Grant Locomotive Works, and Cooke Locomotive Works—as well as a few short-lived firms that contributed to Paterson's international prominence as a locomotive-producing center. The Rogers Locomotive Works was the largest in terms of employees, production, and innovation of design. In locomotive production on a national scale, the Rogers Works was second only to the Baldwin Company in Philadelphia. From its beginning in 1832 as a cotton and textile machinery manufacturing firm, the Rogers Works evolved, in less than 50 years, into a large-scale, integrated manufacturer exclusively of locomotives. By 1881, the firm employed 1800 men, who produced a completed locomotive every second work day. The plant expanded from about six buildings to two and a half blocks of factory buildings, housing a rapidly evolving technology. Because of its early beginnings and long history, the site of the Rogers Locomotive Works encapsulates the development of American manufacturing throughout the nineteenth century.

This chapter is organized in two parts. The first is a more general discussion, describing the 1978–1979 archaeological investigation of the oldest, northernmost portion of the Rogers Locomotive Works (directed by the author), which was undertaken as part of the rehabilitation and adaptive reuse of the 1871 erecting shop. Historical background of the site and a summary of the findings of the investigation are presented. The second part of the chapter is a more specific discussion of selected topics related to the 1978–1979 investigation. The first section, about archaeology and construction, advocates the careful consideration of feasible research questions appropriate to specific construction impact and the development of an anticipatory field approach through extensive use of documentary information. The second section synthesizes the findings of the 1978–1979 investigation for establishing patterns of industrial site-building. The final section points up the problems that can arise from stereotypically interpreting behavior occurring on limited activity sites, such as a locomotive-manufacturing facility.

THE 1978–1979 PROJECT

Beginning in 1975, the City's Department of Community Development embarked on an ambitious project to rehabilitate and rejuvenate the Great Falls Historic District. With Federal and State grant monies, including $11.1 million from the United States Economic Development Administration, the City hoped to attract private developers to adaptively reuse the many attractive but underutilized industrial structures in the district. In addition, the City decided to take direct responsibility for several phases of the project, most notably the rehabilitation and adaptive reuse of the 1871 Rogers Locomotive Works erecting shop as an industrial museum and commercial offices. Other work included the conversion of the uppermost tier (also called raceway) of the water power canal system into a park, the construction of a bike path, and the restoration of the mill facades in the district. To conduct historical and archaeological research related to the Historical District Project, the City created the Paterson Archaeology Project in 1978,[1] consisting of six archaeologists, a historian, an architect, several draftsmen, and about 20 CETA-funded laborers. By the end of 1979, the Archaeology Project completed excavations of the Upper Raceway, part of the Rogers Locomotive Works, and a residential site in the Dublin area; and completed archaeological testing of a block in the Dublin neighborhood, portions of the Swinburne, Smith Locomotive Works, the Essex Mill, the Grant and Cooke Locomotive Company sites, and the route of the bike path.

Much of the Paterson Archaeology Project's work drew on the findings of the Great Falls Development, Inc., Salvage Archaeology Project (directed by Edward S. Rutsch), which identified and recorded all historic resources along the path of a proposed 66 in. (167.6 cm) storm sewer. The 1973–1976 Project established that significant physical remains survive from all phases of Paterson's industrial development, including the locomotive industry, the water power canal system, and the residential area of Dublin (historically associated with the mill district). At the Rogers Locomotive Works, archaeologists excavated a diagonal swath, ranging from

[1]The Paterson Archaeology Project was disbanded June 1981. The Project collections, including all reports and field recordings, are housed in the Passaic County Historical Society, Paterson, New Jersey.

10 ft (3 m) to 100 ft (30 m) in width and extending a full city block in length, through the oldest portion of the locomotive manufacturing plant.[2]

Description of the Project

The City's plans for the Rogers Locomotive Works erecting shop called for the complete restoration of its exterior, and a "deindustrializing" of its interior for a museum of industrial history on the first floor and commercial offices on its upper three floors. Specific work included the installation of new utility and mechanical systems, an internal passenger elevator, and the refurbishing of its interior. Extensive sitework was planned for the use of its rear yard as a paved parking lot, with the installation of a maze of drainage pipes being the most threatening to archaeological remains (Figure 10.1).

Because the rehabilitation had been designed, initially, with little regard for the archaeological richness of the site, many conflicts between known significant archaeological remains and construction activities were anticipated. Therefore, the architects' and engineers' designs and locations of all ground-disturbing construction were considered tentative until their effects on archaeological remains could be assessed, either by archaeological testing or by reference to historical documents and the records of the Salvage Archaeology Project. The 1978 field season consisted of archaeological work in advance and independent of construction activities: testing construction areas for significant archaeological remains, assessing areas for their archaeological potential prior to the final development of construction designs, and recommending alternative construction areas if conflicts with archaeological features were identified. Finally, archaeological data were recovered in those areas where construction could not be relocated or redesigned. This work, conducted primarily in two adjacent areas along the north side (Market Street boundary, against and within the boiler room) of the lot was related to the installation of an electrical transformer, the laying of a network of utility lines, and modifications to the erecting shop boiler room.

Unfortunately, the 1979 archaeological season did not benefit from the leisurely schedule and collaborative design method of the previous season. The rehabilitation project was in its final months and the remaining work was, for engineering reasons, of an inflexible design. Yet, the construction would have grave consequences for the archaeological resources of the site. Ground-disturbing construction included the excavation of a deep, 725 ft (217.5 m) long trench for a site drainage system, a 38 × 60 ft (11.4 × 18 m) area of the erecting shop Middle Annex for a new flooring understructure, and superficial grading for two locomotive viewing pads. Because of an ambitious program that combined construction monitoring and selected ar-

[2]In 1973–1974, H.A.E.R. (Historic American Engineering Record) conducted an architectural and historical survey of the Historic District. H.A.E.R. has been consolidated into N.A.E.R. (National Architectural Engineering Record), part of the National Park Service. Measured drawings were done of the significant structures of the Historic District.

FIGURE 10.1. View of the 1871 Rogers Locomotive Works erecting shop before rehabilitation and of the 1973–1976 Salvage Archaeology Project.

chaeological excavation, the 1979 season was far more involved in recording endangered resources—as in traditional salvage archaeology—than in assessing the historical and archaeological significance of areas to be impacted by construction and then in redesigning the project to avoid or minimize impact to archaeological remains, as was done in 1978. Also, in contrast to the 1978 archaeological crew of five, the Paterson Archaeology Project could spare only the site archaeologist (without a crew). Therefore, the archaeological and construction phases of the rehabilitation project were integrated, both logistically and conceptionally, due to practicality.

Excavation for the site drainage system was accomplished primarily by mechanical means, with hand excavation around archaeological features or in areas of suspected archaeological sensitivity. The site archaeologist directed the backhoe operator and two laborers in all excavation activities, whereas the project supervisor (a carpenter) was responsible for the actual construction work. Every attempt was made to excavate as carefully as possible with the backhoe (optimally in shallow, consistent levels) or to probe areas suspected to be archaeologically sensitive with the backhoe, prior to decisions of whether to intensively excavate by hand or machine. When necessary, the site archaeologist was empowered to stop the backhoe excavation without consulting with other construction project personnel and to proceed with hand excavation to record archaeological features. Time-consuming documentation of features was done as much as possible during lunch and coffee breaks, after the construction work day, and occasionally during holidays. Trenches were left open for as long as a week, so further hand excavation and more detailed documentation could continue. Where necessary, areas adjoining the drainage trench also were exposed and documented to aid in the interpretation of archaeological resources within the drainage trench.

Because primary focus was placed on the drainage system excavation, 85%–90% of the excavation in the Middle Annex was done by the construction crew, with occasional monitoring and additional documentation by the site archaeologist. The construction crew was instructed informally about the basic principles of stratigraphy and superimposition by the site archaeologist. If artifacts or features were found, the crew was directed to call the site archaeologist immediately and note the location, depth, and soil type where the find was uncovered. The progress of the excavation was checked several times a day by the site archaeologist, who maintained daily field notes. As necessary, the site archaeologist spent several hours or occasionally a full day documenting archaeological features.

Historical Background of the Site

In 1832, with the success of his cotton machinery manufactory, the Jefferson Works (located along the Upper Raceway), Thomas Rogers began building a site for his new, small-scale, general iron-working business directly across Spruce Street. Since the site was low-lying and swampy, considerable effort was necessary to make it suitable for industrial use. During a period from the early 1830s to 1869, the site was occupied by about a half-dozen two- and three-storied brick and brownstone buildings, which fronted Spruce Street with their gable ends. Graphic representations depict the earlier plant as initially pastoral, surrounded by planted fields, rolling hills, pine trees, and the 1829 Morris Canal (Figure 10.2). The first structure on the new site was the foundry, built in 1833, as a single-floored edifice with false-front and belltower. A fire in 1845 razed the structure and it was immediately rebuilt.

In 1834 or 1835, a two-storied, brownstone millwright building and adjacent shed were built. Originally L-shaped in plan and 50 × 75 ft (22.5 m) in size, it was fitted with equipment appropriate for the fine machining of general parts and locomotive cylinders: slide, boring, and centering lathes, large planers, screwing machines, and polishing machines. A few years later, an iron-planing shop was constructed immediately south of the foundry. In this three-storied brick building, much heavy iron work was carried out, including slicing, planing, and hammering. To the south of the iron-planing shop, a three-storied brick erecting or locomotive shop was built in 1836, a year before the first locomotive was erected by Thomas Rogers. Reportedly, a single track, on which locomotives were assembled, ran lengthwise through the shop. It was hoped that archaeological evidence of a supporting structure for the track, possibly a variant of the erecting bay, would be found. On its first and second floors, fine machining also was done.

With the success of his locomotives, Rogers seems to have decreased his production of other iron products and concentrated on locomotives. By the 1850s, additional space was evidently needed by the growing locomotive manufactory, and the larger buildings were extended the full 200 ft (60 m) between Spruce and Pine Streets. Numerous subsidiary structures also were built or appended to existing buildings, and several sheds were erected along the east (Pine Street) side of the site. Probably related to the nearby iron-planing shop, a second, small blacksmith building was constructed sometime between 1850 and 1854 along Pine Street.

By the end of the 1860s, the needs of a growing business and a rapidly evolving technology could not be served by the limited space available to the Rogers Company. Between 1869 and 1872, the plant was demolished in a piecemeal fashion, and a new, all-brick plant was constructed. These new structures, about 200 ft (60 m) long, were aligned parallel to Spruce and Pine Streets to allow maximum accessibility of materials and the multiple construction of locomotives and tenders. Where there had been seven structures, three buildings—the blacksmith, the tender, and erecting shop—were constructed (Figure 10.3).

The 1871 erecting shop seems to have been one of the last structures built in the remodeling campaign. Encompassing the area formerly occupied by the 1830's millwright shop, foundry, and iron-planing shop, the imposing brick erecting shop stands four stories high and measures 200 × 58 ft (60 × 17.4 m), with its long dimension fronting Spruce Street. Originally, with only a small, "hazardous construction" boiler room at its northeast corner, it was a long, narrow building with arched openings on its east and west facades to allow for easy movement of raw materials and finished locomotives. Locomotives were assembled on its first or

FIGURE 10.2. An 1836 view of the Rogers, Ketchum, and Grosvenor plant during its very early locomotive manufacturing and general machining period. *A*, Millwright shop; *B*, Foundry; *C*, Iron-planing shop; *D*, Locomotive shop; *E*, Office; *F*, Jefferson Works building; *G*, 1829 Morris Canal.

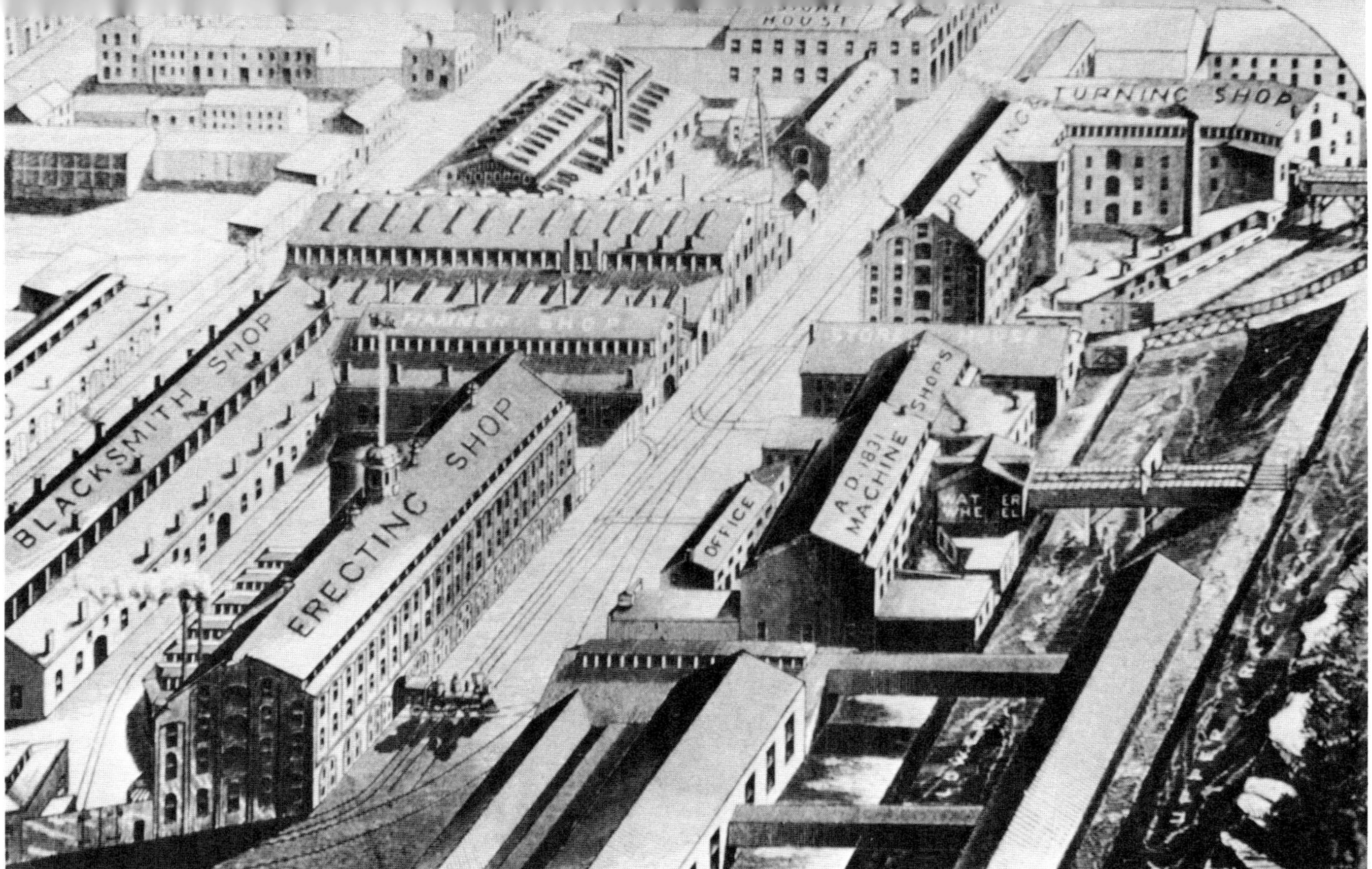

FIGURE 10.3. An 1897 view of the Rogers Locomotive Works, including the erecting shop, blacksmith shop, the head and tailrace of the water-power canal system, and the adjacent 1831 Jefferson Works building dating to the early machining and tool-making period of Paterson's industrialism prior to locomotive manufacturing.

basement-level floor, with machining, sheet iron boxing, and pattern-making in its upper floors. Two other annexes were appended on the east side of the building, south of the boiler room. Sometime before 1874, a middle annex was constructed. This annex, one story high and 80 × 40 ft (24 × 12 m) in size, had a series of now-removed shed dormers, a doorway on the middle of its east facade, and a working basement floor. By 1887, a machine shop occupied the first floor and an iron- and gas-fitting shop was in the basement. Between 1889 and 1899, a south annex, measuring 57 × 40 ft (17 × 12 m), was added to the southeast corner of the erecting shop. Its two stories and basement level accommodated additional space for machining, with locomotive assembly on the first or basement floor (three brick erecting bays are still visible). The boiler room annex of the erecting shop seems to have been reconstructed from the "hazardous construction" to brick by 1881, and continued to shelter two steam boilers in the same location. Between 1884 and 1887, it was extended an additional 20 ft (6 m) east, to its current configuration, to house a total of four steam boilers. Sometime between 1899 and 1906, a 14 ft (4.2 m) wide, iron-clad extension was added to the east side of the boiler room to house a fifth boiler. By the late 1920s, after all locomotive manufacture had ceased, the 1884 boiler room was backfilled and sealed beneath a concrete floor, and the turn-of-the-century extension was demolished.

Only 26 ft (7.8 m) from the erecting shop was the 253 × 80 ft (76 × 24 m) blacksmith shop, which was aligned along Pine Street. It was connected in an L-shaped configuration to the single-storied hammer shop, which fronted Spruce Street beyond the limits of the present erecting shop site. The blacksmith shop is documented as having contained brick forges, steam hammers, and numerous smaller forges. The Salvage Archaeology Project uncovered mounts of gantry cranes; foundations of double- and single-framed steam hammers; a refractory-brick, arched feature (function still unknown); and many drains and pipes.

Located at the corner of Pine and Market Streets was the 1870–ca. 1915 paint and tender shop. It was a smaller, L-shaped, single-storied, brick structure, clad with sheet metal. Photographs show that it had 10 arched openings (along the Market Street side) through which its finished tenders were removed.

Beginning in the early 1870s, shortly after the rebuilding of the locomotive works was finished, labor problems beset the Rogers Works. Strikes slowed and, finally, forced the temporary closing of the Works. Labor tension was continued throughout the succeeding years of the plant. By the late 1890s, the growth of the size of locomotives and the diversification of their types demanded a new technology. Furthermore, the plant had been expanded a full two and a half blocks, the maximum possible. The 1870s' Rogers Locomotive Works facilities were outmoded, and business was going to other builders like Baldwin Company in Philadelphia and the American Locomotive Works (ALCO) in Schenectady, New York. After attempts by local citizens and businessmen to resurrect the beleaguered plant failed, in 1905 the Rogers Locomotive Works was absorbed by the growing ALCO company. ALCO's tenure on the site lasted until about 1913; finally, by about 1915, most of the locomotive buildings were demolished. The erecting shop reverted to a variety of light industrial uses and the rear yard remained barren, except during the 1950s and 1960s, when a cinderblock annex was built there by the Manhattan Shirt Company.

Findings and Conclusions

Rutsch (1978) has hypothesized that, initially, the humus topsoil of the swamp was removed and that traprock and yellow clay was piled as fill to raise the water table of the site. Moreover, he has suggested that the sterile yellow clay will occur beneath all cultural deposits. In the 1979 excavations, no evidence of the humus topsoil of the swamp was found. It is not known if this layer was removed prior to construction, as suggested by Rutsch, or if it remains deeply buried. The 1979 investigations do suggest that the preconstruction preparation of the site was more complex than previously thought. A new stratum of markedly different soil composition was found beneath the ubiquitous layer of yellow clay and traprock. This new soil type—dark brown-to-grey mottled silty sand with small angled traprock fragments—was revealed at a depth of 13 ft (3.9 m) near the northwest corner of the 1870s' blacksmith shop. Its depth seems to correlate with a radical change of soil type at about the same depth under the erecting shop. Its obvious absence of rich organic material does not support it as being the humus topsoil of the swamp. Rather, it seems to be another stratum of fill added to the site before the yellow clay to raise the water table. Furthermore, a careful analysis of the co-occurrence of the yellow stratum with cultural materials opens to question the idea that it occurs uniformly beneath all cultural deposits. In nearly a dozen cases, cultural deposits were found within and beneath the yellow clay. These deposits contained brick rubble, several pipes, slag, a copper drain screen, lenses of mixed mortar, ash, coal, and slag, and even a brick drain.

Remnants of several of the first buildings on the site were found side-by-side and beneath later nineteenth-century development, visibly cross-cut and eclipsed by walls of known 1870-era buildings. The Salvage Archaeology Project uncovered what is thought to be a portion of the southern wall of the 1830s' iron-planing shop, extending west of the 1870s' blacksmith shop. Similar evidence of either the 1830s' locomotive or blacksmith shop was found during the 1979 excavations. A brick wall on a base of coursed brownstone and a working floor of bluestone slabs, sheet iron, and slag were revealed in the area west of the foundation of the 1870s' blacksmith shop. Obscured by more superficial layers of concrete (marking the level of the blacksmith shop), two grindstones and large iron rods were exposed on the bluestone slab floor. Beneath the slabs, a sub-floor was revealed, which consisted of a thin stratum of ash, slag, cinders with glass beverage bottle fragments (no datable sherds), discarded files, and architectural artifacts.

Archaeological remains of structures from the 1850s' expansion of the Rogers plant also were revealed in the drainage line excavations. In general, they appeared as a maze of walls and drains sitting on a thin stratum of tan sand and a deeper layer of yellow clay, all beneath the floor level of the 1870s' blacksmith shop. One brownstone wall and a brick and brownstone trough (FP34/98) were particularly interesting. A sectional view of the trough (after its destruction) showed that it was sitting on a 2 to 3 in. (5 to 7.6 cm) layer of slag and was overlying a deeper stratum of tan silty sand grading to the ubiquitous clay. In the tan stratum, a myriad of seemingly nonindustrial artifacts was found, including sherds of whitewares, banded and finger-trailed annularwares (small bowls or cups), fragments of kaolin smoking pipe bowls and stems, butchered bone, and several thoroughly eroded river

FIGURE 10.4. View of the basement-level working floor of the 1871 erecting shop found in the 1978 investigations prior to the construction of a passenger elevator. Shown are the end of a brick bay, related troughed brick floor, and a grindstone probably used as a base for auxiliary equipment.

cobbles. Closer observation of the east side of the trough revealed that, during its construction, hot liquidous slag had been poured over its brick sides, probably from the nearby foundry. The trough proved to be the eastern extension of a drainage trough that originated in a honeycomb of intersecting walls, pipes, and drains, nearly all predating the 1870s' blacksmith shop. Four tiers of drainage troughs and walls sat above the yellow stratum, of which the trough was the middle tier. The uppermost (most recent) features of the locus were a brick cruciform pier of an 1870-era gantry crane, and the mounts of two, double-framed steam hammers, which eclipsed a wall of earlier construction.

A wealth of archaeological remains of the 1870s' blacksmith shop was revealed within the area encompassed by the drainage line excavations (Figure 10.4). The northwest corner and a limited length of the west wall of the impressive 200 × 80 ft (60 × 24 m) structure were uncovered by both the 1979 work and the Salvage Archaeology Project. The imposing blacksmith shop was supported by a traprock footing that was leveled by two courses of brownstone blocks, sitting on yellow clay and traprock. Along the interior of its foundation, a brick trough covered with bluestone slabs and filled with silts, clays, and greases was found. The blacksmith shop floor was earthen, composed of compacted yellow clay covered by a stratum of various types of slag ranging from a few inches to more than 3 ft (.9 m) in depth, compacted coal dust, and black silty sand.

The inventory of technological remains of the 1870s' blacksmith shop uncovered by the drainage line excavations augmented those previously found by the Salvage Archaeology Project. Amid the labyrinth of remains revealed by the earlier project were the mounts of two double-framed steam hammers, a refractory-brick, arched feature of still uncertain function, and three brick cruciform gantry crane supports. Additionally, the 1979 excavations exposed the base of a third double-framed steam hammer, a single-framed steam hammer, and the eastern extension of the same refractory-brick feature. It is very likely that some of this equipment dated from a late-nineteenth-century upgrading of the shop, possibly with the advent of ALCO. Two of the four hammers were of poured concrete construction, while the other two were of brick, veneered with cement. Several grindstones (which served as the bases for auxiliary machines) were located in strata of slag positioned atop a cruciform gantry crane pier and a brownstone wall. They are, therefore, interpreted as dating from the turn-of-the-century, after the abandonment of the gantry-type cranes for the newer horizontal traveling variety.

INVESTIGATIVE PLANNING AND THEORETICAL ISSUES

Archaeology and Construction

Archaeological and historical investigations at the Rogers Locomotive Works were always inextricably intertwined with the ongoing construction activities. With a construction crew of 80 actively engaged on the site, the 1978 archaeological crew of five and the single site archaeologist in 1979 were clearly outnumbered. A "join 'em, not fight 'em" attitude had to be adopted. The 1978 field season consisted of archaeological testing, assessing areas for archaeological significance, and recommending construction alternatives to avoid or minimize impact. In contrast, the 1979 season entailed the archaeological monitoring of construction, with selected, limited excavation (see previous section for field descriptions). A number of techniques were devised to maximize archaeological information in the face of destructive construction. First, a field approach that was anticipatory, rather than reactive, was essential. This was accomplished with a synthesis of all known documentary and field information. Second, good communication between the construction, design, and archaeological personnel was critical. Third, plans for all archaeological work had to be flexible because construction activities frequently were refined in the field and followed a seemingly irrational schedule. Fourth, research questions or topics had to be based on a realistic assessment of the nature of construction impacts.

With the immediacy of ongoing construction, an intimate knowledge of the site was essential. Prior to 1978 fieldwork, all documentary information was assembled and evaluated. Much was already known, both archaeologically and historically, but it needed to be organized into a new format, from which the archaeological, design, and construction staffs could predict the locations of archaeological features. For this purpose, a "historic composite map" and a standardized building form were developed. On the former, the locations of all documented structures and the outline and main features of the Salvage Archaeology Project excavations were superimposed on historic maps, on the configuration of the 1871 erecting shop, and on an 1854 map (with exact measurements noted). An amazingly accurate "x-ray" of the site was produced, which proved reliable when checked against the location of archaeological remains found by the Salvage Archaeology Project and the 1978–1979 excavations. All architectural, historical, archaeological, and technological information about each known structure was compiled on the standardized building forms. Whereas the composite historic map could be used as a field index to the general shapes, locations, and interrelationships of individual historic structures, the standardized building forms provided more detailed information, such as building dimensions, foundation type, building materials, equipment and processes documented in the structure, noteworthy events (e.g., fires), and the findings of previous archaeological excavations.

Throughout the 1978 field season, it was necessary to maintain a cooperative working relationship between the archaeological, design, and construction staffs. The site archaeologist was involved in all meetings related to any phase of ground-disturbing construction, and freely exchanged information with all project personnel. The findings of the archaeological testing program were constantly communicated to the project personnel through group meetings, informal daily interaction, memoranda, and drawings. Interestingly, by the end of 1978, nearly all aspects of the construction had been modified for archaeological considerations: The oil heating system, which would have impacted an area of 32 × 25 ft (9.6 × 7.5 m), was abandoned in favor of a gas system with only a single fuel line. Also, the electrical transformer, new footings in the boiler room, and an understructure for a new Middle Annex floor either had been shifted in location or substantially redesigned, so as to have less effect on significant archaeological resources.

The monitoring of the 1979 construction activities, with selected, limited excavation, involved a realistic approach to archaeology. Because anticipating archaeological deposits was critical, a prefieldwork "predictive map" was made of the site drainage-system area, synthesizing information from the composite historic map, the standardized building forms, the Salvage Archaeology Project field records, the project engineering drawings, and from other sources. This map showed the expected locations of features, such as walls, machine mounts, and drains, established from projected extensions and patterns of features. This predictive map was used in the field to anticipate the location of features, so that the work schedule could be modified accordingly. The standardized building forms also were referred to for specific, detailed information.

From the predictive map, composite historic map, building forms, and the Salvage Archaeology Project materials, it was possible to formulate research questions or topics appropriate to the vertical, destructive nature of the construction impact. The monitoring technique, with the documentation of features prior to and then after their destruction, afforded an excellent opportunity to examine construction techniques, types of materials, and associated stratigraphy of archaeological features and to uncover earlier features obscured beneath overlying, shallower deposits. A series of research topics about the nature of industrial-site building, appropriate to a narrow, but extensive ground disturbance, was formulated. This investigation emphasized gaining a more refined understanding of the site stratigraphy and the vertical relationships between archaeological features, complementing the horizontal, nondestructive field approach to the Salvage Archaeology Project. Historical evidence suggested a sequence consisting of: the original swamp on the site, the site preparation, the structural and technological remains of the first Rogers Locomotive Works plant (1830s–1870), demolition debris from the 1869–1872 rebuilding of the plant, evidence of the later plant (ca. 1870–1915), a stratum of demolition debris (ca. 1915), and evidence of the light industrial uses of the site (ca. 1920–1970). From this sequence, more detailed questions were posed to guide the field investigation, analysis, and interpretation. Would the humus topsoil of the original swamp be discovered? Related to the initial preparation of the site, would the yellow clay be found to have raised the water table? Would other artificially occurring strata be uncovered? Would it be possible to ascertain types of equipment used in the site preparation? Would there be evidence of little or extensive amounts of site preparation? Would any remnants of the 1830s' or 1850s' buildings be found? Would differences in construction techniques be found between the 1830's, 1850's, 1870's buildings? Would it be possible to identify nonstructural deposits (i.e., by-products) as to their points of origin? Were by-products of the locomotive processes disposed of near their points of origin? Were all earlier structures demolished in the 1869–1872 rebuilding of the Rogers Company plant? In the rebuilding, were earlier deposits demolished to a specific level (i.e., 1870s' blacksmith shop floor), or was fill brought in to bring areas up to a specific level over the earlier deposits? Was there a size that dictated whether a deposit was retained in situ or demolished during the rebuilding? Would archaeological evidence indicate whether locomotive production took place during the 1869–1872 rebuilding?

The 1979 construction monitoring, a less than ideal technique for archaeological investigation, was rationalized as a "last ditch effort," to be used only when the alternative option is to ignore the existence of archaeological remains. The use of the backhoe, however careful, biased the results toward large, usually architectural features (e.g., walls, floors, machine mounts, and slag concentrations), and dislodged from their original contexts smaller artifacts and features (e.g., hand tools, lightweight debitage, and stains and imprints in activity areas). Fortunately, monitoring did prove to be somewhat useful given the intimate knowledge of the site provided by a well-synthesized body of documentary information and well-organized field records from the Salvage Archaeology Project.

Industrial Site Evolution

As more information accumulates from urban archaeological investigations, interest in the processes involved in building the physical fabric of cities seems to be growing. Edward Larrabee's pioneering work (unpublished), which synthesizes the patterns of historical development in New York City and nearby cities of New Jersey, is an excellent example of this important research. A similar approach applied to industrial sites should contribute to an understanding of the nature of relationships between urbanism and industrialism.

The evolution of the Rogers Locomotive Works site illustrates some of the processes involved in industrial-site building. The 1978–1979 investigations revealed that the predevelopment of the site was more complex and extensive than previously thought. Rutsch's (1978) hypothesis that the humus topsoil of the swamp was removed in the initial preparation of the site was not disproven (no evidence of it was found, but it could remain deeply buried). To date, the deepest (oldest?) stratum of the site is the layer of dark brown-to-grey mottled silty sand, uncovered at about a 3 ft (3.9 m) depth in the 1979 construction monitoring. Above the dark soil is a thick stratum of yellow silty clay with angular traprock, found at depths ranging from 2 to 3 ft (.6–.9 m) to 13 ft (3.9 m) below present grade. This stratum, which seems to underlie the entire site, including the erecting shop, likely served to raise the water table prior to the initial development of the block. During subsequent construction, the yellow soil seems to have been superficially manipulated as borrow and was backfilled over earlier deposits, accounting for the dozen cases in which it co-occurs with cultural material. Compacted with large, angular traprock, the yellow stratum was used as a subflooring for all 1830s' and 1870s' buildings encountered.

Structures dating from the 1850s seem to have been constructed on a thin stratum of tan sand filled with artifacts of apparently domestic types, with the ubiquitous yellow clay layer below. Activity appears to have been concentrated in restricted space by the 1850s, judging from the many thin, superficial layers of slag found on floors and within brick joints of a drainage trough, and from many overlapping features.

The 1869–1872 upgrading of the locomotive plant seems to have occurred very rapidly. Remains of the 1830s' and 1850s' buildings were found beneath and next to the 1870s' buildings. The floor levels of the later buildings, apparently, were placed just above the earlier remains, so that little demolition and filling was required. As with the earlier construction, the existing yellow stratum seems to have been manipulated as fill, possibly with soil coming from the excavation of basements (e.g., the tender shop) being reused as the subflooring of other buildings. ALCO, during its short-lived tenure on the site in the first decade of this century, made a few minor modifications, including upgrading the utility systems. With the demolition of many of the locomotive structures around 1915, much building debris was left in situ and was overlain by coal dust and clinker from the erecting shop boiler room. The tradition of using by-products produced on the site to raise the grade of the property to its present level continued until the 1950s. Boiler room clinker and ash from the laundries that occupied the erecting shop during the early twentieth century were deposited over the north portion of the site and in the tender shop basement. In all, the grade was raised a maximum of 7 ft (2.1 m). However, during the 1950s when the building was vacant, brown nonlocal silt was brought in by the Manhattan Shirt Company. This brown soil raised and evened the site grade prior to the construction of a new cinderblock annex.

Thus, a pattern of industrial site evolution can be discerned, which is based on the retention and reuse of existing structural or technological remains and by-products, rather than on the wholesale removal of them and building anew. Using Schiffer's concepts of cultural transformation processes and C-Transform types, the archaeological structure of an industrial site abounds with a variety of C-Transforms (Schiffer 1977). Although there are specific problems in applying Schiffer's types to industrial sites, recycling processes (S-S transformations), primary and secondary refuse discard processes (S-A transformations), and scavenging and removal behaviors (A-S transformations) are apparent. However, the distinction between the S-A and S-S processes is blurred when they are applied to a processual situation. If one views a site as an artifact, then the act of site-building or earth-modification is yet another cultural transformation (S-S). Accordingly, the retention, in situ, of a brick wall or drain and the subsequent backfilling over that feature might be either an S-A or an S-S process. Similarly, should the wall or drain be more accurately classed as disposed material (primary refuse discard) or as convenient fill material used in site building (recycling)? Would the pouring of liquidous slag over the side of the unfinished brick drain be an example of primary refuse discard or of recycling of the slag as a building material? Were the twentieth-century boiler room by-products deposited in the abandoned basement of the tender shop being purposely disposed of in the most convenient location or were they being recycled as fill material to build up the declined north end of the site? In processual discussions, perhaps the building and disposal transformations should be considered together (i.e., primary refuse discard transformation (S-A process) and recycling transformation (S-S process).

Distinguishing between primary and secondary refuse discard transformations (S-A) also is complicated on industrial sites. A range of other factors, most importantly safety and feasibility of disposal, dictates the ultimate disposal location. Obviously, boiler room by-products, such as clinker and ash, could not be discarded at their original locations of manufacture. Similarly, liquidous slag from the foundry casting processing would not be discarded at its point of manufacture. By modifying Schiffer's definitions for primary and secondary refuse discard transformations (S-A) to make them appropriate for industrial sites, we may consider a deposit as having undergone a primary discard transformation if it were disposed of at a location as close as safely and feasibly possible to its point of manufacture or point of usefulness.

The pattern of industrial-site building through primary refuse discard and recycling transformations seems integrally related to efficiency, which can be translated to mean maximum profitability for industrial sites. Profitability is the aggregate of the amount of capital available for site construction, of the pressures of immediate business competition, of the amount of labor and/or time-saving technology available, and of the marketability of available refuse for resale (e.g., iron shavings from planing processes being sold as scarp metal). It is hypothesized that primary refuse discard and recycling transformations occur in high proportions relative to secondary refuse discards, given the profitability of rapid site building. As an immediate example, it was found during the erecting shop rehabilitation that time-consumption was the most effective argument for modifying a project design to allow for the preservation, rather than demolition, of a large archaeological feature. When features were demolished, their remnants were utilized as backfill, rather than being carried away.

Stereotypical Interpretation of Behavior–Material Cultural Relationships on Limited Activity Sites

The discovery of apparently domestic artifacts on a locomotive manufactory illustrates the problem of interpreting a deposit through stereotypical expectations of behavior–material cultural relationships. Initially, the whiteware and banded and finger-trailed annularware sherds of small bowls or cups, kaolin smoking pipe fragments, butchered bone, and river cobbles found beneath an 1850s brick trough (FP34/98) were interpreted as being unrelated to activities on an industrial site and were thought to have been deposited in construction fill. However, closer reflection suggests that this interpretation was based on an assumption that only industrial activities and specialized work occur on an industrial site, and that the types of archaeological material found on such a site will be direct manifestations of those industrial and work activities. A converse assumption would be that domestic-type artifacts can be attributed only to a domestic site, and are "out of context" on any other type of site.

At a fundamentally functional level, ceramic tablewares, butchered bone, and smoking pipe fragments could reflect eating and relaxing activities in an industrial context, though on-the-job smoking was strongly prohibited at the Rogers Locomotive Works, as it was at most plants. Because workers usually were given an hour-long meal break during the middle of the work day, eating and smoking cannot be categorically dismissed on the industrial site, since they may have produced the refuse of meals eaten on the site.

To further explore the meal interpretation, one might ask if work-day meals were eaten at home or at work. If meals were eaten at work, where within the premises were these meals eaten (in specifically designated areas [lunchroom], at the job place, anywhere on the premises, or adjacent to buildings)? Were meals brought by workers or were they delivered at mealtime? What was a meal receptacle like (lunch pail, paper, tablewares)? If the latter, what types of tablewares (common kitchen types [e.g., redwares, salt-glazed earthenwares] or common table types)? Were tablewares carried to the site in good condition, or broken, chipped, or cracked? What foodstuffs might constitute a meal? Was smoking allowed on the work premises and if so, where? Were smoking and eating directly related activities? With whom was the "domestic" debris associated? Is it significant that the artifacts were found under masonry remains? If so, can it be stated with any degree of reliability that the artifacts were associated with a mason? Were the masons part-time locomotive workers and part-time masons or full-time masons? If the latter, were masons working permanently or by the job at the Rogers plant?

Thus far, the documentary record has been of little help in defining the specific nature of meal breaks at the Rogers Locomotive Works or at similar mid-nineteenth-century industrial establishments. Documentary references indicate a variety of types of meal breaks, including having food delivered to the site, eating food brought from home at the job site, and sending out for food to be eaten at the job site. At a Wheeling, Ohio rolling mill, about 1860, a Cornish furnace tender was brought a meal of bread and "flitch," rank salt pork in ceramic receptacles, and a bottle of ale, all carried in a tin lunch pail; however, the accuracy of the source (an historical novel) is questionable (Davis 1972:18). At the New York City shipyards, a ship's carpenter reported a coffeebreak:

> In our yard, at least half-past eight a.m., Aunt Arlie McVane, a clever, kind-hearted but awfully uncouth, rough sample of the "Ould Sod," would make her great baskets, stowed and checked off with crullers, doughnuts, gingerbread, turnovers, pieces, and a variety of sweet cookies and cakes; and from the time Aunt Arlie's baskets came in sight until every man and boy, bosses and all, in the yard had been supplied, always at one cent a piece for any article on the cargo, the pie, cake, and cookie trade was a brisk one. Aunt Arlie would usually make the rounds of the yard and supply all the hands in about an hour, bringing the forenoon up to half-past nine, and giving us from ten to fifteen minutes "breathing spell" during lunch; no one ever hurried during "cake time" [Cross 1974:34].

In 1889, at a New Brunswick cotton mill, Miss Ellen McLean replied to questions about the nature of meal breaks that "a good many young women eat their lunches during the dinner hour at the factory . . . and in the same room that they have been working at [Cross 1974:84]." In the same year, Pierre Pleau, a machinist at a Montreal cotton factory, had the following comments about his meal break:

"When the girls wanted to eat, they were not allowed to go out, and I sent out a little girl of 12 or 13 years, who was employed in changing the work, to get a little lunch, and thus they eat while working [Cross 1974:95]."

CONCLUSIONS

The 1978–1979 archaeological project was closely intertwined with active, ongoing construction activities at the 1871 erecting shop. It was necessary to devise an anticipatory field approach, based on a well-synthesized documentary foundation allowing prediction of artifact and feature locations, good communication with the design and construction personnel, and the development of research questions or topics appropriate to the nature of the construction impacts.

Industrial sites, as illustrated by the archaeological investigations of the Rogers Locomotive Works in Paterson, New Jersey, are fruitful subjects for the study of site-building and site-formation processes, a topic important for understanding the development of the extensively modified urban fabric. Factors particular to industrial sites, such as profitability and the ready availability of refuse, influence some of these processes and require modifications of Schiffer's C-Transforms.

ACKNOWLEDGMENTS

I wish to express my thanks to Edward S. Rutsch, Mary Jane Rutsch, Deborah Goldstein, LuAnn deCunzo, James Lally, Stephen Warfel, Gordon Ash, the construction crew at the Rogers Building, and the staff of the Paterson Archaeology Project.

REFERENCES

Cross, Michael S.
1974 *The workingman in the nineteenth century*. Toronto: Oxford Univ. Press.

Davis,Rebecca Harding
1972 *Life in the iron mills*. Old Westbury, New York: Feminist Press.

Gutman, Herbert G.
1976 *Work, culture, and society in industrializing America*. New York: Alfred A. Knopf.

Ingle, Marjorie I.
1981 Final Report on Rogers Locomotive Works: 1978–1979 Archaeological investigations. In *Report on the historical, architectural, industrial, archaeological research for preservation planning in the Great Falls Historic District; Paterson, New Jersey: 1978–1981*, edited by Preservation Resource Group, Inc. and the City of Paterson, New Jersey, Department of Community Development. Paterson, New Jersey.

Rutsch, Edward S., and Mary Jane Rutsch
1975 Northeast historical archaeology 4(1 and 2). Council for Northeast Historical Archaeology, Paterson, New Jersey. (Spring issue.)

Rutsch, Edward S.
1978 *Salvage archaeology project, Paterson, New Jersey, 1973–1976* 1. Great Falls Development Corporation, Paterson, New Jersey and the New Jersey Department of Transportation. Paterson, New Jersey.

Schiffer, Michael B.
1977 Toward a unified science of the cultural past. In *Research strategies in historical archaeology*, edited by Stanley South. New York: Academic Press.

III

ARTIFACTS ANALYSIS AND INTERPRETATION

Urban archaeologists are recognizing that their analyses and interpretations of artifacts must carefully consider function and context, as well as form and technology, if they are going to be useful in elucidating complex behavioral systems. Such an approach relies heavily on the documentary and oral record.

Bottles, covered in two chapters (Baugher-Perlin; Hill); ceramics, in two chapters (Worthy; Dyson); and faunal remains, in one chapter (Edmiston), represent three important categories of urban material culture. Baugher-Perlin proposes a system for classifying bottle glass, and suggests some potential uses of this system in exploring chronology, site function, and trade networks. Hill develops a method for calculating manufacture-deposition intervals for bottles and bottle assemblages as a means for interpreting site function, as well as specifics of behavior related to health, product consumption, recycling, and solid-waste disposal. Worthy proposes a classificatory system for late historic ceramics that includes formal, functional, and decorative attributes. Using that system, she examines several ceramic assemblages for evidence of eating habits, buying power, status, and distribution networks. Dyson analyzes the ceramics from late-eighteenth- and early-nineteenth-century Middletown, Connecticut, for economic trends and changing world views. Edmiston demonstrates that urban faunal remains require different classificatory and analytical approaches from their prehistoric and early historic counterparts. She treats a collection of bone from an early-twentieth-century site in Atlanta as an indicator of seasonal and special-occasion food habits.

Thompson and Rathje use large artifact assemblages to interpret broad-scale behavioral patterns in modern-day Milwaukee, Wisconsin. They present important findings on purchasing practices and solid-waste disposal as they relate to socioeconomic factors. This last chapter brings the reader, full-circle, back to strategy and method, while demonstrating the importance of a well-ordered data base.

11

Analyzing Glass Bottles for Chronology, Function, and Trade Networks[1]

Sherene Baugher-Perlin

Historical archaeologists seem fascinated with ceramics, sometimes to the exclusion of other important categories of artifacts. Bottle glass, for example, which lacks the visual and perhaps tactile appeal, provides us with data for studying chronology, function of both the individual artifact (such as a bottle to hold wine) and the group use of the object (such as social drinking), and trade networks. However, in perusing site reports, it seems that for the most part we are not utilizing this material. It is hoped that this chapter will demonstrate the importance of analyzing bottle assemblages, and how the data can contribute to a more complete understanding of archaeological sites.[1]

There were major technological changes in the production of glass in the nineteenth and early twentieth centuries. The first section of this chapter focuses on these developments in the glass industry. Emphasis is placed on identifying, for the purpose of dating, characteristic marks left by various molds, pontil marks, and lipping tools. But bottles can reveal much more about a site than simply providing dates. By the early nineteenth century, glass houses were producing bottles in fairly uniform shapes, which makes it possible to recognize a medicine bottle or wine bottle simply by its form. These standardized shapes enable us to quickly determine a bottle's function. The second portion of this chapter classifies bottles into groups that share similar features and functions. Each description of key characteristics is

[1]Portions of this chapter are revisions of material presented in my dissertation (Baugher-Perlin 1978:119–170).

ARCHAEOLOGY OF URBAN AMERICA
The Search for Pattern and Process

ISBN 0-12-214980-7

accompanied by a photograph or drawing. In the nineteenth century, manufacturers embossed bottles with trademarks, company names, and geographic location, that is, city/town and state. The third segment of this chapter focuses on analyzing this embossed information to reconstruct trade patterns. Two late nineteenth, early-twentieth-century sites in the same region are compared to illustrate the importance of studying trade networks. The sites are within 4 mi. (6.4 km) of one another yet their trade patterns, as revealed by the bottle assemblages, are quite different.

In reading site reports from both public and academic archaeologists, too often one finds that the investigators have spent much time measuring bottles, almost as if they were an unknown prehistoric assemblage, and have spent little time analyzing the data that is useful for doing processual studies. Durrenberger (1965), for example, provides very detailed descriptions of all the bottles found at Anderson's Mill, Texas. Even though his presentation is more detailed than is found in many reports, it seems to be typical of the way archaeologists have dealt with bottles in the past. To categorize bottles, he classified (*a*) whole bottles according to their shapes, for example, panel bottles or jars; (*b*) bottle necks according to the presence or absence of wire rims, size of the mouth orifice, neck diameter, and general configuration of the neck; and (*c*) bottle bases according to their shapes and their markings. When I applied Durrenberger's system to bottle assemblages from nineteenth-century sites, I found that bottles of very different functions could fit into the same categories. Furthermore, with this information I could not date the artifacts.

David Brose (1967) and David Rupp took Durrenberger's system a step further. They classified the bottles according to function and "when the function was questionable or not immediately apparent, criteria of shape and size were utilized for typological organization [Brose 1967:118]." Their report provides up to 11 different bottle measurements, such as total height, basal diameter, neck diameter, and rim diameter. Unfortunately, while they have elaborate measurements in centimeters (the American glass industry was measuring its products in inches), little attention is paid to the diagnostic markings on the bottles. They note simply whether there was a pontil mark or if the object was mold-blown, but do not indicate what type of pontil mark or mold was used. I believe that these diagnostic marks, not the size measurements, will provide the most useful data.

In the mid-1970s, a few archaeologists, including myself, turned their attention to articles written by people in the glass industry, such as Julian Harrison Toulouse, and by educated and knowledgeable glass collectors, such as Helen McKearin.[2] We felt that we had to understand the technological changes in glass production and how bottle manufacturers categorized their products. It is this information that must be understood before we can attempt in-depth analyses of our bottle assemblages.

[2]Archaeologists Olive Jones (1971), Dessamae Lorrain (1968), and John White (1978) have written about the diagnostic markings on bottles.

GLASS TECHNOLOGY AND DATING

For almost 6000 years, man has been making glass, which is composed of silica, usually in the form of sand, and alkalies, such as potash, calcium oxide (lime), and sodium carbonate (McLellan 1972:784). The most common type of glass produced today as well as in the past is a silica-soda-lime mixture (Kulasiewicz 1974:89). This soda-lime glass is used to manufacture everyday items, such as bottles and window glass. Fine tableware and cut crystal glass are made from a silica-potash-lead combination (Elville 1968:40). This lead glass has also been mistakenly called "flint glass" because it was thought that "glass of the finest quality could be made only with the silica of burnt flints [McKearin and McKearin 1941:8]." Before the twentieth century, two major combinations for making glass were silica-soda-lime and silica-potash-lead.

Whereas the silica and alkalies affect the overall characteristics of glass, for example, its hardness, brilliance, and durability, other chemicals affect its color. The natural color of glass, due to impurities in the sand, ranges from green to amber (McKearin and McKearin 1941:7). Artificial colors, such as red, orange, blue, yellow, and white, are produced by adding colorants such as copper, cobalt, iron, manganese, tin, gold, and arsenic (Elville 1968:41–42; and Kulasiewicz 1974:143–155). In addition, there are other factors that can influence the color of the glass, such as the heat and the atmosphere in the oven and the number of times an object is reheated (Kulasiewicz 1974:141–142).

Until the mid-1800s, most American bottles were produced in natural colors, for example, amber, olive-green, and aquamarine (McKearin and McKearin 1941:7, 431). However, "the development of the food preservation industry in the last half of the nineteenth century created a need for clear glass for packaging products so that they could be seen [Stewart and Cosentino 1976:15]." Decolorizing agents had to be added to the glass mixture in order to manufacture clear glass.

> From about 1880, when the demand for clear glass forced the manufacturers to perfect the technique of decolorizing with manganese, until approximately 1915, at which time World War I cut off the main source—Germany—manganese was America's most widely used decolorizing agent. By 1916 glassmakers were using the more stable but also more expensive decolorizing agent selenium. . . . The use of selenium continued until around 1930 when arsenic became the popular decolorizer [Munsey 1970:55].

When clear glass contains either manganese or selenium it will change color when exposed to the sun's ultraviolet rays for a prolonged period. Glass containing manganese will take on an amethyst color, whereas bottles made with selenium will turn a light amber (Munsey 1970:55). The degree of color change will depend on how long the bottle was exposed to the sun and how much decolorizing agent it contained. These colors, then, can be of value in dating bottle fragments.

For the most part, it is the method of production and not the color or the composition of the glass that provides the most valuable information for dating the glass. Until the twentieth century, with the advent of machine mold-blown glass, bottles were made in one of two ways, either free-blown or mold-blown.[3]

Free-blown glass refers to all glass that is blown without the aid of a mold. The following is a capsule description of the process of glassblowing. After molten glass is attached to a blowpipe, the glassblower slowly and carefully blows and shapes the glass into the desired form. An assistant places some molten glass on the end of a pontil rod and the rod is then attached to the base of the bottle. The blowpipe is removed, the neck is reheated, and the lip is shaped. When the bottle is completely formed, the pontil rod must be removed before the object can be placed into a cooling oven. The pontil rod leaves a rough circular mark on the glass, which can then be polished (as was done with fine tableware), leaving only a smooth, minute scar.

Mold-blown glass refers to all glass that is blown in a mold. There are two types of molds: (*a*) a dip mold, which is in one piece and is open at the top; and (*b*) a piece mold, which is composed of hinged pieces with a small opening at the top for the blowpipe. Glass is blown in a mold for shape and/or for pattern. Blown-molded glass requires the skill of experienced glass blowers since many pieces are only partially formed in molds and must be finished off in the traditional manner. The glass manufacturer gave both shape and pattern to his wares through the use of molds.

From written records and amateur excavations of nineteenth-century factories, it is known that glass houses were manufacturing bottles for wine, beer, liquors (mainly whiskey), bitters, patent medicine, ink, food, milk, household items, and mineral and soda water (Caldwell 1947; Watkins 1933; and White 1927, 1930). With the growing demand for bottles, molds were introduced both to speed up production and to standardize shapes. Since molds usually leave seams on the bottles, these mold marks can be used for dating purposes. The following are descriptions of eight types of molds[4]:

Dip molds were used in the late-seventeenth through mid-nineteenth centuries. Since the mold formed only the bottom and sides of the bottle, the shoulder, neck, and lip had to be formed by hand (free-blown). Usually there are no seam marks and, therefore, these objects have the appearance of being free-blown. However, if the molten glass was allowed to touch the top of the mold, then a mold seam line will be found around the widest diameter of the bottle (Figure 11.1).

Hinged-bottom molds were used from about 1750 to 1880. Because of the bottom hinge, seam lines are found on the base of the bottle as well as on the sides. The bottom seam goes either straight across the base or makes a half-circle around a push-up in the center. The important thing to remember is that the base seam

[3]These definitions of manufacturing techniques are based on data from the McKearins' *American Glass* (1941:20–26).

[4]This information is based on material from Julian Harrison Toulouse (1969), "A Primer on Mold Seams," Parts I and II, and on personal communication with Olive Jones, Parks Canada.

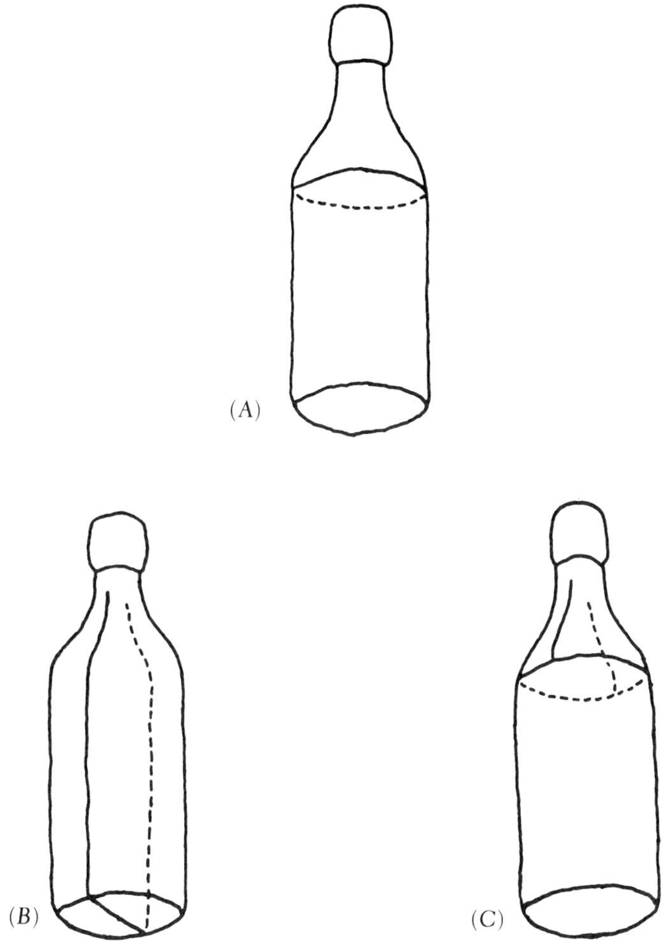

FIGURE 11.1. Mold seams on bottles. The seam lines on these three bottles were made by: (A) dip mold; (*B*) hinged-bottom mold; and (C) three-part mold with a dip body.

crosses the bottom of the bottle. If a pontil rod is used during the finishing process, the bottom seam may be partially obliterated (Figure 11.1).

Three-part molds with a dip body were molds which used a dip body and two hinged sides to form the neck and shoulders. These were patented in 1821 in England and were used up through the 1860s. During the 1870s, use of this mold declined sharply. Bottles made in these molds have a horizontal seam around their widest diameter and two vertical seams extending up the neck to just below the lip. These bottles have no decoration or lettering on the body. However, it was possible (though rarely done) to letter the shoulder area (Figure 11.1).

Three-part mold with three body-mold leaves is a common term for a poly-part mold, which includes a bottom plate which forms a fourth part. Later this mold

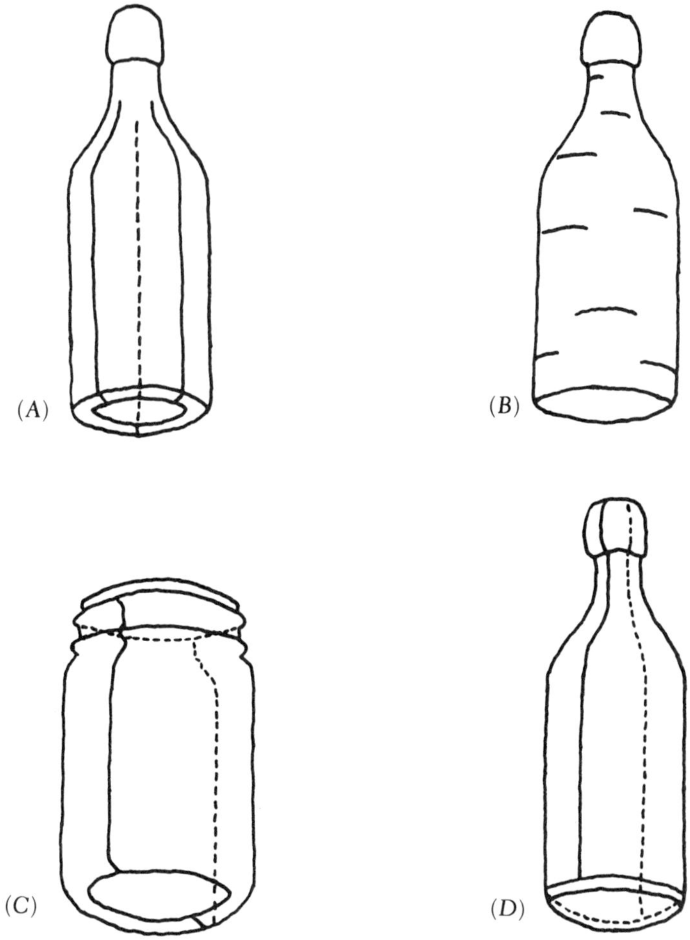

FIGURE 11.2. Mold seams on bottles. The markings on these four bottles were left by: (*A*) three-part mold with three mold leaves; (*B*) turn mold; (*C*) blown-back mold with a post-mold bottom; and (*D*) machine-blown mold with a cup bottom.

style developed to include four to eight side pieces. The poly-part mold was used for making highly decorated bottles and for art glass from 1820 through the rest of the nineteenth century. Deep cut letters and decorations very close to the seams can be made in these molds. There usually are three or more vertical seams from near the base to near the lip. The base is made in either a post or cup mold, although the post design was preferred (Figure 11.2).

Post-bottom molds were used with any of the poly-part molds. The side mold pieces closed about the post bottom and it was easy to align all the parts of the mold. The identifying seam is a centered circle on the bottom of the base. From this circle two or more side seams branch off and continue up the bottle (Figure 11.2).

Cup-bottom mold is the common machine-made base, although occasionally used with the poly-part molds. This mold forms a small depression or cup. The base is more difficult to align by hand with all the side pieces. The characteristic seam is a circle around or just below the point where the heel of the bottle meets the side wall (Figure 11.2).

Turn molds were used from 1870 to possibly as late as the 1920s, when the last of the hand-blown bottle shops closed. They were mainly used to manufacture wine bottles. The metal mold was coated with paste so that the bottle could be turned in the mold. This turning obliterated the seam marks, but the process left slight horizontal marks on the bottle (Figure 11.2).

Blown-back molds are full-height molds, developed in the mid-1800s to produce wide-mouthed bottles with screw threads. In 1858, Mason secured a patent for the process. Bottles made in these molds have seams that run the entire length of the container (Figure 11.2).[5]

Commercial embossments on bottles appeared as early as 1750 (Olive Jones, personal communication). Large companies had lettering and/or designs carved into their bottle molds. However, a more adaptable system of plate molds was developed by 1860 and is still being used today (Toulouse 1969:584). These plates, engraved with the name of the merchant and/or a product, were inserted into a mold in order to emboss the bottle. By using insertable plate molds, a glass blower could utilize the same large mold for many customers, thereby making it financially practical for small companies to purchase personalized containers.

The automatic bottle-making machine revolutionized the bottle industry. The machine was invented by Michael J. Owens and patented in 1903 (Meigh 1960:25).

> By 1914 there were 172 of Owens' machines in operation; each one capable of producing forty bottles a minute or 57,600 per day. The figures are very impressive when it is realized that in the 1800s it took a shop of three men and three boys to produce approximately 1500 bottles a day [Munsey 1970:33].

Machine mold-blown bottles can be distinguished by a variety of marks on their bases and lips.[6] These include:

Suction machine cut-off scars are irregular, often feathered circular marks found on the bottoms of bottles made only in the Owens machines. In heavyweight wares the circle will appear to be nearly round. The circle is more distorted in lighter-weight wares. These marks are the result of the glass being severed from the mold (i.e., when the appropriate amount of glass is sucked from the pot into the mold, the

[5]A variation of this mold was the semiautomatic bottle machine patented in 1881 (Meigh 1960:27). This machine was used to manufacture wide-necked bottles, and the identifying mark was the vertical seam lines that extended up to the lip. Dessamae Lorrain (1968:43) notes that this "machine was not widely distributed however, and the bottles were comparatively few in number."

[6]These descriptions are based on data provided by Munsey (1970:40–41) and Toulouse (1969:582–583 and 585–586).

remaining glass must be severed. The cut-off scar is caused by the sliding action of the knife and the rolling of small slivers of glass against the base of the mold.

A *machine-made valve mark* is an indented circle between .5 in. and .875 in. (1.27 cm and 2.22 cm) in diameter, which is seldom centered and is left on the base of wide-mouthed bottles by the push-up plunger or valve located at the base of the mold. This valve is used to push the completed bottle out of the mold. This mark is found on wide-mouthed containers made between 1930 and 1940, and can still be found on some milk bottles.

Ghost seams are faint, irregular seams beside the normal seams of the bottle. In most machine designs the bottle was blown in a "blank" mold and then transferred to a "finishing" mold. Sometimes the blank-mold seams on the bottle did not line up with the finishing-mold seams, thus leaving faint, irregular seams on the vessel. The ghost seams are found on the side of the bottle and sometimes on the base, where they appear to be a faint, asymmetrical, post-bottom seam.

Automatic bottle tops are one or more horizontal seams found on the tops of bottles produced by machine. These seams are caused by the plunger and guiding collar when they come into contact with the bottle mouth and neck. This method of identification can be applied to all types of machine-made bottles with the exception of beverage bottles. The seams were sometimes obliterated by the fire-polishing that smoothed the mouths of beverage bottles.

In addition to the seam marks, there are other features, for example, pontil marks and lip shape, that can distinguish free-blown or mold-blown bottles from machine-made bottles.

Pontil marks, like mold-markings, can provide the archaeologist with information for dating. McKearin and Wilson (1978:12–14) note that pontil rods were used in the production of both free-blown and mold-blown bottles; the pontils were used to hold the bottle at the base during the finishing process. Four types of pontil rods and the snap case were used in the nineteenth century[7]:

Glass-tipped pontils were used in the 1700s and 1800s, and are still used in hand-manufactured glass. The solid iron bar pontil rod was dipped into molten glass and then applied to the bottle base. The glass on the pontil adhered to the glass of the base. When the finished object was broken from the pontil, a solid, circular scar was left on the bottom of the bottle. When the pontil was removed from the object, either excess glass was left on the bottle or bits of glass were torn out of the base, leaving, in either case, a jagged scar. The scar could be reduced to a shallow depression by grinding it. Since grinding was a costly process, it was only done on expensive bottles, such as decanters. On most bottles, the scar was left untouched unless it interfered with the ability of the inexpensive bottle to stand upright.

Sand-tipped pontils were used in the 1700s and 1800s and are still used in

[7]These descriptions are based on data provided by Jones (1971:68–72) and Munsey (1970:47–49).

hand-blown wares. The pontil, with the molten glass on its tip, is dipped in sand before it is attached to the bottle base. The sand prevents the pontil glass from adhering too closely to the bottle. When this pontil rod is removed, a pebbled surface is left on the bottom of the bottle, and sometimes grains of sand may be embedded in the base.

Blowpipe pontils were used in the eighteenth and nineteenth centuries. When the blowpipe was removed from the bottle neck, the vessel was placed on a V-shaped holder and the blowpipe attached to the bottle's base. When the finished ware was broken away from the blowpipe, a ring-shaped scar was left. As in the case of the glass-tipped pontil rod, when the blowpipe was removed, it either tore glass out of the bottle base or left extra glass on the ware. This uneven surface could be reduced by grinding. With this ring-shaped mark, mold lines or embossments could be seen clearly both inside and outside the ring.

Bare-iron pontils were used from 1845 to 1880. The tip of the rod was not coated with glass. When the iron rod was heated and pressed to the bottom of the bottle, it forced an indentation into the glass. When the complete ware was broken from the pontil, a smooth, circular mark was left on the bottle. The marks, consisting of oxidized iron, either were red to reddish black or were white. The red to reddish-black marks are found on a variety of bottle types during the period 1845–1870.[8] The white marks are found only on soda and mineral water bottles dating from 1870 to 1880.

The snap case was introduced about 1857. By the 1870s, most glass houses were using the snap case instead of the bare iron pontil. A snap case is essentially a pontil split down the middle for about a foot (.3 m) with a cup between the two split ends. The bottle sits in the cup and the pontil ends grip the body of the bottle. The snap case does not leave a basal scar but occasionally leaves a mark on the side of the bottle. The snap case was used until it was replaced by the automatic bottle-making machine, which did not use pontil rods.

Additional data can be obtained from the lips of the bottles. When making free-blown or mold-blown bottles, the lip or mouth is formed after the container has been freed from the blowpipe. Shearing, the process of cutting the bottle from the blowpipe with shears, or wetting off, in which the hot neck glass is weakened with water and then severed from the blowpipe with a sharp tap, are the two ways of producing a simple, straight lip called a sheared lip (Stewart and Cosentino 1976:26). These lips are given a smooth edge by fire-polishing. There is no way to differentiate between bottles produced by these two methods since they both leave the lips in the same condition (Munsey 1970:32). Shearing was done only on wide-mouthed containers (Olive Jones, personal communication). After 1840, most

[8]McKearin and Wilson (1978:220) state that "the black color was caused by oxide from a pontil in a low state of oxidation or what is called a ferrous state; the red resulted when the black oxide turned (through oxidation) into ferric or red oxide."

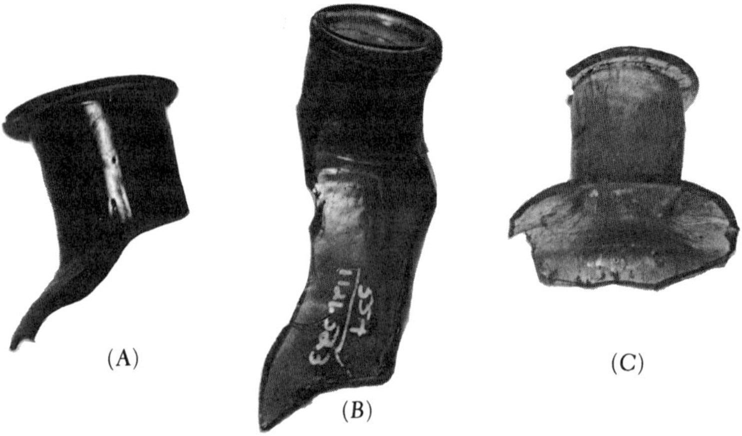

FIGURE 11.3. Hand-blown bottle lips. Left to right: (*A*) flared lip; (*B*) rolled-in (infolded) lip; and (*C*) another flared (rolled-out) lip. These bottle necks are from the Stadt Huys Collection. (Shown at actual size.)

bottles had applied lips, which were formed with lipping tools (Ketchum 1975:34). All of these methods used fire-polishing to smooth out the rough lips.

The laid-on-ring, which is a ring of molten glass laid around the bottle neck, could be used for forming the lip, for additional support to the neck, or for decorative purposes. This is sometimes called an applied lip, but *laid-on-ring*, a term used in the glass industry, more appropriately describes the method of production. A number of lip shapes were formed with the use of finishing tools. In the late 1820s finishing tools were invented in England, but they were not patented in the United States until 1856 (Toulouse 1969:533). White (1978) illustrates a variety of nineteenth-century bottle lips, such as a flared lip, one that is rolled out from the bottle mouth; a sheared lip; and an infolded lip, one that is rolled into the mouth of the bottle (Figures 11.3 and 11.4). The early bottle lips often were crude and rough since these bottles used simple cork closures.

By the 1870s, some major changes had occurred in the glass industry: an improvement in furnaces; the development of more complex finishing tools;[9] and the invention of more elaborate closures.[10] The addition of a separate gas and coal fired "glory hole" to the furnace allowed the glass blower to achieve a smooth neck,

[9]For more detailed information on these technological changes and their effect on glass production see Scoville (1948) and Davis (1970).

[10]See McKearin and Wilson (1978), *American bottles and flasks and their ancestry*, for more information on cork closures, screw caps, and stoppers.

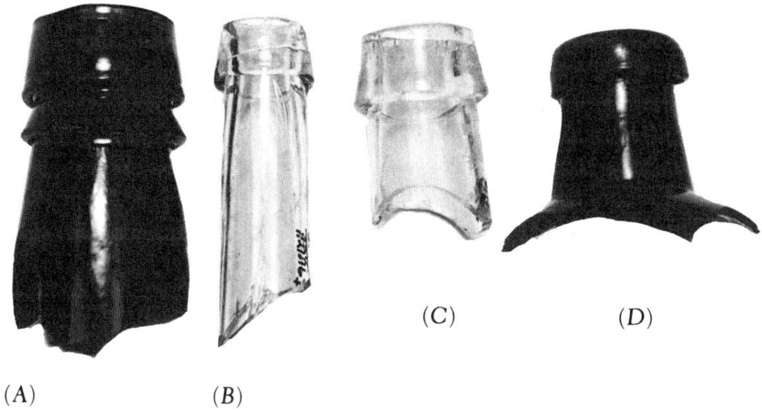

FIGURE 11.4. Laid-on-Rings. The four bottle necks have laid-on-rings (applied lips). Bottle necks (*B*) and (C) clearly show the separation of the two layers of glass. (A) and (*D*), the two dark necks (post-1870), even when held up to a bright light, show one thick layer of glass; the laid-on-ring is virtually undetectable. All four specimens are from the Stadt Huys Collection. (Shown 3/4 actual size.)

mouth, and lip without overheating and perhaps distorting the rest of the bottle; after the late 1870s, "the greater heat made for finishes so smooth that the laid-on-ring was virtually undetectable—the two glasses appear as one [Toulouse 1969:534]."

In summary, the diagnostic features for dating bottles include the color of the glass; the pontil marks or mold marks on the base; the seam lines on the sides, shoulder, and neck; and the shape of the lip and mouth. Taken together, these features can provide an accurate index of the bottle's age.

BOTTLE FUNCTION

Artifacts of glass can be placed into categories based on their shared features and functions. As mentioned earlier, the nineteenth century brought standardization to bottle forms. Of course, there were variations within each type. John Adams' (1971) photographic book on American bottles illustrates the variation in color, height, and width within a genre, such as medicine bottles. Shapes of particular bottles did change through time. Beer bottles, originally quite similar to soda and mineral water bottles, took on their distinctive shape in the 1870s (Munsey 1970:116).

In this section, I provide information on the types of bottles most commonly found on nineteenth- and early-twentieth-century sites. Granted there are other bottles, such as commemorative flasks, that were made in the nineteenth century, but they do not appear frequently in archaeological assemblages. The reader should refer to McKearin and Wilson's (1978) book on American bottles for more detailed information on each bottle type.

Type A: Beer Bottles

Even though beer, ale, and porter had been brewed in America since the founding of the colonies, they were not commercially bottled until the nineteenth century (Ketchum 1975:104). In the 1870s, two developments—the invention of the Lightning Stopper, a cork closure held down by a porcelain stopper and wire; and the discovery of pasteurization—greatly encouraged breweries to bottle their product (Stewart and Cosentino 1976:29). Before pasteurization, it was not practical to do much bottling since beer would spoil two to three days after brewing. In spite of the fact that beer bottles (Figure 11.5) were manufactured in aqua, blue, clear, and

(A)

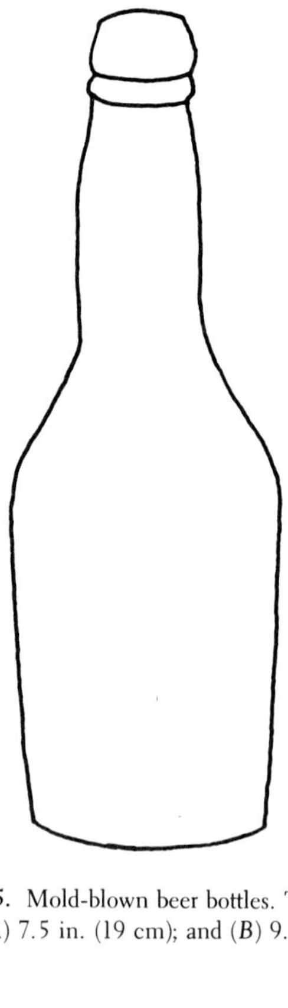

(B)

FIGURE 11.5. Mold-blown beer bottles. The bottles both have laid-on-rings (applied lips). The bottle heights are (A) 7.5 in. (19 cm); and (B) 9.25 in. (23.5 cm).

even yellow glass, amber was the predominant color (Ketchum 1975:109–110). From 1870 to 1920, most beer bottles were embossed, but after Prohibition they carried paper labels (Munsey 1970:116–117).

Type B: Food and Household Bottles

Certain foods that would not readily spoil, such as oil, vinegar, syrup, pepper-sauce, and mustard, were bottled and sold during the nineteenth century. In the early and mid nineteenth century, most food containers used cork closures (Stewart and Cosentino 1976:46). These containers came in a variety of shapes and colors (Figure 11.6). Oil bottles were aqua or green in color and tall and slender in

(A) (B) (C)

FIGURE 11.6. Food and household bottles. (A) Vaseline jar (machine-blown); (B) citrate of magnesia bottle (mold-blown); and (C) Worcestershire sauce bottle (mold-blown). These bottles are from the Prall Site Collection. (Shown one half actual size.)

(A) (B)

FIGURE 11.7. Mold-blown inkwells. (A) umbrella inkwell; and (B) conical inkwell. Both bottles are from the Prall Site Collection. (Shown one half actual size.)

shape (Munsey 1970:152). Peppersauce bottles were narrow with long necks, whereas mustard containers were short and squat (Stewart and Cosentino 1976:45). The common colors of nineteenth-century food bottles were aqua and light green, whereas the early twentieth-century machine-made ones usually were clear (Berkow 1973:112). Household bottles, like food containers, came in a variety of shapes and colors (Ketchum 1975:158). The bottles contained such products as shoe polishes, glues, bleaches, and insect killers (Stewart and Cosentino 1976:45).

Type C: Inkwells

Until the nineteenth century, ink was produced in Europe in ceramic containers. By the early 1800s, American firms such as Maynard and Noles and Thaddeus Davis started to manufacture their own ink in glass bottles (Stewart and Cosentino 1976:65). Inkwells were made in many shapes (Figure 11.7), although two common forms were the "umbrella" and the conical well (Ketchum 1975:134). The umbrella shape was produced in great number by the Whitney Glass Works, the Isabella Glass Works, and Whitall Tatum, during the period from the 1820s to the 1880s (Munsey 1970:120). The conical shape was introduced by Carter's Ink Company in 1858 and was popular until the early 1900s (Berkow 1973:149). Inkwells usually were made of aqua, light green, or clear glass, although some were amber, dark green, or cobalt blue (Stewart and Cosentino 1976:67). Although some inkwells were embossed, many firms used paper labels to identify their products (Munsey 1970:121).

Type D: Medicine Bottles

Bottles for patent medicines, those with their ingredient formulas registered with the government, and proprietary medicines, with only their brand names registered, were produced throughout the 1800s. Even though very few of the potions were

(A) (B) (C)

FIGURE 11.8. Mold-blown medicine bottles. (A) cylindrical bottle with a flared lip; (B) panel bottle with an applied lip (laid-on-ring); and (C) rectangular bottle with a rolled-in lip. The three bottles are from the Prall Site Collection. (Shown one half actual size.)

patented, *patent medicine* has become the generic term for all nineteenth-century medicines sold without a prescription (Munsey 1970:65). Whereas these cure-alls usually contained a high percentage of alcohol, a number of them contained "harmful amounts of codeine, cocaine, morphine, heroin, cannabis indica, and phenobarbitol [Berkow 1973:79]." In 1905, *Colliers* magazine ran a series of articles listing the ingredients in these medicines and exposing the whole medicine fraud. Partly as a result of these articles, the Pure Food and Drug Act of 1906 was enacted (Stewart and Cosentino 1976:89). There was a decrease in the number of patent medicine companies after the companies had both to list ingredients and prove the listing was accurate.

Patent medicines usually were sold in cylindrical or rectangular bottles (Figure 11.8), which were aqua or light green in color (Munsey 1970:69). Most of these bottles were embossed with the marker's name, and had a paper label (Ketchum 1975:92). Over 50,000 medicines were being produced in the United States by the turn of the century (Stewart and Cosentino 1976:89). With so many different medicines, multiplied by the number of bottles per medicine being manufactured, these bottles are common on nineteenth-century sites.

FIGURE 11.9. Machine-blown milk bottles. All three bottles were manufactured for the Borden's Milk Company. These bottles are from the Prall Site Collection. (Shown one half actual size.)

Type E: Milk Bottles

In the early nineteenth century, milk was delivered to the market in large cans or crocks. A customer would bring his or her own pail to the milkman, who would dole out the milk from large containers. By mid-century, "increasing concern with sanitation as well as an expanding urban market encouraged the development of a more efficient method of distribution [Ketchum 1975:154]." In the 1880s, milk was produced in round bottles; from 1936 to 1940, round, squat containers were used; these in turn were succeeded by square, squat containers after 1940 (Munsey 1970:191). Most milk containers were made of clear glass (Figure 11.9), although a few were amber colored. The majority also had embossed designs and lettering (Stewart and Cosentino 1976:72).

Type F: Preserving Jars

In 1810, a Frenchman named Nicholas Appert developed a process of preserving foods by first packing the food in an airtight glass container and then boiling the container to destroy the bacteria (Stewart and Cosentino 1976:53). Until the mid-nineteenth century, preserving jars were fitted with cork closures that were sealed with wax (Ketchum 1975:150). Experimentation with different types of closures

(A) (B)

FIGURE 11.10. Mold-blown preserving jars. Jar *A* has a neck and mouth that uses a Mason screw cap. Jar *B* has a glass lid with a metal clamp. The bottle heights are (*A*) 7 in. (17.7 cm); and (*B*) 7.5 in. (19 cm).

took place in the mid-1800s. In 1858, Mason developed his now famous zinc screw cap, which, however, was not widely used because it was considered unsafe to expose food to zinc (Berkow 1973:121–122). Boyd saved the Mason lid in 1869 by inventing a milk glass liner which prevented contact between the food and the zinc cap (Munsey 1970:146). Other sealing devices were invented during the late 1860s, including glass lids with metal clamps or metal wires (Stewart and Cosentino 1976:55). Even though Mason did not invent the glass preserving bottle, nor were his closures used on all these preserving containers, *Mason* has become the generic term applied to all preserving jars (Munsey 1970:146).

There was a tendency to make all preserving jars in two basic shapes—square or round, straight-sided, wide-mouthed—and they were usually embossed with the manufacturer's name, trade name, or symbol (Stewart and Cosentino 1976:53–56). These jars are commonly found in shades of aqua or clear glass (Figure 11.10), but a few were made in amber, milk glass, emerald green, blue, and black (Ketchum 1975:153).

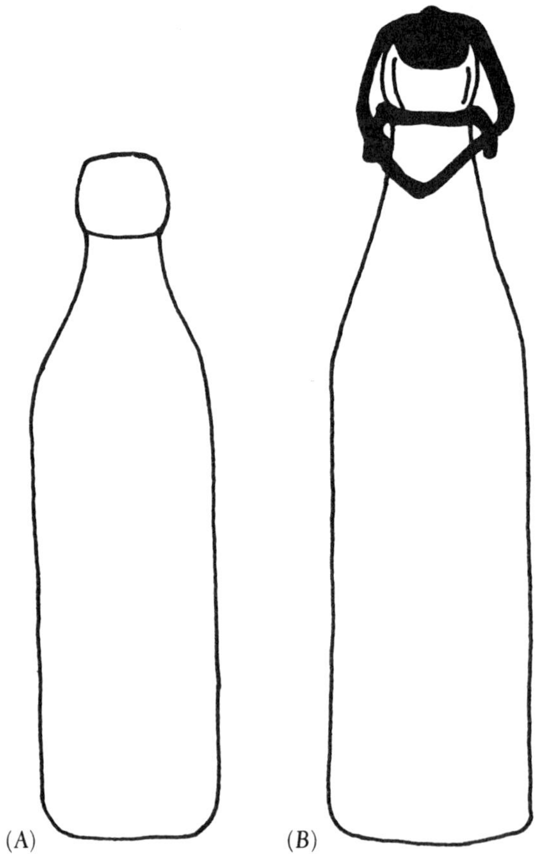

FIGURE 11.11. Mold-blown soda and mineral water bottles. Both bottles have laid-on-rings. Bottle *B* has a metal clamp and cork closure. The bottle heights are (*A*) 7.5 in. (19 cm); (*B*) 9 in. (22.8 cm).

Type G: Soda and Mineral Water Bottles

Natural mineral water, with or without carbonation, was being bottled in America as early as the 1760s (Munsey 1970:101). By 1830, artificially carbonated water with flavoring added was being bottled as "soda water" (Ketchum 1975:117–119). Mineral and soda water containers were generally manufactured in clear, aqua, amber, green, or cobalt blue cylindrical bottles (Stewart and Cosentino 1976:78–79). Since it is often difficult to distinguish the nineteenth-century soda containers from the mineral water bottles, they may be grouped together (Figure 11.11).

Type H: Wine and Champagne Bottles

In the eighteenth century, wine and champagne bottles were free-blown or made in dip molds, whereas in the nineteenth century they were produced in full-sized molds (Olive Jones, personal communication). From 1880 to 1910, wine bottles (Figure 11.12) usually were made in turn molds; after 1910, they were machine-made (Munsey 1970:59). Throughout most of the 1800s, wine bottles were various shades of dark green or black, but in the late 1800s they were also made in other dark colors: amber, red amber, blue, and amethyst (Munsey 1970:60).

Type I: Whiskey Bottles

Pictorial and historical flasks were popular in the first half of the nineteenth century (Stewart and Cosentino 1976:97).[11] In the 1860s, historical and pictorial containers were replaced by plain and heavily embossed flasks (Berkow 1973:29). By 1880, the standardized whiskey containers were cylindrical fifth bottles and oval and rectangular flasks in pint and half-pint sizes (Munsey 1970:125). Whiskey bottles (Figure 11.13) were manufactured in clear, aqua, and amber glass (Stewart and Cosentino 1976:100).

After we have classified bottles according to their function, we should look at the frequency relationships between the artifacts and their cultural contexts. Finding that 40% of the bottles from an inn are whiskey bottles will not raise the same questions as finding the same percentage in the garbage from a single-family home. Before we jump to quick and easy conclusions about behavior, we must determine the provenience of the artifacts. For example, a higher than normal frequency of a certain type of bottle among the kitchen refuse can reveal a preference for a specific food or beverage. In another context, such as a barn or workshop, the presence of numerous small, wide-mouthed food jars may simply mean that the owner was reusing the bottles as containers for nails, bolts, and screws.

The frequency relationships among different bottle types in the same context can provide important behavioral information. To some extent we can gather dietary

[11] See McKearin and Wilson (1978) for more information on pictorial and historical flasks.

FIGURE 11.12. Wine and champagne bottles. The wine bottle (A) has a more narrow neck, mouth, and body. Both bottles are approximately 11.5 in. (29 cm) high and both were blown in molds.

information in regard to percentages of bottled foods and beverages at the site. But again, we must carefully analyze the data in order to interpret correctly the behavior involved. For example, does finding a large number of medicine bottles mean that people were sickly? They may have been overly concerned about their health, involved in preventive medicine, or simply consuming alcohol in a socially acceptable form. We may not find the answer at one site, but by comparing data from a number of sites, we can begin to find patterns of behavior. For instance, do we find different degrees of alcohol consumption between different ethnic or occupational groups? Is there a decrease in medicine bottles at sites when there is an increase of whiskey and other alcoholic beverage bottles? After studying the comparative data

FIGURE 11.13. Whiskey bottles. All three embossed bottles were machine-blown. These bottles are from the Prall Site Collection. (Shown one half actual size.)

we can look again at the original site to see whether the behavior is typical for an ethnic, religious, or occupational group.

Bottles are more than just containers for holding solids and fluids. These objects are also evidence of cultural and personal traits. Some products may have been status or collectors' items, such as commemorative whiskey flasks. Items such as hair lotion from the Seven Southerland Sisters were popular during a specific period of time. Finding beer bottles from only one of three local breweries could represent individual taste, or could result from limited delivery routes in certain areas.

Manufacturers' lists, wholesalers' catalogues, and newspaper advertisements can provide documentary data on popularity trends and status items in bottled products. In addition, we should check these records to see if any companies had deposits on their bottles. If certain bottles, like soda bottles, were returnable, their appearance in small numbers is not an index to actual product use. Since bottle frequency relationships affect our interpretation of behavioral patterns, we must know what types of bottles were commonly discarded and which ones were recycled.

This documentary data will also enable us to plot popularity trends and locate status products that were sold in bottles, thereby defining patterns of conspicuous consumption. Thus far, we have underutilized documentary resources on glass as they relate to the archaeological record.

TRADE NETWORKS

Bottles, as shown earlier, provide information for both obtaining a time framework and determining behavioral patterns from the function, frequency, and cultural context of the artifacts. Bottles can also provide data on trade networks. Embossments on bottles had the product name and sometimes the manufacturer's name and location of the factory (Figure 11.14). By studying these embossments, we can learn about the economic connections between groups and/or communities. To better understand these trade networks, we should know something about the history of the American glass industry and the economic climate surrounding it.

In America, glass manufacturing dates to the founding of the first settlements. In 1608, the first glass house was built at Jamestown; it operated for 1 year and was later reestablished for a brief period in 1622 (Watkins 1949:363). Lura Watkins (1950:21) notes that "strangely enough, although the need for window panes and containers in the pioneer colonies was acute, our first glass was not blown for local consumption, but for export." In spite of the failure of the Virginia venture, other attempts at glassmaking were made in Salem, Massachusetts (1638–1642), in New Amsterdam, New York (1654–1674), and in Philadelphia, Pennsylvania (1683–?) (Hunter 1950:134–142). These later glass houses probably were producing glass for the colonists (Moore 1945:211).

The Wistar family operated America's first successful glassworks from 1740–1780 in South Jersey (Sicard 1926:110–111). Their factory made window glass, bottles, snuff cannisters, and medicine phials, but they are most remembered for their noncommercial wares, for example, bowls, vases, and pitchers (McKearin

(A) (B)

FIGURE 11.14. Embossed bottles. (*A*) mold-blown, rectangular medicine bottle from Staten Island; and (*B*) mold-blown, panel-type, hair tonic bottle from New York. Both bottles are from the Prall Site Collection. (Shown one half actual size.)

1926:275). But it was Steigel, not Wistar, who brought about a major change in American glassmaking. By hiring enamelers and engravers and using lead glass, Steigel was able to produce imitations of fine English tableware at his factory in Pennsylvania (Hunter 1950:185–206). Amelung, who followed Steigel in producing quality glassware, hired skilled blowers and engravers, and his wares, made in Maryland, can be favorably compared to the better-made European glass (Watkins 1950:32–34). By the end of the eighteenth century, some American glass houses had moved from the manufacturing of simple window glass to the production of quality tableware.

Even though the glass houses were capable of producing a wide variety of wares, they could not compete successfully with the imported glass. Steigel started glass production in 1763 and was bankrupt in 1774 (McKearin and McKearin 1941:81–94). Amelung, who started his business in 1788, declared bankruptcy in 1795 (Noël Hume 1964:310). Glass houses failed in America for a variety of reasons: "For one thing there was not enough venture money; for another, when land was free for the taking, no man would work long for another [Davidson 1949:366]." In addition, the early glass manufacturers found it difficult to compete with European imports. American glass remained an infant industry until the nineteenth century.

By the 1820s, the economic climate had changed and conditions now favored the growth of American industries. Along with the invention of the steamboat, the construction of canals and railroads provided new arteries for commerce and larger markets. In addition, immigration provided skilled craftsmen, and the tariff of 1824 protected the glass companies from foreign competition (McKearin and McKearin 1941:132–135). Although only 21 glass houses were established in the seventeenth and eighteenth centuries, 100 new companies were manufacturing glass between 1820 and 1840 (Watkins 1950:52). Many of these factories were built in areas where fuel was abundant and cheap, such as Ohio, western Pennsylvania, and West Virginia (Innes 1948; White 1934).

With the development of removable plate molds, glass houses could produce embossed bottles for a wide variety of small companies. Toulouse (1971) has compiled a listing of over 900 older bottle trademarks and over 311 modern ones, along with a history of each company and its dates of production. Toulouse (1971:8–9) notes that identification marks "came into use in the late 1600s with the development of the 'seal' or portion of glass affixed to the bottle, usually the shoulder, while still hot, and in that condition pressed with a die in the form of initials, dates, or designs (devices) for identification." The seal's value is that it required no mold cutting. In the nineteenth century, some companies had lettering cut into their bottle molds so that their trademarks or name would appear on the side of the bottle. Since this process permanently lettered the mold, it was used only by business that could afford to buy their own molds. With removable plate molds, the same mold could be used to produce bottles for many small companies. The small brewery, dairy, or soda bottler would have to purchase only the plate mold and not the whole bottle mold.

With the widespread use of plate molds, embossed bottles on a given site provide a record of which products were being purchased locally and which ones were being brought in from other areas. To what extent were these trade networks the same or similar for communities in the same locale? This can be answered by studying the bottle assemblages from two geographically related sites.

Both Sandy Ground and the Prall Site are located on Staten Island, one of the five boroughs of New York (Figure 11.15). Staten Island is the most rural of the boroughs, and through most of its history had access to the mainland only by ferries and sloops. The first bridges linking the island to New Jersey were built in 1928. Because of its isolation, the island maintained a small town, rural quality for a long time. In 1964, the Verrazano Narrows Bridge was completed, which provided a link to Brooklyn and opened the way for major land development of the island. After 1964, there was a surge in population growth and a transformation in the socioeconomic composition of the island; it now became a major suburban community for commuters who worked in the other boroughs (Baugher-Perlin 1978:111).

The archaeological comparison of Sandy Ground and the Prall Site is based on a

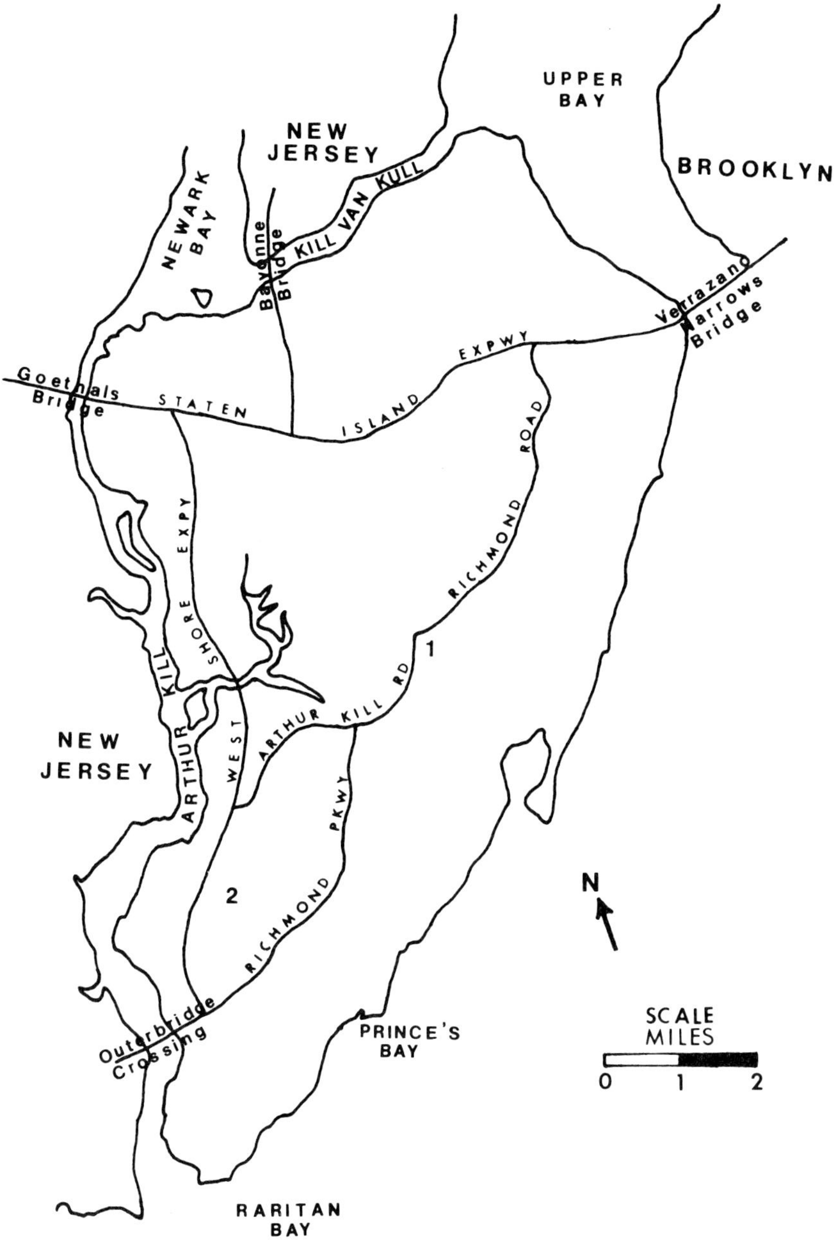

FIGURE 11.15. Map of Staten Island, with the locations of Richmondtown (1) and Sandy Ground (2).

study of data on trade networks presented in Schuyler's (1974, 1977, and 1980) three articles and my dissertation (Baugher-Perlin 1978:141–172).[12] There were major differences between the two areas, even though they were located within 4 miles (6.4 km) of one another. Sandy Ground, a black community, was established in the nineteenth century, while Richmondtown, where the Prall Site is located, was a white community and the county seat from 1729 to 1898.

Sandy Ground is located on the western shore of Staten Island near Lemon Creek. This creek flows into Prince's Bay, an important center for oystering (Figure 11.15). Until the twentieth century, when pollution contaminated the waters, oystering was a major industry on Staten Island. In the early nineteenth century, around the 1830s, these oyster beds were reseeded with oysters brought from the Chesapeake Bay. Schuyler (1977:9) notes that "free blacks, an important segment of the oystering community in Maryland and Virginia, also traveled on the schooners and sloops that carried seed oysters to New York."

By the 1830s, the free blacks in Maryland, a slave state, began to feel the effects of the tension building between the white and black communities throughout the South. Schuyler (1974:18) writes about this persecution in the 1830s, when "a series of laws restricting the freedom of blacks in the oyster industry were passed and this as well as other factors led to the migration of several black families out of Snowhill, Maryland." Since the oystermen of Snowhill had contact with people in New York, the move to Staten Island was not a move to a foreign or unknown territory. By 1850, the black segment of Sandy Ground, which has always been an integrated community, was sufficiently established to found its own church (Schuyler 1974:20). During the second half of the nineteenth century, the community flourished and the blacks maintained a high standard of living from their work in oystering (Schuyler 1974:20). Schuyler (1974:20–21) notes that the period 1900–1965 brought decline and disintegration of the community, because when the oyster industry collapsed, the blacks were forced to take other work. Many of them found jobs in factories in New Jersey.

The Prall Site, located in the heart of Richmondtown, is a microcosm of the village. The owners and occupants of the site were typical in ethnic, vocational, and religious background, of the Richmondtown population from the seventeenth through the twentieth century. Successive occupants included farmer, wheelwright, physician, merchant, innkeeper, carpenter, and barber. In many ways the development of the Prall Site reflected general trends in the socioeconomic evolution of the town as a whole.[13] Richmondtown, from its earliest settlement in the late 1600s, was a community of white people with diverse ethnic and religious backgrounds. Dutch, English, and French settled here (Baugher-Perlin 1978:112). Richmondtown is located in the center of the island, at the crossroads of routes

[12]Due to a variety of factors, I was unable to work with the Sandy Ground bottle assemblage. I used only the data from Schuyler's (1974, 1977, and 1980) articles. This published material does not contain a bottle by bottle breakdown showing functional type, company name, and geographic location; Schuyler presented only the total number of bottles from each town and/or city.

[13]For more details on the specific history of the site and the town see Baugher-Perlin (1978:63–118).

leading to all areas. Merchants traded with the farmers, and products and produce moved between various markets in New York and the neighboring cities in New Jersey, such as Perth Amboy and Elizabeth, which were across the Arthur Kill (Figure 11.15). In 1898, Staten Island became one of the boroughs of New York City, and the county seat was moved from Richmondtown to St. George, a community on the north shore facing Manhattan (Baugher-Perlin 1978:111). The twentieth century brought a period of decline for Richmondtown, as it was out of the mainstream of the island's growth. By the 1950s, land and buildings were being acquired by the city of New York and the Staten Island Historical Society in order to preserve the old town as an outdoor museum. Today the Prall Site is part of the Richmondtown Restoration Center, a restored village. In summary, Richmondtown has undergone the following transformations: seventeenth century—farming community; eighteenth century—expanding, nucleated village; nineteenth century—unincorporated town; early twentieth century—proto-suburb; and mid-twentieth century—outdoor museum and restored village (Baugher-Perlin 1978:112).

The late nineteenth and early twentieth century was the period that ended prosperity for both Sandy Ground and Richmondtown. These communities were dramatically altered by events over which they had very little control, that is, the pollution of the harbor and the change in municipal government.

Schuyler (1974, 1977) studied two contemporaneous bottle assemblages from Sandy Ground, dating from ca. 1890–1910 with a few bottles from 1910–1920. The embossed bottles from the Prall Site range from ca. 1850–1930, with most of the material being late nineteenth and early twentieth century.[14] A comparison of the assemblages from these two sites shows that different trade networks existed for these communities, although there are many similarities.

On both sites, the non–Staten Island bottles are from communities that were located either on rivers or coastal harbors. The Sandy Ground bottles come from as far as Boston to the north; Seaford, Delaware, to the south; Berlin, Germany, to the east; and San Francisco, California, to the west. Schuyler (1977:12) notes that out of "191 specimens only five bottles came from outside of the Middle Atlantic–Northeastern region" and of the remaining 186 bottles "nearly 78% cluster within a tight 20 to 25 mile radius from Sandy Ground." Within the New York metropolitan area, 68 specimens are from Staten Island, 56 are from southern Manhattan, and 33 are from towns in northeastern New Jersey. The remaining 29 bottles are from Boston (1), Lowell, Massachusetts (7), upstate New York (10), Philadelphia (10), and Seaford, Delaware (1).

The number of identified embossed bottles from the Prall Site is only one-third the size of the Sandy Ground assemblage.[15] Of the 59 bottles, 89% are from

[14]Although the provenience of each bottle is known, the site was disturbed and it is impossible to tie individual bottles to their specific owners. The occupants who disposed of these bottles were middle-class whites who worked on Staten Island. See Baugher-Perlin (1978; 1979) for more details on the problems in excavating and analyzing this site.

[15]There are 24 additional bottles that are being analyzed. These broken bottles contain only partial labels, and at this point we have not been able to determine their geographic source. However, most of the 24 bottles are machine-made and come from a deposit that dates from 1911 to 1932.

Table 11.1 Areas of Origin for Bottles Found at Sandy Ground and Richmondtown

Location of origin	Percentage of total specimens	
	Sandy Ground	Richmondtown
Staten Island	35.6	27.0
New York	29.3	25.4
New Jersey	17.3	36.0
Philadelphia	5.2	10.0
Upstate New York	5.2	1.6
New England	4.2	—
Delaware	.5	—
Beyond Mid-Atlantic and Northeast region	2.6	—

communities within 25 mi. (40.2 km) of Richmondtown. Staten Island beer, milk, soda, and medicine bottles represent 16 of the glass containers in the sample. The coastal towns of New Jersey supplied 21 of the specimens, and 15 came from Manhattan. Of the remaining 7 bottles, 1 was from Albany and 6 were from Philadelphia.

If we view the specimens in terms of percentages rather than frequencies, a more meaningful comparison of the two assemblages is possible (Table 11.1). In both cases, more than 75% of the bottles come from sources within 25 mi. (40.2 km) of the two communities. This distribution pattern can be visualized as an arc encompassing Staten Island, Manhattan, and communities in eastern New Jersey. There was a noticeable lack, at both sites, of any bottles from Brooklyn, Queens, or Long Island. The orientation in both cases was toward the western side of New York Harbor. Geographically, Staten Island is so close to New Jersey (at some points only 500 ft or 152.4 m of water separate the two bodies of land) that is is not surprising to find extensive trade between the two areas. From the Colonial period, Staten Island was trading with Manhattan, and again, it is not surprising to find this pattern continued throughout the nineteenth and twentieth centuries.

While Sandy Ground and Richmondtown were different in their ethnic, racial, and occupational composition, they were both lower- and middle-range, middle-class communities. In both cases, their trade patterns reflect a dual local-metropolitan orientation. This similarity might indicate that the Sandy Grounders were adopting the purchasing patterns of white middle-class Staten Islanders. On the other hand, Staten Island was still somewhat isolated and rural in the 1890s, and it is quite possible that the general stores in both communities were purchasing goods from the same distributors.

Even though there is a similar western harbor trade network, there are a number of differences in the percentages of the goods being traded. Schuyler (1977:16) notes that the Sandy Ground pattern forms half an ellipse, with one node for Staten Island (35.6%) and the other for New York (29.3%), and with the two areas connected by the Jersey shore (17.3%). In Richmondtown, the major source of goods is New Jersey (36%), with Staten Island (27%) and New York (25.4%) balancing one another. Since roads from Richmondtown lead to the New Jersey ferries, Richmondtown may have had an easier access to New Jersey commerce than did Sandy Ground. In addition, the Sandy Ground oystermen sailed out of a harbor, Prince's Bay, on the southern shore of the island (Figure 11.15), and their work may have brought them to New York more often than to the Jersey cities.

The major differences between the two sites are seen in the percentages of bottles from outside the New York metropolitan area. Both communities used some bottles from Philadelphia. Since the 1700s, Richmondtown and the Island had trade connections with Philadelphia. Ten percent of the Prall Site bottles are from that city, as compared with 5.2% at Sandy Ground. In Richmondtown, the only other nonmetropolitan area bottle is from Albany, New York. Sandy Ground, on the other hand, had specimens from upstate New York, New England, Delaware, California, and Europe. This difference may reflect the Sandy Grounders' access, via the oyster trade, to goods from areas beyond the general trade and transportation systems available to Staten Islanders.

These brief comparisons of Sandy Ground and Richmondtown leave many questions unanswered. An in-depth examination of the actual bottle assemblages, beyond the limited data available in published form, should be undertaken. An intersite comparison should be made of the specific types of bottles (e.g., medicine, soda, milk, and beer) and the companies that produced them to ascertain similarities and differences between the purchasing patterns in the two communities. From such comparisons, we might gain insights into the degree to which the Sandy Grounders were being assimilated into a Staten Island middle-class life-style and to what extent they were maintaining a tradition from the Chesapeake Bay area. Investigations of free-black sites in the Delmarva Peninsula should be undertaken to determine how this life-style is expressed archaeologically. Clearly, we need to compare Sandy Ground and Richmondtown to other sites on Staten Island and in Maryland to assemble necessary comparative research data.

In analyzing trade networks we must remember that there were differences in purchasing patterns between rural and urban communities and between regional areas. Adams (1976), in his study of Silcott, a small farming community in southeastern Washington, found that the majority of the bottle assemblage originated more than 1000 miles (1609 km) from Silcott. Adams (1976:109–110) notes that people in Silcott may have acquired nationally marketed products from mail-order houses, such as Sears Roebuck and Montgomery Ward. Spencer-Wood (1979), on the other hand, found that in the rural community of Dummerton, Vermont, the majority of bottles were from regional sources. In both Silcott and Dummerton there was a dearth of local industry; Dummerton had access to regional trade, whereas Silcott had to rely on national markets. Spencer-Wood (1979:125) notes that when studying urban sites one may find that there is a high percentage of locally made products; however, many of these items may have been available nationwide. In analyzing the Sandy Ground and Richmondtown bottle assemblages, it is necessary to determine whether the products were marketed through local, regional, or national distributors.

I chose the Sandy Ground–Richmondtown comparison in order to demonstrate the variety of information that can be gleaned from studying embossed bottles. More sophisticated and systematic use of bottle data can contribute to the recognition of other behavioral patterns. However, we must remember that bottles are only one segment of the assemblage from a site. By combining bottle data with ceramic, architectural, and dietary information, we can better interpret the total life-style of the people who lived at a site. Intersite comparisons should be made to assist us in moving beyond the local setting to regional, national, and even international levels. In the end, these patterns should contribute to a greater understanding of the underlying processes of urbanization and industrialization in America.

ACKNOWLEDGMENTS

I wish to thank the following people for their comments and criticisms on the first draft of this chapter: Eloise Beil, Roy Dickens, Meta Fayden Janowitz, Olive Jones, George Miller, and Robert Schuyler. I am grateful to Carl Forster for taking all the photographs. I am indebted to Lorna Baugher for illustrating Figures 11.5, 11.10, 11.11, 11.12, and 11.15; and to Brian Dorph for drawing Figures 11.1 and 11.2. Lastly, special thanks go to Eloise Beil for editing, typing, proofreading, and doing a bit of everything.

REFERENCES

Adams, John P.
1971 *Bottle collecting in America*. Somersworth, N.H.: New Hampshire Publishing Company.

Adams, William H.
1976 Trade networks and interaction spheres—A view from Silcott. *Historical Archaeology* **10**:99–112.

Baugher-Perlin, Sherene
1978 *The Prall Site: A case study in historical archaeology*. Ph.D. dissertation, S.U.N.Y. at Stony Brook. University Microfilms, Ann Arbor, Michigan.
1979 The excavation of a twentieth century site. *Proceedings, Staten Island Institute of Arts and Sciences* **29**(3):63–72.

Berkow, Nancy Pratt
1973 *The Award guide to collecting bottles*. New York: Award Books.

Brose, David S.
1967 The Custer Road dump site: An exercise in Victorian archaeology. *The Michigan Archaeologist* **13**(2):37–128.

Caldwell, Jane Keller
1947 Early Kentucky glass. *Antiques* **52**(5):368–369.

Davidson, Marshall
1949 Foreign influences on American glass, II. *Antiques* **55**(5):356–367.
Davis, Pearce
1970 *The development of the American glass industry.* New York: Russell and Russell (originally published in 1949).
Durrenberger, E. Paul
1965 Anderson's Mill (41 TVI 30): A historic site in Travis County, Texas. *Texas Archaeological Society Bulletin* **36**:1–69.
Elville, E. M.
1968 Techniques of the glassmaker. In *English glass,* edited by Sidney Crompton. New York: Hawthorn Books. Pp. 39–58.
Hunter, Frederick William
1950 *Steigel glass.* Introduction and notes by Helen McKearin. New York: Dover Publications.
Innes, Lowell
1948 Pittsburgh glass. *Antiques* **58**(6):417–419.
Jones, Olive
1971 Glass bottle push-ups and pontil marks. *Historical Archaeology* **5**:63–73.
Jones, Olive, Katherine Sullivan *et al.*
n.d. *Parks Canada, glass glossary.* Manuscript in preparation.
Ketchum, William, Jr.
1975 *A treasury of American bottles.* New York: A & W Visual Library.
Kulasiewicz, Frank
1974 *Glassblowing.* New York: Watson-Guptill.
Lorrain, Dessamae
1968 An archaeologist's guide to nineteenth century American glass. *Historical Archaeology* **2**:35–44.
McKearin, George
1926 Wistarberg and South Jersey glass. *Antiques* **10**(4):274–280.
McKearin, George, and Helen McKearin
1941 *American glass.* New York: Crown Publishers.
McKearin, Helen, and Kenneth Wilson
1978 *American bottles and flasks and their ancestry.* New York: Crown Publishers.
McLellan, G. W.
1972 Glass. *Encyclopedia Americana* **12**:784–792.
Meigh, Edward
1960 The development of the automatic glass bottle machine. *Glass Technology* **1**(1):25–50.
Moore, N. Hudson
1945 *Old glass.* New York: Tudor Publishing.
Munsey, Cecil
1970 *The illustrated guide to collecting bottles.* New York: Hawthorn Books.
Noël Hume, Ivor
1964 The search for New Bremen and the glass of John Frederick Amelung. *Antiques* **85**(3):310–313.
Schuyler, Robert L.
1974 Sandy Ground: Archaeological sampling in a black community in metropolitan New York. *Papers of the Conference on Historic Sites Archaeology* 7(2):12–52.
1977 Archaeology of the New York metropolis. *The Bulletin of the New York State Archaeological Association* **69**:1–19.
1980 Sandy Ground: Archaeology of a black urban community. In *Archaeological Perspectives on Ethnicity in America,* edited by Robert L. Schuyler. Farmingdale, New York: Baywood Publishing. Pp. 48–59.

Scoville, Warren C.
1948 *Revolution in glassmaking: Entrepreneurship and technological change in the American industry*. Cambridge, Mass.: Harvard Univ. Press.

Sicard, Hortense Fea
1926 Sidelights on the Wistars and their glass house. *Antiques* **10**(4):110–111.

Spencer-Wood, Suzanne M.
1979 The national American market in historical archaeology: Urban versus rural perspectives. In *Ecological anthropology of the middle Connecticut river valley*, edited by Robert Paynter. *Research Reports, Department of Anthropology* **18**:117–128 Amherst, Massachusetts.

Stewart, Regina, and Geraldine Cosentino
1976 *Bottles*. New York: Golden Press.

Toulouse, Julian Harrison
1969 A primer in mold seams. *Western Collector* 7(11): Part 1:526–535; Part 2:578–587.
1971 *Bottle makers and their marks*. New York: Thomas Nelson.

Watkins, Lura Woodside
1933 Stoddard glass. *Antiques* **24**(2):52–55.
1950 *Glass and glassmaking*. New York: Chanticleer Press.

Watkins, Malcolm
1949 Foreign influences on American glass, I. *Antiques* **55**(5):363–365.

White, Harry Hall
1927 Keene, New Hampshire. *Antiques* **2**(6):459–463.
1930 New York State glass houses—Mount Pleasant. *Antiques* **18**(1):40–43.
1934 The story of the Montana Glass Works. *Antiques* **26**(6):212–216.

White, John R.
1978 Bottle nomenclature: A glossary of landmark terminology for the archaeologist. *Historical Archaeology* **12**:58–67.

12

An Examination of Manufacture-Deposition Lag for Glass Bottles from Late Historic Sites

Sarah H. Hill

This study proposes a method for determining the manufacture-deposition lag of glass bottles from late historic archaeological sites and suggests some approaches for the use of this method in interpreting past human behavior.[1] *Manufacture-deposition lag* is defined as the difference between the time of manufacture and the time of deposition of an artifact or class of artifacts. It is assumed that the calculated difference, measured in years, reflects not only a segment of time but also a set of behavioral processes.

Consideration of the mechanisms responsible for lag can reveal behavioral patterns related both to the maker and to the user of the artifact. For example, manifestations of behavior inherent in manufacturing and filling include technological innovation, regulatory legislation, and trade and transportation networks. Behavioral factors related to the user of the bottled product include buying power, health needs, consumer habits, and demographics (e.g., population density, distribution, and vital statistics). Finally, aspects of behavior intrinsic to secondary use of bottles include such ecological and economic factors as recycling and garbage disposal practices. By recognizing manufacture-deposition lag in bottles from historic sites and by identifying the reasons for the lag, the historical archaeologist can contribute to an understanding of specific cultural systems of the past and general processes of human behavior.

[1]Only one of the four sites used in this study is urban. However, the method developed here grew out of an effort to date and interpret sites in urban settings.

ISBN 0-12-214980-7

DATING

Traditionally, historical archaeologists have used multiple resources for dating sites. These resources include oral and written histories and the interpretation of artifact styles. Although a single source may be sufficient, several related sources of information are usually integrated to refine the dates for a particular site. At the Edgewood site, a neighborhood garbage deposit in Atlanta, for example, a chronological range of 1908–1912 was provided by several sets of data. Dates obtained from glass artifacts suggested the ravine could not have been used as a trash repository earlier than 1908. Informants from the neighborhood believe the ravine was filled with trash around 1910. And finally, municipal documents, such as Sanborn Insurance maps, indicated that by 1912 a house had been constructed over the ravine, thereby sealing the site (Draper and Gandy 1978).

At the 1972 Conference on Historic Site Archeology, Stanley South introduced a formula for dating sites by the use of ceramic assemblages (South 1972). He stated that there will be a high positive correlation between the manufacturing period of a group of ceramics and the occupation period of the site where the ceramics are found. South's Mean Ceramic Date Formula has been tested on several eighteenth-century British-American sites, and these tests indicate that a relationship does exist between the mean ceramic date derived from the formula and the median occupation date derived from historical documentation (South 1977:221–226).

The first step in the use of South's formula is to identify the ceramics by type and to assign a median manufacturing date to each type. The next step is to multiply the frequency of sherds of each ceramic type by its median date. This step gives greater weight to the artifacts occurring in greater numbers, which assumes that those objects most frequently used are those most frequently represented in the archaeological record. The final step is to find the average of the median-frequency products by dividing the sum of the products by the total frequency of artifact types. The resulting number is the mean manufacturing date of the ceramics and theoretically is the median occupation date of the site.

Use of the Mean Ceramic Date Formula has traditionally been restricted to ceramics, primarily those from eighteenth-century and early nineteenth-century sites. However, this technique can be utilized to determine the mean manufacturing date of *any* class of artifacts for which initial manufacturing dates can be established. Furthermore, it may be assumed that any discrepancy between the calculated mean manufacturing date and the historically documented date is the result of manufacture-deposition lag. When such discrepancies exist, the task of the archaeologist is to interpret the behavioral reasons for the lag. By applying the Mean Ceramic Date Formula to other classes of artifacts and to sites of different periods, it is possible to expand the usefulness of the formula from a dating tool to a method for exploring behavioral processes.

Bottles are suitable artifacts to use as chronological markers on historic sites because they have been extensively used, enter the archaeological record quickly, and have datable attributes. The widespread use of bottles extends through time and across space. Bottles contain a variety of products and are used by virtually everyone in an industrialized society. Furthermore, they tend to survive in the archaeological record. Even though glass may be highly susceptible to breakage while in use, bottles are durable artifacts, resisting corrosion and decay. They are likely, therefore, to appear at every site and in almost every area of a site where human activity has occurred, including areas related to food, drink, health, recreation, and a variety of utilitarian tasks. Bottles appear at industrial sites as well as at habitation sites, although usually in different frequencies.

The reason bottles tend to enter the archaeological record quickly is that they are not functional end-products but are containers for products. The purpose of a bottle is to hold one substance. When that substance is depleted, the bottle is usually discarded. If the substance in the bottle is unsatisfactory or no longer needed, the user may throw away the bottle even before the contents are completely used. Occasionally, a bottle is reused or recycled, but if it has a chip or crack, it may be perceived as an unsafe or useless container, and is even more likely to be discarded.

Manufacturing dates for bottles can be determined with some precision, since changes in bottle form have been traced to recorded changes in manufacturing techniques (Kendrick 1971; Lorrain 1968; McKearin and Wilson 1978; Newman 1970). Variations in the methods for making bottles and closures are documented not only in patent records, but also in advertisements and catalogues, as producers competed for business. Hence, technological changes can provide a *terminus post quem* manufacturing date for many bottles.

A further chronological refinement comes from labeling practices. Some bottles have embossed labels identifying the manufacturer or the product name. Because the manufacturing lives of some bottling companies have been short, their initial and terminal production dates can be found in company records. Paper labels, an increasingly popular alternative to embossing, may be sufficiently well preserved on some bottles to provide information from which dates can be derived. For example, a label that specifies the alcohol or narcotic content probably was manufactured subsequent to the Food and Drug Act (passed in June 1906; effective January 1907), whereas a label listing every ingredient in a substance probably postdates the Federal Food, Drug, and Cosmetic Act of 1938.

These glass chronologies can be used in the Mean Ceramic Date Formula to provide a median occupation date for a site. However, in order to explore manufacture-deposition lag and its causal factors, one must modify the formula. When a bottle's manufacturing dates terminate *prior* to the site's documented closing date, the bottle's median manufacturing date should be calculated as described in the formula. However, if the bottle's manufacturing dates extend beyond the time the site was closed, it is necessary to use the site's documented terminal date as the bottle's terminal manufacturing date. This adjustment acknowledges that the artifact could not have been manufactured after its deposition. The modification is appropriate because the purpose of this study is to explore the behavioral processes responsible for the lag observed in a specific class of artifacts, rather than to provide an occupation date for the site. The final step in this method is to calculate the amount of lag by subtracting the bottle's mean manufacturing date from the site's documented terminal date. It is important to rely on documentation for a site date rather than on dates projected from other classes of artifacts, such as ceramics or coins, because manufacture-deposition lag is likely to affect all manufactured artifacts.

MANUFACTURE-DEPOSITION LAG

To understand the processes responsible for manufacture-deposition lag in bottles, one must consider the possible stages in the production and use of a bottle as well as the functional categories of the bottled products. Eight possible stages can be described for the life-span of a bottle as part of a behavioral system. These stages consist of manufacturing, filling, distributing, selling, purchasing, consuming, recycling, and discarding. Each stage involves the interplay of time and behavior.

The manufacturer was originally the glassblower and, as recently as the mid-nineteenth century, was the person whose behavior was most clearly reflected in the artifact. Processes involved in lag at this stage include technology, transportation, and economics. McKearin and Wilson (1978:68) state that at the beginning of the nineteenth century there were only eight glass factories in America. Skilled glassmakers were few, and whereas one of the main sources for glassmakers was Great Britain, it was a crime in England for craftsmen to be recruited to America. Free emigration of skilled glassblowers was not allowed until the end of the Napoleonic Wars. Furthermore, transportation facilities in America were limited. In 1818, the national road reached only as far as Wheeling, West Virginia, and it was not until 1825 that the Erie Canal crossed New York from Lake Erie to the Hudson River. A nationwide railroad system was not begun until the 1830s (McKearin and Wilson 1978). Bottles from sites of the early nineteenth century, therefore, should express long lags in the early stages (manufacturing through distribution).

In the stage following manufacture, the bottle is transformed to a container and is filled and sealed. The amount of time involved in this transformation depends on how long it will take to manufacture and transport the product as well as the bottle. The kind of closure and the requirements for packing the bottled product may affect the lag time, as the needs of the product must be considered. For example, some products, such as wine, are aged in their bottles and stored at this stage. For this reason alone, wine bottles usually express a significantly longer lag than other bottles.

At the third or distribution stage, the product tends to move quickly, for the successful distributor is the one who makes the fastest delivery, whether it is a milk peddler from the turn of the century or a regional food distributor of today. Lag at this stage may be the smallest percentage of the total lag time, but is nonetheless dependent on behavioral variables and product considerations. Paul and Parmalee (1973:66) point out, for example, that in the early days of the soft drink industry, most bottling plants closed from Labor Day until early spring because distributors would not transport beverages susceptible to freezing. By the middle of the twentieth century, however, packaging and transportation facilities were more efficient. Early soda bottles, therefore, should express a longer lag than more recent ones.

The fourth stage is the marketing of the product. This stage may be considered as beginning the use-life of the bottled product and represents one of the potentially greatest amounts of time in the manufacture-deposition interval. Many behavioral factors affect the selling of a bottled product, including the method of selling (e.g., by door, store, or mail), the size of the community, competition from other products and other stores, and even the personality of the seller. An example of variation at this stage can be found at the Silcott site in the state of Washington, where two general stores, owned by brothers, were located a few hundred meters apart.

> One store moved its merchandise quickly. The other store was a shambles, the candy wormy, the food in boxes either long since eaten by mice, or rotten. One passerby stopped for gas and also bought a box of crackers not opened for several miles—one mouse, no crackers [Adams 1976:106].

It could be assumed that there was greater manufacture-deposition lag at the latter store than at its more successful counterpart.

Purchasing and consuming are components of the fifth and sixth stages, and represent the remaining use-life of the bottled product. The purchaser may be spatially or temporally separate from the consumer, extending the lag time at this stage. Other behavioral factors are related to the size and function of the product. The contents of pint bottles, for example, usually are expended faster than those of gallon bottles, and the containers will express differential lag. Contemporary records of the Coca-Cola Bottling Company indicate that the smallest Coca-Cola bottle moves the fastest in the system; it is purchased more frequently and is used and returned more rapidly (Robert Brown, Coca-Cola Bottling Company, personal communication). The availability of the product to the purchaser includes a number of factors. The product must be marketable, attainable, and portable. Seasonality may affect the lag for food and beverage products, in terms of desirability as well as availability. Additional factors at this stage are related to the individual consumer and his perceived health, nutritional, and social needs. These perceptions may be part of larger behavioral processes, such as family traditions, community reinforcement, or national trends. Prohibition laws, for example, affect the amount of lag expressed by alcoholic beverage bottles.

After its contents have been depleted, the bottle enters the seventh stage, recycling, or goes directly to its place of deposition.[2] Conventional recycling is related to

[2]In his 1975 paper on site formation processes, Schiffer describes three kinds of recycling. The first, called "recycling," he describes as the conversion, within a behavioral system, of the form of an artifact in such a way that it loses its original identity. The second, "secondary use," is where an artifact's form is retained but its function is changed. The third kind, called "lateral cycling," is the transferal of the item, in its original form and function, to another user. In this paper I use the word recycle to mean the reuse, within a behavioral system, of an item in its original form and for its original function. A recycled bottle, then, is one that is reused as a container, although possibly for a different substance.

the function of the bottled product. For example, milk bottles always have been recycled by the bottler. In other cases, recycling occurs when glass resources are scarce or when there is some kind of economic reinforcement for the recycling pattern, such as a discount on additional purchases or a direct refund. Informal recycling involves transforming the bottle to another functional role, as when a wine bottle is made into a candleholder, or a food bottle into a terrarium.

The eighth and final stage in the use-life of a bottle is the stage of deposition, when the artifact enters the archaeological record. Even this stage may involve some amount of lag time because bottles can occur as primary or secondary refuse (Schiffer 1977:19), or as displaced refuse (South 1977:298). The nature, condition, and location of the site, consumer habits, size of the bottle, and garbage disposal patterns can affect this stage.

In addition to obtaining an understanding of the processes responsible for manufacture-deposition lag, the acquisition of behavioral information from glass bottles requires the integration of formal, quantitative, and functional analyses. Initially, bottles from a site should be identified by specific content, such as beer, patent medicine, or ink. Then, the bottles can be counted and grouped in broad functional categories, such as nonalcoholic beverage, alcoholic beverage, food, medicine, and personal-utilitarian. Some demographic and behavioral information may be inferred from this categorization, such as the nature of the site, the buying power of the consumer, and the popularity of a product.

However, in order to explore the behavioral processes producing lag, we should place bottles into functional categories that reflect *probable frequency and immediacy of use*. Frequency refers to how often a product is likely to be used. Those products used most frequently should have a rapid rate of depletion, and their bottles should express a relatively short manufacture-deposition lag. Furthermore, bottles for products that are used frequently should occur in relatively large numbers on the site unless substantial recycling has taken place.

Immediacy of use refers to actions based on a perception by the consumer of the importance of freshness in a product. Those products for which freshness is important should be manufactured, bottled, distributed, bought, and used quickly before they become stale, flat, or spoiled. Therefore, their bottles should express a relatively short manufacture-deposition lag.

In the beverage category, frequency of use is variable and product freshness is important for several types. Milk is used quickly to avoid contamination, and even though milk bottles are now recycled and reused an average of 20 times (R. L. Mathis Dairy, personal communication), they usually are discarded less than 1 year after manufacture. Although frequency of use may vary, milk consumers are likely to use milk regularly. Milk bottles, then, should express a relatively short manufacture-deposition lag.

Juice bottles also would be expected to have short lag. Once a juice bottle is opened, the product is consumed relatively soon, before it spoils. Both juice and milk require refrigeration and, in its absence, are even more likely to be consumed rapidly.

Carbonated beverages, including soda pop, beer, and mineral water, require relatively fast consumption, or they lose their carbonation. Soda and beer are used for recreation and relaxation, and if they are used frequently, their bottles will occur in large numbers on a site and will express relatively short lag. Mineral water, on the other hand, was sometimes considered a medicine. Thus, the amount of lag expressed by mineral water bottles at a site may reveal particular health needs as well as general consumer habits.

For the purpose of this study, the beverages milk, juice, soda, and mineral water are subsumed under one category—fresh beverages. Although beer is also a fresh beverage, because of its alcohol content and behavioral implications, beer bottles should be considered as a separate category. Because of the requirements of freshness for these beverages, it is assumed that they are opened soon after being purchased and depleted soon after being opened. For this reason, bottles for these products should have the shortest lag at a site. An additional factor contributing to the short lag for fresh beverage bottles is that new production techniques have been adopted faster in this category than in others. When manufacturing dates are determined on the basis of form, therefore, it is important to recognize that soda bottles, for example, may reflect new manufacturing techniques sooner than whiskey bottles.

Whiskey and wine bottles are types often found on archaeological sites. There is nothing in the production of whiskey that mandates rapid or frequent consumption, and, therefore, whiskey bottles could be expected to have longer lags than fresh beverage bottles. If whiskey bottles occur in high numbers on a site and express a short lag, special behavioral patterns, such as intensified social activity (e.g., a holiday) or alcoholism may be suggested. On the other hand, wine has been aged in bottles since the rediscovery of the cork in the eighteenth century (Mitchell 1977:344) and, for this reason, wine bottles should express the longest lag at a site. If they express a short lag, economic factors may be implied (e.g., inexpensive wine is not aged). Thus, whiskey bottles should comprise a third category, and wine bottles a fourth.

Bottled foods include spices, oils, condiments, and sauces, products for which freshness is not usually essential. Frequency of use in this category depends on the nature of the site. A domestic site, for example, should reflect regular and moderate use of bottled foods, and the lag should be longer than for fresh beverages, but shorter than for wine. A long lag for food bottles may indicate that the consumers used alternative packaging, such as cans, or alternative food sources, such as homemade products. On the other hand, a short lag for food bottles could suggest a site's having new access to or dependence on bottled foods, or a commercial site. Because of the similar requirements for freshness and frequency of use, all food bottles can be considered a single category.

Until the advent of antibiotics in the mid-twentieth century, medicine had no requirement for freshness or frequency of use. Lag in this category, therefore, should be longer than for food bottles, but shorter than for wine bottles. A short lag in this category may suggest mitigating circumstances, such as communal illness or addiction, whereas a long lag may indicate stable health or reliance on home remedies.

Personal products, those items used for adornment and hygiene, such as powders, lotions, cleansers, and scents, are probably in more frequent use today than at any time in recorded history, and they provide archaeological evidence for the effectiveness of advertising and increasing affluence in America. Freshness, however, is not important in this category. At early sites, then, containers for personal products should have longer lags than at more recent sites. Utilitarian and personal products have comparable requirements for use. Containers for inks, polishes, chemicals, and home cleansers, therefore, should have low to moderate frequency of use, and corresponding lag. For the purpose of this study, these types are combined into a personal-utilitarian category.

Manufacture-deposition lag should vary among sites because it reflects differential behavior patterns. Nevertheless, based on the examination of the factors contributing to lag, three general hypotheses can be proposed. These represent ideal patterns that can be tested with the archaeological evidence. Discrepancies between the patterns and the evidence may indicate behavioral processes.

Hypothesis 1: The length of time between manufacture and deposition of a bottle increases in inverse proportion to the importance of freshness and the immediacy of the product's use.

Hypothesis 2: The length of time between the manufacture and deposition of a

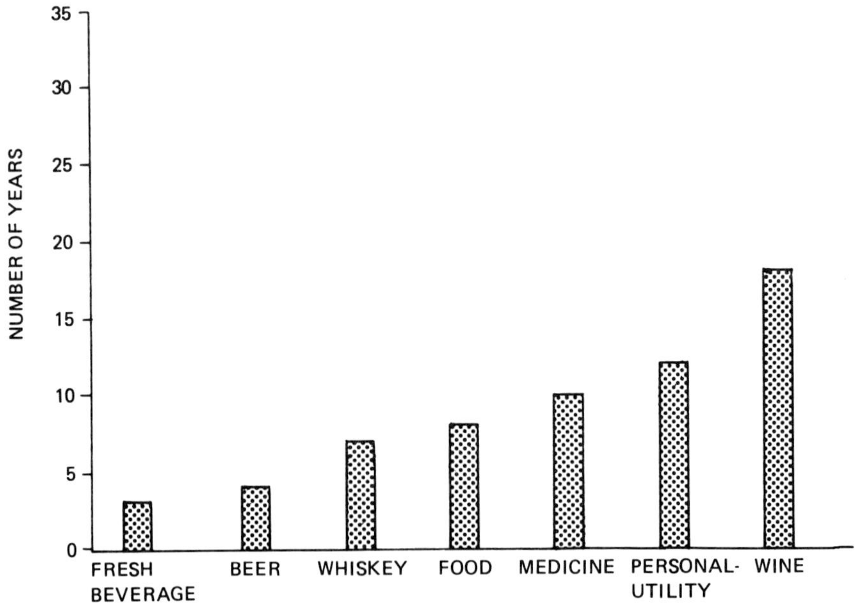

FIGURE 12.1. Idealized lag rates of bottles by category.

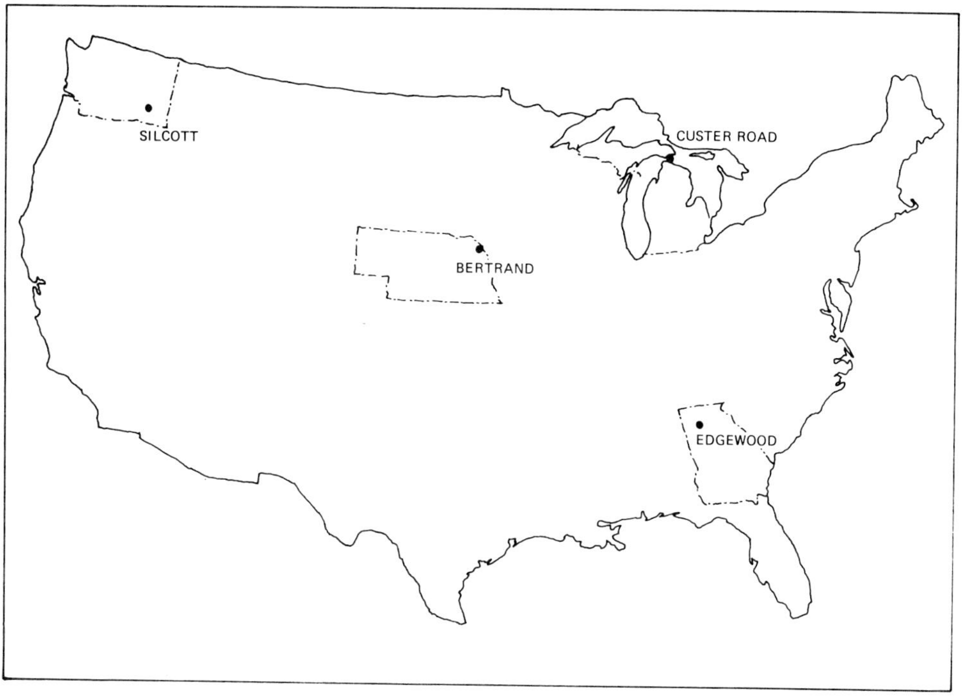

FIGURE 12.2. Locations of sites.

bottle increases in inverse proportion to the frequency of the product's use.

Hypothesis 3: Those bottles expressing the shortest manufacture-deposition lag will be containers for fresh beverages, followed in order by whiskey, food, medicine, personal-utilitarian products, and wine.

The third hypothesis is a corollary of the first two, and is predicated on the expected recurrence and rates of product use, ranging from daily to perhaps yearly use. Figure 12.1 illustrates a model of expected (ideal) lag rates.

To test the above hypotheses, researchers examined the lags of bottles from four historic sites. These sites, the *Bertrand* wreck site, the Custer Road Dump site, the Edgewood site, and the Silcott site, represent considerably different temporal, geographical, and behavioral contexts (Figure 12.2).

SITES

Bertrand Wreck Site

The steamboat *Bertrand* sank in the Missouri River on April 1, 1865, while transporting commercial cargo from St. Louis, Missouri, to Fort Benton, Montana.

Table 12.1 The *Bertrand* Bottles, Whiskey and Ale

Specimen	Median date	Datable attribute	Frequency	Product
III4c	1853	mark	12	22,236
III4b	1850.5	mark	12	22,206
III4a	1838.5	mark	12	22,062
III5	1863	consignee	18	33,534
I3	1837.5	form	19	34,912.5
Total			73	134,950.5

Deposition date	1865.4
Mean manufacture date	1848.6
Lag	16.8 years

In the preceding fall, the discovery of gold in Montana had produced a sudden increase in population and an attendant market for supplies. Steamboats landed at Fort Benton almost daily during navigable months, bringing to the mining towns food, beverages, medicines, and utilitarian products. After the *Bertrand* struck a snag and sank, two unsuccessful attempts were made to recover the cargo. The wreck lay submerged for over 100 years, to be rediscovered and excavated by the National Park Service in 1968 (Switzer 1974). In addition to other cargo, over 6000 bottles were recovered from the wreck.

Mean manufacturing dates could be obtained from 3800 of the *Bertrand* bottles by utilizing published descriptions of the manufacturers' marks, address labels on packing cases, bottle labels and seals, and details of production. Tables 12.1–12.5 show these calculations, and Figure 12.3 illustrates the relationships between the expressed lags.[3]

Based on these calculations, Hypothesis 1 is confirmed for all categories. Although the bottled products were never used, the lags indicate the relative unimportance of freshness in the categories represented. There were no bottles identified in the fresh beverage category on the *Bertrand*, which may mean those products were not usually shipped across the continent but were, instead, manufactured locally, or otherwise were unavailable to inland inhabitants.

[3]In this study I have assumed that datable bottles represent the entire bottle assemblage from a site. Obviously, improved analytical techniques may produce more (and perhaps different) dates for the bottles described here and, therefore, affect my behavioral interpretations. However, this possibility should not detract from the effectiveness of the methods developed in this chapter.

Table 12.2 The Bertrand Bottles, Food

Specimen	Median date	Datable attribute	Frequency	Product
V9f	1857.5	seal	9	16,717.5
V	1857.5	seal	12	22,290
V9g	1857.5	seal	12	22,290
V3	1865	consignee	14	26,110
V4	1850	consignee	22	40,700
V2	1837.5	form	12	22,050
V5	1850	consignee	20	37,000
V6	1852.5	form	22	40,755
V7	1863.5	consignee	45	83,857.5
V9	1843.5	form	24	44,244
V18	1852.5	form	131	242,677.5
V17	1862.5	consignee	38	70,775
V15	1852.5	form	26	48,165
V13	1852.5	form	96	177,840
V16	1852.5	form	65	120,412.5
V14	1837.5	form	24	44,100
V12	1852.5	form	33	61,132.5
V11	1863.5	consignee	95	177,032.5
V9a	1843.5	consignee	4	7,374
Total			704	1,305,523

Deposition date	1865.4
Mean manufacture date	1854.4
Lag	11 years

Table 12.3 The *Bertrand* Bottles, Medicine

Specimen	Median date	Datable attribute	Frequency	Product
III8	1863	label	12	22,356
III6	1855.5	mark	2292	4,252,806
III7	1862.5	label	109	203,012.5
III6c	1863	form	8	14,904
III9	1861	label	69	128,409
III6f	1863	form	48	89,424
III6d	1863.5	consignee	12	22,362
VII2	1852.5	form	133	246,382.5
VII3	1852.5	label	20	37,050
Total			2703	5,016,706

Deposition date 1865.4

Mean manufacture date 1856

Lag 9.4 years

Table 12.4 The *Bertrand* Bottles, Personal-Utilitarian

Specimen	Median date	Datable attribute	Frequency	Product
IV[1,1a,1b]	1852.5	form	22	40,755
VI[1]	1864	case	92	171,488
VII[1]	1852.5	form	4	7,410
Total			118	219,653

Deposition date 1865.4

Mean manufacture date 1861.5

Lag 3.9 years

Table 12.5 The *Bertrand* Bottles, Wine

Specimen	Median date	Datable attribute	Frequency	Product
III[2]	1852.5	form	202	374,205
		Deposition date	1865.4	
		Mean manufacture date	1852.5	
		Lag	12.9 years	

Lags for whiskey (16.8 years) and wine bottles (12.9 years) are the longest, which is appropriate because those products are enhanced by aging. Most of the whiskey bottles were manufactured in glass factories in Connecticut and Pennsylvania, and some of the wine bottles were imported from France (Switzer 1974:25). The process of shipping such distances undoubtedly contributed to the amounts of lag in these categories.

The lag for the food bottles is 11 years, intermediate between the medicine and whiskey categories. Approximately half the identified bottles in this category contained pickled products, which probably could tolerate the lag expressed in Table

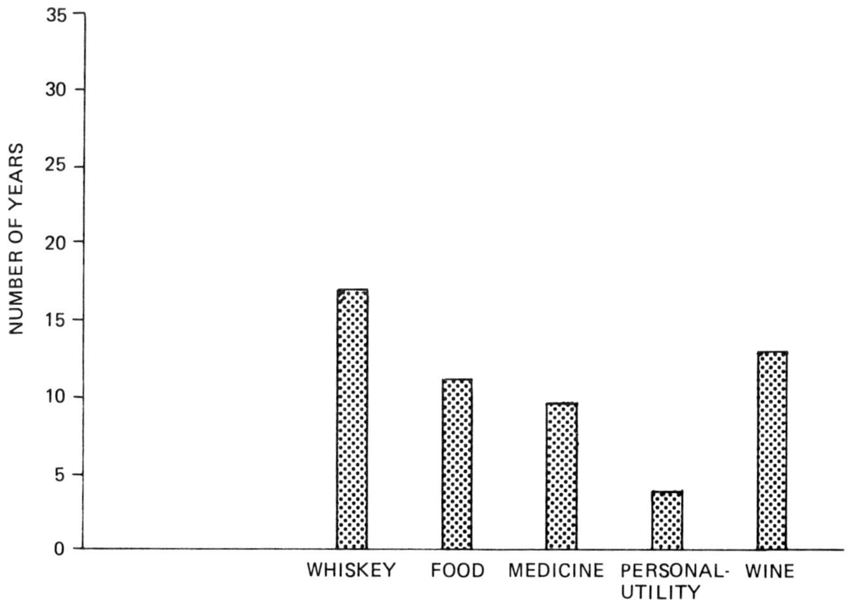

FIGURE 12.3. Differential lag of *Bertrand* bottles.

12.2. The food products and bottles were shipped from places such as Maryland, Ohio, New York, and France. Again, the time involved in shipping the products to the loading dock in St. Louis may account for a significant portion of the total lag.

The lag for medicine bottles, 9.4 years, is appropriate for products that do not require freshness or refrigeration. It should be noted that 94% of the medicine bottles contained bitters. Most of these were one brand, "Dr. Hostetter's Stomach Bitters," a patent medicine known for its high alcoholic content (27%). The alcohol in these medicines not only acted as a preservative but as an intoxicant, making them comparable to whiskey. They are, however, classified as medicine because that is the way they were classified by the manufacturer and consumer.

The relatively short lag in the personal-utilitarian category, 3.9 years, is probably the result of the specialized nature of the sample. Seventy-eight percent of the bottles identified in this category were ink bottles, packed in two cases for shipment to a druggist in Virginia City, Montana. They may represent his inventory of ink for a decade. The remaining bottles in this category contained perfume and chemicals, products that have long shelf lives.

Hypotheses 2 and 3 are not applicable to the *Bertrand* site because the substances were never used. Thus, the information that can be derived from the analysis of manufacture-deposition lag for the *Bertrand* bottles is related to the manufacturing, bottling, and distributing stages of the behavioral process. In 1865, according to the present calculations, a minimum of 1.5 years may have passed between the manufacture and the distribution of certain bottled products. Bottles in the categories of whiskey, wine, food, medicine, and personal-utilitarian products were being manufactured, filled, and shipped long distances. The bottles on the *Bertrand* were manufactured in Europe, Pennsylvania, Kentucky, Connecticut, and New York. After bottling, the products were shipped from Boston, Louisville, Baltimore, Cincinnati, and St. Louis. The amount of lag between the manufacture and deposition of these bottles was the result of geographical distance, transportation networks, economics, and the products' requirements for packing.

Comparisons of the *Bertrand* bottle lags to other sites may indicate the extent to which shipping and manufacturing technology affected lag. The average lag for all of the *Bertrand* bottles is 10.8 years.

Custer Road Dump Site

The Custer Road site, a large refuse mound, is located adjacent to Fort Mackinac on Mackinac Island in Lake Huron, Michigan. The site was used as a dump by civilian and military inhabitants of the post from 1876 to 1896. In 1894, Mackinac Island was declared a National Park, and the following year the fort was abandoned as a military post and turned over to the state. In 1965, the University of Michigan Museum of Anthropology excavated the site under the direction of David S. Brose and recovered 2170 identifiable bottles. Mean manufacturing dates were obtained for 239 bottles by examining the described manufacturers' marks, production techniques, and product names (Brose 1967). The calculations include all functional

Table 12.6 The Custer Road Bottles, Fresh Beverages

Specimen	Median date	Datable attribute	Frequency	Product
12Ap	1868	patent	1	1,868
12Ak	1863.5	mark	1	1,863.5
12An	1886	mark	1	1,886
6R	1873	mark	1	1,873
12Ca	1859	mark	1	1,859
12Cd	1845.5	mark	2	3,691
Total			7	13,040.5

Deposition date	1896
Mean manufacture date	1862.9
Lag	33.1 years

categories. Tables 12.6–12.12 show the calculations of the dates and the manufacture-deposition lag for each category, and Figure 12.4 illustrates the relationships of the lags.

In the fresh beverage category, Hypotheses 1, 2, and 3 are not confirmed. The manufacture-deposition lag for the fresh beverage bottles (33.1 years) at Custer Road is longer than the lags in all other categories. Several behavioral factors may have contributed to this anomaly. A long lag for a relatively low number of fresh beverage containers suggests that the original contents were not popular or readily available, or that the original bottles were returned to the bottler. The identified bottles in this category are soda pop and mineral water. In the early days of the soda industry, bottlers recognized that their products were being recycled by their competitors, and they often embossed warnings on their bottles against such practices (Paul and Parmalee 1973). At least two of the Custer Road bottles have such warnings. Thus, recycling may account for the long lag. However, the low number of fresh beverage bottles (seven) suggests that these beverages were not often used. Since the chronological interval of the dump coincides with a significant growth rate in the soft drink industry (Paul and Parmalee 1973), the low number of soda bottles and their long lag may reflect that the growing popularity of the industry did not impact this military post. If the residents liked soda drinks, perhaps they made their own with powdered extract flavors, or confined their consumption of soda beverages to a local soda fountain.

Alternatively, a long lag for a relatively low number of fresh beverage containers may suggest transformational recycling patterns. Most of the bottles in this category are large, with six of the seven being quart size (19–29 cm or 7.5–11.4 in. tall). It is reasonable to propose that, given a need for or an inclination to reuse glass bottles, those most likely to be recycled for the longest time will be the large ones.

The lag for the beer category (8.6 years) is short relative to the other categories at Custer Road, and confirms Hypotheses 1 and 2. Hypothesis 3 is not confirmed, because the lag for beer bottles is slightly longer than for whiskey bottles. A short lag

Table 12.7 The Custer Road Bottles, Beer

Specimen	Median date	Datable attribute	Frequency	Product
5Aa	1889	mark	7	13,223
5Ab	1888	mark	3	5,664
5Ac	1888.5	mark	1	1,888.5
5Ad	1884	mark	1	1,884
5Ae	1890.5	patent	1	1,890.5
5Af	1878	mark	1	1,878
5Ag	1887.5	mark	1	1,887.5
5Ah	1891	mark	1	1,891
5Ai	1887.5	mark	1	1,887.5
5Aj	1863.5	mark	1	1,863.5
5Ak	1894.5	mark	1	1,894.5
5Aba	1888.5	mark	1	1,888.5
5Acl	1880.5	mark	1	1,880.5
5Da	1891	mark	3	5,673
5Db	1888	mark	5	9,440
5F	1888	mark	1	1,888
Total			30	56,622

Deposition date 1896

Mean manufacture date 1887.4

Lag 8.6 years

Table 12.8 The Custer Road Bottles, Whiskey

Specimen	Median date	Datable attribute	Frequency	Product
3	1887	mark	34	64,158
4A	1891	patent	18	34,038
4B	1891	patent	4	7,564
Total			56	105,760

Deposition date 1896

Mean manufacture date 1888.6

Lag 7.4 years

for a high number of beer containers suggests frequent or recent product use and little or no container recycling. Because of the relatively high number (30) and random distribution of beer bottles identified for the site, it can be assumed that beer was a popular beverage throughout the occupation of the post. However, 25 of the 30 beer bottles have median manufacturing dates after 1888, and, in fact, 18 of the 30 have median manufacturing dates between 1888 and 1889. This suggests that there may have been a change in consumption patterns at that time. Such a change could be related to economic pressures. This interpretation is corroborated by the faunal remains, which show an increase in poor meat cuts in the late 1880s, and by the ceramics, which indicate an increase in soup containers at the same time.

Table 12.9 The Custer Road Bottles, Food

Specimen	Median date	Datable attribute	Frequency	Product
12Cb	1885.5	mark	1	1,885.5
12Cc	1864	mark	1	1,864
16	1886.5	mark	9	16,978.5
12De	1886.5	mark	1	1,886.5
Total			12	22,614.5

Deposition date 1896

Mean manufacture date 1884.5

Lag 11.5 years

Table 12.10 The Custer Road Bottles, Medicine

Specimen	Median date	Datable attribute	Frequency	Product
6T	1888	label	2	3,776
8Ce	1866	label	4	7,464
8Be	1868	label	6	11,208
8Cd,f	1868	label	4	7,472
9d	1876.5	mark	9	16,888.5
10a	1876.5	mark	8	15,012
8Ad	1888	label	2	3,776
Total			35	65,596.5

Deposition date 1896

Mean manufacture date 1874.2

Lag 21.8 years

Table 12.11 The Custer Road Bottles, Personal-Utilitarian

Specimen	Median date	Datable attribute	Frequency	Product
1A	1877	label	3	5,661
1B	1877	label	1	1,877
1F	1877	label	15	28,155
13	1885.5	mark	1	1,885.5
18A	1882	patent	3	5,646
17Da	1871	label	1	1,871
Total			24	45,095.5

Deposition date 1896

Mean manufacture date 1879

Lag 17 years

Table 12.12 The Custer Road Bottles, Wine

Specimen	Median date	Datable attribute	Frequency	Product
6A	1858.5	form	8	14,868
6B,C,D,E, F,G,H,I, K,L,M,N	1870.5	form	64	119,712
6J	1868	form	2	3,736
Total			74	138,316

Deposition date 1896

Mean manufacture date 1869.1

Lag 26.9 years

The amount of lag for whiskey bottles (7.4 years) is the shortest of all categories at Custer Road, which does not confirm Hypotheses 1, 2, or 3. More whiskey bottles were identified at Custer Road than the fresh beverage, beer, and food categories combined. Because of the high number and short lag in this category, it can be assumed that the residents liked whiskey and drank it frequently. The homogeneity of brand and form of the whiskey bottles and their mean manufacturing date of 1888.6 may support an interpretation of changing consumption patterns around 1888.

Furthermore, the unexpected lags in these first three categories suggest a pattern produced by the special behavior one might expect at a military garrison. This behavior includes frequent and rapid use of beer and whiskey and infrequent use of soft drinks and other fresh beverages.

The amount of lag for the food bottles substantiates Hypotheses 1, 2, and 3. The lag of 11.5 years suggests that for these bottled products, freshness was not important and recurrence of use was moderate. The number of food bottles identified is relatively small, which may indicate that the residents prepared many of their food items on the post, or used canned foods. A description of an 1874 menu for the enlisted personnel reveals that the variety of foods was limited:

> A typical bill of fare of the Company Mess in the fall of 1874 featured fresh or salt pork, bread and coffee for breakfast, roast beef, boiled potatoes, a soup, coffee and bread for the main meal at mid-day, and coffee and bread in the evening [Brose 1967:80].

In the medicine category, the lag of 21.6 years supports Hypotheses 1, 2, and 3 and confirms the relative unimportance of freshness and frequency in this category.

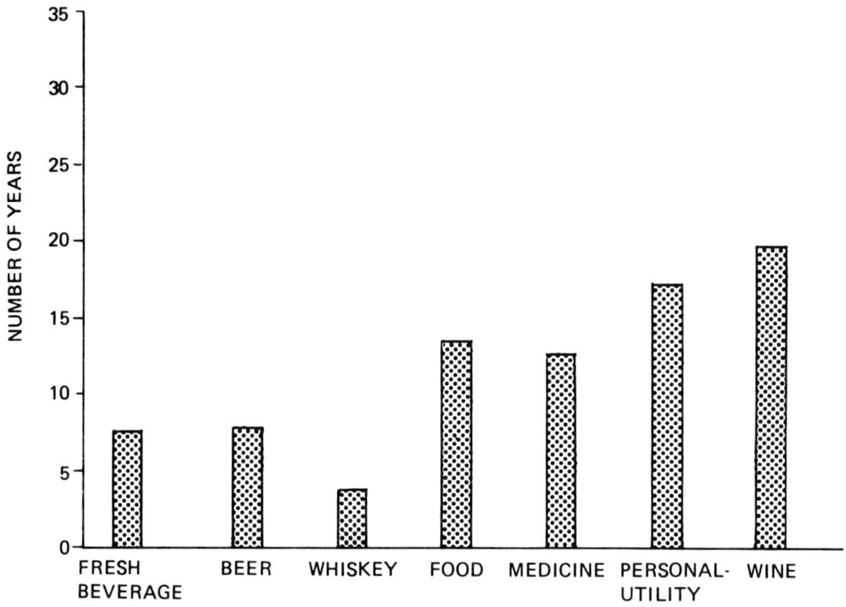

FIGURE 12.4. Differential lag of Custer Road bottles.

However, because the number of identified bottles is high (35) in relation to other categories, this lag should be examined. A long lag for a high number of medicine bottles could mean an early period of communal illness, when the residents purchased, used, and discarded medicine containers. This, however, does not seem likely because of the reported random bottle distribution (Brose 1967). Recycling of containers is another possibility, although medicine bottles are not typically reused. The lag may mean, then, that the Custer Road residents relied on medicinal products that had long manufacturing histories. In fact, 17 of the 35 containers are pharmaceutical bottles with median manufacturing dates of 1876.5. All of these bottles were recovered from the upper excavation level, representing temporally the final change of command and occupation of the post. The distribution, homogeneity, and lag of these bottles suggest either a recent period of illness, or, more likely, a clearing out of old supplies in anticipation of a move. The interpretation of preference for traditional remedies is also supported by the fact that more than half of the medicine bottles with the longest lags are identical to those found in the *Bertrand* inventory 31 years earlier. "Burnett's of Boston" and Dr. Hostetter's were still popular products, which probably means that in the late nineteenth century there was an inclination to rely on traditional medicines (and those with high alcohol content).

Lag for the bottles in the personal-utilitarian category (17 years) confirms Hypotheses 1 and 2, but not 3. Perhaps on a military post in the late nineteenth century, household cleansers were homemade and military hardware cleaners were canned. Examination of the types in this category reveals that the majority are ink bottles. Here, as in the *Bertrand* inventory, the presence of ink bottles has influenced lag.

Wine bottles represent the largest category at the Custer Road site. Their long lag (26.9 years) confirms Hypothesis 1, but not 2 or 3. (Although wine has no product requirement for freshness, it does for frequency, because it sours soon after the bottle has been opened.) Two behavioral explanations can be suggested for this high number of wine bottles expressing long lag. Wine bottlers and bottle manufacturers of the nineteenth century apparently were slow to adopt new production techniques. Accordingly, the manufacturing dates derived from the forms of wine bottles of this period are long and contribute to long lag figures. Furthermore, recycling of the bottles seems likely. Obviously, the Custer Road residents liked wine and drank a lot of it. The bottles are generally quarts and fifths (22–30 cm or 8.6–11.8 in. tall), appropriate sizes for recycling activities. In addition, the random distribution of the bottles and the heterogeneity of types suggest that wine consumption was not limited to a particular time or to a few individuals.

The information that can be derived from the analysis of manufacture-deposition lag for the Custer Road bottles is related to all stages of the behavioral process. According to present calculations, the shortest lag for a bottle from this site was 3 years. Geography was undoubtedly a factor. The Custer Road bottles came from places as distant as Ireland and as near as Detroit, and included New York, Boston, Baltimore, Chicago, Iowa, Pennsylvania, and Ohio.

Brose (1967:81) suggests that the sequence of artifacts recovered from the Custer Road dump demonstrates the impact of improved communications on the Upper Great Lakes area in the late nineteenth century. The bottles support the interpretation that the Custer Road residents had access to products drawn from great distances and diverse areas. The amount of lag expressed by the bottles was, in part, determined by geographic and transportation factors, but was also affected by the personal inclinations of the consumers. Even though the variety of glass bottles increases through time (Brose 1967:119), their random vertical distribution indicates that the consumers did not abandon their traditional preferences. Thus, the recurrence of familiar brands with long manufacturing histories reveals behavioral patterns at Custer Road that were not suggested by the analysis of other artifacts. Furthermore, a military behavior pattern may be indicated by the high number and short lags of whiskey and beer bottles, and the high number and long lags of wine and medicine bottles.

Comparison of the average lag for the *Bertrand* bottles of 10.8 years and the Custer Road bottles of 18 years indicates that the length of time involved in the purchase, consumption, recycling, and deposition stages can extend lag time considerably.[4]

[4]Because of the possibility that the absence of two categories from the *Bertrand* bottle assemblage reduced its comparative value, calculations of lag were also made using only the categories common to both the *Bertrand* and the Custer Road inventories. The relationships between the two assemblages remained the same in the adjusted calculation.

Edgewood Site

The Edgewood site is a small trash deposit that was used by the inhabitants of the Edgewood community on the outskirts of Atlanta in 1910–1911. The deposit, a filled-in ravine, was sealed before the construction of a house early in 1912. A portion of the site was excavated in 1976 by a team from Georgia State University under the direction of Roy S. Dickens, Jr., and 522 whole bottles were recovered (Square 1). Mean manufacturing dates were calculated for 103 bottles in all functional categories. Tables 12.13–12.19 show the calculations for the mean manufacturing dates and the manufacture-deposition lags. The relationships of the lags are illustrated in Figure 12.5.

In the fresh beverage category, the three hypotheses are not confirmed. The lag of 7.5 years is long for these 21 soda and juice bottles, for which freshness and frequency are important. There are several potential behavioral explanations. Recycling, as already suggested for the Custer Road beverage bottles, is a possibility. However, the sizes of the Edgewood soda bottles are relatively small for reuse or transformational recycling, the majority having a capacity of about 7 ounces (.2 liter, between 19 and 21 cm or between 7.5 and 8.2 in. tall). Another possibility is

Table 12.13 The Edgewood Bottles, Fresh Beverages

Specimen	Median date	Datable attribute	Frequency	Product
81	1906	mark	1	1,906
147	1893	mark	1	1,893
203	1907.5	label	1	1,907.5
90, 205	1905	label	2	3,810
197, 206, 62, 136, 137, 138	1907	label	6	11,442
40, 68, 93, 196, 198, 199, 200, 201, 202, 204	1901.5	form	10	19,015
Total			21	39,973.5

Deposition date	1911
Mean manufacture date	1903.5
Lag	7.5 years

Table 12.14 The Edgewood Bottles, Beer

Specimen	Median date	Datable attribute	Frequency	Product
91, 53	1908	mark	2	3,816
96, 58	1905.5	mark	2	3,811
86	1898	mark	1	1,898
60, 80, 124, 135	1901.5	form	4	7,606
Total			9	17,131

Deposition date 1911

Mean manufacture date 1903.4

Lag 7.6 years

that the Edgewood inhabitants did not often purchase bottled soft drinks. Economic factors may have restricted the purchase of products perceived as nonessential or luxury items. This possibility is supported by other research that has placed the Edgewood inhabitants in the lower middle economic class (Dickens and Bowen 1980). Furthermore, the residents of Edgewood may have consumed their soft drinks at a neighborhood drugstore instead of purchasing bottled drinks which were difficult to carry home and which required refrigeration. Paul and Parmalee (1973)

Table 12.15 The Edgewood Bottles, Whiskey

Specimen	Median date	Datable attribute	Frequency	Product
146	1908.5	label	1	1,908.5
83, 67 111, 115, 121, 139	1907	form	6	11,442
Total			7	13,350.5

Deposition date 1911

Mean manufacture date 1907.2

Lag 3.8 years

Table 12.16 The Edgewood Bottles, Food

Specimen	Median date	Datable attribute	Frequency	Product
133	1893	mark	1	1,893
47	1908	patent	1	1,908
57	1909.5	mark	1	1,909.5
153, 154	1890	mark	2	3,780
104, 105, 156, 157, 158, 159, 160	1888.5	mark	7	13,219.5
25, 29, 167, 212, 214, 228	1899.5	mark	6	11,397
208	1907.5	mark	1	1,907.5
51, 112, 155, 161, 162	1907	form	5	9,535
Total			24	45,549.5

Deposition date 1911

Mean manufacture date 1897.9

Lag 13.1 years

point out that the production of liquid carbon dioxide (CO_2) was well established by 1906, making sales of carbonated drinks at soda fountains economically feasible. The existence of neighborhood soda fountains in the Edgewood community has been determined by documentary research (Draper and Gandy 1978).

The 7.6-year lag of beer bottles does not support Hypotheses 1, 2, or 3. Freshness and immediacy of consumption are important for beer. A long lag and low number of beer bottles indicate little product use and little or no recycling of the containers. At least half of the dated beer bottles were manufactured in the same year (1905), which may indicate that the beer was purchased for a single occasion. The relatively small number of bottles and long lag in this category support the interpretation that the Edgewood residents did not drink beer regularly.

The lag in the whiskey category of 3.8 years is the shortest lag at Edgewood and does not confirm Hypotheses 1, 2, or 3. Several behavioral factors may have contributed to this anomaly. A short lag and relatively low number of bottles whose

Table 12.17 The Edgewood Bottles, Medicine

Specimen	Median date	Datable attribute	Frequency	Product
99	1897.5	label	1	1,897.5
28, 66, 85, 132, 172, 177	1898	label	6	11,388
114	1907	form	1	1,907
34, 229	1903.5	label	2	3,807
237, 238	1909	label	2	3,818
39	1905	label	1	1,905
37, 38, 192	1905.5	mark	3	5,716.5
171	1893	mark	1	1,893
69	1908.5	label	1	1,908.5
183	1899.5	mark	1	1,899.5
184, 186	1884	mark	2	3,768
54	1,869	mark	1	1,869
113, 173	1895	mark	2	3,790
Total			24	45,567

Deposition date 1911

Mean manufacture date 1898.6

Lag 12.4 years

contents have no freshness or immediacy requirements suggest the products were not used often but were used recently, and that the containers were probably not recycled. Historical records show that the town of Edgewood had taken the local option to remain dry (Draper and Gandy 1978) and, therefore, consumption of alcoholic beverages would have occurred only in the homes. It also has been suggested that the middle layers at this site represent winter holiday deposition (Dickens and Bowen 1980), a suggestion which is supported by the short lag of whiskey bottles. It can be proposed that the Edgewood residents ordered and used whiskey for a celebration or special occasion, such as Christmas. This interpretation

Table 12.18 The Edgewood Bottles, Personal-Utilitarian

Specimen	Median date	Datable attribute	Frequency	Product
79	1880	label	1	1,880
75, 232	1909.5	label	2	3,819
185	1904.5	label	1	1,904.5
235	1884	mark	1	1,884
77	1910.5	label	1	1910.5
45, 46, 44	1907	form	3	5,721
33, 95, 194, 225	1875.5	form	4	7,502
Total			13	24,621

Deposition date 1911

Mean manufacture date 1894

Lag 17 years

Table 12.19 The Edgewood Bottles, Wine

Specimen	Median date	Datable attribute	Frequency	Product
42, 89, 118, 134	1895.5	form	4	7,582
144	1875.5	form	1	1,875.5
Total			5	9,457.5

Deposition date 1911

Mean manufacture date 1891.5

Lag 19.5 years

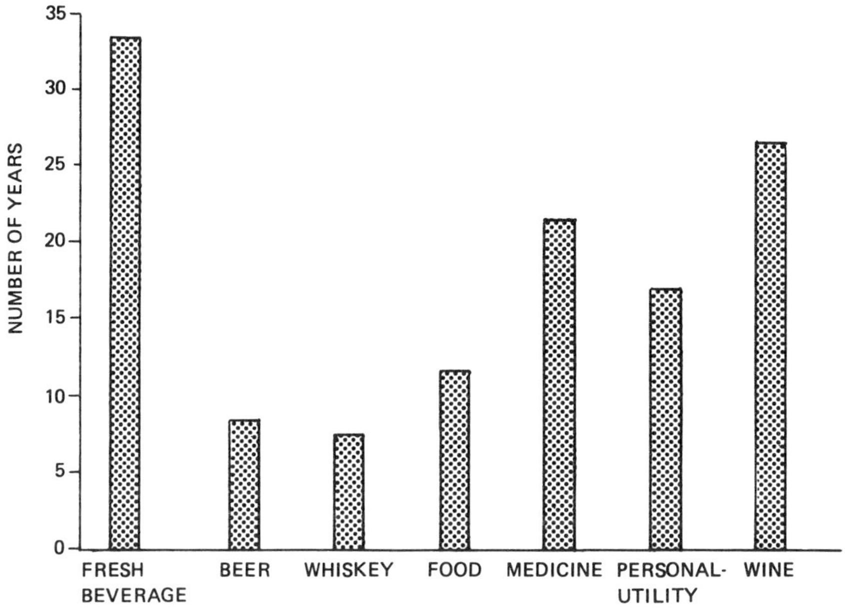

FIGURE 12.5. Differential lag of Edgewood bottles.

is substantiated by the faunal remains, which contain a high frequency of turkey bones, and the ceramics, which contain a high percentage of serving vessels (see Edmiston Davidson, Chapter 15).

The food (13.1 years) and medicine (12.4 years) bottles from Edgewood express similar lag intervals and are represented by the same number of bottles. These lags confirm Hypotheses 1, 2, and 3. Identifiable brands in the food category are well known and long established, extending the lag intervals and suggesting that the Edgewood residents were traditional and conservative in their food buying patterns.

It should be noted that one-third of the 24 identified medicine bottles contained patent medicine, which was subject to scrutiny and harsh criticism in 1904 and 1905, as magazines ran exposés revealing the contents of these preparations (Furnas 1969:907). It is possible that the Edgewood consumers began disposing of their old medicine bottles as they became aware of their high alcoholic content. The remaining medicine bottles are highly variable and include four prescription bottles and three pharmaceutical bottles produced after 1906. These specific lags are relatively short and represent a high percentage of the identified bottles, which provides additional support for the interpretation of a seasonal deposition. (Medicine bottles may be used faster and more frequently in the fall and winter months when people are often in crowds or are confined indoors where infections are spread more quickly.)

A lag of 17 years in the category of personal-utilitarian items confirms the three hypotheses. The most recently produced bottles in this category contained skin creams and shoe polish, products that may be used more often in winter months or at holiday times.

The lag for bottles in the wine category (19.5 years) is the longest at Edgewood and confirms Hypotheses 1, 2, and 3. The identified bottles are old, and one appears to have been free-blown. The appearance of these older bottles at a site where the inhabitants obviously had access to recently produced goods confirms the observation that manufacturers whose products were enhanced by aging were slow to adopt new manufacturing techniques. The number of identified wine bottles is small and, combined with the long lag, indicates the Edgewood consumers did not drink wine often or quickly.

The average manufacture-deposition lag for the Edgewood bottles is 11.6 years. This figure, when compared to the Custer Road lag of 18 years, suggests that the length of time between the manufacture and the deposition of bottles was decreasing through time. This would be expected as transportation networks increased, areas became more populous, advertising more effective, and money more available.

Table 12.20 The Silcott Bottles, Fresh Beverages

Specimen	Median date	Datable attribute	Frequency	Product
A02B	1913.5	label	36	68,886
A08A	1919.5	mark	1	1,919.5
A08D	1916	mark	1	1,916
A70F	1910.5	mark	2	3,821
A70J	1908.5	mark	1	1,908.5
A70N	1914.5	mark	1	1,914.5
A70O	1904	mark	1	1,904
A70R	1913.5	mark	1	1,913.5
A70Y	1922.5	mark	1	1,922.5
A75F	1902.5	mark	1	1,922.5
Total			46	88,028

Deposition date 1928

Mean manufacture date 1913.7

Lag 14.3 years

Silcott Site

Silcott was a small farming community near the Snake River in southeast Washington. Settled by white homesteaders in the 1880s, the community declined in the 1920s as farms and ranches failed. Ultimately, Silcott was abandoned as a social entity. In 1972, a team from Washington State University began excavations at Silcott under the direction of Frank Leonhardy. Several sites were excavated, including Bill Wilson's general store, which was built in 1910 and destroyed by fire in 1928. Ethnographic research shows that the store included a dance hall, a saloon, and second-story living quarters for Bill Wilson and his wife. Archaeological excavations adjacent to the store site revealed a large trash midden, which was compact and had little dirt between the artifacts, indicating short-term deposition. There were 584 bottles recovered (Adams 1975).

Mean manufacturing dates and manufacture-deposition lags were calculated for 163 bottles representing each functional category. Tables 12.20–12.25 show these calculations, and Figure 12.6 illustrates the relationships of the lags.

In the category of fresh beverages, the lag is long (14.3 years) and the number of bottles is high. Therefore, Hypotheses 1, 2, and 3 are not supported and behavioral causes must be sought. A long lag for a high number of fresh beverage bottles

Table 12.21 The Silcott Bottles, Beer

Specimen	Median date	Datable attribute	Frequency	Product
A71A, E14, E13B	1910.5	mark	14	26,747
A73	1905.5	mark	9	17,149.5
E11F	1921	mark	1	1,921
E15	1914	mark	1	1,914
E33S	1916	mark	1	1,916
E33F, E33G, E11D	1923	mark	4	7,692
E11E, E33H	1922.5	mark	2	3,845
Total			32	61,184.5

Deposition date 1928

Mean manufacture date 1912

Lag 16 years

Table 12.22 The Silcott Bottles, Whiskey

Specimen	Median date	Datable Attribute	Frequency	Product
A41A, B, C, D, E, Q, U	1919.5	mark	7	13,436.5
E21B	1908	mark	1	1,908
E23C	1921	mark	1	1,921
Total			9	17,265.5

Deposition date	1928
Mean manufacture date	1918.4
Lag	9.6 years

suggests that either the products were popular or the containers were reused. Of the fresh beverage bottles that can be dated, more than three-fourths are identical, which confirms product popularity. Because their sizes (4 ounce or .12 liter capacity) are small for recycling, it seems likely that Bill Wilson purchased, used, and discarded 36 grape juice bottles at some point early in his occupation of the store.

The long lag for the beer bottles (16 years) does not confirm Hypotheses 1, 2, or 3. Again, potential behavioral factors must be sought. Twenty-four of the 32 beer bottles have median manufacturing dates before 1916, and, in fact, nearly half have a median manufacturing date of 1910. A long lag and a relatively high number of beer containers suggest that the product was popular and the containers were recycled. Adams (1977) notes that Washington enacted a state prohibition law in 1916, but that Bill Wilson sold bootleg whiskey to his customers, and was himself a "drinking man." Furthermore, one-third of the amber beer bottles used cork closures, which would have made refilling and resealing easier. The shape of closure, distribution of the mean manufacturing dates, and overall lag for the beer bottles support Adams' contention about the bootleg sales as well as an interpretation of recycling.

The lag of 9.6 years for the whiskey bottles is intermediate, and confirms Hypotheses 1 and 2, but not Hypothesis 3. The number of whiskey bottles identified is the lowest of all categories at Silcott. A low number of whiskey bottles with a moderate lag indicates little use or reuse of the containers. Because of state, and later, national prohibition, whiskey bottles became less available. If Bill Wilson was utilizing old beer bottles for bootleg, he probably did not need whiskey bottles.

The lag for the food bottles (12.6 years) is intermediate between the fresh beverage and medicine bottles, and therefore Hypotheses 1 and 2 are confirmed.

Table 12.23 The Silcott Bottles, Food

Specimen	Median date	Datable attribute	Frequency	Product
A30A	1902.5	label	1	1,902.5
A30B	1915.5	form	1	1,915.5
A44	1917	label	5	9,585
D22A, D23A, B, C, A46A	1919.5	label	6	11,517
A49A	1926	mark	1	1,926
A52A	1913	label	1	1,913
A54A	1919	label	1	1,919
A60B	1926	mark	1	1,926
D130	1910	mark	1	1,910
A46D, F, G	1911	label	3	5,733
D25	1907.5	label	3	5,722.5
Total			24	45,969.5

Deposition date 1928

Mean manufacture date 1915.4

Lag 12.6 years

Hypothesis 3 is not confirmed. It should be noted that Adams (1975) suggests that Bill Wilson used more commercially produced goods than other Silcott residents because, as a store owner, he had access to them at reduced prices. The lag for food bottles does not support that interpretation, although the percentage of food bottles is not as high as other categories, such as medicine. If Bill Wilson used more commercial foods, apparently they were not bottled.

The lag for the medicine bottles (6 years) is the shortest of all categories. This does not support Hypotheses 1 or 3, but may confirm Hypothesis 2. A short lag for medicine bottles may indicate more frequent use of medicines because of illness or an increasing tendency to rely on drugs. Examination of the medicine bottles shows that the longest lag in this category is 8 years, and that there is an even distribution of lags between 1920 and 1928. Apparently, then, the medicine was being consumed regularly. Further examination indicates that 21 out of 26 medicine bottles

Table 12.24 The Silcott Bottles, Medicine

Specimen	Median date	Datable attribute	Frequency	Product
D51C, D, E, F, J	1922	mark	5	9,610
D06C, D, E, F	1922	mark	5	9,610
D11	1922	mark	1	1,922
D31B, D50F	1919.5	mark	3	5,758.5
E04D	1921.5	label	1	1,921.5
E03H	1921.5	label	2	3,843
E03F, M, J, L, X	1922	label	7	13,454
E03N, O, P, Q, R, S, T, Z	1922.5	label	9	17,302.5
E03U, V	1923	label	3	5,769
Total			36	69,190.5

Deposition date 1928

Mean manufacture date 1922

Lag 6 years

are Dr. Hostetter's patent medicine, which, because of its high alcohol content, was more popular after the enactment of prohibition laws.

Lag for the personal-utilitarian products (8.8 years) is relatively short and does not confirm any of the three hypotheses. The product occurring in highest frequency (one-fourth of the sample) and with the shortest lag (4 years) is library paste. Again, as with the *Bertrand* and Custer Road samples, products associated with record keeping, such as ink and paste, produce short lag and do not support the original hypotheses.

There were no wine bottles recovered from Bill Wilson's store.

The average lag for the Silcott bottles is 11.2 years, which is very close to the Edgewood lag and confirms the trend of decreasing lag through time. Recycling activities at Silcott, not evident at Edgewood, undoubtedly extended the amount of lag.

Table 12.25 The Silcott Bottles, Personal-Utilitarian

Specimen	Median date	Datable attribute	Frequency	Product
A59C	1919.5	label	1	1,919.5
A25A	1915	label	1	1,915
A18	1924	label	4	7,696
A12	1918	label	4	7,672
A16	1914.5	label	3	5,743.5
B23A	1922	mark	1	1,922
D01	1917	label	1	1,917
D02	1922	label	1	1,922
Total			16	30,707

Deposition date 1928

Mean manufacture date 1919.2

Lag 8.8 years

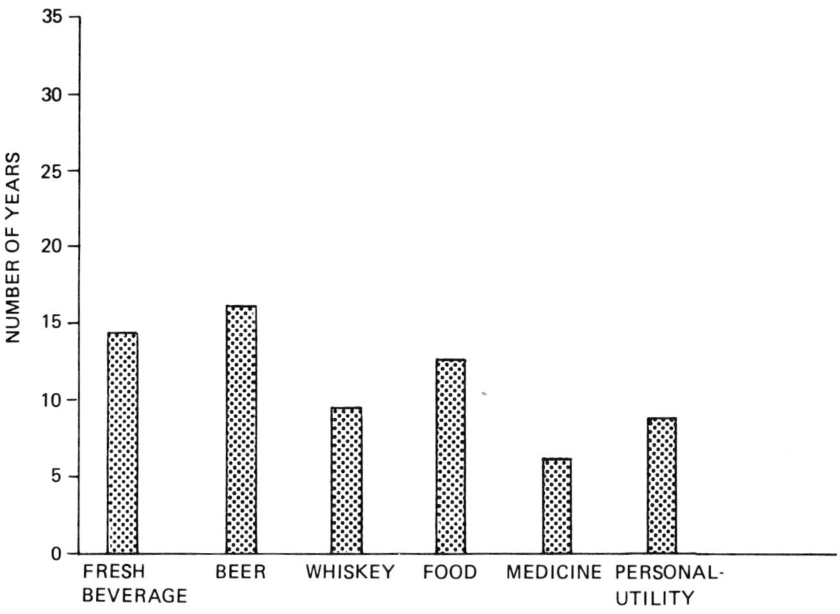

FIGURE 12.6. Differential lag of Silcott bottles.

INTERPRETATIONS

The four sites, represented in time by more than half a century and in space by the breadth of the country, should be expected to manifest different behavioral patterns. The *Bertrand* bottles reflect only the manufacturing, filling, and distributing stages of a bottle's life span in the behavioral system. When the *Bertrand* was carrying cargo to boom towns immediately after the Civil War, manufacturers were operating at maximum efficiency, and the economics of gold mining were hastening the distribution of goods from the plants to the loading docks. However, because ships could not navigate icy rivers, the *Bertrand* cargo may have been held in storage in St. Louis, waiting for spring thaws.

Within 11 years after the *Bertrand* sank, the personnel at Fort Mackinac had begun discarding their trash at the Custer Road dump. It is not known whether all the post's inhabitants used this dump. Nevertheless, the site represents at least some of the trash of a community confined in time and space. The post was destined for abandonment, and the inhabitants may have experienced, over time, a decline in fortune. The increasing frequency of poor meat cuts from the lower to upper levels suggests a deteriorating economy. At the same time, however, rail transportation was improving significantly, and the Custer Road inhabitants seemed to have had access to some commercial products (e.g., ceramics) from increasingly greater distances (Brose 1967:81).

Less than 15 years after Fort Mackinac was abandoned, some of the residents of the Edgewood community were discarding their trash in a neighborhood ravine. Again, it is not known how many families used this dump, or if they used it for all of their trash. The variety in the artifact assemblage, however, indicates residential

Table 12.26 Manufacture-Deposition Lag by Site and Bottle Category

	Bertrand	Custer Road	Edgewood	Silcott
Fresh	—	33.1	7.5	14.3
Beer	—	8.6	7.6	16
Whiskey	16.8	7.4	3.8	9.6
Food	11	11.5	13.1	12.6
Medicine	9.4	21.6	12.4	6
Personal-utilitarian	3.9	17	17	8.8
Wine	12.9	26.9	19.5	—
Average lag in years	10.8	18	11.6	11.2

rather than street discard. At this time, Atlanta was an emerging transportation center, which gave the residents of Edgewood access to a regional and national commercial network. However, since in the early part of the twentieth century private transportation was limited, the Edgewood residents would have relied on home deliveries, mail orders, or occasional streetcar journeys to obtain goods. Furthermore, refrigeration was limited at that time so that preferred food and beverage products would have been those requiring little special treatment.

At approximately the same time that the Edgewood residents were filling the neighborhood ravine, Bill Wilson was building his general store. During the 18 years of the Wilsons' residency at the store, the town of Silcott changed from an isolated rural community to a town dependent on cash crops and external business contracts (Adams 1975). New roads and the automobile extended the range of cultural influence on Silcott. At the same time, the economy of the town and the nation was collapsing. These volatile factors undoubtedly affected the buying power and consumer habits of the Wilsons.

In spite of significant behavioral, temporal, and spatial differences of these sites, some general patterns in the manufacture-deposition lags of their bottles can be discerned (Table 12.26).[5] Overall, the amount of lag declines through time, although the average lag of the Silcott bottles is not significantly different from that of the Edgewood site. However, since the bottled and other products at Silcott came from as far away as 2000 mi. (3218 km) (Adams 1977:83), it still can be postulated that the amount of time required for manufacturing, bottling, and distributing had been considerably reduced between 1865 and 1928. The lag for fresh beverages, both alcoholic and nonalcoholic, decreases from Custer Road to Edgewood, but then increases from Edgewood to Silcott. This unexpected result may be attributable to some of the previously suggested behavioral processes or to sampling error. The amount of lag for beer bottles generally increases from Custer Road to Silcott and, as proposed, is almost certainly the result of recycling at the latter site. This may also be true of the whiskey bottles, whose lag decreases from *Bertrand* to Custer Road and Edgewood, then increases from Edgewood to Silcott. National and local prohibition undoubtedly are reflected in this shift. In the category of food, the lag remains relatively constant through time. Perhaps behavioral patterns related to food are more traditional and resistant to change than other patterns. In the medicine and personal-utilitarian categories, the lags increase from *Bertrand* to Custer Road, then decrease. This probably reflects national trends in increased medicine consumption and use of personal-utilitarian products.

It should be noted that the Custer Road bottles express the longest lags in four of the seven categories. This is probably a material manifestation of the different processes affecting behavioral patterns at a military garrison from a civilian site.

[5]Clearly, national trends cannot be inferred from four sites. However, the patterns described here should provide a comparative basis for other analyses in the expectation of discerning such trends.

CONCLUSIONS

In an effort to make a contribution to the development of theoretical and methodological research strategies in historical archaeology, three proposals have been made in this chapter. They are as follows:

1. Find the mean manufacturing date for a category or type of bottle by adapting South's Mean Ceramic Date Formula. The suggested method is to use the formula to determine the median manufacturing date for any bottle whose manufacturing date terminates prior to the site's documented closing date. In other cases, when the artifact's manufacturing date extends beyond the date of the site, the documented terminal date of the site is used as the *terminus ante quem* manufacturing date. This adaptation provides a mean manufacture date for a class of artifacts at a specific site.
2. Calculate the manufacture-deposition lag by finding the difference between the mean manufacturing date of the artifacts and the documented date for the site. (Documented dates are preferable to artifact dates because all manufactured artifacts reflect some amount of lag.)
3. Examine bottles by integrating analyses of form, function, quantity, probable frequency of use, and probable immediacy of use. Establish categories based on the need for product freshness and frequency of consumption.

Based on the above proposals, three hypotheses were developed and tested at four sites. The hypotheses were confirmed more often than rejected. However, because the purpose of these hypotheses was to investigate assumptions about differential lag and to reveal discontinuities in expected behavioral patterns, they have been productive even when unconfirmed. It appears, for example, that rejection of the hypotheses concerning beverage bottle lag can contribute to a recognition of recycling patterns that otherwise would remain obscure or unknown, and that special behavioral situations, such as holiday or military patterns, can be revealed.

The study of manufacture-deposition lag holds great potential for historical archaeology. It provides a method for analyzing relationships between artifacts, their life-spans, and their behavioral contexts by exploring the interrelated mechanisms of material and technological change. Furthermore, the method permits the establishment of hypotheses set up as models against which archaeological assemblages can be measured. Testing these hypotheses has value in interpreting the remains at a specific site and in elucidating differences between sites. Finally, this type of study can reveal material-behavioral correlates that have applicability to the study of all archaeological remains from prehistoric as well as historic cultures.

ACKNOWLEDGMENTS

I am grateful to Roy S. Dickens, Jr., for sustained encouragement, advice, and critical appraisal of this chapter, from its conception through its completion.

REFERENCES

Adams, William H.
1976 Trade networks and interaction spheres—A view from Silcott. *Historical Archaeology* **10**:99–112.

Adams, William H.
1977 Silcott, Washington: Ethnoarchaeology of a rural American community. *Reports of investigations* No. 54, Laboratory of Anthropology, Washington State University.

Adams, William H., Linda P. Gaw, and Frank C. Leonhardy
1975 Archaeological excavations at Silcott, Washington: The data inventory. *Reports of investigations* No. 53, Laboratory of Anthropology, Washington State University.

Brose, David S.
1967 The Custer Road dump site: An exercise in Victorian archaeology. *The Michigan Archaeologist* **13**(2).

Dickens, Roy S., Jr., and William R. Bowen
1980 Problems and promises in urban historical archaeology: The MARTA project. *Historical Archaeology* **14**:42–57.

Draper, Fontaine, and Gerald Gandy
1978 The Edgewood Site. Unpublished manuscript, Department of Anthropology, Georgia State University.

Furnas, J. C.
1969 *The Americans: A social history of the United States, 1587–1914*. New York: G. P. Putnam's Sons.

Kendrick, Grace
1971 *The antique bottle collector*. New York: Harcourt Brace Jovanovich.

Lorrain, Dessamae
1968 An archaeologist's guide to nineteenth-century American glass. *Historical Archaeology* **2**:33–44.

McKearin, Helen, and Kenneth Wilson
1978 *American bottles and flasks and their ancestry*. New York: Crown.

Mitchell, James (editor)
1977 *The Random House encyclopedia*. New York: Random House.

Newman, T. Stell
1970 A dating key for post eighteenth-century bottles. *Historical Archaeology* **2**:70–75.

Paul, John R., and Paul Parmalee
1973 *Soft drink bottling*. Springfield: Illinois State Museum Society.

Schiffer, Michael B.
1977 Toward a unified science of the cultural past. In *Research strategies in historical archaeology*, edited by Stanley South. New York: Academic Press. Pp. 13–40.

South, Stanley
1972 Evolution and horizon as revealed in historical archaeology. *Conference on Historic Sites Archeology Papers* **6**:71–116.

South, Stanley
1977 *Method and theory in historical archeology*. New York: Academic Press.

Switzer, Ronald R.
1974 *The Bertrand bottles*. National Park Service, U.S. Department of the Interior, Washington, D.C.

13

Classification and Interpretation of Late-Nineteenth- and Early-Twentieth-Century Ceramics

Linda H. Worthy

In the past, most archaeological ceramic studies have emphasized the technical and formal attributes of the wares. Prehistoric and early historic pottery is well documented regarding temper, color, vessel form, rim form, thickness, decoration, surface finish, and so on. A research design for the study of ceramics from late historic (especially urban) sites, however, must go beyond mere technological and formal considerations. Because of the recent nature and extensive documentation of the cultures under consideration, much more is known about the original intended uses of various forms. Therefore, by additionally evaluating the function of vessels and assemblages of vessels, problems relating to such areas as eating habits, buying power, and socioeconomic status may be addressed.

This chapter presents a system for classifying late-nineteenth- and early-twentieth-century ceramics that integrates technology, form, function, and decoration. Furthermore, it suggests some analytical implications of the use of such a format and some directions for the use of ceramic data in interpreting late historic sites. For instance, makers' marks provide a source of information for temporal placement of a site, and they allow for the determination of manufacturing locations for specific items. The latter provides economic network data for a site at a specific point in time. Historical documentation of availability and cost is also obtainable for turn-of-the-century materials. Such documentation is useful when evaluating selection of ceramics, that is, personal preference versus economic status. Differential manufacture-deposition lag in ceramic assemblages can provide insights into the particular behavior which formed the assemblage and which influ-

ARCHAEOLOGY OF URBAN AMERICA
The Search for Pattern and Process

ISBN 0-12-214980-7

enced its use and ultimate deposition. Documentary sources, informants, and personal experience relating to similar artifacts are advantages that archaeologists studying prehistoric and some early historic remains do not have.[1]

Finally, some preliminary results of the analysis of late-nineteenth-, early-twentieth-century ceramics, based on a combined technological-formal-functional system, are presented.

CLASSIFICATION

Nineteenth-century Americans expressed a definite preference for English ceramic tablewares. Even though the last half of the century, specifically the years following the Civil War, brought about major advancements in American ceramic manufacturing, the bias for English wares remained strong. As late as the 1880s, American potters found it necessary to simulate English marks (e.g., lion and unicorn) on their products in order to secure a place in the home market. Through determined efforts, however, domestic wares that rivaled imported ceramics were being produced by the turn of the century. This improved technology resulted in more economical and wear-resistant items. Wider varieties of decoration and special purpose tableservices (e.g., hotelwares) also became available (Ramsay 1976: 109). The diversity of choice provided the American consumer from the last quarter of the nineteenth century to the present is evident in ceramic assemblages from most archaeological sites dating to the late 1800s and early 1900s. The purpose of this chapter is to specify attributes from among this variation that will allow the urban archaeologist to use twentieth-century ceramics as an aid in discerning changing patterns of culture. An example of the data form developed for recording frequencies of sherds according to technology, form, function, and decoration is shown in Table 13.1.

The application of technological categories to the analysis of late historic ceramics allows the researcher to address questions relating to socioeconomic level, based on the assumption that types of wares have basic cost differences and/or status significance.[2] Relative amounts of one type of ware to another present on a site may suggest choice resulting from specific activities at that site. For instance, an as-

[1]The materials recovered from urban archaeological sites are relatively recent, representing a point in time within the continuum of cultural activity that includes the present system. Because of this, comparisons of current ceramic breakage, durability, use habits, etc., are relevant to those under study.

[2]Just before this article went to press, George L. Miller's article on nineteenth-century ceramics appeared in *Historical Archaeology* (1980:1–40). Miller presents a classification for ceramics based on decoration types, and he proposes that earlier classificatory systems based on ware (body) types are not useful for the nineteenth century. While this may be true for early nineteenth-century products, I would argue that from the mid nineteenth century there were marked changes in ceramic preferences that cannot be detected without categorization by body type. Otherwise, "ironstone" would simply be shown as a plain or undecorated type. And if, as Miller supports with his cost data, ironstone was priced slightly higher than the most expensive decorated types, then this cost difference would have to be related to ware-type rather than to decoration. Therefore, for late-nineteenth- and early twentieth-century ceramics, classification combining several attributes, as presented in this chapter, should be utilized.

Table 13.1 Data Form for Classifying Late-Nineteenth- and Early-Twentieth-Century Ceramics

Body type (earthenware, stoneware, porcelaneous stoneware, or porcelain)

Decoration[a]	P	PG	R	RG	F	FR	FG	FRG	GM	GMR	GMG	GMRG	B	SP	SOG	TT	U	Other
I. Food Vessels																		
A. Serving																		
1. Large bowl																		
2. Small bowl																		
3. Gravy boat																		
4. Tureen																		
5. Tureen lid																		
6. Platter																		
7. Butter																		
8. Teapot																		
9. Pitcher																		
10. Miscellaneous																		
11. Vegetable dish with lid																		
B. Eating																		
1. Plate																		
2. Salad/butter plate																		
3. Medium bowl																		

(Continued)

Table 13.1 (Continued)

- 4. Small bowl
- 5. Butter pat
- 6. Breakfast plate

C. Drinking

- 1. Cup
- 2. Saucer
- 3. Mug

D. Utilitarian (kitchen)

- 1. Churn
- 2. Jug
- 3. Crock/jar
- 4. Bottle
- 5. Mixing bowl

II. Nonfood Vessels

A. Decorative

- 1. Vase
- 2. Plate
- 3. Covered jar
- 4. Small dish

B. Utilitarian (household)

- 1. Flower pot

(Continued)

Table 13.1 (*Continued*)

2. Chamber pot
3. Washbowl
4. Pitcher
5. Spittoon
6. Ashtray
7. Soap dish
8. Bottle
III. Unidentifiable
Total

[a] See Table 13.3 for explanation of decoration codes.

semblage of plain white stoneware and/or porcelaneous stoneware suggests a commercial establishment, and presence of the latter indicates a post-1888 deposition (Ramsay 1976:109). Evidence of matched sets of decorated earthenware or porcelain, however, may indicate a domestic site. (One must consider type of body, as well as decoration, in making these interpretations.)

Technology

Because the "fabric" from which an item is formed will help to answer questions relating to its selection and use, "body" or "paste" of ceramics already has been examined and evaluated by historic sites archaeologists (e.g., Cotter 1968; Fontana 1962; Noël Hume 1970; Quimby 1972). These studies have considered hardness of the body, color, and in some cases the actual chemical content of the ingredients used in its formation. Generally, three basic categories (earthenware, stoneware, and porcelain) have been considered as sufficient recognition of variation. Only when applied to early historic ceramics do these divisions seem adequate. Technological developments in the past 100 years have produced greater variation among ceramic bodies, and the distinctions between body types have become less clearly defined. Therefore, the range from crude, opaque earthenware to refined, translucent porcelain must now be updated to distinguish this increased variation along the continuum.

The present taxonomy establishes four technological divisions relating to body: earthenware, stoneware, porcelaneous stoneware, and porcelain (Figure 13.1). These major divisions, further, contain varieties that are critical for interpretive purposes. Definitions for each of these categories were determined using the following criteria: color of the paste, degree of vitrification, opaqueness versus translucence, interface between the body and the glaze, appearance of the glaze, manner in which a break occurs, and smooth versus granular appearance of the paste.

(1) *Earthenware* is pottery with a permeable body.[3] Characteristically, it has a granular texture, is opaque, and breaks irregularly. Because the firing temperatures are in the range of 600°C to about 1150°C (Chandler 1968; Leach 1976), these low-fired clay bodies must be covered by a glaze to be impervious to liquids. (On a continuum, earthenwares are the least vitrified of all ceramic types.) Currently, a transparent alkaline glaze is common to earthenwares, replacing the tinted lead glazes of the eighteenth and early nineteenth centuries. On a cross section of these wares, one can detect a distinct boundary between the glaze and the body. Due to a difference in elasticity of glaze and body, earthenwares are highly subject to crazing (a condition where the glaze breaks into a network of fine cracks). This pottery has a color range from the earthtones to cream or white, depending on the composition of and impurities in the clay.

[3]The absorption quality of a ceramic body may be tested by touching the broken edge of a sherd to the tongue. A porous earthenware body will stick to the tongue, whereas a highly vitrified stoneware or porcelain body will not stick (Spargo 1926:31).

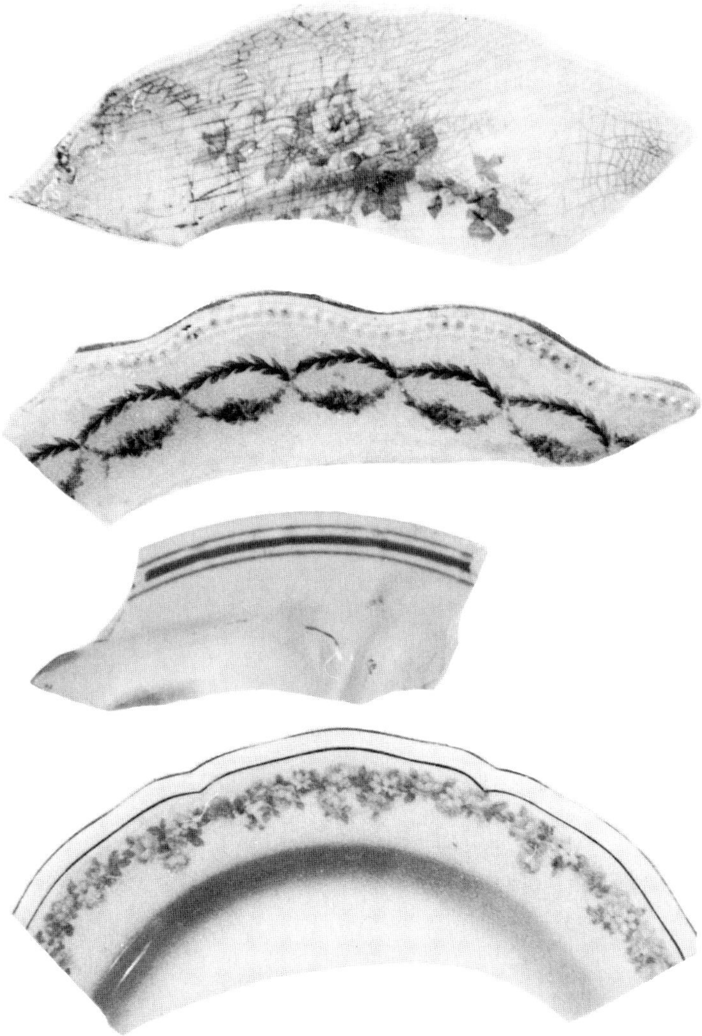

(A)

(B)

(C)

(D)

FIGURE 13.1. Technological categories: (A) earthenware, FR; (*B*) stoneware—white-bodied type—FRG; (*C*) porcelaneous stoneware, and (*D*) porcelain, FG. (Codes for decorative categories are also indicated.)

(2) *Stoneware* is a vitrified pottery that is fired between 1200°C and 1300°C (Spargo 1926:39). The body is opaque, dense, and heavy. When properly fired, glass in the body makes stoneware impervious to liquids, although glazes are commonly added to enhance toughness.

A classification of stoneware for the late nineteenth and early twentieth century must include both a white-bodied type and an earthtone-bodied type. Refinement of

(A) (B)

FIGURE 13.2. Technological variation between a traditional utilitarian stoneware pitcher (*A*) and an industrial utilitarian stoneware jug (*B*).

the white clay paste during the late 1850s resulted in an almost vitreous, heavy white body that was fine-grained, opaque, and dense. The transparent glaze did not craze because the body and the glaze had matured in the kiln at high temperatures. Because of its durability, this body became popular for flatware, although utilitarian and decorative items also were made.

Earthtone-bodied stonewares range in color from red, to tan, to gray. Also, they are dense, heavy, and usually very thick. The texture of the body varies, but is generally granular. Functionally, these are utilitarian hollow-ware items. Two significant variations occur, however, as a result of the method of manufacture: traditional utilitarian and industrial utilitarian.

Traditional utilitarian stoneware (sometimes called "folk pottery") has been described as "that which is traditional in form and construction because it is made according to an inherited tradition, passed on from master to apprentice. It usually consists of handmade, primarily utilitarian hollow-ware vessels," for example, mugs, jugs, pitchers, bowls, and churns (Burrison 1973:66–67). These wares are characterized by finger ridges on the interior walls, types of glazes, thickness, and slight irregularity of shape. Body colors are grays, tans, and browns. Characteristic glazes are salt glazes, slip glazes, and alkaline glazes.[4] Industrial utilitarian stoneware has similar forms to the traditional version, but is more refined (Figure 13.2). For instance, because this ware is formed in molds or by machine, it is regularly shaped; the close-grained body is usually light gray or cream in color; and, due to controlled mixing and firing, the appearance of the glazes is distinctive from the traditional glazes (i.e., they are smoother and the color tones vary).

(3) *Porcelaneous stoneware* is naturally white bodied, highly vitrified, and opaque. (Some late examples have been noted where the body has been stained in pastel colors.) This ware contains those properties that are on the borderline between stoneware and porcelain. Some kaolin in the paste allows very high firing temperatures, 1200°C to 1400°C, but the presence of ball clays in the mixture prevents translucence. By 1888, this durable body began to replace the earlier white stoneware for use in hotels and restaurants and, after the turn of the century, became the accepted institutional ware.

(4) *Porcelain* is pottery that is white, vitrified, and translucent. The kaolin body is fired from 1300°C to 1450°C which eliminates a boundary between the body and glaze. The hard, close-grained texture appears smooth under magnification and breaks in a conchoidal fracture. It is covered with a hard glaze that is melted or fused into the body (Ramsay 1976:155). The level of vitrification prevents absorption of stains from the environment, which facilitates identification of paste color.

Form and Function

Total separation of formal and functional attributes is difficult within the framework of accepted ceramic terminology. Both shape and use, for example, are

[4]For a detailed study of traditional pottery in the South, see Burrison (1973).

included in dictionary definitions (e.g., The G. C. Merriam Company 1967). A *plate* is defined as "a shallow usually circular vessel from which food is eaten or served," a *bowl* as "a concave usually hemispherical vessel used especially for holding liquids," and a *tureen* as "a deep footed vessel with a cover from which cooked foods are served at table." The present taxonomy uses modern names of ceramic pieces to designate form (shape). These forms are then grouped under functional categories that designate the proposed use of the item.

Current use designations for individual pieces of ceramics cannot be transferred indiscriminately to ceramics from the turn of the century. In the late 1800s, for instance, a typical dinnerware set included individual butter servers ("butter pats"). These averaged about 2 in. (5 cm) in diameter and were seldom larger than 2.5 in. (6.3 cm). They came with sets of fine china as well as with inexpensive earthenware, and they could be plain or highly decorated. By about 1900, however, these butter servers had been replaced by the larger bread-and-butter plates (Ray 1974), similar to those still in use. Therefore, even though the ceramics under consideration are only a few generations old, one must be careful not to depend solely on a modern taxonomy. To develop as close an understanding as possible of the contemporary system, one must utilize catalogue descriptions, trade publications, and elderly informants.

Designations for shape are listed individually on the data form (Table 13.1). In some cases, a distinction is made for size or shape within the same general category, for example, large bowl versus small bowl, dinner plate versus salad/butter plate (Table 13.2). These distinctions are important, for bowls and plates in varying shapes and sizes may reflect specific behaviors that would go undetected if general shape alone were considered. Measurements can be made of a reconstructed piece, and the degree of curvature can be matched with a template to determine the size of a vessel.

Another basic assumption followed here is that each ceramic piece was manufactured to serve a specific function or functions. Thus, in the analysis of a site, evidence for divergence from the functional "norm" may identify a particular kind of behavior. When this data is combined with that in other artifact categories, larger behavioral patterns may be identified. For example, at the Edgewood deposit in Atlanta, the number of large bowls and other serving pieces, relative to the number of other pieces of a "typical" dinnerware set, was greater than expected. By combining this information with inventories of faunal remains and glass bottles and by evaluating historical records, a "holiday pattern" was established (Dickens and Bowen 1980:51–52).

The first functional division—food vessels and nonfood vessels—is very general. Food vessels are then separated into serving, eating, drinking, preparation, or storage categories. Nonfood vessels may be decorative (e.g., vases, display pieces, and covered jars), or utilitarian (e.g., soap dishes, ashtrays, spittoons, and flowerpots). As mentioned earlier, some size distinctions can be important. For food vessel categories, sizing allows for quantitative studies by which form-function and size can be related to other aspects of the assemblage. If a larger than expected occur-

Table 13.2 Size Designations for Form-Function Categories

I. Food vessels

A. Serving

1. Large bowl—approximately 20 cm in diameter and 8 cm deep
2. Small bowl—approximately 15 cm in diameter and shallow
3. Gravy boat
4. Tureen
5. Tureen lid
6. Platter
7. Butter dish
8. Teapot and lid
9. Pitcher
10. Miscellaneous (sugar, cream, salt, pepper, mustard jar)
11. Vegetable dish with cover

B. Eating

1. Plate—approximately 23 cm and over
2. Salad/butter plate—approximately 17 cm in diameter
3. Medium bowl (soup, cereal)—18 cm and shallow
4. Small bowl (dessert, fruit)—14 cm and very shallow
5. Butter pat (individual butter)—approximately 6-7 cm
6. Breakfast plate (There is a range which would include dessert and tea plates.)—18-20 cm

C. Drinking

1. Cup
2. Saucer—approximately 16 cm
3. Mug

D. Utilitarian (kitchen)

1. Churn (rim for holding lid, fairly tall, capacity designation)
2. Jug (syrup, whiskey—has small opening and one handle)
3. Crock/jar (preserves, pickles)
4. Bottle
5. Mixing bowl (preparation)

(Continued)

Table 13.2 (Continued)

II. Nonfood vessels

   A. Decorative

      1. Vase (any size)
      2. Plate (display item, any size)
      3. Covered jar (possible candy dish, etc., or display)
      4. Small dish (display—13-16 cm)

   B. Utilitarian (household)

      1. Flowerpot (distinguish size)
      2. Chamber pot
      3. Washbowl
      4. Pitcher
      5. Spittoon
      6. Ashtray
      7. Soap dish
      8. Bottle

III. Unidentifiable

---

rence of soup bowls is accompanied by a large number of soup bones, for example, it may be possible to infer socioeconomic level, seasonality, or a special eating situation. Size is not deemed important for most of the nonfood vessel categories. Exceptions are decorative plates, vases, and flowerpots. Small plates might have been placed on a table, whereas large plates might have been hung on a wall. Likewise the basal diameter of a vase might suggest where it was placed, or the rim diameter might indicate the type of floral arrangements used. These distinctions conceivably could provide information on socioeconomic or ethnic preferences, family traditions, and so on.

Decoration

The final level of classification is by decoration. Table 13.3 is the key for the decoration codes used on the data sheet, as outlined in Table 13.1. Many decorative designs and applications of designs seem to fall within specific time intervals, in a way similar to handpainted and transfer-printed designs of the early to middle nineteenth century (Miller 1980:1–40). For turn-of-the-century ceramics, a chronology for decoration designs and colors has not yet been established. (Much historical and archaeological data needs to be brought to bear on this problem.)

Cost distinctions can be made on the basis of the type of decoration applied to a specific body type. Generally, the simpler the decoration and softer the body, the cheaper the product (Taylor 1950:35). One color application requires one firing, whereas five colors may require five firings, increasing the manufacturing cost. According to Searle (1915:130), "overglaze decoration burned at low temperatures may be rapidly passed through the kiln, affording a simple and relatively inexpensive method of producing large quantities of decorated work in a short time." This process is limited to cheaper dinnerware and ornamental ceramics since the decora-

Table 13.3 Key for Decoration Codes Used on the Data Form

Code	Description
P	Plain = white, smooth, unadorned.
PG	Plain-gilded = gold is added, either as a gold band or as a design.
R	Raised = a design is embossed; otherwise is plain, that is, white-on-white design.
RG	Raised-gilded = embossing highlighted with gold.
F	Floral = a very broad designation, that is, includes a range of floral designs from very delicate to bold, coarse designs.
FR	Floral-raised = embossing and floral design.
FG	Floral-gilded = combination of floral design and gilding.
FRG	Floral-raised-gilded = floral design, embossing, and gilding.
GM	Geometric = geometric design.
GMR	Geometric-raised = geometric with embossing.
GMG	Geometric-gilded = geometric with gilding.
GMRG	Geometric-raised-gilded = geometric design with embossing and gilding.
B	Banded = color (either monochrome or polychrome) applied around the vessel, usually near the edge of the rim.
SP	Sponge = design created by dabbing color onto the ware with a sponge.
SOG	Solid-overall-glaze = one color glaze covering entire vessel with no design.
TT	Two-tone = one color inside, another outside. This category includes those utilitarian wares on which one color covers the inside and the upper portion of the outside, and a second color covers the lower portion of the outside, for example, Albany slip/Bristol glaze combinations (Figure 13.2).
U	Unglazed.
Other	Miscellaneous decorative applications, which appear infrequently, for example, mottled, painted, with logo.

tion is not very durable and easily wears off. Handpainting is more expensive than machine-applied decorations or decalcomania, and gold adds greatly to the cost. In other words, the materials and amount of labor are determining factors in the cost of the finished product. A survey of period advertisements reveals a considerable price range, from the plainest earthenwares to fancy porcelains (e.g., Sears Roebuck and Company 1897; Montgomery Ward and Company 1895).

If sherds are indistinguishable as to form and function, they still might be classified by body type and decoration. It should be noted, however, that the number of undecorated sherds may not be an accurate representation of undecorated vessels, as many plain sherds come from undecorated portions of decorated vessels. Nevertheless, intersite comparisons are useful, assuming that plain wares will be overrepresented and decorated wares underrepresented in similar proportions on every site where other factors remain equal.

INTERPRETATIVE DIRECTIONS

The manufacture of tablewares in America was accelerated after the Civil War (Stillinger 1972:422), when the potteries in East Liverpool, Ohio, stopped making yellow wares and concentrated on white tablewares. This shift in the availability of domestic wares is important to consider when evaluating the effects of product origin on a particular ceramic assemblage. Other changes in the postwar cultural system also provide the researcher with valuable resources for interpretation. By the end of the nineteenth century, for example, mail-order houses were in operation. Through their catalogues, these houses made a variety of goods available to otherwise isolated consumers. Modern reprints of those early catalogues contain information on price, availability, location of manufacturers, and status of the intended consumer (implied in the wording of some advertisements). Also, the practice of listing dinnerware sets by number of pieces and name (function) establishes an "ideal" tableservice, against which the archaeologist can make comparisons relating to selection and use. Newspaper advertisements for ceramics also provide cost and availability information as well as information on the location of retail outlets within the urban context. Trade and popular magazines are other sources of similar information.

A trademark found on an artifact is an obvious aid for interpretation of industrially produced ceramics (Figure 13.3). However, Ramsay (1976:ix) points out that very few potteries marked their entire output, and many never used a formal mark. Therefore, since the number of marked pieces occurring in the archaeological record is very small indeed, the best possible use should be made of this resource. Carefully researched, makers' marks can be used to determine period of manufacture and can help to establish contemporary trade networks. (For approximately 15

FIGURE 13.3. Examples of makers' marks, illustrating the types of information provided: (*A*) pattern name only (USA); (*B*) manufacturer's name and body type (USA); (*C*) manufacturer, country of origin, and body type (ENG); (*D*) manufacturer, country of origin, body type, and pattern (ENG); (*E*) manufacturer and country of origin (FR); and (*F*) manufacturer or decorator and country of origin (AUS).

TACOMA

(A)

MERCER
SEMI-VITREOUS

(B)

JOHN MADDOCK & SONS LTD
ENGLAND
ROYAL VITREOUS

(C)

PARIS
ROYAL
SEMI-PORCELAIN
JOHNSON BROS
ENGLAND

(D)

Haviland
France
Haviland & Co
Limoges

(E)

LS&S
CARLSBAD
AUSTRIA

(F)

years after the American pottery industry began producing tablewares, manufacturers were hesitant to develop marks of their own and copied the marks of English potteries. This duplicity complicates the use of ceramic trademarks as accurate indicators of site age and geographic source.)

Several publications provide line drawings of trademarks and corresponding dates of use. The amount of substantive data varies greatly from one source to another. Geoffrey Godden's *Encyclopedia of British Pottery and Porcelain Marks* (1964) is accepted as an authoritative and easy-to-use source on British marks. It provides details such as when a company was established, subsequent name changes, the various marks used by the company, and the dates of use for each mark. Unfortunately, no such definitive work is available for ceramics made in America. The recent nature of much of the material recovered from urban sites has, up to now, precluded any interest by antique collectors, for whom most of these publications are intended. Several books taken together, however, do provide a minimal source of information (e.g., Cox 1953; Kovel 1965; Ramsay 1976; Thorn 1947). Personal communication with manufacturers still in production also can provide tight dating and source information for recent trademarks. The preciseness of information from current producers allows these late marks to be particularly useful as horizon markers.

The use of dates of manufacture, obtained from trademarks, to establish the date of deposition of a particular site is limited. Taken alone, the only absolute in an unstratified site is that the deposition cannot have been prior to the beginning manufacture date of the earliest item and will be after the beginning manufacture date for the most recent mark. Combined with data from other groups of artifacts at the site, and with available historical documentation, however, dates of manufacture for ceramics often can provide a narrow time range for the deposition.

A method for delineating periods of occupation through the use of ceramic types present on a site was proposed in 1972 by Stanley South. When applied to eighteenth-century sites, the "Mean Ceramic Date Formula" provides dates that reliably correspond to historically documented periods of occupation. Although caution is urged in using ceramic manufacture dates alone to designate the time of deposition for twentieth-century urban sites, there is much potential for use of the formula in interpreting the behavioral processes that produced the artifact assemblage (Turnbaugh and Turnbaugh 1980).

Because ceramics are used over and over, one must recognize that a considerable amount of time might elapse between the date of manufacture and the date of disposal (Schiffer 1972, 1977). For ceramic products, deposition occurs when an item is broken beyond use or is beyond repair for a secondary use. Because "breakage," rather than "wearing out," usually is the reason for discard of ceramics, variables related to technological durability must be considered. For instance, are some body types stronger than others, that is, will stoneware withstand more and rougher use than earthenware? Despite its thin and delicate nature, is porcelain as fragile as it appears? Also, what effect does the form of a ceramic vessel have on the breakage ratio, that is, do cups break more easily than saucers and bowls more easily than plates? Questions such as these should be investigated on an intersite basis. For example, if "standard" (expected) manufacture-deposition lag intervals could be established, researchers would have a "norm" against which to compare the lags of types and forms at specific sites and features within sites. Deviations from the norm could then be examined as material expressions of behavioral processes operating in a given context (see Hill, Chapter 12).

Additionally, manufacture-deposition lag would be useful in studies of changing durability of ceramics. For example, it is likely that technological changes in the fabrics of twentieth-century ceramics will increase the time lag for these shockproof wares. It would follow that assemblages composed chiefly of hotelwares (e.g., a commercial dump) will exhibit a greater time lag than those composed mainly of earthenwares (e.g., a domestic dump). More intensive use, however, might be expected of ceramics in a commercial establishment. Will these two variables—that is, greater durability but more intensive use—cancel each other out, so as to produce a consistent time lag? As more data are forthcoming, comparison of the lags for each technological division (earthenware, stoneware, porcelaneous stoneware, and porcelain) should clarify any assumptions about one type outlasting the others.

Ceramic makers' marks can be used to plot trade networks in which the individual and community participated. In recent studies of the twentieth-century farming community of Silcott, Washington, Adams (1977) has established six levels of trade networks, ranging from "local" to "international" (see also Forsman, Chapter 16). Recognition of the place of a site in a trade network—that is, whether it drew upon local, regional, national, or international sources—is prerequisite to the evaluation of other economic factors in the urban setting. For example, did the local market provide a narrow or broad choice (i.e., was availability the major factor in decisions surrounding purchase and use); were imported wares preferred over domestic wares; what were the relative frequencies of imported, domestic, and local (including folk) wares, and how do these relate to urban cultural processes (e.g., the shift from cottage to industrial manufacture and distribution)?

In summary, the considerable historical documentation on product technology, value, availability, and product origin[5] opens avenues to ceramic analysis for urban sites that are not possible for sites of earlier periods. To follow are some examples of how formal–functional data may be used in conjunction with historical documentation to enhance ceramic interpretation.

PRELIMINARY RESULTS

Development of a formal–functional analysis system evolved during work with materials from the Edgewood site, a small, early-twentieth-century, neighborhood trash deposit in Atlanta, Georgia. The site was exposed by construction activities for

[5]Miller (1980:3) states that for nineteenth-century ceramics, the question of country of origin is not usually asked because of the preponderance of English wares. For turn-of-the-century ceramics, however, the question is an important one. It is during this period that dramatic marketing changes took place, and evidence of these "source" changes in the archaeological record can provide data not available from any other source, e.g., the acceptance and use of domestic wares versus the imported English wares.

installation of the MARTA rapid rail system. Two 10-ft (3 m) squares were excavated in 5-ft (.15 m) arbitrary levels, and the materials were screened through .5-in. (1.2 cm) hardware cloth. All materials recovered were accessioned and catalogued in the Laboratory of Archaeology at Georgia State University. Preliminary analysis of the site suggests a small ravine, used as a short-term depository for trash by residents of the neighborhood. Historic documents provided a probable date of 1910–1911 for the site. The ceramic assemblage from Square 1 was used in the preliminary analysis and is compared in the following discussions with data from other sites in Atlanta and elsewhere.

The non-Atlanta site used for comparison is Silcott, a small farming community in southeastern Washington state. Although white settlement began there in about 1861, the sites excavated in the early 1970s by William H. Adams, Linda P. Gaw, and Frank C. Leonhardy (1975) focused on remains from the period 1900–1930. The relative isolation and rural nature of this community provide an important comparison for assemblages recovered in contemporaneous urban sites.

For the purpose of this study, some basic assumptions were made (*a*) that more usage indicates more breakage, so that frequencies of various categories are assumed to accurately represent frequency of use; (*b*) that body type, combined with the method of decoration, is indicative of expensiveness and thereby offers a basis for evaluating status and/or socioeconomic levels of contributing households; and (*c*) that norms for dinnerware sets were reflected in contemporary advertisements, so that deviations from these expected ratios will indicate greater or lesser usage of specific forms.

Standards

First, in order to establish a typical turn-of-the-century ceramic tableware set with which the Edgewood and Silcott collections could be compared, contemporary advertising sources were evaluated. Reproductions of two popular mail-order catalogues (Montgomery Ward and Sears Roebuck) were selected as containing representative examples of (*a*) types of ceramics being marketed, (*b*) costs to the consumer, (*c*) country of origin, and (*d*) an "ideal" tableservice.[6] Then, by establishing the expected frequencies of formal–functional categories comprising an ideal set, occurrence relationships of the archaeological assemblage with the documented sets could be determined. From these data, questions relating to the eating habits of the neighborhood were addressed. For instance, at the Edgewood site, the numbers of pieces in various functional categories of food vessels were determined and compared with those in the catalogue sets. From this measure, some divergencies from the advertised frequencies were discovered (Table 13.4). A chi-square test was done to determine the statistical significance of these differences. The chi square

[6]Mail-order catalogues from 1915 and 1927 also were considered as documentary resources. The 1895 and 1897 issues were chosen for the analysis, however, because it was felt that those years more closely corresponded to the time of purchase of the Edgewood ceramics.

Table 13.4 Comparison of Food Vessel Form-Function Categories between the Edgewood Assemblage and the "Ideal" Set Represented in Catalogue Advertisements

Source	Serving		Eating		Drinking		Total
	N	Percentage	*N*	Percentage	*N*	Percentage	
Catalogues	148	12	780	63	312	25	1240
Edgewood	159	24	268	40	238	36	665
Total	307		1048		550		1905

obtained was highly significant ($\chi^2 = 95.6$, $df = 2$, $p < .001$), which indicates that the archaeological sample had more serving vessels and fewer eating vessels than would have been expected from the comparative frequencies of the two types of vessels found in the catalogue. What would account for an increase in the use of serving vessels and a decrease in the use of eating vessels? To further explore this question, a comparison of four basic forms—plates, bowls, cups, and saucers—was made for the Edgewood and Silcott sites, using the catalogue set as an example (Table 13.5). There was a higher-than-expected frequency of bowls at Edgewood, whereas cups had a higher-than-expected frequency at Silcott. The frequencies of saucers were about equal and within the expected range at both sites. Plates were underrepresented at both archaeological sites. Whereas the ratios of bowls to other forms at Silcott was similar to the ideal set, Edgewood appears to deviate from the norm.

The predominance of bowl forms at Edgewood suggests a high proportion of foods prepared as soups and stews, which would require the frequent use of bowls. The faunal remains from the site were examined to test this hypothesis. This study produced relatively high ratios of soup bones to other cuts of meat (see Edmiston, Chapter 15). Further analysis of other categories of remains, including bottles (see Hill, Chapter 12), plant remains, and hardware, now indicates that the Edgewood deposit represents fall–winter activities, possibly centering around Thanksgiving and Christmas. One would expect more use of soups and stews in the cold months and at times of greater food consumption. Conversely, the frequent use of bowls should result in the infrequent use of other "eating" forms, as is evidenced in Table 13.5.

Although the lower-than-expected frequencies of plates at both sites suggest that plates were used less than other forms, it may also suggest that tablewares were not purchased in sets. Whereas Edgewood and Silcott both have some evidence for matched sets in the assemblages (i.e., sherds representing various forms which have the same body type and decoration), there is also evidence for unmatched pieces. Individual pieces of ceramics were available from several sources by the end of the nineteenth century. For instance, several companies marketing soap and food items offered individual pieces as premiums with the purchase of their products (Johnson 1961:106; Ray 1974:26).[7] Additionally, the availability of ceramics as open-stock merchandise, both from local merchants and through the mail-order catalogues, allowed the consumer to select only those functional forms most appropriate for his particular eating patterns. This availability through open stock of individual pieces of undecorated ceramics as replacements for broken sets may have been a critical resource. On the other hand, the limited selection of open-stock patterns may have reduced their salability.

Further insight into the value of a combined formal–functional taxonomy is seen in the data for related forms, such as cups and saucers. At both Edgewood and

[7] In 1901–1902, the Buffalo Pottery was established by the owners of the Larkin Soap Manufacturing Company to produce a line of ceramics to be used as premiums with their products. Since 1920, the company has made hotelware exclusively (Ray 1974:26).

Table 13.5 Comparison of Some Basic Forms from Edgewood, Silcott, and the Catalogue Sets

Item	Catalogue		Silcott		Edgewood		Total
	N	Percentage	N	Percentage	N	Percentage	
Plates	24	40	45	30	165	29	234
Bowls	12	20	33	22	168	29	213
Cups	12	20	46	31	112	20	170
Saucers	12	20	26	17	123	22	161
Total	60		150		568		778

Silcott, the frequency of saucers corresponds to the expected, as established by the catalogue sets (Table 13.5). While the same is true for cups at Edgewood, there is a higher-than-expected frequency of these forms at Silcott (Gaw 1976:169). Therefore, the data suggest a pattern of increased "drinking" behavior at Silcott as well as the "style" of that behavior. Does the use of cups without saucers reflect the absence of women (i.e., "refinement"), frugality, or just convenience?

Manufacture-Deposition Intervals

Because of the need to establish "standard" manufacture-deposition lag intervals for late-nineteenth- and early-twentieth-century urban sites, South's (1972:71–116) Mean Ceramic Date Formula was applied to the ceramic assemblage from the Edgewood site. Use of the formula is based on documented dates of manufacture for individual marks as defined in the literature. South's procedure for finding the median manufacture date is followed for each mark or duplicate marks, and the mean date for the assemblage is calculated. By substracting the mean ceramic date from the historically documented *terminus ante quem* date for the site, the calculated manufacture-deposition lag for that particular ceramic assemblage is determined (Table 13.6).

For Edgewood, whereas minimal documentation was established for 23 makers' marks, the most specific temporal data come from those manufacturers who made frequent changes in their trademarks. However, because much of the documentation available for American trademarks is very general (i.e., the name of the pottery and the year it was established often is the only information noted), many of the dates used represent an extended interval for the use of that mark. For marks with no ending use-date noted (i.e., the company is still in business and there are no mark-specific dates given), the historically documented date of the site was used as the ending date for that mark. A median date representing the use of each mark was determined and multiplied by its frequency to arrive at a product. Following South's formula, the sum of the product was divided by the total count (23) of identifiable marks, producing a mean ceramic date of 1892.2 for the Edgewood assemblage. This figure cannot serve as the date of the site, because by definition the use of some identified marks began after this date. However, by subtracting this figure (1892.2) from the documented date of the site (1911), a mean manufacture-deposition interval (lag) can be determined (18.8 years). This average time lag—the time between the manufacture and the deposition of the ceramics used by the residents of the Edgewood neighborhood—can then be used in an intrasite comparison with the calculated manufacture-deposition intervals for other artifact groups, and explanations may be sought for any significant differences. Such a comparison was made between the ceramics and the glass bottles at Edgewood. The 11-year lag calculated for glass bottles (see Hill, Chapter 12) indicates that the bottles were discarded sooner than the ceramics. This temporal dissimilarity may be explained by the fact that ceramics are themselves "products," whereas bottles are merely "containers" for

Table 13.6 Calculated Manufacture-Deposition Lag for the Edgewood Site Ceramic Assemblage

Manufacturer	Inclusive dates	Median date	Count	Product
Cook Pottery Company, USA	1892-1900	1896	1	1,896
D and Company, France	1847-1893	ca.1875	1	1,875
Haviland and Company, France	1893-1911	ca.1889	1	1,889
Henry Alcock and Company, USA	1891-1900	1895.5	1	1,895.5
Homer Laughlin, USA	1879-1911	1895	7	13,265
John Maddock and Sons, England	1891-1896	1893.5	1	1,893.5
John Maddock and Sons, Limited, England	1891-1901	ca.1896	1	1,896
Johnson Brothers, England	1891-1910	ca.1900	1	1,900
KT & K, USA	1872-1911	1890	1	1,890
Knowles, Taylor and Knowles, USA	1872-1911	1890	1	1,890
Knowles, Taylor and Knowles Company, USA	1890-1900	1895	1	1,895
Mercer Pottery Company, USA	1868-1900	1884	3	5,652
Steubenville Pottery Company, USA	1879-1900	1889.5	1	1,889.5

(Continued)

Table 13.6 (*Continued*)

Manufacturer	Inclusive dates	Median date	Count	Product
Theodore Haviland, France	1891-1903	ca.1903	1	1,903
Wedgwood and Company, England	1875-1908	1891.5	1	1,891.5
Total			23	43,521

Deposition date 1911

Mean manufacture date 1892.2

Lag 18.8 years

$$\frac{\text{Total product}}{\text{Total count}} \quad \frac{43{,}521}{23} = 1{,}892.2$$

products and would therefore stand a greater chance of being discarded when the contents were exhausted.

The potential for use of the Mean Ceramic Date Formula extends beyond calculating the temporal placement of a ceramic assemblage, however, to the question of durability of technological types and forms. Determination of the variable life span of ceramic body types, therefore, may be explored by calculating separate time lags for each technological category. Although the Edgewood sample is too small to treat statistically, trends are in the direction one might expect:

1. Porcelain has the greatest lag, 20.25 years. (Assumptions: Porcelain is strong and, because it costs more, is used less and is better cared for.).
2. Earthenware has a lag of 18.72 years (Assumptions: Earthenware is the weakest ware, is the most commonly used, and has been manufactured for a long period of time.).
3. Stoneware has the shortest lag, 17 years. (This is understandable at this point because the product is relatively new.).

There is no porcelaneous stoneware in this assemblage, since this ware did not become available until the late 1880s and then was used mostly in commercial establishments.

As similar data are forthcoming from other archaeological sites, some standards may be established that will allow dating of twentieth-century sites on the basis of a standard manufacture-deposition lag for ceramics, which can be an important tool for temporal placement of a site when there is no available documentary evidence. Furthermore, and perhaps most importantly, once enough data are compiled to establish standard lag intervals, significant deviations should help identify behavioral processes (and technological variables) that were operating within specific spatial and cultural parameters.

Socioeconomic Interpretations

Use of ceramics for interpreting the socioeconomic level of a group contributing to a site is addressed through the analysis of ceramic body and decoration types. Table 13.7 shows the frequencies of these categories at the Edgewood site, with notable absences in two areas. The body type "porcelaneous stoneware" was not present, nor was the decorative category "geometric" and its variations. The most predominant type present is earthenware, which constitutes 58% of the total sherd count. It is followed by porcelain at 26%, stoneware at 16%, and traditional utilitarian stoneware at 2%. The large amounts of earthenware (51% of which were in the "plain" white and "raised" white-on-white decoration categories) are interpreted as representing "everyday" dishes, more utilitarian than stylish. And the smaller amounts of porcelain suggest that it was a "Sunday" or "special occasion" ware, used less and thus broken less. However, because 19% of the earthenware and 19% of the stoneware have some gold included in the decoration, it is suggested that these may represent a third level of social significance for that neighborhood. That

Table 13.7 Body Type and Decoration Frequencies of the Edgewood Ceramics

Code	Earthenware		Stoneware		Porcelaneous stoneware		Porcelain		Total
	N	Percentage	N	Percentage	N	Percentage	N	Percentage	
P	177	26	45	24			65	21	287
PG	20	3	9	5					29
R	172	25	17	9			36	12	225
RG	23	3	14	7			13	4	50
F	37	5	8	4			30	10	75
FR	72	10	26	14			57	19	155
FG	40	6	2	1			28	9	70
FRG	47	7	11	6			36	12	94
GM									
GMR									
GMRG									
B	1		8	4					9
SP	5	1	1	1					6
SOG	18	2	19	10					37
TT			22	12					22
U	68	10					1		69
Other	11	2	6	3			38	12	55
Total	691		188				304		1183

is, the gold-trimmed earthenwares and stonewares may have served as the Sunday-special occasion dishes for some of the contributing households. The small amount (2%) of traditional stoneware (along with the presence of industrial utilitarian forms) suggests that the shift from cottage to industrial manufacture and distribution was well along, but not yet complete, for 1910 suburbanites of Atlanta. This mixed assemblage supports a temporal placement of the site in the early twentieth century.

To summarize, the Edgewood ceramic assemblage represents a modest way of life, demonstrated by the utilitarian quality of the majority of the wares. The amounts of utilitarian vessels, both for the preparation and storage of foods, suggest that the background of the neighborhood had been rural, with the urban transition not yet complete. There was, however, an element of the social importance of the tableservice as shown by the presence of the gold decorated wares and the porcelain.

Identification of Site Function

Another use of technological data, when combined with formal–functional attributes, is in predicting the function of a site. At the Edgewood site, all categories of artifacts suggested a domestic situation. At another small garbage deposit in Atlanta, however, the archaeologists depended almost entirely on the ceramics to identify the context of the materials. Mass-produced, white-bodied stoneware comprised 51% of the assemblage, and porcelaneous stoneware, 26%. Earthenware at 22% and porcelain at 1% completed the assemblage. Because the more durable body types were commonly used by commercial establishments, an interpretation of this site as a public eating establishment was made. The decoration types also supported this interpretation (and logos were included in some of the banded designs). Formal–functional categories included platters, plates, cups, saucers, lids, and miscellaneous serving pieces, some of which were formed to hold oysters-on-the-half-shell. The category that stood out as most distinctive, however, was "lids." Nine percent of the total sherds were lid fragments, the majority of which were from a thick, heavy stoneware, having a raised-ribbon design for decoration. These have been identified as chamber pot lids. Although the tableware pieces would suggest a restaurant, the presence of an unusual number of chamber pot lid fragments suggests a restaurant-and-hotel. Therefore, in this instance, the presence of durable tablewares that were manufactured by the turn of the century as special-use items, and a household utilitarian item appearing in unusually high numbers, combine, in the absence of documentary evidence, to provide a site function identification.

Trade Patterns

Trade patterns reflected in the archaeological record offer the researcher insights into the development of urban–industrial culture and its impact on nonurban areas. For ceramics, designation of the origin of the manufacturer results from analysis of trademarks. As has been mentioned earlier, not all pieces were marked at the time of manufacture, so that only those sherds containing readable marks may be used in this kind of analysis.

The history of the origin of ceramics for the American market is grounded in British colonialism. British ceramic manufacturers were delighted with the new marketplace and were so eager to cater to that market that decorative patterns commemorating American places and events became common export items. In addition, heavier, plain, and inexpensive wares suitable for life on the frontier were developed for export. American manufacturers successfully produced redwares, yellow-wares, and brownwares from the mid-1880s, but it was not until the last quarter of the nineteenth century that these manufacturers were successful in securing a respectable place in the home market. Part of this success lay in the development of wares of added toughness, special-use, and greater variety, all of which were demanded by a culture that rapidly was becoming industrialized. Relative to this history, it is likely that the earlier the site, the higher will be the percentage of tablewares made in England (imported); by the turn of the century, amounts of domestic and imported wares should be about equal; and twentieth-century sites should have greater amounts of domestic wares. Deviations would be explained by isolation from trading centers or special site functions.

Atlanta's location at the intersection of several major rail lines provided the city access to widespread trade outlets, and the archaeological record reflects the availability of varied domestic and imported wares during the late nineteenth and early twentieth centuries (Table 13.8). Of 35 trademarks from the Edgewood assemblage that can be identified by the country of origin, 49% are domestic products and 51% are imported. It is significant, also, that the choice was not limited to American and British goods. Austrian wares comprised 33% of the imports, British wares 28%, French 23%, and German 16%. In addition, the domestic wares reflect access to various producers, for example, five different manufacturers are represented by the 16 domestic trademarks. The latter frequencies suggest the importance of Atlanta's role in turn-of-the-century American trade networks.

By contrast, Silcott, although importing 65% of its ceramics, had a more limited selection (or chose more selectively). Goods from Silcott were almost equally divided between American wares (35%) and British wares (40%), with only 25% coming from other countries. A major source for that isolated area may have been the mail-order catalogue, which included similar amounts of British and American products. Even though the Silcott assemblage represents a later period of occupation, the greater frequencies of British goods suggest limited access to domestic sources and non-British foreign sources.

It is useful to take a similar chronological approach to the relative frequencies of traditional stoneware versus industrial utilitarian stoneware. Early agrarian-based economies in the South used large amounts of traditional stoneware for food-related utilitarian vessels and household utilitarian vessels (Dickens and Worthy 1981). As the mass-produced wares became more available in urban areas, the traditional wares diminished in use. The archaeological record should indicate this chronological shift in form and technology: a shift from all utilitarian stoneware items being

Table 13.8 Geographical Source Areas, Designated by Makers' Mark Analysis

	Archaeological site information					
	Edgewood 1911 urban domestic		Silcott 1900-1930 rural community		Hotel dump 1911-1920 urban special use	
Trademark origin	N	Percentage	N	Percentage	N	Percentage
United States	17	49	7	35	63	94
England	5	14	8	40	4	6
Austria	6	17				
France	4	11				
Germany	3	9	2	10		
Poland			1	5		
Orient			2	10		
Total	35		20		67	

handmade in the late 1800s, to relatively balanced proportions of handmade and mass-produced wares at the turn of the century, to relatively few traditional wares in the twentieth century. As a demonstration of this chronology and the manner in which these sites fit into the domestic-local trade network, the following comparison is offered. At the Brand House site (a rural domestic site of ca. 1860 in Paulding County, Georgia), all of the utilitarian stoneware (25% of total sherd count) was traditional, whereas at the Edgewood site (an urban domestic site of 1911), the utilitarian stoneware (7% of total sherd count) was 29% traditional and 71% industrial. (For more information on the role of cottage manufacture as it relates to the rural–urban culture process, see Faulkner, Chapter 8.)

CONCLUSIONS

In summary, the use of a formal–functional taxonomy for the classification and analysis of late-nineteenth- and early-twentieth-century ceramics is essential if urban archaeologists are to maximize the effectiveness of their behavioral interpretations. This is especially true because of major changes around the turn of the century in ceramic technology, in demands of the market, and in availability of domestic wares. Therefore, through the development of standards (e.g., a contemporary "ideal" tableservice, manufacture-deposition lag intervals, and chronological expectancies for types) to be used in conjunction with various documentary sources and with the quantitative data organized by such a taxonomy, questions relating to eating habits, trade networks, product durability, product use, temporal placement, and site-specific activities may be addressed. And finally, intra- and intersite comparisons, based on data organized in this formal–functional system, will contribute to the elucidation of larger patterns and processes of urban–industrial culture in America.

ACKNOWLEDGMENTS

I wish to express my appreciation to Roy Dickens for his direction of the research on which this chapter was based and for his continued encouragement and advice as the process of developing this classification system progressed.

REFERENCES

Adams, William H.
1977 Silcott, Washington: Ethnoarchaeology of a rural American community. *Laboratory of Anthropology. Washington State University, Reports of Investigations* **54.**

Adams, William H., Linda P. Gaw, and Frank C. Leonhardy
1975 Archaeological excavations at Silcott, Washington: The data inventory. *Laboratory of Anthropology. Washington State University, Reports of Investigations* **53.**

Burrison, John
1973 Georgia jug makers: A history of southern folk pottery. Ph.D. dissertation, University of Pennsylvania. University Microfilms, Ann Arbor, Michigan.

Chandler, Maurice
1968 *Ceramics in the modern world, mans first technology comes of age*. Garden City, N.Y.: Doubleday.
Cotter, John L.
1968 *Handbook for historical archaeology*. Wyncote, Penn.: John L. Cotter.
Cox, Warren E.
1953 *The book of pottery and porcelain*. New York: Crown.
Dickens, Roy S., Jr., and William R. Bowen
1980 Problems and promises in urban historical archaeology: The MARTA project. *Historical Archaeology* **14**:42–57.
Dickens, Roy S., Jr., and Linda H. Worthy
1981 *Archaeological investigations at the Brand house site, Pickett's Mill battlefield, Paulding County, Georgia*. In press.
Fontana, Bernard L., and J. Cameron Greenleaf
1962 Johnny Ward's Ranch: A study in historic archaeology. *The Kiva* **28**(1,2).
Gaw, Linda P.
1976 The availability and selection of ceramics in Silcott, Washington, 1900–1930. *Northwest Anthropological Research Notes* 9(1):166–179.
The G. & C. Merriam Company
1968 *Webster's third new international dictionary* (unabridged). Springfield, Mass.: Merriam.
Godden, Geoffrey A.
1964 *Encyclopedia of British pottery and porcelain marks*. New York: Bonanza.
Johnson, Laurence A.
1961 Something Extra. In *Over the counter and on the shelf: Country storekeeping in America, 1620–1920*, edited by Marcia Ray. Rutland, Vt.: Charles E. Tuttle. Pp. 101–106.
Kovel, Ralph M., and Terry H. Kovel
1965 *Dictionary of marks—pottery and porcelain*. New York: Crown.
Leach, Bernard
1976 *A potter's book*. London: Faber and Faber.
Montgomery Ward and Company
1969 *Montgomery Ward & Company, 1895*, Unabridged facsimile, Catalogue No. 57. New York: Dover.
Miller, George L.
1980 Classification and economic scaling of nineteenth-century ceramics. *Historical Archaeology* **14**:1–40.
Noël Hume, Ivor
1974 *A guide to artifacts of colonial America*. New York: Knopf.
Quimby, Ian M. G. (editor)
1973 *Ceramics in America*. Charlottesville: Univ. Press of Virginia.
Ramsay, John
1976 *American potters & pottery*. Ann Arbor, Mich.: Ars Ceramics.
Ray, Marcia
1974 *Collectible ceramics*. New York: Crown.
Schiffer, Michael B.
1972 Archaeological context and systemic context. *American Antiquity* **37**(2):156–165.
1977 Toward a unified science of the cultural past. In *Research strategies in historical archeology*, edited by Stanley South. New York: Academic Press. Pp. 13–40.
Searle, Alfred B.
1915 *Clays and clay products*. London: Sir Isaac Pitman.
Sears Roebuck and Company
1968 *Sears Roebuck catalogue—1897*. New York: Chelsea.

South, Stanley
1972 Evolution and horizon as revealed in ceramic analysis in historical archeology. *Conference on Historic Site Archeology Papers* **71**(2):71–116.

Spargo, John
1926 *Early American pottery and china.* New York: Garden City.

Stillinger, Elizabeth
1972 *The antiques guide to decorative arts in America 1600–1875.* New York: E. P. Dutton.

Taylor, Sally
1950 *China and other dinnerware.* New York: Fairchild.

Thorn, C. Jordan
1947 *Handbook of old pottery and porcelain marks.* New York: Tudor.

Turnbaugh, Sarah Peabody, and William A. Turnbaugh
1980 New applications of South's mean ceramic date formula. *Pattern and Meaning* **2**(1), Conference on Historic Site Archeology.

14

Material Culture, Social Structure, and Changing Cultural Values: The Ceramics of Eighteenth- and Nineteenth-Century Middletown, Connecticut

Stephen L. Dyson

Since 1974, Wesleyan University archaeological research in Middletown, Connecticut has centered on eight sites located in a downtown area that developed and prospered in the period 1780–1830. This chapter focuses on the analysis and interpretation of ceramics from the eight sites. These studies show some variation in the sites related to social status and occupation, but also many basic similarities related to common behavior patterns. They also show that the ceramics mirror certain general social, economic, and cultural trends of late-eighteenth- and early-nineteenth-century New England.

Middletown is located on the west bank of the Connecticut River about 31 miles (49.8 km) from the mouth of the river. Following its founding in 1650, the community, which then included the present towns of Cromwell, East Hampton, Middlefield, and Portland, began by developing its agricultural hinterland.[1] From the mid-eighteenth century onward, however, the citizens of Middletown turned increasingly toward shipping and established a trade network centered on supplying agricultural commodities to the West Indies. By the last two decades of the eighteenth century, Middletown had become one of the major secondary ports of New England, rivaling such centers as Providence, Newport, and New London (Martin 1938–1939). The growing importance of shipping contributed to the de-

[1]For the history of Middletown in this period, see Field (1819), Beers (1884), and Wallace (1950). Maps and views of Middletown for these years include a 1783 map of Middletown, an 1819 map of Middlesex County, an 1825 map of Middletown in the Wesleyan University library, and a ca. 1800 view of Middletown (painted by Mary Russell) in the Connecticut Historical Society.

ARCHAEOLOGY OF URBAN AMERICA
The Search for Pattern and Process

ISBN 0-12-214980-7

velopment of a section of the city between the principal street (now Main Street) and the river, where many members of the mercantile community began to build their homes. A series of maps and views of Middletown dated from 1783 to 1825 illustrate well this development.

The bustling and diversified shipping community was not destined to last. The embargo of 1807, the War of 1812, the panic of 1819, and the increasing problems of shipping profitably to a relatively small upriver port all doomed Middletown as a major nautical center. The shrewder citizens turned increasingly to manufacturing, taking advantage of the numerous small waterfalls in the area and a developed base of grist, powder, and saw mills. Manufacturing, too, was destined to have a limited future in Middletown, but its rise and fall is beyond the scope of this chapter.

The most important factor in the development of the archaeological research program in Middletown has been the impact of highway construction and urban renewal. The old shipping quarter between Main Street and the river had remained structurally intact although socially and economically drastically altered during the period between 1830 and 1945. The first major change came with the construction of Connecticut Route 9 along the river, which resulted in the destruction of the waterfront area and a severing of the city from its river heritage. Highway construction was followed by the institution of an ambitious urban renewal project, which ultimately leveled most of the central and southern parts of the old shipping district. It was in 1974, during the final phase of this demolition, that the Wesleyan archaeological project was begun.

Most urban archaeology in the United States has been limited to the investigation of a few scattered areas within individual cities, usually where the continual process of destruction and rebuilding has opened random sites. In contrast, the Middletown urban renewal project leveled a whole quarter, one which had developed during a single period and which could provide a cross section of the archaeological remains for an important phase of New England urban development. The main problems have been limited financial resources and limited time.

The early inception of the Middletown urban renewal project meant that no initial archaeological investigation had been required and no mitigation funds were available. In 1974, the city envisioned rapid development of the area, which would have provided only one or two short seasons of limited salvage archaeology. Fortunately, however, a series of complex local factors slowed the pace of development and allowed for additional excavation seasons. Work was carried out on several sites during the spring months of 1974–1980, the fall of 1976, and the summer of 1977, and was resumed in the spring of 1981. Although a reasonable number of sites have been investigated, the uncertain pace of urban renewal has not allowed us to develop research strategies as carefully as we would have liked or to undertake more intensive preseason documentary investigation.

As of the spring of 1981, we have conducted extensive open-area excavations at five sites, done a short salvage dig at one, and cleared trash pits at two others. These sites, located on the accompanying 1825 map of Middletown (Figure 14.1) are (1) the Magill site (1974–1975); (2) the Hall site (1976–1977); (3) the Danforth site

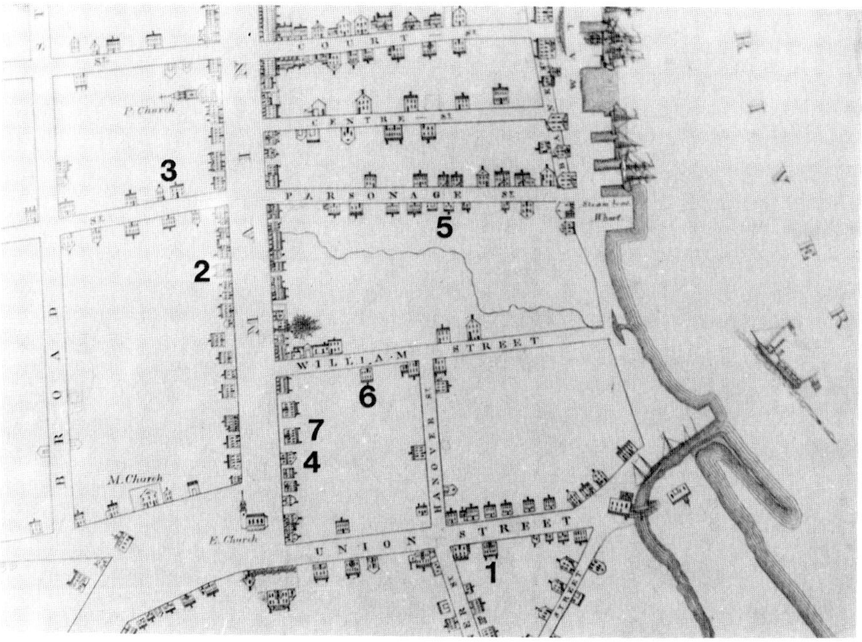

FIGURE 14.1. 1825 map of Middletown, with locations of archaeological sites.

(1979); (4) the White Eagle site (1980–1981); (5) the Metro South site (1978); (6) the Southmayd site (1977); and (7) the Watkinson site (1977). The Phillips-Warner site (1976) is located just to the north of the areas shown in the map. In most cases, the names given to these sites derive from the family name of the most important owner of the property.

All excavations took place in the vicinity of standing or recently razed structures. Usually, they were open-area excavations designed to recover evidence of structures around the house and to obtain a representative sample of backyard artifact scatters. At two of the sites (Southmayd and Watkinson), we concentrated on the excavation of trash pits. The material recovered is currently being stored and processed in the Wesleyan University archaeological laboratory.

The largest and most representative body of material is the ceramics, which will form the basis of the interpretative part of this chapter. Most of these sherds were found in the backyard scatters. Since layers of accumulation were thin and there was much disturbance, the stratigraphic significance of these finds is limited. However, most of the sherds can be identified and dated, and they seem to provide a representative cross section of the pottery in use in the various households over the time span of their occupations. The two trash pits at Southmayd and Watkinson did contain a large number of restorable vessels, which allowed for the comparison of sherd and vessel frequencies.

Table 14.1 Sherd Distributions for the Middletown Sites

	Magill	Hall	Southmayd	Watkinson	Metro South	Danforth	White Eagle
Salt-glazed ware		49		7	47	8	
Scratched blue					5		26
Sgraffito							4
Jackfield			67		7	8	36
Plain creamware	1184	1302	935	1177	668	196	814
Decorated creamware			52	47	3		2
Blue-edged pearlware	114	151	466	116	46	80	76
Green-edged pearlware	174	215	130	396	16	20	152
Hand-painted Chinese pearlware	236	115	24	103	153	16	35
Hand-painted blue flower pearlware	21		134	133			
Multicolored flower pearlware	156	247	160	323	70	42	149
Transparent Chinese pearlware	15	36	74	391	75	9	37
Blue Willow pearlware	38	33	161	21			

Romantic pearlware	65	226	606	130	123		
Miscellaneous pearlware	431	411	122	214	78	151	437
Blue-white porcelain	97	45	1	13	33	36	85
Multicolored porcelain	25	35	48	102	4	9	39
Miscellaneous porcelain	45	101	2	100	92	5	13
Rouen ware	57	5					
Mocha ware	6	7				5	15
Yellow slipped ware	43	56	20	3	12	35	
Black basalt ware	6			42			16
Glazed earthenware	134	306		436	39	72	206
Machine-turned redware	38	1		20			
Stoneware	12	149	228	42	57	49	38
Blue Staffordshire	72	69	215	8	13	36	47
Purple Staffordshire	48	10				6	6
Pink Staffordshire	16	29	18		1	2	8
Green Staffordshire	10	10				2	4
Brown Staffordshire	24	23	293	6	3	58	7
Black Staffordshire	14	14	16		1	44	6
White ware (plain)	168	155			281	297	114
White ware (decorated)	38	4			9	36	15

Table 14.2 Frequencies and Percentages of Ceramic Types by Site

	Creamware	Pearlware	Porcelain	Staffordshire ironstone	Total
Magill	1184(42)	1281(46)	167(6)	181(6)	2813
Hall	1302(42)	1444(47)	181(6)	155(5)	3082
Danforth	196(23)	481(55)	50(6)	148(16)	875
White Eagle	816(39)	1056(51)	137(6)	78(4)	2087
Metro South	668(23)	1436(50)	129(4)	668(23)	2901
Southmayd	935(27)	1889(55)	51(2)	542(16)	3417
Watkinson	1224(36)	1931(57)	215(6)	14(1)	3384
Phillips-Warner	123(18)	515(73)	20(3)	44(6)	702

The sherd frequencies for seven of the sites are given in Table 14.1. The sample from Phillips-Warner was small and the resulting conclusions less secure than those for the other sites. It has, therefore, been omitted. In general, standard historical ceramic designations based on Noël Hume's (1970) have been used in classifying the artifacts. I have divided the blue-and-white transfer-printed pearlwares into two major categories of "Chinese" and "Romantic," based on a change in motifs from the classic chinoiserie to the rural and travel scenes that reflect tastes of the Romantic movement. The former were popular prior to 1820 and the latter in the 1820s and 1830s. In calculating percentages of wares, I have not included the nineteenth- and twentieth-century whitewares, although the frequencies have been included. These later wares vary considerably in quantity by site and distort the results concerning the relative frequency of ceramics in use for the period 1750–1850, which is central to this study. Some evidence on the occupational histories of the sites, as reconstructed from documentary evidence, will be given later. However, for the purposes of ceramic comparison it should be noted that all sites were occupied by the 1780s.

The first comparison can be made in the four major categories of creamware, pearlware, porcelain, and Staffordshire ironstone (Table 14.2). In considering these tabulations, one should keep in mind that Southmayd and Watkinson were trash pits and thus had an accumulation history different from the backyard scatters. Except for sample size, the assemblages from the other six sites are comparable. They show a dominance of creamwares and pearlwares, with small percentages of porcelains and ironstone (as well as small amounts of a few other wares). The high percentage of creamware corresponds well with the known initial occupation of the sites. Although Middletown had been inhabited since 1650, most of the houses we have investigated were built in the last third of the eighteenth century, during the period of greatest shipping prosperity. The Magill house dates to the 1780s. The first record of a dwelling on the Hall property comes from the 1790s; the first Danforth structure dates to 1787; the White Eagle site was developed around 1752–1753; the Southmayd house dates to 1747; the Phillips-Warner house was built 1780–1783; and a house was built on the Metro South site by 1772. Dates for the initial occupation at Watkinson are less clear. The brick house near the trash pit dates ca. 1810 but small amounts of salt-glazed and other earlier wares in the deposit suggest Revolutionary or immediately post-Revolutionary habitation.

Rather unexpected at all sites is the low percentage of ironstone and even the later whitewares. At Magill, Hall, White Eagle, and Phillips-Warner, ironstone represented 6% or less of the total pottery inventory in the four categories under discussion. At Danforth the percentage was 16, and at Metro South it was 23. The Watkinson trash pit had a very low percentage of ironstone (less than 1%), although that is a reflection of the fact that the pit went out of use before these later wares became popular. Considering that all of the sites were inhabited continuously until the post-World War II period, this low percentage is striking and requires explanation. One possibility is that waste disposal practices and attitudes changed during the second quarter of the nineteenth century. By that time, garbage collection certainly became more regular, which meant that backyards were used less as dumping grounds.

It is also possible that the changes are related to the altered socioeconomic character of the neighborhoods. Study of the social history of Middletown is just beginning, and it has not been possible to do the detailed neighborhood analyses that will allow the correlation of archaeology and social history. However, the whole area under investigation certainly declined in relative economic status, which meant fewer ceremonial events, such as teas and dinners, and ultimately fewer sherds of quality crockery.

Pearlwares were the most common ceramics in each excavation. Since occupations at all of the sites spanned most of the period of pearlware use (Noël Hume 1970:128–132), they provide information on changing tastes in pearlwares. The first categories represented in the sites are the three major tea service types: (*a*) hand-painted pearlware with chinoiserie motifs, (*b*) transfer prints with chinoiserie, and (*c*) so-called "Romantic" pearlware with scenes taken mainly from rural life in England and from the "Grand Tour." Table 14.3 shows sherd counts and percentages of pearlware by site.

Since sherd frequencies for many of the sites are relatively small, interpretations must remain tentative. However, significant variations seem to exist. At Hall, Danforth, White Eagle, Southmayd, and Phillips-Warner, the Romantic pearlwares consistently comprise 60% or more of the total pearlware sample. This suggests either an increasing percentage of goods available or rising prosperity, which allowed households to possess more of these status tea-service wares. The manufacture dates of most of these wares are after the 1807–1814 period when Middletown began to decline as a port center. Two sites, Metro South and Magill, have a high

Table 14.3 Frequencies and Percentages of Pearlwares by Site

	Hand-painted pearlware (pre-1780-1790)	Transfer-printed pearlware (1780-1800)	Romantic pearlware (1800-1830)	Total
Magill	236(75)	15(5)	65(20)	316
Hall	115(30)	36(10)	226(60)	377
Danforth	16(9)	9(5)	163(86)	180
White Eagle	35(15)	37(15)	170(70)	242
Metro South	153(44)	75(21)	123(35)	351
Southmayd	24(3)	74(11)	606(86)	704
Watkinson	103(17)	391(63)	130(20)	624
Phillips-Warner	22(16)	19(14)	97(70)	138

percentage of hand-painted chinoiserie wares. At present, however, not enough is known about the inhabitants of Metro South to comment further on the reason for this high percentage.

Historical information on the Magill house is more precise. The site is named after Charles Magill, a Middletown sea captain involved in the West Indies trade. Magill prospered in the period just after the American Revolution, and during the 1780s, he built himself a fine house on what was later to become Union Street (Figure 14.2). However, Magill's fortunes fell equally rapidly, and by 1800, he was bankrupt. His household goods were divided among his creditors and, during the early years of the nineteenth century, the house itself went through a confused period of ownership. The quantities of hand-painted chinoiserie pieces very likely reflect the tea services purchased for this newly constructed house in 1790–1800, whereas the relative lack of transfer prints probably can be attributed to the decline of Magill's fortunes and unstable occupation during the early nineteenth century.

Another unusual feature in Table 14.3 is the high percentage of transfer-printed chinoiserie in the Watkinson group. This is also reflected in the vessel count. The site derives its name from the Watkinsons, a prosperous merchant family whose house stood nearby. There is no absolute proof that the trash pit belonged to the Watkinsons, but that would be a likely supposition. The number of transfer-printed chinoiserie pieces suggests a household that was refurbishing its china cabinet at the turn of the century, perhaps as a result of new-found prosperity. This prosperity also would be reflected in large amounts of broken pottery, the result of frequent social events.

Also popular among the pearlwares were multicolored, hand-painted, floral-decorated pieces. Table 14.4 gives the frequencies and percentages of these multico-

FIGURE 14.2. The Magill site.

Table 14.4 Frequencies and Percentages of Transfer-Printed Pearlwares by Site

	Multicolored floral pearlware	Blue-and-white pearlware	Total
Magill	156(33)	316(67)	472
Hall	247(39)	377(61)	624
Danforth	42(18)	188(82)	230
White Eagle	149(38)	242(62)	391
Metro South	70(16)	351(84)	421
Southmayd	160(18)	704(82)	864
Watkinson	323(34)	624(66)	947
Phillips-Warner	25(15)	138(85)	163

Table 14.5 Frequencies and Percentages of Edged Pearlwares by Site

	Blue-edged	Green-edged
Magill	114(39)	174(61)
Hall	151(41)	215(59)
Danforth	80(80)	20(20)
White Eagle	76(33)	152(67)
Metro South	46(67)	16(33)
Southmayd	466(78)	130(22)
Watkinson	116(22)	396(78)
Phillips-Warner	54(64)	31(36)

lored sherds, which can be compared to the three categories of blue-and-white pearlwares in Table 14.3. Since some of the samples are quite small, caution has to be used in evaluating the relative frequencies. However, it should be noted that two distinct groups seem to be present. In Magill, Hall, White Eagle, and Watkinson, the multicolored sherds form more than 30% of the group. At Danforth, Metro South, Southmayd, and Phillips-Warner, the figures are 18% or lower. The reconstructable vessels from the Southmayd and Watkinson groups show that, whereas the multicolored floral pattern was used on mugs and tea cups, the most popular use was for punch bowls. The different figures in the two groups suggest that the importance of the ritual of communal drinking, symbolized by the punch bowl, varied from household to household.

A final subgroup of pearlwares worthy of separate consideration is the green-edged and blue-edged dining and service plates. Table 14.5 summarizes the frequencies and percentages for this category at the various sites. Again, two distinct groups emerge. Magill, Hall, White Eagle, and Watkinson show clear preference for green over blue, whereas Danforth, Metro South, Southmayd, and Phillips-Warner preferred the blue. In general, the green-edged plates seem earlier than the blue-edged types on American sites (Noël Hume 1970:132; Miller 1980:27–28). Danforth, Metro South, and Southmayd also have high percentages of Staffordshire ironstone. Danforth, Southmayd, and Phillips-Warner also have a higher percentage of the later Romantic pearlwares, but so do Hall and White Eagle. It is possible that more green-edged wares reflect households that built up their ceramic inventories earlier. However, factors of personal and family taste also may be involved.

In contrast to the variation within the pearlware category, porcelain is a consistent 6% of the five major groups at Magill, Hall, Danforth, White Eagle, and Watkinson, and 4% at Metro South. The minor wares are not numerous enough for any statistical commentary. However, the presence or absence of certain material does provide insight into the inhabitants of the sites. Probably the most unexpected ceramic at the Magill site was Rouen ware (Figure 14.3), which was found in some quantity (57 sherds representing several vessels). Magill is the only Middletown excavation to yield Rouen ware in significant quantities, with the only other find being a group of five sherds from Hall. The Rouen ware should date to the last years of the eighteenth century at the latest (Noël Hume 1960). At that time, Captain Magill occupied the house. The presence of these French ceramics as well as other finds, such as a Spanish silver coin of 1788, probably reflects Captain Magill's trade in the West Indies.

It has already been noted that Magill produced a large number of hand-painted

FIGURE 14.3. Rouen ware plate from the Magill site. (Shown one half actual size.)

chinoiserie pearlware sherds and that these can be interpreted as a reflection of the Captain's sudden rise in fortune. Also indicative of this is the considerable quantity of drinking glass fragments of Stiegel-derived types (Hunter 1950:219–220).[2] Finally, the Magill site produced a small amount of Wedgewood black basalt ware, a status ceramic found only on three sites in Middletown. White Eagle also produced some of this ware, but it was most conspicuous at the Watkinson site, where 43 sherds represented at least three distinct vessels.

The relative scarcity of types older than creamware and pearlware at all of the sites has already been noted, and this has been related to the mid-to-late eighteenth-century development of most of the sites thus far investigated. The small amounts of earlier wares that do appear at most of the sites indicate either sporadic earlier occupation, heirloom curation, or late persistence in the markets of some older ceramics. Salt-glazed earthenware was found in quantity (49 sherds) only at Hall, although scattered fragments appeared at Magill, Watkinson, Danforth, and Metro South. Scratched-blue pieces were found at Metro South and White Eagle, and the Southmayd trash pit produced a series of Jackfield teapots.

The total picture of ceramics from the Middletown sites shows market access to most of the major English ceramic distributors. Not only were the major pearlwares and creamwares available in quantities, but lesser wares such as black basalt, mochas, and annular wares (the latter two appearing in very small amounts) were also accessible. Shifts in the popularity of types also indicate a sensitivity to fashion and changing ideology. The best impression of this is obtained from the material found in the two trash pits.

The first and older of the two trash pits was found in the bottom section of a small (2 m or 6.5 ft east–west) stone-lined cellar uncovered during the course of laying a modern building foundation (Figure 14.4). The north wall of the cellar had been destroyed by the construction, and the recovery of the rest of the material was conducted under hasty emergency conditions. Most of the objects originally in the pit, however, seem to have been saved. In quantity and quality, the recovered artifacts represent the richest concentration of material culture found in any of the Middletown sites. As noted above, these artifacts seem most likely to represent debris from the activities of the Watkinson family who lived nearby.

The second trash pit was found on a Williams Street property, which, during most of the period when the dump was in use, belonged to the Middletown merchant family of the Southmayds. The house on the property was built in 1747 by William Southmayd, and the family continued to dwell there until 1825, when the dwelling was sold to a Lot D. Vansand, a rising Middletown manufacturer. Since the whole of the area around the house had been scraped by bulldozers in preparation for the laying out of a parking lot, it was not possible to recover the generalized backyard scatter typical of excavations at other sites. However, the grading did reveal several pockets of concentrated debris including a large, wood-lined trash pit similar

[2]Glass was found in considerable quantities at the Middletown sites. This material is currently being analyzed in the Wesleyan archaeology laboratory.

FIGURE 14.4. The Watkinson trash pit.

to the one found behind the Narbonne house at Salem (Moran 1976:197–201). The pit measured 2.1 × 3 m (6.9 × 9.8 ft), and except for a small amount of material presumably lost when the top soil was removed, all of the contents were recovered. These included large amounts of glass, bottles, and ceramics, as well as bone and shell.

The abundant material from these pits, including a large number of reconstructable vessels, allows a comparison with the finds from sites where only random sherds were recovered and provides a control for such controversial archaeological exercises as the use of sherd counts to reconstruct the ceramic portion of the material-culture universe of individual households. Additionally, the variety of vessels provides an insight into the changing aesthetic and cultural values of two Middletown families from the period just after the Revolution to the eve of the Mexican War. Although the groups overlap slightly in time, they provide a continuum. The Watkinson material begins in the last decades of the eighteenth century, and the Southmayd ceramics continue at least into the 1830s.[3]

On a methodological level, the approach that most interested us was to compare sherd numbers and minimal vessel counts to test the validity of the sherd count approach. From the Watkinson group, 251 vessels could be reconstructed. The Southmayd group produced a total of 233 vessels. Table 14.6 reproduces the counts and percentages for vessels, along with corresponding figures for sherds.

Although the total vessel count is relatively small, the percentage correspondences between vessels and sherds are, on the whole, relatively close. This finding supports the use of sherd counts to make general observations on the relative importance of certain ceramic types in household inventories.

Interesting to the social historian and the anthropologist is the impression the groups provide of changing tastes, ideologies, and world views in the individual households. The Southmayds were middle-class merchant shopkeepers. If the identification of the second group with the Watkinsons is correct, we are dealing with a family that belonged to the Middletown gentry. The latter interpretation is supported by the major functional categories of vessels: (*a*) those connected with drinking rituals (tea and punch drinking), (*b*) those associated with dining (mainly dinner services), and (*c*) those associated with common household functions (stoneware crocks, chamber pots, and kitchen wares). Perhaps the tea services are the most sensitive indicators of social activity and attention to fashion of the Watkinson family during the relatively short period of the hand-painted blue-on-white and Chinese-derived blue-on-white pearlwares. No less than seven sets of these wares can be detected. The family was evidently entertaining widely and buying new tea services in sets as the older dishes were either broken or became less fashionable. Not only was the tea served in the finest porcelain and English earthenware cups and saucers, but it was poured from black basalt teapots.[4]

[3]The terminal date of the Southmayd deposit is based on the multicolored Staffordshire ware, which would require a date in the 1820s at the earliest.

[4]For the importance of tea rituals during this period see Roth (1961). Also, Moran (1976:201) comments on the rarity of black basalt sherds in New England deposits.

For the 1790–1800 period, the Southmayd group has few fine vessels. This is probably due to a later date for the beginning of this deposit, a conclusion which is supported by the lower percentage of creamware. However, the presence of Jackfield ware and decorated creamwares does suggest initial refuse deposition during the last years of the eighteenth century. Another explanation for the limited amount of early fancy wares might relate to status. The Southmayd deposit also had more household glazed earthenware and stoneware vessels, types very poorly represented in Watkinson, perhaps another indicator of difference in social positions in the two families.

If this statement is a true reflection of the position of the Southmayds in the late

Table 14.6 Sherd Frequencies and Minimal Vessel Counts for Each Ceramic Category

		Watkinson	Southmayd
Creamware (all types)	Sherds	1224(35)	935(22)
	Vessels	58(3)	34(15)
Blue-edged pearlware	Sherds	116(3)	466(11)
	Vessels	11(4)	36(15)
Green-edged pearlware	Sherds	396(11)	130(3)
	Vessels	36(15)	5(2)
Hand-painted blue-and-white pearlware	Sherds	236(7)	158(4)
	Vessels	18(7)	6(3)
Transfer-printed Chinese pearlware	Sherds	391(11)	74(2)
	Vessels	30(12)	9(4)
Floral multicolored pearlware	Sherds	323(9)	160(4)
	Vessels	28(11)	5(2)
Romantic pearlware	Sherds	130(4)	606(14)
	Vessels	15(6)	59(25)
Blue Willow pearlware	Sherds	130(4)	161(4)
	Vessels	15(6)	12(5)
Pearlware total	Sherds	1931(55)	1889(44)
	Vessels	154(61)	123(53)
Porcelain total	Sherds	215(6)	15(03)
	Vessels	19(8)	2(1)
Staffordshire	Sherds	14(04)	542(13)
	Vessels	1(04)	37(16)
Others	Sherds	117(3)	752(18)
	Vessels	19(8)	25(11)
Grand total	Sherds	3522	4294
	Vessels	251	233

eighteenth and very early nineteenth centuries, it does not hold for the last years of the deposit. The Romantic pearlware and Staffordshire ironstone are well represented in the Southmayd material. Several distinct tea sets in Romantic pearlware and Staffordshire have been reconstructed. This increase in ceramic elegance may also reflect the transferal in ownership of the house from the Southmayds to the rising manufacturing family of the Vansands. On the other hand, it could reflect the spread downward of gentry life styles during the second and third decades of the nineteenth century. Such intriguing questions will require more investigation, but they suggest possibilities of interchange between ceramic specialists and urban social scientists.

Too often archaeologists stress vessel form at the expense of decoration. The development of the transfer print technique allowed a sensitive interaction between ceramic decoration and changes in visual images of most households of the period. Almost no research has been done on the role of these important objects of daily use in reflecting and shaping cultural attitudes. The Middletown material permits some initial reflections.[5]

The obvious first phase is represented by the hand-painted blue-on-white material with chinoiserie motifs. Whereas these wares originally had an exotic flavor, by the end of the eighteenth century the designs had become conventional and presented the same air of classic stability as the Greek and Roman motifs used in house architecture. The introduction of transfer prints merely allowed greater artistic complexity of these now well-established designs and spawned the long-lasting, but derivative Blue Willow tradition.

By the beginning of the nineteenth century, the classic order based on upper-class British values had given way to the twin movements of local patriotism and European Romanticism. The latter reflected considerable nostalgia for the British world, from which the colonists had so recently separated. At this time, patriotic themes appeared on the Middletown ceramics, but with limited frequency. A series of cups from the Southmayd house shows the Marquis de Lafayette contemplating the tomb of Benjamin Franklin while the sun rises (or sets) in the background (Coyne 1974:24). The White House is shown on one plate, while another depicts the original State House in nearby Hartford (Coyne 1974:54–56; Hill 1953). More general in its reference, but still probably related in the mind of the local buyer to the early nineteenth-century Middletown scene, is a larger brown-and-white Staffordshire ironstone platter showing a river town with boats, a farmer's cart, and small factory buildings, which, during the 1820s and 1830s, were becoming such an important part of the Middletown landscape. Although the scene on the plate is generic, the owner would have associated it with his local world. The impact of this ceramic iconography of a changing urban world was well captured by an anecdote from the Middletown paper, the *Middlesex Gazette*, of January 18, 1826:

[5]Study of the social historical importance of ceramic use in historic sites has focused on the availability of certain types of ceramics and the use of percentages of recovered ceramics as an indication of social status, as in Teller (1968), Feister (1975), Miller (1974; 1980), and Deetz (1973; 1977).

> "O" said a young lady at a party while looking at the picture that was painted on the plate she had in her hand. "What a beautiful cottage, I should admire to live in just such a one all the days of my life." The young gentleman that stood by her, anxious to know what would please her, looked very tenderly at the picture and found it was a steamboat.

However, in this increasingly industrial and commercial world, people were already seeking to escape in their minds to an exotic place or to a fast-disappearing, traditional, rustic paradise. The elegant chinoiserie teacups of the Watkinson group were replaced in the Southmayd group by pearlware pieces showing country scenes with cows and children and thatched roofed villages, and by tea pots with views of northern Italy. The Grand Tour, which during the eighteenth century had been the preserve of the high-status gentlemen, now became a possibility even for the American middle class (Coyne 1974:32–35, 76–79; Hibbert 1969; Piggott 1973:32–34). Chinese-inspired designs survive on Blue Willow plates, but more popular themes from Southmayd are the castles and stately homes of England. An independent, democratic, and increasingly industrialized New England looked back nostalgically to a world of noble and rustic England and to the quaint, ancient cities of Italy (Coyne 1974:88–89; Deetz 1973:32–34). By the time that multicolored Staffordshire wares had become popular in the 1830s, Middletown taste had extended to the exotic world of the Orient and to a pastoral vision set in the days of Renaissance Italy.

A final category of information provided by ceramics relates to the complexity of formal life in the various households under study. Naturally, it would be desirable to make this as family specific as possible and relate certain types of materials to known households. However, social historical research in Middletown still is in its infancy. The records, although abundant, are often imprecise, which makes direct linkages difficult at this stage. Nevertheless, the artifacts do fall into patterns that show similarities and differences among the sites, and this deserves comment.

There is no question that the material from the Watkinson deposit represents the highest level of elegance. This is seen in the presence of high-status wares such as black basalt and porcelain, in the number and diversity of tea sets, in the quantity of dinner plates, and perhaps most strikingly in the almost complete absence of redwares and other humble pottery. The abundance of transfer-printed pearlwares and the almost total absence of Staffordshire whiteware place the major period of use of the trash pit in the first two decades of the nineteenth century, at a time when the property belonged to the John R. Watkinson family. The elegant brick house of Watkinson still survives, and it provides contrast to the even better wooden houses of the other Middletown merchants and tradesmen. The Watkinson family prospered in the early years of the nineteenth century as they turned from the uncertain world of captain merchants to more general mercantile and manufacturing pursuits (Gray 1978:82–84). Comparison of the Watkinsons with the Southmayds has already been made. The more modest wooden house of the latter family further reflects the contrast between the two households.

For the other households studied, the material culture recovered is more fragmentary, but some general observations can still be made. The relation between the rise and fall of Charles Magill and the ceramic inventory from the site has already been discussed. Rouen ware, presumably imported from the French West Indies; hand-painted tea sets; and status pieces of the late eighteenth century, such as black basalt, identify a family with social pretensions as well as shipping connections. This fits with the known historical circumstances of Charles Magill.

Close by the Watkinson house is the White Eagle site. A house was first built on the site during the 1750s. After passing through several hands, it was purchased in 1762 by Deacon Joseph Clark, who lived there until 1778. The house remained in the Clark family until 1795, when it underwent a complex series of ownership changes involving, among others, the neighboring Watkinsons and Southmayds. During much of this period, the house may have been rented. For the years 1762–1795, however, the materials found around the house may be associated with the Clark family. Here, the 1778 probate inventory of Joseph Clark is of interest. Most striking is the limited ceramic holdings. Pewter was evidently the main table ware, since the inventory lists some 46 pewter vessels, whereas the only ceramic entry is a general one for crockery ware. The archaeological evidence suggests that the family of Deacon Clark did not continue this reliance on pewter. Creamwares, hand-painted pearlwares, and black basalt ware all can be attributed to the later years of the Clark occupancy.

A sense of this expanding ceramic inventory can be obtained from the probates of two close neighbors of the Clarks. The first, that of Return Meiggs (dated 1782), lists one china bowl, one set of burnt china cups and saucers (mended), one-half set of blue-and-white cups and saucers, one sugar bowl, one black tea pot, six chocolate-colored earthern plates, and six blue-and-white plates. The second inventory is that of General Samuel Holden Parsons, dated 1790. Mentioned are three small china bowls, four china coffee cups and saucers, one china punch bowl, one broken punch bowl, one pair of glazed salts, three delph plates, one black tea pot, six delph cups and saucers, one blue-and-white pot, 12 china cups and saucers, two cream pots, one delph tea pot, and several ceramic kitchen vessels.

The Hall site is named for Doctor William Hall, a prominent Middletown physician, who occupied the house from 1796 until his death in 1809, and whose family continued in possession of the house until 1822. In the probate inventory of 1809, ceramic items mentioned were one sallet dish, one broken table set of china, one dozen tea cups and saucers, two dozen coffee cups, three bowls, and an undefined amount of old crockery. The ceramics that were recovered archaeologically and can be dated to before 1822 (basically all but the Staffordshire and whitewares) suggest much greater variety and richness in the ceramic inventory than was recorded in the probate inventory. All of the status early-nineteenth-century wares are present, including relatively high percentages of porcelain, Romantic pearlware, and multicolored floral pearlware.

All of the aforementioned sites can be placed in the mercantile professional world of late-eighteenth-century and early-nineteenth-century Middletown. The Danforth house, on the other hand, belonged to a family of pewterers, who represent an important craft tradition in the Middletown of the period. The site was occupied by a house from 1787, which accounts for the scattering of salt-glazed and Jackfield sherds. Although late-eighteenth-century hand-painted blue-and-white pearlware is very sparsely represented, as is Chinese transfer-printed wares, multicolored and Romantic pearlwares and Staffordshire are quite abundant. The general variety of wares at this site is impressive. Tea service items are abundant, suggesting that the families of craftsmen engaged in the same parlor rituals as the merchant-sea captain-professional group.

Space and the incomplete state of social research does not allow us to pursue further connections between status and complexity of material goods. However, some final general observations can be made. Whereas variations appear in the details of the preserved ceramic record, especially among the most expensive goods, what is perhaps most striking is the basic homogeneity in the collective assemblage. This becomes particularly true as we move into the nineteenth century. Prosperous merchant families, professional people, and successful craftsmen all were purchasing a similar range of ceramics. The vessel forms indicate households whose activities centered around similar ceremonies. Tea service of the Danforth family in the years after the War of 1812 would not have been significantly different from that of the Watkinsons.

This relative community homogeneity is evident in other aspects of life. The Watkinsons did build a brick house, and the other families constructed wooden structures, reflecting their relative prosperity. However, the plans were basically similar and the houses were located in the same general area of Middletown. To go from Magill to Watkinson to Danforth was only a walk of three to four blocks. The dead of all families were buried together in the two cemeteries just off the Main Street of Middletown.

All of this expresses a certain community cohesiveness in Middletown in the period between the Revolution and the 1820s. This was soon to disappear as the richest citizens moved up the hill to build more elegant houses near the university and to bury their dead in the family plots and mausolea of the newly established Indian Hill cemetery. It would be interesting to learn whether the later material culture reflects this change.

ACKNOWLEDGMENTS

The archaeological research described in this chapter was conducted with the assistance of various Wesleyan "Introduction to Archaeology" classes. Thanks are due to several generations of students and teaching apprentices who made these results possible. Background information on the sites and the people who lived there comes in part from special research by Brenda Gray, John E. Reynolds, Katherine Cruse, and Karl Rogers, and from the files of the Greater Middletown Preservation Trust. Throughout this project, we have had the active support of the Middletown Redevelopment Agency and its director, Joseph Haze. Finally, I owe many of the insights and ideas in this chapter to conversations with Professor Peter Hall of the Wesleyan University History Department.

REFERENCES

Beers, J. B.
1884 *History of Middlesex County*. New York: J. B. Beers and Company.

Coyne, Arthur W.
1974 *Blue printed earthenware 1800–1850*. Rutland, Vt.: C. E. Tuttle Company.

Deetz, James F.
1973 Ceramics from Plymouth, 1620–1835: The archaeological evidence. In *Ceramics in America*, edited by I. M. G. Quimby. Charlottesville, Va.: Univ. Press of Virginia. Pp. 15–39.
1977 *In small things forgotten*. Garden City, N.Y.: Anchor Press.

Feister, Lois M.
1975 Analysis of the ceramics found at the Vereberg Tavern site. *Man in the Northeast* **10**:2–16.

Field, David D.
1819 *Statistical account of Middlesex County*. Middletown, Conn.: Clark and Lyman.

Gray, Brenda E.
1978 The mercantile community of Middletown, Connecticut 1780–1820. Unpublished honor's thesis, Wesleyan University.

Hibbert, Christopher
1969 *The grand tour*. London: Weidenfeld and Nicolson.

Hill, Nola D.
1953 American history on Liverpool and Staffordshire. *Antiques* **64**:291–293.

Hunter, Frederick W.
1950 *Stiegel glass*. New York: Dover.

Martin, Margaret E.
1938–1939 Merchants and traders of the Connecticut River Valley 1750–1820. *Smith College Series in History* **24**:1–4. Northampton, Massachusetts.

Miller, George L.
1974 A tenant farmer's tableware: Nineteenth-century ceramics from Tabb's Purchase. *Maryland History Magazine* **69**:197–210.

Miller, George L.
1980 Classification and economic scaling of nineteenth-century ceramics. *Historical Archaeology* **14**:1–40.

Moran, Georggrey
1976 Trash pits and natural rights in the Revolutionary Era: Excavations at the Narbonne House in Salem, Massachusetts. *Archaeology* **29**:194–202.

Noël Hume, Ivor
1960 Rouen Faience in eighteenth-century America. *Antiques* **78**:559–561.
1970 *A guide to artifacts of Colonial America*. New York: Alfred A. Knopf.

Piggott, Stuart
1973 *Ruins in a landscape*. Edinburgh: Edinburgh Univ. Press.

Roth, Rodris
1961 Tea drinking in eighteenth-century America: Its etiquette and equipage. *U.S. National Museum Bulletin No. 225. Contributions from the Museum of History and Technology* **14**:61–69. Washington, D.C.

Rural Felicity
1826 *Middlesex Gazette*, January, **41**.

Teller, Barbara G.
1968 Ceramics in Providence, 1750–1800: An inventory survey. *Antiques* **94**:570–577.

Wallace, Willard
1950 *Middletown tercentenary, 1650–1950*. Middletown, Conn.: Scanlon.

15

Patterns in Urban Food Ways: An Example From Early Twentieth-Century Atlanta

Paula Edmiston Davidson

Over the past two decades, interest in recent material culture has grown as archaeologists have moved toward a study of all cultural systems available in the archaeological record. There also has been a recognition that the total material assemblage must be studied if the total system is to be understood. In the realm of American historic sites archaeology, such artifacts as tin cans, bottles, and industrial building materials now come under as close scrutiny as that ever-present artifact, the ceramic sherd. However, historic sites archaeologists as yet seem unaware of the important information available in a data category that may be given only cursory attention at prehistoric sites, the category of faunal remains. Thus, the few faunal analyses available for historic sites usually consist simply of species lists. The potential interpretations to be obtained from archaeological faunal data are numerous (e.g., Lyman 1976; Read 1971; Ziegler 1973), which makes the lack of consideration of this body of data surprising. Chaplin (1971), Daly (1969), Grayson (1973), Olsen (1971), and Ziegler (1973), for example, have outlined specific methodological approaches to prehistoric faunal remains that are easily adaptable to historic faunal data.

The purpose of this chapter is to describe, analyze, and interpret faunal remains from the Edgewood site (9DA89), an early-twentieth-century neighborhood garbage dump in Atlanta, Georgia. Also, I shall attempt to show how this data can be used to interpret seasonality and subsistence patterns in recent urban contexts.

ARCHAEOLOGY OF URBAN AMERICA
The Search for Pattern and Process

ISBN 0-12-214980-7

EDGEWOOD SITE (9Da89)

The Edgewood site is located in suburban Atlanta, about 5.6 km (3.5 mi) east of the center of the city. Salvage excavations were carried out at the site in 1975–1976 under a contract between Georgia State University and the Metropolitan Atlanta Rapid Transit Authority (MARTA). The site originally was a small ravine in the suburban community of Edgewood, later incorporated into the city of Atlanta. The ravine apparently was filled with refuse in 1910–1911 to provide support for planned house construction on the site.

Excavation of the site took place in two 3-m (10-ft) squares, using 15.25-cm (6-in.) vertical increments to a depth of 2.45 m (8 ft). The material used in this study was taken from Square 1, the richest artifact-bearing square. In this square, animal bones were recovered from the surface to a depth of 1.37 m (4.5 ft). Almost all of the animal bones recovered were from food animals (a small amount of worked bone was represented by buttons, tool and utensil handles, etc.).

Small game was present in the assemblage, but the majority of the food remains appeared to be cuts of meat from professionally butchered, domesticated animals. The latter material required an appropriate technique for analysis. For example, instead of calculating the minimum number of individuals present (MNI), as might be employed with prehistoric faunal remains (e.g., Grayson 1978), a taxonomy of meat cuts was developed using standard butchery practices (see Appendix A).

HYPOTHESES

One approach taken by modern archaeologists is to ask what material phenomena are significant for the people under study, and how did they organize these phenomena? One way people organize their material world is by seasonal activities. Prehistoric zooarchaeologists, therefore, might examine migratory habits or seasonal availability of animals in order to determine the season of occupation of a site and the use of specific resources. Since the Edgewood site fauna contained few remains of wild (hunted or trapped) animals, the interpretation of seasonal patterning in urban food remains became a matter of identifying the specific foods that would have been appropriate for the season or seasons represented. The "natural" availability of animals would be much less important than in a prehistoric or early historic context.

Analyses of other artifacts from the site (e.g., plant remains and heating residue) suggested cold weather activity, which yielded Hypothesis 1:

> *Seasonality can be determined from food remains present at the site.*

Tableware, bottles, and personal items, especially in the middle levels of the deposit, suggested the possibility of holiday activity, which produced Hypothesis 2:

> *The food remains at the site will reflect holiday activity (Thanksgiving and/or Christmas).*

Table 15.1 Bones Listed by Class and Excavation Level

	0.0' to 0.5'	0.5' to 1.0'	1.0' to 1.5'	1.5' to 2.0'	2.0' to 2.5'	2.5' to 3.0'	3.0' to 3.5'	3.5' to 4.0'	4.0' to 4.5'	Surface collection	Total	Percentage of total sample
Identified mammal	10	17	25	25	27	61	41	16	5	4	231	16.5
Unidentified mammal	23	27	32	75	93	188	114	25	0	3	580	41.4
Total mammal	33	44	57	100	120	249	155	41	5	7	811	57.9
Identified bird	31	5	19	43	43	150	58	28	0	0	377	26.9
Unidentified bird	1	0	10	15	14	13	13	7	0	0	73	5.2
Total bird	32	5	29	58	57	163	71	35	0	0	450	32.1
Identified fish	0	0	1	0	0	2	0	0	0	0	3	0.2
Unidentified fish	0	2	7	7	2	15	18	3	0	0	54	3.8
Total fish	0	2	8	7	2	17	18	3	0	0	57	4.0
Identified shell	63	12	0	0	1	0	0	1	0	4	81	5.7
Unidentified shell	0	0	0	1	0	0	0	0	0	0	1	0.1
Total shell	63	12	0	1	1	0	0	1	0	4	82	0.1
Total bone	128	63	94	166	180	429	244	80	5	11	1400	100
Percentage of total site	9.1	4.5	6.7	11.8	12.8	30.6	17.4	5.7	0.3	0.7		

The residents of Edgewood lived on the outskirts of a developing urban center and were being affected increasingly by this development. This urbanization process also should be reflected in the foodways, which yielded Hypothesis 3:

> *Foodways (procurement, preparation, and consumption) will reflect the impact of culture change in a turn-of-the-century, middle-class, suburban community.*

FAUNAL DATA

The bone sample from the Edgewood site, totaling 1400 fragments, was recovered from one 3-m (10-ft) square, which was divided into nine 15.25-cm (6-in.) arbitrary levels (Table 15.1). Within this group, the following animals were identified: cow (*Bos tarus*), pig (*Sus scrofa*), rabbit (*Siliagus floridanus*), opossum (*Didelphis marsupialis*), chicken and egg (*Gallus gallus*), turkey (*Meleagris gallopavo*), sheepshead (*Archosargus* sp.), red drum (*Sciaenops ocellata*), and oyster (*Crassostrea virginia*). Land snails found in the upper levels were not food animals and thus were not considered in this study. They probably represented scavengers on the site.

The following is a description of the animals present. Table 15.2 lists the meat cuts and MNI present by level. Identifications of species were made using skeletal collections at Georgia State University, the University of Georgia, and the Florida State Museum. Identifications of the cuts of meat were made using the taxonomy described in Appendix A and through information obtained from interviews with elderly butchers in the Atlanta area.

Beef

Beef cuts, represented by a total of 159 bones, predominated in all levels at the Edgewood site. The cuts of meat present were soupbone (41), steak (39), roast (30), ribs (30), and round steak (17).

Pork

There were 57 pork cuts, the second largest category. They appeared in all of the levels except the surface and the lowest level (4.0–4.5 ft). Pork cuts present in the site were ribs (15), soupbone (14), ham (7), pork chop (5), ham hock (4), sliced ham (2), and pig's head (1). The identification of the pig's head was made on the basis of the presence of one incisor. However, since pig heads were commonly used in the making of several dishes, this probably was a valid identification.

Rabbit and Opossum

Five rabbits and two opossums were identified from the site. The rabbits were represented by three pelves, one mandible, one maxilla, and one humerus. The

Table 15.2 Cuts and MNI Present by Level

Level	Animal	Cut/MNI	Number present	Percentage of total
0.0'-0.5'	cow	rib	3	21
	cow	roast	1	7
	cow	steak	3	21
	pig	ham	2	14
	rabbit	MNI	1	7
	chicken	MNI	1	7
	egg	MNI	1	7
	oyster	MNI	2	14
	total		14	
	Percentage of total site		5	
0.5'-1.0'	cow	rib	3	15
	cow	roast	1	5
	cow	steak	3	15
	cow	round steak	1	5
	cow	soupbone	5	26
	pig	soupbone	3	15
	rabbit	MNI	1	5
	chicken	MNI	2	10
	total		19	
	Percentage of total site		7	
1.0'-1.5'	cow	rib	1	3
	cow	steak	9	31
	cow	round steak	2	6
	cow	soupbone	7	24
	pig	rib	2	6
	pig	ham slice	1	3
	pig	pork chop	1	3
	pig	ham hock	1	3
	rabbit	MNI	1	3
	chicken	MNI	2	6
	turkey	MNI	1	3
	fish	MNI	1	3
	total		29	
	Percentage of total site		10	

(Continued)

opossums were represented by six vertebrae, two humeri, and one scapula. These represent wild species, which presumably were obtained by hunting or trapping.

Chicken and Egg

There were 30 individual chickens and five eggs. Like pork, chicken was present in every level except the surface and the lowest level. Although it was the third largest group, it was never represented in large numbers.

Table 15.2 (Continued)

1.5'-2.0'	cow	rib	4	14
	cow	roast	4	14
	cow	steak	1	3
	cow	round steak	4	14
	cow	soupbone	5	17
	pig	head	1	3
	pig	ham slice	1	3
	pig	pork chop	2	7
	pig	soupbone	1	3
	rabbit	MNI	1	3
	chicken	MNI	3	10
	egg	MNI	1	3
	total		28	
	Percentage of total site		10	
2.0'-2.5'	cow	rib	5	16
	cow	short rib	1	3
	cow	roast	3	10
	cow	steak	8	26
	cow	soupbone	3	10
	pig	ham	2	6
	pig	ham hock	1	3
	opossum	MNI	1	3
	chicken	MNI	5	16
	oyster	MNI	1	3
	total		30	
	Percentage of total site		11	
2.5'-3.0'	cow	rib	1	1
	cow	short rib	2	2
	cow	roast	10	14
	cow	steak	4	5
	cow	round steak	3	4
	cow	soupbone	13	16
	pig	rib	8	11
	pig	ham	3	4
	pig	pork chop	2	2
	pig	ham hock	1	1
	pig	soupbone	7	10
	opossum	MNI	1	1
	chicken	MNI	10	14
	egg	MNI	1	1
	turkey	MNI	3	4
	fish	MNI	1	1
	total		70	
	Percentage of total site		26	

(Continued)

Table 15.2 (Continued)

3.0'-3.5'	cow	rib	10	22
	cow	steak	11	25
	cow	round steak	5	11
	cow	soupbone	4	9
	pig	rib	3	6
	pig	ham hock	1	2
	pig	soupbone	3	6
	rabbit	MNI	1	2
	chicken	MNI	3	6
	egg	MNI	1	2
	turkey	MNI	2	4
	total		44	
Percentage of total site			16	
3.5'-4.0'	cow	roast	6	27
	cow	round steak	2	9
	cow	soupbone	3	15
	pig	rib	1	4
	pig	ham	3	13
	pig	ham hock	1	4
	chicken	MNI	4	16
	egg	MNI	1	4
	oyster	MNI	1	4
	total		22	
Percentage of total site			8	
4.0'-4.5'	cow	rib	1	20
	cow	roast	3	60
	cow	soupbone	1	20
	total		5	
Percentage of total site			1	
Surface collection	cow	rib	1	16
	cow	roast	2	33
	pig	ham	1	16
	oyster	MNI	2	33
	total		6	
Percentage of total site			2	

Turkey

There were six turkeys. All but one of these were found in the sixth and seventh levels, the middle portion of the deposit.

Oyster and Fish

There were six oysters and two fish identified from the site. The oysters were a Gulf Coast variety; the fish were sheepshead and red drum, both salt-water species.

The fish were difficult to identify. Out of 54 bones recovered, only three could be classified as to species (the sheepshead was identified by one vertebra, and the red drum was identified by one vertebra and one operculum). One reason for this difficulty in identification was the absence of cranial bones. Almost all of the fish bones recovered were vertebrae, the most ambiguous of fish bones. Elizabeth Wing (personal communication) suggested that the fish probably were shipped from the coast beheaded, which might explain the lack of cranial bones.

ETHNOGRAPHIC DATA

One of the advantages of archaeology on recent historic sites is the addition of the dimensions of documentation, ethnography, informants, and observations of contemporary society. With these resources, the archaeologist has at his command a potential far greater than that provided by the material record alone (South 1977).

In the fall of 1977 and the winter of 1980, I conducted a series of interviews with Mrs. Rebecca Cooper (name changed to protect informant's privacy), an early resident of the Edgewood neighborhood. She gave me the following information on the acquisition and use of food during the period that the dump was in use. Mrs. Cooper's family, like most of their neighbors, kept a cow for milk and chickens for meat and eggs. Most of the meat cuts (beef and pork) were purchased at retail establishments in downtown Atlanta. The residents of the Edgewood community traveled by trolley into town for most of their shopping. Mrs. Cooper remembered beef being the most expensive meat, followed by pork and fish. Chicken was not expensive since they raised their own.

When questioned about family preference for different meats, Mrs. Cooper listed the following, in descending order: beef, chicken, pork, and fish. She went on to explain that whereas beef and chicken were favored in all seasons, pork was eaten more in the winter months. This was due to the lack of refrigeration and the rapid spoilage rate of pork. In the course of one conversation, Mrs. Cooper mentioned a change in the butchering techniques that she has noticed through the years. She said rump, ham, and shoulder cuts now seem to be cut smaller, as if to eliminate the articulating ends of the bones. She laughed and suggested that people are more squeamish these days and do not like to be reminded of where their food actually comes from. When the bones from the Edgewood site were rechecked, many of the pig bones did include more of the articulating ends of long bones, especially on cuts such as hams.

Residents of the community obtained chickens either from a meat market or raised them at home. Mrs. Cooper's family raised their own chickens, as did most of their neighbors. However, chickens and turkeys could be purchased intact and sometimes alive. According to Mrs. Cooper, turkey was eaten by her family and neighbors only at Thanksgiving and Christmas and was viewed as a "holiday bird."

Fish and other seafood were the least available items to Mrs. Cooper's family. Some local residents fished the Chattahoochee River, but the Cooper family bought their fish downtown. Seafood came into Atlanta packed in ice on trains. Seafood was considered a special food because of its general unavailability; however, it was not particularly expensive. Oysters were shipped in barrels from Mobile, Alabama, and were available in months with "r."

Mrs. Cooper remembered that some people in the community ate rabbits and opossums, but her family did not. When questioned about seasonal activity, Mrs. Cooper stated that there were no hunting seasons; people hunted when they "felt like it." She also mentioned that people usually hunted near home. During the period that the dump was in use, the Edgewood community was surrounded by woods that were full of small animals.

When asked about eating habits in general, Mrs. Cooper said that meat was eaten at every meal and was the focal dish. Mrs. Cooper also remembered that soup was very popular and that a pot of soup was always kept simmering on the stove. The same kinds of soup were eaten year round, but more soup was eaten during the winter when hot dishes were preferred.

ANALYSIS

In the archaeological collection, the most prevalent meat was beef (Table 15.3). It comprised 58% of the cuts recovered. Next was pork, which made up 20% of the food remains. Chicken was the third largest category present, comprising 11%. Rabbit and opossum together comprised 2%, and turkey and oyster each accounted for 2%. Chicken eggs accounted for 1%, and fish for .7%. Beef cuts predominated in all but one level (Table 15.2).

Census data for 1910 indicates that the per capita consumption of foods was similar to the archaeological findings and establishes that turkey consumption was very small from 1909 through 1928 (United States Department of Commerce, Bureau of the Census, 1976). Mrs. Cooper remembered that her family preferred chicken over pork. In this case the inconsistency between the informant's memory and the material record may be affected by the season of the year in which the bones were deposited. If the site does reflect winter activity, a larger than usual number of pork cuts might be expected. Mrs. Cooper did point out that pigs were more often available and eaten in the winter, when lack of refrigeration was less important.

The large number of roast and steak bones was somewhat puzzling for a lower middle-class community. If the site did reflect a lower economic group, as evidenced by the soupbones, then how could the large amounts of relatively expensive cuts be accounted for? An explanation began to emerge from an examination of the

Table 15.3 Distribution of Animals (Cuts of Meat and MNI) by Level

	Beef		Pork		Other mammal		Chicken	
Level	N	Percentage	N	Percentage	N	Percentage	N	Percentage
Surface	3	(50)	1	(16)	0		0	
0.0'-0.5'	7	(50)	2	(14)	1	(7)	1	(7)
0.5'-1.0'	13	(66)	3	(15)	1	(5)	2	(10)
1.0'-1.5'	19	(65)	5	(17)	1	(3)	2	(7)
1.5'-2.0'	18	(64)	5	(17)	1	(3)	3	(10)
2.0'-2.5'	20	(66)	3	(10)	1	(3)	5	(16)
2.5'-3.0'	33	(47)	21	(30)	1	(1)	10	(14)
3.0'-3.5'	30	(66)	7	(15)	1	(2)	3	(6)
3.5'-4.0'	11	(50)	5	(22)	0		4	(16)
4.0'-4.5'	5	(100)	0		0		0	
Total	159		52		7		30	
Percentage of total	55		20		2		11	

pattern of overall bones distribution. Figure 15.1 depicts the distribution of all bones by level. It is obviously not a consistent distribution. The middle section (1.5–3.5 ft) had large numbers of bones, whereas the upper and lower sections had comparatively small numbers.

The botanical analysis of the site revealed that there were very few edible vegetable species present. In examining a household refuse dump, one would certainly expect to find, along with animal remains, some vegetable foods represented by seeds and fruit pits. The negative evidence from the botanical inventory seems to reflect the activities of people during a cold season, when vegetables would not be as available as during the warm growing season. The vegetable remains that were available probably were placed in mulch piles for the spring gardens. It is also possible that most of the vegetables that were available at this time were canned, which would produce a minimum of waste.

In the winter it is sometimes common for people to eat soups and stews, as they are hot and nourishing. This tradition could explain the presence of the large number of soupbones. Another indication of winter activity is the presence of turkey bones. Turkey, according to Mrs. Cooper, usually was reserved for Thanksgiving and Christmas dinners. If this is the case in the Edgewood site, the overall bone

Egg		Turkey		Oyster		Fish			
N	Percentage	N	Percentage	N	Percentage	N	Percentage	Total	Percentage of total
0		0		2	(33)	0		6	2
1	(7)	0		2	(14)	0		14	5
0		0		0		0		19	7
0		1	(3)	0		1	(3)	29	11
1	(3)	0		0		0		28	10
0		0		1	(3)	0		30	11
1	(1)	3	(4)	0		1	(1)	70	26
1	(2)	2	(4)	0		0		44	17
1	(4)	0		1	(4)	0		22	8
0		0		0		0		5	2
5		6		6		2		267	100
1		2		2		.7			

distribution pattern also could be explained. Possibly the lower section (3.5–4.5 ft) represented preholiday activity, in that there were fewer bones overall and no turkey bones. The middle section (1.5–3.5 ft) reflected the holiday season; there was more bone overall because people gave large dinners with many relatives to feed. Also, turkey was present, as was a greater variety of types and cuts of meat. The upper section represented post-holiday activity, when there were fewer people to feed and less need for variety and special dishes.

An obvious difference between the faunal assemblage of the Edgewood site and that of a prehistoric or early historic site is the ratio of game animals to professionally butchered, domesticated animals. Table 15.3 presents the distribution of animals, as cuts of meat and MNI, by level. The category "Other Mammals" includes those animals defined as game and is composed of rabbit and opossum. As the outer reaches of the Edgewood community were sparsely populated in 1910, it is reasonable to expect that some hunting was practiced. Thus, although an urban procurement system predominated, aspects of the rural pattern still were present.

The residents of the Edgewood site could obtain professionally butchered cuts of meat from several commercial establishments (this has been documented by historical research of the neighborhood), and therefore did not need to raise or hunt much

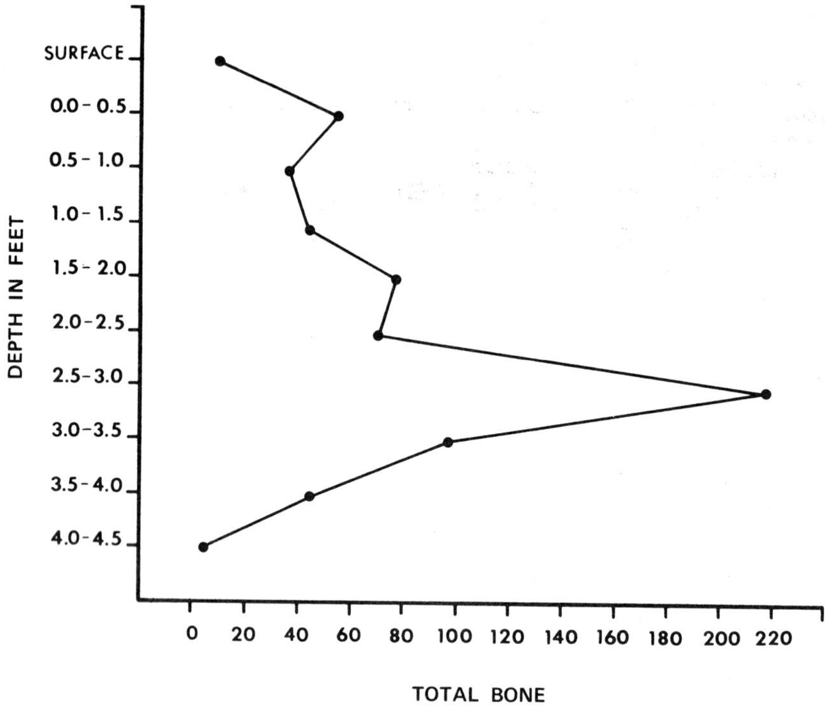

FIGURE 15.1. Distribution of identified bone by excavation level.

of the meat they consumed. Neither did they have to eat the entire animal, but could purchase that portion desired at any specific time and for any specific meal. Purchasing food at commercial establishments in a major transportation center also made available nonlocal foods, such as fish and oysters.

INTERPRETATIONS

The faunal remains from the Edgewood site probably reflect the activities of several lower middle-class suburban families during a winter season. The period of time involved seems to cover the several months immediately before, during, and immediately following Thanksgiving and Christmas. Thus, the hypotheses stated at the beginning of this report can be reasonably supported by the faunal record. The presence of soupbones in large numbers as well as the absence of vegetable remains supports an interpretation of cold-weather subsistence activity. The informant data also support this hypothesis, especially the reference to seasonal preference for pork. Pork as a seasonal-indicator seems even more important in light of the census data on per capita meat consumption.

The presence of turkey remains, along with the overall bone distribution pattern, and the ethnographic data, are indicative of holiday activity for a portion of the period involved.

The methods of butchering domesticated animals, the absence of significant numbers of game animals, and the presence of imported seafoods all suggest a well-developed urban economic-subsistence pattern. Residents of Edgewood no longer had the need to raise and butcher animals for food; they simply went to a store where selected portions of animals were packaged and sold. This is signifi-

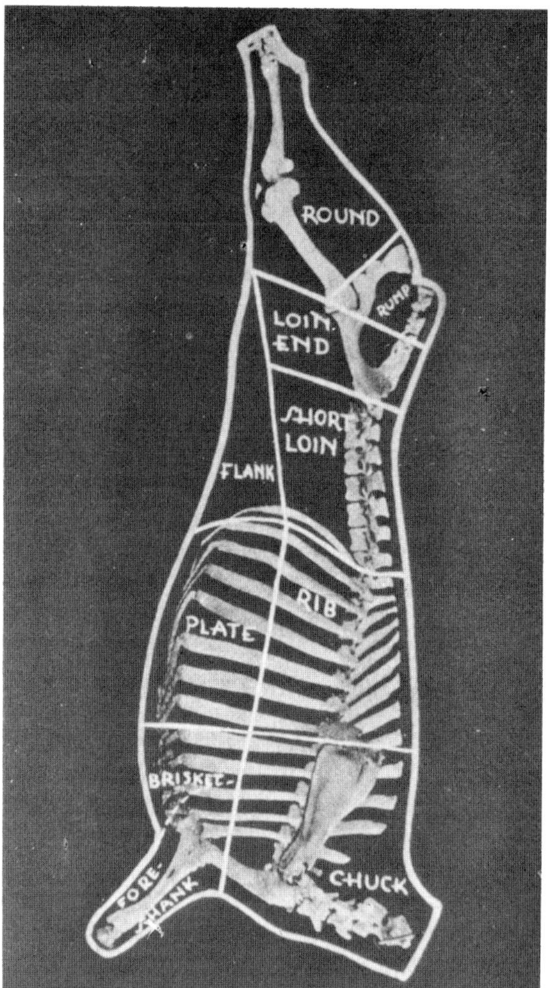

FIGURE 15.2. Wholesale meat cuts (from Halliday and Noble 1928).

cantly reflected in the material record by the variety and abundance of professionally butchered meat cuts.

CONCLUSIONS

Zooarchaeology has earned an important place in archaeology as a resource for behavioral interpretation. In addition to its uses as illustrated in this chapter, zooarchaeology can be used in the historic context to determine social status as well as

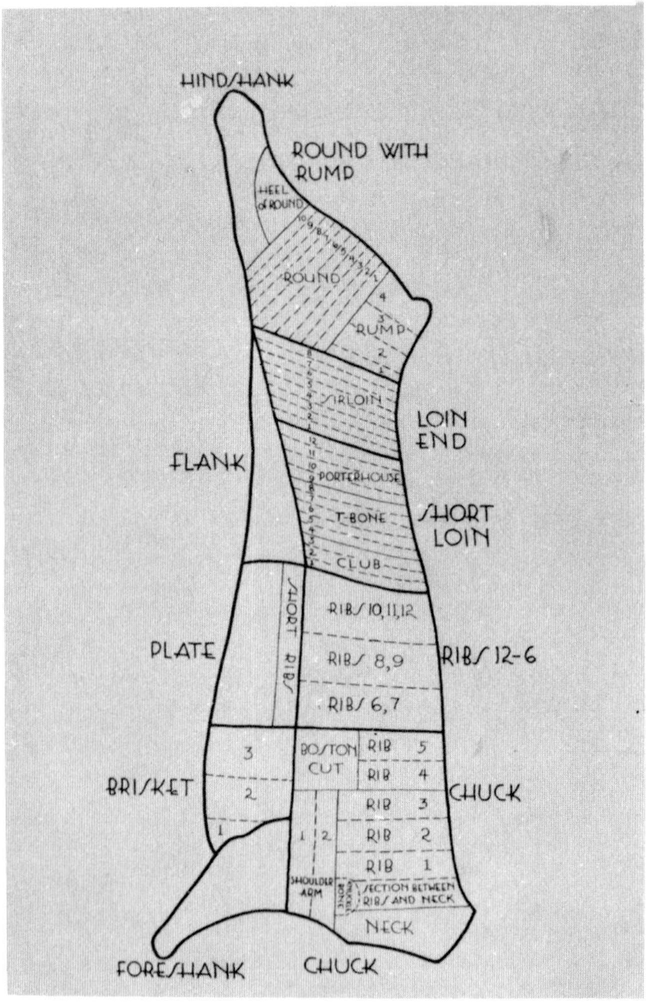

FIGURE 15.3. Retail meat cuts (from Halliday and Noble 1928).

serving to develop cross-cultural economic comparisons. Coupled with documentary and ethnographic research, studies of foodway patterning should provide significant insights into the diverse and complex cultural processes of urban America.

APPENDIX A

In the historic context, and especially at late historic sites, there is likely to be a majority of domesticated animals present, possibly professionally butchered and sold through commercial establishments. The presence of bones of wild animals at these sites usually means that they were a supplement to the diet, and in some cases, a seasonally specific resource.

Modern butchering methods have been standardized into patterns that show little regional differentiation. Halliday's and Nobel's *Hows and Whys of Cooking* (1928) is an excellent source of early twentieth-century butchering techniques.

Figure 15.2 is a line drawing of the skeleton of a cow with the wholesale cuts superimposed. The wholesale cuts are sold to butchers who divide them further into retail cuts for sale to the general public (Figure 15.3). Cows and pigs are butchered in a similar fashion. Butchers have their own terminology for the bone elements. The scapula is called the "blade bone," the humerus the "arm bone," the femur the "round bone," the ulna and tibia the "shank bones," and the pelvis the "rump bone." When counting ribs, some butchers refer to the twelfth rib as the first and number toward the neck (Halliday and Nobel, 1928). The cuts with the highest meat value come from the humerus and femur; these are the beef steaks and the pork chops. "Soupbones" are discarded bone. They include bones not used in any cut (e.g., the pelvis and shanks) and the articular ends of long bones trimmed from the cuts.

The following is an outline of meat cuts and the bones contained in them. This outline can be applied to pigs and sheep since they are butchered in comparable ways.

Beef Cuts

Chuck:
- cervical vertebrae
- scapula
- humerus (except distal articulation)
- first 5 ribs at articulation with vertebrae
- first 6 thoracic vertebrae

Foreshank:
- ulna/radius
- distal humerus

Rib:
- 7–13 thoracic vertebrae
- 6–12 ribs, proximal end

Plate:
- 6–12 ribs, distal end with sternal ribs

Shortloin:
- lumbar vertebrae

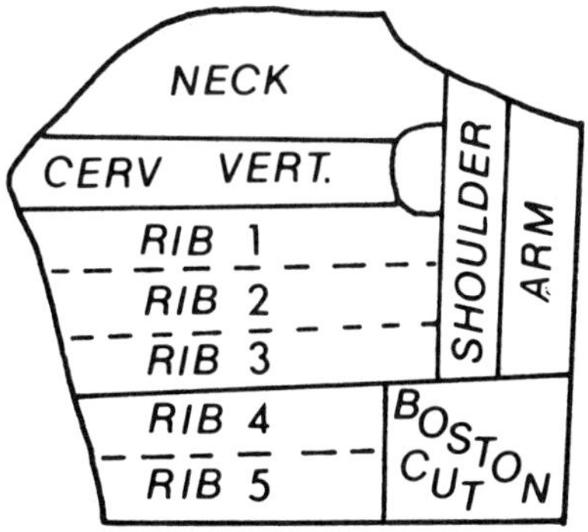

FIGURE 15.4. Forequarter cuts (after Halliday and Noble 1928).

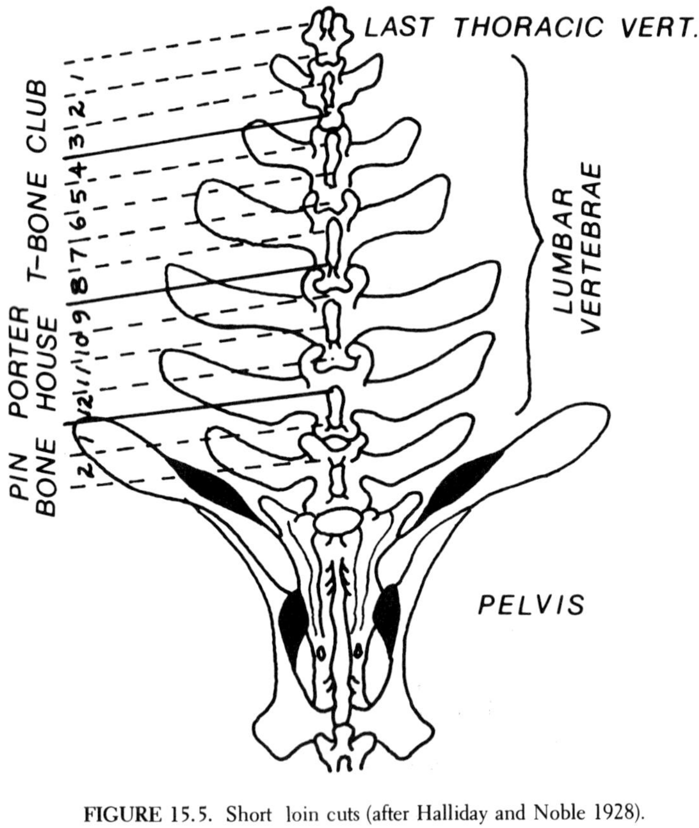

FIGURE 15.5. Short loin cuts (after Halliday and Noble 1928).

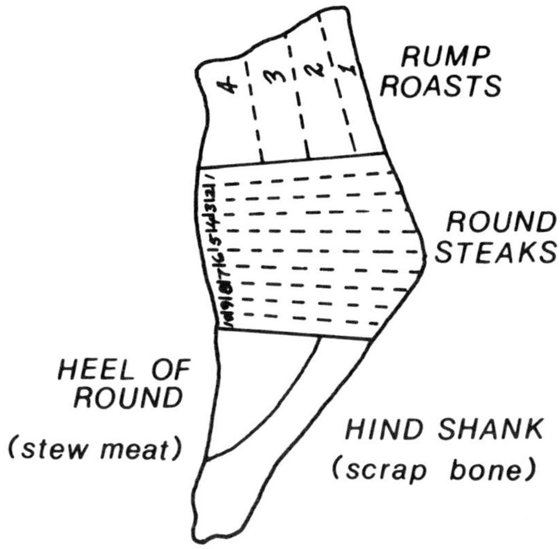

FIGURE 15.6. Hindquarter cuts (after Halliday and Noble 1928).

Loin end:
 sternum
 ilium (wedge bone, rump)
Rump:
 coccygeal vertebrae
 ischium
 proximal articular end of femur
Round:
 femur
Shank:
 tibia/fibula
 manus and pes

Retail butchers receive sides of meat from wholesalers. These are often divided further into quarters—the forequarters and hindquarters. The aforementioned cuts of meat are retail cuts, which are further divided into roasts and steaks. Figures 15.4, 15.5, and 15.6 show how the quarters are divided into retail cuts.

Shoulder arm pot roast: humerus (cross section) and
 scapula (7 in.)
Steaks
Chuck ribs: rib roasts or steaks
Plate: distal ribs 1–5 distal ends are cut for short ribs
Short Loin: (as follows)
Club (Delmonico) steak: first 1 in. (2.5 cm) short loin steak (beginning to number from the last thoracic vertebra). Also contains the 13th rib.
T-bone steak: next six 1 in. (2.5 cm) steaks (first 3 lumbar vertebrae)
 Porterhouse steak: next five 1 in. (2.5 cm) steaks (distal 3rd lumbar and 4, 5)
Pin bone steak: next two 1 in. (2.5 cm) steaks (6 lumbar, tip of the ilium)

Loin cuts: femur and pelvic bones, some coccygeal vertebrae
Rib roasts (not shown in Figure 15.3): ribs 12, 11, 10
ribs 9, 8
ribs 7, 6

Hind Quarter: (as follows)
Rump roast: sections of the shaft of the femur
Round steaks: cross sections of the femur
Scrap bone ("dog bones"): tibia/fibula

ACKNOWLEDGMENTS

I would like to thank Charles Wharton of the Department of Biology at Georgia State University for use of his comparative skeletal collection. I would also like to thank Josh Laerm and Gary Shapiro of the Departments of Zoology and Anthropology, respectively, at the University of Georgia for allowing me access to their skeletal collections, and Elizabeth Wing of the Florida State Museum for identifying the fish and rabbit bones.

I am also grateful to Preston Johnson of the Avondale Food Store for his help in making identifications of cuts of meat, and to my informant, Mrs. Rebecca Cooper, for sharing with me her childhood memories of the Edgewood community.

Special thanks are due to my professor, Roy S. Dickens, Jr., who introduced me to the fascination of urban archaeology.

REFERENCES

Chaplin, Raymond E.
1971 *The study of animal bones from archaeological sites.* New York: Seminar Press.

Daly, Patricia
1969 Approaches to faunal analysis in archaeology. *American Antiquity* **34**:146–153.

Grayson, Donald K.
1973 On the methodology of faunal analysis. *American Antiquity* **38**:432–438.
1978 Minimum numbers and sample size in vertebrae faunal analysis. *American Antiquity* **43**:53–65.

Halliday, Evelyn G., and Isabel T. Nobel
1928 *Hows and whys of cooking.* Chicago: The Univ. of Chicago Press.

Lyman, R. Lee
1976 A cultural analysis of faunal remains from the Alpowa locality. Unpublished MA thesis. Department of Anthropology, Washington State University, Pullman.

Olsen, Stanley J.
1971 *Zooarchaeology: Animal bones in archaeology and their interpretation.* Reading, Mass.: Addison-Wesley.

Read, Catherine E.
1971 Animal bones and human behavior: Approaches to faunal analysis in archaeology. Unpublished Ph.D. dissertation, University of California, Los Angeles.

South, Stanley
1977 *Method and theory in historical archeology.* New York: Academic Press.

United States Department of Commerce, Bureau of the Census
1976 *Historical statistics of the United States: Colonial times to 1970, part 1.* U.S. Government Printing Office, Washington, D.C.

Ziegler, Allen C.
1973 *Inference from prehistoric faunal remains.* Reading, Mass.: Addison-Wesley.

16

The Milwaukee Garbage Project: Archaeology of Household Solid Wastes[1]

Barry E. Thompson
William L. Rathje

ARCHAEOLOGY AND MODERN MILWAUKEE GARBAGE

Archaeology is founded on a simple premise: Differences in behaviors will result in differences in material remains and discards. Regardless of time and place, this proposition should be valid when considering the resource management practices of society's most basic behavioral unit—the household—and its most common material discards—household garbage.

In 1978 and 1979, to answer some questions of importance to organizations responsible for managing modern municipal solid wastes (see Rathje and Thompson 1981), members of the Garbage Project studied the solid wastes discarded by house-

[1]The Milwaukee Garbage Project was a joint project of the Departments of Anthropology of the University of Arizona and the University of Wisconsin, Milwaukee, with additional cooperation of the Marketing Department of Marquette University. It was jointly funded by the Solid Waste Council of the Paper Industry, the Can Manufacturers Institute, the National Food Processors Association, the Society of the Plastics Industry, the U.S. Brewers Association, the National Soft Drink Association, the Glass Packaging Institute, and the Solid and Hazardous Waste Research Division of the U.S. Environmental Protection Agency.

Dr. William Rathje (U of A) and Dr. Barry Thompson (UWM) were co-directors, Dr. Patrick Murphy (Marquette) served as a consultant, and Wilson Hughes was Assistant Director and Field Coordinator. Field Supervisors were John Bourschied, Margaret Nowak, and Mark Ryan. This chapter was written with the assistance of Martin Senour, Garbage Project Data Manager, and Wilson Hughes.

The statistical procedures utilized in this chapter (with the exception of cluster analysis) are from SPSS, Versions 7.0 and 8.0 (Hohlen 1979; Hull and Nie 1979; Nie, Hull, Jenkins, Steinbrenner, and Bent 1975).

ISBN 0-12-214980-7

holds in five Milwaukee neighborhoods. The primary objective of the Milwaukee Project was to investigate the effect of general income level of groups of households on the solid wastes they discard. Five neighborhoods, characterized by households with generally different socioeconomic standings and cultural backgrounds, were chosen for study.

Based on archaeology's founding premise, it seems reasonable to expect that different garbage should be discarded in the five different Milwaukee neighborhoods. The differences in garbage, in turn, should point out important differences in the behaviors of households in the five sample areas. In this chapter, three research questions will be explored.

1. What are the comparative weights of solid wastes discarded weekly by sample households in the five Milwaukee neighborhoods?
2. Do some of the five Milwaukee neighborhoods discard different kinds of garbage?
3. If there is variability in discards, what household behavior patterns are most likely responsible for the different kinds of garbage discarded in the five neighborhoods?

Answering these questions will provide a test of the founding premise of archaeology and insights into the resource management activities of a variety of modern urban households. Hopefully, both will be used in the continued development of urban archaeology.

MILWAUKEE GARBAGE PROJECT METHODS

To answer its research questions, members of the Milwaukee Garbage Project established a set of basic logistic and analytic procedures. Permission to sort household solid wastes was obtained from the City of Milwaukee's Department of Public Works and the Americology Division of the American Can Company. These two organizations also furnished analysis space for garbage sorting. The Milwaukee Bureau of Sanitation Services collected garbage pickups from households in five sample neighborhoods.

To allow for statistical analyses of variability within and between sample areas, we established the *garbage pickup*, that is, all of the garbage set out by an *individual household* each week for city collection, as the basic unit of data collection. Sanitation Bureau foremen randomly selected samples from households with garbage containers clearly separated from those of other residences. Thus, project data were collected from individual housing units and do not represent the behaviors of people living in duplexes and apartment complexes.

Sample Neighborhoods

Milwaukee is a large, industrial, ethnically diverse, Midwestern city. In 1981, its 640,000 people, living in an estimated 240,000 households, produced the 265,000 tons (240,355 metric tons) of refuse collected by the city's Sanitation Bureau. Five sample neighborhoods in Milwaukee were picked to represent three different income groups. They were initially chosen through the analysis of census data and verified through data from an interview survey.

1970 Census Data

Sample areas were first selected on the basis of a study of 1970 U.S. census data, consisting of information on income, family size, and other characteristics. These data were aggregated by *enumeration districts,* divisions of census tracts with average populations of around 800 persons. Cluster analysis was used to stratify the enumeration districts into classes. Seven clusters were identified. Actual sample neighborhoods were chosen for study based on several constraints:

1. For logistic purposes, the number of sample areas to be selected was limited to five.
2. Sample areas were chosen to represent a cross section of the most common types of Milwaukee neighborhoods, as identified by the cluster analysis of enumeration districts.
3. Specific sample neighborhoods were chosen from clustered groups of enumeration districts because the separate garbage containers of individual households easily could be identified. This selection process was accomplished by visual inspection.

Milwaukee has a large number of apartment complexes and duplexes. Because of this, enumeration districts often have only a few houses with clearly separated garbage containers. Thus, the actual sample areas chosen were portions of census tracts and included more than one enumeration district.

The socioeconomic characteristics of the five sample neighborhoods as recorded by the 1970 Census are presented in Table 16.1.[2] Areas MID.1 and MID.2 generally represent middle-income households, area M.LOW represents moderately low-income households, and areas LOW.1 and LOW.2 represent low-income households.

1978 Interview Survey Data

Since the initial census data used to choose sample areas were 9 years out of date, it was necessary to confirm that the sample areas still were made up of households with the same matrix of socioeconomic characteristics. This confirmation was provided by an interview survey conducted by phone in the fall of 1978. A total of 432 interviews was completed.

A bias was introduced by interviewing by phone. Since lower-income families are more likely not to own phones, they are more likely to be underrepresented in the interviews. This underrepresentation can be seen in Table 16.2, which presents the

[2]A code will be used to identify the sample areas by income. *MID* will signify the two middle-income areas, *LOW* the two low-income areas, and *M.LOW* the moderately low-income area.

sampling frequencies of total "collectible" households, the number of households with phones, and the number of interviews completed for each sample area. The low-income areas as identified by 1970 Census data have a very low percentage of households with phones. Those households with phones may be mainly those which are better-off financially. Thus, in the sampled "low-income" areas there are probably even more low-income families than represented in the completed telephone interviews.

Table 16.1 Milwaukee Sample Neighborhood Socioeconomic Characteristics from 1970 U.S. Census Data

	Family size by percentage of households					
	One	Two	Three	Four	Five	Six
MID.1	12.4	22.5	18.1	17.6	13.8	15.6
MID.2	23.3	31.0	17.5	14.6	7.8	6.1
M.LOW	48.3	19.1	9.9	7.1	4.6	10.7
LOW.1	36.9	19.3	11.8	10.0	7.2	17.8
LOW.2	41.0	18.8	10.3	8.2	7.7	13.6

	"Race" by percentage of households		
	White	Black	Spanish
MID.	1100.0	0	0
MID.2	100.0	0	0
M.LOW	83.9	8.4	5.2
LOW.1	9.0	91.0	0
LOW.2	72.1	0	26.0

	Annual income by percentage of households					
	$3000	$3000 4999	$5000 6999	$7000 9999	$10,000 12,499	$12,500
MID.1	11.8	13.0	14.0	25.2	35.0	1.0
MID.2	13.3	11.8	10.5	21.0	42.4	0
M.LOW	28.3	13.7	15.3	21.0	21.0	0
LOW.1	34.6	22.8	15.0	13.1	14.2	0
LOW.2	37.0	15.0	8.2	22.8	15.1	1.0

Table 16.2 Milwaukee Garbage Project, Interview Survey Sampling Frequencies

Sample neighborhoods	"Collectible" households	"Collectible" households with phones	Completed interviews	Percentage of households with phones	Percentage of "collectible" households interviewed
MID.1	279	213	98	76.3	35.1
MID.2	348	239	147	68.7	42.2
M.LOW	175	114	78	51.2	44.6
LOW.1	140	76	49	54.3	35.0
LOW.2	249	149	60	59.8	24.1
Total	1191	791	432		

Three basic variables were evaluated from the interview survey data: income of the head of household, family size, and ethnic affiliation.

Income

The variable of income for the head of household showed statistically significant differences (at the .05 level) between sample areas (Table 16.3). The major patterns for each group are

MID.1: large numbers relative to other areas in class 4, upper income, $15,000 and up per year
MID.2: large numbers relative to other areas in class 4, upper income, $15,000 and up per year
M.LOW: large numbers relative to other areas in class 2, lower income, $7500 to $10,000 per year
LOW.1: large numbers relative to other areas in class 1, low income, less than $7500 per year
LOW.2: large numbers relative to other areas in class 1, low income, less than $7500 per year

Thus, the interview samples from areas MID.1 and MID.2 both display relatively high incomes, LOW.1 and LOW.2 relatively low incomes, and M.LOW moderately low incomes.

Family Size

There are also statistically significant differences (at the .05 level) in the distribution of family sizes among sample areas (Table 16.3). The main patterns between sample areas and family sizes are

MID.1: large numbers relative to other areas of 3- and 4-person households
MID.2: low numbers relative to other areas of 1-person households
M.LOW: large numbers relative to other areas of 1-person and also 5- or more person households
LOW.1: large numbers relative to other areas of 1-person households
LOW.2: large numbers relative to other areas of 1- and 2-person households, low numbers relative to other areas of 5- or more person households

Therefore, the interview sample population frequencies show more large family sizes for study areas MID.1 and MID.2, more small family sizes for LOW.1 and LOW.2, and a mixed situation for area M.LOW.

Ethnic Affiliation

Informants were asked to state their "dominant ethnic origin." Several ethnic backgrounds were found in high frequencies in the study areas—German, Polish, Negro, and Hispanic (Mexican-American, Puerto Rican, or Spanish). The percentages of individuals who responded to the survey with these descriptions are presented in Table 16.3. Based on these interview data, the families in area MID.1 are

Table 16.3 Milwaukee Sample Neighborhoods—Socioeconomic Characteristics and 1978 Interview Survey Data

	Annual income of head of household by percentage of households			
	below $7500	$7500 9999	$10,000 14,999	$15,000 and above
MID.1	25.8	14.9	23.6	42.7
MID.2	19.8	14.3	23.8	42.1
M.LOW	32.3	21.5	24.6	12.0
LOW.1	51.5	10.3	20.5	6.0
LOW.2	73.1	7.7	9.6	9.6

	Family size by percentage of households				
	1	2	3	4	5 or more
MID.1	9.2	32.7	26.5	17.3	14.3
MID.2	8.8	38.1	17.7	14.3	21.1
M.LOW	23.1	26.9	15.4	10.3	24.4
LOW.1	26.5	28.6	12.2	10.2	22.4
LOW.2	26.7	41.7	18.3	6.7	6.7

	Reported ethnic origin by percentage of households				
	German	Polish	Black	Hispanic	Other
MID.1	61.0	4.2	2.1	—	32.6
MID.2	15.3	77.1	—	.7	6.9
M.LOW	35.6	4.1	6.8	2.7	50.7
LOW.1	4.1	2.0	79.6	—	14.3
LOW.2	23.3	8.3	—	13.3	55.0

largely German, MID.2 largely Polish, M.LOW of mixed ethnicity, LOW.1 heavily black, and LOW.2 are of mixed ethnicity with a significant percentage of Hispanics.

It is clear from this analysis that the socioeconomic groups, as represented by the interview data, contain the same "type" of households as were recorded in the 1970 Census. The socioeconomic characteristics of the households in the sample areas can be summarized as:

MID.1: middle income, relatively more large families, largely German
MID.2: middle income, relatively more large families, almost entirely Polish
M.LOW: moderately low income, mixed family sizes, mixed ethnicity
LOW.1: low income, relatively more small families, almost entirely black
LOW.2: low income, relatively more small families, mixed ethnicity with a significant number of Hispanics

Because of a growing distrust of government intervention and of interviewers in general, the validity of our neighborhood socioeconomic data is questionable. Recent experience indicates that "reactive bias" is likely to be especially high among low-income respondents. Reported household sizes in low-income areas are suspiciously small (Raymond Caplan, personal communication). Since both federal census and interview survey information agree, household sizes may be accurately reported. On the other hand, it is important to keep in mind that they may be the result of biased reporting.

Refuse Data Bases

Refuse from the five sample areas was recorded during fall 1978, spring 1979, and fall 1979, using standard "Le Projet du Garbage" methods (McGuire 1980; Rathje and Hughes 1975, 1978). This work resulted in three separate data bases being collected at the same time. The first data base, *total pickup weights*, consists of the total weights of 598 individual household refuse collections.

The second data base, *weight sorts*, consists of refuse samples whose contents were sorted into 15 categories based on material composition. The weight of refuse in each of the 15 material categories was then recorded (Figure 16.1). The 15 classes of material composition used in the weight sort are

1. (IRON) Ferrous Metal
2. (ALUM) Aluminum
3. (IRAL) Ferrous/aluminum combinations
4. (METOTH) Other metals
5. (NEWS) Newsprint
6. (MAGS) Magazines
7. (PACKP) Packaging paper
8. (NPACKP) Nonpackaging paper
9. (PLAST) Plastic
10. (NRGLAS) Nonreturnable glass
11. (RETGLS) Returnable glass
12. (FOODRL) Food debris
13. (YRDWST) Yard debris
14. (TEXT) Textiles
15. (OTHER)

Weight sorts are similar to most solid waste analyses, except the paper component is subdivided into *packaging paper* and *nonpackaging paper*. *Packaging paper* in-

M

B02	1	16 NOV 78	Nowak / Ryan
Tract	# Houses	Date	Recorders

METALS	Ferrous	1 LB. 8 OZ.
	Aluminum	
	Ferrous/Aluminum Combinations	
	Other	
	Specify	////////////////////////////////
PAPER	Newsprint	5 LB. 2 OZ.
	Magazines (glossy)	
	Packaging (and packaging related)	2 LB. 2 OZ.
	Nonpackaging (mail, tissues, etc.)	1 LB. 15 OZ.
		////////////////////////////////
	PLASTIC	13 OZ.
		////////////////////////////////
GLASS	Nonreturnable	2 LB. 15 OZ.
	Returnable	
		////////////////////////////////
ORGANIC	Food Related	1 LB. 10 OZ.
	Yard Wastes	3 LB. 2 OZ.
		////////////////////////////////
	TEXTILES	Trace
OTHER	Specify Wood	4 LB. 8 OZ.
	Specify	
		////////////////////////////////
	TOTAL	23.7 LB.

FIGURE 16.1. Garbage Project weight recording form.

M

25.2 TOTAL HH WEIGHT (LBS.)

CENSUS TRACT (16 17 18): 807 | COLLECTION MO. (19 20): 10 | DAY (21 22): 31

Freidel / Hughes — NAME OF RECORDER

11/16/79 — DATE OF ANALYSIS

MATERIAL COMPOSITION CODES

CODE (LIST MOST PREVALENT MATERIAL FIRST)

A PAPER	H RETURNABLE GLASS	R COPPER AND BRASS
B FERROUS (STEEL/TIN)	J AEROSOL CANS	S BIODEGRADABLE PLASTIC
C ALUMINUM	K WOOD	T TEXTILES
D PLASTIC (CELLOPHANE)	M CERAMICS	V CORRUGATED CARDBOARD
E NONRETURN GLASS	P LEATHER	X OTHER (SPECIFY ON BACK)
	Q RUBBER	

TRACT: 807 PAGE 1/5 TOTAL PGS.

	ITEM CODE (23–25)	NO. OF ITEMS (26–28)	FLUID OUNCES (29–33)	SOLID OUNCES (34–38)	COST (39–44)	WASTE (GRAMS) (45–48)	SPECIAL IND. (49)	BRAND (50–57)	TYPE (58–65)	MATERIAL COMPOSITION CODE (66–68)
1	086	6	72.0	.	.			STROHS	BOHEMIAN	C
2	011	1	128.0	.	.			WILKES	WHOLE	AD
3	075	1	64.0	.	1.65			TROPICAN	ORANGE	ED
4	079	1	67.6	.	.			COCACOLA	COLA	DC
5	140	14	.	.	.				PAPER	A
6	140	4	.	.	.				PLASTIC	D
7	022	3	.	7.5	.20			MARTHAWH	MUFFIN	A
8	079	1	16.0	.	.			MOUNTAIN	CITRUS	H
9	079	1	16.0	.	.			SPOT	ORANGE	E
10	027	1	.	24.0	.	70		WONDER	ENRICHED	D
11	005	1	.	3.8	.			SPIRITOF	SARDINE	CD
12	027	1	.	24.0	.			JAEGER	ENRICHED	D
13	020	2	.	16.0	.98			PATRICKC	BACON	DA
14	086	1	12.0	.	.			PABST		CB
15	131	1	.	7.0	.83			GLADE	AIRFRESH	BD
16	057	2	.	14.0	.49			HEINTZ	CATSUP	EB
17	003	1	.	56.0	1.35			KOHLS	FRYING	D
18	017	1	.	12.0	.88			JIFF	CREAMY	EB
19	042	1	.	8.0	.17		G		TOMATOSA	BA
20	030	1	.	20.0	1.25			KELLOGGS	FROSTEDF	A

FIGURE 16.2. Completed Garbage Project recording form.

BEEF *.................... 001
OTHER MEAT (not bacon)*.... 002
CHICKEN.................... 003
OTHER POULTRY.............. 004
FISH (fresh, frozen, canned, dried)*......... 005
CRUSTACEANS & MOLLUSKS (shrimp, clams, etc.)... 006
T.V.P. TYPE FOODS *........ 007
UNKNOWN MEAT............... 008
CHEESE (including cottage cheese)......... 010
MILK *..................... 011
ICE CREAM (also ice milk, sherbet)*......... 012
OTHER DAIRY (not butter)... 013
EGGS (regular, powdered, liquid)*................ 014
BEANS (not green beans)*... 015
NUTS....................... 016
PEANUT BUTTER.............. 017
FATS: Saturated *.......... 018
Unsaturated *........ 019
Bacon, saltpork *.... 020
Meat trimming........ 021
CORN (also corn meal and masa)*.............. 022
FLOUR (also pancake mix)*.. 023
RICE *..................... 024
OTHER GRAIN (barley, wheat germ, etc.)............ 025
NOODLES (pasta)............ 026
WHITE BREAD................ 027
DARK BREAD................. 028
TORTILLAS *................ 029
DRY CEREALS:
Regular................ 030
High Sugar (first ingredient only)..... 031
COOKED CEREALS (instant or regular)............ 032
CRACKERS................... 033
CHIPS (also pretzels)...... 034
UNKNOWN PRODUCE *.......... 040
FRESH VEGETABLES *......... 041
CANNED VEGETABLES (dehydrated also)*...... 042
FROZEN VEGETABLES *........ 043
POTATO PEEL *.............. 044
FRESH FRUIT *.............. 045
CANNED FRUIT (dehydrated also)*...... 046
FROZEN FRUIT *............. 047
FRUIT PEEL *............... 048
RELISH, PICKLES, OLIVES *.. 049
SYRUP, HONEY, JELLIES, MOLASSES............... 051
PASTRIES (cookies, cakes and mix, pies, etc.) *.. 052
SUGAR *.................... 053
ARTIFICIAL SWEETENERS...... 054
CANDY *.................... 055
SALT *..................... 056
SPICES & FLAVORINGS (catsup, mustard, pepper, etc.)*.......... 057
BAKING ADDITIVES (yeast, baking powder, etc.)*... 058
POPSICLES.................. 060
PUDDING.................... 061
GELATIN.................... 062
INSTANT BREAKFAST.......... 063

DIPS (for chips)........... 064
NONDAIRY CREAMERS & WHIPS................... 065
HEALTH FOODS *............. 066
SLOP *..................... 069

REGULAR COFFEE (instant or ground)*............. 070
DECAF COFFEE............... 071
EXOTIC COFFEE *............ 072
TEA *...................... 073
CHOCOLATE DRINK MIX OR TOPPING................. 074
FRUIT OR VEG. JUICE (canned or bottled)..... 075
FRUIT JUICE CONCENTRATE.... 076
FRUIT DRINK, pdr. or lqud. (Tang, Koolaid, Hi-C)*.. 077
DIET SODA.................. 078
REGULAR SODA............... 079
COCKTAIL MIX (carbonated).. 080
COCKTAIL MIX (non-carb. liquid)................. 081
COCKTAIL MIX (powdered).... 082

PREMIXED COCKTAILS (alcoholic)............. 083
SPIRITS (booze)............ 084
WINE (still & sparkling)... 085
BEER *..................... 086

BABY FOOD & JUICE *........ 087
BABY CEREAL (pablum)....... 088
BABY FORMULA (liquid)*..... 089
BABY FORMULA (powdered)*... 090
PET FOOD (dry)............. 091
PET FOOD (canned or moist)................. 092
TV DINNERS (also pot pies). 094
TAKE OUT MEALS............. 095
SOUPS *.................... 096
GRAVY & SPECIALTY SAUCES *. 097
PREPARED MEALS (canned or packaged)*.............. 098

VITAMIN PILLS & SUPPLEMENTS (commercial)*........... 100
PRESCRIBED DRUGS (prescribed vitamins)... 101
ASPIRIN *.................. 102
COMMERCIAL STIMULANTS & DEPRESSANTS *........... 103
COMMERCIAL REMEDIES *...... 104
ILLICIT DRUGS *............ 105
COMMERCIAL DRUG PARAPHERNALIA........... 106
ILLICIT DRUG PARAPHERNALIA. 107
CONTRACEPTIVES:
MALE................... 108
FEMALE................. 109

BABY SUPPLIES (diapers, etc.)*........ 111
INJURY ORIENTED (iodine, bandaids, etc.)......... 112
PERSONAL SANITATION *...... 113
COSMETICS *................ 114

CIGARETTES (pack)*......... 124
CIGARETTES (carton)*....... 125
CIGARS..................... 126
PIPE, CHEWING TOBACCO, LOOSE TOBACCO........... 127
ROLLING PAPERS (also smoking items).......... 128

HOUSEHOLD & LAUNDRY CLEANERS *............. 131
HOUSEHOLD CLEANING TOOLS (not detergents)....... 132
HOUSEHOLD MAINT. ITEMS (paint, wood, etc.).... 133
COOKING & SERVING AIDS.... 134
TISSUE CONTAINER.......... 135
TOILET PAPER CONTAINER.... 136
NAPKIN CONTAINER.......... 137
PAPER TOWEL CONTAINER..... 138
PLATIC WRAP CONTAINER..... 139
BAGS (paper or plastic)*.. 140
BAG CONTAINER............. 141
ALUMINUM FOIL SHEETS...... 142
ALUMINUM FOIL PACKAGE..... 143
WAX PAPER PACKAGE......... 144

MECHANICAL APPLIANCE (tools)................ 147
ELECTRICAL APPLIANCE & ITEMS................ 148
AUTO SUPPLIES............. 149
FURNITURE................. 150
CLOTHING: CHILD *......... 151
ADULT *......... 152
CLOTHING CARE ITEMS (shoe polish, thread).. 153
DRY CLEANING (laundry also)......... 154
PET MAINTENANCE (litter).. 155
PET TOYS.................. 156
GATE RECEIPTS (tickets)... 157
HOBBY RELATED ITEMS....... 158
PHOTO SUPPLIES............ 159
HOLIDAY VALUE (nonfood)*.. 160
DECORATIONS (nonholiday).. 161
PLANT & YARD MAINT........ 162
STATIONERY SUPPLIES....... 163
JEWELRY................... 164

CHILD SCHOOL RELATED PAPERS *............... 171
CHILD EDUC. BOOKS (nonfiction)........... 172
CHILD EDUC. GAMES (toys).. 173
CHILD AMUSEMENT READING... 174
CHILD AMUSEMENT TOYS (games)................ 175
ADULT BOOKS (nonfiction).. 176
ADULT BOOKS (fiction)..... 177
ADULT AMUSEMENT GAMES..... 178

LOCAL NEWSPAPERS *........ 181
NEWSPAPERS (other city, national)*............. 182
ORGANIZATIONAL NEWSPAPERS OR MAGAZINES (also religion)*............. 183
GENERAL INTEREST MAGAZINES *............ 184
SPECIAL INTEREST MAGAZINE OR NEWSPAPER *......... 185
ENTERTAINMENT GUIDE (TV Guide, etc.)....... 186

MISCELLANEOUS ITEMS (specify on back of sheet)*................ 190

*Special Notes Used in Recording Procedures, see Appendix.

FIGURE 16.3. Garbage item code list.

cludes any item used in the packaging or transport of any commodity except mail. Cereal boxes, paper rolls from paper towels, shopping bags, containers from take-out meals, and most cardboard boxes fall into this category. *Nonpackaging paper* includes paper towels, napkins, paper plates and cups, cigarette filters, and disposable baby diaper papers. Mail, with the exception of boxes, also is in this category. This weight-sort format is designed to record the actual weights of the major material components of household solid wastes. The weight-sort data base consists of 224 pickups.

The third data base, *regular sorts*, is composed of refuse samples whose contents, including food debris and packaging, were recorded item by item. This data base was compiled in order to identify the specific commodities that compose the solid wastes from different sample areas. For each identifiable item, the following data were recorded when available (see Figure 16.2):

1. Garbage Project item code (refer to Figure 16.3)
2. Number of items
3. Original net weight in solid ounces or volume in fluid ounces
4. Cost
5. "Waste" in grams
6. Specific type of item
7. Brand name
8. Material composition code

If a set of identical items was being recorded, number of items, net weight or volume, and costs were added together. If data, such as cost, were not marked directly on packages or commodities, they were left blank. The regular-sort data base consists of 179 household refuse samples.

The sample sizes of refuse pickups recorded from the five Milwaukee study areas

Table 16.4 Milwaukee Garbage Project, Household Pickup Sample Sizes

Sample neighborhood	Total pickup weight	Weight sort	Regular sort	(Interview survey)
MID.1	118	45	31	98
MID.2	141	57	47	147
M.LOW	108	41	32	78
LOW.1	103	38	35	49
LOW.2	128	43	34	60
Total	598	224	179	432

are presented in Table 16.4. Weight sorts and regular sorts provide independent lines of evidence on the nature of household solid wastes. The weight sorts record the weight of items in household pickups by material composition. The deficiency of weight sorts is that they do not provide information on how much weight each commodity and package type adds to the total weight of household refuse. Regular sorts do provide this information in the form of counts of specific items that can be sorted by size and material composition.

Analysis Limitations

It is important at this point to emphasize the limitations imposed on analysis by the methods used in collecting data. All of the information on the socioeconomic characteristics of sample neighborhoods was recorded in interview surveys and is subject to possible informant bias. Another possible bias comes from the method of collecting refuse for study. Random samples of household refuse were collected within selected neighborhoods without additional background on the specific households sampled. As a result, specific patterns in recorded refuse can be related only to overall neighborhood characteristics, not to the characteristics of individual households. This limitation on data analysis was necessary to protect the anonymity of the residents of study households.

INCOME AND SOLID-WASTE BACKGROUND STUDIES

A number of studies from cities other than Milwaukee have developed socioeconomic models of residential solid waste generation. Most have come to the same conclusion: Rates of residential solid waste production are directly related to household income—Chicago (Tolley, Hastings, and Rudzitis 1978), Baltimore (Winfield 1974:2,44), Detroit (Wertz 1976), Indianapolis (Richardson and Havlicek 1974, 1975, 1978), and Lafayette–West Lafayette (Havlicek and Saleh 1974; Saleh 1974; Saleh and Havlicek 1975). The income elasticities are relatively small (.279–.272 for Detroit, .242 for Indianapolis, and .50–.55 for Chicago), indicating that "waste generation increases less than proportionally with income [Tolley *et al.* 1978:97]." Nevertheless, the conclusion remains: Differences in family income can explain a portion of the variation in per capita solid waste discard. The relation between income and solid wastes, however, is not simple.

Upon further examination, it is clear that income does not correlate directly with all of the components of solid waste. In fact, it correlates only with a few. One component is newspapers. Most studies have found that the weight of discarded newspapers in residential solid wastes rises in direct relation to income (Richardson and Havlicek 1978:108; Saleh 1974:126; Winfield 1974:2, Table 5).[3] The strongest

[3]This income–newspaper relationship was not found to hold for the Milwaukee neighborhoods sampled in this study. The relation, if it does exist, may have been masked by the high participation of Milwaukee residents in newspaper recycling programs.

Table 16.5 Per Capita Weekly Household Solid Wastes, Indianapolis, Indiana, 1972[a]

Component	Per capita disgard rate (lb.)		
	High income	Medium income	Low income
Glass	1.37	1.57	1.6
Aluminum	.04	.07	.08
Other metals	1.07	1.12	1.28
Other paper	2.37	1.83	1.72
Plastics	.45	.50	.59
Textiles	.23	.34	.45
Garbage/other	1.37	3.05	3.25
Newspaper	1.84	1.37	.86
Grass	10.05	2.57	.86
Total	18.77	12.41	11.29
Total without grass	8.72	9.84	10.43

[a]From Table II in Richardson and Havlicek (1978).

direct relationship between income and solid wastes, however, is with "yard wastes" (Richardson and Havlicek 1974:152, 1975:7, 1978:108; Tolley *et al.* 1978:88,95; Winfield 1974:2,44).[4] The yard waste linkage is expected since upper-income households have the largest yards. The degree to which this affects solid wastes is less expectable and even rather amazing. In Baltimore, for example, seasonal yard wastes account for 10% of all residential residuals (Winfield 1974:44). In Indianapolis, the weekly yard wastes ranged from less than 1 lb. per capita in low-income areas to more than 10 lb. per capita in high-income neighborhoods (Table 16.5; Richardson and Havlicek 1978:Table 2). Seasonal volumes are so high, in fact, that where income has been compared to rates of solid waste generation, the relationship is almost totally explained by yard wastes alone. For example, when yard wastes are added into total weekly refuse in Indianapolis, the high-income per capita discard rate of 18.77 lb. completely outweighs the low-income rate of 11.29 lb. When yard wastes are subtracted, however, the rates are reversed. The low-income rate of 10.43 lb. per week is higher than the high-income rate of 8.72 lb. per week. One report of the Indianapolis study states that yard wastes accounted for 90% of the seasonal variability in residential residuals (Havlicek and Saleh 1974:10).

[4]This income–yard waste relationship also was not identified for sample Milwaukee neighborhoods. One reason may be that all samples were collected in the spring and fall rather than during the summer when yard wastes would be most consistently discarded in large quantities.

Given that yard wastes are seasonal and are by far the most important element in the income and solid-waste relation, income should have a less significant effect on waste volume in the winter than during the rest of the year. As expected, those researchers who checked their data for this relationship reported that the correlation between higher income and higher solid wastes generation was much stronger during the summer (Richardson and Havlicek 1974:152; Tolley *et al.* 1978: 88,95,97). As Tolley *et al.* (1978:88) conclude, "There is a basic year-round volume of wastes, represented by the mid-winter volume, that is relatively less sensitive to income than 'excess' volumes in other parts of the year." Packaging and related consumer products are a large part of this basic material flow that does not fluctuate with season.

Few significant differences in the packaging discard patterns of different income groups have been identified. What differences there are tend to indicate that packaging is discarded at a higher rate in lower-income neighborhoods. In Baltimore, lower-income groups discarded more glass containers and more paper, both packaging and otherwise, than other groups (Winfield 1974:Table 5). In Indianapolis, low-income households discarded more glass, more aluminum, more other metals, and more plastics than other households (Table 16.5; Richardson and Havlicek 1978:Table 2).[5]

Most of these observations fit with the general summary of Milwaukee's residential solid wastes provided by the Milwaukee Department of Public Works, Bureau of Sanitation: "Observation and weights tell us the garbage in outer sections of the city has a greater seasonal variation due primarily to yard wastes. The inner sections of the city have a lesser variation in weight and remain heavier than the outer sections of the city for the entire year [Raymond Caplan, personal communication]."

Thus, income level often has been directly related to the discard of yard wastes and sometimes to the discard of newspapers. The effect of income level on the discard of packaging and other consumer products is still largely unstudied (Saleh 1974 and Saleh and Havlicek 1975 are exceptions). The residential solid waste data collected in Milwaukee provide some potentially useful insights into the nature of the income and solid-waste relationship, especially the relationship involving the discard of packaging.

Research Question 1: *What are the comparative weights of solid wastes discarded weekly by sample households in the five Milwaukee neighborhoods?*

Answer 1: *Sample households in the two low-income, small family areas and in one middle-income area discarded more refuse overall than households in the other two areas. This indicates that income and family size probably cannot be used in a simple manner to explain the quantity of solid wastes discarded.*

[5]In addition to the income relationship, a number of studies have concluded that household size is directly correlated with the discard of solid wastes. Generally the relationship has been stated in a simple form: the larger the household, the more solid wastes (Richardson and Havliceck 1978; Saleh 1974; Saleh and Havlicek 1975; Tolley *et al.* 1978; Winfield 1974).

Table 16.6 Milwaukee Garbage Project Weekly Household Pickups[a]

Sample neighborhood	$\bar{X}$	Standard deviation	Percentage of pickups 20 lb. or less	Estimated lb./year/household[b,c,d,e]
MID.1	27.2437	15.0957	38.13	1416.67
MID.2	21.4418	12.3398	53.57	1114.97
M.LOW	23.1851	13.6470	47.22	1205.62
LOW.1	29.4590	17.1734	39.80	1531.87
LOW.2	26.9180	19.5846	38.76	1399.74
Milwaukee total	25.5673	15.9730		

[a] Total number of pickups recorded was 598.

[b] Kendall Correlation, the likelihood that the five data sets are patterned in the same way is .004; correlation coefficient .0738.

[c] Spearman Correlation, the likelihood that the five data sets are patterned in the same way is .007; correlation coefficient .1005.

[d] Kruskal-Wallis 1-Way ANOVA, significant at the .0005 level.

[e] Breakdown ANOVA, significant at the .0006 level.

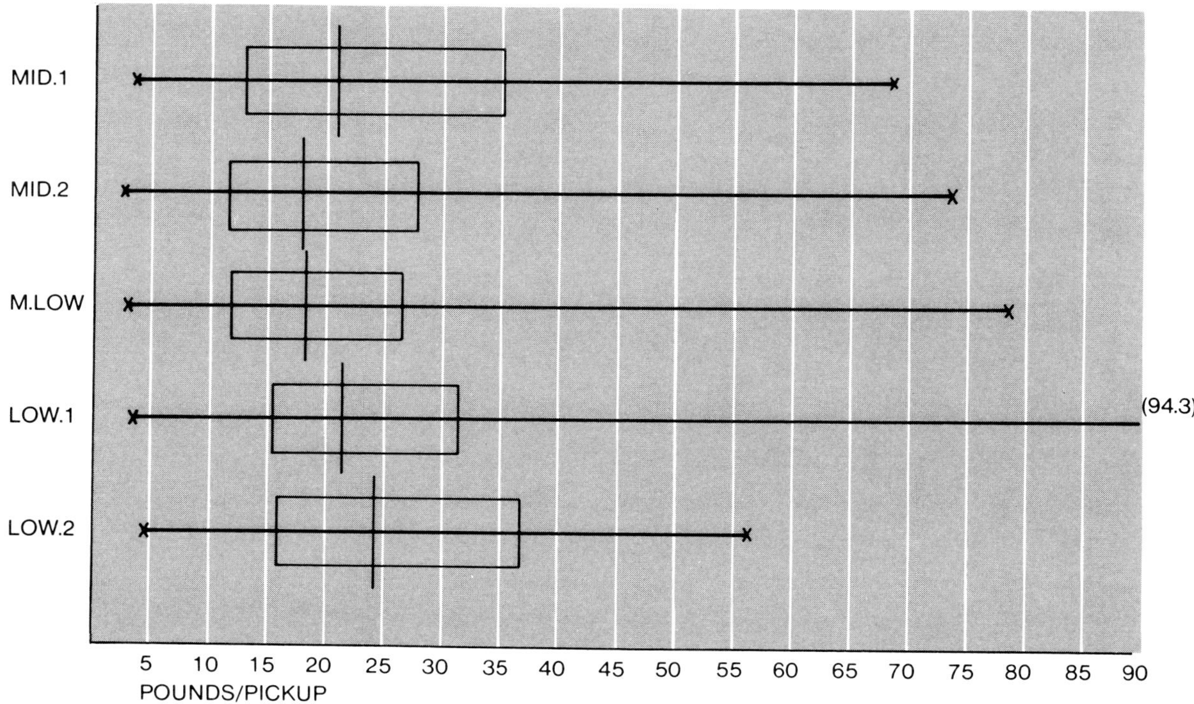

FIGURE 16.4. Total pickup weights.

MID.1

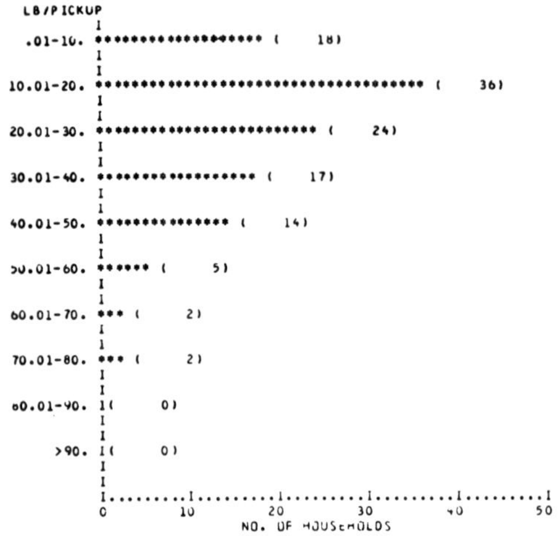

MEAN	25.796	STD ERR	1.430	MEDIAN	22.405
MODE	9.700	STD DEV	15.537	VARIANCE	241.410
KURTOSIS	.541	SKEWNESS	.950	RANGE	73.260
MINIMUM	3.740	MAXIMUM	77.000	SUM	3043.920
C.V. PCT	60.232	.95 C.I.	22.963	TO	28.629

VALID CASES 118 MISSING CASES 0

M.LOW

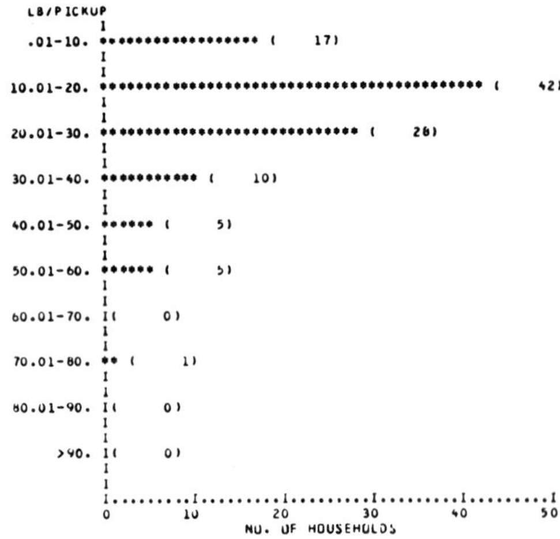

MEAN	21.573	STD ERR	1.323	MEDIAN	18.200
MODE	23.900	STD DEV	13.751	VARIANCE	189.078
KURTOSIS	2.716	SKEWNESS	1.469	RANGE	76.160
MINIMUM	2.900	MAXIMUM	79.060	SUM	2329.910
C.V. PCT	63.734	.95 C.I.	18.950	TO	24.196

VALID CASES 108 MISSING CASES 0

MID.2

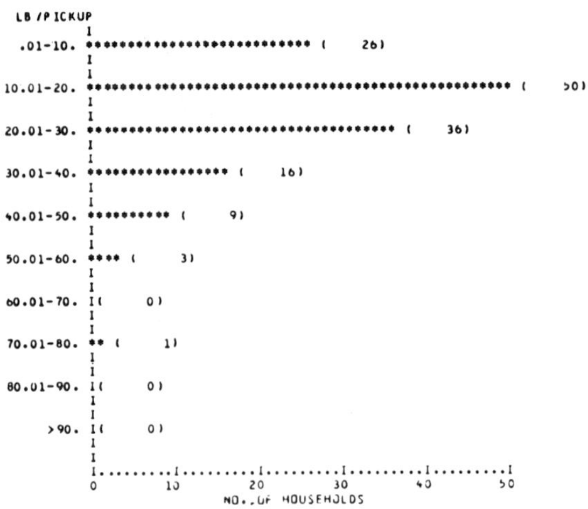

MEAN	20.797	STD ERR	1.036	MEDIAN	18.870
MODE	22.500	STD DEV	12.299	VARIANCE	151.276
KURTOSIS	1.915	SKEWNESS	1.102	RANGE	71.610
MINIMUM	2.390	MAXIMUM	74.000	SUM	2932.350
C.V. PCT	59.141	.95 C.I.	18.749	TO	22.845

VALID CASES 141 MISSING CASES 0

FIGURE 16.5. Total pickup weights by sample neighborhood.

LOW.1

```
LB/PICKUP
           I
 .01-10.   ************** (    13)
           I
           I
10.01-20.  ********************************** (    33)
           I
           I
20.01-30.  ******************************* (    30)
           I
           I
30.01-40.  ************* (    12)
           I
           I
40.01-50.  ********** (     9)
           I
           I
50.01-60.  **** (     3)
           I
           I
60.01-70.  I(     0)
           I
           I
70.01-80.  I(     0)
           I
           I
80.01-90.  *** (     2)
           I
           I
     >90.  ** (     1)
           I
           I
           I.........I.........I.........I.........I.........I
           0        10        20        30        40        50
                          NO. OF HOUSEHOLDS
```

MEAN	25.133	STD ERR	1.561	MEDIAN	21.650
MODE	15.200	STD DEV	15.844	VARIANCE	251.043
KURTOSIS	5.391	SKEWNESS	1.936	RANGE	90.690
MINIMUM	3.620	MAXIMUM	94.310	SUM	2588.710
C.V. PCT	63.042	.95 C.I.	22.036	TO	28.230

VALID CASES 103 MISSING CASES 0

LOW.2

```
LB/PICKUP
           I
 .01-10.   ************* (    12)
           I
           I
10.01-20.  ****************************************** (    41)
           I
           I
20.01-30.  ***************************** (    28)
           I
           I
30.01-40.  ************************** (    25)
           I
           I
40.01-50.  ************* (    12)
           I
           I
50.01-60.  ****** (     5)
           I
           I
60.01-70.  ** (     1)
           I
           I
70.01-80.  **** (     3)
           I
           I
80.01-90.  I(     0)
           I
           I
     >90.  ** (     1)
           I
           I
           I.........I.........I.........I.........I.........I
           0        10        20        30        40        50
                          NO. OF HOUSEHOLDS
```

MEAN	27.758	STD ERR	1.457	MEDIAN	24.205
MODE	13.500	STD DEV	16.486	VARIANCE	271.789
KURTOSIS	2.895	SKEWNESS	1.384	RANGE	94.530
MINIMUM	4.900	MAXIMUM	99.430	SUM	3552.970
C.V. PCT	59.393	.95 C.I.	24.874	TO	30.641

VALID CASES 128 MISSING CASES 0

FIGURE 16.5 (*continued*)

MILWAUKEE TOTAL PICKUP WEIGHTS

The first and most obvious difference between the five Milwaukee sample neighborhoods is in the total weights of individual household pickups. Whereas the average weight of a refuse pickup for the five areas was a little more than 25 lb. a week, the MID.2 and M.LOW areas had much lower mean weights than the MID.1, LOW.1, and LOW.2 neighborhoods. The difference was determined to be significantly well below the .05 level on the basis of four separate statistical tests (Table 16.6). The difference is clear in the distribution of refuse pickup weights (Figures 16.4 and 16.5). For example, although about half the pickups in the MID.2 and M.LOW areas were below 20 lb. in weight, only a little over a third of the pickups from MID.2, LOW.1, and LOW.2 households were below 20 lb. The difference is also clear in absolute weight. Over a year period, single households in MID.1, LOW.1, and LOW.2 areas are likely to discard almost 300 lb. more than households in MID.1 and M.LOW areas; more specifically, a single household in the LOW.1 areas is likely to discard 400 lb. more solid wastes than a single household in the MID.2 area.[6]

These results at first seem a little confusing. The two middle-income areas are about equal in solid waste weights and the two lowest-income areas with relatively more small families produce heavier solid wastes than an area with a higher percentage of large families (MID.2). These findings indicate that income and family size alone do not explain the discard of solid wastes. A search for other factors begins with the material composition of household garbage pickups.

Research Question 2: *Do some of the five Milwaukee neighborhoods discard different kinds of garbage?*

Answer 2: *The material composition breakdown of household solid wastes indicates that sample households in the two low-income areas discarded more packaging by weight than sample households in the other areas.*

MILWAUKEE WEIGHT SORTS—DETAILED VIEW

If income is an important factor in solid waste discard patterns, there should be differences between the material composition of household refuse from low- and middle-income sample areas. We should also expect differences in the refuse between neighborhoods with relatively more small families and those with relatively more large families. The second step in the Milwaukee analysis used nonparametric tests to determine if there were statistically significant differences in the *weights* of material composition categories when compared between sample neighborhoods.

There are no clear differences in refuse weight patterns among the five sample neighborhoods for most of the material composition categories (Table 16.7; for the

[6]These calculations may be overestimates by 20%, as households do not always place refuse pickups out for collection. The 20% figure comes from a prior study of household refuse disposal patterns in Tucson, Arizona.

Table 16.7 Milwaukee Garbage Project, Statistical Test of Differences in Discard Patterns between Sample Neighborhoods

Material composition category	Breakdown ANOVA significance level (total sample)	Breakdown ANOVA significance level (only pickups with occurrences)	1-way ANOVA significance level (total sample)	1-way ANOVA significance level (only pickups with occurrences)
IRON	.9976	.9650	.4084	.3688
ALUM	.0982	.1087	<u>.0282</u> (2.7694)[c]	.1353
IRAL	.8151	.7383	<u>.0006</u> (5.1505)[c]	<u>.0788</u>
METOTH	.6248	.9327	.9038	.5506
NEWS	.3087	.4964	.3914	.6181
MAGS	.2939	.2213	.2939	.2162
PACKP	<u>.0214</u> (2.9407)[c]	<u>.0327</u> (2.6787)[c]	<u>.0597</u> (2.30009)[c]	<u>.0863</u>
NPACKP	.3929	.5120	.4641	.2554
PLAST	<u>.0365</u> (2.6099)[c]	<u>.0504</u> (2.4084)[c]	<u>.0750</u> (2.1558)[c]	<u>.0504</u>
NRGLAS	<u>.0002</u> (5.7869)[c]	<u>.0011</u> (4.7804)[c]	<u>.0000</u> (6.9549)[c]	<u>.0002</u>
RETGLS	.3725	.7016	.5159	.7016
FOODRL	.8242	.9562	.9319	.9766

(Continued)

Table 16.7 (*Continued*)

Material composition category	Breakdown ANOVA significance level (total sample)	Breakdown ANOVA significance level (only pickups with occurrences)	1-way ANOVA significance level (total sample)	1-way ANOVA significance level (only pickups with occurrences)
YRDWST	.1568	.5344	.2015	.6215
TEXT	<u>.0165</u> (3.0994)[c]	.1901	<u>.0064</u> (3.6739)[c]	<u>.0235</u>
OTHER	.4516	.8043	.4450	.6363

[a] Levels of significance $\frac{\alpha}{2} \leq .05$; modified approach $\frac{\alpha}{10} \leq .01$.

[b] For full category names see page 406.

[c] F values.

specific weight breakdowns by neighborhood see Tables 16.8A and 16.8B). There are, however, statistically significant differences by weight in six categories: aluminum, ferrous/aluminum combinations, nonreturn glass, paper packaging, plastics, and textiles.

Textiles were discarded at high rates in all three low-income areas, M.LOW, LOW.1, and LOW.2 (Figures 16.6 and 16.7). One possible explanation is that middle-income households buy more of their clothing new and turn in their used clothes to thrift shops, Salvation Army stores, and other similar outlets. The poor may buy more used clothes and discard them when they are worn out (Richardson and Havlicek 1978:108). Although this explanation seems probable, it has not been tested in this study. The other differences between sample areas involve packaging materials.

Nonreturn glass discards form the most significant pattern (Figures 16.8 and 16.9). LOW.1 households discard nonreturn glass at more than double the rate of

Table 16.8A Discriminant Analysis: Five Sample Neighborhoods, Packaging Solid Wastes Group Means and Standard Deviations in Pounds per Pickup

Material composition category[a]		Sample areas				
		MID.1	MID.2	M.LOW	LOW.1	LOW.2
IRON	$\bar{X}$	1.74	1.56	1.11	1.60	1.84
	SD	1.78	1.67	1.24	1.81	2.35
ALUM[b]	$\bar{X}$	.29	.22	.30	.41	.65
	SD	.49	.39	.79	.62	1.03
IRAL	$\bar{X}$	.09	.05	.26	.64	.20
	SD	.26	.17	.58	1.31	.64
PLAST[b]	$\bar{X}$	1.81	1.24	.97	1.51	1.83
	SD	2.17	1.29	1.03	1.69	2.43
NRGLAS[b]	$\bar{X}$	1.82	2.24	2.23	5.21	2.14
	SD	1.64	2.99	3.45	5.44	2.42
RETGLS	$\bar{X}$	.12	.03	.46	.06	.10
	SD	.69	.19	2.83	.27	.58
PACKP[b]	$\bar{X}$	2.96	2.98	2.42	3.99	3.64
	SD	2.31	2.99	1.85	3.22	2.59
(Total packaging)		(8.83)	(8.41)	(7.75)	(13.42)	(10.40)

[a] For the full category names see page 406.

[b] Key variables for the discriminant analysis.

Table 16.8B Discriminant Analysis: Five Sample Neighborhoods, Nonpackaging Solid Wastes, Group Means and Standard Deviations in Pounds per Pickup

Material composition category[a]		Sample areas				
		MID.1	MID.2	M.LOW	LOW.1	LOW.2
NPACKP	$\bar{X}$	2.76	1.90	2.12	2.40	2.69
	SD	2.85	2.09	2.49	4.76	3.02
NEWSP	$\bar{X}$	3.88	1.98	3.56	3.30	3.92
	SD	4.16	3.65	6.33	5.13	8.40
MAGAZ	$\bar{X}$	.20	.04	.11	.14	.24
	SD	.60	.15	.36	.60	.65
METOTH	$\bar{X}$	.04	.06	.06	.00	.03
	SD	.15	.42	.39	.02	.19
TEXTL[b]	$\bar{X}$	.33	.34	.40	.83	1.66
	SD	.72	.62	1.16	1.57	4.00
FOODRL	$\bar{X}$	5.96	5.61	5.02	5.83	5.25
	SD	6.16	5.44	4.82	7.07	4.21
YRDWT	$\bar{X}$	2.23	3.65	2.83	.42	2.35
	SD	5.91	7.70	8.18	1.18	5.83
Other	$\bar{X}$	1.23	.81	1.31	1.29	2.25
	SD	3.04	2.01	3.62	3.47	5.87
(Nonpackaging total)		(16.63)	(14.39)	(15.41)	(14.21)	(18.39)
Total pickup weights		25.46	22.80	23.16	27.63	28.80

[a] For the full category names see page 406 .

[b] Key variables for the discriminant analysis.

all four other neighborhoods; over a 1-year period a single LOW.1 household is likely to discard 150–170 more pounds of glass than a single household in another area (Table 16.9). Thus, a low-income area is generating double the glass-packaging solid wastes per household of other neighborhoods.

The discard of *aluminum* seems to increase as income decreases (Figures 16.10 and 16.11). The most aluminum is discarded in the two lowest-income areas. Households in the LOW.1 neighborhood throw out more aluminum than households in the higher-income areas; those in the LOW.2 neighborhood throw out twice as much aluminum as households in the higher-income areas. As a result,

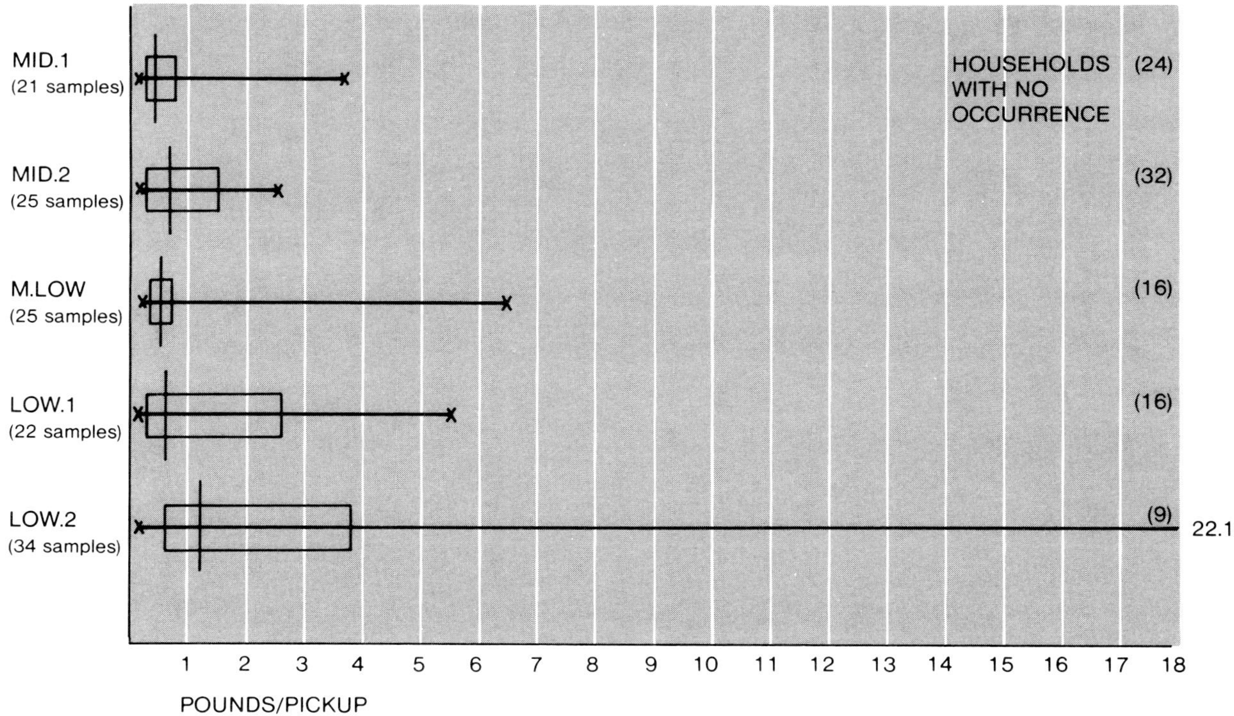

FIGURE 16.6. Textiles.

MID.1

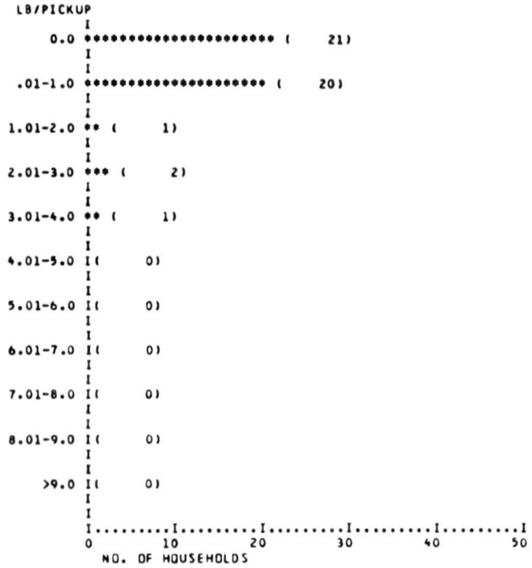

MEAN	.327	STD ERR	.107	MEDIAN	.010
MODE	0	STD DEV	.721	VARIANCE	.520
KURTOSIS	10.620	SKEWNESS	3.142	RANGE	3.600
MINIMUM	0	MAXIMUM	3.600	SUM	14.730
C.V. PCT	220.285	.95 C.I.	.111	TO	.544

VALID CASES 45 MISSING CASES 0

M.LOW

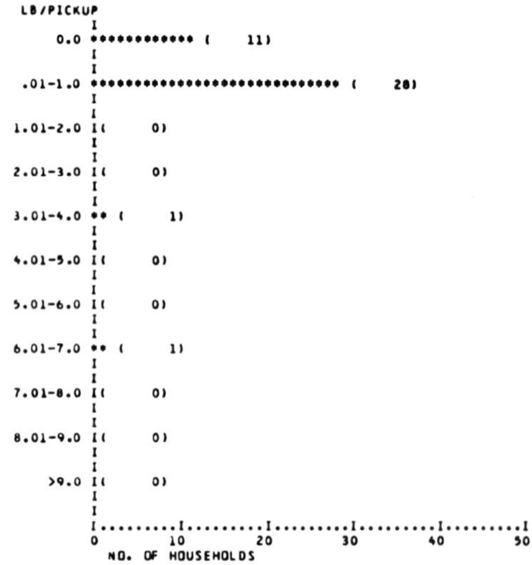

MEAN	.403	STD ERR	.181	MEDIAN	.064
MODE	0	STD DEV	1.162	VARIANCE	1.350
KURTOSIS	21.306	SKEWNESS	4.522	RANGE	6.500
MINIMUM	0	MAXIMUM	6.500	SUM	16.520
C.V. PCT	288.327	.95 C.I.	.036	TO	.770

VALID CASES 41 MISSING CASES 0

MID.2

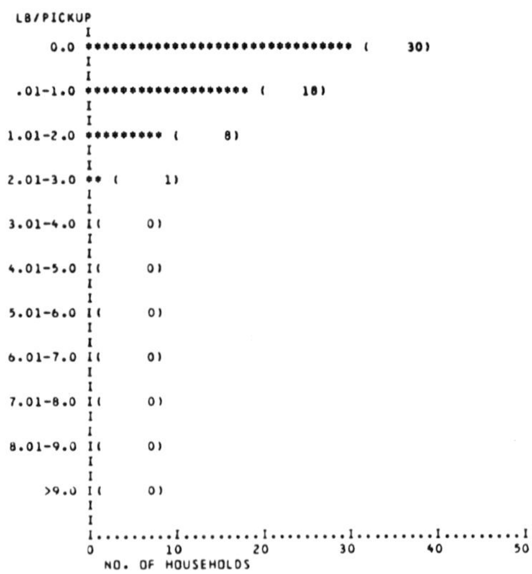

MEAN	.342	STD ERR	.082	MEDIAN	.004
MODE	0	STD DEV	.619	VARIANCE	.383
KURTOSIS	2.647	SKEWNESS	1.920	RANGE	2.500
MINIMUM	0	MAXIMUM	2.500	SUM	19.520
C.V. PCT	180.701	.95 C.I.	.178	TO	.507

VALID CASES 57 MISSING CASES 0

FIGURE 16.7. Textiles by sample neighborhood.

LOW.1

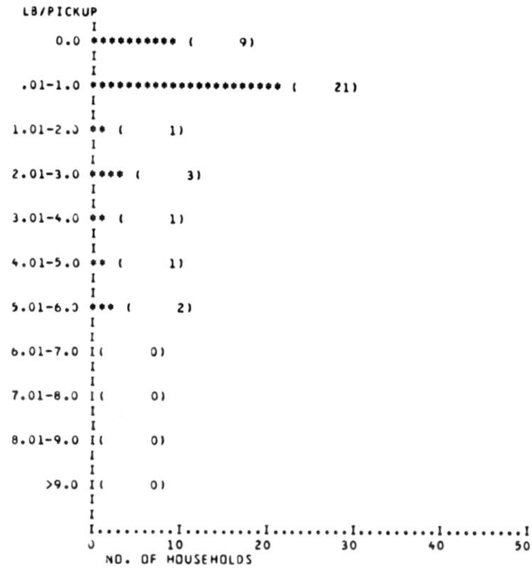

MEAN	.833	STD ERR	.255	MEDIAN	.098
MODE	0	STD DEV	1.571	VARIANCE	2.470
KURTOSIS	3.227	SKEWNESS	2.081	RANGE	5.500
MINIMUM	0	MAXIMUM	5.500	SUM	31.660
C.V. PCT	188.620	.95 C.I.	.317	TO	1.350
VALID CASES	38	MISSING CASES	0		

LOW.2

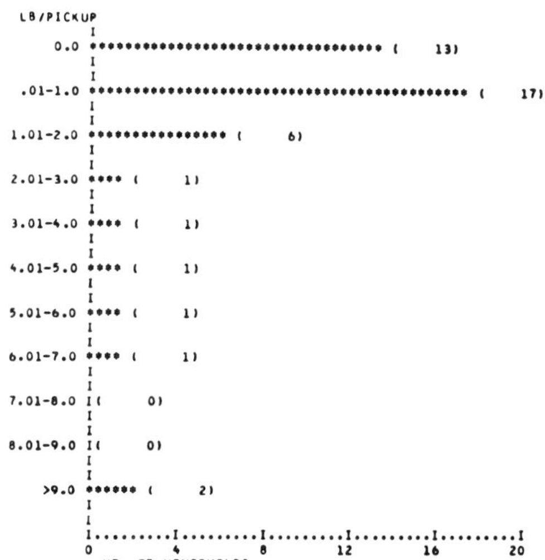

MEAN	1.665	STD ERR	.610	MEDIAN	.300
MODE	0	STD DEV	3.999	VARIANCE	15.995
KURTOSIS	17.729	SKEWNESS	3.989	RANGE	22.190
MINIMUM	0	MAXIMUM	22.190	SUM	71.580
C.V. PCT	240.251	.95 C.I.	.434	TO	2.895
VALID CASES	43	MISSING CASES	0		

FIGURE 16.7 *(continued)*

Table 16.9 Material Composition Categories with Different Patterns of Discard among Milwaukee Sample Neighborhoods[a]

Sample Area	Average lb./week	SD	Yearly	Average lb./week	SD	Yearly
		Textiles			Nonreturn glass	
MID.1	.3273	.7211	17.02	1.8169	1.6377	94.48
MID.2	.3425	.6188	17.81	2.2446	2.9829	116.72
M.LOW	.4029	1.1617	20.95	2.2288	3.4467	115.90
LOW.1	.8332	1.5715	43.33	5.2153	5.4367	271.19
LOW.2	1.6647	3.9993	86.56	2.1447	2.4231	111.52
Total	.6875	2.0303		2.6405	3.5057	
		Paper packaging			Plastics	
MID.1	2.9622	2.3133	154.03	1.8093	2.1716	94.08
MID.2	2.9023	2.9836	150.92	1.1477	1.1344	59.68
M.LOW	2.4159	1.8542	125.63	.9739	1.0262	50.64
LOW.1	3.9911	3.2239	207.54	1.5076	1.6939	78.39
LOW.2	3.6447	2.5852	189.52	1.8305	2.4341	95.19
Total	3.1525	2.6797		1.4409	1.7759	
		Aluminum			Ferrous/aluminum	
MID.1	.2949	.4916	15.33	.0924	.2642	4.80
MID.2	.2153	.3850	11.20	.0507	.1656	2.64
M.LOW	.3046	.7907	15.84	.2602	.5811	13.53
LOW.1	.4124	.6215	21.44	.6429	1.3057	33.43
LOW.2	.6484	1.0271	33.72	.1984	.6366	10.32
Total	.3642	.6950		.2263	.6942	

[a] See also Table 17.11.

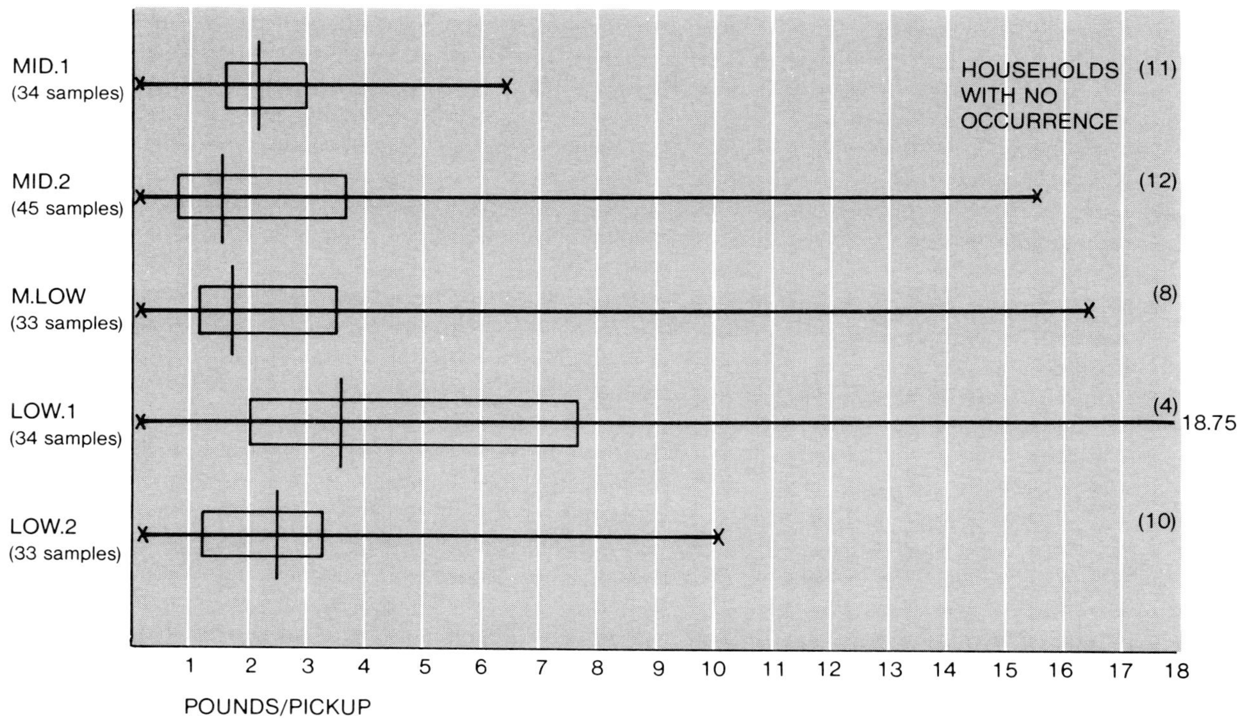

FIGURE 16.8. Nonreturn glass.

MID.1

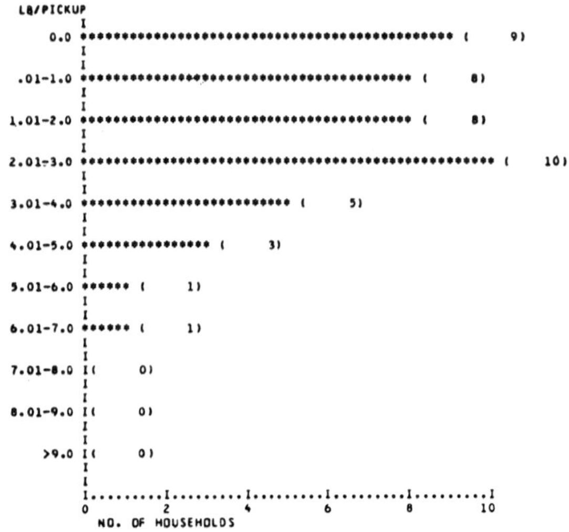

MEAN	1.817	STD ERR	.244	MEDIAN	1.752
MODE	0	STD DEV	1.638	VARIANCE	2.682
KURTOSIS	.062	SKEWNESS	.737	RANGE	6.430
MINIMUM	0	MAXIMUM	6.430	SUM	31.760
C.V. PCT	90.137	.95 C.I.	1.325	TO	2.309
VALID CASES	45	MISSING CASES	0		

MID.2

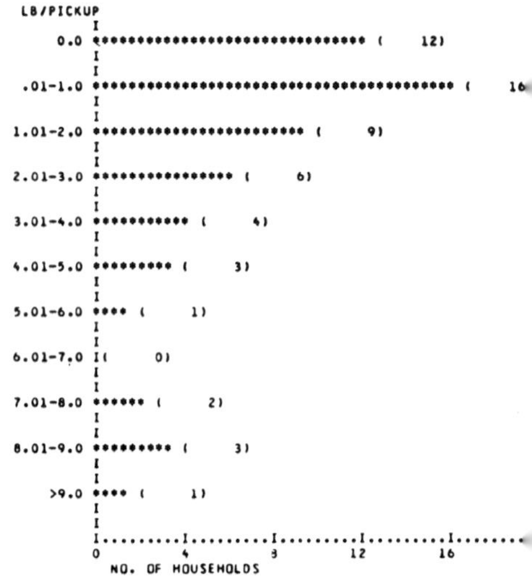

MEAN	2.245	STD ERR	.395	MEDIAN	1.[illegible]
MODE	0	STD DEV	2.983	VARIANCE	8.[illegible]
KURTOSIS	6.507	SKEWNESS	2.261	RANGE	15.6[illegible]
MINIMUM	0	MAXIMUM	15.620	SUM	127.9[illegible]
C.V. PCT	132.894	.95 C.I.	1.453	TO	3.0[illegible]
VALID CASES	57	MISSING CASES	0		

M.LOW

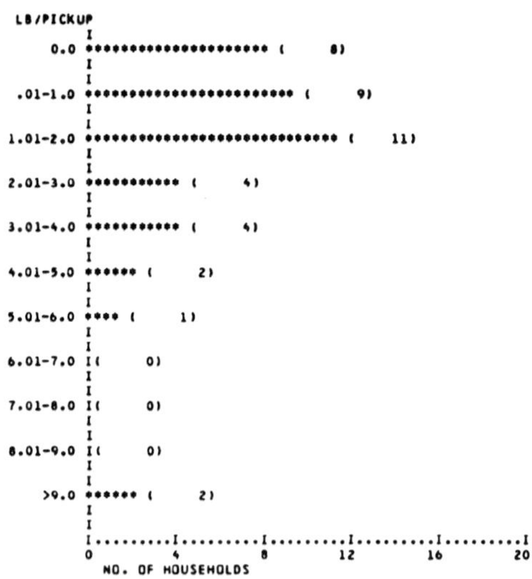

MEAN	2.229	STD ERR	.538	MEDIAN	1.250
MODE	0	STD DEV	3.447	VARIANCE	11.880
KURTOSIS	11.523	SKEWNESS	3.264	RANGE	16.500
MINIMUM	0	MAXIMUM	16.500	SUM	91.380
C.V. PCT	154.647	.95 C.I.	1.141	TO	3.317
VALID CASES	41	MISSING CASES	0		

FIGURE 16.9. Nonreturn glass by sample neighborhood.

LOW.1

```
 LB/PICKUP
            I
   .   0.0  ********************* (      4)
            I
            I
   .01-1.0  ********************* (      4)
            I
            I
  1.01-2.0  ************************** (      5)
            I
            I
  2.01-3.0  ************************** (      5)
            I
            I
  3.01-4.0  ********************* (      4)
            I
            I
  4.01-5.0  *********** (      2)
            I
            I
  5.01-6.0  **************** (      3)
            I
            I
  6.01-7.0  ****** (      1)
            I
            I
  7.01-8.0  *********** (      2)
            I
            I
  8.01-9.0  I(      0)
            I
            I
      >9.0  ******************************************* (      8)
            I
            I
            I.........I.........I.........I.........I.........I
            0         2         4         6         8        10
              NO. OF HOUSEHOLDS

MEAN            5.215     STD ERR         .882     MEDIAN          3.195
MODE                0     STD DEV        5.437     VARIANCE       29.557
KURTOSIS         .779     SKEWNESS       1.312     RANGE          18.870
MINIMUM             0     MAXIMUM       18.870     SUM           198.180
C.V. PCT      104.245     .95 C.I.       3.428           TO        7.002

VALID CASES        38     MISSING CASES      0
```

LOW.2

```
 LB/PICKUP
            I
       0.0  ****************************************************** (     10)
            I
            I
   .01-1.0  ******************************************* (      8)
            I
            I
  1.01-2.0  ******************************** (      6)
            I
            I
  2.01-3.0  ******************************************* (      8)
            I
            I
  3.01-4.0  ************************** (      5)
            I
            I
  4.01-5.0  ****** (      1)
            I
            I
  5.01-6.0  I(      0)
            I
            I
  6.01-7.0  *********** (      2)
            I
            I
  7.01-8.0  *********** (      2)
            I
            I
  8.01-9.0  I(      0)
            I
            I
      >9.0  ****** (      1)
            I
            I
            I.........I.........I.........I.........I.........I
            0         2         4         6         8        10
              NO. OF HOUSEHOLDS

MEAN            2.145     STD ERR         .370     MEDIAN          1.252
MODE                0     STD DEV        2.423     VARIANCE        5.871
KURTOSIS        2.228     SKEWNESS       1.570     RANGE          10.060
MINIMUM             0     MAXIMUM       10.060     SUM            92.220
C.V. PCT      112.983     .95 C.I.       1.399           TO        2.890

VALID CASES        43     MISSING CASES      0
```

FIGURE 16.9 (*continued*)

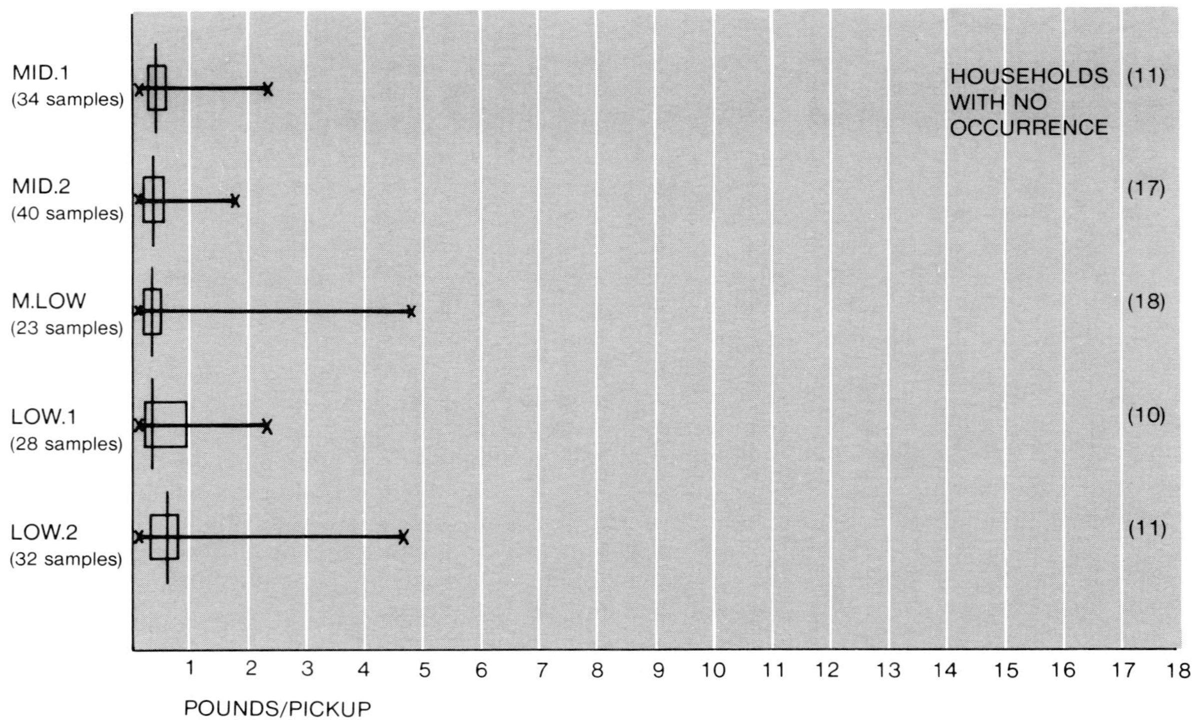

FIGURE 16.10. Aluminum.

LOW.1 and LOW.2 households are likely to discard between 20 and 34 lb. of aluminum in a year.

Although the weights are small, LOW.1 and M.LOW households discard more bimetal *ferrous/aluminum* commodities (Figures 16.12 and 16.13). In fact, LOW.1 households throw out three times more ferrous/aluminum items by weight than MID.1, MID.2, and LOW.2 households.

The next pattern of importance is the discard of *packaging paper* (Figures 16.14 and 16.15). LOW.1 and LOW.2 households discard quantities well above the total mean, while MID.1, MID.2 and M.LOW discard well below the mean. As a result, each year LOW.1 and LOW.2 households are likely to discard between 35 and 80 lb more of paper packaging than MID.1, MID.2, or M.LOW households. Thus, two low-income areas are associated with high rates of packaging discard.

The final significant pattern is the discard of *plastics* (Figures 16.16 and 16.17). MID.1, LOW.1, and LOW.2 households discard plastics at high rates, MID.2 and M.LOW at low rates. Higher rates are likely to add up to almost 35 lb more of plastics in MID.1, LOW.1, and LOW.2 household refuse each year. Again, two low-income neighborhoods are associated with high rates of discard of packaging.

In sum, the LOW.1 neighborhood is characterized by high rates of discard of five types of packaging (glass, aluminum, ferrous/aluminum combinations, paper, and plastic) and the LOW.2 neighborhood by high rates of discard of three types (aluminum, paper, and plastic). These patterns are especially significant because LOW.1 and LOW.2 areas are characterized by these higher rates of discard even though they have the lowest incomes and the largest proportions of small family households.

These differences in packaging discard are not only significant when viewed category by category, but they also are important to the overall pattern of solid wastes in a neighborhood.

MULTIVARIATE WEIGHT SORT ANALYSES

Since the values for each of the 15 material composition variables are the product of a continuous event (discard behavior over a week period), they should be analyzed together as a unit. Discriminant analysis was used in an attempt to determine how distinctive overall solid waste patterns are among the sample neighborhoods. Specifically, discriminant analysis first defines those material composition variables (called "key variables") that set the neighborhoods furthest apart. Next, it tries to reallocate individual refuse collections into their proper neighborhood designations simply on the basis of differences in the weights of key material composition variables.

The first discriminant analysis reallocated refuse pickups into their initial five neighborhood categories. There was a 20% chance that any individual allocation would be correct. In the end, 40% of the pickups were properly reassigned, double what would be expected by chance alone (Table 16.10). The key variables were nonreturn glass, textiles, plastics, aluminum, and packaging paper (Tables 16.8A

MID.1

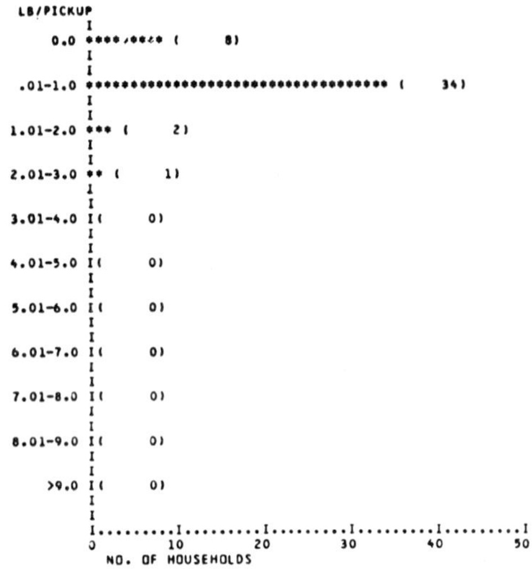


```
MEAN          .295    STD ERR      .073    MEDIAN       .124
MODE             0    STD DEV      .492    VARIANCE     .242
KURTOSIS     8.268    SKEWNESS    2.899    RANGE       2.180
MINIMUM          0    MAXIMUM     2.180    SUM        13.270
C.V. PCT   166.691    .95 C.I.     .147          TO     .443

VALID CASES     45    MISSING CASES    0
```

MID.2

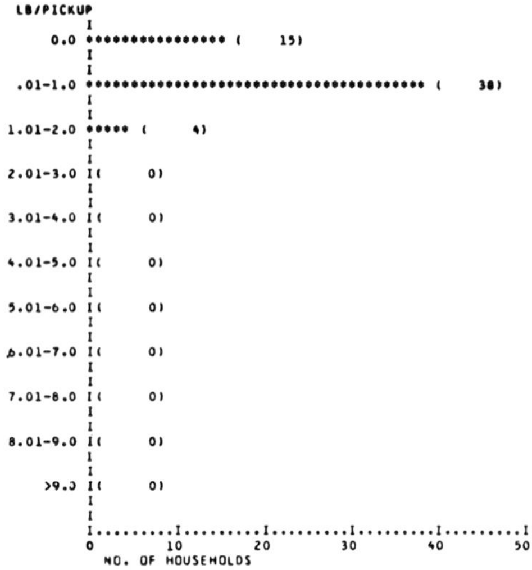


```
MEAN          .215    STD ERR      .051    MEDIAN       .061
MODE             0    STD DEV      .385    VARIANCE     .148
KURTOSIS     6.439    SKEWNESS    2.573    RANGE       1.750
MINIMUM          0    MAXIMUM     1.750    SUM        12.270
C.V. PCT   178.866    .95 C.I.     .113          TO     .317

VALID CASES     57    MISSING CASES    0
```

M.LOW

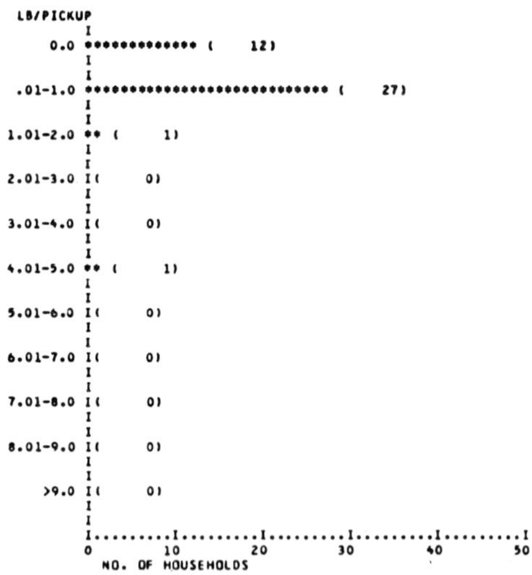


```
MEAN          .305    STD ERR      .123    MEDIAN       .060
MODE             0    STD DEV      .791    VARIANCE     .625
KURTOSIS    26.066    SKEWNESS    4.806    RANGE       4.750
MINIMUM          0    MAXIMUM     4.750    SUM        12.490
C.V. PCT   259.541    .95 C.I.     .055          TO     .554

VALID CASES     41    MISSING CASES    0
```

FIGURE 16.11. Aluminum by sample neighborhood.

LOW.1

```
LB/PICKUP
          I
      0.0 ********* (      8)
          I
          I
  .01-1.0 ************************** (      25)
          I
          I
  1.01-2.0 **** (      3)
          I
          I
  2.01-3.0 *** (      2)
          I
          I
  3.01-4.0 I(      0)
          I
          I
  4.01-5.0 I(      0)
          I
          I
  5.01-6.0 I(      0)
          I
          I
  6.01-7.0 I(      0)
          I
          I
  7.01-8.0 I(      0)
          I
          I
  8.01-9.0 I(      0)
          I
          I
      >9.0 I(      0)
          I
          I
          I.........I.........I.........I.........I.........I
          0        10        20        30        40        50
            NO. OF HOUSEHOLDS

MEAN            .412    STD ERR          .101    MEDIAN         .125
MODE               0    STD DEV          .621    VARIANCE       .386
KURTOSIS       3.618    SKEWNESS        2.054    RANGE         2.370
MINIMUM            0    MAXIMUM         2.370    SUM          15.670
C.V. PCT     150.710    .95 C.I.         .208          TO       .617

VALID CASES       38    MISSING CASES       0
```

LOW.2

```
LB/PICKUP
          I
      0.0 **** (      3)
          I
          I
  .01-1.0 ********************************** (      33)
          I
          I
  1.01-2.0 *** (      2)
          I
          I
  2.01-3.0 **** (      3)
          I
          I
  3.01-4.0 ** (      1)
          I
          I
  4.01-5.0 ** (      1)
          I
          I
  5.01-6.0 I(      0)
          I
          I
  6.01-7.0 I(      0)
          I
          I
  7.01-8.0 I(      0)
          I
          I
  8.01-9.0 I(      0)
          I
          I
      >9.0 I(      0)
          I
          I
          I.........I.........I.........I.........I.........I
          0        10        20        30        40        50
            NO. OF HOUSEHOLDS

MEAN            .648    STD ERR          .157    MEDIAN         .200
MODE            .010    STD DEV         1.027    VARIANCE      1.055
KURTOSIS       5.572    SKEWNESS        2.379    RANGE         4.620
MINIMUM            0    MAXIMUM         4.620    SUM          27.880
C.V. PCT     158.411    .95 C.I.         .332          TO       .964

VALID CASES       43    MISSING CASES       0
```

FIGURE 16.11 (*continued*)

Table 16.10 Discriminant Analysis: Five Sample Neighborhoods, Prediction Results

Actual group	Number of cases	Predicted group membership				
		MID.1	MID.2	M.LOW	LOW.1	LOW.2
MID.1	45	 28.9%	12 26.7	11 24.4	2 4.4	7 15.6
MID.2	57	6 10.5	30[a] 52.6%	7 12.3	9 15.8	5 8.8
M.LOW	41	6 14.6	11 26.8	13[a] 31.7%	6 14.6	5 12.2
LOW.1	38	3 7.9	12 31.6	3 7.9	17[a] 44.7%	3 7.9
LOW.2	43	7 16.3	7 16.3	7 16.3	5 11.6	17[a] 59.5%

[a] Overall 40.2% of known cases were correctly allocated.

and 16.8B). The largest problem in classification occurred within middle- and moderately low-income areas, where 27% of the MID.1 pickups and 27% of the M.LOW pickups were misallocated as MID.2.

A second discriminant analysis reallocated pickups into three income groups: (*a*) middle income, MID.1 and MID.2; (*b*) moderately low income, M.LOW; and (*c*) low income, LOW.1 and LOW.2. Some 50% of the cases were correctly allocated (Table 16.11), a result higher than would be expected by chance alone (33%). The key variables were textiles, paper packaging, and aluminum (Table 16.12). The

Table 16.11 Discriminant Analysis: Income Groups, Prediction Results

Actual group	Number of cases	Predicted group membership		
		MID.1, MID.2	LOW.1, LOW.2	M.LOW
MID.1, MID.2	102	64[a] 62.7%	17 16.7	21 20.6
LOW.1, LOW.2	81	25 30.9 PCT	38[a] 46.9%	18 22.2
M.LOW	41	23 56.1 PCT	8 19.5	10[a] 24.4%

[a] Overall 50.0% of known cases were correctly allocated.

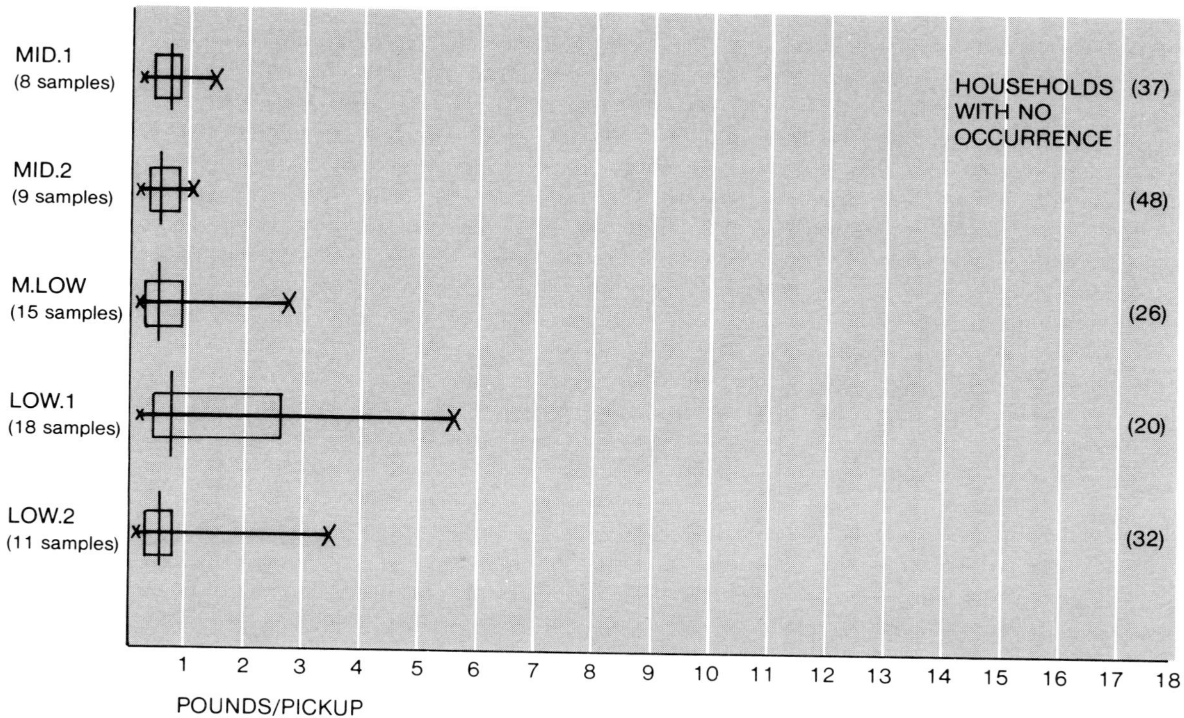

FIGURE 16.12. Ferrous/Aluminum.

MID.1

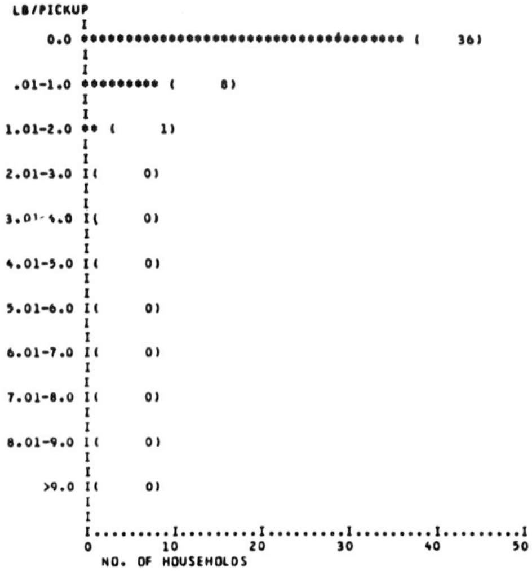

MEAN	.092	STD ERR	.039	MEDIAN	.001
MODE	0	STD DEV	.264	VARIANCE	.070
KURTOSIS	11.677	SKEWNESS	3.357	RANGE	1.310
MINIMUM	0	MAXIMUM	1.310	SUM	4.160
C.V. PCT	285.773	.95 C.I.	.013	TO	.172
VALID CASES	45	MISSING CASES	0		

MID.2

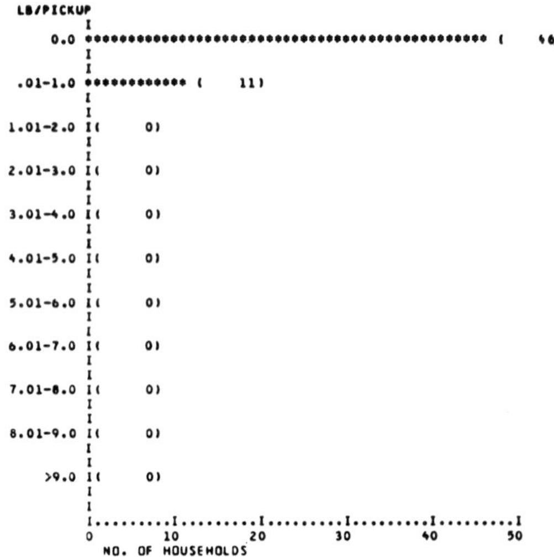

MEAN	.051	STD ERR	.022	MEDIAN	.000
MODE	0	STD DEV	.166	VARIANCE	.027
KURTOSIS	15.928	SKEWNESS	3.938	RANGE	.900
MINIMUM	0	MAXIMUM	.900	SUM	2.890
C.V. PCT	326.686	.95 C.I.	.007	TO	.095
VALID CASES	57	MISSING CASES	0		

M.LOW

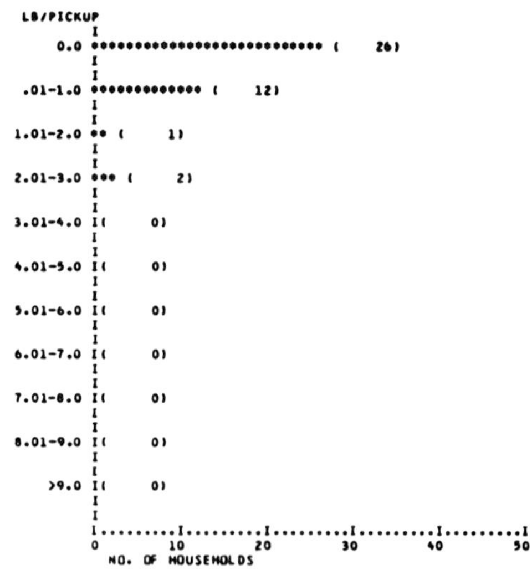

MEAN	.260	STD ERR	.091	MEDIAN	.003
MODE	0	STD DEV	.581	VARIANCE	.338
KURTOSIS	8.900	SKEWNESS	2.949	RANGE	2.680
MINIMUM	0	MAXIMUM	2.680	SUM	10.670
C.V. PCT	223.276	.95 C.I.	.077	TO	.444
VALID CASES	41	MISSING CASES	0		

FIGURE 16.13. Ferrous/Aluminum by sample neighborhood.

LOW.1

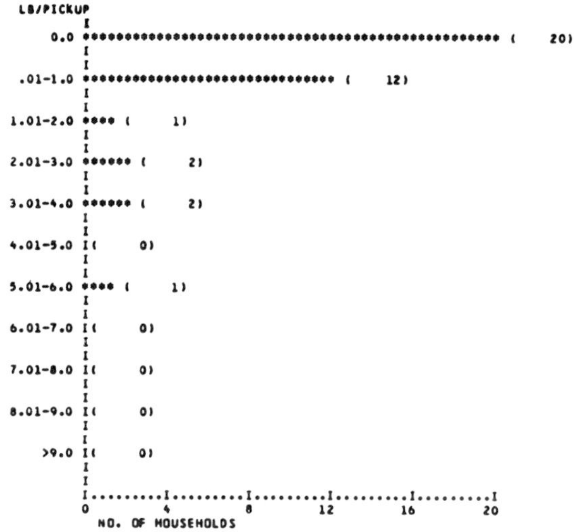

MEAN	.643	STD ERR	.212	MEDIAN	.004
MODE	0	STD DEV	1.306	VARIANCE	1.705
KURTOSIS	6.718	SKEWNESS	2.609	RANGE	5.750
MINIMUM	0	MAXIMUM	5.750	SUM	24.430
C.V. PCT	203.101	.95 C.I.	.214	TO	1.072
VALID CASES	38	MISSING CASES	0		

LOW.2

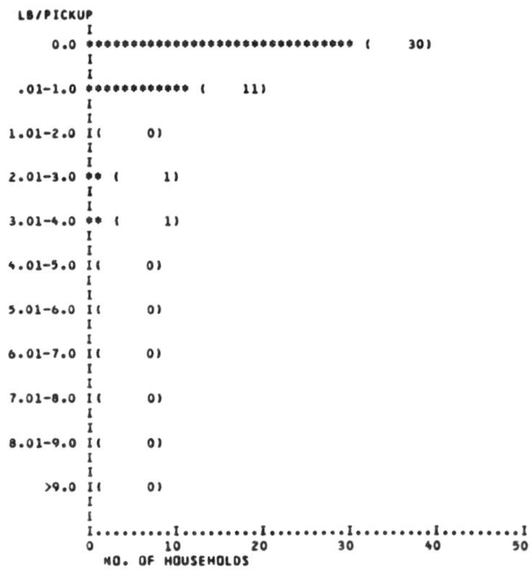

MEAN	.198	STD ERR	.097	MEDIAN	.002
MODE	0	STD DEV	.637	VARIANCE	.405
KURTOSIS	17.218	SKEWNESS	4.122	RANGE	3.310
MINIMUM	0	MAXIMUM	3.310	SUM	8.530
C.V. PCT	320.935	.95 C.I.	.002	TO	.394
VALID CASES	43	MISSING CASES	0		

FIGURE 16.13 (*continued*)

Table 16.12 Discriminant Analysis: Income Groups, Group Means and Standard Deviations in Pounds per Pickup, Income Groups

Material composition category[a]	MID.1, MID.2 $\bar{X}$ SD	LOW.1, LOW.2 $\bar{X}$ SD	M.LOW $\bar{X}$ SD
IRON	1.64/1.71	1.72/2.10	1.11/1.24
ALUM[b]	.25/ .43	.54/ .86	.30/ .79
IRAL	.07/ .22	.41/1.02	.26/ .58
PLASTC	1.44/1.70	1.68/2.11	.97/1.03
NRGLAS	2.06/2.70	3.58/4.37	2.23/3.45
RETGLAS	.06/ .48	.08/ .46	.46/2.83
PACKP[b]	2.93/2.70	3.81/2.99	2.42/1.85
(Total Packaging)	(8.45/35.6%)	(11.82/41.8%)	(7.75/33.4%)
NPACKP	2.21/2.42	2.55/3.91	2.12/2.49
NEWSP	2.82/3.98	3.63/7.01	3.56/6.33
MAGAZ	.11/ .42	.19/ .62	.11/ .36
METOTH	.05/ .33	.02/ .14	.06/ .39
TEXTL[b]	.33/ .66	1.27/3.12	.40/1.16
FOODRL	5.77/5.74	5.52/5.70	5.02/4.82
YARDWT	3.12/6.97	1.44/4.41	2.83/8.18
OTHER	1.00/2.51	1.80/4.89	1.31/3.62
Total pickup weights	23.76	28.26	23.19

[a] For the full category names see page 406 .

[b] Key variables for the discriminant analysis.

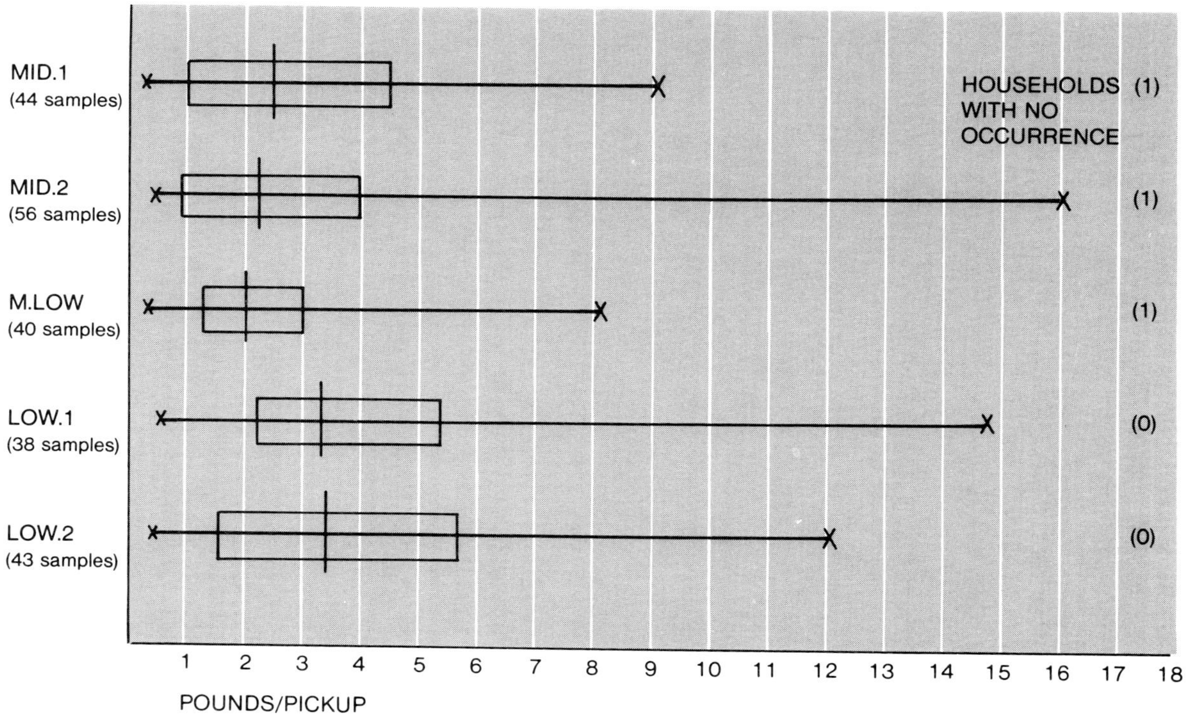

FIGURE 16.14. Packaging paper.

MID.1

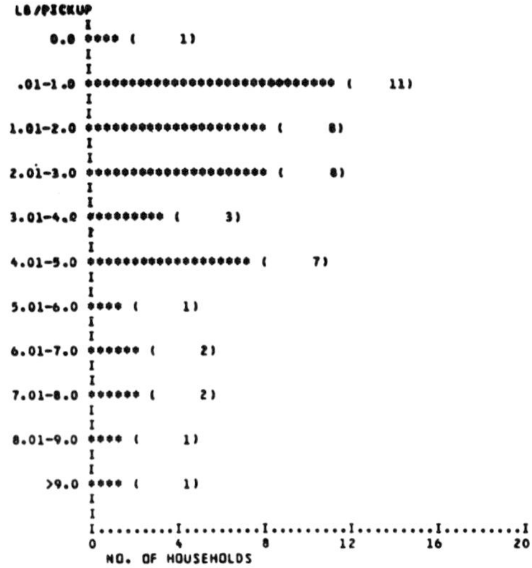

MEAN	2.962	STD ERR	.345	MEDIAN	2.620
MODE	.560	STD DEV	2.313	VARIANCE	5.352
KURTOSIS	.185	SKEWNESS	.934	RANGE	9.100
MINIMUM	0	MAXIMUM	9.100	SUM	133.300
C.V. PCT	78.095	.95 C.I.	2.267	TO	3.657
VALID CASES	45	MISSING CASES	0		

MID.2

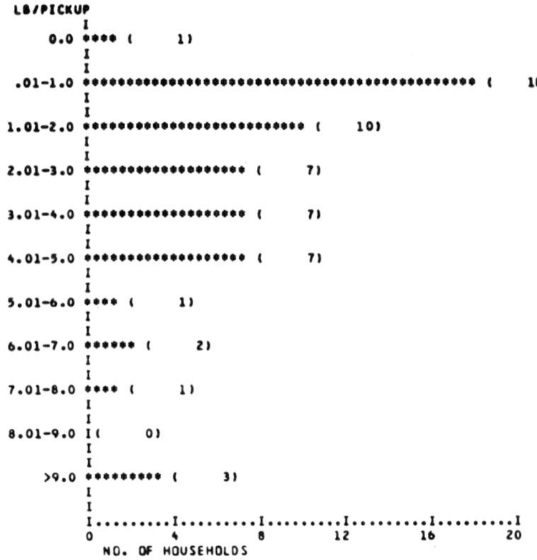

MEAN	2.902	STD ERR	.395	MEDIAN	1.872
MODE	.500	STD DEV	2.984	VARIANCE	8.902
KURTOSIS	7.283	SKEWNESS	2.409	RANGE	16.120
MINIMUM	0	MAXIMUM	16.120	SUM	155.430
C.V. PCT	102.803	.95 C.I.	2.111	TO	3.694
VALID CASES	57	MISSING CASES	0		

M.LOW

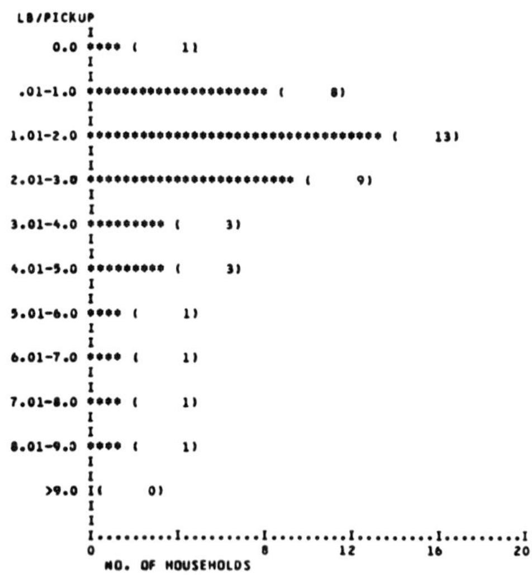

MEAN	2.416	STD ERR	.290	MEDIAN	1.880
MODE	1.000	STD DEV	1.854	VARIANCE	3.438
KURTOSIS	2.473	SKEWNESS	1.592	RANGE	8.120
MINIMUM	0	MAXIMUM	8.120	SUM	99.050
C.V. PCT	76.750	.95 C.I.	1.831	TO	3.001
VALID CASES	41	MISSING CASES	0		

FIGURE 16.15. Packaging paper by sample neighborhood.

LOW.1

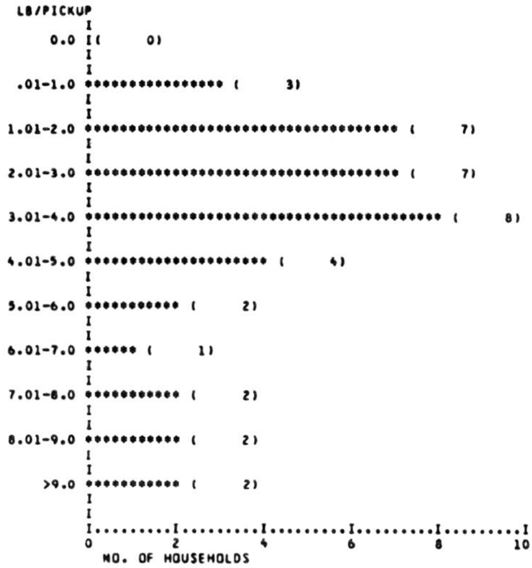

MEAN	3.991	STD ERR	.523	MEDIAN	3.320
MODE	2.120	STD DEV	3.224	VARIANCE	10.393
KURTOSIS	3.424	SKEWNESS	1.717	RANGE	14.920
MINIMUM	.010	MAXIMUM	14.930	SUM	151.660
C.V. PCT	80.777	.95 C.I.	2.931	TO	5.051
VALID CASES	38	MISSING CASES	0		

LOW.2

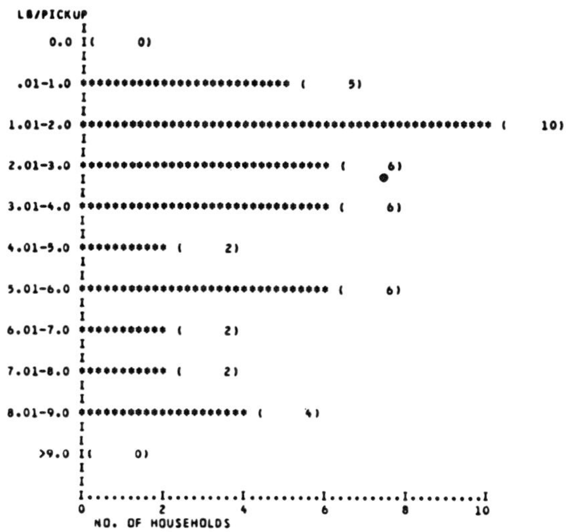

MEAN	3.645	STD ERR	.394	MEDIAN	3.060
MODE	.800	STD DEV	2.585	VARIANCE	6.683
KURTOSIS	-.633	SKEWNESS	.655	RANGE	8.700
MINIMUM	.300	MAXIMUM	9.000	SUM	156.720
C.V. PCT	70.930	.95 C.I.	2.849	TO	4.440
VALID CASES	43	MISSING CASES	0		

FIGURE 16.15 (*continued*)

major confusion again was with the middle- and moderately low-income areas, where 56% of the M.LOW pickups were classified with the MID.1 and MID.2 pickups in the middle-income set.

WEIGHT SORT ANALYSIS SUMMARY

All of these studies of the weights of the contents of Milwaukee household pickups reinforce two propositions:

1. Many patterns of solid waste discard are shared among different socioeconomic groups, which makes the few differences that do exist more important to understand.
2. At least for Milwaukee sample households, higher income does not mean a higher rate of discard of packaging; if anything, income may be inversely related to the quantity of packaging discarded in solid wastes. This does not negate earlier studies that have related income to the disposal of yard wastes and newspapers. It does expand on these studies by better identifying the relation between income and packaging solid wastes. It also leads to further questions and possible factors that influence this relationship.

THE POOR AND SOLID WASTES: TWO POSSIBLE FACTORS

Milwaukee data on household solid wastes raise an important question about the generation of residential refuse. In Milwaukee, the two lowest-income areas have the largest proportion of small households. If the rate of per capita generation is the same for different socioeconomic groups, these neighborhoods should discard lower levels of packaging solid wastes. Since they do not, and in some cases they discard at significantly higher rates, the question is: What is causing these high rates of packaging discard in low-income neighborhoods with relatively more small family households? At least two possible factors provide likely answers.

Possible Factor 1: Low-income households may buy more preprepared foods and beverages per capita for use at home and, therefore, throw out more packaging.

The first possible factor is that the higher discard of packaging by low-income households is due to specific food consumption patterns. Some studies of food expenditures indicate that upper-income families tend to eat more meals away from home than low-income families (Saleh 1974). Thus, it would seem reasonable that households in low-income areas have more packages to discard because they buy greater quantities of food for home use.

All types of packaging are not discarded at a higher rate in low-income neighborhoods, and households in all sample areas discard food-related debris (preparation remains and waste) at approximately the same rate. Based on these findings, factors other than the quantity of food eaten at home may play a part in the high discard of packaging by households in low-income neighborhoods. For example, the use of more preprepared foods than fresh produce and/or high consumption of beverages

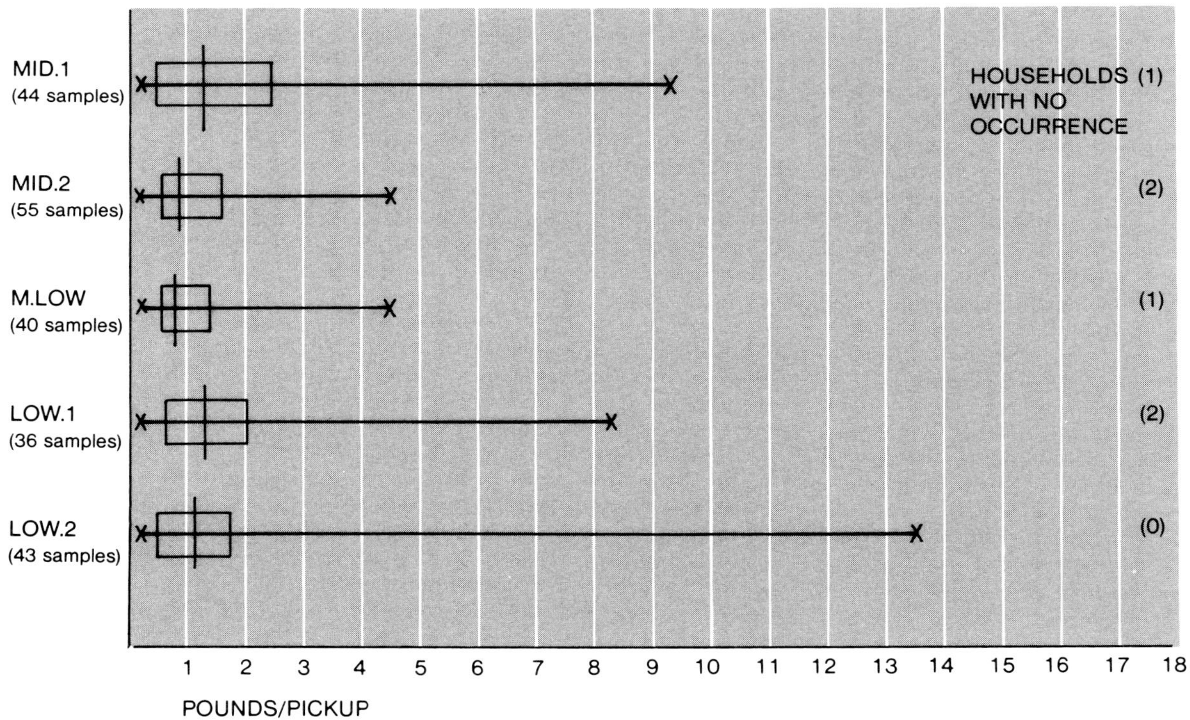

FIGURE 16.16. Plastics.

MID.1

```
LB/PICKUP
           I
       0.0 I(       0)
           I
           I
  .01-1.0  ************************* (       24)
           I
           I
 1.01-2.0  *********** (       10)
           I
           I
 2.01-3.0  **** (       3)
           I
           I
 3.01-4.0  ** (       1)
           I
           I
 4.01-5.0  ** (       1)
           I
           I
 5.01-6.0  ***** (       4)
           I
           I
 6.01-7.0  ** (       1)
           I
           I
 7.01-8.0  I(       0)
           I
           I
 8.01-9.0  I(       0)
           I
           I
     >9.0  ** (       1)
           I
           I
           I.........I.........I.........I.........I.........I
           0        10        20        30        40        50
             NO. OF HOUSEHOLDS
```

MEAN	1.809	STD ERR	.324	MEDIAN	.933
MODE	.560	STD DEV	2.172	VARIANCE	4.716
KURTOSIS	2.762	SKEWNESS	1.787	RANGE	9.360
MINIMUM	.010	MAXIMUM	9.370	SUM	81.420
C.V. PCT	120.025	.95 C.I.	1.157	TO	2.462
VALID CASES	45	MISSING CASES	0		

MID.2

```
LB/PICKUP
           I
       0.0 *** (       2)
           I
           I
  .01-1.0  ************************************ (       35)
           I
           I
 1.01-2.0  ********** (       9)
           I
           I
 2.01-3.0  ******** (       7)
           I
           I
 3.01-4.0  *** (       2)
           I
           I
 4.01-5.0  *** (       2)
           I
           I
 5.01-6.0  I(       0)
           I
           I
 6.01-7.0  I(       0)
           I
           I
 7.01-8.0  I(       0)
           I
           I
 8.01-9.0  I(       0)
           I
           I
     >9.0  I(       0)
           I
           I
           I.........I.........I.........I.........I.........I
           0        10        20        30        40        50
             NO. OF HOUSEHOLDS
```

MEAN	1.148	STD ERR	.150	MEDIAN	.703
MODE	.560	STD DEV	1.134	VARIANCE	1.287
KURTOSIS	1.059	SKEWNESS	1.339	RANGE	4.430
MINIMUM	0	MAXIMUM	4.430	SUM	55.420
C.V. PCT	98.837	.95 C.I.	.847	TO	1.449
VALID CASES	57	MISSING CASES	0		

M.LOW

```
LB/PICKUP
           I
       0.0 ** (       1)
           I
           I
  .01-1.0  **************************** (       27)
           I
           I
 1.01-2.0  ********* (       8)
           I
           I
 2.01-3.0  **** (       3)
           I
           I
 3.01-4.0  I(       0)
           I
           I
 4.01-5.0  *** (       2)
           I
           I
 5.01-6.0  I(       0)
           I
           I
 6.01-7.0  I(       0)
           I
           I
 7.01-8.0  I(       0)
           I
           I
 8.01-9.0  I(       0)
           I
           I
     >9.0  I(       0)
           I
           I
           I.........I.........I.........I.........I.........I
           0        10        20        30        40        50
             NO. OF HOUSEHOLDS
```

MEAN	.974	STD ERR	.160	MEDIAN	.598
MODE	.430	STD DEV	1.026	VARIANCE	1.053
KURTOSIS	4.045	SKEWNESS	1.946	RANGE	4.370
MINIMUM	0	MAXIMUM	4.370	SUM	39.930
C.V. PCT	105.373	.95 C.I.	.650	TO	1.298
VALID CASES	41	MISSING CASES	0		

FIGURE 16.17. Plastics by sample neighborhood.

LOW.1

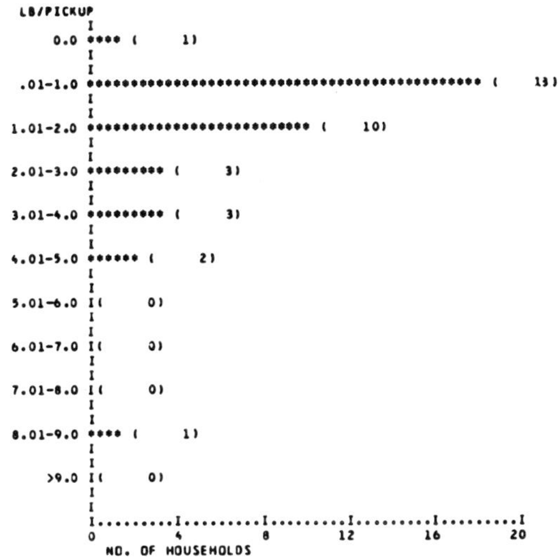

MEAN	1.508	STD ERR	.275	MEDIAN	.905
MODE	.250	STD DEV	1.694	VARIANCE	2.869
KURTOSIS	6.027	SKEWNESS	2.184	RANGE	8.310
MINIMUM	0	MAXIMUM	8.310	SUM	57.290
C.V. PCT	112.354	.95 C.I.	.951	TO	2.064

VALID CASES 38 MISSING CASES 0

LOW.2

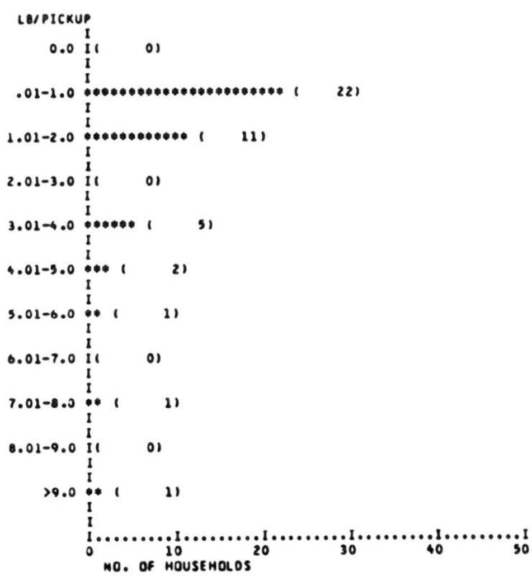

MEAN	1.830	STD ERR	.371	MEDIAN	1.003
MODE	1.000	STD DEV	2.434	VARIANCE	5.925
KURTOSIS	12.977	SKEWNESS	3.215	RANGE	13.570
MINIMUM	.060	MAXIMUM	13.630	SUM	78.710
C.V. PCT	132.975	.95 C.I.	1.081	TO	2.580

VALID CASES 43 MISSING CASES 0

FIGURE 16.17 (*continued*)

(which come in relatively heavy packages), could account for the higher rate of packaging discards. Identifying the reasons for these possible preferences is beyond the scope of this chapter. Nevertheless, studies by Saleh (1974) and others indicate the possibility of such patterns of use.

Possible Factor 2: Low-income households may buy what they consume in large numbers of small packages, which will result in high weights of packaging discards.

This second factor is based on the rationale that low-income households may discard more packaging due to the position of low-income and small-family populations within American consumer society. An explanation begins with the *economy of scale* that exists within most types of packaging. As one buys food or drink in larger and larger packages, fewer solid wastes are generated relative to the amount of product purchased. For example, if one buys 32 ounces of soft drink in one large bottle, he will discard less total glass than if he buys only 24 ounces in two smaller bottles. If he buys one 181-ounce box of laundry detergent, he will throw out less paper than if he buys the same quantity of soap in nine 20-ounce boxes.

Not only is an economy in solid wastes achieved by purchasing products in larger-size packages, there also is a direct monetary incentive. The products in large packages usually are cheaper per ounce. Thus, both for the sake of household finances and the environment, everyone should buy in "giant economy" sizes. But everyone does not and there often are good reasons why.

First, the low-income areas in question in Milwaukee contain a large number of one-person and two-person households. These households may buy in small sizes to avoid spoilage and waste, which will result in a high rate of packaging discard relative to the amount of product purchased. Second, many low-income families do not have the resources to buy consumer products in large quantities. Because of limited cash-flow, limited home storage facilities, and limited access to cars to transport large quantities of groceries, disadvantaged families are likely to buy for immediate needs in small packages (Gladwin 1967; Rathje and McCarthy 1977:268–270). The result is likely to be a relatively high price per ounce for a product and a high rate of packaging discard relative to the amount of product purchased. Thus, the same limited resources that may make the poor inefficient consumers in terms of the costs of products may also make them inefficient in the discard of solid wastes.

In summary, two possible factors have been presented here to account for the high rate of packaging discarded in low income neighborhoods.

1. The poor may purchase more preprepared foods and beverages per capita for home use.
2. The poor may buy their products in large numbers of small packages.

In the next section, detailed item-by-item garbage records will be examined to determine patterns in the rates of household consumption and in the purchase and discard of different package sizes (for further discussion of packaging discard rates see Hill, Chapter 12).

Research Question 3: *Since there is variability in discard, what household behavior patterns are most likely responsible for the different kinds of garbage discarded in the five neighborhoods?*

Answer 3: *Differences in discarded packaging are the result both of high rates of consumption of some preprepared foods and beverages and the purchase of some products in large numbers of small containers. Thus, the heavy discard of packaging is the final outcome of behaviors with economic and nutritional implications that deserve more study.*

MILWAUKEE REGULAR SORTS—PRODUCT CATEGORIES AND PICKUP WEIGHTS

This set of analyses was designed to determine what consumer behaviors are related to the observed significant differences in the material composition of pickup weights from the five sample neighborhoods. The first step was to place the individual items recorded in regular-sort data into an aggregate array suitable for analysis. In this process, the specific code list categories were collapsed to form 19 general product categories (Table 16.13 and Figure 16.3). All of the items that had a net weight or a fluid volume, indicating that they were containers, were separated for study.[7] The total from the sampled garbage of the five neighborhoods was 5781 containers, 3732 with net weights and 2049 with fluid volumes. These items were grouped by general product category, weight or volume (rounded off to the nearest ounce), and neighborhood. A package's material composition was defined as whatever material was most abundant in the package. As a result, bimetal cans were categorized as steel and paper–metal fruit juice concentrate containers as paper.

Two statistical testing procedures were used to identify significant patterns in the distribution of package–product configurations among the five sample neighborhoods. *Statistic 1* is a 1-Way ANOVA test (significance at .05). *Statistical Set 2* uses three separate tests—χ^2, Kendall's τ, and Pearson's r—all of which were applied to the same data arrays of container configurations as found in the five sample areas. To be defined as significant by Statistical Set 2, all three significance values had to be less than .05.

To assure that these statistical tests could recognize significant patterns, we applied them to package configurations (Table 16.14). First, product categories were compared to package volumes. This analysis tested whether different products were packaged in different sizes. As expected, both statistics found that this indeed was the case. Second, product categories were compared to package material composition (Table 16.14). Again, both statistics found that there was a high correlation between product categories and the material compositions of their packages. Thus,

[7]Note that this process excludes packages without a recorded weight or volume, such as cigarette packs and cartons or toilet paper or paper towel rolls and wrappers.

Table 16.13 Garbage Project Aggregate Product Categories

Aggregate	Garbage project item codes product categories (see Figure 17.3)	Net weight recorded	Fluid volume recorded
Foods:			
Protein foods	1-10, 14-17	638	—
Dairy foods	12, 13, 61-65	63	85
Fresh fruit and vegetables	40, 41, 44, 45	125	—
Processed fruit and vegetables	42, 43, 46, 47	294	—
Fats	18, 19	240	34
Grains and chips	22-30, 32-34	725	—
Nonnutritive foods	49, 54, 56-58	142	28
High-sugar foods	31, 51-53, 55, 74	678	32
Baby foods	87-90, 111	2	40
Preprepared foods	94-98	309	—
Pet foods	91-92	157	—
Beverages:			
Milk	11	—	292
Fruit beverages	75-77	—	274
Caffein beverages	70-73	57	—
Soft drinks	78-82	—	417
Wine and spirits	83-85	—	94
Beer	86	—	674
Household products:			
Personal care	113, 114, 151-154, 164	155	—
Health care	100-104, 106, 108, 109, 112	52	—
Household care	131-144, 149, 162	95	79
Total items		3732	2049

Table 16.14 Significance Tests of Package Configurations

	Statistic 1 ANOVA significance	Statistical Set 2 χ^2 Kendall's τ Pearson's R
Item by volume:		
Solid	SIG .0000 F= 8.7451	SIG. .0000 .0000 .0000
Fluid	SIG. .0000 F= 11.1003	SIG. .0000 .0000 .0000
Item by material:		
Solid	SIG. .0000 F= 46.8718	SIG. .0000 .0000 .0000
Fluid	SIG. .0000 F= 42.8718	SIG. .0000 .0000 .0000

Note: SIG = significance level; F = F values.

our statistical tests confirmed the obvious, that different products generally come in packages of different sizes and different material composition.

Next, the statistics were used to determine if there were overall significant differences in (*a*) the quantity of containers from different areas, (*b*) the material composition of containers from different areas, and (*c*) the volume of packaged goods from different areas (Table 16.15). The results showed that differences in material composition are pronounced between neighborhoods only for containers of solid food, and that package volume–weight differences are pronounced only for fluids. Although these results are interesting, they are highly abstract.

To give the results more substance, we applied the statistical tests to determine if there were differences in the distribution of container quantities and sizes within product categories when compared by sample area (Table 16.16). Such differences were confirmed by both Statistic 1 and Statistical Set 2 for five product categories: two solid—nonnutritive foods (spices, condiments, etc.) and high-sugar foods (Table 16.17); and two fluid—milk and highly processed beverages (Table 16.18).

Nonnutritive foods: LOW.1 and LOW.2 households consume significantly larger quantities of spices, condiments, and other cooking aides. LOW.1 households buy these in small packages, as do M.LOW households which consume few such products in total. A large portion of these containers (20%) found in LOW.2 refuse

Table 16.15 Significance Tests of the Overall Distribution of Packages by Milwaukee Sample Neighborhood

	Statistic 1	Statistical Set 2
	ANOVA significance	χ^2 Kendall's τ Pearson's r
Number of items by area:		
Solid	SIG. .0000 F= 9.3613	NON-SIG.
Fluid	NON-SIG.	SIG. .0000 .1926 .0304
Material composition by area:		
Solid	SIG. .0000 F= 15.0261	SIG. .0000 .0000 .0724
Fluid	NON-SIG.	NON-SIG.
Volume by area:		
Solid	NON-SIG.	NON-SIG.
Fluid	SIG. .0000 F= 6.5392	SIG. .0000 .0113 .0013

Note: SIG = significance level; F = F values.

were 26-ounce salt packages made of paper. Nonnutritive food containers represent 4% of the containers and 4% of the net weight of solid foods purchased by sample households.

High-sugar foods: LOW.1 households consume extremely large quantities of cakes, pies, pastries, pastry mixes, candies, and cookies, many of which are purchased in relatively large containers. MID.1 households consume large quantities purchased in similar container sizes; MID.2, M.LOW, and especially LOW.2 households buy smaller container sizes. This category seems important as it accounts for 13% of the net weight of solid foods and 20% of the solid food containers.

Milk: Milk is a high-volume item, usually bought in large containers. It represents 42% of the fluid volume, but only 14% of all containers of fluids. LOW.2 households consume large volumes of milk; LOW.1 households consume far less than the average and buy it mainly in small containers.

Highly processed beverages (soft drinks, beer, wine, and spirits): LOW.1 and

LOW.2 households consume large volumes of highly processed beverages. LOW.2 households buy these beverages in larger containers, and LOW.1 households buy them in greater numbers of small containers than the households in other areas. Containers of highly processed beverages account for 65.4% of all fluid containers and 84.8% of all glass containers, but only 35% of the fluids purchased.

Although these patterns are significant, most products involved come in a variety of material composition types. For example, high-sugar foods come packaged in

Table 16.16 Significance Tests of the Overall Distribution of Package Sizes within Product Category and Milwaukee Sample Neighborhood

	Statistic 1		Statistical Set 2	
	ANOVA	χ^2	Kendall's τ	Pearson's r
Foods:				
Protein Foods	—	.0227	.0793	—
Dairy Foods—Solid	—	.0019	—	—
—Fluid	.0357(2.7121)[a]	.0074	—	.0554
Fresh Produce	—	.0007	—	—
Processed Produce	—	.0187	.0408	.0663
Fats	.0526(2.3781)[a]	.0539	—	—
Grains	—	.0000	—	—
NONNUTRITIVE FOODS—SOLID	.0776(2.1531)[a]	.0022	.0670	.0313
—FLUID	—	—	—	—
HIGH-SUGAR FOODS	.0000(7.8517)[a]	.0000	.00000	.0000
Baby Foods	—	—	—	—
Preprepared Foods	—	.0208	.0561	—
Pet Foods	—	.0000	.0169	—
Beverages:				
MILK	.0023(4.2532)[a]	.0000	.0175	.0426
Fruit Beverages	—	.0000	.0172	—
Caffein Beverages	—	—	.0347	—
HIGHLY PROCESSED BEVERAGES[b]	.0070(3.5620)[a]	.0000	.0000	.0006
SOFT DRINKS	.0236(2.8518)[a]	.0000	.0240	.0002
WINE AND SPIRITS	.0003(5.8710)[a]	.0000	.0002	.0002
Beer	—	.0000	.0000	—
Household Products:				
Personal Care	—	—	—	—
Health Care	—	—	—	—
Household Care				
Solid	—	—	—	—
Fluid	—	—	—	—

[a] F values

[b] Sodas, beer, wine, and spirits.

Table 16.17 Product Categories with Significant Differences among Milwaukee Sample Neighborhoods by Net Weight and Number of Occurrences

Solid foods				
	Average weekly Consumption (in ounces)	Average package size (in ounces)	SD	Total number of containers recorded
Processed product:				
MID.1	26.7	14.56	7.75	57
MID.2	13.2	14.44	7.23	43
M.LOW	34.0	15.12	8.90	72
LOW.1	26.4	14.90	8.78	62
LOW.2	26.3	14.88	7.62	60
7.9% of solid food containers				
7.0% of total solid food weight				
Nonnutritive food:				
MID.1	4.0	15.50	11.55	8
MID.2	6.8	13.83	20.20	23
M.LOW	4.8	7.00	9.16	22
LOW.1	8.5	5.27	8.66	51
LOW.2	13.5	12.13	21.31	38
4.3% of solid food containers				
4.1% of total solid food weight				
High-sugar foods:				
MID.1	49.0	12.34	20.47	123
MID.2	22.9	7.68	11.67	140
M.LOW	32.6	8.69	9.56	120
LOW.1	75.8	19.22	41.27	201
LOW.2	29.5	6.39	6.89	157
20% of solid food containers				
13% of total solid food weight				

both paper (cereal boxes) and plastic (pastry containers), and milk is sold in both paper and plastic cartons. Thus, in order to draw meaningful results for solid waste concerns, it is useful to step down one more level and look at the distribution of total package configurations—including material composition—among sample areas (Table 16.19). Paper is the first material composition type to analyze by product–package configuration and by area (Table 16.20).

Grains and chips in paper containers: Households in the three low-income areas buy large quantities of grain products (flour, noodles, bread, cereals, chips, and crackers) in paper packages. M.LOW and LOW.2 households buy them in relatively large sizes, and LOW.1 households buy them in small sizes (Table 16.20). In fact, 90% of the packages in LOW.2 refuse were 8 ounces or over in net weight, while 30% in LOW.1 refuse were less than 4 ounces in net weight.

High-sugar foods in paper containers: The consumption of pastries in paper packages in different neighborhoods is extremely varied (it does, however, match the pattern of consumption in plastic containers) (Table 16.20). In this case, LOW.1 households are buying in large packages, while LOW.2 households are buying smaller ones. Both sets of households, together with MID.1 households, are buying and discarding pastries in relatively large numbers of paper containers.

Table 16.18 Product Categories with Significant Differences among Milwaukee Sample Neighborhoods by Fluid Volume and Number of Occurrences

	Fluids			
	Average weekly consumption (in fluid ounces)	Average package size (in ounces)	SD	Total number of containers recorded
Milk:				
MID.1	120.8	64.60	49.65	58
MID.2	113.6	79.67	45.50	67
M.LOW	122.0	84.87	43.50	46
LOW.1	78.6	55.06	42.11	50
LOW.2	157.0	59.79	47.53	71
14.0% of fluid containers				
41.9% of total fluid volume				
Highly processed beverages:[a]				
MID.1	67.6	12.86	7.56	163
MID.2	39.5	15.61	12.96	119
M.LOW	66.7	14.23	8.92	150
LOW.1	156.6	13.84	12.99	396
LOW.2	109.5	17.08	16.73	218
65.4% of fluid containers				
34.7% of total fluid volume				
Sodas:				
MID.1	21.3	14.69	11.49	45
MID.2	16.1	15.41	13.06	49
M.LOW	23.4	15.94	13.53	47
LOW.1	71.5	13.45	8.39	186
LOW.2	50.8	22.07	21.09	90
20.3% of fluid containers				
11.4% of total fluid volume				
Wine and spirits:				
MID.1	6.3	19.50	13.26	10
MID.2	9.4	27.62	11.25	16
M.LOW	2.0	21.33	12.22	3
LOW.1	20.3	13.69	11.08	52
LOW.2	13.3	22.07	21.09	13

[a] Sodas, beer, wine, and spirits.

Table 16.19 Significance Tests of the Distribution of Specific Package/Product Configurations among Milwaukee Sample Neighborhoods

	χ^2 Kendall's τ Pearson's r					
	Paper		Plastic		Glass	
	Solid	Fluid	Solid	Fluid	Solid	Fluid
Foods:						
Protein foods	—	—	—	—	—	—
Dairy foods	—	*[a]	—	—	—	—
Fresh produce	*	—	—	—	—	—
Processed produce	—	—	—	—	—	—
Fats	—	—	—	—	—	—
Grains	.0017 .0016 .0868	—	.0000 .0314 .1625	—	—	—
Nonnutritive foods	—	—	—	—	—	—
HIGH-SUGAR FOODS	.0000 .0000 .0002					
Baby foods	—	—	—	—	—	—
Preprepared foods	—	—	—	—	—	—
Pet foods	—	—	—	—	—	—
Beverages:						
MILK	—	.0000 .0003 .0034	—	—	—	—
Fruit beverages	—	—	—	—	—	—
Caffein beverages	—	*	—	—	—	—
HIGHLY PROCESSED BEVERAGES[b]	—	—	—	—	—	.0000 .0072 .0105
Soft drinks	—	—	—	—	—	—
WINE AND SPIRITS	—	—	—	—	—	.0000 .0006 .0003
Beer	—	—	—	—	—	—
Household products:						
Personal care	—	—	—	—	—	—
Health care	—	—	—	—	—	—
Household care	—	—	—	—	—	—
Overall			.0340[c] 2.6808[d]	.0011[c] 4.7671[d]	—	—

[a] Asterisk means may be significant, but the frequencies are too low to tell.

[b] Sodas, beer, wine, and spirits.

[c] ANOVA results.

[d] ANOVA F values.

Paper milk cartons: The quantities of milk purchased per week in paper cartons in all five areas is extremely consistent, with LOW.1 households just below the other four. MID.1, LOW.1, and LOW.2 households seem to buy a few more small containers (Table 16.20).

Three paper package–product configurations emerge as significant: grains and chips, pastries, and milk. Of these, the main differences seem to rest in grain products and chips and pastries. LOW.1 neighborhoods discard a high number of paper grain and chips packages and large paper pastry packages. LOW.2 discards a large number of small paper pastry containers as well as large paper grain and chips packages. These discards might help account for the higher rate of discard of paper packaging in LOW.1 and LOW.2 neighborhoods.

Plastic: Plastic is another material where differences between neighborhoods were observed.

Grains and chips in plastic: The highest consumers of these products, mainly bread and chips, are MID.2, LOW.1, and LOW.2 households. LOW.1 households buy small packages, LOW.2 households buy larger packages, and MID.1 and MID.2 households purchase still larger packages. The large number of packages discarded by LOW.1 and LOW.2 households may be important (Table 16.21).

Although no other significant patterns were found for specific product categories, the overall distribution of plastic containers of both solids and fluids was found to be

Table 16.20 Paper Package-Product Configurations with Significant Differences among Milwaukee Sample Neighborhoods

	Average weekly consumption (in ounces)	Average package size (in ounces)	Total number of containers recorded	Number of containers discarded per pickup
Grains/chips in paper				
MID.1	15.9	9.9	50	1.6
MID.2	6.0	10.0	29	.6
M.LOW	29.3	20.9	46	1.4
LOW.1	31.0	12.4	87	2.5
LOW.2	33.5	23.9	48	1.4
High-sugar foods in paper				
MID.1	26.3	10.9	75	2.4
MID.2	9.1	5.7	74	1.6
M.LOW	17.6	8.8	64	.2
LOW.1	61.0	29.0	73	2.1
LOW.2	14.0	5.0	95	2.8
Paper milk cartons				
MID.1	48.1	39.4	38	1.22
MID.2	48.2	63.4	36	.76
M.LOW	47.5	60.9	25	.78
LOW.1	43.8	45.1	34	.97
LOW.2	48.2	44.2	37	1.09

Table 16.21 Plastic Package/Product Configurations with Significant Differences among Milwaukee Sample Neighborhoods

	Average weekly consumption (in ounces)	Average package size (in ounces)	Total number of containers recorded	Number of containers discarded per pickup
Grains in plastic				
MID.1	19.7	13.1	47	1.5
MID.2	24.8	13.0	88	1.9
M.LOW	20.7	9.9	68	2.1
LOW.1	25.8	9.2	98	2.8
LOW.2	33.2	11.1	102	3.0
Plastics with solid contents				
MID.1	140.2	20.5	212	6.84
MID.2	100.5	16.7	283	6.02
M.LOW	161.8	20.3	255	7.97
LOW.1	126.5	15.6	284	8.11
LOW.2	121.6	15.2	272	8.00
Plastics with fluid contents				
MID.1	98.9	68.2	45	1.45
MID.2	83.1	100.1	39	.83
M.LOW	85.7	94.2	29	.91
LOW.1	60.1	60.1	35	1.00
LOW.2	105.3	74.7	48	1.41

significant by an ANOVA Statistic 1 test. In the case of solids, LOW.1 and LOW.2 households discarded smaller packages and more packages overall (Table 16.22). In the case of fluids, MID.1 and LOW.2 households discarded more plastic containers than households in other areas. The plastics with solid contents represent 87% of all plastic containers. The high LOW.1 and LOW.2 household discard of small plastic packages may explain the higher overall weights for plastics in their refuse. In the case of fluids, the major difference is the higher purchase of soda in large plastic containers in LOW.1 and especially LOW.2 neighborhoods.

Aluminum and bimetal: No significant differences were found in the discard of aluminum and bimetal ferrous/aluminum packaging. Nevertheless, these items are associated with a limited number of commodities: aluminum—foil, foil wraps on frozen foods, and soft drink and beer cans; and bimetal—soft drink and beer cans. It may be important, then, that LOW.1 households (high for aluminum and bimetal) and LOW.2 households (high for aluminum) purchase significantly more highly processed beverages, especially soft drinks, than households in the other three areas (Table 16.18).

Highly processed beverages in glass (soft drinks, beer, wine, and spirits): The pattern for glass containers of highly processed beverages is extremely clear (see

Table 16.22 Glass Package/Product Configurations with Significant Differences among Milwaukee Sample Neighborhoods

Highly processed beverages in bottles[a]	Average container size (in ounces)	SD	Average number of containers discarded per pickup	Average weekly consumption (in ounces)	Total number of containers recorded
MID.1	15.292	9.091	.77	11.8	24
MID.2	17.367	12.409	.85	14.8	40
M.LOW	25.429	9.761	.44	11.2	14
LOW.1	14.300	9.423	2.77	39.6	97
LOW.2	27.273	13.956	.59	16.0	20

[a] Not including dry mixes, fruit juices, milk, or caffein beverages.

Table 16.22). More than 49.7% of all such bottles were discarded by LOW.1 households. LOW.1 households also discarded the smallest bottles on the average. This behavior, which seems to fit well with the weight data, indicates that LOW.1 households throw out much more glass than households in any other area. In fact, the preference for glass containers occurs with all types of beverages. Overall, LOW.1 households account for 36% of all beverage bottles, a rate one-third higher than what would be expected if glass containers were evenly distributed among households in the five neighborhoods. The high discard of glass by LOW.1 households, then, may relate both to the consumption of beverages (Table 16.18) and to a general preference for beverages in glass containers (Table 16.22).

REGULAR SORT ANALYSES SUMMARY

The weight-sort data analysis indicates that LOW.1 and LOW.2 households discarded significantly higher quantities by weight of paper, plastic, and aluminum, and that LOW.1 households also discarded significantly more glass and ferrous/aluminum combinations by weight. Detailed regular-sort records of the distribution of specific package–product configurations in the refuse of the five sample neighborhoods were studied to account for these patterns.

Higher paper discards seem to be the result of the consumption of grain products, chips, and pastries, either because large quantities are bought in large packages or because the product is purchased in large numbers of small packages.

Grain products and chips again figure in the discard of plastics. In this case, however, the overall purchasing patterns of LOW.1 and LOW.2 households seem most important, especially in their purchase of products in small plastic packages.

The high discard of glass by LOW.1 households seems best explained by the high consumption of, and general preference for, beverages in glass containers.

Finally, the high discard of aluminum and bimetal is most likely due to a heavy consumption of soda, although this proposition is not fully substantiated.

An examination of these results indicates that both possible factors seem to be at work:

Factor 1: Low-income households do purchase large quantities of some preprepared foods and beverages. LOW.1 and LOW.2 households buy more highly processed beverages and more grain products and chips in paper and plastic packages; LOW.1 households buy much more pastry and consume more highly processed beverages in bottles.

Factor 2: Low-income households do purchase larger quantities of small packages. LOW.1 households buy grains and chips in small paper and plastic packages; LOW.2 households buy pastry in small paper packages; LOW.1 households buy highly processed beverages in relatively small bottles; and both LOW.1 and LOW.2 households buy more items in small plastic containers than other households.

In Milwaukee, low-income sample households discarded more packaging of various types than middle-income groups. These low-income households do not consciously decide to buy products so that they can discard more packaging. They buy packaging–product configurations based on food preferences and the economic and physical realities of shopping and food storage. Thus, purchasing patterns are not frivolous. They seem to be the result of the use of relatively inexpensive high-bulk foods, such as breads, chips, and pastries as well as certain bottled beverages, and limited cash-flow, limited storage space, and small family sizes. Following this line of reasoning suggests that the heavy discard of packaging in low-income areas is the final outcome of behaviors with economic and nutritional implications that deserves more study.

Thus, through the analysis of actual refuse, we have not found the neat patterns of theory, but the complicated face of reality: The solid wastes of poor households are the result of a mix of consumer strategies that will take considerably more research to document fully and explain.

CONCLUSIONS

The Milwaukee Garbage Project has provided tentative answers to the three research questions at the beginning of this chapter:

1. The average weight of solid wastes discarded weekly by sample households was a little over 25 lb. Sample households in the two low-income, small family areas and in one middle-income area discarded more refuse overall than households in the other two areas. This indicates that income and family size alone cannot be used to explain the quantity of discarded solid wastes.
2. The material composition breakdown of household solid wastes indicates that sample housebolds in the two low-income areas discarded more packaging by weight than sample households in the other areas.
3. Differences in discarded packaging are the result both of high rates of consumption in the home of some preprepared foods and beverages and of the purchase of some products in large numbers of small containers. This heavy discard of packaging is the final outcome of behaviors with potentially important economic and nutritional implications.

Overall, archaeology's founding premise has been supported—households with different behavioral characteristics generate different discards. In addition, an archaeological approach to modern solid wastes has provided some insights into differences in basic resource management behaviors among household groups. These are important because of their economic and nutritional implications for the household occupants.

Although the validity of these results is limited to only those households sampled, the patterns described in this report do seem quite supportable for those households. This study has not explained all of the observed patterns of residential solid waste generation. In fact, the major portion of the variability in household solid wastes remains to be carefully described and explained in behavioral terms. This study has succeeded in taking an archaeological look at solid waste questions—from *inside* the garbage can. The quantitative data generated raise the potential of direct comparisons with the solid waste of urban households of earlier times and a chance to evaluate our current material life styles against those of our past. That is a major goal in the Garbage Project's future.

ACKNOWLEDGMENTS

The members of Garbage Project would like to extend special thanks to Herb Goetsch, Director of the Milwaukee Department of Public Works, Raymond Caplan, Superintendent of Sanitation Services, and Ignatius A. Balistrieri, Sanitation Supervisor 3. The same gratitude goes to the student volunteers, who now know what "garbology" really means, and without whose help the Milwaukee Garbage Project would never have happened. Special thanks also go to Doris Sample who patiently typed the drafts of this chapter.

REFERENCES

Gladwin, T.
1967 *Poverty U.S.A.* New York: Little Brown.

Havlicek, J., Jr., and A. A. Saleh
1974 Quantity, composition and seasonality of residential solid wastes. Paper presented at the annual meeting of the American Agricultural Economics Association, College Station, Texas.

Hohlen, M.
1979 *SPSS-6000 release 8.0 update manual.* Northwestern University, Evanston, Illinois.

Hull, C. H., and N. H. Nie
1979 *SPSS update: New procedures and facilities for releases 7 and 8.* New York: McGraw-Hill.

McGuire, M.
1980 The logistics of solid waste analysis: The Garbage Project Manual. Manuscript on file at Le Projet du Garbage, Department of Anthropology, University of Arizona, Tucson.

Nie, N. H., C. H. Hull, J. G. Jenkins, K. Steinbrenner, and D. H. Bent
1975 *SPSS: Statistical package for the social sciences,* 2nd ed. New York: McGraw-Hill.

Rathje, W. L., and W. W. Hughes
1975 The Garbage Project as a nonreactive approach. In *Perspectives on attitude assessment: Surveys and their alternatives,* edited by H. W. Sinaiko and and L. A. Broedling. *Smithsonian Institution, Technical Report* 2. Washington, D.C.: Smithsonian Publications, p. 151–167.

Rathje, W. L., and W. W. Hughes
1978 *Socioeconomic correlates of household residuals: Phase* 2. Report to the National Science Foundation. Directorate for Applied Science and Research Applications.

Rathje, W. L., and M. McCarthy
1977 Regularity and variability in contemporary garbage. In *Research strategies in historical archeology,* edited by Stanley South. New York: Academic Press. Pp. 261–286.

Rathje, W. L., and B. E. Thompson
1981 The Milwaukee Garbage Project. *Report of the Solid Waste Council of the Paper Industry,* New York.

Richardson, R. A., and J. Havlicek, Jr.
1974 An analysis of seasonal household waste generation. *Southern Journal of Agricultural Economics,* December, 143–155.
1975 An analysis of the generation of household solid wastes from consumption. *Purdue University Agricultural Experiment Station, Research Bulletin,* No. 920.
1978 Economic analysis of the composition of household solid wastes. *Journal of Environmental Economics and Management,* 5:103–111.

Saleh, A. A.
An analysis of consumer food expenditures and consumption waste. Unpublished Ph.D. dissertation, Department of Agricultural Economics, Purdue University, Lafayette, Indiana.

Saleh, A. A., and J. Havlicek, Jr.
1975 Household solid waste associated with food consumption activities. *Southern Journal of Agricultural Economics*, December, 9–18.

Tolley, G. S., V. S. Hastings, and G. Rudzitis
1978 Economics of municipal solid waste management: The Chicago case. "*Special*" *Report Series*, EPA-600/8-78-013. Solid and Hazardous Waste Research Division, U.S. Environmental Protection Agency, Cincinnati, Ohio.

Wertz, K. L.
1976 Economic factors influencing household's production of refuse. *Journal of Environmental Economics and Management* 2:263–272.

Winfield, G. L.
1974 *Solid waste samplings: Baltimore City*. Department of Public Works, Baltimore, Maryland.

Subject Index